学汇中外 语通世界

YUYAN · WENXUE · FANYIYANJIU

语言·文学·翻译研究

——电子科技大学外国语学院研究生论文

（第三辑）

主 编 楚 军

副主编 王爱华 邹 涛 廖 敏 尹永顺

电子科技大学出版社
University of Electronic Science and Technology of China Press

·成都·

图书在版编目（CIP）数据

语言·文学·翻译研究：电子科技大学外国语学院研究生论文. 第三辑 / 楚军主编. —成都：电子科技大学出版社，2018. 12

ISBN 978-7-5647-6704-4

Ⅰ. ①语… Ⅱ. ①楚… Ⅲ. ①英语－语言教学－文集 Ⅳ. ①H319.3-53

中国版本图书馆 CIP 数据核字（2019）第 001656 号

语言·文学·翻译研究

——电子科技大学外国语学院研究生论文（第三辑）

主　　编　楚　军

副 主 编　王爱华　邹　涛　廖　敏　尹永顺

策划编辑　谢应成
责任编辑　谢应成

出版发行　电子科技大学出版社
　　　　　成都市一环路东一段 159 号电子信息产业大厦九楼
　　　　　邮编　610051
主　　页　www.uestcp.com.cn
服务电话　028-83203399
邮购电话　028-83201495

印　　刷　成都市火炬印务有限公司
成品尺寸　185 mm×260 mm
印　　张　20.25
字　　数　530 千字
版　　次　2018 年 12 月第 1 版
印　　次　2018 年 12 月第 1 次印刷
书　　号　ISBN 978-7-5647-6704-4
定　　价　68.00 元

树立精英意识·优化育人环节·培养精英人才

电子科技大学外国语学院　冯文坤

学生主动选择一所大学，意味他们认同一所大学的价值，意味他们对“我将成为什么样的人”有了一种期待，尽管这种期待在一个大学生那里还十分朦胧，但他们却从此接受这所大学对他们未来的一种承诺。“我是谁？从哪里来？到哪里去？”这是古希腊哲学家苏格拉底提出的问题。古希腊哲人认为，人活着就是为了弄清楚这三个问题。“我是谁？”“从哪里来？到哪里去？”这三问不仅是哲学中询问“人”的意义的问题，也可以是一所大学应该首先思考“培养什么人”和“如何培养人”的问题，因为大学是青年人自我塑型和自我形成的地方，是向社会许下未来和承诺美好价值的地方，因此，大学责无旁贷，应率先帮助学生去思考“我从哪里来”“我是谁”“我将到哪里去”这三个问题，并在教育过程中回答学生对人生的建构。

两年前，言荣校长在“关于我校本科人才培养的思考”的报告中，全面总结了学校人才培养所取得的成绩、存在的问题和今后人才培养的目标与实现路径，至今令人振奋，发人深思，催人改进和革新，尤其是言荣校长直逼大学“要培养什么人”和“如何培养人”的发问，并立足电子科技大学，提出了未来电子科技大学精英人才培养目标定位，体现了言荣校长枕于忧患、着眼于未来的教育战略思维和一位教育家的人才培养观，更体现了秉持科大“追求卓越，大气大为”之校训精神的办学理念自信、发展自信和责任自信。精英培养，引领大众，服务于社会是大学的崇高使命，更是对电子科技大学几代人崇高使命的继承和发扬。根据校长讲话，结合外语学院办学实际，围绕精英人才培养定位谈几点愚见和忧思。

一、创新人才培养模式，孕育精英人才成长

要成就精英人才之办学目标，要明确人才培养的模式定位。要使学生明确知道“我成为谁？”“我要到哪里去？”，要以学生成才或培养效果或标准为终极目标。也就是说，效果或标准重于环节，环节推动人才成长，要把**有效教学、有效学习和有效评估**统一起来。今天，我们的教学管理过程，学习管理过程，似乎每个环节都做到了，有的环节还非常严苛，我们的精力都用来应付这些环节，形式大于内容，学生成长实际效果如何却没有给予充分重视，因为对人才终端之效果如何担责的问题十分模糊，也是十分复杂，但背后折射出的却是大学之全体责

任。法不责众，更何况是一个庞大的机构。生产线上的不合格产品可以退回，可人不同于物。拿外语人才培养来说，一个学生通过 4 年学习，他是不是实现了当初选择的专业人才愿望，是不是达到该专业人才所应有的要求，如外语交际能力、外语写作能力、系统的学科知识以及认知能力等，还是仅仅入了大学，遵循了每个环节，蹲满了学分，最后成为“毕了业的人才”。就我个人愚见，大众教育重通识，精英教育更重研究能力和创新思维。大众教育造就学生“成人”，精英教育造就学生“成为杰出的人”或成为具有精英意识的人。

二、创新课程体系，适应精英人才培养

要培养精英外语人才，就要遵循外语学科的系统性和人文人才培养规律，要实现语言的人文性和工具性的高度统一，要实现中国情怀和国际视野在一个外语人才身上的结合，要在把握语言工具性的过程中含化人文教育，要实实在在把语言转化为学科性学习和向外拓展的工具理性。由此，应该反思我们现有的外语课程内容体系：缺乏学科系统性、内容片段化、破碎化和随意性；操作性、技能训练占到接近 80%、内容倒转为技能服务；课程体系性不衔接，课程层级不分明，课程目标不清楚；特色原本是学科体系中的特色，却一言以蔽之，外语加特色，其结果是特色性遮蔽专业学科属性，不伦不类。

由此产生三大后果、引发三大整改：外语人才学科定位不清楚，专业兴趣游移，效果不明确，标准不清楚，不利于杰出专业人才成长，因此，应强化学科专业定位和人才培养目标的课程体系建设；仅仅为技能而设计的课程体系就如有“矛”无“盾”，有驾照无车开，开花不结果，因此，应将操作性、技能性训练溶于内容系统性传达、素养含化和学科培养目标之中；目前课程体系只具有指标意义，如专业基础课、专业核心课程和专业选修课，它们在多大程度上是服务于外语学科专业人才“成才”是值得我们思考的，因此，应以人才效果和标准为鹄的，加强以“人才培养为中心，以成才为目标”的专业课程体系建设，应推进课程内容调整，建设由 How to Speak English 向 What to Speak with English 转变的课程内容体系。

今天，略举一例，一个十分怪异的事实是：外语文学专业的学生少有读完一本英文原著，一个较长时间从事文学课教学的老师却鲜见他或她读完读透几本原文著作。我一直觉得由体系性课程教学推动学科性研究，进而推动学科人才培养和学科平台建设是自然而然的。可事实则是，一批教师应急而上课，且续且止，留下许多僵死课程，到头来，科研与教学二元对立，元音与辅音永远靠不近。作为学院派的外语学科教学，我们不能让外语教学内容在浅层次上循环，我们的教

师不能在浅层次上经年循环，最后自我矮化，语言用语格式化。我们虽然不能教会学生像奥巴马那样讲英语，但我们可以培养像奥巴马那样运用思维的人。总之，精英人才有各样的，但精英人才一定是有内涵的。大学中的外语专业应该培养“精通外语的精英人才”，不是培养“没有内涵的外语人才”。这是大学院系外语学科人才培养体制与新东方语言培训方式的本质区别。

三、创新人才培养评估体系，适应精英人才成长效果评估

要培养精英人才，反思和调整现有评估机制非常迫切。“以人才培养为中心，以学生成才为目标”，重在成才效果，重在学生“成为谁？”“到哪里去？”这一目标对学校、教师要求特别高，心理压力特别大，因为这意味教与学之间无间隙的接触、无间隙的全员投入和无间隙的关怀。这不仅仅是一个规定教授每周在指定时间与学生面谈所能完成的，或循规蹈矩，完成教学各环节，因此做到无教学事故了事。“以学生成才为目标”，把老师的日常意识变成日常责任，时时牵挂，萦于心际，教师就如参加大赛的领队，直到最后一刻，方才身心委地。优化生源，减少师生比，小班授课是完成学生成才的路径，同时还要有若干系统路径，如创新目前的评估体系：建立以学生成才为依据的有效学习路径体系与有效教学综合效果指标体系，如课程内容体系、教/学环节（硬性与灵活结合）、资源体系、学科教学团队；建立以学生成才为目标的“一体两翼”的培养机制和评估机制（学生选、育、评一体化），教师个体（遴选、考核、评价）和教学团队（团队考核个人）；采取内部和外部相结合的评价和测试办法——内部评估指学科体系评估、教、学评估、课程和课程内容评估；外部评估指学生外语水平认证评估、行业用人评估、国际化水平评估等。

四、建立全程导师制，落实全员育人

建立全程导师制，形成贯穿四年的学业指导、科研训练、成人成才“三位一体”的引导学生全面发展的指导制度；形成教师团队与学生班级相融合的团队式教与学模式；形成学生（思想工作）与教学一体化的学业、成长、成才体系。从2013年开始，外语学院在全体本科生中落实导师制，对学生的学业过程、学业规划发展、成人成长等进行指导。接下来，学院将实施班级教授导师制，专业教学团队责任制（探索中），基于“基础、提高和发展”的大学外教学团队责任制，以及已经实施并取得显著效果的指导各类外语大赛的“外语实践教育团队”等。

五、学、研、训一体化，在思辨与运思中成长

建立贯穿学生培养全过程的研究方法论课程群、学期论文、学年论文、科研训练等一体化研训机制，培养具有方法论的思维模式与批判性思维能力；根据本科学生毕业走向（直接就业或继续深造）进行差异化的论文或毕业环节训练等；实施“外语写作课程”贯穿四年不下课，培养学生规范写作，独立思考，考量心理变化历程。

今天的大学生似乎并不缺乏知识，一键网络天下，大数据时代的一个重要特征是我们只需要知道“what it is”，而不需要知道“why it is”，可这恰恰指出我们大学在当今的使命：更应该去培养学生的判断能力、逻辑思维能力，从相似性、类似性、联想性和模糊性中去培养学生的选择能力和判断能力。

据观察，大多数具有创新思维能力的人都具有类似性思维、联想性思维和关联性思维等特征，能从两件表面上毫无联系的事情上发现其关联性，一般被人戏称“发散思维”，其实是他们省略了线性逻辑，而直接地领悟到其内隐逻辑。人们常说，有些人无学历却能干大事，如知名企业家，而那些搞量化经济学的却并非能够对市场做出准确的预测，也没有成为企业家。问题的关键是，做出的固化数学建模尽管来源于经验观察所取得的数据分析，却永远也取代不了直观洞察力、类似性思维、关联性思维以及想象力，后者的所有者就是创新性人才。

六、“学科内培养，学科外发展”

人们常讲，育人者应“授人以渔”，要育人者授人可以临深渊而渔之的本领。“授人以渔”与“授人以鱼”是对操作型人才和社会适应性人才的暗喻式诠释。言荣校长讲，当今社会发展，产业更新，变化快于规划，今日就业明日失业，我们的教育应为学生的第二次转岗打下基础，这话讲得简单却深刻，说出了一个教育家“道术合一”的崇高信念和面向未来、与时俱进的责任感和发展观。大学既要培养满足社会行业阶段性需要的应用性人才，又要使学生具有应对变化挑战、掌控变化以及人生变化的适应性人才。前者是学科内培养，后者需要通过培养学生的综合人文素质，厚基础、宽口径，以培养学生的持续再生产能力。前者是培养学科专业精英，后者是造就具有精英意识的商界精英、政治精英和社会贤达。一言以蔽之，培养精英人才，以造就学科领域大师、专业方向领军和行业界翘楚，而培养具有精英意识的大学生则惠及全体学生之终生和全社会之发展，这或许就是我们对大众中的精英教育的最好诠释。

学院组织和推动研究生和本科生文集出版，这是一种记载和书写学生成长中的记忆。湖泊中的涟漪总是由振荡而来，微风过林，七窍玲珑心。我相信这里记录的是同学们的认知自信、成长自信。

前　言

电子科技大学外国语学院从2016年起在在读研究生中广泛征集、遴选，编辑出版研究生论文集，目的是保障研究生的培养质量和学术论文的发表质量，锻炼研究生的批判性思辨能力、学术创新能力和独立从事学术科研的能力，为研究生学术研究提供成果展示平台。

即将付梓的《语言·文学·翻译研究》（电子科技大学外国语学院研究生论文集（第三辑））主要包括以下三方面的研究：

“语言学研究”部分收录了9篇论文。隋智帆的“国内隐喻论文可视化分析研究”运用可视化的研究手段对近期国内的隐喻研究状况进行了较为深入的分析。宋艳梅以“Doubt”和“Suspect”两词为例运用语料库的研究方法进行了辨义性探讨。王筝从合作原则的角度探析了小说《大饭店》的会话含义。温淑婧从隐喻分类和因素层次分析研讨了科技发展与日常生活的相互关联性。汤朝菊教授指导的张晗同学对互联网环境下英汉混合四字格流行词语做了模因解析。罗时乾以“菜鸡”一词为例运用概念整合理论分析了汉语网络语的在线意义构建。余悦运用关联理论对《虬髯客传》的两个译本中文化负载词英译做了对比研究。江露对基于中介语的初中英语学习者的写作偏误进行了分析阐释。最后，钱思颖探讨了汉字的理据性及对外汉语教学的影响作用。

“文学研究”部分收录了21篇论文。王蕾、常红、王若岚、张玲等同学从不同的视角分析研究了诺贝尔文学奖得主库切创作的《耻》和《等待野蛮人》两部作品。严肖肖、谢诗阳两位同学对卡夫卡作品《变形记》进行了初步的探讨。曹宇、王若岚两位同学从不同视角分析研讨了作品《别让我走》。陈玥含、廖梦园对经典名著《老人与海》，李静、夏谦滢对作品《幽暗之地》分辨做了不同视域的分析讨论。常红运用文本世界理论对作品《青春咖啡馆》中的露姬形象做了初步的探析。郭佼从巴赫金的“对话理论”解读了《小王子》。谢诗阳对作品*YELLOW BACK RADIO BROKE-DOWN*中的魔幻现实主义创作手法进行了分析。黄丹从原型-神话批评角度分析了《最蓝的眼睛》中男性形象的神话原型。常红对非洲作家阿依·克韦·阿尔马赫的国内外研究做了述评。黄玉珊、何露、韩文丽三位日语语种的同学分别对夏目漱石的作品《心》中的“先生”形象、察谷崎润一郎的审美情趣和日本传统文学进行了较为深入的分析研究。

“翻译研究”部分收录了 14 篇论文。毛晓燕从存异伦理视角分析了莫言小说《蛙》的葛浩文英译本中的文化负载词的翻译问题。张玲从“音美”角度探析了古诗英译问题。伍永晔、杨亚婷、施瑞、于晶四位同学从不同视角对《虬髯客传》英译本进行了初步研讨。詹廷运用操纵论探讨了《诗经》的英译问题。李文瑾和詹廷、刘夏、刘芸均项目组分别分享了《二十世纪的女性》和《十大探险胜地》两个英译汉项目实践报告。吴崔娟运用目的论对《伊豆的舞女》的两个中译本进行了比较研究。张娇研讨了励志性人物自传的翻译策略。李杨红对《罗生门》的中文译本做了初步的比较分析。樊一霖浅析了日本电影片名的翻译方法。邓雨洁分析研讨了《母亲的初恋》的叶渭渠译本的翻译特点。

由于时间仓促，加之所辑“论文集”中的文章都是出自外语专业在校硕士研究生之手，文中错误和不当之处在所难免，诚望读者批评斧正！

《语言·文学·翻译研究》研究生论文集（第三辑）得以出版，感谢电子科技大学外国语学院王爱华教授、邹涛教授、廖敏副教授、尹永顺副教授以及所有研究生导师的悉心指导和辛勤付出，感谢电子科技大学出版社编辑们的辛勤劳动。

编　者

2019 年 1 月 24 日

目　录

语言学研究

国内隐喻论文可视化分析研究……隋智帆 2
基于语料库的动词近义词辨析
——以“Doubt”和“Suspect”为例……宋艳梅 10
从合作原则的角度来研究小说《大饭店》的会话含义……王　筝 22
从隐喻分类和因素层次分析看科技发展与日常生活……温淑婧 38
互联网环境下英汉混合四字格流行词语模因解析……汤朝菊　张　晗 45
概念整合理论下汉语网络语在线意义构建
——以“菜鸡”一词为例……罗时乾 50
《虬髯客传》两个译本中文化负载词英译对比分析
——基于关联理论视角……余　悦 56
基于中介语的初中英语学习者写作偏误分析……江　露 63
汉字的理据性及对对外汉语教学的影响……钱思颖 71

文 学 研 究

库切《耻》的精神分析学解读
——库切和他的白日梦……王　蕾 77
酷儿理论视阈下的《耻》……常　红 82
霸权帝国的崩塌：库切《等待野蛮人》中二元的解构与重构……王若岚 87
《等待野蛮人》中的暴力与救赎……黄　丹 92
沉默中他者的爆发：福柯权力与话语理论视角下《耻》的解读……张　玲 97
《变形记》—卡夫卡自我理想与本能的博弈……严肖肖 103
被女性化的男人的困境
——从《变形记》中析出的卡夫卡……谢诗阳 107
An Analysis of Tommy’s Personalities in *Never Let Me Go* from the Perspective of Personality Structure Theory……曹　宇 116
石黑一雄《别让我走》替罪羊原型下的主题分析……王若岚 128
《活着》与《老人与海》中主人公的认知模式对比研究
——在“独立”与“互立”间寻求生存希望……陈玥含 136
新批评视域下的《老人与海》的结局合理性分析……廖梦园 141
自我与他者的消解：解构视域下的《幽暗之地》……李　静 147
“边缘者的孤独”：《幽暗之地》中的自我他者化……夏谦滢 153
文本世界理论视野下《青春咖啡馆》中的露姬形象探析……常　红 159

从巴赫金的“对话理论”解读《小王子》
——聆听大自然的教导……郭 佼 166
Magic Realism in Yellow Back Radio Broke-Down……谢诗阳 172
从原型-神话批评分析《最蓝的眼睛》中男性形象神话原型……黄 丹 186
非洲作家阿依·克韦·阿尔马赫国内外研究述评……常 红 191
社会心理学视角下“先生”的形象分析
——以夏目漱石《心》为对象……黄玉珊 198
从《刺青》来考察谷崎润一郎的审美情趣……何 露 203
日本人缩小意识中隐含的扩大心理研究
——以日本传统文学为例……韩文丽 211

翻译研究

存异伦理视角下文化负载词的翻译研究
——以葛浩文英译《蛙》为例……毛晓燕 218
从“音美”角度看《古诗十九首》的英译
——以《青青河畔草》和《迢迢牵牛星》为例……张 玲 226
《虬髯客传》英译本中主要人物肖像描写比较研究……伍永晔 231
《虬髯客传》两种英译本中李靖人物形象和传统礼仪对比分析……杨亚婷 237
从文学文体学视角评析《虬髯客传》两译本的可读性和灵活性……施 瑞 243
动态对等在人物形象翻译中的适用性探讨
——以《虬髯客传》为例……于 晶 251
从操纵论看《诗经》英译
——以《桃夭》三个译本为例……詹 廷 258
《二十世纪的女性》英译汉实践报告……李文瑾 265
《十大探险胜地》英译汉项目报告……詹 廷 刘 夏 刘芸均 275
目的论视角下《伊豆的舞女》两个中译本的比较研究……吴崔娟 282
目的论视域下的励志性人物自传翻译策略探析
——以路英勇译《五体不满足》为例……张 娇 289
从《罗生门》中文译本看翻译策略和原因
——比较鲁迅译本和林少华译本……李杨红 295
浅析日本电影片名的翻译方法……樊一霖 301
论叶渭渠译《母亲的初恋》的翻译特点
——兼论谭晶华的中译本……邓雨洁 308

语言学研究

国内隐喻论文可视化分析研究

隋智帆

摘　要：本文运用 Excel 分析了国内隐喻文献发文的主要时间段及其变化、主要发文期刊及领域分布、高产学者及发文机构分布。同时，本文采用文献计量学的可视化技术，运用 CiteSpace 考察了接近 40 年来发表收录于 CNKI 上与隐喻研究相关的论文，以呈现国内隐喻的研究现状和趋势。其重点进行了关键词分析，总结出国内隐喻的主要研究领域和受人关注的热点问题，并通过各时间段的对比，梳理了国内隐喻研究热点的演进，指出了国内隐喻研究的整体发展趋势

关键词：隐喻；可视化分析；研究热点；发展趋势

Abstract：This paper, using EXCEL, analyzes quantity change along with the time line, and demonstrates majorjournals and fields, representative researchers and institutions in the field of domesticmetaphors. At the same time, using the visualization technology of bibliometrics, this paper uses CiteSpace to examine the papers published on CNKI in recent nearly forty years to show the research status and trends of metaphor in China. It focuses on the analysis of key words, and summarizes the main research fields of metaphor in China as well as the hot issues that have been paid attention to. Through the comparison of various time periods, it combs the evolution of the hot spots in the domestic metaphor research, and points out the overall development trend of metaphor research in China.

Key words：metaphor；visualized analysis；research hot issues；trend of development

1 引　言

自 Lakoff 和 Johnson 于 1980 年出版《Metaphors We Live By》一书后，隐喻的概念便由此被引入国内。经过近 40 年来的发展壮大，国内隐喻研究呈现出新的研究热点和发展趋势。王文斌主要探讨了隐喻性词义的生成（2007）和演变以及隐喻中的相似性（2006）；束定芳则着重论述了隐喻的认知功能（2001）、本质及语义特征（1998）以及与换喻的差别和联系（2004）。国内对隐喻的研究多是集中于定性研究，利用数据分析的定量研究很少，虽然也有一些关于隐喻研究的述评类文章，如张全生（2004）的中国隐喻研究十年综述，张杰（2010）的国内隐喻研究状况述评，但大部分内容皆是简单数据的整合和罗列以及基于专家学者经验性的判断，且分析的文献时间跨度短，数量亦较少。总体来看，以往的研究定量分析涉及较少，且都没有应用专业的分析软件对国内隐喻的总体发展历程做一个完整的可视化分析研究。本文基于前人对于国内隐喻研究的缺陷和不足，借助文献计量学分析工具 CiteSpace，考察分析了 1980—2018 年（截至 2018 年 7 月 13 日）收录于 CNKI 上的各类国内隐喻研究的论文，以期更为全面、直观地展示国内隐喻研究领域的重要学者、文献、研究热点及其发展趋势，为未来的国内隐喻研究更好地指明了方向。

2 研究问题与方法

2.1 研究问题

本研究将回答以下问题：（1）国内隐喻研究的论文在时间分布、来源期刊及其涉及领域等方面呈现出怎样的特征？（2）国内隐喻研究领域有哪些发文量居多且极具代表性的学者？（3）国内隐喻研究的研究热点及其发展趋势是怎样的？

2.2 研究方法及数据来源

本文以“隐喻”为篇名检索词，检索 CNKI 来源中的所有期刊，时间设置为 1980—2018 年，对相关数据进行筛选，获得 19 340 篇论文，并导出相关文献记录。

本文首先利用 Excel 对国内隐喻研究论文进行描述性统计和分析，在梳理其时间分布、来源期刊、涉及领域、高产作者及机构等特征基础上，采用可视化分析工具 CiteSpace 绘制关键词共现网络图谱，发现并梳理国内隐喻研究领域的主要研究热点及其发展趋势。

3 国内隐喻研究描述性统计

3.1 时间序列分布

如图 1 所示，近 40 年来，国内隐喻研究的发文数量呈现出显著增长的趋势，论文涉及的范围及水平亦有相应的扩展和提升。回顾这些年来隐喻的发展可将其分为以下四个阶段。

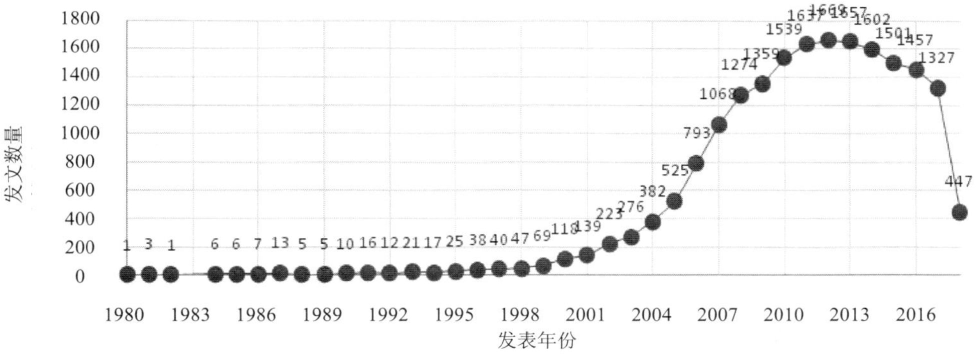

图 1 国内隐喻文献时间分布

（1）1980—1990 年是萌芽期。CNKI 中关于隐喻研究方面的论文最早见于 1980 年肖联冰的《隐喻的妙用》，此年仅此一篇而已。这种境况的存在是由于 1980 年 Lakoff 和 Johnson 首次提出隐喻的概念，而国内当时人文交流相对闭塞，科研氛围不够浓厚，且国外隐喻研究的论文发表数量在当时也十分匮乏，以至于国内鲜少有学者注意隐喻这一研究热点。直到 1990 年，共发文 57 篇，这 11 年间年均发文 5.2 篇。在此期间，论文多是对国外隐喻及其相关领域的介绍和描述，以 metaphor、simile、literal 等关键词占比居多，也有不少论文涉及文学作品。发文涉及领域主要集中于哲学与人文科学，共 53 篇文献，占比 70.7%，这为后来隐喻研究涉及的主要领域奠定了基础，也为隐喻的进一步发展提供了理论支撑。

（2）1991—1999 年是初步发展期。年均发文 31.7 篇，发文数量为 285 篇，较上一时期增长率为 400%。这九年间每年发文量皆为两位数，皆总体呈现较为稳定的小幅增长趋势，由此可见，国内隐喻进入初步发展时期。这一时期的研究主要集中在隐喻意义，隐喻理论及隐喻性等方面，同时涉及结构隐喻、概念隐喻、语法隐喻、修辞效果等方面，范围逐渐开始拓宽，发文领域仍以哲学与人文科学为集中之地，共计 192 篇文献，占比 66.4%，不过隐喻研究开始拓展到信息科技，医疗卫生科技等新领域，学术氛围渐趋浓厚。

（3）2000—2007 年是成熟期。文献数量逐年上升，且呈现出最大上升态势。在此期间，年均发文 440.5 篇。这八年间发文的关键词转变为认知与文化领域、概念隐喻、语法隐喻亦涉及较多。发文总体上依旧集中于语言文学领域，且以上海外国语大学为首发机构，发文数量居首，为 73 篇。纵览各位学者专家，尤以束定芳教授发文最多，共计 9 篇。此阶段涵盖领域繁复庞杂，视角多样，且出现较多的述评类文章，对前期相关的研究成果进行了系统理论性的总结，为之后的隐喻研究指明了研究方向。

（4）2008 年至今是稳定发展期。此阶段年均发文 1406 篇，且于 2012 年达到峰值 1669 篇，发文数量略有起伏（因截止时间为 2018 年 7 月 13 日，故而 2018 年的发文数量不可计入总体态势），但每年依然保持千位数的发文量。在此期间，随着涉及领域的不断拓展，隐喻研究亦随之深化，成功地在当今学术研究领域占据十分重要的一席之地。但近年来，大部分隐喻研究未能发现新的视角，据分布曲线推测，2018 年国内隐喻的发文数量较 2017 年会有所减少，这也为未来的隐喻研究提出了新的挑战与契机。

3.2 期刊及领域分布

国内隐喻发文数量接近 20 000 篇，其中载文 50 篇以上（>50）的期刊有 43 种，如图 2 所示。载文前五位的期刊为海外英语、电影文学、民主协商报、安徽文学及外语学刊，占比 4.7%，可见文献分布的各类期刊数量较为均匀，从侧面反映出国内开办的期刊数目繁多。专业类期刊在这 43 种期刊中数量为 14 种，占比约为三分之一，可见虽然各类报刊均有所涉猎隐喻研究，但仍以专业期刊为引领旗帜，形成以专业带动旁支的浓厚的学术研究景象。广泛的期刊种类分布和相对集中的专业期刊群反映出隐喻研究已得到国内学术界的广泛重视且形成纵深研究。

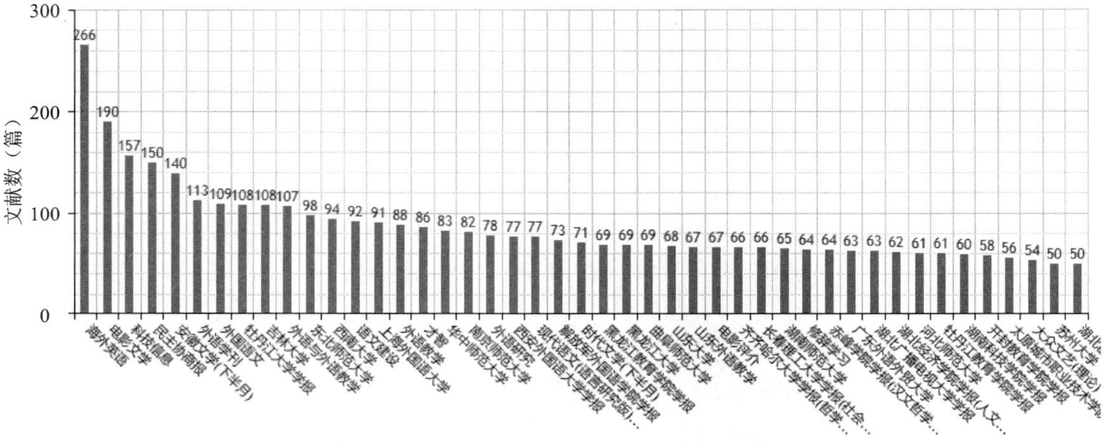

图 2　国内隐喻文献来源期刊分布

至于隐喻文献涉及领域的分布则主要集中于语言文学领域（外国语言文学最多，其次为中国语言文学、世界文学、中国文学），占比为 87.2%。随着隐喻研究的不断深入及多样化视角的逐渐挖掘，隐喻研究逐渐与其他领域的研究交相融合，不断渗透，如心理学、宗教、戏剧等领域，也展现出较为丰富的隐喻研究成果，具体涉及领域如图 3 所示。

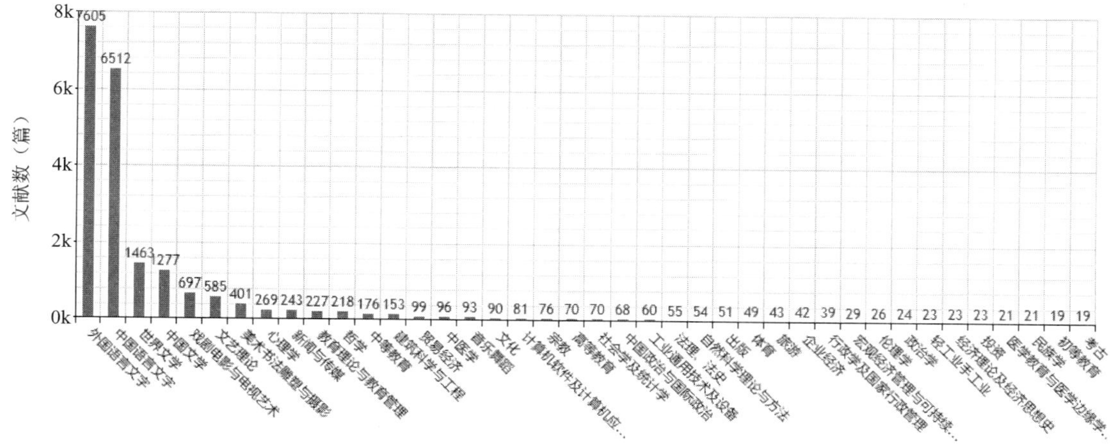

图 3　国内隐喻文献涉及领域分布

3.3　作者及机构分布

1980—2018 年，发文数量最多的学者是来自渭南师范学院中文系的王炳社，发文量位居前五的学者依次有贾春华（北京中医药大学）、孙毅（西安外国语大学）、陈清（湖南第一师范学院）、谢世坚（广西师范大学）。总体来看，这五位学者在语言文学界的影响力较小，由此可见，学者们发文数量虽多，但未能对专业学术领域带来极大的改变与影响。而学术界一些知名学者，如束定芳、胡壮麟、汪少华、刘振前等，虽然其发文数量不在前列，但却一直致力于隐喻研究的热点和发展，并在学术界产生了良好的影响，这也从一定程度上说明，发文数量不等于发文质量。值得庆贺的是，国内隐喻发文量在 8 篇及其以上的学者共有 48 位，可见隐喻研究之狂热，具体情况如图 4 所示。

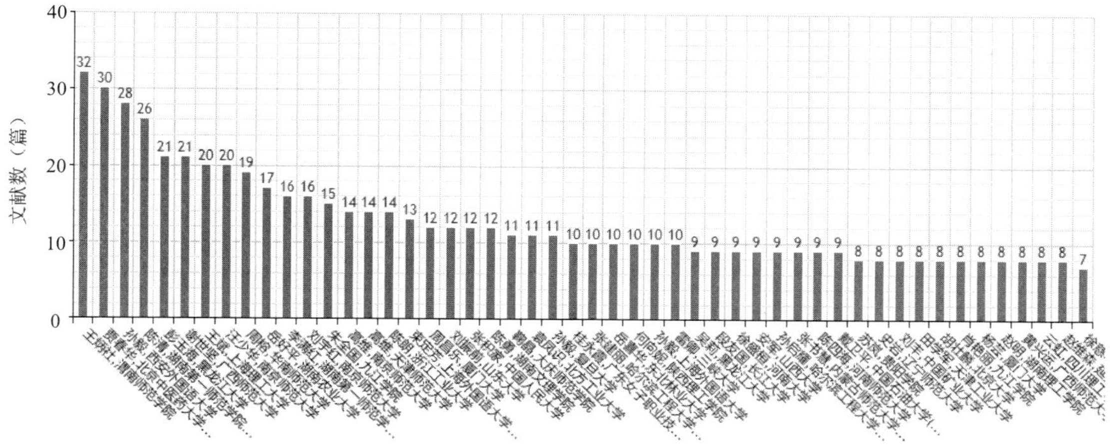

图 4　国内隐喻文献发表作者分布

在 1980—2018 年期间，CNKI 收录的隐喻文献发文量在 80 篇以上的机构共有 49 家，尤以师范类院校居多，共有 20 家，占比 40.8%（如图 5 所示）。发文量前五的机构依次为南京师范大学、广西师范大学、上海外国语大学、吉林大学和华中师范大学。由此可见，国内隐喻研究领域师范类院校占据重要地位，综合类院校力量雄厚，专业类院校发文数量有待提升，且发文量居多的机构皆以东部院校为主，西部院校影响较为薄弱。

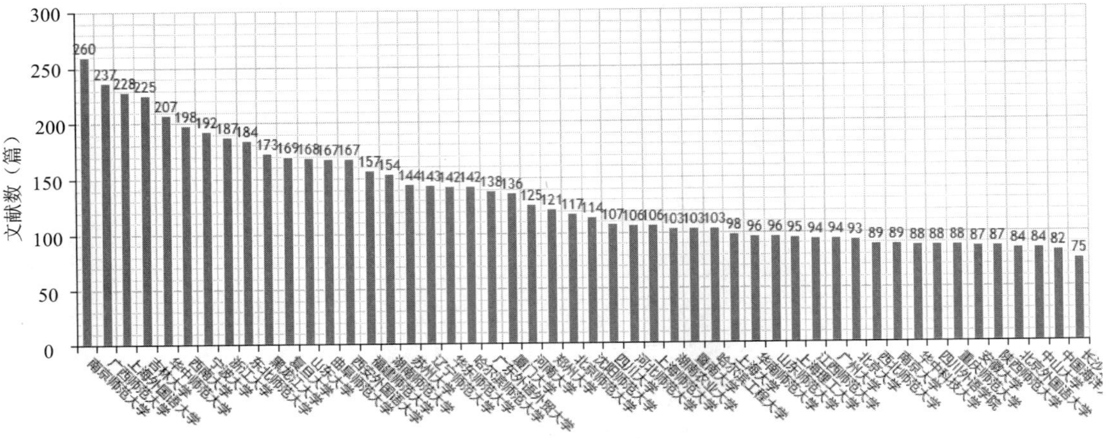

图 5　国内隐喻文献发表机构分布

4　国内隐喻研究可视化分析

因涉及论文数目众多，可视化分析工具处理速度受限，故而将其分为三个阶段以此进行关键词共现分析。

关键词是从论文的题名、摘要和正文中提取出来的，是对表述论文的中心内容有实质意义的词汇，是文献主旨内容的概括精炼，是考察文献核心观点的可信指标。关键词共现关系显示文献研究主题之间的密切联系，而关键词的集中出现能显示特定时期内的研究热点。通过分析国内隐喻文献关键词频次分布及其共现关系，可以客观反映该领域研究热点及其动态趋势。

第一阶段：1980-2000 年。此阶段综合了萌芽期和初步发展期两个时期，因其涉及的文献数量较少，故而将其统一分析。

在 CiteSpace 中设置节点类型为“Keywords”，每 3 年为一个时间分区，筛选每时间片出现频次最高的 30 个关键词，选择路径寻踪为简化网络结构的算法。由于使用了关键词显示的方法，最明显的关键词已经呈现在图中。图中的节点代表关键词，如图 6 所示，排名前五的关键词依次为喻体、小说、隐喻、军事术语、时间。由此可知，那一阶段的隐喻研究多是以文学作品为依托，军事术语方面的应用也十分突出，而纯正的语言学领域隐喻研究的影响力较小。

第二阶段：2001—2007 年，此阶段为成熟期。在 CiteSpace 中设置节点类型为“Keywords”，每 2 年为一个时间分区，筛选每时间片出现频次最高的 30 个关键词，选择路径寻踪为简化网络结构的算法。由于文献检索词是“隐喻”，因此隐喻作为最大的节点存在。如图 7 所示，排名前五的关键词分别是：概念隐喻、意象、词汇教学、隐喻翻译、思维方式。此阶段内，隐喻研究的视角拓展到认知与思维领域，翻译领域亦不断展现出隐喻研究的活力。同时，概念隐喻和语法隐喻作为隐喻研究的两大触角也在不断延伸发展。

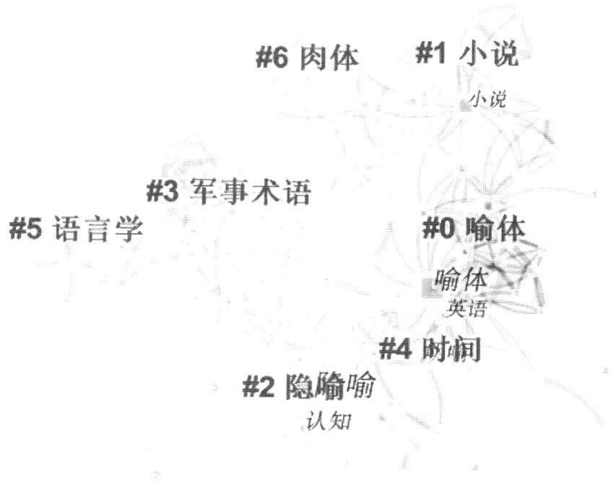

图 6　1980—2000 年文献关键词共现图谱

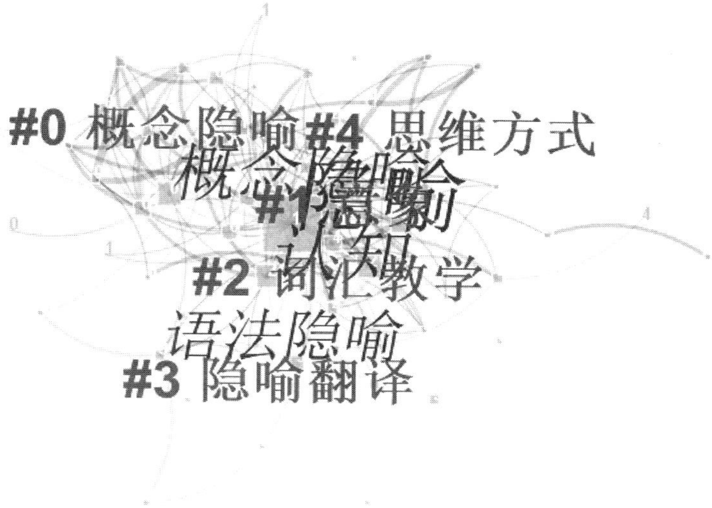

图 7　2001—2007 年文献关键词共现图谱

第三阶段：2008 年至今，此阶段是稳定发展期。在 CiteSpace 中设置节点类型为“Keywords”，每 3 年为一个时间分区，筛选每时间片出现频次最高的 30 个关键词，选择路径寻踪为简化网络结构的算法。如图 8 所示，隐喻研究将触角延伸到认知语言学和文化方面，并提出隐喻能力这一新的名词。除隐喻外，排名前五的关键词依次为空间隐喻、概念隐喻、转喻、语法隐喻以及隐喻思维。

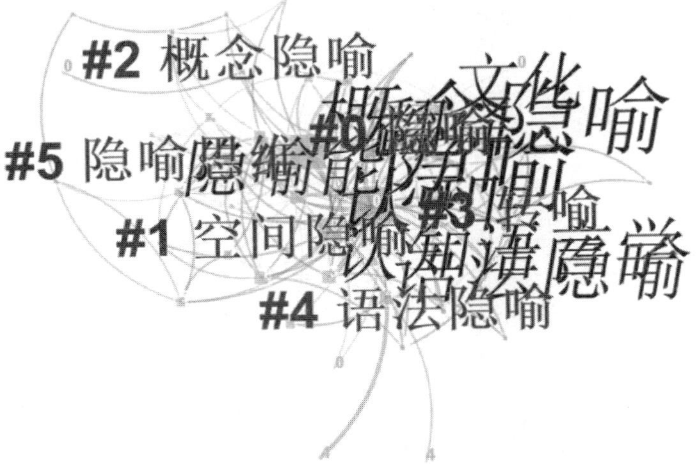

图 8　2008 年至今文献关键词共现图谱

4.1.1　研究热点

通过对上述三个发展阶段所呈现的关键词的归类分析，隐喻研究的热点可主要概括为以下几点。

（1）认知语言学视角方面的隐喻研究；

（2）概念隐喻的相关研究；

（3）空间隐喻的相关研究；

（4）语法隐喻的相关研究；

（5）转喻的相关研究；

（6）外语教学实践领域的隐喻研究；

（7）翻译领域的隐喻研究。

4.1.2　研究的发展趋势

从整体上来看，对概念隐喻、语法隐喻以及认知语言学的追求与研究始终占据国内隐喻研究的重要位置，可以推断它们是现今国内隐喻研究的核心话题。同时，国内隐喻研究呈现视角多样化的特征，认知语言学视角和哲学思维与隐喻研究日益密切，文献综述类文章数量逐渐增多，多模态研究也日渐壮大。虽然隐喻研究仍以定性研究为主，但数据分析等定量研究方法也在慢慢渗透到隐喻研究领域，如语料库隐喻研究等。定量研究方法对于国内隐喻研究而言，是不可或缺的研究工具。

5　结　　语

本文以 CNKI 数据库中，1980—2018 年收录的 19 340 篇隐喻研究文献为对象，首先用 Excel 对文献的时间序列分布、来源期刊、涉及领域、高产作者及机构等进行计量分析；在此基础上，运用可视化分析软件 CiteSpace 绘制出隐喻研究领域的关键词共现网络图谱，研究发现：

（1）国内隐喻研究成果在时间分布上总体呈增长趋势，共分为 4 个阶段：经历了 1980—1990 年萌芽期、1991—1999 年初步发展期以及 2000—2007 年成熟期后，自 2008 年起进入稳定发展期，年均发文1503篇，跨学科研究、应用研究不断深化；期刊和学科分布上，隐喻研究领域已经形成以专有期刊为引领的、稳定的核心期刊群，研究所涉及的学科领域多样化分布，呈现多学科交融发展态势，主要涉及新闻学、心理学、教育学、医学和语言文学等领域；高产作者和机构方面，国内隐喻领域核心作者分布较广，高产机构主要分布于东部院校，以南京师范大学、广西师范大学、上海外国语大学为主要代表。

（2）王炳社（渭南师范学院）、贾春华（北京中医药大学）、孙毅（西安外国语大学）、陈清（湖南第一师范学院）、谢世坚（广西师范大学）是国内隐喻研究领域发文位居前五的学者，但客观而言，他们在学术界的影响力并不显著，可见发文数量并不一定和学术影响力呈正比；相对而言，束定芳、王斌、胡壮麟等学者发文量虽然不是遥遥领先，但他们却是隐喻研究领域较有影响力的重要学者，他们关注、追踪隐喻的相关研究，并致力于隐喻研究的新视角。

（3）隐喻研究热点包括认知与文化、概念隐喻、空间隐喻、语法隐喻、转喻、语言学习与教学、哲学基础、语料库研究、多模态研究等。

参考文献

[1] Cameron，L. & R. Masle, 2010. *Metaphor Analysis*. London：Equinox.

[2] David，O.，G. Lakoff & E. Stickles, 2016. Cascades in metaphor and grammar：A case study of metaphors in the gun debate. *Constructions and Frames* 8（2）：214-253.

[3] Deignan，A.，J. Littlemore & E. Semino, 2013. *Figurative Language，Genre and Register*. Cambridge：Cambridge University Press.

[4] Domínguez，M. , 2016. The metaphorical new synthesis：Toward an eco-evolutionary theory of metaphors. *Metaphor and Symbol* 31（3）：148-162.

[5] Lakoff，G. & M. Johnson, 1980. *Metaphors We Live By*. Chicago：University of Chicago Press.

[6] 李杰，陈超美. CiteSpace：科技文本挖掘及可视化[M]. 北京：首都经济贸易大学出版社，2016.

[7] 林书武. 隐喻研究的基本现状、焦点及趋势[J]. 外国语，2002（1）：38-45.

[8] 刘启元，叶鹰. 文献题录信息挖掘技术方法及其软件 SATI 的实现——以中外图书情报学为例[J]. 信息资源管理学报，2012（1）：50-58.

[9] 石磊，刘振前. 隐喻能力研究：现状与问题[J]. 外国语，2010（3）：10-16.

[10] 束定芳. 论隐喻的本质及语义特征[J]. 外国语，1998（6）：11-20.

[11] 束定芳. 论隐喻的认知功能[J]. 外语研究，2001（2）：28-31.

[12] 束定芳. 隐喻和换喻的差别与联系[J]. 外国语，2004（3）：26-34.

[13] 孙亚，钱玉彬，马婷. 国外隐喻研究现状及发展趋势[J]. 现代外语，2017（5）：695-704.

[14] 王文斌. 再论隐喻中的相似性[J]. 四川外语学院学报，2006（2）：125-130.

[15] 王文斌. 隐喻性词义的生成和演变[J]. 外语与外语教学，2007（4）：13-17.

[16] 王寅. 隐喻认知理论的新发展——语言体验性论文之六：从神经学角度论证隐喻和语言的体验性[J]. 解放军外国语学院学报，2006（5）：1-5.

[17] 曾广，梁晓波. 国际期刊认知语言学论文可视化分析研究[J]. 外语教学，2017（6）：30-36.

[18] 张杰. 国内隐喻研究状况述评[J]. 西安文理学院学报（社会科学版），2010，13（1）：34-37.

[19] 张全生. 中国隐喻研究十年综述[J]. 新疆师范大学学报（哲学社会科学版），2004，25（3）：173-176.

[20] 钟兰凤，陈希卉. 隐喻识别研究现状述评[J]. 外语研究，2013（5）：40-44.

[21] 周运会，吴世雄. 国外语料库隐喻研究综述[J]. 外语学刊，2015（1）：72-78.

基于语料库的动词近义词辨析
——以“Doubt”和“Suspect”为例

宋艳梅

摘　要：近义词辨析一直是英语学习的重难点。传统的近义词辨析教学或是通过词典释义来进行，又或是依靠直觉经验、采用内省的定性方法。与之相比，语料库在近义词的辨析上有着不可比拟的优势。本文基于美国当代语料库（COCA）和英国国家语料库（BNC），分别从语域、类链接、搭配和语义韵四个方面，对易混淆的近义动词 doubt 和 suspect 进行了辨析。在得出结论的同时，本研究也论证了利用语料库辅助教学、学习难辨英语近义词的可行性和必要性，探讨了基于语料库的认知分析在该领域的可延展性，力图使得英语近义词教学更加行之有效。

关键词：近义词；语料库；“doubt”；“suspect”

Abstract: Synonym discrimination is consistently an important and difficult point in English learning. Compared with traditional methods that discriminates synonyms by dictionaries or by intuition from qualitative analysis, corpora are endowed with some incomparable advantages. Using the 560+ million-word Corpus of Contemporary American English (COCA) and the 100 million-word British National Corpus (BYU) as its data, this study examines the semantic and usage differences between “doubt” and “suspect”, two near-synonymous verbs notorious for their confusing usage patterns. The data analysis eventually yields an informative delineation of the synonym pair regarding their 1) use and frequency in different registers, 2) colligation, 3) collocation and 4) semantic prosody revealed by their occurrences in both COCA and BYU. Finally, the study also demonstrates the viability and necessity of using corpora to help teach and learn difficult-to-distinguish English synonymous words, and the possibility of a corpus-based cognitive analysis in this research field, to make language learning/teaching more engaging and effective.

Key words: Synonyms；corpus；“doubt”；“suspect”

1　Introduction

According to statistics, the number of near-synonyms[①] in English accounts for approximately 60% of the total vocabulary. (He, 2003) Synonymy is an important, but also intricate and challenging linguistic feature (Taylor 2002, Divjak, D. 2006, Liu, D., & Espino, M. 2012) : synonymy is

① Here, “near-synonymous” instead of “synonymous” is used because true synonyms are extremely rare unless cross-dialect synonyms are considered (Edmonds &Hirst, 2002; Liu, 2010; Taylor, 2002). In other words, all synonyms are really near-synonyms. For the sake of simplicity, however, I will use the term “synonym” in the rest of the paper.

important because it is ubiquitous and necessary for precise and effective communication. Yet, it is difficult because while synonyms convey essentially the same or nearly the same meaning, they are not completely and indiscriminately interchangeable because synonyms in a pair/set typically express the same concept in different manners, for different contexts, and/or from different perspectives. There are subtle nuances and variations in their meaning and usage. Added to the difficulty is the fact that often some L2 synonyms are not lexicalized or differentiated in learners' L1 (i.e., they are translated as the same word in their L1) . Consequently, how to help students learn the appropriate use of synonymous words has been a must and a great challenge for L2 teachers.

Traditionally, synonym discrimination mainly relies on dictionaries, intuitionistic experience and adopts introspective qualitative method. Definitions and examples from dictionaries are taken to illustrate shades of differences between synonyms. However, a lot of examples are collected by the lexicographers; they do not necessarily conform to the usage habits of native English. Even the specialized synonyms dictionaries, for example, Thesaurus, generally fail to provide a comprehensive description of these differences for students to distinguish synonyms. In brief, they are far from satisfactory. Compared with traditional methods, corpora are endowed with some incomparable advantages, providing a useful and necessary supplementation. By taking use of corpus' large volume, authentic materials, fast and convenient retrieval, the corpus-based synonym discrimination method can make an all-around description of synonyms.

2 Literature Review (selection of the words)

2.1 The unique nature of verbs: Reasons for studying synonymous verbs

Thanks to the advancements in corpus linguistics, there have been some corpus-based studies on synonymous words at home and abroad. They could be divided into four categories in terms of part of speech of their research objects:

（1）synonymous verbs: develop vs. improve vs. advance vs. enhance vs. progress, (Cui, 2007) wish vs. hope vs. want, (Lv, 2008) obtain vs. get vs. achieve vs. gain vs. acquire, (Yue, 2009; Wang, 2012) insist vs. persist, (Liu, 2010a) cause vs. generate, (Zhan & Zhang, 2011) demand vs. request vs. require, (Liu, D., 2013b) suspect vs. doubt, (Yang, 2014) learn vs. study, (Yang, 2015) confess vs. admit vs. acknowledge, (Feng & Wu, 2016) choose vs. Select, (Wu & Jiang, 2016) raise vs. rise ... (Jiang & Huang, 2018)

（2）synonymous nouns: convention vs. regulation, (Wang, 2012) event vs. affair, (Huo, 2013) authority vs. power vs. right, (Liu, D., 2013b) duty vs. obligation vs. responsibility ... (Liu D. &Zhong, 2016)

（3）synonymous adjectives: big vs. large vs. great, (Biber& Conrad, 2000) true vs. real, (Wang, 2009) chief vs. main vs. major vs. primary vs. principle, (Liu, D., 2010b) beautiful vs. pretty, (Wang, 2011) important vs. significant, (Liu, D., 2013b) confused vs. puzzled ... (Qing, 2017)

（4）synonymous adverbs: largely vs. broadly, (Tognini-Bonelli, 2001) almost vs. nearly, (Kjellmer, 2003) awfully vs. bitterly, (Yang, 2007) rather vs. quite, (Zhang, 2012) actually vs.

genuinely vs. really vs. truly, (Liu, D., 2012) erroneously vs. inaccurately vs. incorrectly vs. mistakenly ... (Liu, D., 2013b)

These studies have significantly enhanced our understanding of the synonyms examined and synonymy in general. All the foregoing research taken into consideration, one can easily observe that synonymous verbs have been mostly researched. But why? Verb has its unique nature: verbs instinctively represent different situation types: states, activity, accomplishment, semelfactive, achievement; (Smith 1991, cited in Saeed, 2003) verbs could be stative or dynamic; (durative/punctual or telic/atelic) tense and aspect makes verbs standout; verbs can be used differently to express different modality; a verb actually corresponds to an event frame ... (Wu & Xiao, 2016)

The reason for selecting "doubt" and "suspect"① (their verbal occurrences) for such a close analysis is threefold. Firstly, as mentioned, verb is one of the most common type of English synonymous research and the focus of most studies on the teaching of English synonyms. Secondly, "doubt" and "suspect" appear to be puzzling (even the writer herself may feel confounded and sometimes make mistakes) ; it is very interesting to know whether they are indeed interchangeable in meaning and usage. Thirdly, there is a paper about these two verbs, in which sense the differentiation between "doubt" and "suspect" worth exploring and can indeed reveal something.

2.2 Existing descriptions of the examined verbs

Regarding the meanings and usage of the two verbs of concern in this study, existing dictionaries offer some helpful information. In *Macmillan English Dictionary for Advanced Learners*, "doubt" is termed as "to think that something is probably not true or that it probably does not exist; to think that something is unlikely; to feel that you cannot trust or believe someone". Meanwhile, the dictionary defines "suspect" as meaning "to believe that something is true, especially something bad; used for stating an opinion to make it sound less direct ('I doubt') ". *Thesaurus* defines "doubt" as "lack confidence in; question", "suspect" as "distrust; guess". When it comes to their collocation, in *Oxford Collocations Dictionary for Students of English*, "doubt" is said to be used with "sceptic" as the subject, with "ability, accuracy, authenticity, correctness, feasibility, judgement, loyalty, truth ..." as the object; it is often modified by adverbs such as "highly (*esp.*AmE) , seriously, privately, very much". "suspect" is recorded to be used with "conspiracy, foul play, motive" as the object; it is often modified by adverbs such as "rightly, wrongly, strongly, rather, always, immediately".

While these descriptions offer us some valuable information about the complex semantic functions of the two verbs, they are inadequate in a few important ways: there aren't enough examples and no precise provenance; the explanations for their meaning and usage to some extent overlap; which one is more formal and frequently-used is unknown. While attempting to uncover all the missing information, the present study will also try to test many of the aforementioned existing descriptions of the two verbs.

---

① "doubt" and "suspect" in the present study are all searched and analyzed by their verbal occurrences in both COCA and BNC, all these ensured by retrieving [doubt].[v*] and [suspect].[v*] in the two corpora. So all "doubt" and "suspect" in the rest of the paper respectively represents "doubt (v.)" and "suspect (v.)".

3 Methodology

3.1 Corpus-used Method

In the literature, most scholars (Zhan & Zhang, 2011; Yang, 2014; Feng & Wu, 2016; Wu & Jiang, 2016; ...) used a single corpus to study synonym discrimination, and only a few to use two or more corpus. (Wang, 2009; Jiang & Huang, 2018) To this end, the present study draws on two corpora: the 560+ million-word Corpus of Contemporary American English (COCA) and the 100 million-word British National Corpus. (BYU)

3.2 Corpus query and analytical procedures

Zhang and Liu (2005) proposed that the corpus-based method of synonym discrimination includes the statistics of the word frequency distribution of synonyms in different registers; the span of the node word taken as the reference, the mutual information value (MI value) of the synonyms and their collocation words were calculated, thus its closely related lexical collocates (MI value > 3) can be found; (Yang, 2002) by observing and retrieving the collocations of synonyms in the concordance lines, one can also know the linguistic features such as colligation and semantic prosody of the research word. Following this train of thought and taking advantage of the versatile search functions of the COCA and BNC, this study differentiates "doubt" and "suspect" as regard to their 1) frequency in different registers, 2) colligation, 3) collocation and 4) semantic prosody. Furthermore, it is imperative to note that, in many cases, to truly understand the semantic differences between two synonyms, we will need to read and analyze the concordance lines of the result tokens (the actual sentences in which the synonym is used) , thus the writer also manually perused some of the tokens in context, making some "concordance contextual analysis" to ensure the accuracy of the analysis.

4 Results and Discussions

4.1 Frequency in different registers respectively in COCA and BNC

Register is a variety of a language used for a particular purpose or in a particular social setting. Its distribution reflects the use of words in the actual language environment. To understand the general usage patterns of the two verbs, the writer first queried COCA and BNC for the overall and cross-register frequency information for "doubt" and "suspect".

When comparing corpora of different volumes, the frequency (per million) is usually standardized. (Yang, 2015) According to the CHART function of COCA and BNC, "doubt" and "suspect" are input respectively, and word frequency distribution as shown in Table 1 is obtained.

Table 1 General overall and cross-register distributions* of "Doubt" and "Suspect"

	Doubt (v.)		Suspect (v.)	
Register	COCA	BNC	COCA	BNC
SPOKEN	21.73	7.33	43.38	17.16
FICTION	44.79	25.52	53.95	35.77
MAGAZINE	20.21	19.42	39.83	32.64
NEWSPAPER	21.86	23.50	35.38	31.72
ACEDEMIC	17.44	31.89	27.28	28.83
NON-ACAD	0	24.73	0	30.25
MISC	0	23.23	0	23.61
ALL	24.81	22.47	39.49	27.42

*: per million

The results (reported in Table 1) can be interpreted as follows:

In COCA (American English), "doubt" is often used in fictions, "suspect" in fictions and spoken English. They are not so often used in academic writing. And in each register, "suspect" is used more than "doubt";

In BNC (British English) , "doubt" is mostly used in academic writing, and "suspect" is often used (from high to low) in fictions, magazines and newspapers. It is important to note that "suspect" seldom occurs in spoken English, and "doubt" even much less.

On the whole, "suspect" is used more often than "doubt", either in American English or in British English. What needs more illustration is that in spoken English, fictions and magazines, both "doubt" and "suspect" are favored in American English than in British English.

Thus, by investigating the frequency of the distribution of synonyms in different registers, the principle of which word is preferential in a certain register can be found. And this is right beyond the reach of the traditional discrimination of synonyms that relies on the definitions or syntactic functions of synonymous words most of the time.

4.2 Colligation revealed by COCA and BNC

It is Firth (1957) who first proposed the concept of colligation and defined colligation as "the interrelation of grammatical categories in syntactical structure". According to him, colligation refers to the relations between words at the grammatical level, i.e. the relations of 'word and sentence classes or of similar categories' instead of 'between words as such'. Simply speaking, colligation is the collocation relation between words at syntactic or grammatical level, which is very essential for one to master the use of words, especially those synonymous ones that are nearly the same in their definitions and even their tie-in words. And the patterning with grammatical words, of course, can be observed and computed using a raw corpus.

To simplify the analysis of the present study, the author uses the KWIC function of COCA and BNC, extracts the first 100 concordance lines (100 in COCA, 100 in BNC) by random extraction, then calculates the percentage of each of them to represent the frequency one by one. The statistical colligation of "doubt" and "suspect" in COCA and BNC are shown in Table 2.

According to Table 2, we can see that when used as verb, "doubt" and "suspect" have little difference with respect to their colligation. "Doubt" can work with kinds of nouns, prepositions (about/as to), pronouns (it, sb., that, oneself), adverbs (seriously, very much) and subordinate clauses including those leaded by "if", "that", "whether". And in American English, under certain condition (1 out of 100), "doubt" is used solely as intransitive verb. As for "suspect", it can work with kinds of nouns, pronouns (it, sb., that, oneself), and subordinate clauses with some specific ones leaded by "that" (mostly) and "how" (rarely). Compared with "doubt", suspect" is more likely to be used as intransitive. In addition, "suspect" can draw forth "sb. of doing sth", while it not the case for "doubt".

Table 2　Colligation of "Doubt" and "Suspect"

Doubt (v.)			**Suspect (v.)**		
Colligation	Frequency		**Colligation**	frequency	
	COCA	BNC		COCA	BNC
doubt+n.	9	9	suspect+n.	10	14
doubt+prep.	2	0	suspect sb. of doing sth.	3	2
doubt+pron. (it, sb., that, oneself)	30	27	suspect+pron.	14	10
doubt+subordinate clause (normal clause, if-, that-, whether-)	52 (24+9+15+4)	56 (25+5+21+5)	suspect+subor-dinate clause (normal clause, that-, how-)	59 (31+27+1)	61 (28+33+0)
doubt+adv.	6	8			
doubt (vi. without prep.)	1	0	suspect (vi.)	14	13
All	100	100	All	100	100

By and large, "doubt" and "suspect", in most of the time (52%～61%), elicit subordinate clauses. And more importantly, "if-clause" and "whether-clause" are leaded by "doubt" rather than "suspect".

4.3　Collocation revealed by COCA and BNC

Since the two synonymous verbs have little difference concerning their colligation, differentiating them asks for a further understanding for their collocations. As Liu, D. (2013) has put it, despite its importance and intricacy, synonymy has not garnered the scholarly attention it deserves until the 1980s when experimental and corpus-based studies began yielding empirical evidence for the Firth/Halliday/Sinclair lexical semantic theory that the meaning of a word is largely shaped by its collocates, a theory arguably best articulated by Firth's (1957, p.11) now famous quote: we "know the word by the company it keeps".

The ability of COCA and BNC to generate both frequency and the mutual information (MI) for lexical collocates is especially helpful for a query of collocates of a word. MI (developed/introduced by Church & Hanks, 1990) is a statistical procedure that determines how likely two words may co-occur by comparing "the probability of observing x [word] and y [word] together (the joint probability) with the probabilities of observing x and y independently (chance) " (p. 23) . Also and importantly, when MI value is larger than three, the collocates can be acknowledged as a typical one, as we've mentioned before.

"To distinguish synonymous verbs often requires us to examine their typical object and subject collocates as well as their common modifying adverbs (Liu, D., 2013) ". Thus the collocation condition comparison of "doubt" and "suspect" is conducted from this three aspects by utilizing the COLLOCATES function.

Table 3 Ten most frequent object nouns of Doubt /Suspect in COCA (n+5)

Doubt			Suspect		
Object Noun	F*	MI	Object Noun	F*	MI
Ability (ies) **	0.25/0.07	4.09/4.95	*involvement****	0.13	4.09
*sincerity***	0.11	8.18	*murder****	0.11	3.07
*existence***	0.08	4.00	crimes	0.07	3.49
*wisdom***	0.07	4.50	terrorism/sts	0.07/0.06	3.34/3.71
*commitment***	0.06	3.30	*motive/s****	0.03/0.05	3.80/4.70
veracity	0.05	8.55	*fraud****	0.04	3.36
intentions	0.04	4.53	arson	0.04	6.22
*accuracy***	0.04	3.99	conspiracy	0.03	3.50
authenticity	0.03	5.48	wrongdoing	0.03	4.93
efficacy	0.03	4.47	theft	0.03	3.63

*Frequency (per million)

** An *italicized* word with one ** on the noun list of "doubt" also appears in that of "doubt" in BNC

*** An *italicized* word with one *** on the noun list of "suspect" also appears in that of "suspect" in BNC

Table 4 Ten most frequent object nouns of Doubt /Suspect in BNC (n+5)

Doubt			Suspect		
Object Noun	F*	MI	Object Noun	F*	MI
*ability***	0.49	4.94	*involvement****	0.20	4.60
validity	0.21	6.46	offence	0.15	4.35
*existence***	0.15	3.71	*motives****	0.10	5.63
*commitment***	0.14	3.82	*murder****	0.10	3.18
faith	0.13	3.85	foods	0.09	4.42
*sincerity***	0.09	7.44	abuse	0.09	3.65
*wisdom***	0.08	4.88	variability	0.08	6.59

（续表）

Doubt			Suspect		
Sanity	0.07	7.32	witchcraft	0.07	6.93
*accuracy***	0.07	4.55	bias	0.06	4.42
willingness	0.06	4.86	*fraud****	0.06	4.10

*Frequency (per million)

** An *italicized* word with one ** on the noun list of "doubt" also appears in that of "doubt" in COCA

*** An *italicized* word with one *** on the noun list of "suspect" also appears in that of "suspect" in COCA

Judged from Table 3 and Table 4, the most typical (top ten) object nouns of each verb are thus clearly observable. For "doubt", they are words like "ability, sincerity, existence, wisdom, commitment, accuracy, validity, authenticity, efficacy ... " that share some kind of good quality/trait. For "suspect", they are words "involvement, motives, murder, fraud, offense, crimes, conspiracy, theft ... " that are often deemed as wrongdoings, whether in American English or in British English.

In the same way, the writer summarized the typical subjects (n-1) of "doubt" and "suspect" as well as their common modifying adverbs (n-1/n+1) , and there are few differences detected. Usually the subjects of "doubt" are "people, sceptics, experts, observers, critics, officials, scholars, beholder, optimists ... " the subjects of "doubt""police, people, officials, critics, investigators, researchers, scientists, authorities ... " As for their common collocate adverbs, they can both be modified by various adverbs of degree (seriously, very, really, highly, strongly, somewhat ...) those of frequency (never, sometimes ...) those of emphasis (even, rather, still ...) and some other adverbs like "already, immediately, sincerely, initially, reasonably... " Exactly, those results high correspond to the ones displayed in 2.2, now we can say the entries in dictionaries are to some extent motivated.

4.4 Semantic prosody embedded

Semantic prosody is an important concept and, since Sinclair (1987) first noticed its existence in the collocational behaviors of lexical items, has become a primary research interest in corpus linguistics. It represents that words may habitually collocate with other words from a definable semantic set. Stubbs (1996) classified semantic prosody into three types: positive, negative and neutral/mixed prosody, and this categorization is widely admitted.

The introduction of this concept plays a good role in explaining the attitude marking function of synonyms. It can be identified by examining concordance lines for a pragmatic function or meaning that is spread across an extended unit of meaning.

As mentioned above (in the collocates part) , it is concluded that:

"Doubt" often co-occurs with words like "ability, sincerity, existence, wisdom, commitment, accuracy, validity, authenticity, efficacy ... " that share some kind of good quality/trait. All these words have positive colors, and taking the fact that "doubt" is often used in negative sentences into consideration, we can easily draw the conclusion: doubt is often used in the context to express "something having positive sense is not doubted", so the word has a positive semantic prosody.

"Suspect", however, often appears together with words like "involvement, motives, murder, fraud, offense, crimes, conspiracy, theft ... " that are often deemed as wrongdoings. They "diffuse" a kind of "violent crime" atmosphere, making "suspect" have negative semantic prosody. Even the more neutral collocations, such as "food" and "involvement", are found to be stained with negative meanings. Take the following concordance lines as examples:

"Keeping a food diary can be helpful in identifying potential headache triggers. Once you suspect a food may be to blame, try eliminating it from your diet and see." (COCA)

"# SUSPECT FOODS Any foods that you suspect are causing problems during the course of Stage II." (BNC)

"There was genuine cause to suspect his involvement in the drug traffic, any actual proof of which would help justify." (COCA)

"He suspects our involvement with the rebel militia. He knows we will not cower and hide." (BNC)

5 Conclusions and Future Work

Using the query functions offered by COCA and BNC plus some manual checking and tabulation of the results, the present study yields an informative delineation of the synonymous verb "doubt" and "suspect" regarding their 1) use and frequency in different registers, 2) colligation, 3) collocation and 4) semantic prosody revealed by their occurrences. The above data analyses have elucidated many of the fine-grained semantic and usage differences of the two examined verbs:

（1）By investigating the frequency of the distribution of synonyms in different registers, we can sum up the principles of which word is preferential in a certain register. The present study suggests that in American English, "doubt" is often used in fictions, "suspect" in fictions and spoken English. In British English, "doubt" is mostly used in academic writing, and "suspect" is often used in fictions, magazines and newspapers. On the whole, "suspect" is used more often than "doubt", either in American English or in British English. In spoken English, fictions and magazines, both "doubt" and "suspect" are favored in American English than in British English.

（2）By summarizing use patterns of synonyms, we can know their colligation association with other words at syntactic or grammatical level. "Doubt" and "suspect", in most of the time, elicit subordinate clauses, with "if-clause" and "whether-clause" often leaded by "doubt" rather than "suspect".

（3）By calculating the collocability (MI value) between synonyms and their different collocations, we can conclude their collocation behavior in practical language use. The most typical object nouns of "doubt" and "suspect" differ. For "doubt", they are words like "ability, sincerity, existence, wisdom, commitment, accuracy, validity, authenticity, efficacy ... " that share some kind of good quality/trait. For "suspect", they are words "involvement, motives, murder, fraud, offense, crimes, conspiracy, theft ... " that are often deemed as wrongdoings, whether in American English or in British English. But their subject collocates as well as their common modifying adverbs are nearly the same.

（4）By analyzing concordance lines of the synonyms about their semantic prosody, we can sense their positive/negative/neutral attitudes that are displayed in the context of collocation. “Doubt” often has a positive semantic prosody, while “suspect” often a negative semantic prosody.

In a nutshell, these important fine-grained semantic/usage differences uncovered in this study test many existing reference books’ descriptions of the synonymous pair, but also highlight some noticeable deficiencies. Of course, more work in this area is still needed. And corpus, as a burgeoning research resource and platform, has already had a profound effect on the development of the various ramifications of the linguistic research. It is necessary to use corpora to help teach and learn difficult-to-distinguish English synonymous words. And in recent years, Liu, D. (2010a, 2010b, 2012, 2013a, 2016) has strongly appealed to conduct language research by combining Cognitive and Corpus Linguistic Approaches; also, Wu and Xiao (2016) made a corpus-based cognitive analysis of English synonymous verbs and worked out its discrimination mechanism. All these pioneering papers are promising and worthy efforts in our quest for more valid and informative research findings and more engaging and effective language teaching and learning.

参考文献

[1] Biber, D., & Conrad, S, 2000. Corpus Linguistics. Cambridge: Cambridge University Press.

[2] W. Church, & P. Hanks, 1990. Word association norms, mutual information, and lexicography, Computational Linguistics, 16: 22-29.

[3] Divjak D. , 2006. Ways of intending: delineating and structuring near-synonyms[M]. Mouton de Gruyter.

[4] Edmonds, P., &Hirst, G. , 2002. “Near synonyms and lexical choice.”Computational Linguistics, 28（2）: 105-144.

[5] Firth, J. R. , 1957. Papers in Linguistics, 1931-1951. New York: Oxford University Press.

[6] John I. Saeed, 2003. Semantics (2nd ed)[M]. Blackwell Publishing Ltd.

[7] Kjellmer, G., 2003. Synonymy and corpus work: on almost and nearly. ICAME, 27: 19-27.

[8] Liu, D. , 2010a. Going beyond patterns: Involving cognitive analysis in the learning of collocations. TESOL Quarterly, 44: 4-30.

[9] Liu, D. , 2010b. Is it a chief, main, major, primary, or principal concern: A corpus-based behavioral profle study of the near-synonyms. International Journal of Corpus Linguistics, 15（1）: 56-87.

[10] Liu, D. , 2012. Combining cognitive and corpus linguistic approaches in language research and teaching: Theoretical grounding, practices, and challenges. Contemporary Foreign Languages Studies, 12: 18-33.

[11] Liu, D. , 2013a. Describing and explaining grammar and vocabulary: Key theories and effective practices. New York: Rortledge.

[12] Liu, D. , 2013b. Using corpora to help teach difficult-to-distinguish English words. English Teaching, 68（3）: 27-50.

[13] Liu, D., & Espino, M., 2012. “Actually, Genuinely, Really, and Truly: A corpus-based Behavioral Profle study of near-synonymous adverbs” International Journal of Corpus Linguistics, 17（2）: 198-228.

[14] Liu D., & Zhong S., 2016. L2 vs. L1 Use of Synonymy: An Empirical Study of Synonym Use/Acquisition[J]. Applied Linguistics, 37（2）: 239-261.

[15] Sinclair, J. , 1987. Looking up. London and Glasgow: Willian Collins.

[16] Smith, Carlotta S. , 1991. The Parameter of Aspect. Dordrecht: Kluwer.

[17] Stubbs, M. , 1996. Text and Corpus Linguistics [M]. Oxford: Blackwell Publishers.

[18] Taylor, J. R. 2002. “Near Synonyms as Co-extensive Categories: ‘High’ and ‘tall’ revisited”. Language Sciences, 25（3）：263-284.

[19] Tognini-Bonelli, E. , 2001. Corpus Linguistics at Work. Amsterdam: John Benjamins.

[20] 崔薇. 基于语料库的近义词辨析——对 develop、improve、advance、enhance 和 progress 的对比研究[J]. 新乡师范高等专科学校学报，2007（4）：104-107.

[21] 冯恩玉，吴蕾. 基于 COCA 语料库的英语近义词差异性研究——以 confess 等近义词为例[J]. 西安航空学院学报，2016，34（2）：25-28+59.

[22] 贺晓东. 英汉双解英语同义词典[M]. 北京：商务印书馆，2003.

[23] 霍艳娟. 基于 BNC 语料库的近义词用法对比研究——以“event”和“affair”为例[J]. 长春大学学报，2013，23（10）：1334-1337.

[24] 姜敏，黄蕾. 基于 COCA、BNC 语料库的近义词辨析——以 raise 和 rise 为例[J]. 长春教育学院学报，2018，34（6）：39-41+46.

[25] 刘丹丹. 基于语料库数据的近义词辨析——以 insist 和 persist 为例[J]. 湖北广播电视大学学报，2010，30（5）：103-104.

[26] 吕俊梅. 中国学生的英语同义词使用研究——基于语料库的方法[J]. 四川教育学院学报，2008，24（11）：75-80.

[27] 卿尧. 基于 COCA 语料库的英语同义词辨析——以 Confused 和 Puzzled 为例[J]. 才智，2017（24）：208.

[28] 王春玲. 对近义词 beautiful 和 pretty 的区分讨论——一项基于 Brown 和 CLEC 语料库的对比研究[A]. . 语言与文化研究（第八辑），2011：6.

[29] 王春艳. 基于语料库的中国学习者英语近义词区分探讨[J]. 外语与外语教学，2009（6）：27-31.

[30] 王大鹏. 基于 COCA 语料库的英语同义词辨析——以 obtain 等同义词为例[J]. 渤海大学学报（哲学社会科学版），2013，35（1）：72-74.

[31] 王静. 基于语料库的“convention”和“regulation”近义词对比研究[J]. 辽宁工程技术大学学报（社会科学版），2012，14（6）：633-636.

[32] 汪兴富，Mark Davies，刘国辉. 美国当代英语语料库（COCA）——英语教学与研究的良好平台[J]. 外语电化教学，2008（5）：27-33.

[33] 吴琳，蒋虹. 基于 COCA 语料库的近义词辨析——以 choose 和 select 为例[J]. 湖南工业职业技术学院学报，2016，16（6）：93-97.

[34] 吴小芳，肖坤学. 基于语料库的英语动词近义词辨析的认知语言学研究[J]. 外语研究，2016，33（5）：46-51.

[35] 杨春霞. 基于语料库的近义词辨析研究——以 suspect 和 doubt 为例[J]. 西南科技大学学报（哲学社会科学版），2014，31（5）：45-49+86.

[36] 杨惠丽. 基于 COCA、BNC 和 CLEC 语料库辨析同义词——以 learn 与 study 为例[J]. 洛阳师范学院学报，2015，34（7）：112-116.

[37] 杨惠中. 语料库语言学导论[M]. 上海：上海外语教育出版社，2002：112-117.

[38] 杨元媛. 基于语料库的 awfully 和 bitterly 两词用法研究[J]. 宁波教育学院学报，2007（6）：56-61.

[39] 岳迎光. 关于中国大学生同义词使用情况的研究[D]. 大连海事大学，2009.

[40] 张传琪. 基于语料库的近义词 rather 和 quite 使用研究[D]. 山东财经大学，2012.

[41] 张继东，刘萍. 基于语料库同义词辨析的一般方法[J]. 解放军外国语学院学报，2005（6）：53-56+100.

[42] 展雪梅，张发祥. 基于语料库近义词辨析：以动词 cause 和 generate 为例[J]. 黑龙江教育学院学报，2011，30（11）：148-151.

从合作原则的角度来研究小说《大饭店》的会话含义

王　筝

摘　要：此论文是对英国加拿大籍小说家阿瑟·黑利的作品《大饭店》的研究。阿瑟的小说情节以各种各样的工业为背景。《大饭店》是其最成功的作品之一，其中描述了在新奥尔良一家奢侈的格雷戈里饭店中的职员和房客在五天内所发生的事情。《大饭店》通过紧凑连贯的故事情节向我们展现了格雷戈里饭店中所发生的几个故事，尤其是饭店侦探奥格尔维勒索的情节。本论文基于格里斯的合作原则，从语言学角度对《大饭店》的会话含义进行详细分析。通过个案研究，尽力找出违反合作原则会话的真正意图。通过回顾国内外对于合作原则和小说《大饭店》的研究，论文论证从违反合作原则的角度来研究会话含义。小说通过对语言以及会话含义分析每个人物的性格特征表现得淋漓尽致。例如，奥格尔维的自大，狡猾和贪婪被清晰地刻画出来，这也说明为什么人们要违反合作原则，以便大家更好地理解《大饭店》中的每一个人物。

关键词：合作原则；会话含义；《大饭店》；性格特征

Abstract：This thesis studies on *Hotel* which was written by a British-Canadian novelist—Arthur Hailey whose plot-driven story lines were set against the backdrops of various industries. *Hotel* was the most successful writing of Authur Hailey which followed five days in the lives of employees and residents of New Orleans' luxurious St. Gregory hotel. It characterizes with continuous and compact plots，which shows us several stories happened in the St. Gregory hotel，especially the blackmail done by Ogilvie，a detective of this hotel. Based on the theory of Grice's cooperative principle，this essay will make an elaborate analysis of the conversational implicature of *Hotel* from the perspective of pragmatics. With the method of case study，this thesis is trying to find the real intentions of the conversations by violating the maxims of cooperative principle，and thus provides a new angle for the study of utterances. This paper reviews the research of cooperative principle and this novel both at home and abroad，then it proves the availability of analyzing the conversational implicature from violating the cooperative principle. The language selection and and conversational implicature of this masterpiece completely shows the characteristics of every person in it，such as how arrogant，tricky and greedy Ogilvie is，and the reason why they violate this theory，so as to make a better understanding of the characters in *Hotel*.

Key words：Cooperative principle；conversational implicature；*Hotel*；characteristics

1　Introduction

Arthur Hailey was born in England in 1920，and then moved to Canada in 1947. His works have been translated into 38languages，among which，*Hotel* was a masterpiece published in 1965. It talks about the management of the St. Gregory hotel during five days. *Hotel* is mainly made up by short or long conversations implying the characteristics of speakers, which can be analyzed by cooperative principle through the perspective of pragmatics. This novel is not long, but Arthur Hailey uses short and precise sentences to show us vivid and graphic figures, such as the manager Peter McDermott, the proprietor Warren Trent, the Duke and Duchess of Croydon and the house detective Ogilvie and so on. From the beginning to the end, *Hotel* is filled with a sense of nervousness. In the beginning, it shows that the St. Gregory hotel maybe took over by others due to financial crisis, therefore, people from manager to cleaner are facing with the choice of exist and work. Except for the staff in the St. Gregory hotel, the novel mainly centers on the action of the house guests. The Duke and Duchess of Croydon are the guests in the presidential suite who killed a child by driving, and they were blackmailed by the house detective Ogilvie. The conflict between them is the highlight of *Hotel*. Christine Francis is the secretary of Warren Trent who is warm-hearted and judicious, and her relationship with the manager Peter McDermott adds the romantic feeling to this novel.

Hotel is worthy of study because many topics are involved, of which the conversational implicature and the characteristics of the characters are mostly studied. This thesis aims to study the conversational implicature in *Hotel* through the perspective of Grice's cooperative principle. In order to attain the goal, the author is going to explain the theory of the cooperative principle and analyze the violation of it to find out the conversational implicature of every conversation, which can help us make a better understanding of this novel.

2 Theoretical Framework

This chapter aims to introduce the theories applied in the paper, those are the definition of conversational implicature and the classification of cooperative principle.

Conversational Implicature

The theory of conversational implicature was first raised by Grice in 1967 in the William James Lectures at Harvard University. Grice thinks that when the meaning of words cannot be interpreted by logic semantics, then the implied meaning will be required for a better understanding of the words. There are not only one types of implied meanings, and the most popular one is conversational implicature. Conversational implicature reveals that the conversation that one expresses may not be the real intention of the speaker, therefore, the actual intention of the speaker may be misunderstood or misinterpreted by the hearer. Conversational implicature is obviously an implicit speech act rather than a direct speech act. Specifically, the meaning of conversational implicature refers to what is intended by a speaker's utterance, which is not entirely what is said, this is also called implicature in pragmatics. Thus, it is necessary for us to figure out the difference between literal meaning and the actual meaning. That is what is said and what is implicated. The most important point made by Grice about the theory of conversational implicature is the distinction between what is said and what is implicated. As for what is said, it means that the speaker provides the utterances without any considerations of circumstantial factors, which can be understood in accordance with its original meaning or sentence meaning. When it comes to what is implicated, it means that the expressions carries more meaning than its original meaning, and take a lot of circumstantial factors into consideration.

Here are two examples to show what is said and what is implicated:

Example1:

A: What day is it?

B: It's Friday.

From this example, we can see that B provides enough and concise information that A requires. "It's Friday." is what is said by B without any special implicature or any considerations of circumstantial factors. People cannot analyze anything such like B's mood or circumstance by this accurate and actual reply.

Example2:

A: Do you know where your mom is?

B: She is not at home.

Here B does not give a definite answer for A's question, namely, B does not supply enough information for A's question but only a vague reply. What is said by B is only "She is not at home.", but what is implicated by B is that her\his mom is at somewhere else. Thus, this essay is able to deduce that the external factors which lead to giving vague answers must be B is unwilling to tell A where is her\his mom is or he\she has no idea where her/his mom actually is.

In a nutshell, Grice analyzes the implicature of the conversation with a brand new method, which is integrating the meaning of people's intention into the analysis of implicature, and thus finds a new way to understand the intended meaning. The theory of conversational implicature has turned to an important part of pragmatics. And it is applied in analyzing our daily conversations more often.

The Cooperative Principle and Four Categories

In 1975, the language philosopher H. P. Grice published a seminal article entitled "The Cooperative Principle" which created quite a stir in the linguistic world and generated a large number of linguistic publications that are built on Grice's postulates. According to Grice, in conversational exchange, people usually try to reach a common goal by mutual efforts or at least make the conversation develop in the direction of their expectation. To achieve this, people need to cooperate with each other. Grice' theory of the cooperative principle explains how it is possible for the speaker to convey more than what is literally said and force the hearer to understand. In short, as Grice put it for the cooperative principle, "make your conversational contribution such as is required, at the stage at which it occurs, by the accepted purpose or direction of the talk exchange in which you are engaged". (Hu Zhuanglin, 2001) Though phrased as a prescriptive command, the principle is intended as a description of how people normally behave in conversation. Put more simply, people who obey the cooperative principle in their language use will make sure that what they say in a conversation furthers the purpose of that conversation. Obviously, the requirements of different types of conversations will be different. Grice put forward four maxims of cooperative principle, which are the maxim of quantity, the maxim of quality, the maxim of relation and the maxim of manner. In other words, these four maxims guarantee that communications are able to be smoothly performed.

Since Grice put forward the cooperative principle, it has been applied to many fields. Foreign scholars apply the theory to different areas. The most effective one is from the field of education; they apply the cooperative principle to analyze the class rules. Edwards and Mercer (1987, P18) explain Questions &answers in the class based on the cooperative principle. Kleifgen (1900) finds that Grice's cooperative principle is pretty useful in understanding the game rules among children. When the children violate the maxim of quality, she gets the core rule of the game, which creates a sense of humor. Her theory of "pre-determined point" plays a vital and substantial part in teaching strategy, which is able to help teachers judge how much the children understand and when we should deliver the knowledge. In addition, the cooperative principle is used to analyze cross-culture communication and the difference between male and female.

Since1979, Sperber and Wilson began to publish a series of essays and then put forward the theory of relevance. The key of the theory of relevance is the maxim of correlation, namely, every word should be envisaged as behavior and has the optimal relevance. This theory is actually an amplification and development of the maxim of relation in the cooperative principle. The "three principle" of conversation is raised by Levinson in 1987. It is the core of "new Grice's theory of conversational implicature", which includes Q-Principle, I-Principle and M-Principle three principles. This theory can also be regarded as a complement to the maxim of quantity in the cooperative principle. Then, Leech raised the polite principle which is also a complement of cooperative principle. The principle of politeness consists of six main criteria, they are the tacit maxim, generosity maxim, approbation maxim, modesty maxim, agreement maxim and sympathy maxim. (Leech, 1983)

The Cooperative principle has four maxims; they are the maxim of Quantity, the maxim of Quality, the maxim of Manner and the maxim of Relation. (Hu Zhuanglin. 2001)

The maxim of quantity

The maxim of quantity requires the participants to make their words conform to the degree of required information. In other words, both sides should provide sufficient information as is required from the current situation. Generally, both the speaker and the hearer in a conversation should possess the attitude of cooperation and offer the information as is required in order to make the conversation goes smoothly. However, in some cases, speakers will violate the cooperative principle to achieve some purposes. The maxim of quantity has two sub-maxims that require the cooperative speaker to say as much as but no more than is required for his particular purposes in the talk exchange, the two sub-maxims are: (1) understatement: to provide less information than required. (2) Overstatement: to provide more information than required. Then, the author will show three examples among which the first one without violating the maxim of quantity, and the other two violating the maxim of quantity. (Song Xiaodi, 2017)

Example 1:

A: Do you know where Rose is?

B: Yes.

A: Where is she?

B: She is in the classroom.

This conversation obviously happens in the school. Student A is asking whether student B knows where is Rose. Student B's response is satisfactory, because student B provides adequate information not more or less. And the implicature student B wants to express is general. Student B may observe the principle strictly out of the following two reasons: on the one hand, student A may has something important to tell Rose and he is in a hurry, therefore, student B answers quickly without hesitation; on the other hand, student B is a kind person, so he would like to help others like student A.

Example 2:

In a bus station, a person forgot wearing his watch, and he is in a hurry for the exact time of the next bus, so he asks a woman near him,

Man: Excuse me, would you mind telling me what time is it?

Woman: nearly 5 o'clock.

The woman does not offer adequate information but only a rough time. Maybe she thinks a rough time is enough for the man, or she does not like the man who is nearing her or some other reasons we cannot guess without any circumstance factors. Anyway, she just gives a rough time to the man and violates the rule of maxim of quantity on purpose or not, but the man would be confused. Thus, this is a typical example of understatement.

Example 3:

A: Which one is your favorite book?

B: *Hotel* is my favorite book. It costs me nearly one week to read it, and I do believe Arthur Hailey is a fabulous writer because he can apply the short sentences and easy words to illustrate fascinating stories. I like his writing style.

In example3, A's question is only "Which one is your favorite book?" B can just answer with the book he likes best. But he provides lots of information more than this to explain his emotions. B provides overstatements implicates that he intends to emphasize that he likes this book very much as well as its writer. Therefore, B provides more information than that is required, and he violates the maxim of quantity.

The maxim of quality

The maxim of quality also has two sub-maxims, which demands that the speaker say only what he believes to be true and for which he has sufficient evidence. However, in some cases, people are inclined to violate this maxim by this or that reason, in which must contain some special conversational implicature. Let's look at the examples listed below.

Example 4:

In a very noisy classroom, a teacher speaks to the students: please be quiet, you are breaking my nerves.

In this example, the teacher intends to get these students quiet and she uses a metaphor to emphasize that their voices are too high. But we know it is possible to break the nerves, therefore, it is just a metaphor and not the truth. The teacher violates the maxim of quality by exaggerating the truth to blame the students, which shows her way of speaking. The conversational implicature here is "I cannot stand you any more, can you behave yourselves".

The maxim of relation

The maxim of relation urges the speaker to make his contribution relevant to the communication context. This principle demands both sides in a conversation to obey the cooperative principle and to express the things related to the ongoing conversation to make the dialogue go smoothly. However, people often violate the maxim of relation to convey their implicature in daily conversations.

Example 5:

Mary: Do you want to go out with us today?

Jack: I have to finish my homework.

In this conversation, it is obviously that Jack does not answer Mary's question and he does not want to answer it, so he changes the topic to unrelated things. So the implicature here is that Jack does not want to go out today with Mary.

The maxim of manner

The maxim of manner requires the speaker to be methodical and to avoid ambiguity, prolixity, and obscurity. It requires that the speaker should provide concise and systematic information in a conversation. The maxim of manner is about the manner of expression. The general request is that the expression should be clear and specific. In daily life, people tend to apply obscure, ambiguous or prolix utterances to generate implicature for their purposes.

Example 6:

Wife: What should we buy for children?

Husband: Except I-C-E-C-R-E-A-M.

From this conversation, we can see the husband uses the letters to avoid children understanding what they are talking about. This sentence violates the maxim of manner, because it is too prolix.

The Cooperative Principle and Conversational Implicature

The cooperative principle defined by Grice is: once we begin to have a conversation, we will follow the principle of cooperation without realizing it- we will cooperate to achieve mutual conversational ends. This cooperation even works when we are in a conversation that does not need cooperation. For example, we can argue with one another fiercely, and at the same time we still comply with the principle a lot to achieve the argument goal. This principle is juat a set of hypothetical theory, which conveys one idea that if the speakers want to understand each other better, they need to follow the cooperative principle in the course of a conversation.

However in the actual conversational environment, this principle is hardly obeyed totally, people are inclined to break this principle or it's sub-principle to convey a potential intentions. Grice (1975) considers there are two approaches to generate the conversational implicature: one is that the communicators conduct the conversations by adhering to the principles of cooperation and its maxims strictly, in this process some general conversational implicature will be generated; another one is that the communicators proceed the conversations on the basis of the principles of cooperation, but at the same time, they purposely violate some of the principles to convey conversational implicature and to express their mood, just like humor, irony, score, disdain on something else.

3 Research Methodology and Research Procedure

This chapter mainly introduces the methodology to be applied for the analysis of the conversational implicature in *Hotel*. It shows how the data collected first of all, and then presents what procedures are included in the analysis of the conversational implications. Finally, this part goes like this step by step and achieves the goal.

Thesis Statement

Based on the theory of cooperative principle, the thesis aims to prove the availability of analyzing the conversational implicature of utterances in *Hotel* from the violation of cooperative principle. In this way, we can have a better understanding of this novel as well as the theory of cooperative principle which benefits to our daily conversations.

Data Collection

The data collection in *Hotel* is collected in the following steps. First and foremost, all the conversations are identified and there are 118 conversations altogether; then the author examines them carefully to exclude those without violations of the cooperative principle to obtain 32 conversations with violations. Therefore, these 32 conversations are the targets we are going to make a analysis. The next step is to classify the conversations which violate the cooperative principle into four different categories according to each of the four maxims. The last step which is also the most important step, is to analyze the 32 conversations which violate the cooperative principle in order to identify what kind of conversational implicature will be expressed by violating different maxims of the cooperative principle, namely, the violation of the maxim of quality, the violation of the maxim of quantity, the violation of the maxim of relation and the violation of the maxim of manner. They can all illustrate how the characters violate the principle of cooperation and generate conversational implicature. In addition, based on the analysis, we are able to get to know what kinds of people intend to violate the cooperative principle and what their characteristics are. Therefore, we are able to make a better understanding of the characters as well as this novel.

Research Procedures

Qualitative research is the main approach to this study. *Hotel* is a novel which is not long, so the qualitative research is suitable and available for this study to collect data and information.

This thesis attempts to adopt the cooperative principle and its four maxims to analyze the conversational implicature of these 32 conversations in which the characters intend to violate one or two of the four maxims deliberately. Then the same procedures will be followed in the analysis of the 32 conversations chosen from the dialogues in *Hotel* and they will be analyzed one by one in order to find out the real purposes hidden behind the words.

The conversational implicature include four categories according to the cooperative principle, and it will be analyzed according to three steps as follows: the thesis will analyze the superficial conversational meaning at first, then based on which maxim it violates, the example will be categorized into four types, the violation of the maxim of quality, the violation of the maxim of quantity, the violation of the maxim of relation and the violation of the maxim of manner. In the final step, the thesis will analyze the conversational implicature of each example according to the maxim it violates.

4 Analysis of the Violation of the Cooperative Principle in *Hotel*

This chapter plans to analyze the conversational implicature in details by violating the cooperative principle. First and foremost, the thesis will introduce the overall situation of the violations of the cooperative principle in *Hotel* and then detailed analysis of the conversational implicature in the examples is presented. It concludes with the brief summary of the characters that are more inclined to violate the cooperative principle and what conversational implicature are conveyed.

Violation of the Cooperative Principle in *Hotel*

In *Hotel*, there are various conversations happening among all kinds of people, and these conversations provide adequate research data for language study. This thesis attempts to calculate the total number of the conversations happening in this novel firstly, and then to make out among all the conversations, how many of them violate the cooperative principle. At last, this thesis will analyze the 18 chosen conversations which violate the principle of cooperation. Of course, they will be classified into the four maxims of the cooperative principle they are violating, which are the maxim of quality, quantity, relation and manner. The author has done a calculation as follows.

Table　Violation of the maxims of CP

	Violation of the maxim of quantity	Violation of the maxim of quality	Violation of the maxim of relation	Violation of the maxim of manner
Times	11	11	7	5
Percentage	32%	32%	21%	15%

From the above table, we can see that the number of the violations of the maxim of quality and quantity are relatively higher than the other two and account for a large proportion. This indicates that in *Hotel*, the characters are more inclined to violate these two maxims. This thesis is going to analyze the conversations which are violating the cooperative principle one by one. In addition, the thesis will talk about the conversation according to the sequence of the violation of the maxim of quality, the violation of the maxim of quantity, the violation of the maxim of relation and the violation of the maxim of manner.

Violation of the Maxim of Quantity

People often say more or less information than that is required in order to express their conversational implicature, and in these cases, they will violate the maxim of quantity. Moreover, the maxim of quantity can be divided into two types: overstatement (more information) and understatement (less information). (Hu Zhuanglin, 2001)

Overstatement: it refers to the speaker tells more information than that is required.

There are some examples in Hotel that offer more information than that is needed in order to convey characters' intentions. From these cases, we can know more about the characteristics of the characters.

Example 1：

> Mr. Wells: "You can get one for me，can't you，Miss"?
>
> Christine: "Well, yes, I suppose so". Christine wondered if Mr Wells could afford the cost of a nurse. He was a humble man and he did not appear to have much money.
>
> （Arthur Hailey，1997：23）

This conversation happens in the room of Mr. Well's. Mr. Well was ill，as a staff of the hotel; Christine cared about the situation of him. In this conversation，we can see that Mr. Well asks Christine to look for a nurse to look after him. Looking for a nurse is easy for Christine，but she offer more information that is "I suppose so"，the reason why she adds more information than that is needed，because she thinks Mr. Well does not have the money to employ a nurse. So she violates the maxim of quantity to express her doubt of the power of Mr. Well.

Example 2：

> Marsha looked worried. "You won't tell my father，will you？"
>
> "No one will tell him，" Peter promised her.
>
> （Arthur Hailey，1997：53）

This conversation happens after Marsha was insulted by four young men. She asks Peter not to tell this to her father. Peter answers "No one will tell him"，here "no one" violates the maxim of quantity，because Peter tells more information than that is required. Marsha just asks him not tell her father，but Peter says no one will tell him. The conversational implicature is that don't worry any more，her father won't know this thing. From here we can see Peter is a warm man who is good at comforting others.

Example 3：

> The Duchess's lips tightened，"You have not come here to discuss our rooms."
>
> The fat man laughed piddly. "No. You are right. But I like nice things." He paused. "I like your car—the one in the hotel garage，" he said. "It's a Jaguar，isn't it？"
>
> （Arthur Hailey，1997：69）

This conversation happens in the presidential suite of the Duchess and the Duke. From the answer of Ogilvie we can see that he offers much more information than that is needed. The Duchess's question is only he does not come here only for their rooms. The first sentence of Ogilvie's response is enough，but he adds the next sentences which are not required. Therefore，Ogilvie violates the maxim of quantity on purpose. The detective directly answers that he comes here not only for talking about the rooms，but he also not make clear why he come here，instead， he talks about the car which implies the accident. The excessive information is used to lay a foundation for his blackmail. From here we can see Ogilvie is crafty and cunning guy.

Example 4:

> "How do you know this?" the Duke asked in a trembling voice.
>
> "I've been in this town a long time," Ogilvie told him. "I've got a lot of friends. I help them and they help me. They tell me everything of importance that happens in this city. People who stay in this hotel can keep no secrets from me."
>
> (Arthur Hailey, 1997: 71)

This conversation happens between Ogilvie and the Duke. From the answer of Ogilvie we can know that he provides more information than the Duke's quotation required, therefore, it is obviously Ogilvie violates the maxim of quantity. Ogilvie is proud of his reliable information resources, and he shows off it on purpose by violating the cooperative principle, which is a stupid action revealing his rudeness and arrogance. From this case, it is easy to figure out that Ogilvie is a man lacking of politeness, not noticing the social rules and not to mention being modest. The conversational implicature of this conversation not only for Ogilvie to show off his abundant information but also reveal Ogilvie is a man who tends to ignore others' emotions and refuses to cooperate with others. (Kang Xiangying, 2011)

Example 5:

> Warren Trent did not listen. "Get out of my hotel and never come back again," he cried.
>
> Earlshore lost his temper. "All right! I'll go," he roared. "And you will soon go, too—prond Mr Trent. You are going to lose your hotel. When that happens, the people who work in this place will laugh! You've always behaved as if you owned your employees. Well, they've been laughing at you behind your back and cheating you. Everyone has been cheating you."Tom turned and quickly left the room.
>
> (Arthur Hailey, 1997: 100)

This conversation happens in the bar where Earlshore works. Earlshore's response is far more than that is required, he just needs to say "All right! I'll go", but he adds so much information about his attitudes towards Mr. Trent. Thus, Earlshore violates the maxim of quantity for the intention to express his complains about Mr. Trent. From here we can see, as a owner of the hotel, Mr Trent is not qualified because he does not really care about his employees but just regards them as workers. From here we can draw a conclusion that the relationship between the boss and employees is a vital factor for the development of the hotel.

Understatement: it refers to the speaker tells less information than that id required.

Example 6：

> Peter said firmly. "Let him have the room at the same price. I'm going to move Mr. Wells from 1439 to 1410. Please send up a porter with the key of that room."
>
> "Wait a minute，Mr. Dermott，" the clerk said rudely. "Mr. Trent has given orders that—

In this conversation，it is obviously that the clerk does not finish his conversation and he does not offer enough information. Therefore，he violates the maxim of quantity. The reason why he does not offer enough information may be that he just wants to refuse the demand of Mr Dermott and he make up a lie, or he wants to express his unsatisfactory emotions to Mr Dermott, so he does not want to complete his words.

According to the above analysis，it is not hard to see that the times of violating the maxim of quantity is much many，and from the analysis，we can see the characters that have something to express or show off，they tend to break the maxim of quantity to add or ignore some information.

Violation of the Maxim of Quality

In Hotel，there are some conversations which violate the maxim of quality，the reason why people violate it because they have to hide something in mind or based on the daily experience of metaphorical conception they may violate subconsciously. Then，this thesis will make an analysis of chosen conversations among these targeted conversations.

Example 1：

> "The Waldorf would not have allowed this behavior，" the Duchess said. "Do you know that your waiter poured soup over my husband？"
>
> "Our evening has been ruined，" the Duchess cried. " My husband and I wanted to enjoy a quiet evening alone in our rooms. We took a walk around the square and came back for dinner. Then this happened！"
>
> （Arthur Hailey，1997：16）

After reading the next part of this novel，it is not difficult to figure out that the Duchess is lying, because they didn't take a walk before supper, instead, the Duke was driving and killed a child. So the Duchess violates the maxim of quality，in order to hide some clues of their crimes.

Example 2：

> "I was doing my best to hide your foolishness，" the Duchess went on. " I pretended that we both spent a quiet evening in the hotel. I even invented that story about our walk in case anyone saw us come in. Then you stupidly appeared and said that you have left your pipe in the car."
>
> "That manager fellow didn't notice."
>
> （Arthur Hailey，1997：26）

This conversation happens after Mr. Dermott leaving out of the Duke's room between the Duke and the Duchess. The Duke's stupid words reveal his track, but he says "That manager fellow didn't notice." From here, we can see the Duke is talking about something he does not have enough evidence. But out of self-comfort or shameless, he makes up the situation where he does not sure. Therefore, he violates the maxim of quality to conceal his worries. (Liu Baoyan, 2009)

Example 3:

> "Excuse me, sir. I was passing the room and I heard someone cry out, " said the man outside the door. He was Warren Trent's young manservant, Aloysius Royce.
>
> "My wife was having a bad dream, " Dixon explained. " She's all right now."
>
> (Arthur Hailey, 1997: 30)

This conversation happens outside the room of Dixon's. Aloysius Royce was asking whether there was a person crying, but Dixon answers that his wife was having a bad dream. Actually, Dixon has no wife, and it was Marsha who was shouting because te four young men intended to insult her. Therefore, Dixon does not tell the truth but make up a lie, and he violates the maxim of quality to hide his incorrect behavior.

Example 4:

> "Your hotel is all alike. They have no character, " Trent replied, "Look at the bedrooms! They are like boxes. Your hotels are cold and unfriendly."
>
> "My hotels make money, " O'Keefe said with a smile.
>
> (Arthur Hailey, 1997: 77-78)

This conversation happens in the office of Mr. Trent. It is obviously that mar Trent uses a simile to describe the style of O'Keefe's hotel. Therefore Mr. Trent violates the maxim of quality, maybe out of sub consciousness. "They are like boxes" implies the disgusting of MrTrent towards the O'Keefe's hotel.

Example 5:

> "What do you mean? " he said in a rough voice.
>
> "This is not your room. It's mine. Yes—mine. You're in my bed." Keycase moved closer and breathed whisky into the man's face.
>
> (Arthur Hailey, 1997: 85)

This conversation happens in the 641 room between the house guest and Keycase. From the context we can know Keycase wants to steal money from this guy, but unfortunately, he was catched on occasion. Therefore, he pretends to be a drunken man and walked into the wrong house. So he violates the maxim of quality deliberately and lies that this is his room to escape from been arrested.

Violation of the Maxim of Relation

In common conversations，if the hearer likes the conversation topic，he or she will continue it; but if the hearer does not interested in the topic， he or she would change to another topic to replace the previous one or make no response about it. Therefore，the changed topic maybe not related to the previous one. There are some such examples in Hotel，the thesis will make an analysis of the conversational implicature next.

Example 1：

> Royce looked at Dixon. " I'd like to come in，please，" he said firmly.
>
> "I tell you—my wife is having a dream." Dixon repeated.
>
> "I'm sorry， sir. I don't believe you."

（Arthur Hailey，1997：31）

This conversation happens outside the Dixon's room. Royce is asking to go into the house， but Dixon does not answer whether he can or not. Instead， he answers that his wife was having a bad dream. From here， we can see that Dixon does not want to answer this question， so he changes the topic and talks about his "wife". This conversation implies that Dixon intends to hide his crimes.

Example 2：

> Ogilvie followed the Duchess into the living room. He was smoking a big cigar. The Duchess looked at the cigar in the fat man's mouth and said coldly： " My husband and I hate the smell of cigars. Kindly put that out."
>
> The detective looked at her and blew out a cloud of smoke. He looked around the room. "You people have a very comfortable place，" he said. He knocked some ash from his cigar on to the floor.

（Arthur Hailey，1997：69）

The conversation happens in the living room of the Duchess. From the dialogue we can see that the Duchess is talking about putting out the cigar, but Ogilvie just ignores the Duchess's demand and talks about the living room. Therefore， the answer is not related to the question and Ogilvie violates the maxim of relation. Ogilvie's violation of the maxim of relation reveals his emotional condition at the beginning of the negotiation which is arrogant and self-important. The Duchess asks him to put out the cigar， and he refuses to do so and violates the maxim of relation deliberately， which shows Ogilvie is a man who is used to ignoring and refusing others and lack of politeness. Ogilvie's arrogant attitude is due to his birth， he comes from a family in the low social class.

Example 3：

> The Duchess looked Ogilvie in the face. "How much money do you want？"
>
> The sudden question took the detective by surprise. "Well，I imagine that you people are very rich."
>
> （Arthur Hailey，1997：74）

In this conversation，the Duchess comes straight to the question and asks the detective how much money he wants. However，the detective is astonished about this direct question，so he makes a response that is not related to the question，then，he violates the maxim of relation. This conversation shows the detective is a greedy man who intends to be controlled by money.（Chen Yanqing，Zhou Qiaohong，2014）

Example 4：

> The old man shook his head again. "I'll keep this note—in case there is any trouble.
>
> Ogilvie didi not argue. He did not want to give the man cause for suspicion. He pointed to a paper bag that he was carrying：it contained the lamp and some tools. "I'm going to put this in the car，" he said. "I'll take the car out in about two hours."
>
> （Arthur Hailey，1997：123）

This conversation happens between the detective and Kulgmer. From the conversation we can see that the old man just says he would keep the note. But the detective talks about something not relating to the topic；therefore the detective violates the maxim of relation to conceal his own fear.

Violation of the Maxim of Manner

As mentioned above，the maxim of manner requires people in a conversation to offer concise and organized information to avoid ambiguity nad obscurity. In Hotel，some people tend to speak in a prolix and repetitive way. The thesis is going to analyze the conversation which violates the maxim of manner.

Repetition：it refers to the speaker talks about one thing again and again.

Example 1：

> Peter Mcdermott agreed. He went straight to the telephone and spoke to the room clerk on night duty. " Is there a room free on the fourteenth floor？" he asked.

> There was a pause. The clerk—another of Warren Trent's favorites—did not like Peter and he objected to people interfering his job.
>
> "Well，" Peter said. "Have you a free room or not？"
>
> "Room 1410 is free，" said the clerk，" but I'm about to give it to a gentleman who has just arrived."
>
> （Arthur Hailey，1997：24）

This conversation happens between Peter Mcdermott and one of the clerk. From the conversation we can see that Peter repeats his question and violates the maxim of manner deliberately，because he wants to catch the attention of the rude clerk and emphasize his demand. After repeating the question，the clerk just answers.

Example 2：

> "Sorry！" His wife's voice was bitter. "This trouble tonight might ruin us."
>
> "I know，old girl. It's serious—extremely serious." The Duke lay back in his deep armchair and looked miserable.
>
> （Arthur Hailey，1997：25-26）

As we know，the Duke has killed one child and his mother by driving，so the Duchess tries her best to hide the truth. However，the Duke's foolishness betrays their lies，and the Duke comes to realize the seriousness of his behaviour so that he uses repetition to express his shamefulness.

Prolix：it refers to the speaker talks about one thing too by using too much useless words.

Example：

> Peter laughed. "You talk like a woman"
>
> "I'm a woman."
>
> "I know，" Peter said. "I've just begun to notice." He said with a little hesitation："I had no dinner tonight. I was too busy. Would you care to come out with me and have a late supper？"
>
> （Arthur Hailey，1997：28）

This conversation happens between Peter and Charistine. Peter wants to go out with Charistine，and he could only talk about the last sentence that would she care to come out with him and have a late supper. But Peter says more words to show he maybe a little nervous and afraid that Charistine would not go out with him. Therefore，he says more information.

5 Conclusions

Cooperative principle is used in the analysis for a better conversation for both the speaker and the hearer.

This thesis analyzes the conversations in *Hotel* violating the four maxims of cooperative principle respectively. Meanwhile, those conversations violating the cooperative principle must convey some special potential meanings. And sometimes we have to break the maxims out of some reasons to express ourselves by some conversational implicature. That is, the analysis of the violations of the maxim of quality, the maxim of quantity, the maxim of relation and the maxim of manner contributes to show the vivid images of the figures in front of the readers.

In conclusion, the violation of the four maxims of cooperative principle is a useful way for us to express ourselves better. And this thesis can help people to come to realize the conversational implicature of the conversations and make a better understanding of this novel.

参考文献

[1] Arthur Hailey, 1997. *Hotel* [M]. Beijing: Foreign Language and Teaching Research Press.

[2] Edwars, D. & Mercer, *Common Knowledge: the Development of Understanding in the Classroom*[N]. 1987.

[3]Grice, H. P. *Studies in Syntax and Semantics III* [R] Speech Arts. 1975. New York: Academic Press.

[4] Kleifen, J. *Pre-kindergarten Children's Second Discourse Learning. Discourse Processes* [A]. 1990（13）: 47-52.

[5] Leech, Geoffery. *Principles of Pragmatics*[M]. New York: Lingman Group Limited.

[6] 陈彦青，周巧红. 从合作原则看“讹诈”中奥格尔维的形象塑造[J]. 湖南人文科技学院学报，2014（6）: 12-15.

[7] 胡壮麟. 语言学教程[M]. 北京：北京大学出版社，2001.

[8] 康响英. 论《讹诈》中隐含作者的隐性建构[J]. 池州学院学报，2011（10）：23-27.

[9] 康响英. 论模糊限制语在《讹诈》中所反映的人际关系[J]. 外语学刊，2008（1）：53-57.

[10] 刘桂香. 从话轮转换看《大饭店》“敲诈”片段中任务的权势关系[J]. 新乡教育学院学报，2009（1）：33-37.

[11] 刘宝岩. 论《讹诈》中语式对语旨的建构作用[J]. 外语学刊，2009（4）：45-47.

[12] 宋晓笛. 合作原则视角下小妇人中的会话含义分析[D]. 大连海事大学，2017.

[13] 张璟. 从言语行为看交际中的权势关系：浅析《讹诈》中的人物关系[J]. 语言文字，2001（1）：36-41.

从隐喻分类和因素层次分析看科技发展与日常生活

温淑婧

摘　要：本文基于 Lakoff 和 Johnson 在《我们赖以生存的隐喻》中提出的隐喻的概念模型和分类及因素分层分析了隐喻是如何在描述科技及其演变过程中起作用的，并进一步分析了科技和隐喻对我们日常生活感知方式的影响。

关键词：因素分层分析；隐喻；科技

Abstract：This paper is based on the conceptual model and classification of metaphors proposed by Lakoff and Johnson in "Metaphors we live by", and on CLA（Causal Layered Analysis） to analyze how metaphor take action in the description of technologies，in their evolution，and the impact of technologies and metaphors on the way we perceive our daily life.

Key words：CLA；metaphors；technology

1 引　言

Lakoff 和 Johnson 在 2008 年对隐喻再解释，将其视为认知问题而非语言问题，在语言与认知过程的关系上树立了一个里程碑。《我们赖以生存的隐喻》也成为学术和科学界对隐喻的重要参考。其理论已经广泛应用于不同的领域，包括认知心理学、数学、社会学、政治学、神经理论、市场营销、传播学、句法学等。

在因素分层分析（Causal Layered Analysis）方法（Inayatullah，1998）中将隐喻看成“基础”层，设想了一种解构方法，一个从最明显的现象信号考虑隐藏的动机的过程，这些动机通常在文化中根深蒂固，但大多数时候却被人们忽视。因此，它使用四个层次的模型（平述、系统原因、话语/世界观、神话/隐喻），其中平述型包含现象最明显的信号，神话和隐喻移动则是行为的深层动机。通过这种方式，Inayatullah 和 Lakoff 超越了隐喻对于理解我们对现实的看法是至关重要的这一观点，他们认为隐喻为我们的行为预设了一种倾向。这种方法在一定程度上与萨皮尔-沃夫假说一致，即我们所说的语言决定了我们思考和行动的方式。

社会中的隐喻和主导价值体系正在发生变化，原因在本质上十分多样：科学发现，人口变化，文化冲突，天气变化，科技……前人对于隐喻和科技之间的联系的研究中，大多数情况，他们将隐喻与交流联系在一起；（Christidou，Dimopoulos，&Koulaidis，2004）但其他研究则超越了这一范畴，研究了隐喻在科技应用中的影响（Stevenson，2008）或隐喻在科技应用中定义现实的影响。（Walsham，1991）

本文根据 Lakoff 和 Johnson 的分类来描述隐喻，并将它们与因素分层分析的图层相联系。也将展示我们感知现实、科技和隐喻的方式之间的关系以及隐喻之间的冲突如何影响科技的采用。

2 隐喻的分类

参考《我们赖以生存的隐喻》（Lakoff& Johnson，1980）第一版中提出的隐喻的高级分类，本文将隐喻分为方位隐喻、实体隐喻和结构隐喻三类。方位隐喻是一种将概念相互联系起来的系统，大多数都与空间定位有关；实体隐喻解释我们如何从自身经历理解物质；结构的隐喻是将一个概念从另一个概念的角度构造出来。

多年来，这种分类并不是一成不变的，也不是没有争议的。9 年后，Lakoff 和 Turner（1989）增加了一个新的范畴，图像隐喻，即那些将图像映射到意象上的隐喻。Szwedek（2007）认为实体隐喻、结构隐喻和方向隐喻的区别是不正确的，他认为定向隐喻本质上是本体隐喻。其他的分类，例如，根据源领域的性质，或者根据主隐喻和复合隐喻的区别（Grady，1997）已经有合理解释。Ruiz de Mendoza Ibanez&Perez Hernandez（2011）也对这些分类进行了很好的评估。

然而，最初的分类是有意义的，无论是基于空间方向的隐喻，还是暗示概念结构的隐喻，都让我们理解隐喻的不同性质，因此，本文依旧采用方位隐喻、实体隐喻和结构隐喻三分法。

3 关联 Lakoff 的隐喻观点和因素分层分析

对隐喻的分类可以了解它的丰富性，也是一个很好的起点，供我们思考它们解释的不同层次。但从未来的角度思考，需要在一个更一般、更面向未来的框架内考虑隐喻方法。因素分层分析可以起到这样的作用，因为因素分层分析提供了一个整体分析现象的框架，考虑了四个层次的深度，神话/隐喻是最深层的，平述包含一种最浅显的表达，即可见的信号，例如新闻或事件。在这两者之间还有另外两个层次，系统原因和话语/世界观，其性质如表 1 所示。

表 1　因素分层分析层级

平述	数量趋势，问题所在，经常被夸大，经常被用于政治目的。例如，人口过剩，通常由新闻媒体呈现
系统性原因	包括社会、技术、经济、环境、政治和历史因素（例如，出生率的上升、计划生育的缺失）
话语/世界观	支持和合法化系统原因（人口增长和家庭的文明观点；缺乏女性的力量；缺乏社会保障。例如，关于人口/消费的辩论）
神话/隐喻	深层的故事，集体的原型——问题或悖论的无意识和经常情绪化的维度

本节将探寻 Lakoff 和 Johnson 对隐喻和层级分类之间的关联。Lakoff 和 Johnson 的结构隐喻与概念模型有关，这些概念模型使我们能够理解另一个概念。通过观察因素分层分析的理论和实践研究中所展示的例子可以发现，迄今为止，在因素分层分析的神话/隐喻层中所考虑的大多数隐喻都是结构性隐喻（Inayatullah & Milojević，2015）。例如，在由 Saliv Bin Larif 撰写的《隐喻与因素分层分析》一章中，作者在神话/隐喻层面上使用隐喻，用于战争隐喻，或者用身体来识别概念（经济、国家）。这些都是结构隐喻，因为它们用其他概念来定义概念，而这些概念的结构是公认的。

方向隐喻在一定程度上与层次化话语/世界观相吻合，因为最常见的方向隐喻具有向上和向下的性质，与修饰的“好”“坏”相关，所以它们代表我们的价值观和世界观。

实体隐喻使我们能够把不同的元素和抽象概念看成是资源和物质，并以这种方式与它们进行运用。因此，从系统的角度分析现象是很重要的。例如，我们可以说，每个居民的健康成本在上升，因为我们把健康看成一种物质；我们可以说，将会有能量分解，因为我们把能量看成一种资源。

根据这一推理，三个因素分层分析阶层（系统、世界观、神话）直接与隐喻相关，而不仅仅是神话/隐喻层，它们与不同类型的隐喻相关。

平述反映了社会中发生的事件/问题，这些事件/问题通常被社会的底层所过滤，也因此被他们的隐喻所过滤。例如，2015 年 9 月发布的一条新闻中写道：“专家警告说，人类平均寿命延长三至十年，可能会促使国家在 2050 年将退休年龄提到 70 岁。”我们可以设想另一个层级的隐喻将会是：生活是一种物质，因此越多越好，生活是一个旅程，不同阶段……

综上所述，Lakoff 与 Johnson 模型和因素分层分析之间的高层关系如表 2 所示。

表 2　因素分层分析与 Lakoff&Johnson 的隐喻间的关系。

因素分层	Lakoff 和 Johnson 的隐喻分类
平述	事实，由底层的隐喻过滤
系统性原因	基于实体隐喻
话语/世界观	方向隐喻
神话和隐喻	结构隐喻

4　科技隐喻及其对现实进化和感知的影响

人们通过心灵的透镜来感知现实。这些透镜或过滤器以这样或那样的方式依赖于内部认知知识结构：一个信号可以是一个旁人并未注意到的施事者或者事物“认知系统与环境相互作用，是认知系统而非环境决定如何交互”。（Seidl，2004）本文认为，隐喻在配置这些过滤器以及我们对现实的感知中扮演着中心角色。

一项科技，至少当它是新兴技术时，可以看成是一种新的现实。例如，当计算机被发明的时候，这被认为是一个新的物理元素。作为一个新的概念，用大家都知道的概念的隐喻来解释它是有必要的。

通过分析来自高德纳（Gartner Group 公司成立于 1979 年，它是第一家信息技术研究和分析的公司）的新兴科技报告的炒作周期中所包含的新兴科技，可以说明，为了理解科技，在它们出现的时候，必须使用隐喻。选择这份报告有两个主要原因。首先，它是一个享有盛誉的文件，得到了所有创新和研究部门的认可，并得到主流公众的认可。其次，它从社会影响的角度考虑新兴科技。报告开头提到这种方法：“这种炒作周期汇集了高德纳研究领域最重要的科技。它提供了对新兴科技的深入了解，这些科技具有广泛的、跨行业的相关性，具有转型和巨大的潜力”。

我们从 2014 年报告中的描述中识别出这些隐喻。它们作为一个框架来定义和解释正在出现的问题，并对表 3 中描述这些问题的语言产生影响。

表 3　新兴科技首次被纳入 2014 年新兴科技炒作周期表达

新兴科技	隐喻	新兴科技的炒作周期表达
数据科学	数据是资源	大量数据，数据准备
软件——定义一切	软件是新型建筑材料	软件定义的存储、基础设施的可编程性
虚拟加密货币	软件是钱	虚拟货币、硬币、价值、货币
混合云计算	计算是一种云；计算是一种混合	云服务、集成、云服务组合、由多个集合组成的云
智能顾问	计算系统是智能的	为用户的问题提供最好的答案，个性化的建议
连接的家庭	家是连接设备的容器，多个设备相互连接	家是服务和产品的筒仓
数字安全	数字是一种资源	数字资产，易于处理的表单
智能工作区	空间智能	帮助员工提升表现，与情绪、压力相关的反馈……

通过这张表，能看出很多与新兴科技相关的隐喻都具有实体隐喻性质，将数据、数字或软件等抽象概念视为资源和物质就可以将这些抽象概念当成材料来管理。这种新科技将自然元素视为物质和资源的力量在过去是很普遍的，主要是在西方文化中，社会深受理性主义的影响。例如，因为电的发现而产生的隐喻中“光”是一种资源，因为“光”成为一种独立于太阳的资源，而且第一次有可能购买、使用它……工业革命后的人们也是如此，这场革命带来工厂中工人的可替代性，而隐喻中的“人”是一种资源，被认为是我们经济模式最坚实的基础之一。这个比喻使我们的工作语言充满了诸如“这项活动需要 5 个小时”之类的表达。其他科技将其他自然元素转化为资源，例如，风力涡轮机将风能转化为资源，或者电信技术将通信转化为物质。我们可以得出这样的结论：本体论隐喻在新科技的定义中是至高无上的，而这些隐喻具有双重含义：它们可以描述新科技，并以一种新的方式体验现实，在这种情况下，自然概念被视为材料。

结构隐喻在新兴科技的描述中也很常见，例如，系统是智能的，空间是智能的，这为理解智能顾问和智能工作区提供了一个复杂而丰富的框架。这种以隐喻为基础的概念化不仅在这些科技的定义中有用，而且在科技的发展和对现实的感知中继续作为一个框架。再以高德纳炒作周期的新兴科技为例，在这种情况下，2004 年发布的产品，在人们使用前，强调它们的未来作用，我们看到，用在新兴科技上的隐喻是处于“上升期”，此时的影响，不仅在这些科技的进化，也是我们对现实看法的进化。例如，新兴科技“维基”用的隐喻基础是知识是开放的，新兴科技增强现实是基于其他隐喻，如感官定义现实或虚拟世界。这些隐喻在当时听起来很奇怪，但现在它们已经成为我们思维模式的一部分。

科技和社会隐喻之间的联系不止于此，社会中的一些主导隐喻也有科技基础。例如，“世界是一个村庄”，因为通信传输科技减少了时间从一个地方到另一个地方，和与人沟通的另一边的世界。这些隐喻是基于实体隐喻“时间是一种资源”“交流是一种资源”，在最后一种情况下，资源是一种渠道，让我们能够接近人，尽管他们离我们很远。另一个隐喻是，社会是自然保护者，这是基于这样一个事实，一些科技有能力破坏我们的环境。例如，核能，排放二氧化碳的内燃机，或过度开发自然资源的科技，既然它们存在，社会就有保护地球的新角色。虽然在某些文化中，自然被认为是一个生态系统，在犹太-基督教文化中，隐喻“人是自然之王”是根深蒂固的，在这种情况下，残酷的现实迫使西方观念发生转变。

所有这些例子都表明，隐喻是一种框架，也是一个双向过程：科技隐喻来源于日常生活的现实，而这些隐喻也塑造了人们对现实的演变和感知。

5　科技发展中的影响：隐喻的冲突

如前所述，现实、新科技和隐喻之间存在很强的内在联系，这三个术语之间的关系将标志它们的演变。

原则上，大多数国家都对科技持积极态度，因为很少有事物像科技一样对人民的生活水平和进步产生如此大的影响。因此，大多数国家和组织都鼓励使用科技，例如，根据联合国教科文组织宽带数字发展委员会的数据，世界上有 148 个国家有国家宽带计划从这个角度来看，与科技是好的相关的定向隐喻科技在过去两个世纪主导了科技的视野。这些隐喻与这样一个事实相一致：科技意味生产力的提高，这些提高意味更多的数量，而且几乎在所有文化中，越多越好。（Lakoff & Johnson，1983）然而，当这些隐喻和其他公认的隐喻之间存在摩擦时，这种设想就受到质疑。比如在 19 世纪初的勒德分子抗议中科技进步与工作进步相撞。在关于“科学反对宗教”的争论中，它与圣经的说法相抵触。在一些社区，例如一些和尚社区，隐喻越少越好。在这些情况下，科技只能用于某些目的，例如卫生目的。有些宗教团体甚至不接受为此目的使用科技。这样，文化差异对采用的程度或科技的发展有重要的影响。

关于科技的好处的这场辩论质疑了这样一个前提，即科技已经上升，至少超过一个门槛，而且目前在不同的领域还在继续。例如，信息通信科技（Information and communication technologies）正在经历一个巨大的增长时期，大多数专家认为基于信息通信科技的新服务具有极大的潜力对社会产生积极的影响。然而，它们的大量利用引起人们对它们的限制以及对人口可能产生的消极影响的若干关注。皮尤研究中心（Pew Research Center，该组织研究影响美国和世界的问题、态度和趋势）2014 年 9 月至 2015 年 9 月发表的 29 篇关于互联网的报告中可以看出，有 8 篇报告关注互联网的使用。如表 4 所示，关注的是数字鸿沟、骚扰和隐私，它们非常重要，以至于该组织已经发表了几份关于这些问题的报告。

这种方法意味将现象视为互联网的格式塔，即一种基于不同深度层次的复杂结构的形式，从而允许我们检测层次之间和其他格式塔之间的关系和摩擦。例如，隐喻“老大哥”反乌托邦与隐喻“国家是保护者”相冲突。最后，当两种隐喻发生冲突时，就会出现一种谈判，例如，西班牙电话公司（Telefonica）的一份报告称，“在互联网上共享数据，是为了获得互联网使用的好处而付出的代价，如果你想在这个世界上生存，你就必须参与其中”。

这些冲突也发生在其他层面，例如在世界观层面，隐喻“平等上升”，与“市场上升”的冲突。在信息通信技术趋势的情况下，需要对这些摩擦和关系进行详细分析，以了解这些现象的动态并做出决定。（Carbonell，Sanchez-Esguevillas & Carro，2015）

表 4　由皮尤研究中心发布的关于互联网相关问题的报告。

关注	日期	报告标题	隐喻
数字鸿沟	2015 年 7 月 28 日	15%的美国人不使用互联网。他们是谁？	方向：平等上升； 实体：信息通信技术是墙； 结构：阶级斗争
数字鸿沟	2015 年 4 月 30 日	种族和民族差异在人们如何使用移动技术	
数字鸿沟	2015 年 4 月 20 日	宽带“家庭作业鸿沟”背后的数字	
数字鸿沟	2014 年 9 月 19 日	人口普查：计算机拥有率、互联网连接在美国各地差异很大	
骚扰	2015 年 6 月 1 日	网络骚扰最黑暗的一面：威胁行为	方向：尊重程度上升； 实体：信息通信技术是武器； 结构：人类作为掠食者
骚扰	2014 年 11 月 20 日	大约五分之一的网络骚扰受害者说，这是在评论区发生的	
隐私	2015 年 5 月 20 日	美国人对隐私、安全和监视的态度	方向：隐私程度上升； 实体：信息通信技术是眼睛； 结构：反乌托邦老大哥
隐私	2015 年 4 月 14 日	为什么有些美国人没有改变他们的隐私和安全行为	

虽然我们将此分析集中在信息通信技术上，但对其他科技的深入研究，例如，遗传学或能源科技也会引起伦理或社会关注。就遗传学和其他与生物学相关的领域而言，这些摩擦的重要性是如此之高，以至于它们催生一个新的研究领域——生物伦理学，它试图讨论和规范这些科技可能引发的隐喻冲突。在学术数据库 ProQuest 中有超过 80k 的参考文献，一些关于这个主题的期刊展示了这个概念的相关性，并作为一个例子，说明不兼容的隐喻之间的摩擦如何塑造和限制了科技的发展。

6　结论及展望

科技对人们生活的影响超越了其工具作用——提高活动的“绩效”。新科技，尤其是那些具有颠覆性潜力的科技改变了社会规则、人们的行为，最终改变了人们对生活的看法。本文展示了隐喻在社会中是如何支配科技的进化以及科技的进化是反向塑造社会中的隐喻的。在某种程度上，这一过程与马歇尔·麦克卢汉（Marshall Mcluhan）的观点相似，他认为科技产生了新的感觉和感知结构，因此根据这种哲学，我们可以表述为“我们创造科技，然后科技创造我们”。

本文还将隐喻方法与更一般的方法因素分层分析相结合，以提供一个更全面的视野和对现象的未来导向，将内部动机、系统原因和外部信号联系起来，以提出进化的场景和简化预见活动。

然而，这只是研究隐喻在思考未来时的潜力的一个起点。在进一步的研究中，除了 Lakoff 和 Johnson 的比较适合因素分层分析的隐喻分类外，也应当考虑其他的隐喻分类。例如，深入研究神话/隐喻（内部动机）和其他层次之间的关系，比如系统原因、世界观或外部信号（平述）。研究隐喻在一种文化中的支配地位对社会发展的影响以及对隐喻的社会发展影响的内在机制，可以为隐喻的创造和演变提供一个新的视角。

参 考 文 献

[1] Carbonell，J.，Sánchez-Esguevillas，A.，&Carro，B. , 2015. Assessing emerging issues：the external and internal approach. Futures，73，12-21.

[2] Christidou，V.，Dimopoulos，K. & Koulaidis，V. , 2004. Constructing social representations of science and technology: the role of metaphors in the press and the popular scientific magazines. Public Understanding of Science，13（4）：347-362.

[3] Grady，J. E., 1997. Foundations of meaning：primary metaphors and primary scenes. Berkeley：University of California.Inayatullah，S. 1998. Causal layered analysis：poststructuralism as method. Futures，30（8）：815-829.

[4] Inayatullah，S. & Milojevic，I. 2015. CLA 2.0 transformative research in theory and practice. Tamkang University Press.

[5] Lakoff，G. & Núñez，R., 2003. Where mathematics comes from. Santa Fe Institute.

[6] Lakoff，G. & Turner，M., 1989. More than cool reason：a field guide to poetic metaphor. Chicago，IL：The University of Chicago Press.

[7] Ruiz de Mendoza Ibáñez，F. J. & Perez Hernandez，L., 2011. The contemporary theory of metaphor：myths，developments and challenges. Metaphor and Symbol，26（3）：161-185.

[8] Seidl，D., 2004. The concept of "weak signals" revisited：a re-description from a constructivist perspective. In H. Tsoukas & J. Shepherd（Eds.），Managing the future：developing strategic foresight in the knowledge economy（153-170）.Oxford：Blackwell.

[9] Stevenson，I., 2008. Tool，tutor，environment or resource：exploring metaphors for digital technology and pedagogy using activity theory. Computers &Education，51（2）：836-853.

[10] Walsham，G., 1991. Organizational metaphors and information systems research. European Journal of Information Systems，1（2）：83-94.

互联网环境下英汉混合四字格流行词语模因解析

汤朝菊　张　晗

摘　要：互联网环境下，社会经济文化以及语言都随之而产生各种变化，词汇是语言中最活跃的因素，词汇的变化主要反映在新生的流行词语上面。而互联网让世界变成“地球村”，因而流行词汇也对此进行了认知的折射和反映，一个比较突出的现象就是英汉混合式的网络流行词语的出现。本文以英汉混合式四字格流行词语为例，从语言模因论视角对其进行认知探讨，主要从词语的产生机制、结构特点、语音特点和语用环境等方面进行讨论。

关键词：语言模因论；流行词语；英汉混合式四字格；产生机制

Abstract: Under the Internet environment, social economy, culture and language have undergone various changes. Vocabulary, as the most active element of language, its changes are mainly reflected in new catchwords. It can be seen that internet has turned the world into a “global village”, as a result, catchwords are supposed to reflect and cognizes it accordingly. One of this prominent phenomena is the emergence of English-Chinese mixedcatchwords.This paper taking English-Chinese mixed four-character catchwords as an example, tends to explorethe cognition of them from the perspective of linguistic memetics. It mainly discusses the generating mechanism, structural characteristics, phonetic characteristics and pragmatic contexts.

Key words: Linguistic memetics; catchwords; English-Chinese mixed four-character words; the generating mechanism

1　引　　言

流行语作为一种新兴的语言现象，具有动态性和开放性的特点，是语言研究不可忽视的一种语料，同时也是社会经济、政治、文化和思维方式的一种折射，将社会生活中出现的新事物、新现象和新观念呈现在我们面前。人类使用的语言就其本质来说是一种音义结合的符号，其产生发展与社会生活息息相关，流行语以形式的创新、内容的丰富和传播的快捷使其渗透力与影响力日益扩大，广泛运用于各领域，频繁地出现在报刊、网络、电视，因此引起学者们的讨论。（仓理新，2011；崔蓬克，2012；孙曼均，1998；杨建国，2004；邹嘉彦、游汝杰，2008）

英汉语码混合也是流行词语的一大特点，近几年，出现了诸如“book 思议”（不可思议）、“贪生 pass”（贪生怕死）、“半 tou 废”（半途而废）、“鱼香 rose”（鱼香肉丝）等英汉双语混合式短语，这类短语因其特殊的结构、双语码的形式，更因其语音音节的韵律而类似于汉语的四字格成语模式而一时爆红，在短时间受到广泛追捧，并一度入选网络热词。用百度搜索引擎搜索“半 tour 而废”，相关词条高达 38 100 个，仅仅同类词语的一个就有如此高的搜索量，可见这类词语在网络流传甚广。

然而这些词语为什么在红极一时之后，又迅速消退，快速淡出人们的视线呢？这种“速食”词汇现象其背后的理据是什么？我们在下面进行讨论。

2　语言模因论下流行词语的消长

2.1　语言模因论

“模因”（meme）一词本身就是受生物学领域的术语“基因”（gene）的启示而被命名的一个新词汇，主要用来指文化传播的机制和原理，（Dawkins，1976；Blackmore，1999）也是文化信息传播的一个模仿单位。模因一般被定义为“能够通过广义上称为‘模仿’的过程而被复制的信息单位”。（Dawkins，1982：109）模因作为大脑里的信息单位是存在于大脑中的一个复制因子，而在现实世界里，模因的表现型是词语、音乐、图像、服饰格调，甚至手势或脸部表情。（Blackmore，1999）提到信息复制传递就必须涉及社会信息复制传递的载体，也称其为宿主，那就是人。“模因”就是借助人脑的机制由这一宿主传递到那一宿主，任何信息只要经历了广义上被称为“模仿”的过程就可以成为“模因”。简单地说，任何可以被复制的信息单位都可以成为“模因”。（陈琳霞、何自然，2006；何自然，2014）因此，模因论很快被应用在语言的传播中，尤其是语言中新词新语的产生机制，这个视角被称为“语言模因论”。语言模因观认为，语言模因作为一种信息储存于人脑之中并随时可能被激活并传递出去，在语言交际中，语言选择和使用的过程就是各种模因相互竞争的过程，也是一个模因宿主传递、接收、接受或拒绝模因的过程。“语言模因就是语言中的模因，它带着模因宿主的意图，借助语言结构，以重复或类推的方式反复不断传播信息的表征。”（陈琳霞、何自然，2006；何自然，2016）

2.2　语言模因论视角下流行语的产生机制

语言模因观照下，流行词语的诸多现象都能得到解释，首先，模因要竞争就要不断创新，并就要求语言有一定的宿主众体，因而就必须具备新奇性。（夏中华，2012）作为语言发展过程中的现象，流行语不仅反映社会现实，传播社会热点，更是可以改变本族语原有结构，将外语中的语音音调以及词汇短语与本族语相结合，创造出新词汇。而英汉混合式类成语就是这样结合的产物。以“半 tour 而废”（半途而废）为例，我们可以看出，在结构上，完整的一个英语单词，因其发音与汉语的字或者字的组合相似而替代它们出现，形成了结构上中英双语的特色，造成了书面内容上的新颖性。同时，这种创造也是时代发展的产物，具有时代性。随着互联网和全球化的快速发展，语言之间的碰撞不可避免，而英语作为我国基础教育中的外语，使得新兴一代在其长期的学习生活中对其产生依赖，并渴望将其用于生活中，其渗透力也随着人们英语的普及日渐加深，成为人们生活中的一部分，在网络语言中而成为汉字的替代品。因此，可以说，英汉双语四字短语的产生是时代的产物，有着时代性和新颖性。（杨建国，2004；胡培安，2012）此外，变异性也是其重要特征。（郑荣馨，1994）其“洋词”中用，或中西结合的创意给这类网络词语带上了“特别”的标签，在“追新逐异”的思维模因下，自然就流行起来。最重要的是，这类词语在语音韵律上，像极了汉语的四字格成语，而成语本身在汉语中其语义的高度浓缩性和结构的稳定性就决定了其在使用中的高端性和文化性，因此，这类网络“类成语”或“伪成语”在流行语言中有一定的传播性和流行热度。

这类短语中，英语词往往只起替代汉语字或者字的组合发音的作用，并没改变整个短语所要表达的语义，在使用的过程中，“半 tour 而废”依然表达“做事不能善始善终，比如事情没有做完就停止不能坚持到底”。这类短语往往用于书面语中，由于其独特的结构组合而引起读者注意，造成双语组合的独特性和适时使用英语读音的快感。我们可以看出，这类流行语从发音上与原短语基本一致，以“book 思议”为例，其发音和模因元表征信息“不可思议”一样，只是用了英语词汇“book”来替代汉语“不可”，由此创造了英汉混合语码的新颖形式，但其语义并没有发生改变，其内容也别无二致。这种流行语以成语变异或者短语变异的形式形成并传播，由于其宿主在特定的语境引起某种联想，就该类流行语的宿主来说，常常为接受过英语教育并有一定英语基础的群体，他们接收到网络视频博主 papi 酱所发微博“半 tour 而废”的信息，借由流行语广泛传播和网络宽松环境下的自由创造的启发，形成了该类流行语的认知语境，由此他们在大脑形成可以由相同发音的英语词汇替代汉语字或者字的组合的信息，并发挥宿主自身的主体性，借助大脑中的汉语和英语信息储存检索，将汉语成语或者四字短语中的字或者字的组合用相同发音的英语单词替代，形成了英汉混合四字格短语。

我们可以由此总结出英汉混合四字格短语的创造传播机制，首先是汉语成语或者短语引发以英语为二语的汉语者利用某一成语或者短语（这里是“半 tour 而废”）的元表征信息，结合其英语知识将该成语或者短语中的字或者字的组合由英语单词来代替，用类推的方式完成模因的变异，并借助网络快速地传递出去，引起以英语为二语的汉语者的兴趣，他们接收到这种内在语用特性，并接受这种特性，再利用其自身知识加以创造，造成此类流行语的广泛流传。

就其使用群体而言，使用英汉混合式四字短语的大多是接受过英语教育并拥有一定英语基础的人，在使用和创造此类短语的过程中，使用者可以发挥主体性，根据所学英语知识对汉语成语或者短语进行改造，由此产生适时应用英语单词的错觉，从而带来使用外语的快感。然而，这类词语为什么在一定的生命周期后很快就消亡了呢？

2.3 语言模因论视角下流行语的发展与消亡

根据模因论，模因分为强势模因和弱势模因。（陈琳霞、何自然，2006）简单来说，那些广泛被接收的模因被称为强势模因，那些由于各种原因不能被接受的模因称为弱势模因。强势模因和弱势模因也是一个相对较量的概念和过程，在一段时期内可以相互转化，流行语言尤其如此，在强势语言模因一段时间之后，就逐步成为弱势模因，其传播也就停止了，语言的使用也就消亡了。而二者之间的优胜劣汰受很多因素的影响。

语言作为反映人类社会的表现形式处在动态变化和不断丰富的过程中，社会的快速发展不可避免地会造成语言的更新退跌，基于社会现象所产生的大量新型词汇也层出不穷，丰富着语言的同时也对语言造成了不同的影响。这些词汇有的日渐发展强化成为普通词汇并纳入词典字典，有的逐渐淡化退出人们的视线。有些词汇以其自身特点被人广泛传播成为所谓的流行语，有的则自行消亡。（何自然，2005）

首先，流行词语本身就有一个生命周期，“流行语指的是在某些人中间，主要是在青少年中间，在某个时期广泛流行，过了一段时间又为新流行的词语所代替而悄然消失的词语”，（胡明扬、张莹，1990）并有时效性和阶段性。（葛本仪，2003；杨文全，2002；杨建国，2004）

就英汉双语四字短语来说，虽然流行一时，其网络浏览量和点击率也高，但是由于其不符合客观规律，违背大众认知心理和有限的传播语境，其最终会沦为弱势模因并消失在人们的视野中，就其创造传播机制而言，主要利用英语单词来替代同音的汉语字或者字的组合，而这种组合并没有对其本身的语义产生影响，造成语义的变异，因而违背了语言发展的客观创新规律。人们说话交际更多的是信息的交换，只是形式上的创新而未改变其语义特征的流行词是无法从根本上撼动原成语或者短语的语言地位的。我们可以看到，很多模因之所以成为强势模因是因为其本身增添了一定的语义特征，改变了原模因的语义，因此有存在的价值和意义。另外，就文化传播的角度而言，很多英汉双语四字短语都是由汉语成语改编而来，而其无法替代汉语成语的文化渊源，并在一定程度上造成了汉语文化的恶性发展，不符合民族文化的发展趋势。与此同时，此类流行语也违背了大众的认知心理，由于其传播流行是由网络恶搞开端，借助诙谐幽默的形式在以英语为外语的汉语使用者中传播，这种形成机制无法满足更广大的群体，导致大部分人无法理解这种流行语的存在机制，因而无法再认知上接受此类流行语。最后，我们可以看出，此类流行语因为借助语音变化，往往很多时候存在于书面表达，使用语境有限而限制了其广泛传播。可以看出，英汉双语四字短语因其自身对汉语语言文化的恶性影响以及本身违背规律，有沦为弱势模因并逐渐消失的潜势。

此外，语言的广泛受众性和结构及语义要受到正统语言语法规则的检验，混合式四字短语作为新兴现象，其存在和发展不仅改变了原有词汇短语本身所特有的文化渊源和使用语境，更是对汉语造成了许多负面的影响，其极强的渗透力使汉语中传统的成语短语遭到破坏，以其对中国传统成语的腐蚀而最终失去了生命力。

3 结　论

本文以英汉混合式四字格流行语为案例，通过语言模因论对其产生和消亡的原因进行探讨，中英混合四字格流行语在特定时间产生，快速在网络媒介流行并传播，持续过一段时间后，又被其他流行语替代。就其语体特征而言，由于英语单词的加入，破坏了此类成语的传统文化传承和文化意境，造成了由正式规范的语用情景到诙谐幽默的转变，破坏了传统成语所形成的文化意义。由于英汉混合四字格流行语不符合客观规律，违背大众认知心理和存在于有限的传播语境，其对汉语语言文化存在消极影响，会发展成为弱势模因并消失在人们的视野里。我们可以看出，流行语作为社会文化的产物，有其存在的内在原因和机制，但是并不是所有的流行语都对语言发展产生积极的影响。在日常生活中，我们要注意加以甄别，并采取积极的态度来对待各种流行语。

参考文献

[1] Blackmore，S., 1999. The Meme Machine [M]. Oxford：Oxford University Press.
[2] Dawkins，R., 1976. The Selfish Gene[M]. New York：Oxford University Press.
[3] Dawkins，R., 1982. The Extended Phenotype：The Geneas the Unit of Selection[M]．Oxford：Freeman.
[4] 仓理新. 研究流行语的社会文化意义[J]. 北京师范学院学报（社会科学版），2010（2）.
[5] 陈琳霞，何自然. 语言模因现象探析[J]. 外语教学与研究，2006（3）.
[6] 崔蓬克. 当代汉语流行语概念的再界定[J]. 当代修辞学，2012（2）：27-31.
[7] 葛本仪. 汉语词汇学（第 3 册）[M]. 济南：山东大学出版社，2003：703.
[8] 何自然. 语言中的模因[J]. 语言科学，2005（6）.
[9] 何自然. 流行语流行的模因论解读[J]. 山东外语教学，2014（4）.
[10] 何自然. 语言模因及其变体的应用[J]. 语言学研究，2016（2）.

[11] 胡明扬，张莹. 70—80 年代北京青少年流行语[J]. 语文建设，1990（1）.
[12] 胡培安. 流行语的语言学界定及特征[J]. 华侨大学学报（哲学社会科学版），2012（1）.
[13] 孙曼均. 北京的流行词语与当地北京城市文化[J]. 语言文字应用，1998（3）.
[14] 夏中华. 关于流行语性质问题的思考[J]. 语言文字应用，2012（1）.
[15] 杨建国. 流行语的语言学研究及科学认定[J]. 语言教学与研究，2004（6）.
[16] 杨文全. 流行语的界说与初步描写[J]. 新疆大学学报（社会科学版），2002（2）.
[17] 郑荣馨. 略论社会流行语[J]. 三峡学刊，1994（2/3）.
[18] 邹嘉彦，游汝杰. 汉语新词与流行语的采录和界定[J]. 语言研究，2008（2）.

概念整合理论下汉语网络语在线意义构建
——以“菜鸡”一词为例

罗时乾

摘　要：汉语网络语凭借其独特的创新性、诙谐性、流行性在我们的日常生活用语中占有一席之地。随着认知语言学的蓬勃发展，越来越多的学者从概念整合的角度对网络词语进行分析。本文亦从概念整合理论出发，分析了网络流行语“菜鸡”一词在线意义构建的方式，并从仿拟的角度分析了“菜鸡”一词的来源，为类似的仿拟网络语的研究提供了一个新的视角。

关键词：“菜鸡”；概念整合理论；在线意义构建

Abstract: Chinese network language, featuring on unique innovation, humor and popularity, is an important part in our daily expression. With the vigorous development of cognitive linguistics, more and more scholars analyze network language from the perspective of conceptual blending. Based on the conceptual blending theory, this paper discusses how to construct the online meaning of the network word – “vegetable chicken” (incapable people), and analyzes the origin of the word “vegetable chicken” (incapable people) from the perspective of parody. This paper provides a new perspective for the study of network words parody.

Key words: “Vegetable Chicken” (Incapable People); Conceptual Blending Theory; Online Meaning Construction

1 引　言

随着互联网的飞速发展以及微信、微博、QQ 等信息传播平台的普及，诙谐幽默、新颖简洁的网络词语也如雨后春笋般地出现在人们眼前，如凤凰男、妈宝、扶弟魔、不明觉厉等。这些网络词语不仅生动形象而且感情色彩丰富，让我们在缺少表情、手势或者语气聊天时能准确把握住谈话人的态度和其所传达的信息，在我们的日常生活中扮演不可或缺的角色。

网络语言的流行很大程度上依赖于简单明了、生动活泼、寓意深刻的独特词汇和语句。（沈梅英，2012）网络语言因其别具一格的语言形式和生动形象的意义内涵而备受修辞学家和语言学家的青睐。目前语言学界对网络词语的研究也从早期的“不屑一顾”迈入了“研究探讨”阶段，对网络语言的研究层出不穷。研究角度和研究理论多种多样，从社会语言学、语用学、语义学、词汇学等角度对网络语言的构成、功能、语用特征、在线意义构建等进行多层次多方面的分析。随着认知语言学的兴起和不断壮大，越来越多的学者从概念整合的角度来研究网络语言意义的动态生成。谢颖梅（2015）利用概念整合理论来分析各类网络流行语的特点，探讨网络语言的社会成因、建构过程。宋雨涵（2017）分析出网络新词的概念整合类型有糅合型整合和截搭型整合，网络新词概念整合的层次更多地集中于次低和次高两个等级上，鲜有高层级整合的出现。罗雪（2017）对网络语言“一言不合就 XX”进行概念整合解析，从动态、静态两个方面来分析“一言不合就 XX”运用的过程及广为流行的原因。

阚安捷（2017）讨论了以“X 客”为代表的网络新词词族在相同的构词方式下不同的概念整合过程，发现“X 客”网络词族的产生和发展历史以及读者的背景知识在其意义建构的过程中起着一定的作用。张玮玲（2017）从概念整合的角度，通过分析网络流行语的运作流程归纳出其意义建构的两种模式，即类比赋义和联想赋义。沈梅英（2012）用概念整合理论来阐释网络语仿拟的认知机制。

随着网络游戏近年来的蓬勃发展，一个新的网络词语“菜鸡”出现在人们的视野中，还由“菜鸡”一词衍生出“神仙打架，菜鸡互啄”这句网络流行语。看到“菜鸡”，我们首先可能会想到“菜鸟”一词，“菜鸟”这个词已经被大众熟悉并且接纳，目前对“菜鸟”也有学者进行过研究。钟惠尧（2006）通过语素分析和近义比较来考察“菜鸟”的读音和意义。宋兴甫（2005）从仿词的角度探讨了“菜鸟”一词的来源、组合方式及语汇意义。但目前还没有学者对“菜鸡”一词及其衍生句子“神仙打架，菜鸡互啄”进行分析。为了让读者对“菜鸡”一词有更深入的认识，本文将对其词汇来源、词汇构成和语义特征从概念整合理论出发对其在线意义构建进行探讨。

2　概念整合理论

概念整合理论由认知语言学家 Fauconnier 和 Turner 提出，认为人们在加工和融合概念时，会从各种来源中提取相关概念，并将它们进行短期记忆的概念整合处理。概念整合理论建立在心智空间理论的基础上。“心智空间是人类进行范畴化、概念化和思维的媒介”。（王寅，2006）心智空间理论存在一定的局限性，它只揭示了意义建构的一些基本原则，并未对各意义概念之间的联系及工作机制等做出进一步研究。（刘正光，2002）因此，在此基础上建立起来的概念整合理论建立起详尽的模型来揭示人们的语义认知工作机制。

“概念整合”是人类有选择地提取来自不同空间的输入信息并将其意义整合成一个新概念结构的一系列认知活动。（张玮玲，2017）它是心理空间之间的一种普遍的认知操作，一般来说，概念整合理论关注四个心理空间（类属空间、输入空间 1、输入空间 2、合成空间）之间的概念投射。空间之间能进行跨空间的对应连接映射，两个输入空间的共有结构及其共有的抽象信息被投射到第三个空间即类属空间里；而同时，在这两个输入心理空间的基础上，通过“组合（composition）”“完善（completion）”和“扩展（elaboration）”三个彼此关联的心理认知过程的相互作用，（刘正光，2002）跨空间的部分映射、匹配并有选择地投射第四个空间——合成空间，合成空间再从两个输入空间中有选择地提取部分结构，形成层创结构。这样，四个空间通过投射链彼此连接起来，形成一个概念整合网络，如图 1 所示。Fauconnier 和 Turner（2002）认为，要得到合理的合成空间，概念整合必须遵守整合（integration）、构造（toplogy）、网络（web）、解包（unpacking）、充分理由（good reason）五条优化原则，建立合理的概念整合网络。Fauconnier 和 Turner（2002）还指出概念整合网络的最基本类型有：镜像网络（mirror network）、简单网络（simplex networks）、单域网络（single-scope network）以及双域网络（double-scope network）。

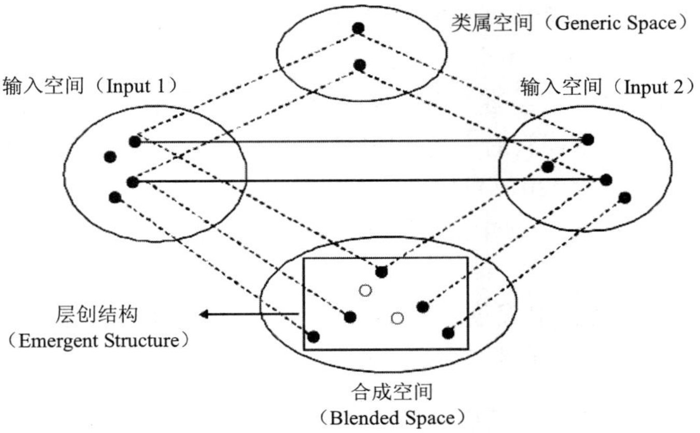

图 1　概念整合理论动态示意图

3 “菜鸡”一词具体分析

“菜鸡”这个网络词目前还未收纳进词典，一般认为该词表示贬义，指那些在某方面既不擅长又特别差劲的人，比“菜鸟”还不如。“菜鸡”一词在网络上已广泛使用，从网络游戏拓展到其他领域，下面三个例子可以很好地证明“菜鸡”一词使用领域广泛并且其衍生语“菜鸡互啄”也受到网友们的认可和使用。

例 1　A：我今天排位赛遇到几个“菜鸡”，又输了！

B：我也是，排位老输，最近可能不适合打游戏！

例 2　湖人和骑士这比赛是真实的“菜鸡互啄”，一个瞎打，一个瞎投。

例 3　我的 pre 怎么越做越差，现在简直是“菜鸡”一个，我要好好学英语。（引自微博网友评论）

目前人们对“菜鸡”的来源以及产生途径也各执一词，其主要原因是网络语言的发明者一般都是“随手拈来”，使用者也不拘一格，并且“发明人”及其源头初衷也无从考证。很多人看到“菜鸡”的第一眼或许会以为它是指一道菜，还有人认为“菜鸡”就是“菜鸟”的意思，但鸡比鸟更低等，它表达的意思可能是指某人连“菜鸟”都不如。但本文认为“菜鸡”一词极可能是由于修辞格——仿拟中的仿词造成的。仿词是根据表达的需要，更换现成词语的某个语素或词，临时仿造出新的词语，改变原来特定的词义，创造出新意的修辞手法。由此可知仿词是在现有词语的基础上进行仿拟，既在形式上还保持与原有词语近似的特点，又在内容上赋予新的意义。

从仿词的角度来看，“菜鸡”这个词和“菜鸟”一词缘分颇深。首先这两个词都是偏正结构，由“菜”和“鸡”以及“菜”和“鸟”这两个语素组成，“菜”在这个词语中对“鸡”和“鸟”起修饰或限制作用。“菜”字在《现代汉语大词典》中有 5 种解释：①蔬菜类植物的总称；②肴馔的总称；③指素食，斋食；④专指油菜；⑤方言。懦弱无能，差劲。与上文中的例子相联系，从具体语境中进行分析。我们认为“菜鸡”或“菜鸟”中的“菜”表达的是第五种意思“懦弱无能，差劲”，且表示贬义。下面再来看“鸡”这个语素。“鸡”在《现代汉语大词典》中有 3 种解释：①家禽；②十二生肖之一，与十二地支的酉相配；③娼妇。从第三个释义可以推测出，“鸡”这个字可以表达一定的贬义，这也可以从一些与“鸡”有关带有一定贬义的词语或成语中看出来，如“鸡犬不宁”，“鸡飞狗跳”，“鸡犬不留”，“鸡鸣狗盗”等。“菜”和“鸡”合起来就是贬上加贬，更能表达出贬低的意味。

《现代汉语大词典》并没有“菜鸟”或“菜鸡”两词的具体解释，但我们一般认为“菜鸟”用来戏称刚进入一个新环境而对诸事不熟或愚蠢的人。宋兴甫（2005）指出，“菜鸟”一词极可能是在北方方言词汇“菜货或菜包子”（“菜货”在《现代汉语大词典》表示下等货、劣货，而“菜包子”则比喻无用的人，两者都带有贬义）及这类现有词的基础上，借了“菜”的意义，把“菜”后面“货或包子”这些无生命的实物变换为乖巧可爱的“鸟”，不仅在视觉上给人以冲击，且含有几分喜爱的情感因素，即使用其来损人和贬人也比“菜货”之类的词更文雅、更含蓄。从“菜鸟”对“菜货”和“菜包子”的仿拟中可以推测出“菜鸡”也是对“菜鸟”的仿拟，但“菜鸟”仿拟“菜货”和“菜包子”是为了显得更文雅含蓄，而“菜鸡”对“菜鸟”的仿拟则偏离了这个目的，只为了显示出贬低的意味，表达出对对方或者对自身的不满或嘲笑。而且“鸡”为家禽，“鸟”为飞禽，在普通人的认知中，“鸡”看上去要比“鸟”低等一些，并且鸡一般都比较弱小，任人宰割，所以“菜鸡”的贬斥意味可能比“菜鸟”更深。

还有一种猜测是认为“菜鸡”是对“弱鸡”一词的仿拟。“弱鸡”一词在《现代汉语大词典》中也没有解释，但一般我们认为是指在某方面能力比较弱的人，把“人”比喻为“鸡”，表达出人就像小鸡仔一样弱小，任人宰割。“弱”这个字在《现代汉语大词典》上有 6 种解释：①气力小，势力不强；②差，不如；③削弱；④年幼，年少；⑤丧失，失去；⑥表示略少于某个数值。从以上释义可以看出，“弱”表达的贬义没有“菜”那么浓，并且因为“菜”的引申义已经被大家所熟练运用及广泛接受，所以“弱鸡”就被仿拟成“菜鸡”。

最后一种猜测是“菜鸡”一词可能是对“辣鸡”一词的仿拟。“辣鸡”现在也是比较“火”的网络语言，主要是运用在网络游戏中。“辣鸡”其实就是“垃圾”的谐音仿拟词，因为有很多网站会屏蔽骂人的关键词，所以网友们就想出用《舌尖上的中国》里面的“辣鸡”来取代“垃圾”一词。因为在游戏里面经常会吐槽别人的技术很“菜”，很“辣鸡”，然后用着可能就合并起来出现“菜鸡”一词。

“菜鸡”一词的真实来源已经无从考证，但我们可以推测出“菜鸡”可能是对“菜鸟”“弱鸡”或“辣鸡”进行仿拟得来的，它既保持原词的特点，也增加了自己独特的意味，为网络语言增添了一丝新的色彩。

4　概念整合理论下“菜鸡”的在线意义构建

从概念整合理论来看，“仿词”一词本身就是一个合成空间，“仿”一词说明存在两个输入空间，一个心理空间和一个心智空间。（沈梅英，2012）因此用概念整合理论来分析仿词“菜鸡”十分恰当，从中我们可以发现“菜鸡”的在线意义构建方式。以概念整合理论来分析，四个心智空间均参与了“菜鸡”一词概念的认知过程，如图 2 所示。输入空间 1 包含的是“菜”字的引申义：懦弱无能，差劲；输入空间 2 则包含“鸡”的比喻义：弱小，低等；然后两个空间通过跨空间投射到类属空间得出“菜”和“鸡”的共同特点：弱小，差劲；通过组合、完善并扩展在合成空间里就得到一个新的词“菜鸡”，表示那些弱小又差劲的人。同理我们也可以分析出“菜鸟”“弱鸡”以及“辣鸡”的概念整合方式。

图 2 将对由“菜鸡”衍生出来的一句网络流行语“神仙打架，菜鸡互啄”进行概念整合的认知分析。这句话也属于仿拟的其中一类——仿句。这句话的原句子是“神仙打架，小鬼遭殃”，其字面意思是：神仙们起了争斗，反而是底下的小鬼遭了倒霉；引申义：地位高的几

方人在争权夺利，倒霉的往往是那些说不上话的底下人。原话强调的是“神仙打架”的后果，而仿句更多的是形成对比，把“神仙打架”和“菜鸡互啄”的场面、气势、姿势、整体形象等进行对比，形成画面上的反差，更加突出“神仙”的“神”和“仙”以及“菜鸡”的“菜”。

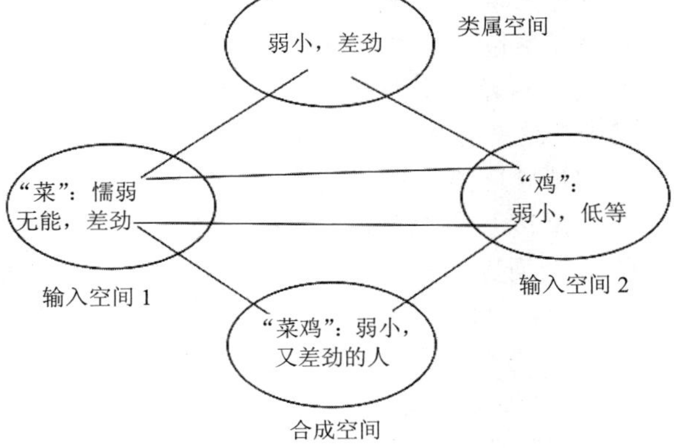

图 2 “菜鸡”的概念认知模型

以概念整合理论来分析，四个心智空间参与“神仙打架，菜鸡互啄”一句的概念认知过程，如图 3 所示。输入空间 1 包含的是“神仙打架”的属性：强者对决，气势恢宏，场面大，整体感观较好；输入空间 2 则包含的是“菜鸡互啄”的属性：弱者对决，无气势，场面小，整体感观较差；两个空间通过跨空间投射到类属空间得出“神仙打架”和“菜鸡互啄”的共同特点：争斗，比拼；然后在合成空间里对两个输入空间的内容进行对比，最终通过组合、完善和拓展得到层创结构：“神仙打架”有看头，“菜鸡互啄”没看头。对“菜鸡”和“神仙打架，菜鸡互啄”的概念整合解读过程也遵循 Fauconnier 语义理解的认知程序：确定其字面意义→对照其隐含意义的相似性→推断出实际意义。（梁艳春，2003）通过这种认知推理方式，人们不难理解类似的网络新词。

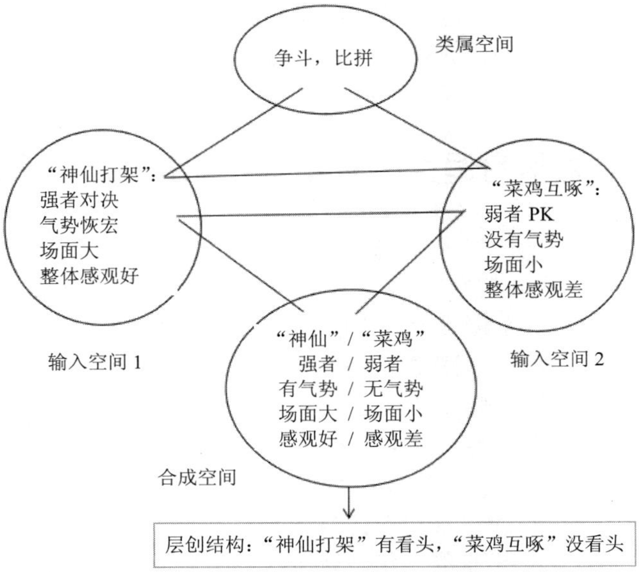

图 3 “神仙打架，菜鸡互啄”的概念认知模型

5 结　语

网络语言是互联网和信息传播平台发展的产物，其创新性及诙谐性给我们的日常生活带来了便捷与乐趣。概念整合理论作为认知语言学的研究热点之一，将语言特别是语义的研究带入到一个新的时代。Fauconnier 和 Turner（2002）指出通过概念的整合，人们理解了其所生活的物质世界、心智世界和社会世界。在概念整合的引领下，本文不仅探索了“菜鸡”一词的来源，还结合概念整合理论，利用其强大的解释力破解了“菜鸡”一词的认知奥秘，让我们能够从一个新的角度去解读网络流行语的在线意义构建，也有助于揭示类似“菜鸡”这样的网络语仿拟表面下隐含的语义，为网络语言认知研究提供了新的视角和新的途径。

参考文献

[1] Fauconnier，Turner. G. M.，2002. *The Way We Think：Conceptual Blending and the Mind's Hidden Complexities* [M]. New York：Basic Books.

[2] 梁艳春. 合成空间理论对委婉语的阐释力[D]. 暨南大学华文学院学报，2003（2）：53-61.

[3] 刘正光. Fauconnier 的概念合成理论：阐释与质疑[J]. 外语与外语教学，2002（10）：842.

[4] 沈梅英. 概念整合理论对网络语仿拟的阐释力[J]. 西安外国语大学学报，2012，20（2）：48-51.

[5] 宋兴甫. 浅析“菜鸟”[J]. 郧阳师范高等专科学校学报，2005（2）：143-144.

[6] 王寅. 认知语言学[M]. 上海：上海外语教育出版社，2006.

[7] 现代汉语大词典编委会. 现代汉语大词典[M]. 上海：上海辞书出版社，2010.

[8] 张玮玲. 概念整合对网络流行语的阐释力[J]. 商丘师范学院学报，2017，33（1）：107-109.

[9] 钟惠尧.“菜鸟”小议[J]. 湖南冶金职业技术学院学报，2006（4）：514-515+532.

《虬髯客传》两个译本中文化负载词英译对比分析
——基于关联理论视角

余　悦

摘　要：唐传奇作品中，《虬髯客传》被认为是中国武侠小说的开山之作，对后世的武侠小说产生了深远影响，同时，也吸引众多学者对其进行研究和翻译。正确理解和翻译《虬髯客传》中的文化负载词，不仅有助于向国外读者传播中国优秀的文化作品，展示中国传统民族文化及特性，还能丰富英语语言文化。本文旨在关联理论的指导下，对杨宪益、戴乃迭译本，William H. Nienhauser Jr. 编著的 *Tang Dynasty Tales: A Guided Reader* 中 Wang Jing 译本进行对比分析，并提出一些文化负载词翻译方面的看法和建议。

关键词：《虬髯客传》；关联理论；文化负载词

Abstract：The Tang dynasty tale - *The Man with the Curly Beard*，as the forerunner of Chinese material arts fictions，has exerted great influence on literary creation in the later generations and intrigued researches and translators. It is conducive to disseminating an excellent Chinese literary work，demonstrating traditional Chinese folk cultures and enriching English culture when dealing accurately with culture-loaded words and translated version of *The Man with the Curly Beard.* Based on the relevance theory，comparative analyses of two different translated versions - one is translated by Yang Xianyi and Dai Naidie and another by Wang Jing，in a book called *Tang Dynasty Tales：A Guided Reader* compiled by William H. Nienhauser Jr. - have been produced in this paper. Meanwhile，it offers some views and suggestions about translating culture-loaded words.

Key words：*The Man with the Curly Beard*；the Relevance Theory；Culture-loaded Words

1　《虬髯客传》简介

1.1　内容介绍

隋末时乱，平民李靖向当时权倾天下的大臣杨素进言献策，不俗的谈吐吸引了侍妓红拂女，毅然随李靖私奔。二人逃往太原的路上结识了虬髯客。虬髯客从二人口中得知太原有“异人”李世民，并通过李靖的朋友刘文静见到该人，顿时对争夺天下心灰意冷，但又不死心，约道兄再次与李世民见面，经道兄证实之后，虬髯客便将自己的财产悉数送给李靖夫妇，以助他们辅佐李世民建功立业，自己则和妻子离去。贞观十年，李靖担任左仆射平章事，虬髯客在扶馀国称帝。

1.2　作者介绍

关于《虬髯客传》的作者不能确指。后世多认为作者为杜光庭。杜光庭，字宾圣（或宾至），号东瀛子，唐末五代著名道教学者，勤奋好学，博览群书。唐懿宗时期弃儒从道，后隐青城山白云溪，潜心修道。宋代洪迈《容斋随笔》卷十二《王珪李靖》称有杜光庭《虬髯客传》。《宋史·艺文志》著录杜光庭《虬髯客传》，明代《顾氏文房小说》本署杜光庭撰（宋良宏，2009）。

2 相关理论简介

2.1 关联理论概念

关联理论是学者 Dan Sperber 和 Deidre Wilson 在其合著《关联性：交际与认知》（*Relevance: Communication and Cognition*）中提出的概念。关联理论认为人们在语言交际过程中，包含明说和暗含两种意义，明说表达一种信息意图，听话人可以从中获得语境假设，而暗含则传达一种交际意图，即让听话人明白说话人试图传递信息。（余丽雯等，2010）因此，人们的语言交际是一个明示——推理的过程。具体来说，在交际过程中，明示就是说话人通过语言或非语言的形式传达出听话人能够直接理解的信息或意图，而推理就是听话人需要根据已经理解的明示部分，结合语境进行一定的推理从而明了说话人暗含的部分。

关联理论的另一观点认为，语言交际目的在于追求最佳关联，这是交际成功的核心因素。话语最佳关联性的条件是：话语使听话人不必付出不必要的努力就能得到说话人想要传达的意思；说话人想要传达的意思值得听话人付出努力，即对听话人产生“积极的语境效果”（Gutt，2001）。因此说话人要为听话者提供充分的语境，并且使听话者在正确理解信息意图时付出最小努力。

2.2 关联理论对翻译的指导作用

关联理论是对人类认知交际的解释，同样可以解释为交际的翻译。如此，翻译的整个过程就可以做如下解释：首先，原作者（说话人）需要向原文读者（听话人）明示并提供一定的交际语境，从而使原文读者能够明确理解作者意图。而译者作为听话人的一种，需要利用自己的语言、专业能力等从原作者的明示中推理出作者暗含的意图，寻求话语与语境之间的最佳关联；其次，译者（说话人）需要在译文中向译语读者（听话人）转达原文作者意图，并且因原文读者和译文读者的认知环境有较大差异，这就要求译者应运用自己的知识与技能为译文读者构建语境，使其能够通过最小的努力达到对原作者意图的理解。

由于不同的语言文化背景，即使是原作者明示的信息有时候也会因认知差异难以让译语读者理解，而原作者暗含的意图对于译语读者来说会因“文化缺失”产生理解上的困难。因此对于译者来说，首要任务便是具有扎实的原语言能力，了解原作者与原文读者的文化、认知语境等。同时，译者也要在最佳关联原则的引导下去搜索作者想要其读者（译者）获得的语境假设，推理得到作者想要其读者得到的最佳关联的交际效果；（孙正峰，2008）其次，译者需要充分考虑译语读者的认知水平与审美期待，通过运用灵活的翻译技巧为其提供充足的语境。不过，提供充足语境并不代表赋予译文所有的信息，译者应该有重点地突出重要的信息，以减少译语读者了解作者意图时所做的努力，这也是满足最佳关联的必要条件之一。

3 《虬髯客传》两个译本中文化负载词英译对比分析

3.1 文化负载词的含义及分类

因历史背景、地理位置、文化底蕴、思维方式等多方面的不同，英汉两种语言存在诸多差异，这些差异体现在词汇方面就是文化负载词。文化负载词是指标志某种文化中特有事物的词、词组和习语，这些词汇反映了特定民族在漫长的历史进程中逐渐积累的有别于其他民族独特的活动方式。（廖七一，2000）文化负载词又称词汇空缺，指源语词汇包含的文化信息无法在译入语中找到相对应的词汇。（余立霞，2016）可以说，文化负载词是不同文化之间交流的重要桥梁，因此在翻译过程中，准确恰当地译出文化负载词对译者来说是一项必需的任务。

美国翻译理论家尤金•奈达（E. A. Nida）对语言中的文化因素进行分类，将文化负载词分为五类：生态文化负载词、物质文化负载词、社会文化负载词、宗教文化负载词和语言文化负载词。（Nida，1993）参照这种划分方式，《虬髯客传》中出现的文化负载词同样可以划分为五类：生态文化负载词、物质文化负载词、社会文化负载词、宗教文化负载词和语言文化负载词。

3.2 《虬髯客传》中出现的文化负载词

3.2.1 生态文化负载词

不同国家或民族因地域环境、气候特点、自然条件等因素的不同，对大自然与生态环境的认知也会有所不同。生态文化负载词就是反映某一语言描述生态环境的文化词汇，主要包括动物、植物、天气、地理等。《虬髯客传》中出现的生态负载词以地理文化词汇为主，主要有江都、西京、太原、灵石、汾阳桥、马行东酒楼、扶馀国等。

3.2.2 物质文化负载词

物质文化负载词指的是特定语言文化团体下的人们创造出的能反映其日常生活的食物、服饰、居住、出行、产品的文化词汇。《虬髯客传》中出现的物质文化负载词主要有红拂、轩、闼、胡饼、衫、履、裘、东厅、中堂等。

3.2.3 社会文化负载词

不同语言文化的群体，其生活方式、风俗习惯、历史文化背景等也会有所不同，这些不同反映到社会礼仪称呼、休闲娱乐名称、社会习俗等方面的词汇或短语就是社会文化负载词。《虬髯客传》中出现大量的社会文化负载词，主要有：隋炀帝、司空、卫公、布衣、妾、妓、五更、拜、李郎、三兄、州将、天子、十数巡、贞观十年、左仆射平章事等。

3.2.4 宗教文化负载词

宗教文化是人类文化不可缺少的一部分，影响人们的思维方式、伦理标准、意识形态等。而宗教文化负载词则是承载特定语言团体的特定宗教传统的词汇和短语。受道教思想的影响，《虬髯客传》中出现一些宗教文化负载词，主要有望气者、奇气、善相者、道兄、龙虎之状等。

3.2.5 语言文化负载词

汉语和英语属于不同的语系，因此在语音、字形、语法、语用等多方面存在很大差异。

语言文化负载词就是承载特定语言团体、语言系统的音系、语法和形式等特征的文化词汇。《虬髯客传》中出现的语言文化负载词主要有“丝萝非独生，愿托乔木”、尸居余气、神气扬扬、虎啸风生、龙吟云萃等。

3.3 两个译本中文化负载词英译对比分析

本文选取两个译本中的文化负载词进行对比分析，分别是杨宪益、戴乃迭在《唐代传奇选》一书中的译本，William H. Nienhauser Jr.编著的 *Tang Dynasty Tales: A Guided Reader* 中 Wang Jing 译者的译本。下文分别简称为杨和 Wang。

3.3.1 生态文化负载词英译对比

《虬髯客传》中出现的生态文化负载词大多为地理名称，选取其中典型的词汇进行对比分析，可以总结出合适的翻译方法。

（1）原文：隋炀帝之幸江都也，命司空杨素守西京。

译文：

（杨）When Emperor Yang of the Sui Dynasty（605-618）visited Yangzhou，Councillor Yang Su was ordered to guard the West Capital.

（Wang）When Emperor Yang（r. 605-616）of the Sui（569-618）Dynasty favored Jiangdu with a visit，he entrusted Yang Su（d. 606），Minister of Works，to guard the western capital.

“江都”是古代城市的名称，现今称为扬州。比较两个译本，其共同点是都采用了音译的翻译方法，不同之处在于，杨的译本中直接呈现“江都”现今名称“扬州”的音译 Yangzhou；Wang 的译本中除去音译为 Jiangdu，还在脚注处用近一百个单词解释了“江都”的地理位置及历史发展（因篇幅所限没有附上脚注内容）等信息。

从译语读者实施最小努力获取信息的角度来看，Wang 的译本尽管能够让读者了解到更多中国地理文化，但是读者要花费时间去理解这些信息，并不利于读者的阅读效率，也不利于故事情节的推动，显然阻碍了对交际最佳关联的追求。相比之下，杨的译本中更符合关联理论所倡导的理念。

（2）原文：李郎宜与一妹复入京，某日午时，访我于马行东酒楼。

译文：

（杨）You two go back to the capital，but meet me one afternoon at the wineshop east of Mahang.

（Wang）At the seventh watch 31 of a certain day，visit me at the wineshop east of the horse market.

“马行东酒楼”概念有些模糊，不过既然在原文中是作为一个地理标识，可算作是一个特殊的生态文化负载词，也可讨论一下类似的词汇如何翻译。三个译本中，杨和 Wang 都将其理解为马行东侧的酒楼，不过对“马行”一词的理解有差别，在此可猜测杨的译本中将“马行”理解为一个店名或是其他跟马不相关的指称，译为“Mahang”，而 Wang 则将其理解为卖马的地方，因此译为“the horse market”。

从最佳关联的效果来看，显然，Wang 的译本更为恰当：杨的译本中“Mahang”一词过于模糊，一定程度上会阻碍读者的阅读；相比之下，Wang 的译本解释更清楚。

3.3.2 物质文化负载词英译对比

《虬髯客传》中的物质文化负载词相对较少，且两个译本中的表达整体较为接近，此处只选择一个表达差异较大的例子进行分析。

原文：公出市胡饼。

译文：

（杨）While Li went out to buy bread…

（Wang）Li Jing went out to buy some tartar bread.

“胡饼”在现代更通行的叫法是馕，是由少数民族流传而来，其中“胡”就是代表少数民族。根据古书记载，胡饼在汉代就传入中原，唐代更是盛行，对中原的饮食文化产生了一定的影响。两个译本中都运用意译的方法选用了“bread”一词，不同的是，Wang 在前面加了修饰词“tartar”。

比较两个译本，杨的译本略胜一筹：尽管没有体现胡饼一词背后的饮食文化，但是更加简洁明了，容易让译语读者理解；而 Wang 的译本尽管呈现了一定的文化内涵，但是“tartar”即“鞑靼的”，该词最早在唐朝时期出现的，是对北方游牧民族的称呼，并不能完全表达出少数民族的意思，另外也会给读者带去阅读上的困惑，这个在行文中显然是不必要的。

3.3.3 社会文化负载词英译对比

《虬髯客传》中的社会文化负载词很多，以人物的社会头衔或礼仪称呼为主，通过对两个译本的分析，可以探知称呼背后的社会文化，并了解相关的翻译方法。

（1）原文：其夜五更初，忽闻叩门而声低者，公起问焉。

译文：

（杨）That night，just before dawn，there was a soft knocking at Li’s door…

（Wang）That night，at the beginning of the fifth watch，he suddenly heard someone knocking softly on the door.

“五更”：受科技水平和计时手段的限制，我国古代把夜晚分成五个时段，用鼓打更报时，分别是一更，二更，三更，四更，五更，五更即为现代时间的凌晨 3：00—5：00。杨的译本中根据原作者所表示的时间段采用意译的方式，译为“just before dawn”；Wang 则是采取了与“江都”同样的处理方式——直译，并用加注的方式对该词进行了解释。

从读者付出最小努力获取作者意图的角度来讲，杨的译本简单，容易被译语读者所接受；而 Wang 的译本虽然忠实原文，但如前所说，容易造成读者的困惑，影响读者的阅读效率，且不利于小说情节的推动。

（2）原文：张氏遥呼：“李郎且来见三兄！”

译文：

（杨）“Come and meet my cousin，” she called to Li，who bowed to…

（Wang）Miss Zhang called out from a distance：“Master Li，come to bow to our third brother！”

首先讨论“李郎”这个称谓。张氏，即红拂女与李靖情投意合，因此“李郎”的称呼更像是妻子对丈夫的呼唤。杨的译本中虽然巧妙地避免了“李郎”的翻译，但在某种程度上弱化了二人之间的亲密关系，甚至容易有命令他人的嫌疑，略有不足；Wang 的译本中选用“Master”一词，在英语文化中，主要用于中层，即小贵族和新兴资产阶级和一些高收入的职业阶层（刘齐方，2011）。使用该词能体现张氏对李郎一定程度的崇敬态度，也符合李郎目前正待干一番事业的状态。

“三兄”是张氏得知虬髯客的姓氏及在家中排行之后对虬髯客的称呼。杨的译本中以“cousin”表示，而 Wang 则直译了“三兄”一词。

从译语读者的接受度来讲，显然杨的译本更能让读者理解：汉语中的亲属称谓系统繁复多样，此外，用亲属称谓语称呼非亲属成员是现代汉语口语中十分普遍的现象，我们将这种现象称为亲属称谓语的泛化。（潘攀，1998）此处的“三兄”就是泛化使用的表现，相比之下，英语的亲属称谓就比较笼统模糊，一词多义，覆盖面广。cousin 一词更是万能，对年龄、父系、母系，甚至连性别都不分。因此 cousin 更符合译语读者的习语习惯。

3.3.4 宗教文化负载词英译对比

如前所说，《虬髯客传》有一定的政治目的，赋予了李世民命中注定的“天子”身份。文中从道教的思想着手，出现一些与道教相关的宗教文化负载词。

原文：望气者言太原有奇气，使吾访之。

译文：

（杨）An astrologer told me there had been a strange portent at Taiyuan, and I should look into it.

（Wang）A man who [excels in] observing the air [for heavenly signs] said that Taiyuan had an extraordinary emanation and asked me to investigate it.

“望气”是我国历史上一种较为独特的文化现象，主要是将人事的某种变化和天象及自然界的变化联系起来。英语文化中的星座研究也是同样的道理。中国的“望气”主要体现在政治方面，人们认为，有天子的地方会出现所谓的天子气，非常重要的贵人所在之地也会有对应的气。两个译本中，杨采取意译的方式，选取了英语中有类似意思的词语表示“望气者”；而 Wang 的译本则是采取直译加释意的方式。

从最佳关联及读者实施最小努力两个方面来说，杨的译本很容易使读者理解“望气者”的职能或作用，但是某种程度上没有诠释完整作者的原意及这个身份的具体操作情况，在最佳关联的达成方面略有不足；Wang 的译本加入了解释的部分，且笔墨不多，不影响读者的阅读效率，还解释出何为“望气”，更符合关联理论指导下的翻译标准。

3.3.5 语言文化负载词英译对比

《虬髯客传》中出现的语言文化负载词以四字词语、习语等为主，这样的词语很少能在英语中找到对等的表达，因此分析三个译本的翻译是很有必要的。

原文：尸居余气，不足畏也。

译文：

（杨）Never mind him – he’s an old imbecile.

（Wang）He lives like a corpse with only one breath left and is not to be feared.

“尸居余气”指像尸体一样但还有一口气，指人将要死亡。也比喻人暮气沉沉，无所作为。原文中，这句话是红拂女用来形容大势已去的杨素，用的是该成语的比喻意。杨的译本采取意译的方式，并以名词形式展现出来；而 Wang 则是采取直译的方式，遵从字面意思上进行翻译。

从最佳关联角度来看，杨的译本明显表达出作者想要传达杨素已不能成气候的意图；而 Wang 虽然忠实原文，但是没有译出“尸居余气”的比喻意，没有成功表达出作者的意图。

4 结　语

4.1 两种译本文化负载词的翻译特点

通过对比分析，在满足最佳关联及译语读者付出最小认知努力角度来讲，两个译本的文化负载词翻译各有优劣。杨宪益、戴乃迭的译本关于文化负载词的翻译大部分采取意译的方式，专注于文本内部的一致性，以服务目标语读者为目的，保留了作品文化负载词的原有味道，将一部分文化负载词转化成容易被目标语读者接受的文化意象。但译本在一些文化负载词承载的文化信息传递方面有不足之处。Wang Jing 的译本基本上以直译或直译加注的方式呈现给读者，力图将小说中文化负载词承载的文化信息原原本本地展现给目标语读者。这种方法能很好地保持语际间的一致性，有助于中国文化传播，但同时，该译本也在一定程度上影响了读者的阅读效率，增加了读者的阅读负担。

4.2 文化负载词的翻译建议

结合前文所做的分析与比较，可以发现，两个译本中的译者关于文化负载词的翻译，以意译、直译、直译加注（释意）三种方式为主。那么，究竟依据什么选择合适的翻译方法呢？以下是笔者基于关联理论所做的分析。

如果文化负载词在上下文中所传递的意义主要是其基本含义，所承载的文化信息并非是作者想要重点突出的，宜采用意译的方式，在译语中能够找到可替代相关概念的词汇。如“胡饼”在文中属于一带而过的信息，其翻译更推荐符合译语读者习惯的“bread”，而非直译“tartar bread”；又比如“五更”在作者的笔下只是提供一个大致的参照时间，如果直译的话会造成读者的困惑。

如果文化负载词在上下文中有一定的文化内涵，宜采用直译加注（释意）的方式，在保证文本顺畅的同时将文化信息传递给读者。如“望气者”是中国特有的文化，虽可以类比为英语国家的占星家或预言家，但仍有其独特之处，且含有一定的宗教信仰在其中。再如涉及中国的地理名称，如果含有一定的历史意义，也适合采用直译加注的方式，但加注部分不宜过长，否则会影响读者的阅读（主要针对小说一类的文本）。

参考文献

[1] Gutt E.A. , 2001. *Pragmatic Aspects of Translation：Some Relevance-theory Observations*，In Leo Hickey（ed.）. The Pragmatics of Translation. Shanghai：Shanghai Foreign Language Education Press，43.

[2] Nida. E. , 1993. *Language，Culture，and Translating*. Shanghai：Shanghai Foreign Language Education Press.

[3] 廖七一. 当代西方翻译理论探索[M]. 南京：译林出版社，2000.

[4] 刘齐方. 汉语通称比较研究[D]. 内蒙古大学，2011.

[5] 宋良宏.《虬髯客传》作者考[J]. 黑龙江教育学院学报，2009（12）：131-133.

[6] 孙正峰. 翻译过程的关联理论视角[J]. 内江科技，2008（5）：23.

[7] 余丽雯，全红. 从关联理论看归化和异化翻译的对立和统一[J]. 科技信息，2010（29）：24.

[8] 余立霞. 毛泽东诗词英译本中文化负载词翻译的对比研究[J]. 外语学刊，2016（6）：106-109.

[9] 潘攀. 论亲属称谓语的泛化[J]. 语言文字应用，1998（2）.

基于中介语的初中英语学习者写作偏误分析

江 露

摘 要：本文以偏误分析理论和中介语理论为指导，以成都市郊区某中学初一年级 2 个班共 110 名学生所撰写的 280 份英语作文为语料，对其中的中介语偏误进行定量和定性分析。统计结果显示错误共计 1431 处，其中偏误为 1242 处，失误为 189 处。定性分析发现，偏误以局部偏误为主，局部偏误又以动词偏误为中心，共计 569 处。研究发现：（1）英语二语初学者的局部错误和全局错误占比与二语学习时间长短无关。（2）局部错误以实词错误为主，实词错误主要是动词错误和名词错误，虚词错误占比较小，但比例会随二语学习时间的延长而上升。（3）母语为汉语的英语二语初学者犯错原因主要在于母语负迁移。

关键词：写作偏误；偏误分析；中介语；初中英语学习者

Abstracts: Guided by Error Analysis Theory and Interlanguage Theory，this thesis adopts a corpus of 280 compositions of 110 students from 2 classes of Grade 7 in a Junior High school located in the suburb of Chengdu. Both qualitative analysis and quantitative analysis are involved With 1431 errors in all. 1242 errors and 189 mistakes are identified. The qualitative analysis reveals that errors are mainly local errors，in which 569 verb errors are found. Based on the data analysis，the interlanguage model is built.（1）The ration of partial error and global errors is not connected with the time for SL learning.（2）Lexical word errors cover the most part of local errors，and verb errors and noun errors cover the most part of lexical errors. The ration of functional word errors，which covers a small part，increases with a deep learning in SL.（3）The main reason why students commit such errors lie in the negative mother-tongue transfer.

Key words: written errors；error analysis；interlanguage；Junior High school students

1 引 言

偏误理论最早提出于 20 世纪 60 年代。（Corder，1967）由于对比分析不能解释所有的语言错误，逐渐被适用范围更广的偏误分析理论所替代。自 20 世纪 80 年代偏误分析理论引入中国以来，已取得不小的研究成果。罗晓杰和孙琳（2003）对偏误理论进行了全面的介绍，提出了一些对于偏误的纠正策略。而从近 30 年所发表的论文看，其研究对象主要集中于大学生群体，（冯巧丽，2010；于景梅，2010）偏误分析语料大多来自语料库，只有少部分学者以中小学生为研究对象、收集实时语料，基于偏误理论，对其中介语错误进行横向分析和研究。还有部分学者对二语学习者的中介语偏误特点进行分类和归纳。（章宜华，2012）通过分析不同水平的英语学习者的中介语偏误得出二语学习的偏误实际上是有规律可循的。（王晓燕，2006）本文收集了 280 份初中生考试作文为语料，对其中出现的 1242 处偏误进行纵向分析。

中介语是指二语学习者居于本族语与目标语之间的语言状态，这一状态是随着学习的深入，由接近本族语水平逐渐提升到接近目标语水平。中介语假说出现于 20 世纪 60 年代末和

70 年代初。（Selinker，1972）后有研究证明中介语会话对外语学习具有促进作用。（Long & Porter，1985；Long，Adams，McLean & Castanos，1976；Li，1989；Pica，1992）近年来国内学者基于中介语理论的研究主要集中在对中介语石化现象的描述及其出现的原因，（杨文秀，2000；杨连瑞，2014）还有部分综述性文章，（李炯英，2003；白凤欣，2007；杨连瑞等，2015）对中介语理论、现象、产生原因、研究背景和前景进行了梳理和说明。中介语石化现象主要出现在中高水平二语学习者中，因此国内有关中介语的研究多以初中高年级、高中、大学学生为研究对象。本文以英语二语低水平学习者为研究对象，前后进行了两次语料收集，通过对错误类型及数量的分析，旨在构建英语二语初学者的中介语模型。

2 研究设计

本文选取了成都市区县某附属中学初一年级 110 名学生作为研究对象。该校学生皆从周边各街区小学通过中考或自主招生考试考入该校，随机分班。本文的研究对象既不至于对英语太过陌生，也不至于英语水平过高而影响初中英语初学者的中介语普遍水平。研究语料分前后两次收集，分别来自半期考试、月考和部分学生的家庭作业。学生事先并不知道其作文会作为中介语研究语料，考试形式正式，内容具有涵盖度，研究对象不会过于紧张或放松而影响其写作水平。前后两次语料收集间隔 5 个月，在此期间，研究对象的中介语水平有显著提高，对于构建英语初学者的中介语模型具有指导意义。收集语料后采用 James 的错误分类法（James，1998）对研究对象作文中的错误进行分类，并统计错误数量。数据统计结束后，所有统计数据以人工加手动的方式转换为 SPSS18.0 格式进行各项相关分析和检验。

3 结果与讨论

3.1 英语二语初学者的局部错误和全局错误占比与学习时间无关

本小节首先检验分析收集语料中局部错误和全局错误数量表征的特点，然后考察英语二语初学者的局部错误和全局错误占比是否随着学习时间的延长而变化（如表 1 所示）。

表 1 局部错误、全局错误*时间交叉制表

			Time		Total
			1	2	
Type	Local Error	Count	620	430	1050
		Expected Count	627.3	422.7	1050
		% of Total	49.9%	34.6%	84.5%
		Residual	-7.3	7.3	
	Global Error	Count	122	70	192
		Expected Count	114.7	77.3	192
		% of Total	9.8%	5.6%	15.5%
		Residual	7.3	-7.3	
Total		Count	742	500	1242
		Expected Count	742	500	1242
		% of Total	59.7%	40.3%	100%

表 2　局部错误、全局错误*时间卡方检验

	Value	df	Asymp. Sig.（2-sided）	Exact Sig.（2-sided）	Exact Sig.（1-sided）
Pearson Chi-Square	1.363[a]	1	.243		
Continuity Correction[b]	1.183	1	.277		
Likelihood Ratio	1.376	1	.241		
Fisher's Exact Test				.263	.138
Linear-by-Linear Association	1.362	1	.243		
N of Valid Cases	1242				

a. 0 cells（.0%）have expected count less than 5. The minimum expected count is 77.29

b. Computed only for a 2x2 table

由表 2 可以看出：局部错误和全局错误数量与学习时间无显著关联（P=0.263 > 0.05），即错误占比不受时间的影响。由表 1 可以看出：局部错误与全局错误在英语二语初学者所犯错误中有稳定占比，大约为 85%和 15%。

局部错误按词类进行分类，包括名词性错误、动词性错误、介词性错误等。人教版七年级上下册英语教材（2011 年修订版）课程大纲不要求学生掌握系统的语法知识，只要求掌握一定数量的词汇、培养一定的英语交际能力、了解文化背景知识等，因此缺乏系统语法框架的英语二语初学者在英语输出中出现语法错误必不可免。二语习得初期，学习者只需掌握简单句和少量由逻辑连词连接的复合句。因此，对于英语二语初学者来说，最容易犯的错误就是词类错误。根据课程大纲的要求，考试内容也大多测试学生的词汇量，对此按词类分类的局部错误数量将远远超过按影响句子成分因素分类的全局错误数量。

全局错误包括逻辑关系不当、语序不当、成分残缺和表达不当。逻辑关系不当主要是句子的逻辑连词赘余，即在一句话中同时出现 because…so，though…but 等在汉语中成对出现的逻辑连词。语序不当主要是学生关于中英中定语、状语的位置不了解，如将时间状语放在句首位置 this afternoon I will go to the movie。汉语中对于定、状语的位置没有严格约束，而英语中则对定、状语的位置做了明确要求，因此上述例子需改为 I will go to the movie this afternoon。成分残缺主要包括主语和谓语的缺失。汉语造句注重隐形连贯（covert coherence），注重逻辑事理顺序，注重功能、意义，注重以神统形。（连淑能，1993：53）英语造句注重显性接应（overt cohesion），注重结构完整。（连淑能，1993：48）因此对于母语为汉语的英语二语初学者写作中出现成分缺失错误也是情有可原。表达不当主要指中式英语（Chinglish），如 I very like basketball。出现这种错误的原因在于初学者只熟悉词意，不熟悉词类用法。上述例子中 very 是程度副词，可以修饰形容词和副词，但是不能修饰动词，所以不能使用 very like，应改为 I like basketball very much。英语二语初学者的全局错误原因主要在于中英两种语言的语法规范不同，这种不同具体是指刚柔性的不同，即中文语法更柔和，似有若无，而英语语法更刚直，要求严格。

3.2　英语二语初学者的局部错误中实词错误多、虚词错误少

本小节首先检验分析了局部错误中实词错误与虚词错误的比例，然后考察了实虚词错误占比是否随着学习时间的加长而变化。

表 3　实词、虚词*时间交叉表

			type		Total
			lexical	functional	
time	semester1	Count	452	168	620
		Expected Count	434.6	185.4	620
		% within time	72.9%	27.1%	100%
	semester2	Count	284	146	430
		Expected Count	301.4	128.6	430
		% within time	66%	34%	100%
Total		Count	736	314	1050
		Expected Count	736	314	1050
		% within time	70.1%	29.9%	100%

表 4　实词、虚词卡方检验

	Value	df	Asymp. Sig.（2-sided）	Exact Sig.（2-sided）	Exact Sig.（1-sided）
Pearson Chi-Square	5.695[a]	1	.017		
Continuity Correction[b]	5.372	1	.020		
Likelihood Ratio	5.660	1	.017		
Fisher's Exact Test				.020	.010
Linear-by-Linear Association	5.689	1	.017		
N of Valid Cases	1050				

a. 0 cells（.0%）have expected count less than 5. The minimum expected count is 128.59

b. Computed only for a 2x2 table

由表 3 可知：局部错误中实词错误多，占比大、虚词错误少，占比小。实虚词错误数量与时间有明显关联（由表 4 可知：$p=0.02<0.05$），即随着学习时间的延长，实虚词错误的数量与占比都发生了变化。在第一学期，实词错误占比远远超过虚词错误占比；第二学期，局部错误总数相比第一学期急剧下降，并且实词错误占比下降，虚词错误占比上升。实词错误大于虚词错误说明受新课标课程大纲影响，英语二语初学者学习初期以词汇学习为主，而到了第二学期，实词错误占比下降说明语义词汇错误是可以通过反复练习或者继续学习避免的；虚词错误占比提升，说明随着学习时间的增加，课程逐渐要求学生掌握功能性词汇的用法，例如介词、代词等。

3.2.1　英语二语学习者实词错误以动词错误为主、名词错误为辅

由表 5、图 1 可知，实词错误以动词错误为主、名词错误为辅；随着不断地学习，动词错误与名词错误占比有些许下降。

表 5　局部错误数据统计表

	1st semester	2nd semester
	Cases（%）	Cases（%）
Noun	103（16.6）	37（8.6）
Verb	346（55.8）	223（51.9）
Adjective	2（0.3）	17（4）
Pronoun	65（10.5）	63（14.6）
Adverb	1（0.2）	7（1.6）
Preposition	15（2.4）	38（8.8）
Conjunction	68（11）	20（4.6）
Article	20（3.2）	17（4）
Phrase	0（0）	8（1.9）
Total	620（100）	430（100）

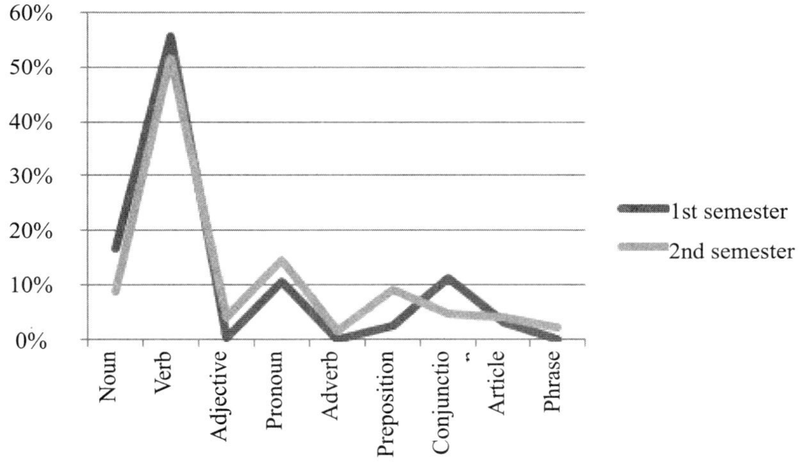

图 1　局部错误频率分布图

首先，英语二语初学者的动词错误主要是主谓不一致。对于英语二语初学者而言，动词错误由主语人称和数的变化造成，主要是第三人称单数的谓语词尾变化。错误原因也在于中英意合与形合的区别。汉语作为一种意合语言，其动词没有任何语法标记，即谓语不随主语人称和数的变化而变化；反之，英语作为一种形合语言，其特征就是有许多语法规则，例如谓语动词的形态要与主语的人称和数保持一致。所以，主谓不一致错误也就成了英语二语初学者的一种常见错误。例如 she think it is terrible，应改为 she thinks it is terrible。其次，英语倾向于多用名词，因而叙述呈静态（stative）；汉语倾向于多用动词，因而叙述呈动态（dynamic）。（连淑能，1993：104）在汉语中，说话人或作者倾向于使用动词来描述事物的发展变化，并且作为一种意合语言，汉语也允许在同一个句子中出现多个动词，只需句子意义正确表达；英语倾向于将动词名词化来描述事物的变化过程，同时作为一种形合语言，英语不允许一句话中有多个动词出现。那么，学生作文中出现一句话中多个动词的现象也就不难解释了。例如 she is my sister，her name is Nancy，应改为 she is my sister，and her name is Nancy。

英语二语初学者实词错误中也出现了大量的名词错误。这些名词错误主要为复数形式错误。对此，必须再次提到中英两种语言是意合与形合的区别。在汉语中，名词复数标记为“们”“之类的”等，这类标记只有在强调集体的场合才会出现，一般情况下，只要能够清楚地表达句子意思，不使用复数标记也是可以的。例如：我们是电子科技大学学生；我是电子科技大学学生。但是英语作为一种形合语言，必须处处注意语法标记。除了第三人称单数的谓语语法标记，可数名词复数词尾的语法标记也很常见。因此英语二语初学者的作文中出现名词复数形式错误就有迹可循了。

对于形容词错误和副词错误，其数量和占比就小得多。因为英汉语言中形容词和副词的用法相似，且拥有固定的词性标记。如：英语形容词词尾多为-ful，-able，-ing，-ed，ive 等，语义性副词词尾多为-ly；汉语形容词词尾一般为“的”，副词词尾一般为“地”。学生作文中出现的形容词错误主要为语义错误，即以-ing 结尾的形容词修饰物，-ed 结尾的形容词修饰人。除此之外，形容词比较级、最高级也是容易出错的地方。

3.2.2 英语二语学习者虚词错误以介词错误、代词错误为主

由表 5 可知：虚词错误主要为介词错误和代词错误；介词错误和代词错误占比随学习时间延长而升高。

英语代词包括人称代词、物主代词、指示代词等。在收集的语料中，学生所犯的代词错误不外乎上述三种。人称代词错误是混淆人称代词的主格与宾格，如：him does the dishes after dinner，此处 he 做主语，应该用主格，应改为 he does dishes after dinner。物主代词错误是混淆形容词性物主代词和名词性物主代词，如：she only has 3 minutes to brush hers teeth，此处句意为她只有 3 分钟刷“她的”牙，强调的是物的所有者，应该是形容词属性的，而不是强调名词属性的所有物，应改为 she only has 3 minutes to brush her teeth。指示代词错误主要是因为there，their，these 三个词的发音或写法相近引起的，如：I don’t like there rules，应改为 I don’t like these rules。

介词错误增多主要是因为不及物动词的学习。中学语法对及物动词和不及物动词的区分为：及物动词后可直接加宾语，不及物动词后必须先加介词再加宾语。英语介词总量不多，但用法广泛且多样，对于英语初学者来说，介词使用错误或缺失错误是比较常见的。汉语为意合语言，及物动词与不及物动词没有明显的用法区别，只要能表达说话人的意思即可；英语是形合语言，及物动词与不及物动词有明显的用法区别。因此英语初学者在写作中混淆及物与不及物动词，出现介词错误主要是由母语负迁移造成的。

3.3 英语二语初学者犯错原因主要在于母语负迁移

从 3.1 中可看出，全局错误原因主要在于中英刚柔性不同；3.2.1 中，虚词错误主要原因在于中英语言的及物性不同；3.2.2 中实词错误主要为动词错误，原因在于中英语言动静态偏好不同，名词错误也较多是因为中英两种语言有意合和形合的不同。因此，我们可以大胆猜测：母语为汉语的英语二语初学者犯错主要是由于母语负迁移。因此，在教学中应注重中英两种语言的对比，从二者的区别入手，让学生在学习之初就明白汉语和英语是两种有巨大差异的语言。明白二者的差异后，学生在使用英语时就能尽量避免由母语负迁移造成的语法错误，提高自身的英语输出能力，即英语写作能力。

由 3.2 可知，局部错误与学习时间有显著关联，这说明通过词汇的不断积累，英语二语初学者的大部分错误都能避免，使二语学习者的中介语水平更接近目标语。大量的局部错误，即词类使用错误，说明在英语作为二语的学习初期，教师可以重点关注词汇使用和词汇积累，以此来避免局部错误的出现。

4 结　论

本研究对英语二语初学者作文出现的错误数量及类型进行了详细对比和分析，结果表明：（1）英语二语初学者的局部错误和全局错误占比与学习时间长短无关。中介语模型形成初期，局部错误与全局错误占比是稳定的，教师和学生应致力于减少总体错误数量，而不只是减少某类错误。（2）局部错误以实词错误为主，实词错误主要是动词错误和名词错误，虚词错误占比较小，但比例会随着学习时间的延长而上升，主要包括介词错误和代词错误。中介语形成初期，应通过反复练习和深入学习减少实词错误，尤其是动词错误和名词错误。虚词错误会随着学习的加深占比越来越大，教师在教学期间可以加强引导，通过练习和难点讲解来加深学生对于功能性词汇用法的认识，学生也可以在课余时间进行反思，加深印象。对于错误，教师不必全部讲解，只需讲解那些十分重要的或者特别难的，学生自身很难改正的错误。（冯巧丽，2010）（3）母语为汉语的英语二语初学者犯错原因主要在于母语负迁移。对此，教师在教学过程中可以加强英汉两种语言的比较和区别，尽量减小母语负迁移出现的概率。

参 考 文 献

[1] Corder，S., 1967. The Significance of Learners' Errors[J]. *International Review of Applied Linguistics*，5：161-169.

[2] Li，X., 1989. Effects of contextual cues on inferring and remembering meanings of new words[J]. *Applied Linguistics*，（10）：402-13.

[3] Long，M.，L. Adams，M. Mclean &F. Castanos, 1976. Doing things with words：verbal interaction in lockstep and small group classroom situations. [C] // J. Fanselow &R. Crymes. *On TESOL*. Washington，D. C.：TESOL.

[4] Long，M. &P. Porter, 1985. Group work，interlanguage talk，and second language acquisition[J]. *TESOL Quarterly*，（19）：207-28.

[5] Pica，T., 1992. Questions from the language classroom：research perspectives[J]. *TESOL Quarterly*，（28）：49-79.

[6] Selinker L., 1972. Interlanguage[J]. *IRAL - International Review of Applied Linguistics in Language Teaching*，（10）：37.

[7] Šesták Z. James，C., 2000. Errors in Language Learning and Use. Exploring Error Analysis[J]. *Photosynthetica*，38（4）：235-236.

[8] 白凤欣. 国内第二语言习得中介语及其石化现象理论研究综述[J]. 河北师范大学学报（哲学社会科学版），2007，30（4）：115-119.

[9] 冯巧丽. 高职学生写作中的错误分析及其对教学的启示[D]. 西南大学，2010.

[10] 李炯英. 中介语石化现象研究 30 年综观[J]. 外语教学理论与实践，2003（4）：19-24.

[11] 连淑能. 英汉对比研究[M]. 北京：高等教育出版社，2010.

[12] 罗晓杰，孙琳. 偏误理论与二语习得[J]. 外语学刊，2003（2）：103-105.

[13] 王晓燕. 中介语会话的偏误分析[J]. 解放军外国语学院学报，2006，29（6）：39-43.
[14] 杨连瑞，尹洪山，赵昌芝，等. 中介语石化现象研究的进展[J]. 外语与外语教学，2014（1）：36-40.
[15] 杨连瑞，纪璐，李绍鹏. 中介语石化现象研究综述[J]. 天津外国语大学学报，2015，22（3）：36-40.
[16] 杨文秀. 中介语石化现象与口语教学[J]. 外语与外语教学，2000（9）：33-35.
[17] 于景梅. 基于中介语的大学生非谓语动词使用错误分析[D]. 东北师范大学，2010.
[18] 章宜华. 中介语偏误特点与学习词典理想作用机制探讨[J]. 外语教学与研究，2012（2）：233-245.

汉字的理据性及对对外汉语教学的影响

钱思颖

摘　要：现代语言学把任意性原则作为语言的一个最基本原则之一，但这并不代表各种语言在发展完成体系之后仍然只是无理的符号。任何实用的文字都是有理据的。不同民族的语言受其历史文化等因素的影响，其文字符号的拼写与其语言成分之间存在一定的内在联系，有的是显性的，有的是隐性的难以察觉的。简单来说，即文字符号和语言成分之间的关系能体现出某些具有规律性的特征，这一点不仅体现在英语中，在汉语中的体现更是尤为明显。掌握汉字的理据性会对汉语学习者受益匪浅，同时对对外汉语教学有着很长远的影响。

关键字：理据性；汉字；对外汉语教学

Abstract：Modern linguistics regards the principle of arbitrariness as one of the most basic principles of language，but that does not mean that various languages are still just irrational symbols after the completion of the language system and any practical writing is based on evidentiality. The language of different nationalities is influenced by its historical and cultural factors，and there is a certain internal connection between its spelling and its linguistic components. Some are explicit，while others are invisible and imperceptible and put it simply，the relation between text symbols and language components reflects some regular features，not only in English，but also in Chinese. Knowing evidentiality could benefit the Chinese leaners a lot and it also has great influence on TCSL.

Key words：evidentiality；Chinese；TCSL

1 引　言

汉语作为一种缺乏形态，并不严格地要求外在形式标记的语言，其句法结构比起形态丰富的语言更加明显地具有一种概念和象似的原则。20 世纪的结构主义语言学大师们，包括索绪尔、萨丕尔等人都分别指出语言的任意性是一条普遍规律。基本思想都表明语言能指（signifier）和所指（signified）之间的关系是任意的，不存在任何逻辑证明，不过索绪尔认为象声词和语音论证比在整个语言系统中占极小一部分。虽然语言本身已经成为一个体系，但是却并不是一个完备的科学体系，加之语言主要是为交际服务的，在使用过程中会呈现出各种各样的无理性，无法用科学的手段来研究或者给汉字的理据性下定义，而是应该搜集和分析从古至今汉字发展的大量事实，着眼于汉字的发展历程来说明汉字内在的理据性。这样也可以发挥汉字的理据性对汉语发展的影响，运用到对外汉语教学中，增强我们本民族对汉文化的认同感，进而扩大汉语在世界范围内的影响力。有专家指出：对外汉语教师应重视汉语语法理据特点在教学中的运用；外国学生了解和掌握汉语的理据性会提高学习汉语的信心；抓住理据性进行教学，可以取得事半功倍的教学效果。

2 研究背景

中国是汉字的发源地，对汉字理据性的研究从未间断。世界范围内，“汉语热”已经迅速扩散开来，越来越多的留学生渴望能够学习汉语，了解中国的文化。中国历久悠久绵长，文化博大精深，而文字作为中国历史文化传承的载体，让留学生们对汉语有望而却步之意。这对汉语和中国文化在全球范围内的传播都很不利。由于汉字是表意文字而非拼音文字这一特点，汉字成为他们在汉语学习过程中的最大困难。而对于来自汉字文化圈的留学生来说，表面上他们似乎比较容易掌握汉字的书写技巧，但是在偏误分析中发现，他们比非汉字文化圈的学生更容易出现偏旁误用现象。而以上诸多问题都是可以利用汉字理据性的相关知识得到改善和解决的。

3 研究目的

在对外汉语教学中，词汇教学是基础教学阶段中与语法教学同样重要的内容之一，随着语言学习的深入，词汇学习则会变得越来越重要。因为掌握充分的词汇量、理解词语的意义、掌握词的用法是学习语言成功的关键因素之一。同时，词汇学习也是留学生学习汉语时感觉最吃力、最难以攻克的难关。对外汉语教学历来重视语法知识的传授，甚至可以说把语法的结构框架教学作为对外汉语教学的终极目标，但却忽视了留学生言语交际能力的培养。目前，对外汉语的词汇教学主要是通过词的句法组合来介绍给学生，目的主要是培养学生的言语交际能力和汉语表达能力。这在一定程度上使得目前的对外汉语词汇教学更注重词的字面意义的讲解，而忽视了词的理据意义和引申意义。造成的结果是：留学生理解了一个词的词义却不知道这个词的使用条件，从而造成了很多不必要的语言错误。这客观上要求学习中文的外国学生要能准确地理解汉语词汇的理据意义，才能更准确地在语言环境中正确使用汉语。

4 汉字的理据性

对认知语言学而言，认为“语言要么是‘可预测的’，要么是‘任意的’”这种传统的语言学观不够全面。语言中还存在一个第三选择，即“有理据的”（Lakoff1987：107）语言形式和意义之间除了任意的关系之外，还有更为重要的理据关系。

理据性是指语言形式和意义之间的一种非任意的，可以论证的，意义激发形式且形式反映意义的关系。（李福印，2008：43）客观事物的名称与事物本身没有必然的本质的联系，人在交际中给事物取名称时，用什么语言形式代表该事物是任意的，语言符号与客体之间复制式的象似是极其偶然的个别现象，语言单位及其系列与客体及其关系之间没有必然的一一对应，任何语言单位及其组织规则一旦为社会公认就可约定俗成。但是，语言的意义与人的认识过程紧密联系，它与语音形式的联系虽然大部分都是任意的，但在一种语言内部往往具有理据性。

现代汉字的理据性要从分析研究汉字的内部结构开始。苏培成（2001）指出，内部结构是指与字音、字义有联系的汉字构成成分的组合，字符是其基本单位。现代汉字有意符、音符和记号三类字符，其中意符、音符和整字的字义、字音有联系，是有理据的；记号和整字的字义、字音没有联系，是无理据的。因此，在由意符、音符、记号组成的六类字中，会意字、形声字是有理据字，半意符半记号字、半音符半记号字是半理据字，独体记号字、合体记号字是无理据字。

4.1 语音理据

汉语词汇中具有语音理据的词具体表现在词的语音形式和词的意义的联系上。他们是以模拟声音给事物命名为主要造词手段的一类特殊词类，包括拟声词和叹词。拟声词是模拟自然声音为主的特殊词类，又叫象声词，如“叭、叮当、哗啦”。叹词是一种模拟人类自己的声音，表示感叹、呼唤、应答等情感为主的特殊词类，如“咦、哎呀、啊、嗯、哦”。词的语音理据以上面两类中的拟声词为主。如汉语中的“鸭子嘎嘎叫、关门的声音是砰的一声……”从以上分析可以看出，中国人在感知外界事物时，就从自己汉语语音系统中找一个与自然界声音相似的语音来模拟，并非是声音的物理属性。另一方面，拟声词和叹词的理据性虽然很强，但是其在汉语词汇系统中所占的比例不多，对外汉语教学中如能适当展开，与留学生母语中相应的拟声词作对比分析，这样可能会引起学生更大的学习兴趣，取得更好的词汇教学效果。

4.2 形态理据

形态理据就是指人们可以通过某一个词的形态构成进行分析，进而得出词义的词特点。汉语中具有形态理据的词有复合词和派生词两类。比如，留学生知道了一个构词语素“车”是一种交通工具的话，那么他们就可以知道由“车”这个语素构成的一批词：汽车，卡车，自行车，房车……；同样，如果他们知道两个语素：“手”和“表”，那么他们就能知道“手表”是表示“戴在手腕上的计时工具”。

汉语词汇的形态理据主要体现在复合词上，因为复合词是由两个及以上语素构成的。他们内部就形成了一定的形态关系，这主要体现在语素义与词义之间的关系上，一方面表现在汉语复合词的两个语素是直接复合的：

词的意义是两个语素意义之和：席卷（像席子那样卷）

词的意义是两个语素意义之和或者之一：学习（学和习、学或习）

词的意义大于两个语素意义之和：领袖（是领导的意思）＞领子和袖口

词的意义小于两个语素意义之和（即汉语中的偏义复词）国家（国）＜天子之国和诸侯之家。

另一方面表现在汉语复合词的两个语素是提示复合的：

前一个语素提示事物的形状特点：蛤蟆镜、八字胡；

前一个语素提示事物的功能特点：茶杯、水壶、肉鸡；

前一个语素提示事物的制作方法：烧饼、蒸饺、水煮鱼；

前一个语素提示事物的时间特点：腊八蒜、春风、端午节；

前一个语素提示事物的原材料特点：花生油、米酒、瓷砖；

前一个语素提示完成事物所用的工具：皮影戏、篮球、粉笔画。

在对外汉语复合式合成词的教学过程中，教师如果能较好地利用以上提到的这些形态理据，外国留学生就能较快地理解词的意义，并准确地进行运用。汉语的词汇较少用形态变化，所以汉语中只有少量的附加词，但是这些附加词可以很好地帮助留学生成批的掌握汉语词汇。

4.3 语义理据

词的语义理据是指一个词的语义之所以形成的道理，是词的意义构成的根据。词的词义理据研究属于语义范畴，是人们构词心理的反映，不是词的结构形式的问题。

4.3.1 直接理据词

直接理据词的词义是由词素间的相互联系和相互作用构成的。从词素的意义和词素间的关系就可以理解词义形成的道理。汉语中有很多词都是直接理据词，这些词把两个事物之间的相似点在人脑中建立了一定的关系后通过词汇反映出来的。

4.3.2 间接理据词

间接理据词的词义不是由其构成成分决定的，而是由词义形成的语用环境决定的，也可以说是词源理据。这是从历史的角度来观察词的来源、解释词的形态和意义的演变的。如汉语的“染指”一词，词义是“想得到不应得到的利益”。

4.4 文字理据

文字理据表现为词的词形与词义之间的联系。汉语最突出的一个特点就是汉语是语素文字，而汉语的一个语素往往对应的是一个汉字。同时，汉字又有很强的表意性，对汉语这种语义型的语言，其基本结构格局隐含在传统的字中。如果在对留学生的语素教学中对一些汉字进行现代意义上的解读，比如告诉他们中国人感情丰富，光和竖心旁有关的字就有两百多个。如果能把这些字拆解开来解释，会发现很有意思。比如：“憔悴”就是心焦、心快死了；“慎”就是心里认真一点，就谨慎了；心里一解放，就不认真了，就变成松懈的“懈”了……这样的解释固然有望文附会的不足之处，但是汉字的表意特征给留学生在词汇学习上的巨大启发也是毋庸置疑的。

5 小　　结

伴随中国的经济振兴，汉语也伴随国家发展的脚步走向了世界，近年来对于对外汉语教学的研究越来越多，但是作为对外汉语教学中重要一环的对外汉字教学，专家学者所给予的关注度却并不是很高。而有关本文所提到的把固有的汉字理据性理论应用到对外汉字教学中的这一方法，研究的学者更是屈指可数。许多外国人在汉字学习中感到困难，主要是因为他们没有认清汉字的理据性和学习规律。若把汉字当成没有联系、毫无意义的符号，一个个地死记硬背，势必造成学习困难。如果我们采用理据性，通过对汉字字形的分析为学生指明字形与字音、字义的联系，使他们懂得字符的特定意义，那么学生不但易学易记，而且会越学越有兴趣。汉字理据性教学，不仅能够增强外国人的学习信心，发扬民族传统文化，还有助于汉语的国际推广。因此，我们要重视理据性的运用，在教学中不断探索，进一步提高对外汉字教学的水平。

参 考 文 献

[1] Lakoff，George, 1987. Women，Fireand Dangerous Things：What Categories Revealabouthe Mind. Chicago：The University of Chicago Press.

[2] 戴浩一. 时间顺序和汉语的语序[J]. 国外语言学，1988（1）：10-20.
[3] 杜文礼. 语言的象似性探微[J]. 四川外语学院学报，1996（1）：60-65.
[4] 李宝贵. 汉语语法的理据性与对外汉语教学[J]. 汉语学习，2004（5）：64-71.
[5] 李福印. 认知语言学概论[M]. 北京：北京大学出版社，2008.
[6] 苏培成. 现代汉字学纲要[M]. 北京：北京大学出版社，2004.
[7] 王寅. 论语言符号象似性[J]. 外语与外语教学，1999（5）：4-7.
[8] 严辰松. 语言临摹性概说[J]. 国外语言学，1997（3）：21-25.
[9] 张敏. 认知语言学与汉语名词短语[M]. 北京：中国社会科学出版社，1998.

文学研究

库切《耻》的精神分析学解读
——库切和他的白日梦

王　蕾

摘　要：诺贝尔文学奖得主库切的《耻》是一部主题丰富的小说。不少学者已从历史、后殖民、文化等若干个视角对耻的多重主题进行讨论，而小说中的精神分析学现象却少有人关注。为了弥补这一空缺，本文采取弗洛伊德的精神分析学理论和传记研究的方法，通过对库切的童年经历的分析，探究库切和《耻》中的两个主人公（卢里和露茜）的精神分析学联系，从恋母情结和同性恋倾向等多个维度来表明卢里和露茜在心理学层面上也是库切压抑的本能（比如性欲）升华的产物。把作品与作者的经历联系起来为《耻》提供了新的阐释空间。

关键字：库切；《耻》；精神分析学

Abstract: Written by Coetzee，the winner of Nobel Prize，*Disgrace* is a novel rich in meanings. Many literature researchers have probed into the themes of the novel from multiple perspectives such as historicism，post-colonialism，and culturalism. However，people seem to turn a blind eye to the psychoanalytic hints in *Disgrac*e. In order to make up for this vacancy，this paper adopts Freud's psychoanalytic theory and biographical research methods and explores the psychoanalytic relationship between the two heroes（Lurie and Lucy）and Coetzee through the analysis of Coetzee's childhood experience，and demonstrates that fact that both Lurie and Lucy are the products of Coetzee's suppressed Ego（e.g.sexual desire）from dimensions of the Oedipus Complex and homosexual tendencies. Linking the work with the author's experience provides a new interpretation for *Disgrace*.

Key words: Coetzee；Disgrace；psychoanalytic theory

1

对于南非小说家库切的《耻》来说，相关研究已经颇具广度与深度。研究主题跨越生命体认、族裔身份、历史文化，视角大多涉及解构主义，后殖民批评解读、女性主义等。主要讲述教授卢里诱奸自己女学生后被迫逃到乡下跟女儿生活，后经历抢劫和女儿强奸的耻辱等一系列的变故，卢里又回到城里。在小说中，性欲是卢里所有耻辱的导火索，我们如果把焦点放在小说主人公卢里上，不难得出这样一个结论：卢里是一个被情欲所支配的人，即书中所说的“爱欲的仆人”（61）。从妓女索拉娅到学生梅拉妮在到后来农场妇女，为满足欲望，卢里甚至跨越道德界限。“事实上，在库切的所有主人公里，卢里是唯一一个被身体本能控制而带来麻烦的人。在库切的作品中，身体是受折磨的，饥饿的，远离性爱的。（Neimneh，173）”为什么库切会在他的小说中塑造这样一个被性本能主导生活的人物？基于这个问题，考虑到性欲对人带来的影响，我们便可发现这本小说的一个新的阐释方向——弗洛伊德的精神分析学。弗洛伊德主张艺术作品是作者压抑性欲的升华，在他看来，“在所利用的本能力量中，性冲动起到了重要的作用；在这个过程中它们得到升华，也就是说，他舍弃性的目标，而转向其他的较为高尚的社会目标”。（弗洛伊德，9）这启示我们将《耻》和库切本人联系起来，从殖民主义的历史大背景中抽离出来，以一个全新的视角探究书中的主人公，将弗洛伊德精神分析理论运用于文学研究实践。

在阐释文学作品时，作者的地位一直是文学批评界争论的一个问题。一方面，作者的生平、兴趣、感情被认为应该排除在其作品之外，另一方面，有人认为作者的生平与作品有密切的联系，作者的个人经历可以被看作是艺术作品的心理学支撑。“作者一旦除去，解释文本的主张就变得毫无益处。给文本一个作者，是对文本横加限制，是给文本以最后所指，是封闭了写作”。（赵毅衡，511）和传记研究不同，精神分析强调研究心理性欲上的决定因素，而这些因素正是艺术家创作的灵感启发。“在精神分析研究控制下的材料是由一个人生活的历史组成的：一方面是事件的偶然情况和背景的影响，另一方面是这一对象被记叙的反应”。（Freud，Leonardo Da Vinci，85）换言之，用精神分析学的方法研究文学就是“运用精神分析学概念分析作者的主体性怎样影响他所塑造的主人公”。（Obaid，190）如法国精神分析学派的主要创始人玛丽·波拿巴特在研究爱伦·坡的短篇小说时参考了大量的生平事迹，并得出坡的创作灵感主要来源于其母亲早年死亡的经历。而在研究南非小说家库切的作品时，我们更有理由倾向于参考他本人的人生经历。库切在接受采访时谈道：“你写作的任何东西，包括文论和小说，都在你书写他们的同时，也在书写着你本人”。（Attwell，17）所以，他以第三人称的手法创作他的“自传三部曲”《男孩》《青春》《夏日》。这三部作品中的主人公经历和库切本人的人生经历基本重合。除此之外，库切的早期作品《幽暗之地》也包含自传元素：不同的人物都有库切这样的姓氏。这些证据都足以证明，把库切本人的经历与其作品联系起来，并非封闭了作品，而是扩大了作品的阐释空间。本文在参考他人为库切所做的个人传记和他本人的“自传三部曲”的基础上，探讨小说《耻》的心理学基础，主要分析小说中的主人公卢里和露茜与库切本人经历的关系，尤其是童年经历，研究库切如何将他的白日梦和幻想投射到这两个主人公身上。

2

弗洛伊德一直强调童年经历对人后期的影响，他在《创作者与白日梦》一文中提到：“现时的一个强烈经验唤起作家对早年某个经历（通常是同年时代）的记忆，在此记忆中又产生一个在其作品中可以得到满足的愿望。其作品本身能够显示出近期的诱发事件和旧时的记忆这些因素”。（11）（也就是说，我们在研究小说《耻》和探究其中主人公的心理时，不妨考虑作者本人库切的心理经验与人生经历，尤其是童年经历。从他的早年经历看来，库切是有恋母情结的。“他非常喜欢他的母亲。库切家族的人都知道她是一位聪明、谦逊，且极为爱儿子的母亲”。（坎尼米耶，23）在他的第一部自传小说《男孩》以一个疏离的叙述者约翰讲述了他的童年经历，在他的叙述中我们可以了解到约翰的母亲在他的生命中扮演的重要角色。童年时，母亲维拉就独自带着他到处奔波，所以约翰对母亲有着近乎狂热的迷恋之情。“她是他生命中的最坚实的东西。她是他脚下的基石。没有她，他就失去了一切”。（40）弗洛伊德曾写过一篇文论《达·芬奇对童年的回忆》，分析达·芬奇的名作蒙娜丽莎。他指出达·芬奇的恋母情结“自然地外射到他的绘画作品中，使他的绘画中出现女性的所谓‘达·芬奇’的嘴唇，这是一种长弓形的带着谜一般的静的微笑的嘴唇”。（鲁枢元，55）在《耻》中，库切花了不少笔墨从卢里的视角对书中女性的生理特点进行描写，他对女性的身体有着近乎狂热的迷恋之情。如果说对跟他发生过关系的女性的身体的迷恋是性欲在作祟的话，那对女儿露茜和梅拉妮的父亲的女性特质的一瞬间迷恋一定是某种超越性欲的东西的驱使。在去梅拉妮家道歉时，他在梅拉妮父亲的身上“察觉到一丝梅拉妮的味道：嘴和嘴唇线条很好看……光滑的皮肤上摸不到汗毛的感觉”。（194）结合作者库切本人的经历，我们可以把这些超乎常理的描写视作他自己的恋母情结的一种投射。根据弗洛伊德的理论，有恋母情结的人都有着“弑父”倾向。虽然库切没有“弑父心理”，但在《男孩》有提到他的“仇父心理”，对于约翰来说，“丈夫倒成了一种附属的角色”；（13）“他不喜欢父亲……她不想要一个父亲，或者至少不想要一个同处在一片屋檐下的父亲”。（49）这在卢里身上表现为丈夫和父亲的角色被削弱。对于卢里的前妻，文中提到的次数很少，但每次提到她都是因为卢里的生活遭遇到难题。他也承认“罗萨琳依然住在附近，这使他感觉有些安心……最糟糕的事情发生时，总还有个人可以商量商量”。（51）首先，卢里作为父亲的抚养者的角色被削弱。对卢里来说，他不明白为什么长大后的露茜会选择经营农场来作为自己的事业，他搞不懂为什么“他和她母亲都是城里人，生下来的却是一个返祖的孩子”。（71）卢里作为父亲的主导的角色被削弱。按理说，在当时男权至上的社会背景下，卢里作为一位父亲应该主导他和露茜的关系，他却经常在与女儿相处的过程中显得无能为力。他按照露茜的指示照料生意，“女儿成了他第二个救星，是他重生的年轻的新娘”；（102）在露西被强奸之后，他没有办法让露茜对他敞开心扉；就算他极不理解露茜继续留在农场嫁给黑人佩特鲁斯并生下孩子的决定，他也没有办法干预他的想法。最后，卢里作为父亲庇护者的角色被削弱。与其说卢里可以保护他的女儿露茜，不如说露茜才是卢里的庇护者。卢里在露茜受到黑人伤害的时候没有能力保护她，反而自己受了伤。在那之后，他也不能为露茜提供心理和身体上的庇护。在他劝露茜离开的时候，露茜对他说：“我知道你是一片好心，但你却不是我所需要的领路人”。（187）相反，当他在文明社会中受到谴责，丢掉工作后，他逃向在乡下的女儿寻求庇护。除了卢里，文中还有另外一名父亲，即梅拉妮的父亲。和卢里不同，梅拉妮的父亲在他女儿受到伤害时站出来代表女儿谴责卢里，展现出的是一个可靠的父亲的形象。不过值得注意的是，库切却在最后对梅拉妮的女性特质进行了刻画。

3

弗洛伊德在《创作者与白日梦》一文中写道：“现代作家倾向于凭借自我观察，将他的主人公分裂成许多部分自我，结果是作家将自己心理生活中相冲突的几个倾向在几个主角身上体现出来。”（10）所以，在《耻》中我们也可以在另外一个主人公露茜身上找到库切的影子。弗洛伊德在分析达·芬奇的童年经历时提到，同性恋倾向也是恋母情结的一种体现：“孩子压抑了他对母亲的爱，他把自己放在母亲的位置上，使自己被母亲同化（identify），他以自己为模特儿，选择与自己相像的作为他的新的爱慕对象。这样，他变成了一个同性恋者。”（Freud，48）根据《男孩》描述，库切的少年时代展现出对男孩子的倾慕。他跟被称为娘娘腔和可能是同性恋的男孩西奥交朋友，“他喜欢西奥的样子，喜欢他光洁的皮肤、红润的脸色和无可挑剔的发式，还有他文雅的着装”。（175）在他的第二部传记类小说《青春》中，提到与他发生过关系的各个女人，但与这些女人之间的情感却不能被称之为爱情。他在这本书中写道：“可能他生来就不适合去爱女人……如果他是个同性恋就能从头到尾解释他的苦恼。”（92）库切有过一个妻子菲利帕，后来他与菲利帕离婚。在菲利帕得乳腺癌死去时库切在朋友的信中写道：“我和她结婚17年，并不是很开心的17年（这绝不是她的错）。”（坎尼米耶，234）这些信息中判断，我们有充分理由认为库切有同性恋的倾向。在小说《耻》中，库切把卢里的女儿露茜塑造成一个有同性恋倾向的女人，露茜20多岁的时候就开始“穿没有性别特征的衣服”。（105）并且，与库切更为相似的是，露茜最后也选择嫁给一个自己不爱的人。而对于卢里来说，也有着跟《青春》的库切有着相似的情况，虽然他迷恋女性的生理特质，却从未与她们产生过真正的爱情，他“没有感情冲动”。（6）

4

我们还可以从露茜和卢里身上发现库切其他的“白日梦”。比如说库切儿时对农庄的喜爱与露西相吻合。农庄把库切与过去联结在一起，“因为农庄他才有了实质的存在”。（J.M.库切，《男孩》 24）然而，库切对农庄的爱恋也给他带来了苦恼，他不是农庄主人的孩子，在农庄将永远不会拥有属于自己的房间。所以，他把自己对农庄的喜爱移植到他笔下的露茜身上。《耻》中没有特别指明，甚至没有暗示，为什么她有作为教授的父亲，可是还是决定生活在乡下。甚至在她受到侮辱之后，她也没有改变心意。库切对农庄的热情在露茜身上被放大了，她认为“乡下的灰土：那是光荣”，（71）为了继续待在农庄，她可以付出任何代价。对于卢里来说，他和库切本人一样喜爱诗歌和音乐。在库切刚满15岁时，他说服父母让他学音乐课，他“本人成为音乐家的雄心要大得多”。（库切，《青春》18）而卢里一直在创作关于浪漫诗人拜伦和他的情人特蕾莎的歌剧，“他在创造着音乐（或者说音乐在创造着他）”。如在本文开篇提到的一样，艺术是性欲升华的产物，压抑的欲望特别是性欲会激发作者的创作灵感。对于库切本人而言，他欣赏艾略特的名言：“诗不是放纵感情，而是逃避感情，不是表现个性，而是逃避个性。”（库切，《青春》71）他的自传体小说《青春》和《夏日》都在或明或暗地向我们揭示这个事实。在《夏日》中，库切虚构了一个采访者在他死后要搜集资料为他作传，试图构建库切在南非的一段经历。他的朋友认为，“他为艺术保留自己”，（84）库切的这一方面和后期的卢里如出一辙。卢里离开露茜回去之后沉迷于艺术创作。他把他的激情和热情都赋予他的主人公。“他整天整天地生活在特蕾莎和拜伦之中，就靠不加糖的咖啡和早餐麦片度日”。（213）他试图将压抑的欲望转化为艺术创造：“那么这样的感情又怎么可能加之变形使之成为诗歌呢？”（207）

5

根据弗洛伊德精神分析学理论思路，我们可以说库切在书写卢里和露茜的同时也在书写他自己。库切认为，“所有自传都在讲故事，所以写作都是自传”。（庄华萍，58）自传多是在讲述真正发生过的事实，而作者的写作过程是在潜意识的驱使下完成的。忽略作者的主体地位或者过分强调作者的地位都容易造成作品的误读或者过度解读。不过，对于库切这样强调作品中的自传元素的作家，为了获得作品更广更准确地阐释，我们在关注他的后殖民作家的身份的同时，也必须探究他的写作心理成因。

参考文献

[1] Attwell，David. Ed, 1992. *Doubling the Point：Essays and Interviews.* Cambridge：Harvard UP.

[2] Freud，Sigmund, 2002. “Leonardo Da Vinci：A Memory of his Childhood.” Trans. Alan Tyson. *The International Library of Psychology：Leonardo Da Vinci*. Taylor & Francis e-Library.

[3] Freud，Sigmund, 2013. “Creative Writers and Day-Dreaming.”*On Freud's “Creative Writers and Day-Dreaming”*. Ed. Ethel Spector Person，Peter Fonagy and Servulo Augusto Figueira. London：Karnac Books Ltd.

[4] Obaid，Francisco Pizarro, 2016. “The Dead-Living Mother：Marine Bonaparte's Interpretation of Edgar Allan Poe's Short Stories.” *The American Journal of Psychoanalysis*，76：183-203.

[5] Neimnesh Shadi, 2013. “J. M. Coetzee's Disgrace：Eros，（Dis）grace，& the Body.” *International Journal of Applied Linguistics &English Literature.* 2.2：172-178.

[6] 坎尼米耶. J. M. 库切传[M]. 王敬慧译. 杭州：浙江文艺出版社，2017.

[7] J. M. 库切. 耻[M]. 张冲译. 南京：译林出版社，2010.

[8] J. M. 库切. 男孩[M]. 文敏译. 杭州：浙江文艺出版社，2013.

[9] J. M. 库切. 青春[M]. 王家湘译. 杭州：浙江文艺出版社，2013.

[10] J. M. 库切. 夏日[M]. 文敏译. 杭州：浙江文艺出版社，2010.

[11] 鲁枢元. 文学的跨界研究：文学与心理学[M]. 张冲译. 上海：学林出版社，2011.

[12] 西格蒙德·弗洛伊德. 精神分析引论[M]. 张爱卿译. 南京：江苏文艺出版社，2010.

[13] 赵毅衡. 符号学文学论文集[M]. 天津：百花文艺出版社.

[14] 庄华萍. 库切“自传三部曲”中的人称，时态与自我[J]. 外国文学，2013（3）：53-60.

酷儿理论视阈下的《耻》

常　红

摘　要：2003 年度诺贝尔文学奖得主库切（Coetzee）以“后殖民主义”为主题而闻名于世。他的小说《耻》是这种文体的典范。但是小说中涉及的酷儿因素却甚少有人研究。本文以朱迪思·巴特勒的“性别操演理论”为基础，通过质疑同性恋机制内在的一致性：生理性别、社会性别和性取向，分析酷儿对异性恋霸权的解构，并且结合南非后殖民时代社会生活角色的转变以及殖民主义带来的心理障碍与创伤，运用酷儿理论对《耻》进行重新阐释，分别从三个方面说明：（1）《耻》挑战了同性恋和异性恋的二分法；（2）它挑战了男人和女人的二分法；（3）酷儿们的异装政治行为，旨在揭示酷儿们在异性恋霸权与父权制社会中既抗拒又服从主流社会规范的矛盾心理。

关键词：库切；《耻》；酷儿理论；解构

Abstract: Coetzee, the winner of the 2003 Nobel prize in literature, enjoys a high reputation in the literary world for his theme of “post-colonization”, and his novel *Shame* is the model of this style. Unfortunately, the queer factors involved in the novel are rarely studied. Based on queer theorist Judith Butler's “Theory of Gender Performativity”, this paper analyzes the “Cool” in the text by questioning the basis of heterosexual mechanism: physiological sex, gender and sexual orientation to reveal the deconstruction of heterosexual hegemony. Combined with the social life role transposition in the post-colonial era of South Africa and the psychological disorder and trauma brought by colonialism, the paper uses Queer Theory to reinterpret the Shame and explain it in three ways respectively: Shame challenges the dichotomous structure of heterosexuality and homosexuality; It challenges the dichotomy between men and women; Queer's cross-dressing political behavior, aiming to reveal that queer in heterosexual hegemony and patriarchal society is filled with the ambivalence of resistance and obedience to mainstream social norms.

Key words: Coetzee; *Shame*; Queer Theory; deconstruction

1 引　言

酷儿理论是 20 世纪 90 年代西方兴起的性别研究理论，著名女权主义者特蕾莎·洛利茨（Teresa Lolitz）于 1990 年首次使用“酷儿”一词来指那些在性取向方面不符合主流、主流的性别规范或性规范的人。它指的是文化中所有的异常表达。这一类别不仅包括男同性恋、女同性恋和双性恋的位置，还包括所有其他潜在的未分类的异常位置。从国内学者对酷儿理论的观点看，存在将两者等同起来的现象。例如，华中师范大学文艺学系列教材《女性主义文学批评导论》第六章将酷儿理论等同于 LGBT 研究，即女同性恋、男同性恋、双性及跨性研究。（魏天真　梅兰，2011）《简析作为文学批评方法的“酷儿理论”》一文的作者认为，“20

世纪90年代，男女同性恋研究逐渐融合成一个相对独立的理论体系，即酷儿理论”。（傅树琴 李红，2009）很多人都对酷儿理论有所误解，认为它是在宣扬同性恋、否定异性恋。实际上，酷儿理论强调批判传统的男性气质和霸权，试图建立一个尊重个体性别发展和创造平等社会氛围的自由空间。

库切的小说《耻》充满了酷儿因素。瑞典皇家颁奖委员会指出库切获奖的理由是：“在人类反抗野蛮和无知的历史中，库切通过写作表达了他对弱势个人奋斗经历的坚定支持。”瑞典文学院认为库切的作品主要描写种族隔离下的人们的生活。他也是一个审慎的怀疑者，在他的作品中无情地批判了西方文明的残酷理性主义和伪善的道德。受到这些主题的影响，以往关于这部作品的研究大多集中在后殖民主义话语特征、白人的生存困境与宿命、身份认同的转变等等，国内各式评论亦层出不穷，有学者将其精辟地概括为“八大说”，即“越界说”“耻说”“施暴者说”“历史说”“现实—历史说”“种族问题说”“族裔政治说”和“白人知识分子精神空虚和道德沦丧说”。（仵从巨，范蕊，2006）而小说《耻》的女主人公露茜和其父亲卢里的性恋明显的非常态，这是一个动态变化的过程，复杂的情感纠葛。事实上，异性恋、同性恋或双性恋是人类不同的性倾向，但异性恋本身是人为地自然化，使之成为人类性行为的基础。在异性恋的规范下，一旦人们偏离了异性恋的标准，他们就会受到社会排斥。所以研究小说中的酷儿因素也给小说研究打开了新的大门，给小说研究提供了新的思路和方法，在后殖民主义的背景下，本文研究了社会和政治冲突中个体性别身份的演变。

酷儿理论的实质之一是挑战异性恋和同性恋的结构。著名社会学家朱蒂斯·巴特勒认为，一个人的性恋是不固定的，在很多时候，人们的性倾向模糊不定，常常会发生变化。酷儿理论的实质之二是挑战性别的两分结构。根据酷儿理论，个人的社会性别和生理性别不完全对等，女性有时候会表现出男性的特质，而男性也可能会具备女性的特点。

2 挑战性向的两分结构

酷儿理论的第一个重要内容是对同性恋和异性恋的双性恋结构和异性恋霸权的挑战。福柯在他的《性的历史》中指出欲望是社会的一种普遍形式，而不是天生固有的。酷儿理论批评家提出，人类爱的定义可以基于对年长或年轻人、对人或动物、对物体或多重物体的爱或者对自己的爱恋。库切小说《耻》中的露茜和其父亲卢里带有明显的反叛色彩。

“露茜的一生中并没有受到什么人的保护。”（库切，2002）“对露茜我早就放手了。做父亲，我可算是最没有保护好孩子的。”（162）“你从来没和我说过你第一个太太的事，露西也从未提起过她。露西和她的继父相处得不好，她提出来想回南非。”（187）在露茜的成长过程中，父母的婚姻和爱情消失，父亲不负责任，父母经常吵架。在这个充满爱心的父亲缺席的不完整的家庭里，露西长期生活在代表男人的父亲的阴影下，所以她害怕所有代表父权制的男人，所以即使她的母亲再婚，其父亲的缺席造成露茜精神上永远的伤痛和永远无法摆脱的记忆，最后甚至要逃离继父，去一个完全陌生的新环境生活。受父母男女关系的影响，她没有看到男女之间健康完美的爱情，而是看到无尽的争吵和背叛。这样，来自男性中心主义的压力，或者直接来自男性的压力，使得露西逃到同性别那里寻求安慰和支持。“也许他把露西归类为同性恋是不对的。”“也许她更喜欢和女人交往。或者说，所谓女同性恋就是这样一些男人：有些男人不需要男人。”（70）在这种情况下，女人之间的爱成为女人栖息在她们心中的一种方式。对异性失望后，她们同性之间的情感就变成一盏明灯，这是女性在遭受男性伤害、厌倦男性欺骗和生活纠缠之后，逃离到女性同伴身边，给予彼此安慰和同情的一种方式。

但是，我们可以看到露西对海伦的感情并没有在男性社会的环境中得到永久的保持。小说也没明确告诉读者海伦因为什么原因而离开露茜，选择到约翰内斯堡，而且已经离开很长时间。尤其是那场意想不到的强奸，预示女性之间纯洁的心理情感随时都会被男性社会渗透和瓦解。“所以男人应该被允许按照他们的本能行事，不需要任何控制就做任何他们想做的事？”（106）“当谈到男人和性时，没有什么让我吃惊。……你是个男人你应当知道。”（184）在露茜被无情残忍的蹂躏之后，在她逃离父亲和继父为代表的男权压力之后，又再次遭受到来自男性的伤害，她对男性已经彻底失去了信心。那次事件后，露茜怀孕了，但是她并没有选择去做人流手术，而是决定要把孩子生下来，这让其父卢里既担心又费解。在露茜看来，她自己现在无依无靠，没有兄弟，父亲也是什么都做不了，毫无力量来对抗这里的一切，她唯一能依赖的人只有佩特鲁斯。而且露茜很明确地知道自己对佩特鲁斯没有什么幻想，她内心一直保持自己想过的生活。佩特鲁斯原先是露茜农场雇佣的助手，露茜虽然知道佩特鲁斯要追求她是为了农场，她还是选择嫁给他。因在遭受了如此多的男性伤害之后，同性恋的姐妹关系可以看作是治愈男性创伤的港湾，这注定了同性恋爱的暂时性质。女性之间的情感因其不稳定结构而时时面临离散的状态。因为一旦有了能够保护、庇护女性的男性，他们会选择这些人来保护他们的安全。从这个角度来看，同性恋爱只是一些女性角色的权宜之计。

而男主卢里依赖于让身心得到慰藉的异性欢愉，在欲望面前无法摆脱梅拉妮、索拉娅、贝芙肖等女性的性吸引力和爱抚。小说第一章交代了卢里是一位传播学副教授，所开设课程为论浪漫主义诗人。他饱读浪漫主义诗歌且深谙浪漫主义，因此他自称是华兹华斯的信徒，浪漫主义诗人拜伦的追随者。拜伦在生活中一直处在感情的漩涡中，除了在诗作上的成就，拜伦也因其放荡不羁的私生活以及同性恋、乱伦等惊世骇俗的绯闻红透英伦。卢里与拜伦确有相似性：二者是冷漠的、浪漫的，崇尚自由和充满反叛。更为巧合的是二者都由于丑闻缠身而出逃，因此有些学者把他视为拜伦式的英雄，并把卢里前往女儿露西的农场寻求庇护比作“拜伦式流放”。（姜小卫，2007）酷儿理论将个体性取向定义为一种动态的零星的可能性取向的集合。在我们的一生中，甚至在一周的不同时期，性取向都有可能有所不同，因为性取向是一系列动态的欲望。（Tyson，2006）除此之外，卢里和拜伦一样，他们的性恋不再是大众所拥护的“异性恋”常态，而是一个变化、流动的过程。

当卢里看到梅拉妮的爸爸艾萨克斯时，被其身上具有的女性特质而吸引：“他第一次从他身上觉察到一丝梅拉妮的味道：嘴和嘴唇线条很好看。……凉凉的，光滑的皮肤上摸不到汗毛的感觉。”（194）“那父亲的手摸上去丝绸般的凉……”（197）。因此，我们可以看到卢里在异性恋和同性恋爱情之间徘徊和犹豫。他的复杂而矛盾的男性欲望恰恰说明了酷儿的性别认同和性取向理论是多元的、动态的。

3　挑战性别的两分结构

巴特勒认为，我们通常用性别来区分身体。她也认为，在性化过程之前或之后，没有原始的主体，而主体正是从性化过程中产生的。为了说明这个观点，在1990发表的《性别麻烦》（Gender Trouble），巴特勒提出了著名的性别操演理论（Theory of Gender Performativity）。简言之，巴特勒的性别操演理论强调了三点：（1）性别不是一种存有，而是一种行为，这是性别操演的戏剧维度。（2）性别身份的形成不是人们可以自由控制、有意为之的行为，而是在不断重复性别规范的过程中逐渐形成，因而一定需要时间的演进。这是性别操演的仪式维度。（3）规范和话语生成性别化的主体，生产关于性别的现实，这是性别操演的语言维度。（都岚岚，2015）

生理性别是指由生殖生理定义的两种人类性别，即男性和女性。酷儿理论认为，男性和女性之间的界限并不清楚。性别角色认为男性是主动的、支配性的、理性的、坚强的、保护性的和果断的，而女性是被动的、顺从的、害羞的和非理性的。“天生就是一个重生的孩子，一个年轻而坚强的移民。她的指甲永远不会干净。”（71）“她冲他做了一个他只能用甜蜜来形容的微笑可美丽，她却有许多许多。”（91）在传统的社会性别描述中，我们是不会用“健壮”或“壮实”来描述一个女孩的。在露茜被强奸后，卢里也深刻地认识到自己的无能为力，连自己的女儿都保护不了，从原先作为白人殖民者的优越感也被现实无情地吞噬，只能“像狗一样”活在这里。露茜既有社会性别角色设定的女人的脆弱，也有男人的刚毅，卢里既有社会性别角色设定的男人的坚毅，也有女人的无助。

酷儿理论研究的异装行为：服装是体现传统性别不同的重要标志，两性在着装上的笔墨倒置是对男女二元对立的质疑。“到了二十五六岁上，她开始表现出不同了。护养狗，忙菜园，看星相书，穿没有性别特征的衣服。这每一个现象，他都感觉是一份经过深思熟虑的、有目的的独立宣言。同时也是与男性世界决裂的宣言。过自己的生活。”（105）“露茜穿着一件下摆及膝的中长上衣，脚蹬高跟鞋……这不是她通常的穿着打扮。”（149）酷儿理论家摧毁了性的本质主义，提出人类在性向上的模糊性与自由性。每个人都有权利选择成为男人或者女人，有在不同性别之间进行转换的自由。因此，一个人虽然在生理上曾被命名为“男性”，但是可以在社会性别中扮演女性的角色，而一个生理上的“女性”也可以选择扮演男性的社会角色。

4　个人身份的重新定位

在宗主国文化大势已去，殖民地本土文化反噬的大背景下，前殖民者及其后代往往在此消彼长的文化冲突中失却了方向和归属感，陷入霍米·巴巴所说的“无家状态”（unhomeliness），即“文化和身份认同危机造成心理层面的流亡者”。（Tyson，2006）后殖民时代的前殖民区已发生翻天覆地的变化，旧式殖民结构被摧毁或削弱，导致“后殖民话语自然而然地随社会政治的变化而变化”，西方文化渐显式微之势，殖民者角色也就被注入新的含义（Loomba，1998）。库切曾在访谈录中一针见血地指出：“种族隔离在南非结束引起了一系列富有挑战的问题的语言、文化和故事会具有权威，这些问题可归结为：做一个南非人意味着什么？”的确，对于被殖民者和殖民者及后裔来说，身份认同在已经变革的环境下都是一个不小的挑战。

在库切笔下，对卢里的论述有多重角度。笔者认为，从酷儿的角度来看，卢里与其学生梅拉妮和索拉娅的性经历代表了白人曾经的强势文化，体现出其作为一个白人与生俱来的优越感。面对自己日渐弱势的状况，卢里要想证明他仍然是一个坚强的人，只有在一个弱势群体中，才能实现这一希望。索拉娅和梅拉妮都是有色人种，他们曾经是弱势群体，能够使他具有强烈的心态和征服意识。就像卢里说的三个黑人像狗一样，他也认为黑人是劣等的野蛮人。当露西被强奸后怀孕，即将生下一个黑白混血孩子时，露西的决定让卢里非常沮丧。从过去到现在，其他种族对白人来说总是意味着恐怖和卑贱。降低身份和他人和平共处是不容易的，婚姻是绝对不可接受的。

而露茜的名字虽然是光明之意，但是其身份却有着神秘感。萨莱姆镇附近的地方是作品故事情节展开的主要地点，而露西曾经独自居住在这里，就连她唯一的女性伴侣海伦也离开了此地，这使得露西的身份有了一层神秘性。露茜的异装行为和憎恨男性、偏爱女性的性恋趋向也使得其性别身份多了一层神秘性。而《耻》中的露茜让我们不由得联想起华兹华斯所刻画的露西。《耻》中的露茜是神秘而奇怪的，连她的父母都无法理解她；而华兹华斯《露西》组诗中也没有说明露西的身份，她的真实身份无从知晓。华兹华斯在组诗《露西》中用简单的表达方式对露西这一形象进行了刻画，但是表达的含义却模糊不清。唯一可以确定的是诗歌的主题是对他者、改变和死亡的探讨。对作者而言，《耻》所要处理的是，如何去理解并构建露西这一带有神秘色彩的人物。对读者而言，理解露西的神秘身份则是一个重要的问题，事实上读者很难完全理解她。佩特鲁斯说道："可在这里，那很危险，太危险了。女人必须结婚。"（234）异性恋、生儿育女被人为地自然化、优等化，这体现了一种规范化的异性恋霸权。无奈屈于现实，露茜不得不依附于佩特鲁斯生存，这是酷儿群体对现实的逃避，也是对自己的保护，他们得不到正常人应有的生活，只能蜷缩在角落被排斥被压迫，但露茜也坚定地保持自己的立场。或许可以这样理解，露西的神秘在于她只是朴实无华的存在于自己的世界，存在于自我简单的生活中。

身份政治是酷儿运动无法逃避的议题。如果酷儿们不能超越现有政治体制的束缚，就会被死死地限制在身份标签内难以超脱，最终成为体制中的"正常成员"。但这种身份的获得，却是以牺牲其他性向为代价。酷儿们只有打破权力话语、意识形态强加在人类身上的最后一道枷锁——性的枷锁，才能打破社会权力复杂而牢固的控制网络，实现人的自由生存，这或许就是库切赋予露茜这个人物的最后希冀吧。

5 结　语

从性向政治到身份政治，酷儿理论表现出鲜明的层进性。在库切的小说里，性别不再是永恒不变的事物，性别变得模糊与不稳定，每一个人物都可以具有与生理性别不相符的性别气质。此外，库切打破了传统文学中对性取向的桎梏，不仅描述了异性恋的感情生活，还描绘了同性恋、双性恋的感情生活，甚至把它们交织在一起。在《耻》中，库切刻画了白人酷儿殖民者后裔在后殖民南非的现实和精神遭遇。在黑人力量重新崛起的环境下，白人的文化和个人的重新定位迫在眉睫。

参考文献

[1] J. M. 库切. 耻[M]. 张冲，郭整风译. 南京：译林出版社，2002.

[2] Loomba，Ania，1998. Colonialism/Postcolonialism [M]. London：Routledge.

[3] Tyson，Lois，2006. Critical Theory Today [M]. New York：Routledge.

[4] 都岚岚. 酷儿理论等于同性恋研究吗？[J]. 文艺理论研究，2015（6）：184-191.

[5] 傅淑琴，李洪. 简析作为文学批评理论的酷儿理论[J]. 时代文学，2009（5）：212-13.

[6] 姜小卫. 库切小说《耻》中的忏悔、宽恕与和解[J]. 当代外国文学，2007（3）：31-37.

[7] 魏天真，梅兰. 女性主义文学批评导论[M]. 武汉：华中师范大学出版社，2011.

[8] 仵从巨，范蕊. 三重主题及其完成：关于库切之《耻》[J]. 当代外国文学，2006（1）：64-72.

霸权帝国的崩塌：库切《等待野蛮人》中二元的解构与重构

王若岚

摘　要：约翰·马克斯韦尔·库切发布于1980年的《等待野蛮人》被定位为政治恐怖小说，讲述了虚构背景下的帝国对所谓的野蛮人发起征战的历史，而这一历史对现今仍有很强的关照意识。在国内对《等待野蛮人》的研究涉及方面较广，本文则主要根据王敬慧在《两种帝国理念的对照：论库切寓言体小说“等待野蛮人”》一文中所提出的“建立一个更有包容性的帝国”观点进行延伸，拟进一步从后殖民的角度利用拉康的“小写他者”理论，通过解构文中的现有二元对立再重构中心的方法来探索库切的人文关怀表达以及想表达的核心，即：通过帝国传达出的不是绝对的非黑即白，而是一种对一种更具有包容性、求同性的社会的追求和呼吁。

关键字：《等待野蛮人》；库切；他者理论；解构；重构

Abstract：Written by Coetzee，*Waiting for the Barbarians*，published in 1980，was positioned as political horror fiction. It tells an invading history of the Empire against the so called Barbarians in fictional context， which still has something strongly related to nowadays. In China， the relevant research on *Waiting for the Barbarians* involves a wide range of topics，among which，this article is mainly based on the opinion of “reconstructing a more open and tolerant society” published in Contrast of Two Empires：Reading Coetzee’s Allegorical Waiting for the Barbarians by WangJinghui. From the perspective of post-colony，using the “other” theory of Lacan，this article attempts to deconstruct the binary oppositions in the novel and reconstruct a new core which accords with the humanistic thoughts of Coetzee，that is，the empire conveys the pursuit and appeal of a more inclusive and homogenous society.

Key words：*Waiting for the Barbarians*；Coetzee；the “other” theory；deconstruction；reconstruction

1　引　言

《等待野蛮人》是一部被瑞典学院的教授们誉为“继承了约瑟夫·康拉德的手法的政治恐怖小说”。（2003年诺贝尔文学奖颁奖词）从1980年发表至今，仍可以产生令人振聋发聩的效果，而且更给人留下掩卷之余深思的余地。对其的解读中，王敬慧在《两种帝国理念的对照：论库切寓言体小说“等待野蛮人”》中将库切理想中的帝国阐释为一种与乔尔上校所代表的霸权帝国相对立的具有强大包容性的后殖民主义帝国，文敏在《库切及其作品“等待野蛮人”》中将野蛮人阐释为所谓文明人的自省，而浙江大学俞晓红在《权力的写作——解读J.M.库切的“等待野蛮人”》对小说中权力、身体和知识的关系进行重新解读，指出小说对西方文明欺凌异族野蛮本质的揭露，从而反驳外界评论对小说的不公正批评，上海外国语大学段宇杰在《从“等待野蛮人”中管窥库切的道德评价》分析了库切对帝国的道德行为规范及主人公的道德选择。本文的目的是针对王敬慧提出的“更具包容性的帝国”中帝国的概念进行延伸，利用拉康的“小写的他者”理论，对文中两组鲜明的二元对立“文明与野蛮，等待与被等待”解构，并试图重新建构一个库切对理想世界的定义。

小说中的帝国没有具体的指代，但通过帝国代表乔尔上校可以看出，此时帝国的唯一目的就是“如何确保政权的长治久安，避免分崩离析。”（《等待野蛮人》文敏译）然而“偏执狂是《等待野蛮人》中那个帝国的基本状态。”（用人生写作的库切：与时间面对面，p. 103）因而，处于偏执状态的帝国为了达到政权的长治久安的方法就是消灭一切与自己为敌的对面或者使他们归顺。所以，本文认为，库切理想中的世界既非强硬地以彼之道还彼之身的报复，从而使自己变成施暴者，也非逆来顺受的接受霸权帝国的独裁和物化。相反，正如王敬慧在《两种帝国理念的对照：论库切寓言体小说“等待野蛮人”》所阐释的一样，真正直击霸权帝国核心的是建立一种更为包容的帝国，而本文针对包容做进一步衍生，将帝国概念泛化。

拉康把失落的欲望对象称为 object petit a（小写的他者客体）。“小写的他者客体”也可以用于指称一切事物，只要它能够重新激发起我对失落对象的被压抑的欲望，他者来源于主体的虚幻映射，主体本是虚无，万物皆幻象。本文主要采用拉康这一理论进行分析，将文本中的二元对立进行解构。小说中以乔尔上校为代表的文明人想要用文明去征服处于边境地带的野蛮人，他们认为他们一直在等待野蛮人的入侵，也在等待去救赎被野蛮人困扰的群众。然而库切在小说中则通过无名的行政长官之口，将所谓的文明与野蛮以及等待者与被等待者从内部解构，从而瓦解霸权帝国主义所建构的他者。所以本文认为作者所想要表达的是希望构建一个具有包容性的世界，没有所谓的非黑即白而是在混沌中找到各自的意义，互相尊重。

2　野蛮：文明的黑暗之花

根据拉康的小写“他者”来看，他者来源于主体的虚幻映射，主体本是虚无，万物皆幻像。罗世平在“殖民（主义）文学的主体性建构”一文中指出，“我思他故我在”，这是对笛卡尔“我思故我在”说的修正，说明“自我”通过“他者”建构自身，并指出殖民（主义）文学建构西方主体性的过程本质上是“我”思“他”故“我”在的过程。据此，在小说中，一直缺位的野蛮人其实在根本上就是以乔尔上校为代表的“文明”帝国所建构的存在，他们的存在只是为了帮助来证明“文明”的存在。除此之外，小说《等待野蛮人》的名字源于康斯坦丁·卡瓦菲的同名诗：“参议员立法何用之有？一旦野蛮人来这里，他们会立法。”“因为野蛮人今天到来，皇帝等待接见他们的领袖。”“为什么我们两个领事和裁判官今天出来穿着刺绣的，鲜红宽大衣袍？因为野蛮人今天到来”“现在没有野蛮人了。现在没有野蛮人我们该怎么办？那些人似乎是一种权宜之计。”诗歌几个连续的自问自答也讽刺了所谓的文明其实根本就是帝国掌权者的自我标榜，而野蛮也只是为了成全他们的文明而被建构的存在而已。所以这些内部的自我解构其实表达出文明和野蛮的本质并不是对立的存在，只是人为的构建而已，因此他们的差异也并不科学。

此外，在小说中对文明和野蛮的描写也充满了讽刺意味。“我派了一个士兵去厨房弄点食物。他带来昨晚剩余的一块面包，他把这面包交给了囚犯中最年长的一个。这个老人虔诚地用两只手接过面包，先用鼻子嗅了嗅，然后掰开来。把面包分给周围的人。他们都狼吞虎咽地大口吃起这‘吗哪’来，快速地咀嚼着，他们都没有抬起眼睛。一个女人把嚼过的面包吐进手掌里喂她的孩子。”（文敏译《等待野蛮人》，p. 24）作为野蛮人的代表，他们对待同伴和亲人的关怀和分享是显而易见的，可是反观作为文明人的行为：“一个女孩被她的朋友推上前来，咯咯地笑着，捂着自己的脸。‘去嘛，别害怕！’他们鼓动她。一个士兵把警棍递到她手里领她上前。她站在那儿直发愣，一只手还掩在脸上。叫嚷声、玩笑声、暧昧的喊唆向她扑来。她举起了警棍，猛地一下砸在囚犯臀部，扔下警棍跑回欢呼的人群中去。人们开始竞相争夺警棍，士兵们几乎难以维持秩序，人们一拥而上或是自己上去动手或是等着警棍传过来，我看不见地上的囚犯，站在那里忘了脚下的水桶。（p. 143）”“我蹦蹦跳跳地跑过去，撞在绳子上，傻站在那里。我闻到了屎臭。他们不准我去洗。苍蝇总是围着我，很有兴趣地叮着我脸上的伤处，我稍一停下来就会叮上来。（p. 156）”这些文明人，他们对别人冷漠，对同伴无情，在他们身上表现出的一切都毫无文明所标榜的人性存在。同时，作为叙述者的执行长官在小说中曾发问：我想：“许多年以后的某一天，当人们在这个地方挖掘废墟时，他们会对沙漠居民留下的文物更感兴趣而不是我可能留下的什么东西。”（p. 205）这表明，“其实文明人和野蛮人在文明的链条上并没有固定的序列，在不同的历史阶段上，二者的位置也许正好颠倒过来。”（文敏）

但是，小说对野蛮人除了正面的叙述也包含对野蛮人的嫌恶。“边境地区的妇女们，没有一个不梦到有双黝黑的野蛮人的手从床底下伸出来握住她的脚踝；也没有一个男人不被想象中这样的景象吓住：野蛮人跑到他家来闹宴，打碎盘子，放火烧帘子，强奸他的女儿。”（p. 11）“几天下来，人们对这些捕鱼人的看法拐了个弯儿，那是因为他们那些让人听不懂的含糊不清的语言、他们健硕的胃口、他们像动物一样没羞没耻的举止、他们动不动就乱发一通的脾气……后来，所有的事情都使我们失去了对他们的同情心：肮脏、熏臭，还有他们争吵的喧哗声和咳嗽声也越来越大……一种流言开始在镇上传播，说这帮人都是有病的，会把疾病传染给镇上的人。（p. 26）”这样的描述也比比皆是，野蛮人似乎也确实有不及文明人的地方，他们粗俗、好逸恶劳还缺乏思考。但这正如在《文化定位》一书开头，霍米·巴巴引用海德格尔的一句名言：“界线不是某物中止的标志，相反，按照希腊人的说法，界线正是某物开启其存在的标志。”文明和野蛮其实之间并没有存在明显的界线，它们总是在相互转化中。所以不难看出，作者借用小说自相矛盾的叙述，将文明和野蛮的对立自我瓦解。

霸权帝国下的人制造了劣于他们的“他者”野蛮人们，可是这样的劣等野蛮人其根本就是一种建构，再者，这样的建构在其存在过程中也发生了自我解构，他们的存在使文明人的行为变得野蛮，使文明人不断出于向野蛮人转化的过程，将两者的边界不断迷糊甚至消除。

3 等待：潘多拉的魔盒

库切将《等待野蛮人》作为小说的标题，一方面借鉴了康斯坦丁·卡瓦菲的同名诗，另一方面也向读者提出一个问题，等待者到底是谁？等待的过程又究竟是怎样的？同样用等待命名的戏剧《等待戈多》中，等待者是两个流浪汉，在全剧快要结束时，其中的一个流浪汉说：“咱们明天上吊吧。除非戈多来了。”另一个说：“他要是来了呢？”“咱们就得救啦。”最后他们等待的戈多还是没有来，他们还需要等下去。很明显，在《等待戈多》中等待者就是两个流浪汉所代表的人类，而所等待的戈多则是唯一被留在潘多拉魔盒中的希望，他们主动在等待的一直都是他们的精神支撑。那么反观在《等待野蛮人》中的等待，若将等待者看成是文明人，将等待的过程看成是主动的期盼，那么这样的等待便是一种消极而无意义的等待，也和小说中整个剧情的走向相悖。所以小说的等待者其实是被文明人所定义的野蛮人，他们被动地等待着文明人的离开，文明人离开之后他们才能在他们的土地上去重建自己的家园，去重新等待希望。所以在这一方面来说，小说本来所设定的等待者与被等待者被解构，随着其被解构所表现出的对希望的等待也随之浮现。

在大卫·科特维尔所著的《用人生写作的 J. M. 库切：与时间面对面》中，他写道："《等待野蛮人》写了一年之后，他意识到这本书是关于'等待一个没有出现的欲望，虽然人正在等。《等待戈多》描写的是等待一个主题'。等待的心理状态也表现在这部小说倾向于隐藏它的本意。当结尾逐渐明朗时，库切在笔记中这样描述行政长官：'他之所以困惑，关键就在于他从来没弄明白自己生活的象征意义，即使在生活的紧要关头也是如此。跟野蛮人的会面没有实质内容，也没有语言交流，警察也并非都是坏人，女孩儿拒绝向他透露自己的想法，最后野蛮人也没有来……这是一部在表情达意时一直闪烁其词的小说'。"总的来说，悬而不决和含而不露是《等待野蛮人》的两个基本特色，这和看似即将土崩瓦解的偏执狂社会状态息息相关。（大卫·科特维尔）

正如康斯坦丁·卡瓦菲的同名诗中所描写的一样：

为什么这样突如其来的困惑，这样的混乱？
（人们变得如此庄重。）
为什么街道和广场空得如此迅速，
每个人都在回家路上陷入了沉思？
因为夜幕降临，而野蛮人还没有来。
刚刚从边境回来的男人说
现在没有野蛮人了。
现在没有了野蛮人我们该怎么办？
那些人似乎是一种权宜之计。

当野蛮人已经不是等待的对应物之后，所谓的文明人又该用什么来麻痹自己，又该用什么来支撑那个霸权帝国主义下的野心勃勃？

在等待野蛮人的过程中，文明人自我将等待的意义解构，凸显出其霸权帝国主义下的勃勃野心，也表现出小说最终等待的其实是人类自我之思，对希望和信仰的重构。

4 混沌：孕育出尊重与包容的种子

荷兰学者兼作家弗兰斯·凯伦敦克曾评论过："如果将库切的作品过于狭窄地与他的祖国的悲剧相联系，那是错误的。他所描述的种族隔离是非政治的，是存在主义的。种族是一种迷信，种族主义与反种族主义都是错误的陈述。它实际上在讲述承认与尊重真正的差异，这是文化的问题。人只有在保持不同的情况下，才是平等的。"小说中逐步将文明与野蛮解构，让读者渐渐明白所谓的文明其实并不优于野蛮，只不过是一者对另一者怀有目的的臆想；而所谓的文明对野蛮的等待也不过是恶意的扭曲。而这样的霸权帝国最终的结局也是落荒而逃。整本小说中最具有代表性的行政长官则是经历了从霸权到包容和尊重的转换。所以他选择了解救女孩，但是在经受帝国的残害之后仍旧坚守在自己的岗位上，因为他知道，文明与野蛮都没有错，错的是将它们泾渭分明的态度。他也知道，面对不同的文化，最重要的态度是尊重，以包容的眼光去对待才不会让自己囿于一家之见而有失偏颇地站边。

5 结　语

通过以上对《等待野蛮人》的分析可以得知，以乔尔上校为代表的霸权帝国主义想要通过构建一个劣于自我的野蛮人“他者”来建构自我的文明形象，从而达成帝国的侵略与掠夺。但是通过对小说中为建构低劣的帝国“他者”而塑造的文明和野蛮，等待与被等待的解构，不难看出，霸权的帝国主义自身也无法合理存在。想通过掠夺的方式获得扩张的帝国最终以失败告终，而野蛮人也一直没有出现，一切似乎又回到起点，甚至有一种会将野蛮人和文明人置换再卷土重来一次的意味。这也就意味，霸权帝国主义从本质上来说是不合理的存在，它虚构了“他者”来衬托自己的优越，从而将他者物化与低劣化。那么将一切都解构之后，剩下的是什么呢？将绝对的文明与野蛮剥开，剩下的不是非黑即白，而是一种混沌。在这样的混沌中去区分优劣与好坏是无用而自我矛盾的。所以本文认为库切真正提倡的并不是优劣而是包容以及对一种尊重差异的社会的呼吁。

参考文献

[1] 大卫•阿特维尔. 用人生写作的 J. M. 库切：与时间面对面[M]. 哈尔滨：黑龙江教育出版社，2017.
[2] 段宇杰. 从《等待野蛮人》管窥库切的道德评价[J]. 名作欣赏，2011（21）.
[3] 黄丽娟. 从拉康“镜像说”解读“他者”的含义[J]. 沈阳师范大学学报（社会科学版），2008（6）.
[4] J. C. 坎尼米耶. J. M. 库切传[M]. 王敬慧译. 杭州：浙江文艺出版社，2017.
[5] 库切. 等待野蛮人[M]. 文敏译. 杭州：浙江文艺出版社，2004.
[6] 库切访谈录，https://www.douban.com/group/topic/38184297/.
[7] 卡卡瓦菲斯诗全集[M]. 黄灿燃译. 石家庄：河北教育出版社，2002.
[8] 拉康. 拉康选集[M]. 上海：上海三联书店，2001.
[9] 刘立辉. 等待戈多：信仰和理性真空状态下的等待行为[J]. 英美文学研究论丛，2010（1）.
[10] 罗世平. 殖民（主义）文学的主体性建构[J]. 外国文学评论，2007（3）.
[11] 王敬慧. 两种帝国理念的对照：论库切寓言体小说《等待野蛮人》[J]. 外国文学研究，2016（6）.
[12] 文敏. 库切及其作品《等待野蛮人》[J]. 文学教育（下），2009（6）.

《等待野蛮人》中的暴力与救赎

黄　丹

摘　要：《等待野蛮人》是南非作家库切第一部为自己赢得国际声誉的长篇小说，受到学界的广泛关注。自“9·11”事件以来，学界对暴力的讨论不断深入。库切在该书中大量详尽描写“文明人”暴力行为和老行政长官的救赎，这一矛盾行为对分析文章的主题有重要意义。本文从后殖民主义角度追溯文明人的暴力和老行政长官救赎行为之源，并分析救赎行为的有效性，结合作者库切的写作背景和写作过程，认为部分积极觉醒的白人殖民者的救赎力量是有限的，只有被压制者主动对抗才是行之有效的救赎，呼吁广大被压迫者团结起来积极抵抗殖民者。

关键词：后殖民主义；库切；《等待野蛮人》；暴力；救赎

Abstract: It is agreed that *Waiting for Barbarians* through which the author J.M.Coetzee has won his international reputations has been paid much attention by scholars. The scholars has done more discussions and researches on violence since “9 • 11”event in 2001. In this novel, many pages are focused on the violent behaviors of “the civil” and the salvations of the old administer, which are contradictory two sides, in turn, helping to analyze the meaning of the theme. From the perspective of Post-colonism the essay will search the source of the violent acts and salvations, then analyze the effectives of the salvations and combined with the Coetzee’s writing background and process conclude that the power of salvations from part of pioneered white people is limited and only that of the oppressed is the way to save themselves so that the novel calls for the unity of the suppressed to revolt.

Key words: Post-Colonism; J. M. Coetzee; *Waiting for Barbarians*; Violence; Salvation

1 引　言

《等待野蛮人》是“让世界对这位文坛（指库切，作者注）新秀刮目相看”（董亮，2018）的作品。《等待野蛮人》是设定在某帝国统治之下的边塞，帝国第三局听信“野蛮人”即将进攻的谣言，派驻以乔尔上校为首的帝国军队前来镇压，边塞老行政长官协助。之后帝国军队使用各种残暴的手段多次围剿“野蛮人”，他们最终狼狈而归，离开边塞。边塞回归平静。

目前国内外对库切的研究关注较多。据不完全统计，从2009—2017年，英语世界国家至少举办过八次大型的库切国际研讨会，出版了19本研究库切作品的专著，3本对比库切和其他作家的论著，8本研究库切的论文集。（董亮，2018）“9·11”事件是西方文学界和学术界的分水岭，此后暴力、战争、道德、历史及文化等因素愈加受到重视。（于琪，2015）库切在《等待野蛮人》中大量详尽描写“文明人”的暴力行为，因此，有必要对《等待野蛮人》中的暴力行为进行讨论。目前已有论文对库切小说的暴力讨论主要是与南非当时的种族隔离制度背景相结合，以探讨历史背景对作家书写的影响，例如，“outrageous meaning：the fiction of J.M.Coetzee” by Lars Engle。国内对该小说的暴力探究大体上集中于暴力话语与与伦理道德的关系，如谢菲、杨辉“库切小说《等待野蛮人》中的国家与暴力话语”等。这些对暴力的探讨较少涉及对“暴力”自身在小说中的探讨。所以，本文根据齐泽克对“暴力”的定义观察暴力行为，从后殖民主义角度追溯文明人的暴力和老行政长官救赎行为（应对暴力的方法）之源，并分析这种救赎行为的有效性，结合作者库切写作背景和写作过程，认为部分积极觉醒白人殖民者的救赎力量是有限的，只有被压制者主动对抗才是行之有效的救赎，呼吁广大的被压迫者团结起来积极抵抗殖民者。

2 暴力行为表现

暴力是库切小说必不可少的元素。Lars Engle 认为：“库切小说的三个特征即：散体风格，对暴力痛苦的关注和对社会制度的冷峻态度，以及对现代历史恐慌中个体复杂性抑或者天真性的巧妙处理。”（1986）那么，暴力定义是什么呢？哪些是暴力行为？哪些是攻击行为呢？从词义来说，暴力是指使用武力或人身攻击或指国家与国家之间的纷争。齐泽克认为斗争和攻击性为生命所必需时，可以通过区分“攻击”与“暴力”来解决问题，即处于“求生驱力”的攻击只叫“攻击”而不叫“暴力”，作为“死亡驱力”的攻击才叫“暴力”。（2012）他指出，“暴力不是单纯的攻击，而是攻击过剩。暴力的定义不是罪与恶的区分上，而是欲望与需要的区分上”。（2012）因此，本文所讨论的“暴力”是指基于欲望之上的攻击过剩的暴力。由此分析《等待野蛮人》中乔尔上校为代表的帝国第三局对“野蛮人”和“叛国者”所实施的一系列残酷行为，这些行为都是基于彻底消灭野蛮人的欲望之上的，且对野蛮人的攻击是以“杀死野蛮人”为目的，所以这些行为都属于暴力行为。暴力是帝国用以统治蛮族的工具。（赵修伟，2010）然而，野蛮人对第三局的抵抗行为只能算是“攻击”，这是基于求生驱力之下的行为。

《等待野蛮人》中以乔尔上校为代表的第三局对“野蛮人”所实施的酷刑，对老行政长官所进行的拷问，这些流血血腥的事件都是主观暴力行为。所谓主观暴力，“由某个非常明确的行为为人展现出来的……并表现我对事物‘正常’的平静状态的扰乱”。（Zizek，2008），也就是指犯罪行为，战争等从主观意志出发，打乱社会正常状态的行为。各种歧视行为和煽动仇恨的演说等都是其具体表现。（于琪，2015）小说的发酵素就是帝国军队到边塞镇压野蛮人，对他们发动战争。接着就是在边塞的一系列暴力行为，他们实施这些暴力行为的宗旨正如老行政长官所总结的“痛就是真相；所有其他人都值得怀疑。”（库切，2004）他们用尽一切手段折磨所谓“敌人”，而目的就正如福柯所言：“折磨就是为直达被折磨者的灵魂，从而消除最后一丝反抗。”（《规诫与惩罚》）这使他们无力反抗，更好地统治帝国。除了对人的暴力，书中还充满对动物的主观暴力。小说中多次对狩猎行动的描写和对动物惨状的描写。例如，乔尔上校对“我”兴高采烈谈论最近一次大狩猎，“当时成百上千的鹿、猪和熊被杀死，漫山遍野都是动物尸体，多得没法收拾，只好让她们去烂掉。”（2004）

在分析暴力时，不能只看到血淋淋的主观暴力，隐藏在生活中的客观暴力也是值得注意的。“对暴力行为的过度恐惧以及受害者的同情，将冷酷无情地成为阻碍我们思想的诱饵。”（Zizek，2008）仅注意直观的主观暴力行为使我们容易忽视对潜藏的客观暴力思想的思考。《等待野蛮人》中贯穿始终的矛盾都是野蛮人与文明人的对立。那么首先在提及所谓“野蛮人”与“文明人”概念时已经是一种符号暴力（客观暴力的一种表现）。齐泽克认为符号暴力就是以语言等符号来施加的暴力，且“每个符号暴力都建立在某种”暴力的“伦理-政治性上”。（齐泽克，2012）帝国占据的主导地位使它拥有话语权，他们划定什么才是“文明人”，老行政长官在看到俘虏遭遇时，一连串的问话“没有人告诉他这些人的区别就在于捕鱼的用渔网，野外骑马打猎的用弓箭吗？没有人告诉他这些人甚至讲的都不是同一种语言吗？”（库切，2004）这说明帝国标准主要是在使用工具和语言上。还有在这个情节之前所反映的生活习惯上，这种符号化过程就是典型的“非理性”暴力强加过程。（于琪，2015）这些都是帝国统治者强制加给野蛮人的意识形态。

3 暴力来源

以上种种暴力无论主观与客观都源自社会意识形态。社会学家鲍曼认为：“对残酷的纵容并非源自参与者的邪恶，而是源自邪恶社会的安排。”（2002）也就是说各类残酷行为来自于社会意识形态。本文所说的源自意识形态主要是指源自意识形态的思想渗透和对意识形态的空间秩序建构。Steven Waltson 认为，“库切在他作品中都具体的提及殖民主义”，（1986）并且认为“库切的书最大广泛地涉及了殖民主义”。（1986）殖民主义通过强力占有殖民地的土地与财富，他们的霸权“也是通过无以数计的文化形式，通过文化象征层面上的炫耀和展示，才得到肯定、认可和合法化的。”（博埃默，1998）帝国神话以文本的方式将帝国中心意识灌输给读者，为殖民主义以及后来的隔离制度的存在做了意识形态的铺垫与固化。（邵凌，2010）“自 16，17 世纪始，西方‘文明’的概念与帝国扩张与历史发展紧密联系。”（Paul Rich，1987）在《等待野蛮人》中，帝国统治者文化层面上灌输的思想一直都是“野蛮人”是“懒惰，没有道德感，肮脏，愚蠢。”（库切，2004）“文明人”是先进的和聪明的。野蛮人应该臣服于文明人，完全无条件避让，这与殖民者美化自己的殖民思想而提出来的——东方主义思想紧密相关。赛义德认为东方主义就是西方殖民者，想象出的一套有利于殖民统治的规则，企图在被殖民者的头脑中内化成一种“殖民思维”：即被殖民者生来就是下等的、落后的，就应该臣服于殖民者，接受殖民者的奴役和驯化。如果不按他们的规则行事就会被施以酷刑。（1999）书中男孩、蛮族女孩以及其他贴着野蛮人标签的人都遭受来自文明人的酷刑，因为“痛才是真相”。“这不是人与人的交往，只有支配和屈从，殖民统治等于将人物化，强迫输入一种惧怕，绝望，被奴才化。”（张德明，2009）恋族女孩的死和男孩爷爷的死是例证。用他们的死和对死亡的惧怕，促使他们编造出帝国想要的“真相”。且老行政长官提出这样最简洁的方法处理所有异类，“让她们挖一个坑，用他们最后一点力气挖掘，挖到他们所有人都能躺进去那么大（这个坑就是为他们而挖），就把他们永远永远地埋葬在那里”，（库切，2003）活埋极其残忍和非人道，却能被理所当然地提出来，就是为了达到所谓和平，不惜一切手段。殖民者构建意识形态空间秩序主要的手段就是划界，正如张明德所认为的“划界是现代化谋划的一个标志性行为。通过划界，流变种的自然物被纳入人的规范，消除不了他的稳定性，混乱的世界有了秩序和理性，现代性就此产生。通过划界，为自己构建一个以自我为中心的空间，将它与蛮荒取分开来。界线之内，代表着安全、秩序、文明和理性；界限之外，则是危险的、混乱的、野蛮的，‘他者’触摸的自然，于是，现代性的空间秩序就如此被构建和生产出来了。”（2009）小说开篇就提到“边界”“城墙”等界限的标志，一直都在提到围墙内和围墙外，“今年没有野蛮人到来。往年入冬后，游牧部落的人通常陈群结队地来到居民点，在城墙外支起帐篷跟居民进行物品交换的易货贸易。”（2003）这些围墙标签进一步划开了殖民者与被殖民者的空间范围，构建了帝国自身的殖民空间秩序，在空间内殖民意识得到统一。

4 暴力救赎

"在库切的作品——《幽暗之地》《国家中心》《等待野蛮人》和《迈克尔 k 的时代和生活》中都存在着一个殖民者主人公叙述，他的叙述还比较客观。去理解库切作品这种非常规之处最重要的一点就是知道主人公是知识分子殖民者，但他并不愿意成为殖民者。"（Stephen，1986）这是对老行政长官（《等待野蛮人》主人公，叙述者）真实的写照。作为管理帝国边境的行政长官，他一直兢兢业业守着这片平静的小镇，自己过着优哉游哉的生活，不过问世事。甚至在最开始乔尔上校虐打的时候，不愿打破自己的平静生活去掺和。但从他"为着自己的良心"去看小男孩开始，他一路见证了帝国第三局的种种血腥暴力，并且开始用自己的行动救赎。从悄悄关怀小男孩，收留并送回蛮族女孩，到自己被贴上"叛国者"标签遭到酷刑，再到他自己用身体为受虐者挡住大锤。他"内心忍受着作为殖民者的愧疚"，（274）用实际行动瓦解暴力，救赎自我。老行政长官的行为与乔尔上校为代表的第三局帝国殖民者（施暴者）的行径大相径庭，因为他在选择着，寻找着自己的本质。萨特在存在主义中说道："存在的第一原则'如果上帝并不存在，那么至少总有一个东西先与其本质就已经存在了，先要有这个东西的存在，然后才能用什么概念来说明它。这个东西就是人。"（1987）存在的第二原则就是人有绝对自由，人有选择的权利。"这些哲学精神鼓励人们相信自己完全可以创造他自己，只要勇敢的行动，就会寻找到人的本质，从而实现完全的自我救赎。"（郑亚萍，2012）因此，老行政长官的转变是对人本质的追寻，通过对暴力的瓦解，以实现自我救赎。但这种单个努力的救赎效果是有限的。老行政长官救赎结果是：男孩爷爷死去，男孩被迫领着第三局去找所谓的野蛮人；蛮族姑娘走后，他被免职受讯；大锤之后，受尽酷刑，遭到周围人的围观和嘲弄。

库切借老行政长官的口诉说着对南非种族隔离制度的批评和不满以及救赎之道。《等待野蛮人》写于南非种族隔离制度后期，在那期间，黑人觉醒运动领袖斯蒂夫比科在拘押期间离奇死亡，这也对小说的主题和内容产生了影响，正如《J.M》所写："这正是库切要寻找的'欲望的落脚之地'。""库切本人曾经说过，一切书写都是自传。"（王卫平，2017）他的作品都是对自己生活的写照，"老行政长官可以看作库切批评南非社会状况的代言人"，（谢琼，2013）他自己也认为："自我存在于作品当中，不是作为原材料，而是存在于叙事本身中，在讲述故事的过程中。"（库切，2004）库切自己就存在于老行政长官讲述帝国故事的过程中。库切自己作为一个南非白人殖民后代，"他的小说作品都呈现了一系列现代南非白人的类似处境"，（Lars engle，1986）老行政长官展现了以他为代表的南非白人后裔内心所遭受的折磨，希望结束种族隔离制度，但却因个人力量的有限，只能做出自己的贡献。"小说让库切在种族隔离制度孤雁残喘之际，为祖国刮骨去毒。"（131）因此，被压制者也要有所行动，就如《等待野蛮人》中野蛮人利用自己的智慧赶走帝国统治的军队一样，将这种力量与觉醒白人殖民者的力量相结合，才能改变南非现状，从而实现对暴力的救赎，找到人的本质。

5 结　论

《等待野蛮人》对暴力的直接和间接呈现较多，联系当今对"暴力"话题的讨论。本文首先根据齐泽克对暴力的定义和分类分析了《等待野蛮人》中暴力的具体表现；其次，结合萨义德对东方主义思想的批评，找出了暴力的来源，源于殖民意识形态，主要是意识形态的渗透和空间秩序的构建。最后，从萨特存在主义角度分析老行政长官的救赎有效性，再根据库切经历和创作观，说明个体救赎力量有限，被殖民者也要觉醒起来反抗，两股力量的结合才能改变种族隔离制度的现状，从而实现自由。

参考文献

[1] Foucault，Michel, 1991. Discipline and Punish：The Birth of the Prison，Alan Sheridan（tran.）. New York：Vintage-Random.

[2] Lars Engle，1986. “Outrageous Meaning：The Fiction of J.M.Coetzee”，The Threepenny Review. No. 24，p5-7.

[3] Zizek Slavoj, 2008. Violence：Six Sideways Reflections，New York：Picador. Print.

[4] Stephen Watson，1986. “ Colonialism and the Novels of J.M.Coetzee”，Research in African Literatures，Vol.17，No. 3，Special Focus on Southern Africa，370-392.

[5] Zizek，Slavoj，2008. Violence：Six Sideways Reflections. New York：Picador. Print.

[6] Rich，Paul，Autumn 1984. “Apartheid and the Decline of the Civilization Idea：An Essay on Nadine Gordimer’s “July’s People” and J.M.Coetzee’s “Waiting for the Barbarians”，Research in African Literatures，Vol.15，No.3，pp365-393.

[7] 董亮. “库切研究的新动向：关注作家的作者身份建构”[J]. 外国文学研究，2018（1）：165-169.

[8] 艾勒克·博埃默. 殖民与殖民文学[M]. 盛宁译. 沈阳：辽宁大学出版社，牛津大学出版社，1998.

[9] J. M. 库切. 等待野蛮人[M]. 文敏译. 杭州：浙江文艺出版社，2004.

[10] 齐格蒙鲍曼. 现代性与大屠杀[M]. 杨渝东，史建华译. 南京：译林出版社，2002.

[11] 齐泽克，斯拉沃热. 暴力：六个侧面的反思[M]. 唐健，张嘉荣译. 北京：中国法制出版社，2012.

[12] 萨特，保罗让. 存在于虚无[M]. 北京：三联书店，1987.

[13] 萨义德. W. 爱德华. 东方学[M]. 王宇根译. 北京：生活·读书·新知三联书店，1999.

[14] 邵凌. “库切的政治观与文学创作”[J]. 外国文学，2010（6）：78-84.

[15] 王卫平. “‘作者意识’和 J. M. Coetzee 写作的自传性——J. M. 库切及其书写的一生：与时间面对面评介”[J]. 外国文学。2017（5）：163-172.

[16] 谢琼. “走出困境自我救赎——《等待野蛮人》中男主角心路历程分析”[J]. 作家杂志，2013（18）：33-34.

[17] 于琪. “齐泽克论暴力”. 学术月刊，2015（47）：70-77.

[18] 张德明. 西方文学与现代性的展开[M]. 北京：中国社会科学出版社，2009.

[19] 赵修伟. 《等待野蛮人》中显性暴力的作用[C]. 库切研究与后殖民文学国际学术研讨会文集，2010.

沉默中他者的爆发：福柯权力与话语理论视角下《耻》的解读

张　玲

摘　要：库切的小说《耻》深刻地揭示了沉默中他者为了追求与主体相抗衡的平等权利与话语而进行的爆发与反抗。透过福柯权力与话语理论视角，本文剖析了男性与女性、白人与黑人、殖民者与被殖民者之间权力与话语如何置换与转位，认为曾经的他者——女性、黑人以及被殖民者——通过爆发与反抗，在后殖民，后种族隔离时代的新南非成为新兴的主体，展示了沉默中他者逐步崛起，人们趋向和谐的社会倾向。

关键词：库切；《耻》；福柯；权力话语

Abstract: Coetzee's novel *Disgrace* profoundly reveals the outbreak and resistance of the other in silence in pursuit of equal rights and discourse to compete with the subject.From the perspective of Foucault's theory of power and discourse, this paper analyzes how the power and discourse of men and women, white and the African-Americans, colonizers and the colonized are substituted and translocated and thinks that the former others—women, the African-Americans and the colonized—became a new subject in the post-colonial and post-apartheid era through outbreak and resistance, which shows the gradual rise of the other in silence and people's tendency towards a harmonious society.

Key words: Coetzee; *Disgrace*; Foucault; Power and Discourse

1 引　言

权力与话语理论是米歇尔·福柯（Michel Foucault）的代表性理论。“权力观念及其分析方法，堪称福柯一生中最有价值的理论遗产。”（汪民安，2002）“对话语轮阐述得最精到的要数法国哲学家福柯，影响最大者也非他莫属。”（周宪，2013）对于权力，福柯在《权力/知识》中说道：“权力必须为循环的东西，或能以链条形式运作的东西。权力通过网状组织运行。个体是权力的工具，而不是施用对象。”（Foucault，1980：98）“福柯的自下而上的权力模式，关注的是渗透在社会所有关系中的权力关系，它描述了权力在世俗生活中的建立和竞争，并用以分析个体作为能动的主体，作为行动者（agents）而不是被动的傀儡。”（Sara Mills，34）对于话语，福柯在《知识考古学》中表示，他用“话语”指“所有陈述的一般领域，有时指个体化群体的陈述，有时指解释陈述的秩序化实践。”（Foucault，1972：80）他说到“所有陈述的一般领域”，福柯表示“话语”可以用来描述所有具有意义且有影响的表达和陈述。此外，他有时也用这个词来描述“个体化群体的陈述”，即话语形成小团体，例如，女性气质的话语或种族主义的话语。（Sara Mills，53）

小说《耻》是南非当代著名作家，2003 年诺贝尔文学奖获得者——库切（John Maxwell

Coetzee，1940—）的一部代表性力作。小说出版当年便获得英国文学最高奖——布克奖，被《纽约时代书评》评为年度最佳图书。小说叙述了52岁的南非白人教授戴维•卢里（David Lurie）因与一位女学生的性丑闻而被逐出学界。出于无奈，卢里来到农村，与在那独自谋生的女儿露茜（Lucy）共同生活，却无法与女儿沟通；从此还不得不与从前不屑一顾的人打交道，干从前不愿干的活，不得不生活在他们中间。在女儿露茜遭到农场附近三个黑人的抢劫和蹂躏之后，面对这样的耻辱，权力与话语的位移，卢里痛苦不堪。此后，为了生存，露茜做了当地黑人佩特鲁斯（Petrus）的小老婆，卢里作了护狗员，帮助人们处理那些被淘汰的小动物。

这部内涵丰富的小说引起国内外读者和学术界的广泛关注和解读。目前国内研究主要集中在小说主题、叙事特色、女性主义、后殖民主义以及精神分析等方面。比如，张冲、郭整风、姜小卫等学者主要从小说的主题入手，分析了越界的代价和忏悔、宽恕、和解等主题。国外研究主要关注小说的主题、文化、女性主义、结构主义等方面。但鲜有论文从福柯权力与话语理论角度进行解读。本文透过福柯权力与话语理论视角，深入剖析男性与女性、白人与黑人、殖民者与被殖民者之间权力与话语如何置换与转位，认为曾经的他者——女性、黑人以及被殖民者——通过爆发与反抗，在后殖民和后种族隔离时代的新南非成为新兴的主体，展示了沉默中他者逐步崛起，人们趋向和谐的社会倾向以及作者库切对弱者的关注，为被边缘化的他者代言所体现出的人文关怀。

2 男性与女性的权力与话语

在权力与话语的关系中，福柯强调话语与权力有关。他认为话语不仅仅是一套强加于个人的想法。在《性史（第一卷）》，福柯说：话语不会一直屈从于权力或反对它，也不会沉默。我们必须意识到话语的复杂性和不稳定性，话语既可以是权力的一种手段和效果，也可以是一个障碍、一个绊脚石、一个反抗点和一个对立策略的起点。话语传递并产生权力；它强化权力，但也损害它并将其公开，使得它十分脆弱并且能够阻止它。（Foucault，1978：100-101）

上述引文中，福柯主张话语既是压迫的方式也是反抗的方式。这种既具有压迫性又具有反抗性的话语生动形象地体现在小说《耻》中男性与女性的权力与话语关系中。这部小说中男性与女性间权力与话语的置换与转位主要体现在卢里和索拉娅，卢里和梅拉妮·艾萨克斯以及卢里与露茜这三组人物关系上。

首先，在卢里和索拉娅的关系中，卢里的童年是一个在全是女性的家庭中度过的。“在女人身边长大的经历，使他成为爱女人的人，甚至在一定程度上使他成为善于玩弄女人的人。……这就是他的生活；几年来，几十年来，这就是他生活的真谛。”（库切，8）作为一个52岁，结过婚又离了婚的男人来说，他一直为自己的性生活解决得不错而自豪。每周四下午，他都会去温莎公寓与索拉娅发生性关系。然而，随着时间的流逝，“他的吸引力在毫无预兆的情况下消失了。”（库切，8）卢里由一开始对索拉娅的控制、玩弄、施虐，到后来索拉娅找理由拒绝出现，拒绝满足卢里的欲望，再到后来她说道，“你在骚扰我。我明令你从今往后不要再往这里打电话，永远不要。明令。她是想说命令。她的声音十分尖利，这使他有点吃惊，她以前从来不是这样的。”（库切，11-12）卢里作为一位大学教授，如此小心谨慎地请求一位妓女，得到的却是强硬的命令，而且无任何话语来应对。如果卢里仍处于男权占统治地位的殖民统治时代，这种女性反抗男性权力与话语的现象是不可能发生的。但是，在后殖民时代的新南非，明显以卢里为代表的男权统治地位正在被削弱。索拉娅在这里用话语和实际行动来反抗卢里以及男性主导的南非社会，为女性的自由、平等发声。语言作为一种交流的媒介和方式，通过谈话的音调、语调以及节奏，语言的使用者可以表述自己内在状态或情绪，达到自我表述的目的。海德格尔就将语言看作是“生存之道”“存在之家”。语言作为话语权的表现方式，在塑造自我和表达自我方面具有极大的社会现实意义。

其次，在卢里与其学生梅拉妮·艾萨克斯的关系中，卢里作为老师而且比梅拉妮大了整整32岁，无论在身份地位，还是社会阅历上，卢里都处于占统治的强势地位。在这样的统治地位和男权的支配下，卢里对处于弱势地位的梅拉妮进行为所欲为的施虐和控制，是握有权力的一方，而学生梅拉妮则处于没有权力与话语的弱势地位。

“别走了，和我过一夜吧。”

她的目光从杯口的另一端朝他瞪过来。“为什么？”

“因为你应当这么做。”

“为什么我应当这么做？”

“为什么？因为女人的美丽并不属于她们自己。那是她带给这个世界的恩惠的一部分。女人有责任与别人分享这美丽。”（库切，19）

这不是强奸，不完全是，但不管怎么说也是违背对方意志的，完完全全违背了对方的意志。（库切，30）

从上面引文可以看出卢里和梅拉妮之间的关系是完全违背了学生梅拉妮的个人意志的，是男性对女性为所欲为的控制与压迫。此外，小说中的卢里，不顾梅拉妮的反对往她的饮料里加烈酒，私闯梅拉妮的住处来体现自己作为男性的权力与话语。但这一切由于学校举行的反抗强暴活动而终止。校园里正在进行警觉强暴周活动。一个名为“女性反抗强暴”——简称“女抗暴”——的组织宣布进行 24 小时静立，声援“最近的受害者”。从他门缝下有人塞了份传单进来：“女性的呼喊。”传单下方用铅笔潦草地涂着这样的字眼：“卡萨诺瓦，你末日到了！”（库切，50-51）随着卢里对梅拉妮的施害行为被举报、揭发，卢里与梅拉妮的性侵行为终止了，而且他由于引诱了自己的学生，事后又拒绝公开悔过，结果被解除教职。这种传统的男性凌驾于女性之上，占统治地位的权力与话语被颠覆，女性也有了为自己的自由与平等发声的权力与话语。

最后，小说中男性与女性间权力与话语的置换与转位也深刻地体现在卢里和女儿露茜的关系中。为了躲避性丑闻的各种困惑与干扰，出于无奈，卢里来到位于乡下女儿露茜的农场，与在那独自谋生的女儿露茜共同生活。然而，由于与女儿的常年疏远以及露茜自立自强意识的觉醒，露茜使他觉得“做父亲是件相当抽象的事。”（库切，73）露西与卢里之间传统父权制下的顺从关系被彻底颠覆了。

“因为我不想听你来一阵爆发，戴维，我不能根据你喜欢或不喜欢我做的事来过自己的生活，再也不能了。你的所作所为就好像我的生活只是你生活的一部分似的。你是主角，而我只是个小角色，直到故事讲了一半才出现。哼，同你想象的正相反，人是不能被分成主角和小角色的。我不是个小角色。我有自己的生活，这生活对我十分重要，就像你的生活对你十分重要一样。而在我的生活中，做决定的人只能是我。”（库切，228）

在这段露茜对父亲卢里所说的话语中，体现了卢里失去了传统家庭父权制对露茜的控制与支配。正如福柯认为的那样，谁拥有了某种话语，谁就拥有了某种权力。露茜的话语充满了对父系权威的挑战意味，强调了自我的决定作用，而且坚持自己的立场和话语。卢里面对女儿的申诉却丧失了自己的话语权，这一切皆是社会变革给卢里带来的权力的削弱甚至删除的表现。

上述三组人物关系中，都深刻地体现了在后殖民后种族隔离时代的新南非，小说中男性与女性间权力与话语的置换与转位。

3 白人与黑人的权力与话语

在历史上，白人在南非实行了种族隔离制度。1948 年南非实行了对白人与非白人进行分隔，并在政治上、经济上予以歧视、区别对待的种族隔离制。1991 年废除该项制度。在种族隔离制实施期间，白人不管在经济上，政治上，还是社会地位上都处于绝对的统治地位。在小说《耻》中，女儿露茜被三个黑人强暴以泄愤来反抗白人对黑人的压迫，从而颠覆了白人昔日的中心地位和主导话语权。“大学传播学副教授卢里在特权丧失后因昔日看上去微不足道的性丑闻而失去教职，不得不与等级低下的黑人共事，而且失去话语权，沦为默默无语的传递工具的帮手。”（石云龙，2011）此外，露茜的农场在偏僻的乡村，相当于处于黑人的包围之中。露茜和卢里处在被黑人包围之中尤为明显地体现在佩特鲁斯庆祝建新居的晚会上，“他俩是仅有的白人。有人在跳舞，伴奏的音乐是他曾经听到过的旧时的非洲爵士乐。他总觉得有人朝他们两人投来好奇的目光。”（库切，149）在聚会上，卢里和露茜是唯一的两个白人，形影相吊，其处境十分尴尬，和周围的环境格格不入，极不协调。更重要的是，在聚会上，主人佩特鲁斯刚开始并没有欢迎他们的到来。后来，“佩特鲁斯出现在他们身边。他没有做出万分热情的样子，也没有请他们喝点什么。”（库切，150）这种现象在之前是不可能发生的，但在后殖民后种族隔离时代的新南非，白人与黑人的权力与地位却完全倒过来了。白人曾经凌驾于黑人之上的地位发生了质的变化与置换。

此外，黑人佩特鲁斯原本是露茜农场上的雇工，后来不仅经济发达了，而且还收购了露茜的地，成为农场主，实现了经济的提升和社会地位的上升，达到了可以与白人相抗衡的地位。露茜为了自己的安全，为了能在被黑人包围的地方生存下去，不得不以自己的身体和尊严为代价，做佩特鲁斯的第三个老婆。“你低估了佩特鲁斯。……没有佩特鲁斯，露茜不可能有今天的情况。我不是说露茜完全靠佩特鲁斯，但她有赖他的地方还的确不少。”（库切，162）由此观之，黑人不仅不像以前那样是白人的奴隶，时时刻刻都依附于白人，而是成为白人依附的对象，成为白人的保护者。这种白人与黑人之间权力与话语的置换与位移，表明了在后殖民后种族隔离时代的新南非，白人话语与权力的丧失，黑人作为他者的爆发与反抗正逐步崛起。

4 殖民者与被殖民者的权力与话语

在《性史（第一卷）》，福柯指出：“哪里有权力，哪里就有反抗。”（Foucault，1978）“有权力运行的地方就有关系，就必然有人反抗。就福柯而言，如果权力关系不生效，那么就不存在反抗。因此，福柯认为反抗‘写在’权力的行驶中。”（Sara Mills，40）小说《耻》中，在后殖民后种族隔离时代的南非，曾经的殖民者沦为被殖民者，相反，曾经的被殖民者上升为殖民者。这种殖民者与被殖民者权力与话语的置换与位移尤为明显地体现在小说中露茜被农场附近三个黑人所强暴的事件中。事后，露茜回想起来，“那完全是在泄私愤，她说道，那时候带着那么多的私愤。那才是最让我震惊的。”（库切，181）在强暴事件中，让露茜感到最可怕的是那三个黑人强暴者似乎并不是在宣泄情欲，而是那种让人震惊的仇恨。对于这种仇恨和泄愤行为，卢里认为“他们的行为有历史原因，一段充满错误的历史。……这事看起来是私怨，可实际上并不是。那都是先辈传下来的。”（库切，181）这样看来，露茜成为殖民主义的替罪羊，而曾经的被殖民者，在后殖民后种族隔离时代，由于权力与话语权的上升，他们有能力与曾经的殖民者相抗衡，甚至让曾经的殖民者沦为如今的被殖民者。这种殖民者与被殖民者权力与话语的置换与转位，正如露茜自己所明白的那样：“在他们眼里，我什么都不是，一文不值。我能感觉到这一点。”（库切，183）

小说中，伴随白人殖民者的衰落，而黑人——曾经的被殖民者在种族隔离制度废除后经济上的崛起，深刻体现了殖民者与被殖民者权力话语的转位与置换。佩特鲁斯作为曾经的被殖民者，如今的殖民者的显著代表，他原本是殖民者后代露茜农场上的雇工，但是凭着他的智慧和勤劳以及新政府政策的帮助，他得到一笔贷款，拥有了土地，并盖起自己的新房子。此外，露茜为了在被黑人包围的乡下生存下去，也不得不将她自己的土地转让给佩特鲁斯，“告诉他我放弃土地。告诉他他可以得到这土地，包括所有权和所有的一切。他听了一定非常高兴。”（库切，236）佩特鲁斯个人光荣的发家历程在某种意义上，代表了在后殖民后种族隔离的新南非，曾经被殖民者的崛起。而曾经的殖民者竟然沦落为黑人保护的对象。“‘这多让人丢脸，’他开口说道。那么高的心气，到头来落到这个地步。”（库切，236）对此，殖民者发现，自己的身份与地位和从前的被殖民者换了位置。而现在，曾经的殖民者不得不“从起点开始。从一无所有开始。……没有武器，没有财产，没有权利，没有尊严。”（库切，237）这凸显了白人农场主露茜和雇工佩特鲁斯之间殖民者与被殖民者地位的转换，权力与话语的置换。

此外，曾经是大学教授的卢里，“听惯了‘老爷’一类的称呼”，（张冲，郭整风，2001）以前一句话就能让佩特鲁斯丢了饭碗。而在后殖民主义时代的新南非，这一切都颠倒过来了。白人的农场朝不保夕，白人的社会地位也悄悄发生了质的变化。黑人种植经验丰富，农业装备良好。作为曾经是殖民者的卢里，现在只能给曾经的被殖民者佩特鲁斯打下手。卢里的权力与话语的缺失与被颠覆尤为明显地体现在其女儿露茜被三个黑人强暴之后，佩特鲁斯对卢里追查凶手时的问话和要求的沉默与冷淡。卢里虽然对此极其愤怒和不满，但却无能为力。

英语在特定环境中，代表着殖民者权力和话语的力量，但是在后殖民后种族隔离时代的新南非，英语失去了它原有的权威和作用。相反，真正能表达后殖民后种族隔离时代新南非曾经被殖民者思想情感的恰恰是当地原有的语言——“索托语”和“科萨语”。但作为曾经是殖民者的卢里却一句也听不懂。卢里的英语、西班牙语、意大利语等西方语言，在他女儿露茜遭遇强暴，需要请求警察帮助时，却一点用也没有。这深刻地体现了在后殖民后种族隔离时代的新南非，殖民者与被殖民权力与话语的置换与位移。

5 结　语

面对南非新语境下白人主体地位的丧失和特权生活的不复存在，作为后殖民时代白人的代表——露茜，选择了接受现实，“向前看。”（库切，158）此外，露茜打算把由黑人强暴所产生的孩子生下来，“这孩子？不。我怎么会爱他！不过我会的。爱会滋长起来——得相信大自然母亲。戴维，我决心要做个好母亲。好母亲，好人。你也应该努力做个好人。”（库切，249）通过这样的方式，作者在小说的后半部分对于主体与他者的权力与话语之争提出了可能和解的解决方式。

在此小说中，库切打破了性别、肤色、种族以及殖民者与被殖民者的界限，关注了被权威压迫、折磨、束缚的他者的生存状况。库切展现出对处于压迫之下并遭受痛苦的人们极大的人文关怀以及他对人类最终打破权力与话语界限并能真正融合的一种期许。

本文透过法国哲学家、社会思想家福柯的权力话语理论，深入阐释了小说《耻》中男性与女性、白人与黑人、殖民者与被殖民者之间权力与话语如何置换与转位，展现了在后殖民后种族隔离时代的新南非，曾经的他者——女性、黑人以及被殖民者——通过爆发与反抗，拥有了与主体相抗衡的权力与话语，而曾经的主体随着权力的丧失导致话语的丧失，展示了沉默中他者逐步崛起，人们趋向和谐的社会倾向。

参 考 文 献

[1] Beyad，Maryam & Hossein，Keramatfar, 2018. Subjection and Survival in J. M. Coetzee’s. *Disgrace*[J]. Journal of Black Studies，Vol. 49（2）：152-170.

[2] Foucault，Michel, 1972. The Archaeology of Knowledge[M]. London：Routledge.

[3] Foucault，Michel, 1978. The History of Sexuality，Vol. I：An Introduction[M]. Harmondsworth：Penguin.

[4] Foucault，Michel, 1980. ‘Two lectures’，in C. Gordon（ed.），Power/Knowledge[M]. Brighton：Harvester.

[5] Kalua，Fetson, 2012. “Seeing the entire world as a foreign land”：the exilic intellectual in JM Coetzee’s *Disgrace*[J]. University of South Africa Press，（1）：49-60.

[6] Kissack，Mike & Michael，Titlestad, 2005. The dynamics of discontent：containing desire and aggression in Coetzee’s *Disgrace*[J]. African Identities，（1）：51-67.

[7] Lopez，Maria, 2010. Can We Be Friends Here？Visitation and Hospitality in J. M. Coetzee’s *Disgrace* [J]. Journal of Southern African Studies，Vol. 36（4）：923-938.

[8] 福柯. 权力眼睛——福柯访谈录[M]. 严锋译. 上海：上海人民出版社，1997.

[9] J. M. 库切. 耻[M]. 张冲译. 南京：译林出版社，2010.

[10] 萨拉·米尔斯. 导读福柯[M]. 潘伟伟译. 重庆：重庆大学出版社，2017.

[11] 隋欣彤. 权力压迫下的属下——库切作品中小人物的分析[D]. 东北师范大学，2009.

[12] 石云龙. 他者·他性——库切研究[J]. 外语研究，2011（2）：95-100.

[13] 陶国山. 批判性话语理论：福柯的人文学科话语型研究[J]. 文艺理论研究，2011（6）：107-112.

[14] 汪民安. 权力[J]. 外国文学，2002（2）：81-89.

[15] 张冲，郭整风. 越界的代价——解读库切的布克奖小说《耻》[J]. 外国文学，2001（5）：86-89.

[16] 周宪. 福柯话语理论批判[J]. 文艺理论研究，2013（1）：121-129.

《变形记》—卡夫卡自我理想与本能的博弈

严肖肖

摘　要：弗兰兹·卡夫卡的《变形记》自出版以来一直受到广泛的讨论和深度研究，其中更不乏从精神分析的角度进行探讨的文章。此文以卡夫卡的生平经历及其日记、书信和谈话录等为基础，结合弗洛伊德提出的强迫重复原则、自我理想（超我）概念及其形成根源，探讨《变形记》如何在现实与虚拟世界的角色错位与重叠中展示出卡夫卡在意识和潜意识层面的欲望，并且在痛苦的精神拉锯中找到了唯一的出路——死亡。

关键词：卡夫卡；《变形记》；自我理想；强迫性重复

The Metamorphosis—A Game between Kafka's Ego Ideal and Instinct

Abstract: Franz·Kafka's *The Metamorphosis* has been widely discussed and studied intensively since published, and there've been plenty of articles exploring it from the perspective of psychoanalysis. Based on Kafka's life story and his diaries, letters and discourses, combining what Freud proposed as compulsion to repeat, the concept of ego ideal (superego) and the source it comes from, this paper explores that how *The Metamorphosis* indicates Kafka's conscious and unconscious desire in the dislocation and overlap of characters in the fictional world and in reality, and finds the only way out of the painful psychological seesaw battle—death.

Key words: Kafka; *The Metamorphosis*; Ego ideal; Compulsion to repeat

1 引　言

目前关于《变形记》的精神分析解读，主要从格里高尔即卡夫卡的俄狄浦斯情结以及作品中混乱的同性欲、乱伦欲和受虐欲等方面进行分析，其中研究俄狄浦斯情结的尤甚，但绝大部分都是从父子冲突这一角度入手；有的则是将《变形记》看作一个精神分析案例，发现格里高尔有回归婴儿期的倾向、阉割焦虑及其幻想的解决途径（雌雄同体甚至是女性化）；还有研究者从《变形记》中发现了卡夫卡对变老的焦虑；大多数研究者都将重心放在父与子（小说和现实）的关系上。相反，笔者则通过有关卡夫卡的文献资料来分析作品中卡夫卡的心理投射，试图从另一个角度来解读《变形记》。

2 自我理想与强迫重复原则

卡夫卡的俄狄浦斯情结是一个不可避免的话题，这也是自我理想形成的最主要的原因，但目前分析俄狄浦斯情结的论文主要是从小说中父亲对儿子的仇恨或者父子间的冲突（现实与小说中）来体现的，与笔者要入手的角度截然不同。

首先引入弗洛伊德提出的本我、自我与超我的概念。简而言之，本我是人最原始的、潜意识的、非理性的心理结构，充满着本能和欲望的强烈冲动，受着快乐原则的支配；自我代表理智和常识，按照现实原则来行事；超我则是人格中高级的、道德的、超自我的心理结构，它以良心、自我理想等至善原则来规范自我，其中，自我理想的定义如下：

"在我们的自我中形成了某种这样的能力，使自己从其余的自我中分离出来，并与它们发生冲突，我们称之为'自我理想'（ego ideal）""它从环境的影响那里逐渐收集环境施加给自我而自我又总是不能达到的各种要求。……显露了它在优势力量（尤其是父亲）的影响方面的根源。"[1]

为避免误解，这里要说明本我、自我与超我并不是完全对立的关系，自我来自于本我，超我则来自于自我，是一种逐层升华的关系。虽然在超我的定义中，自我理想只是它遵循的原则之一，但弗洛伊德曾直接用自我理想指代超我[2]，因此本文也沿用这一用法。

那么自我理想是如何形成的呢？自我理想的起源是童年最早期的第一次认同作用的影响，这一影响是普遍和持久的；自我理想是俄狄浦斯情结在自我中形成的沉淀物，它永远反映着父母的影响，它是我们和父母关系的代表，是一种代替做父亲的渴望。值得注意的是，俄狄浦斯情结对父亲产生敌对态度，但又存在认同作用，关于敌对态度这一点的研究已不计其数，本文将重点着眼于卡夫卡对其父亲的认同如何体现在《变形记》的文本中。

上文提到本我受快乐原则的支配，但在人的本能中，存在一种超越快乐原则的冲动，即强迫性重复（compulsion to repeat），它是一个比它超越的快乐原则更原始、更基本、更具有本能的东西，表现生物的惰性，体现为要求重复以前并回归到过去的状态[3]，其中恢复原初的无机状态的倾向就是我们熟知的死的本能。

3　小说与现实的角色错位与重叠

那么《变形记》这一文本是如何体现卡夫卡的自我理想以及强迫性重复呢？关于自我理想这一点，笔者在查阅众多关于卡夫卡的生平资料之后，发现卡夫卡的现实生活与《变形记》中的角色发生了颠倒或错位，可能有人会说这只是作家创作的虚拟世界，可以与作家毫无关联，但就卡夫卡而言，其作品具有一贯的自传性，而他自己也在《致父亲》里写到"我写的书都与您有关，我在书里倾诉了在您面前无法说出的话"[4]。既然与父亲有关，现在我们进一步观察卡夫卡的父亲与格里高尔的父亲这一角色是如何颠倒的。

在《变形记》中，读者都注意到墙上挂着格里高尔参军时的照片，"照片中的他脸上带着无忧无虑的笑容，手按在剑上，仿佛要别人对他的军人风度和制服表示尊敬似的"[5]，并有不少读者将格里高尔参军和工作的状态进行对比来反映格里高尔为家庭做出的牺牲，然而现实中的卡夫卡并没有参过军，而其父赫尔曼年轻时却服过三年的兵役，并凭借这一经历获得了一定的社会声望；格里高尔在变形前一直承担养家的重任，而现实中的很长一段时间却是卡夫卡的父亲在养家；现实中赫尔曼身强体壮，卡夫卡一直体弱多病，而小说里格里高尔的父亲被描述成一个年迈体弱的老人，不难想象承担养家重任的格里高尔在变形前才是年轻力壮的那个；同时，赫尔曼是一位暴躁多疑的商人，在小说里对应的则是格里高尔的老板这一角色，此处值得一提的是现实中卡夫卡所工作的工伤保险公司的上司相当信任他，同事也很尊重和喜欢他；关于卡夫卡的母亲，在她的原生家庭的成长经历中，她一手抚养五个弟弟长大，担任了他们的“代理母亲”，在《变形记》中，格里高尔在变形前则扮演着全家人的“代理父亲”这一角色。

在格里高尔变形成一只甲虫后，只能被关在一间小屋子里受家人的照顾，并且丧失了与家人沟通的能力，在这一方面与现实中卡夫卡的家庭生活无异：后来卡夫卡在保险公司上班有一定的经济来源之后，仍然一直住在家中，从未长久离开父宅，也不建立自己的家庭，不积极存钱，甚至不谋求普通意义上的自己的生计[6]，且因身体原因一直受着家人的照顾。

4 自我理想与本能的博弈

在格里高尔变形前，卡夫卡所塑造的是一个兢兢业业养家糊口的年轻职员的角色，然而是建立在父亲赫尔曼的人物基础之上，上文已经罗列出现实和虚拟的角色错位，笔者认为这是卡夫卡潜意识中“代替做父亲的渴望”的体现。卡夫卡的母亲一直对其丈夫言听计从，关系亲密，在卡夫卡看来，父亲霸占了他应该享受的母爱[7]，他一生都在与其父争夺母亲，虽然未能成功，可以说卡夫卡身上具有典型的俄狄浦斯情结。俄狄浦斯情结不仅使卡夫卡对其父产生敌对态度，也产生认同作用，实际上弑父娶母本身就包含对父亲的崇拜和认同，因此才有了取代的欲望。在《致父亲》中，卡夫卡在控诉其父在他成长期的暴戾和专横的同时，尊敬和仰慕也是显而易见的，实际上这也是卡夫卡无论在选择另一半还是选择朋友时，往往被具有其父某一方面的气质的人所吸引的原因所在。在小卡夫卡的童年时期，父亲的影响就已经深深扎根，而卡夫卡一直以来的焦虑也正是因为达不到父亲的期望所产生的，他想要成为父亲那样的人，但被父亲压抑的天性又限制了他的能力，那么擅长写作的卡夫卡就在自己的小说中实现了这一自我理想。为了更大限度地靠近父亲，做到像父亲一样在艰苦卓绝的环境中创业成功，他在小说中将格里高尔的工作环境描写得同样辛酸，虽然这与卡夫卡实际的工作条件并不相符。代替父亲还不够，卡夫卡还将父亲（实际上是全家人）这一角色塑造成寄生虫，这也是受俄狄浦斯情结影响的自我理想的一种具现。

然而格里高尔变形成一只甲虫，在这之后父亲又重新承担起养活家人的重任，母亲和妹妹也开始自立，此时他与家人的角色颠倒，不少研究者将此看作卡夫卡对自己压抑的家庭生活的披露和控诉，但了解了强迫重复原则以及卡夫卡的生平之后，再重新审视这部作品，或者卡夫卡的每一部作品都是以主人公的失败或死亡告终，可以发现卡夫卡的退化本能。这一结论来源于对卡夫卡生平的研究，卡夫卡一生都未摆脱“儿子身份”，在他自己看来，是由于强势的父亲对其产生的终身的影响；但纵观卡夫卡的一生，他三次订婚又三次退婚、无数次想搬离这个家却从未真正实现以及对自己身体状况的长期主观臆断，从中可以发现卡夫卡身上所体现出的强迫性重复。看着父亲“成功”建立的家庭，卡夫卡认为只有建立自己的家庭才能真正脱离父母，因此一直以成家为目标，却多次订婚又自己主动退婚，退婚的时候甚至感到解脱；想从空间上远离父母，但即使是有经济来源之后也未能实现；卡夫卡总是认为自己躯干弯曲、长相丑陋，这与他的真实形象严重不符，除了晚期病重的时候，他也一直认为自己身体孱弱，并以此作为无法在外奔波的理由。这些都是典型的强迫性重复，作为一种生物本能，卡夫卡自己也并未意识到。在变形之后，甲虫的生活很贴近卡夫卡本人的现实生活，但甲虫这一形态本身就是生命退化的表现，Silhol Robert 在 *Franz Kafka's « The Metamorphosis »: A case study* 中也分析了甲虫的形象实际上是卡夫卡内心退化到婴儿时期的欲望的表现（四肢爬行、没有牙齿以及丧失与父母交流的能力）[8]，这是每个人与生俱来的生物惰性。通过重复过去表现对回归到过去的渴望。

5 结论：唯一的出路——死亡

格里高尔变形前反映的是卡夫卡的自我理想，变形及变形后则是其强迫性重复本能的投射，但在变形之后，格里高尔仍处于自我理想践行失败的焦虑和痛苦中，这也是卡夫卡本人所面临的焦虑，而结束这种痛苦的唯一出路就是死亡。读者通常将格里高尔的死归咎于家人的冷漠和嫌弃，不可否认此为外部原因，更重要的是卡夫卡的死亡本能的驱动，这也是他每部作品都是以主人公的死亡为结局的根本原因。“我们假设有两类本质不同的本能：一类是在最广泛意义上所理解的性本能——假如你喜欢，也可叫作爱的本能（eros）；另一类则是攻击性本能，其目的在于破坏”[9]。这两类本能在格里高尔身上也体现得很明显，并已有不少研究，但弗洛伊德进一步指出，一方面，攻击性本能也会将自身当作攻击对象，也就是我们通常理解的自残甚至自杀倾向，另一方面，强迫重复原则的终极目的就是恢复到原初的无机状态，即死亡。研读过卡夫卡传记和他本人日记的都知道，卡夫卡有严重的自杀倾向，也有研究者发现卡夫卡由于理想的自我与实际的自我差距过大而产生明显的自虐倾向（周何法，卡夫卡的自虐狂倾向及其触发因素），无论是出于本能的攻击性还是超我与自我的悬殊差距所产生的自我憎恨，卡夫卡的自我毁灭倾向都是毋庸置疑的；但理智使他意识到“自杀者只是由于无能而自杀”[10]，因此没有勇气自杀的卡夫卡就将死亡本能投射到作品中，并给予人物各种各样骇人的死法。

超我与本我、压倒性的自我理想与生物本能之间的博弈带来了巨大的痛苦，无论是对作品中可怜的格里高尔，还是现实中抑郁一生的卡夫卡，解脱的唯一出路只有死亡，而这一出路也正好满足了生命最根本的本能——死亡本能。

参 考 文 献

[1][2][3] 弗洛伊德. 自我与本我[M]. 车文博主编. 北京：九州出版社，2014.
[4] 卡夫卡，等. 致父亲[M]. 郜志云等译. 南京：江苏文艺出版社，2014.
[5] 卡夫卡. 变形记[M]. 王宏，王翠译. 武汉：长江文艺出版社，2011.
[6][7] 邵嘉骥. 卡夫卡传：墓地里的寒鸦[M] 北京：新世界出版社，2015.
[8] Available http://www.clas.ufl.edu/ipsa/journal/articles/psyart/2008%5fsilhol01.s shtml.Feb. 24，2018.
[9] 弗洛伊德. 精神分析新论[M]. 郭本禹译. 南京：译林出版社，2014.
[10] 雅诺施. 卡夫卡谈话录[M]. 赵登荣译. 桂林：漓江出版社，2014.

被女性化的男人的困境

——从《变形记》中析出的卡夫卡

谢诗阳

摘　要：卡夫卡的作品《变形记》通过异化主题记录了悲剧主人翁——甲虫格里高尔从诞生到死去的荒诞事迹。小说充满了卡夫卡的女性主义思想，体现了作者作为被女性化的男人复杂矛盾的两性观——对自我的定位、对强势女性的希望和恐惧以及对强健男性的崇拜和敬畏。

关键词：弗兰兹·卡夫卡；《变形记》；女性主义

Abstract: Using the alienation theme，Kafka's work *Metamorphosis* records the grotesque deeds of the tragic master—beetle Gregor. This novel is full of Kafka's feminist thoughts，as a feminine man，embodying the author's complex and contradictory gender perspective. With such a pair of colored glasses，Kafka's feminism is showed up.

Key words: Franz Kafka；*Metamorphosis*；feminism

1 引　言

卡夫卡的《变形记》讲述了主人公格里高尔异化变形为甲虫后，被社会抛弃、被家人抛弃，最终自我抛弃而痛苦死去的故事。作为一部经典的异化主题小说，小说受到评论家的高度赞扬，较早评论《变形记》的专家有瓦尔特. H. 索克尔，其《反抗与惩罚——析卡夫卡的〈变形记〉》中认为“变形便把反抗与惩罚两层意思联系了起来。”（叶廷芳，253）日本学者平野嘉彦在其著作《卡夫卡——身体的位相》中表达了“是由人退化成‘毒虫’，蕴含了使所谓生物‘进化’逆转的倾向性。”（平野嘉彦，67）诺贝尔文学奖得主埃利亚斯·卡内蒂（Elias Canetti）如此称道：“在《变形记》中，卡夫卡已达到大师的高度：他写出了一部自己再也不能超越的作品，因为再没有任何东西能超越《变形记》这部本世纪伟大完美的著作。”（石海霞，18）

《变形记》采用第三人称全知视角，以主人公格里高尔为叙述中心讲述了他变形后生活周遭主要成员心理、态度、行动等方面的变化，刻画了父亲传统父权制一家之主的专横自私、冷酷无情、自高自大，母亲传统父权社会操控下软弱无能、毫无主见，妹妹一方面渴望表现自我，一方面无力挣脱家长制等形象，刻画过程中，作者的性别观、女性化倾向以及由此陷入的困境也得以呈现。

从 1729 年玛丽·沃斯通克拉夫特写下《女权辩护》，到 1929 年弗吉利亚·伍尔夫发表《一间自己的房间》，再到 1949 年西蒙娜·德·波伏娃创作《第二性》（泰森，93/102）产生，并以压迫为滋养，得以发展蔓延，至今已分流出各门各派。在女性主义看来，所有的感知都不可避免地受到主观因素的影响：大到社会性别、政治倾向、宗教信仰、种族等，小到自身优缺点、情绪波动等，而我们不应回避主体性，而要尽可能意识到它的存在。（泰森，95/104）

维斯也提到，自女性主义理论开始问世，"'父权制'（patriarchy），或一些人称之为性别体系（the sex/gender system）或'性别体制'（'genderregimes'）的理论，一直是其核心部分"。（伊瓦-戴维斯，7）卡夫卡在创作《变形记》的过程中将个人的女性主义思想投射到整部作品的宏大结构中，作品对两性角色的塑造析出他对两种不同性别的复杂矛盾情感，以他为代表的被女性化的男人的困境在读者面前铺展开来。

2　被女性化的男人的自我定位：心理与生理上的无能

小说中格里高尔是家中的长子，五年前父亲破产后，他成为整个家庭的顶梁柱，承担起供养一家四口的责任。从普通职员到旅行推销员，在不懈努力下，他使双亲和妹妹重新过上了有尊严的生活。然而，除了忍受老板无情的剥削，回归家庭的他一切均以家人为中心，俨然成了赚钱的机器，毫无自我可言。而格里高尔的尴尬地位与卡夫卡的艰难处境具有极大的相似性。

2.1　被女性化的男人的家庭定位

2.1.1　作为父亲的父亲

格里高尔的父亲在五年前公司破产后就不再上班，尽管没能给家庭带来经济收入，但他一如既往地专制专断、自高自傲、冷酷无情，俨然一副传统家长制一家之主的样子。发现格里高尔表现异常时，他的反应是粗暴冷漠的："在侧边的一扇门上立刻就响起了他父亲的叩门声，很轻，不过用的却是拳头。"（李文俊，62）带有的情感更多的是焦急与不耐烦，而原因是：儿子的反常行为可能会对家庭的经济来源受影响——被老板开除。在察觉格里高尔发出的信号——说话声音没人能理解时，父亲的反应是吩咐人赶紧去请个锁匠，强行开门，一探究竟。格里高尔在家中的地位，在父亲眼中，与其说是一个家庭成员，不如说是一台印钞机，出毛病了需要的是修理。随着事实越来越明晰，变成甲虫的格里高尔在父亲眼中越发不值一钱，甚至成了敌对的"他者"。在把格里高尔赶回房间的过程中，父亲"从后面使劲地推了他一把……使他一直跌进了房间中央，汩汩地流着血。在他后面，门砰的一声用手杖关上了，屋子里终于恢复了寂静。"（李文俊，69）在粗暴冷血的父亲看来，格里高尔仅仅是一只令人作呕的虫子，不是人类，更不是儿子。尽管父亲对格里高尔如此冷酷，格里高尔依然持理解的态度，甚至在家庭事宜上，仍旧承认父亲统筹全局的地位："当然，本来他也可以用这些多余的款子把父亲欠老板的债再还掉些，使自己可以少替老板卖几天命，可是无疑还是父亲的做法更为妥当。"（李文俊，74）宁愿自己多辛苦一点，都一味认可父亲的决策地位。

父亲的冷血与专制在"搬家具事件"中一览无余。格里高尔无意中使母亲和妹妹受到惊吓，父亲对两位女性的举动的反应是"'果然不出我的所料'，他父亲说，'我不是告诉过你们吗，可是你们这些女人根本不听'。"（李文俊，78）在父权思想占主导地位的意识形态里，女性毫无逻辑理性可言，她们还没说话就被认定是错的。对于"犯错的"格里高尔，父亲用苹果恶狠狠地砸他，有一个"正好打中了他的背并且还陷了进去"，"那个苹果还一直留在他的身上……仿佛这是一个公开的纪念品似的"。（李文俊，79）苹果成了父亲专制独裁路上的里程碑，也成了被父亲定义为毫无用处甚至充满恶意的甲虫格里高尔被边缘化的深深印记。

作者卡夫卡一生都没能与父亲和解，并且一生都活在父亲的影子下。在父亲眼中，这个不争气的儿子就像个无能的小姑娘，正如卡夫卡自己说的那样："我瘦削、柔弱、羸小，而您强壮、高大、宽阔。在更衣室里，我自惭形秽，不仅是在您面前，也是在全世界面前，因为您是我衡量一切的标准。”（卡夫卡，致父亲，7-8）因为卡夫卡不够强健的体魄以及与父亲截然不同的秉性，父亲总是不赞同他，甚至是否定他的一切，将他置于形同父权制下女性的位置上——天生的弱者。格里高尔在还能养家糊口的时候尚得一丝尊重，在失去作为人的行为能力以后，地位甚至不如父权制下的女性，并且还自卑自轻，仍没有自我意识。格里高尔就是现实中父亲眼中的卡夫卡，在生物性别男性和社会性别女性化的泥淖中挣扎。

2.1.2　母亲

格里高尔的母亲是一位传统父权制压抑下的女性，温和善良，但却几乎是软弱无能的。在格里高尔变形事件中她是对儿子始终保有温情的一方，现实中卡夫卡的母亲充当和事佬的角色，因为她的付出能够得到回馈。也是因为这一点，相对于父亲，卡夫卡更爱母亲。卡夫卡在父亲从他身边几乎夺走一切后仍然写道：“小时候，父亲战胜了我。但是这么多年来，虽然他还是不断地战胜我，我还是对这片战场抱着收复之心。”（邵嘉骥，18）对于夺回母亲这场战争，他一直耿耿于怀。

面对生病的格里高尔，母亲的反应与父亲要求请锁匠的举动截然不同，她吩咐妹妹：“你得马上去请医生。格里高尔病了。去请医生，快点儿。”（李文俊，66）在与格里高尔正面撞见时，母亲的表现将对儿子爱的天性和软弱无能的脾性的矛盾表现得淋漓尽致，她“一面又低下头来，仿佛想把格里高尔看得更清楚些，同时又偏偏身不由己地一直往后退”。她爱儿子，而面对作为甲虫的儿子，更多的是把格里高尔看作异类而非儿子。在“搬家具事件”中，母亲首次提出自己的见解与看法——不同意妹妹搬空房间的主意，表明她有做决策的心力，但性格软弱不坚定，容易动摇——“事实上自始至终她都几乎是用耳语在说话，她仿佛连声音都不想让格里高尔听到。”（李文俊，76）在妹妹无法被动摇的情况下，母亲不再发声，在父权制压抑下已养成一味服从的习惯。尽管在行动上没能有效帮助儿子，但母亲的话提醒了格里高尔作为一个人而不是异形的身份。作为在生理和心理上都十分脆弱的母亲，“患有气喘病，在家里走动都很困难，隔一天就得躺在打开的窗户边的沙发上喘得气都透不过来”，（李文俊，74）却扮演着儿子避风港的角色，以自己的方式来想办法稍稍维护儿子。从角色功能看来，格里高尔的母亲就是卡夫卡的母亲，虽然卡夫卡意识到母亲太爱父亲了，对父亲过于忠贞、过于顺从，以致在孩子的斗争中，母亲不可能成为一种“独立的、持久的精神力量”。（卡夫卡，致父亲，22）但他却始终处于母亲的庇护下，作为男人，却始终处于软弱、顺从的母亲的庇佑下，这一事实不仅塑造了卡夫卡“洛维式（卡夫卡母亲娘家姓氏，译者注）的固执、敏感、正义、不安”，（卡夫卡，致父亲，24）相悖于传统男性刚毅果敢的性格，而且使他“早熟地意识到，自己融不进同龄男孩当中”，（邵嘉骥，27）母亲希望把儿子拉入正常人的圈子，而儿子却在自我异化。母亲对儿子潜移默化的影响，不仅促进了格里高尔的变形，还滋养了卡夫卡的女性气质。

2.1.3　妹妹

格里高尔的妹妹格雷特“只是个十七岁的孩子……关心的只是怎样穿得漂亮些，睡个懒觉……出去找些不太花钱的娱乐。”（李文俊，74）因为妹妹的上进，格里高尔打算送她去音乐学院深造，这一点在相夫教子是主流的社会里可以算是女性的一大进步。现实中的卡夫卡有三个妹妹，他最偏爱小妹妹奥特拉，就因为这位妹妹在信心、自信、体魄以及无所顾忌等方面的素质都胜于卡夫卡。因为父亲破产，格里高尔不得不早早工作，以家庭为中心为一切行动的指南已成为一种习惯，因此他将自我梦想的实现寄托在妹妹格雷特身上，以此弥补没能获得作为男人的自我这一缺憾。卡夫卡认为小妹妹奥特拉“纯洁又宽容、谦卑又自信、羞怯又勇敢”。（邵嘉骥，84）她敢于违抗父亲甚至与父亲决裂，在他的潜意识里，他本应该如同妹妹一样敢于反抗父亲，但他做不到，所以他支持甚至是崇拜妹妹的反叛行为。他写信对朋友说：“她比我更有信心，更充满自信，体魄更健壮，更无顾忌。”（邵嘉骥，84）格雷特和奥特拉的希望给了格里高尔和卡夫卡的希望，妹妹们的不断强大也让哥哥们意识到了自己不如女性的事实，格里高尔采取的举措是自甘卑微、暗自神伤，卡夫卡则是让小说戏剧性地以夫妇俩互相会意的眼光结尾，伴随格里高尔的死亡，妹妹格雷特的音乐梦想最终屈服于传统女性定位。

变形前，家人对格里高尔的供养行为固然感激，而和他最亲的只有妹妹；变形后，妹妹承担起照顾他的任务，从“似乎她来看望的是一个重病人，甚至是陌生人”，（李文俊，71）到“她工作中不太愉快的那些方面，她显然想尽量避免”，（李文俊，74）到主张搬空格里高尔的房间，再到“对他又是挥拳又是瞪眼”，（李文俊，77）最后到成为赶走格里高尔的带头者。妹妹也因为照顾格里高尔的大胆行为受到父母的感激，“而以前他们是常常骂她，说她是个不中用的女儿”。（李文俊，75）随着妹妹地位的提升，格里高尔的地位从面包赚取者跌到比父权制下女性还卑微的非人地位，这一地位正是卡夫卡面对比自己强大的妹妹时的切身感受。奥特拉身上积聚了卡夫卡在别处徒然寻找的种种可能性，“她因为‘具有如此充沛的力量’而让他满意”。（代马盖斯，162）瘦削的男性躯体包裹着阴柔、敏感的灵魂，而这些特点在传统父权社会里是被视为女性特有的，“女性化”这个标签成了卡夫卡挥之不去的阴影。

2.1.4 佣人/老妈子

格里高尔从变形到死去，接受了使女、女仆、老妈子三位女性的“照顾”。在他需要人帮忙翻身的时候，他想到了父亲和使女，因为他认为这两者“身强力壮”，后面也证实了使女不仅身体强健，也有一定的心理承受能力——女仆走后她留了下来，只是“求主人赐给她一个特殊的恩惠，让她把厨房门锁着，只有在人家特意叫她时才打开”；（李文俊，75）而女仆在事发第一天就“来到母亲跟前，跪下来哀求让她辞退工作”，并且“当她一刻钟之后离开时，居然眼泪盈眶感激不尽，仿佛得到了什么大恩典似的”。（李文俊，73）这二者都采取了冷眼相待的态度。使女辞退后请来一早一晚帮忙干粗活的老妈子，在格里高尔眼中，“这个老寡妇”身体“经受了漫长的一生中所有最最厉害的打击”，变得“结实精瘦”，（李文俊，81）最为重要的是，她根本不怕格里高尔，甚至挑衅他，“用自以为亲热的话招呼他，比如：‘来呀，嗨，你这只老屎壳郎！’或者是：‘瞧这老屎壳郎哪，吓！’”（李文俊，82）格里高尔不屑搭理她，认为她是粗俗。正是这样一个令人厌恶的女性恰恰成了格里高尔死亡的第一见证人——发现格里高尔死亡时，她“睁大眼睛，吹了一下口哨”，（李文俊，87）继而大呼以告知其父母。主动请缨收拾好格里高尔的尸体后立马邀功：“‘哦，’老妈子说，简直乐不可支，都没法把话顺顺当当地说下去，‘这么回事，你们不必操心怎么样弄走隔壁房间里的东西了我已收拾好了’。”（李文俊，89）她对格里高尔生命的践踏一目了然，而对冷血仆从的塑造并不是偶然。

卡夫卡的父亲是一位成功商人，整日围着生意转，母亲是父亲最忠实的贤内助，整日围着父亲转，作为至亲，根本无暇顾及卡夫卡。妹妹们太过年幼，无法给童年的卡夫卡需要的温暖与体贴，陪伴他成长的便是家中仆人。而照顾卡夫卡的仆人只把他当作薪水的象征。她们认为自己是为了薪水而不得不服侍他，因此有时候还要恐吓他。“长久以来，如果仆人们报酬微薄、劳累过度，就会把气撒在最弱小的成员，也就是他的身上。在这样的环境中，除了生存的权力，他几乎什么也得不到”。（邵嘉骥，24）在父亲的呵斥、母亲的忽视、仆人们的恐吓中成长的卡夫卡胆小怕事、懦弱无能，作者卡夫卡被家中地位卑微的人凌辱，正如甲虫格里高尔到最后甚至虚弱到能被女仆踩在脚下，失去了作为主人甚至是作为男人应有的尊重，卡夫卡短暂的一生都在被对自己的定位所困扰。

2.2 被女性化的男人的社会定位

2.2.1 经理/秘书主任（作为老板/商人的父亲）

格里高尔的经理是一个名副其实的“吸血鬼”，虽然从未出场，通过格里高尔之口以及其代理人——秘书主任，可以了解到，他总是“居高临下坐在桌子上面对职员发号施令”，（李文俊，62）职员生病，他会带去质问而不是问候。格里高尔五年来第一次迟到，经理便将携公款私逃的嫌疑扣在他头上，格里高尔坦言：“如果不是为了父母亲而总是谨小慎微，我早就辞职不干了，我早就会跑到老板面前，把肚子里的气出个痛快。”（李文俊，62）在利欲熏心、自私自利、专断独裁的经理面前，格里高尔长期忍气吞声，地位卑微。经历的代言人秘书主任出场只是为秉公问罪，在格里高尔看来，他“既无骨气又愚蠢不堪”，而且还“总是那么偏袒女性”。（李文俊，68）这些剥削者企图将格里高尔压这样的小职员压榨得片甲不留。

卡夫卡作为保险公司职员的职业生涯是安逸的，因为他的温和认真，老板善待他，同事尊重他，在他生命的最后两年，公司常常允许他请假修养，甚至最后同意他提前退休。他对剥削阶级血淋淋的揭露得益于商人父亲与雇员间的日常。父亲对雇员的狠毒霸道与反复无常使卡夫卡感到战栗，固化了他多愁善感、优柔寡断的性格。更糟糕的是，父亲将对雇员的粗暴专制态度沿用到卡夫卡身上，父亲的商人作风不断打压渴望成为真正男子汉的卡夫卡，在他看来，世界也因此分成三个部分：“一个部分是我这个奴隶居住的，必须服从种种专门为我制定的法律，而我不知为什么，从来不能完全符合这些法律的要求。然后就是第二个部分，它离我的世界无限遥远，那是您的世界，您行使着统治权，发号施令并因命令得不到执行而大发雷霆。最后是第三个部分，其余的人都在那儿幸福地、无拘无束地生活着，不受命令和服从的制约”。（卡夫卡，致父亲，10-11）长此以往，在感性层面，卡夫卡太过多愁善感；在理性层面，卡夫卡坚忍不拔，他不会草率地放弃人生，因此躲避、迂回、纾解都是他的抗议方式。这些秉性使他在与人相处中把自己放得卑微，默默无闻，温和谨慎，内化一切不安，在放肆男子气与收敛如处子之间徘徊犹豫。

2.2.2 同事（以挣钱为宗旨的作家/出版商）与情人

格里高尔在回复秘书主任的话中提到：“旅行推销员在公司里不讨人喜欢……大家以为他们赚的是大钱，过的是逍遥自在的日子……旅行推销员几乎长年不在办公室，他们自然很容易成为闲话、怪罪和飞短流长的目标。”（李文俊，67-68）对同事的提及虽然只有寥寥几句，但却充满不信任与距离感，并且小说中的格里高尔仿佛没有朋友，只是太阳下的一个影子，在周围看来，毫无存在感。这种消极情绪来源于卡夫卡的切身体会。在与同学的交往中，他同样表现出极强的逃避性。尽管在卡夫卡的中学同学看来，他并不是个孤僻的人，参与集体活动，毫不落单，也不凸显个性，但他在人群里却毫无存在感，当他的同学们回忆起他，记忆中的卡夫卡“穿着干干净净的衣服，我们都很喜欢他、尊敬他，但无法和他有亲密无间的关系，他常常微笑着，与他人保持距离”。（邵嘉骥，40）这种对所有人都持远距离观望态度的个性发展成了日后他对作家同行的质疑以及对出版商的不信任。谨小慎微的有意疏远将他囿于自己的文学世界，亢奋于绝佳的创作环境，也痛苦于过于女性化的小心翼翼。

在成为甲虫的无聊日子里，格里高尔开始回想起过去的时光，他想起曾经邂逅的一个乡村侍女，并把这称作“一闪即逝的甜蜜的回忆”。（李文俊，81）一个女帽店里的出纳，格里高尔提到自己曾殷勤地向她求过爱，“但是让人家捷足先登了”。（李文俊，81）没有过度热烈的感情经历，殷勤求爱也以失败告终，这样的安排也透露着卡夫卡的情感经历。卡夫卡一生邂逅了不少女性，《变形记》是在他与菲丽丝来往期间创作的，两次订婚、两次取消，他需要的只是精神的寄托，一想到婚后重复单调的生活和作为丈夫的责任，恐惧使他止步不前，逃避男性的传统角色。

3 被女性化的男人对女性的态度

《变形记》塑造了三类女性：传统父权制操控下软弱无能的母亲，怀揣音乐梦想实现未果的妹妹，庸俗不堪的底层女仆。卡夫卡在塑造她们的同时，穿插着他对女性复杂矛盾的情感——即他厌恶低俗而无所作为的女性，欣赏追寻自我的新女性；一方面希望女性强大起来，另一方面又恐惧她们过于强势而颠覆自己作为男人的性别地位。

3.1 无能的女性（庸俗/不寻求改变）：厌恶

格里高尔的母亲身体虚弱，“患有气喘病，在家里走动都很困难，隔一天就得躺在打开的窗户边的沙发上喘得气都透不过来”。（李文俊，74）精神上也脆弱不堪，在家的职责就是服从丈夫的一切命令，贴身服侍一家之主；在当格里高尔变甲虫之后，不仅顺从父亲还协助女儿。在“搬家具事件”中，母亲第一次提出反对意见，得不到认可后“旋即不作声了，只是竭力帮她女儿把柜子推出去”。当父亲变得越发固执倔强时，母亲婉言款语相劝，黑夜里往往和妹妹“涕泗交流起来，或是眼眶干枯地瞪着桌子”，（李文俊，81）无能为力的传统女性跃然纸上。现实中卡夫卡认可自己母亲的善良与忠诚，却反感她的无主见和对父亲的绝对顺从。卡夫卡认为母亲“太爱您了，她对您太忠贞、太顺从，以致在孩子的斗争中，她不可能成为一种独立的、持久的精神力量”。（卡夫卡，致父亲，21-22）柔弱无能的母亲形象时时在提醒卡夫卡个性里的软弱，提醒他身上“洛维家族的刺激，它比较神秘羞怯”，（卡夫卡，致父亲，5）而他憎恨这样阴柔的自己。

格里高尔家的女仆们要么脆弱不堪，无法忍受格里高尔变甲虫的事实，要么俗不可耐、自以为是。尤其是老妈子，她非但不害怕格里高尔，还粗俗地挑衅他。在一次冲突中，她“把刚好放在门旁的一张椅子高高举起，她的嘴张得老大，显然是要等椅子往格里高尔的背上砸去才会闭上”。（李文俊，82）卡夫卡厌恶这样不求上进还沾沾自喜的女性，正如他厌倦家中庸俗可恶的仆人一样，这些无能为力的角色太让他想起自己。在写给父亲的信中，他提到自己的妹妹艾莉时，如此直言道：“……她那时可是个迟钝、疲倦、胆小、易怒、有负罪感、低声下气、恶毒、懒惰、贪吃、吝啬的孩子。我简直不能看到她，更不会跟她说话，她太使我想到自己”。（卡夫卡，致父亲，23）

3.2 有改变可能性的女性（喜欢有自我的女性、希望女性强大和恐惧女性强大）

格里高尔爱好小提琴的妹妹格雷特，梦想进入音乐学院，尽管父亲认为她一无是处，母亲也没有提供任何支持，哥哥却始终为身上洋溢着希望的她感到欣慰，因而更加努力赚钱以实现妹妹的梦想。格里高尔对格雷特音乐事业的支持反映了作者卡夫卡对妹妹或者是对女性的期许，他欣赏有自我意识的女性，支持并鼓励女性追求自己的事业，甚至在男人世界里取得一席之地。格雷特在承担起照顾哥哥的任务后自我意识不断增强，不仅成为“搬家具事件”的发起者，还为母亲私自打扫格里高尔的房间大发脾气，她“怒不可遏地冲进起坐室，而且不顾母亲举起双手苦苦哀求，竟号啕大哭起来”。（李文俊，81）在她看来，母亲无意的举动侵犯了自己在父权统治下找到的一席领地。卡夫卡的女性主义观点在对格雷特的塑造中得以充分体现。

三个妹妹中，卡夫卡最喜欢小妹妹奥特拉。这位妹妹拥有和卡夫卡截然不同的个性，她敢于公然反对父亲的专断。卡夫卡认为她继承了父亲的一部分个性，因此她固执又强大，甚至可以公然与父亲决裂。这个妹妹和卡夫卡一样热爱大自然并且不顾父亲反对，把对农业的痴情投到了实处。“她果敢冲决了一切障碍，并以某种方式实现了兄长的梦想。她不顾父亲发怒的眼睛，毫不畏惧地与商场职员，那些‘下属’来往，甚至违反习俗，爱上并嫁给一个捷克非犹太人”。（代马盖斯，163）妹妹坚毅勇敢、敢于反抗，这些品质都是卡夫卡缺少的，得益于这些品质，她部分实现了哥哥的愿望，卡夫卡支持她，甚至崇拜她，常常带她一同旅游，给她推荐自己喜欢的书籍，以弥补文化教育上的缺憾。

卡夫卡对强大女性的偏爱还体现在他的择偶标准上。他的未婚妻菲丽丝是一个世俗的女强人，是柏林一家留声机公司的销售代表；随后爱上菲丽丝的朋友格雷特·布洛赫同样是个女强人，只是性格上相较于菲丽丝稍内向；红颜知己密伦娜·耶森斯卡是一个与父亲断绝关系的反叛者、女生领袖，她对卡夫卡的爱带有“母性的怜爱”。（邵嘉骥，231）她在文学上的天赋也让卡夫卡另眼相待：“写出这些作品的人，并不是一位平凡的女作家。”（卡夫卡，给米莲娜的信，26）对于他总是被强势的人所吸引，他直言不讳：“因为我的尊严，因为我的骄傲，我只能够爱上置于我之上的东西，爱上那些我无法获得的东西。”（邵嘉骥，160）

而作为男人的卡夫卡恐惧女性过于强大而颠覆自己的男性地位。于是《变形记》中的妹妹格雷特在稍稍得到父亲的认可后开始变得盲目自大，为自己照顾格里高尔的斐然成绩沾沾自喜，在唯一支持自己梦想的哥哥死后，成为父母延续传统的目标。她的音乐梦想在父母“不自然地交换了个互相会意的眼光”（李文俊，89）中被“找个好女婿”（李文俊，89）所替代，而她充满讽刺意味的“仿佛要证实他们新的梦想和美好的打算似的”，（李文俊，89）在旅途终结时，第一个跳起来，“舒展了几下她那充满青春活力的身体”。（李文俊，89）生活中的卡夫卡喜欢读书给心爱的人听，于是《变形记》里的父亲平日里也喜欢“大声地把晚报读给母亲听，有时也读给妹妹听”。（李文俊，70）卡夫卡认为朗诵是他建立与少女们最可靠联系的途径。他以这样的方式把她们置于自己的控制之下。有书籍这位最好的同盟军，他驯服年轻的姑娘，“用文学来使她们服从，进而喜欢她们：卡夫卡全身心地做出了这种亲热表示”。（代马盖斯，167）卡夫卡理想中的女强人是在他控制能力以内的强势女性，他羸弱的躯体和不振的精神使他无法以传统男性的方式来征服少女们，书籍成了他最好的武器。

4 被女性化的男人对男性的态度

作为被女性化的男人，卡夫卡对男性也有着复杂的观点。《变形记》中的格里高尔对独裁专制的经理怒不敢言；对暴躁的一家之主——父亲，从遵从到心寒；对世俗傲慢的伪君子——绅士们嗤之以鼻。

4.1 代表父权统治地位的父亲：遵从/恐惧

格里高尔认为自己在一个“所有的职员全是无赖的公司”，（李文俊，64）因为在经理看来，所有员工都会趁机为自己牟利。父亲驱赶甲虫格里高尔时，“无情地把他往后赶，一面嘘嘘叫着，简直像个野人”；（李文俊，69）众人劝父亲喝点酒时，“父亲断然地说一个‘不’字，大家就再也不提这事了”；（李文俊，73）变成甲虫的格里高尔在听到父亲对余款的安排时，仍旧认为“无疑还是父亲的做法更为妥当”，（李文俊，74）甚至贴心地“在大白天，考虑到父亲的脸面，他不愿趴在窗子上让人家看见”（李文俊，75）……《变形记》中父亲、经理形象灵感源于生活中卡夫卡的父亲，而卡夫卡对父亲的情感一面像格里高尔一样遵从，一面是无尽的恐惧。卡夫卡的父亲轻视儿子，尤其是逐渐发现儿子身上没有任何他需要的才能以及值得他称赞的秉性，这种失望随着卡夫卡的成长与日俱增。卡夫卡坦言：“……许多年后我还会惊恐地想起这个画面：那个身影巨大的人，我的父亲，至高无上的权威，半夜三更将我从被子里拉出来，赶到阳台上，在他眼里就是这样无足轻重……这在当时只是一个小小的开端，但这种无足轻重的自卑感却经常笼罩着我，这都来自于您的影响。”（卡夫卡，致父亲，7）面对暴戾专横的父亲所代言的父权形象，个性和身体同样软弱的卡夫卡恐惧、遵从、躲避。

4.2 绅士们（崇拜男子汉/厌恶伪君子）

卡夫卡在《变形记》里塑造了三位绅士租客，“什么都要井井有条，不光是他们的房间里得整齐……他们无法容忍多余的东西，更不要说脏东西了”。（李文俊，82）三个男人吃饭时“大模大样地坐在桌子的上首”“就餐之前要细细察看一番”。（李文俊，82）举止高雅的面纱很快就被撕破，他们不屑欣赏格雷特的小提琴演奏，在发现甲虫格里高尔后立即耍赖要求退租并声明不给房租。活脱脱的伪君子面孔得以呈现。卡夫卡憎恶虚伪之人，崇拜真正的男子汉。

卡夫卡一直以来都容易被强势的人吸引，他的父亲、恋人、朋友、上司，只要他们足够强势，就能让他产生崇拜之情。这样的情结不仅体现在他对强势女性的偏爱上，还体现在他对朋友的情感上。在朋友贝尔格曼身上，卡夫卡看到了很多吸引他的东西，“强壮、有力、坚韧、独立、领导力、生存能力”。（邵嘉骥，200）这些品质和他在父亲赫尔曼身上感受到的相似，因此而使他崇拜、畏惧。卡夫卡的朋友几乎都有赫尔曼的某些特征，这样的特征让他恭顺地服从这段友情。他的崇拜有时甚至有越界的嫌疑，朋友波拉克的坚毅让卡夫卡感觉获得了人生的力量，这种影响既来自这位朋友的鼓励，也来自耳濡目染。在与波拉克的深交中，卡夫卡感到自己身体越来越健康，性格也越来越坚强，他强烈地认为自己“长大了”。（邵嘉骥，204）除了在人群之中不再害怕，卡夫卡也逐渐变得能轻松地和女人交谈。他把这一切都归功于波拉克。而他对作为朋友的感情甚至有某种恋爱成分，他说：“这么多年轻人，我只跟你说过话，我跟其他人说话都是应酬。”（邵嘉骥，205）卡夫卡因为先天的羸弱而自卑，加上长期笼罩在父亲的阴影下，正如他作品中的男人，“只不过是太阳底下一个可怜的影子，在那个荒谬的世界里，一切活动都注定要失败”，（杜瓦尔，152）缺乏男性的阳刚之气，因此而崇拜男子汉，既为男子气概着迷，又为自己的无能而苦恼。

5 结　论

卡夫卡的作品里往往有他身边男男女女以及他自己的影子，比如《审判》里的K和勒妮，《城堡》里的K和仕女弗里达，《美国》里的卡尔和保姆、悍妇克拉拉、黛莱丝、任性而专横的布鲁纳达以及打扮成天使模样的法妮格。他将对女性和男性的复杂矛盾情感注入这些作品。因此，一位被女性化的男人对自我的定位、对强势女性的希望和恐惧以及对强健男性的崇拜和敬畏在《变形记》中得以体现。卡夫卡的女性气质使他向往力量的同时又为之苦恼，为之苦恼之后退而采取迂回、纾解的抗议方式，面对困境，他只能喃喃道："世界的有声'残酷地回应着'我生命中的无声。"（代马盖斯，237）

参考文献

[1] 陈顺馨，戴锦华. 妇女、民族与女性主义[M]. 北京：中央编译出版社，2004.

[2] 达尼埃尔·代马盖斯. 卡夫卡与少女们[M]. 管筱明译. 郑州：河南人民出版社，2006.

[3] Kafka，Franz, 2016.The Metamorphosis and Other Stories[M]. Trans. Crick，Joyce. Nanjing：Yilin Press.

[4] 弗兰兹·卡夫卡. 变形记[M]. 李文俊译. 北京：北京燕山出版社，2000.

[5] 弗兰兹·卡夫卡. 给米莲娜的信[M]. 彤雅立，黄钰娟译. 上海：上海文艺出版社，2015.

[6] 弗兰兹·卡夫卡. 致父亲[M]. 郜志云译. 南京：江苏文艺出版社，2014.

[7] 平野嘉彦. 卡夫卡—身体的位相[M]. 刘文柱译. 石家庄：河北教育出版社，2002.

[8] 雅克琳娜·拉乌-杜瓦尔. 恋爱中的卡夫卡[M]. 彭怡译. 深圳：海天出版社，2014.

[9] 邵嘉骥. 卡夫卡传：墓地里的寒鸦[M]. 北京：新世界出版社，2016.

[10] 石海霞. 碎裂的家庭影像——解读《变形记》中的兄妹关系[J]. 重庆教育学院学报，2005，18（2）.

[11] 洛伊斯·泰森. 当代批评理论实用指南（第2版）[M]. 赵国新等译. 北京：外语教学与研究出版社，2014.

[12] 叶廷芳. 论卡夫卡[M]. 北京：中国社会科学出版社，1988.

An Analysis of Tommy's Personalities in *Never Let Me Go* from the Perspective of Personality Structure Theory

曹 宇

摘　要：石黑一雄的小说《别让我走》讲述了人类制造克隆人以捐献其器官的故事。汤米、凯西和露丝是《别让我走》的主人公。迄今为止，评论家们更多的是从叙述者凯西而非其他人物的角度解析这本小说。本文结合弗洛伊德的人格结构理论分析小说中汤米的性格特点，旨在探讨一条新的解读之路。

论文主要分为四个部分。前两部分分别介绍作者石黑一雄、《别让我走》及弗洛伊德的人格结构理论。第三部分结合弗洛伊德的人格结构理论，重点分析了汤米在三个不同地方的性格特点分别对应他性格中的本我、自我和超我。最后一部分对汤米在生死观、价值观和爱情观上的成长进行了解析。

基于上述研究，本文指出汤米在三个不同地方的性格表现最终促成其成长；他成为一个自信且有担当的人，无畏困难，学会珍爱生命及所爱之人。故本文的分析能让读者对《别让我走》有更深层次的理解并领悟汤米积极对待生活的态度，也能让读者从汤米身上汲取力量，学会珍惜已有的一切，积极面对困境。

关键词：《别让我走》；汤米；本我；自我；超我

Abstract: Kazuo Ishiguro's novel *Never Let Me Go* tells a story that clones are createdas organ donors. Tommy, Kathy and Ruth are the three protagonists in *Never Let Me Go*. Up to now, most critics interpret this novel from the point of the narrator Kathyinstead of other characters, while this thesis analyzes Tommy's personalities through Freud's Personality Structure Theory so as to find a new way to interpret this novel.

This thesis is divided into four parts. The first two parts introduce the author Kazuo Ishiguro, *Never Let Me Go* and Freud's Personality Structure Theory separately. The third part, combined with Freud's Personality Structure Theory, mainly analyzes Tommy's personalities in three different places which correspondsto his id, ego and superego respectively. Finally, Tommy's growth is discussed through his changes in view of life and death, life value and love concept.

Therefore, Tommy's personalities in three different placesultimately catalyze his growth and finally he grows up into a confident and responsible man who deals with problems intrepidly and treasures life and the people he loves.In this sense, readers can gain a better understanding of *Never Let Me Go*and of Tommy's positive attitude towards life. From the analysis of Tommy's personalities, Tommy has thus been molded by Ishiguro to be a model for readers to cherish what they have possessed andconfront plightoptimistically.

Keywords: *Never Let Me Go*; Tommy; id; ego; superego

1 Introduction

Never Let Me Go is the sixth novel of Kazuo Ishiguro who won the Nobel Prize in 2017 for his works have uncovered the abyss beneath our illusory sense of connection with the world.As an international writer, Ishiguro often incorporates emotional force and memory into his works which contain deep thinking and profound meaning. Although Kazuo Ishiguro has been acknowledged more widely after his winning Nobel Prize, there is still large space in his works to be studied.In *Never Let Me Go*, one of his most bewildering and acclaimed novels of recent years, Kazuo Ishiguro portrays the lives of a group of students growing up in a darkly skewered version of contemporary England. Narrated by Kathy H, *Never Let Me Go* hauntingly dramatizes her efforts and attempts to come to terms with her childhood atHailsham, and with the fate that has always awaited her and her closest friends Tommy and Ruth in the wider world.

This novel has been widely discussed both by the domestic and foreign critics after its publication in 2005. In 2011, it has been adapted into a movie in London. Many western critics have voiced their views towards this novel. American scholar Cynthia F. Wong in his book review considersthe narrator of *Never Let Me Go* as "often slips in a reflection offered by other characters that might contest the narrator's perspective or understanding", (Wong, 2015) while Deborah P. Britzmanand Titus Levy believe that this novel can be regarded as a "kind of allegory". (Britzman, 2006; Levy, 2011) Both of them classify *Never Let Me Go* as an anti-Utopia novel. YuginTeo combines this novel with the theory of memory supported by "Paul Ricoeur's*Memory, History, Forgetting*". (Teo, 2014) Meanwhile critics at home mainly put emphasis on those themes including clones' submission probed by PuLixin, paradox of Hailsham system by Gu Wei, traumatic memories and identity narration by LiJueyun and etc.Furthermore, GuoGuoliang and Li Chun have analyzed this novel from the perspective of existentialism. They hold that "Ishiguro is utilizing the eye of clone to explore modern human existence, unclosing the inescapability of the tragic individual life, the relativity of freedom, and the courage to seek freedom and value of existence". (郭国良、李春, 2007)

Although those themes have been extensively discussed by critics, most critics put emphasis on Kathy, the narrator in *Never Let Me Go*, rather than on other characters. They emphasize the important role Kathy plays or the construction of her identity. Nevertheless, this thesis chooses to analyze this novel through the point of another protagonist, Tommy, from the perspective of Freud's Personality Structure Theory which up to now is regarded as a new way to elucidate this novel.More specifically, this thesis points out that the changes in Tommy's personalities arerevealedthroughthree separate stages in which Tommy gradually unfolds his id, ego and superego in this novel. At Hailsham, his id is demonstrated from his self-preservation, unconventionality and his physical love with Ruth. Then at the Cottages, his ego is reflected fromhis obedience, painting awareness and love dilemma. At recovery center, Tommy grows up into a man withstrong responsibility and self-affirmation and pursues his love bravely, which unfolds his superego. Finally, Tommy's growth is manifested through his changes in his view of life and death, life value and love concept. As a result，readers can see the changes of Tommy's personalities and better understand Kazuo Ishiguro's intention of inspiringpeople to lookforward to this world and to be positive when they are trapped in dilemma.

2 Kazuo Ishiguro and *Never Let Me Go*

As a contemporary immigrant writer， Kazuo Ishiguro is concerned with the identity of diaspora group and has advocated the new writing concept.According to the Swedish Academy，the themes of memory，time and self-delusionweave through his works.*Never Let Me Go* is his sixth novel which was shortlisted for the 2005 Man Booker Prize. Meanwhile，the *Time* named it the best novel of 2005 and classified the novel in its *TIME 100 Best English-language Novels* from 1923 to 2005.

2.1 Kazuo Ishiguro

In 1954，Kazuo Ishigurowas born in Nagasaki in Japan but moved to Guildford in the UK with his parents and two sisters when he was five years old. His first novel，*A Pale View of Hills*，was published in 1982. After graduation，he worked for a homeless charityin Notting Hillwhere he met and married his wifeLorna MacDougall.Although Kazuo Ishiguro moved to Britain when he was young，which was referred to his "placelessness"，（Shaffer，1998）his experience asimmigratewas conducive tothe exploration of estrangement that had little to do with any particular time or place. His second novel *An Artist of the Floating World*won the Whitbread prize and his third，*The Remains of the Day*，won the Man Booker Prize.The narrator of *The Remains of the Day* is a butler who recalls his past life in the form of a diary. At 54，he remained a "literary phenomenon"（Sim，2010）that his sixth novel，*Never Let Me Go*，a philosophical investigation into mortality and meaning，writes about the clones who slowly realize the fact that they had been created as organ donors.

There's a persistent note of quiet enjoyment at the ironies of the human comedy presented throughout Ishiguro's works. He describes the themes thathe has spent his life thinking about and painstakingly unpicking："The way countries and nations and communities remember their past and how often they bury the uncomfortable memories from their past".（李春，2005）In Ishiguro's novels，according to Barry Lewis，what Ishiguro has written on paper is only the tip of the iceberg：so much is happening underneath，usually beyond the characters' own knowledge. Ishiguro's novels illuminate reality in a profound and surprising way worthy of a Nobel and are acclaimed for the spare elegance of the writing，a testament to the power of what is left unsaid.

2.2 Never Let Me Go

Up to now，*Never Let Me Go* has won many awards. Kazuo Ishiguro considers it as his most pleasant and inspiring novel. He holds that *Never Let Me Go* allows him to "see the positive side of human beings although they have some flaws such as jealousy and baseness".（Wong and Yildiz，2015）Kazuo intends to demonstrate three upright characters in this novel-Tommy，Kathy and Ruth. When they three are at the end of their life，they care about others and correct errors instead of minding their own status or property. Therefore，this novel aims to reveal the positive side rather than the weak side of human beings. This novel can be interpreted through many ways. On the one hand, it is often defined as a dystopian science fiction since Ishiguro depicts a dark society where human beings create clones in order to transplant their organs to the patients. On the other hand, some critics interpret this novel through a traumatic perspective and they analyze it from the theme of remembering and forgetting.

The story revolves around three Hailsham students: Kathy, Ruth and Tommy, who develop a close but intricate friendship. Tommy and Ruth start a romantic relationship when they are at Hailsham, which continues when they leave for the Cottages.At the Cottages, they get to know the deferral from veterans. Then Kathy becomes a carer and leaves the Cottages. 11 years later, they three reunite at the recovery center. Ruth and Tommy have donated twice and they break up after Kathy's leave. Ruth persuades Tommy and Kathy to apply for deferralwhich at last is proved to be a failure when Madame tells them the news is not true. Finally, Tommy completes his four donations and Kathy is ready to face her destiny bravely.

3 Brief Introduction to Personality Structure Theory

Personality Structure Theory, one of the main constituent in Psychoanalysis established in the early 1890s by Austrian neurologist Sigmund Freud, can be explained through three aspects including id, ego and superego. According to Freud, the id is primitive and emotional, which is governed only by the most basic principle of mental dynamics.The ego is an organized and realistic part that represents consciousness, and the superego serves to repress the desires of the id while taking the responsibility of censoring agency.

3.1 Freud and Psychoanalysis

Sigmund Freud, an Austrian neurologist, is the founder and leading pioneer of psychoanalysis. Psychoanalysis is a method used for treating psychopathology through conversation between a psychoanalyst and a patient.Freud was born in 1856 and his parents were Jewish. In 1881, he was qualified as a doctor of medicine at the University of Vienna. In 1886, Freud set up his clinic in Vienna and lived there. Then he became an associate professor in 1902. In order to escape from the persecution of Nazis, he left Austria but died in the UK in 1939.

In creating psychoanalysis, Freud resorts to combining practice and theory by means of establishing the association between sexuality and human action.According to Freud, most individual's mental processes are unconscious and many of our desires and memories are repressed because of the powerful social taboos attached to certain sexual energy. On this basis heassigns the mental processes to three psychic structure comprising id, ego and superego.

Up to now, psychoanalysis remains influential within the fields of psychology, psychotherapy, and psychiatry, and even across every aspect of human life.His contributions have suffused contemporary western opinion and popular culture.Although there are some changes in psychoanalysis today and some critics even deem his theory as being out-of-date, Freud's achievements in psychoanalysis should never be underestimated.

3.2 Personality Structure Theory

Freud suggests that the human psyche be divided into three parts: id, ego and superego. According to Freud, the id is the set of uncoordinated instinctual trends which follows the "pleasure principle", avoiding any pain or discomfort. It is the disorganized part of the personality structure that contains a human's instinctual desires.Freud holds that the id is the only component of personality that is "present from birth and it is the source of our bodily wants and impulses, particularly our aggressive and sexual drives".（何爱平，2011）Unchecked, it would lead us to any lengths, destruction or even self-destruction. Safety for the self and for others does not lie within the boundary of the id.

The ego is the realistic and organized part that mediates between the desires of the id and the superego. Abiding by "reality principle", the egorefers to the coherent organization in psychological process. If the id represents sexual and irrational desire, then the ego means reason and wisdom. Therefore, it depends on the surface of the id without definite boundary and the depressing part is annexed by the id. Humans' perceptual system grows up from the core of ego and it takes the part of communicating information with the outside.

The superego, also called "self-paradigm",（Storr, 1989）plays a critical and moralizing role.The superegoacts as an internal censor that is dominated by the "morality principle". Freud develops its conception from an earlier combination of the ego ideal. He explains that the superego bases on the Oedipus Complex. For instance, the superego can be demonstrated in a little boy who, on the one hand, attaches to his mother and models his father, and on the other hand, hopes to replace his father.It is originally derived from parental prohibitions and criticism.

4 Analysis of Tommy's Personalities

In the three places, Tommy has his personalities displayed differently, which corresponds to his three stages of id, ego and superego respectively at Hailsham, the Cottages and recovery center. At the beginning of his stay at Hailsham, Tommy presents his id through his self-preservation, unconventionality and desire for physical satisfaction. When he moves to the Cottages, Tommy's ego gains the upper hand. Acknowledging and accepting the rules imposed on clones, he begins to obey these regulations. Several years later, when he meets Kathy at recovery center, Kathy's support and love help him further realize his life goal.

4.1 Tommy's Id at Hailsham

During Tommy's stay at Hailsham, his id is mainly presented through his self-preservation when he is mocked by other students at Hailsham. Besides, his rebellion against the rules at Hailsham incurs the isolation from others. Unlike them, he has no painting works selected into Madame's gallery and he is the only one who does not paint at Hailsham. Moreover, the love between Tommy and Ruth is a kind of physical attraction which demonstrates the sexual desire of his id.

4.1.1 Self-preservation

At the very beginning, Kathy begins to reminisce about the time when they are in the Juniors. It is in the pavilion that Kathy watches students' tricks imposed upon Tommy. After Tommy realizes he is made fun by other boys, he bursts into bellowing, but the boys, laughing openly, run off from the ground. Tommy stands there, glaring at these boys, and his face scarlet. Then he begins to scream and shout, which is "a nonsensical jumble of swear words and insults". (9; ch. 1)

In fact, it is not the first time that those boys play tricks on him. Almost every day, there are pranks that have been played on him. Therefore, those boys'tricks are one of the reasons for his self-preservation at Hailsham. On the one hand, his instinctual impulsedrives him to pour out his anger. Even when Kathy tries to comfort him, he rejects her help. On the other hand, Tommy reveals his id through his ignorance of those tricks. Gradually, there is a real change both in Tommy's personality and others' attitude towards him.

Later, Kathy finds that things seem to be going much better for Tommy. Tommy tells her that he really does not want to be the person who does the same thing with others. What he really minds is his instincts for pleasure without regard to social conventions or school rules.Freud denotes that the id is the source of all our aggressions and desires, which can be used to explain Tommy's self-preservation.

4.1.2 Unconventionality

At Hailsham, those students have a big exhibition called the Exchange for four times a year. They can sell all the things they have created like paintings, drawings, pottery, or even all sorts of sculptures in the three months since the last Exchange. For students, the Exchange becomes so important to them since how they are regarded at Hailsham or how much they are liked and respected is so closely linked with the Exchange. It is the Exchange that makes Hailsham special. Apart from the Exchange, every week, Madame comes to Hailsham and takes away their best works. Then they begin to imagine that there is a gallery for storing their best pictures.

However, Tommy does not have a picture or painting for the Exchange or the gallery, which has started in one of Miss Geraldine's art classes. He finishes a particular watercolor -an elephant standing in some tall grass. Nevertheless his paintingis mocked by other students. After this elephant painting, the whole thing has been brought into the open that once Tommy starts on something, there are sneers and giggles all around him. As a result, he refuses to paint or to be a creative student. Most students take him as a crank since he is the only one who does not care about the Exchange and the gallery.

Tommy's unconventionality can be attributed to his unconscious psyche. Freud explains that safety for the self and for others does not lie within the province of the id: its concern is purely for instinctual satisfaction, regardless of consequence. In Tommy's inner heart, no matter how important the Exchange is for other students, he still goes on his own way. Those paintings cannot bring him the pleasure or gratification but to sting his nerve all the time. Naturally, he knows no good and evil, and his unconventionality becomes more obvious.

4.1.3 Physical Love with Ruth

In their last years at Hailsham, when they are from thirteen to sixteen, Tommy and Ruth become a couple. Miss Emily gives a lot of the sex lectures to those students, and she tells them they have to be extremely careful about sex. Even though guardians tell students the truth, they make it actually impossible to do such without breaking rules, which is "for all the talk of sex being beautiful, we had the distinct impression we'd be in trouble if the guardians caught us at it". (95; ch. 8)

But for Tommy, his love for Ruth is completely from his desire for satisfying the physical needs, which can be taken as sexual attraction. About having sex, these students do not know whether or not the guardians want them to have sex or not. Ruth gives an explanation that the guardians want students to have sex appropriately with the person they like and without getting diseases, but students do break the rules and have sex including Tommy and Ruth even though they'd never been a proper couple.

It is known that the id is the reservoir of libido which is the primary source of all psychic energy, especiallythe sexual drive. When Tommy and Ruth are in the period from thirteen to sixteen, all of their knowledge about sex is from their guardians. While they have instinctual desire and curiosity, then their libido drives them to eat the forbidden fruit. In fact, the love between Tommy and Ruth is purely body attraction since they always have serious conflicts. They cannot clam down and care about each other once they have bust-ups.

4.2 Tommy's Ego at the Cottages

In *Freud*, Anthony Storr elucidates Freud's theory that the ego is the conscious part which employs the reason and common sense. It is at the Cottages that Tommy starts to restrain his irritable personalities through obeying the rules and accepting the reality. His ego "works as a mediator between the world within and the world without". (Storr, 1989) Besides, the veterans'referring to deferral arouses Tommy's painting awareness that he finds how important a selected picture means. Meanwhile, the love dilemma he confronts also reveals his ego which mediates between his physical love and spiritual love.

4.2.1 Obedience

When students are at sixteen, they have to leave Hailsham and be dispatched to different places in Britain. In *Never Let Me Go*, Tommy, Kathy and Ruth are sent to the Cottages which are "the remains of a farm that had gone out of business years before". (116; ch. 10) The Cottages is completely different from the Hailsham- no courses, no rigorous rules even no guardians.

These environmental and realistic changes to some extent reverse their recognition of the outside world, especially for Tommy. He begins to imitate the veterans at the Cottages and think over his future. Tommy notices those changes, trying to adjust himself and adapt to the reality. Like the veterans, the intimate behavior of him and Ruth are copied from the television: the way they gesture to each other and the way they argue with each other. Moreover, Tommy graduallyacknowledges his ego and obeys the rules at the Cottages.

Because of the veterans at the Cottages, He begins to accept the reality and knows that there is a bigger and totally different world outside Hailsham. As clones, they have no privileges than others, let alone they can share the same future with human beings. Once they leave the Cottages, they have only two choices-either to be carers, which can provide them with more time before donations, or to be donors directly. Tommy's ego regulates his instinctual drives of the id, which helps him integrated into clones' circle. His rational psyche serves as a mediator balancing his inner desire with social rules. Therefore, the ego of Tommy can be seen from his accepting the reality and obeying the rule at the Cottages.

4.2.2 Painting Awareness

It is at the Cottages that Tommy arouses his painting awareness which can be illustrated from two aspects. In the first place, Kazuo Ishiguro denotes that when they go to Norfolk to find Ruth's "*possible*", (139; ch. 12) they stand outside a gallery called "The Portway Studios". (162; ch. 14) And all of them including Tommy are fascinated by the pictures. When the owner of this place asks Tommy whether he is an art student, Tommy subconsciouslyresponds that he is just keen about art and the pictures. In the second place, Tommy tells Kathy his speculation of Madame's gallery that the selected pictures reveal what a student is like inside and reveal one's soul. Tommy believes the point of testing a couple is that Madame or others need something to prove their soul. Therefore, he starts to paint pictures and finishes a dozen of his fantastic creations.

It can be seen how resistant Tommy is about the art, the gallery and painting at Hailsham. However, his stay at the Cottages changes his attitude towards painting that he increasingly realizes how significant the pictures are. Even when he responds to the lady of "The Portway Studio", his ego controls his consciousness and reflects his painting awareness. He tells Kathy the pictures can explain why the gallery is so important and why the guardians want them to work so hard on their art, through which Tommy's initial purpose of painting can be understood.

According to Freud, the ego can be viewed as a psychic agency to protect the individual. It is the rational part of the mind, representing consciousness and employing the reason and common sense. Tommy's ego in painting awareness reflects his individual protection that he can postpone his donations through proving his creativity. Besides, he becomes more rational about his behaviors at the Cottages that he conceals his intention in front of other veterans and students.

4.2.3 Love Dilemma

Although Tommy and Ruth still keep their relationship as a couple, their conflicts and misunderstanding are hidden below the peace. Despite Tommy is satisfied with his sexual relationship between Ruth, he struggles to restrain his love and admiration for Kathy. In their journey to Norfolk, when Ruth decides to go with the veterans to visit a carernamed Martin, Tommy chooses to stay with Kathy, which irritates Ruth. Then, Tommy helps Kathy retrieve her lost tape-Judy Bridgewater's *Songs After Dark.* After Ruth's returning back, both of them do not mention the tape Tommy has bought for Kathy since they know Ruth cannot tolerate that.

What's more, Tommy tells Kathy his idea and plan about deferrals, but he conceals those in front of Ruth. For one thing, his intimate talks with Kathy are often rumored by other students that they are actually in love, and then his ego drives him to be more rational and more sensible about his behaviors. For another, his unconscious partgains upper hand in terms of his unconditional trust for Kathy. Tommy eagerly shows Kathy his pictures, desiring for her approval and support. Unlike Ruth, Kathy brings more spiritual power to Tommy.

Trapped by the love dilemma, Tommy faces his inner conflicts even though he tries to restrain his real love. Freud explains that the ego is a special organization andis closely connected with the organs of perception. For Tommy, Ruth can be taken as physical satisfaction while Kathy conforms to his spiritual attraction.Though a large part of the ego is unconscious, the ego nevertheless comprises the conscious mind. Tommy's love for Kathy embodies both his unconscious actions and conscious recognition.

4.3 Tommy's Superego at Recovery Center

When they three meet again at recovery center, all of them experience different life. Kathy becomes a respectable carer, Ruth has begun her donations and Tommy is facing his third donation. Since they know what the fourth donation means for clones, they all treasure the limited time they have. Although Tommy is not sure whether his speculation about Madame's gallery is right or wrong, he still continues his painting career and enjoys its pleasure. After so many years, Tommy becomes more confident and affirms what he has done. In addition, he grows up into a responsible man who is brave to pursue his love.

4.3.1 Perseverance

When Kathy meets Tommy again, she is amazed that Tommy perseveres in painting. Once Tommy has told Kathy his initial purpose of drawing his animals, "it's not only because of all that I'm doing the animals. I just like doing them". (188; ch. 16) After so many years, Tommy does not give up his drawings. He does not forget, even though he and Kathy hardly discuss anything openly. Then Ruth tells them they should visit Madame, applying for a deferral as there is no more time for Tommy after his third donation.

Nevertheless, their visit to Madame turns out to be a failure. What Madame has told them shatters their promising vision of the future. As for the gallery, Madame indicates that the art works of student can reveal their inner selves and display their soul. That's the main reason to explain her collecting pictures at Hailsham. In fact, there is no deferral, no gallery and no truth in the rumor. Ishiguro denotes that due to the "Morningdale scandal", (263; ch. 22) the climate changes and the Hailsham education has to be stopped. Tommy's expectations and hopes are dampened thoroughly with the end of their talks. However, after that trip, Kathy is surprised to find Tommy still carries on his animal pictures.

In his limited time at recovery center, Tommy starts to value his dreams and future. His superego works unconsciously, serving to inhibit or repress the drives of the id. Guided by the morality principle, he builds his confidence based on his painting and expectation for future. Although what he has hoped falls short, he has not been defeated by reality. On the contrary, his self-recognition has been strengthened.

4.3.2 Self-affirmation

Tommy finally grows up into a confident and thoughtful man in his stay at recovery center. He is not just a new man in his thoughts, but also a new man in his actions. He is less likely to experience distress and react defensively when confronted with contradictions or threats.In the past, Tommy would ask Kathy for advice about his pictures and think highly of her comments. Now, his experiences and thoughts support him to be more independent and be a man with self-affirmation. When he shows Kathy his animals at recovery center, he never asks Kathy again for advice about those pictures.

On the one side, Tommy has suffered from three donations, which has brought force and great changes in his personalities and life values that he cares about his life without concerning others' comments or judgements. On the other side, for those clones, few of them can get over the third donation and very few of them can finish their fourth donation. Most clones cannot wait for their third donation. Therefore, Tommy's previous donations render him the honors of being the lucky donor. His respectable fame increases his confidence of himself, which drives him to protect his self-integrity and dignity.

Experimental investigations of self-affirmation suggest that self-affirmation can help individuals cope with threat or stress and that it might be beneficial for improving performanceand reducing defensiveness. Tommy's self-affirmation helps him face his inescapable life bravely and accept what has been already arranged for him. According to Freud, the superego helps human beings adapt to society by getting them to act in socially acceptable ways.Then Tommy's superego forms the unconscious part of the personality structurethat includes his ego ideals, spiritual goals, and the psychic agency.

4.3.3 Spiritual Love with Kathy

Finally, Tommy and Kathy reunite together at recovery center. Tommy is so happy to see Kathy again. After all the years, they can still touch the soft part in their heart and come close together again. Ruth asks for Kathy's forgiveness because of her intervention between Tommy and Kathy, although she knows Tommy really loves Kathy. In their last happy days, Kathy brings Tommy energy and forces to move forward. That is a spiritual support and inspiration for Tommy.

Tommy admits that he always loves Kathy which can be traced back to their days at Hailsham. Kathy remembers that time Ruth tells her Tommy does not see her like the usual friend. Yet he always conceals his feelings and emotions. When Kathy decides to take care of him, the way they get along with each other seems like they have been together for a long time. Kathy usually sits in the chair and read to him from various paperbacks. Tommy stretches out on the bed and listens to her quietly. Otherwise, they talk about the old days, the Hailsham and other things.

In general, as the main driving force in Tommy's last days, Kathy brings him abundant happiness and hope for future. To a large extent, it is Kathy's company that reignites his passion for arts and for life. No matter what has happened or what will happen, Tommy has already prepared for that. Anthony Storr illustrates that "the superego acts as the conscience, maintaining the sense of morality and proscription from taboos". (Storr, 1989)

5 Significance of Tommy's Growth

The analysis of the changes in Tommy's personalities allows thereaders to understand this novel as well as this character in a comprehensive way. Tommy, through a completely different perspective compared with his previous view, finally confronts death intrepidly and seizes the limited time. At the same time, his attitude towards life also changes for he admits those meaningful things and affirms his efforts. In addition, Tommy's pursuit of real love motivates readers to cherish the people they love. Accordingly, Tommy's growth provides a significant mode for readers if they come into predicament.

It is known to all that one requires tremendous courage to face the end of life, let alone his death has been decided by other people. From the initial innocence to his awareness for basic right, Tommy understands how treasurable life is. Therefore, in his last days at recovery center, he cares more about the present instead of the past. When he and Kathy reminisce about the old Hailsham people, hesooner or later transfers the conversation to his current friends or donors. This is one of his changes about his view of life and death.

Tommy makes use of his limited time drawing his pictures before his fourth donation. Kathy believes he always knows his future and his goals, so he decides to fulfill his commission in advance after five years'career of being a carer. With time goes by, Tommy grows into a mature man full of responsibilities. Therefore, readers can be inspired by Tommy's active life value and hold positive attitude towards the problems in life.

The ideal love is that one can gain happiness and pleasure from the person he loves. For Tommy, Kathy is the one who brings him belief of life and energy to move on. Their love encompasses strong emotions and mental states, positively experienced and ranging from their common interests for reading, their deepest interpersonal affection to the simplest pleasure. Henceforth, the ideal love is such a cozy state for both sides that they learn from it and support each other.

6 Conclusions

This thesis analyzes the male character Tommy'spersonalities in Kazuo Ishiguro's *Never Let Me Go* based on Freud's Personality Structure Theory. Tommy's personalities have been unfolded gradually in threedifferentplacesatHailsham, the Cottages and recovery center, which at the same time reflects his stages of theid, ego and superego respectively. This thesis focuses on the analysis of the significant impact upon his personalities in his whole life. Consequently, readers can be inspired from his growth in his view of life and death, life value and love concept.

Then there are three main findings of this thesis. First of all, Tommy's growth and attitude towards death encourage readers to be more positive when theyget into trouble. As a clone, Tommy understands he has no more right or chance to choose the life he wants, but he treasures what he has already possessed and cherishes the limited time and the people he loves. He has no complaint or grievance. Secondly, he grasps the time to paint his pictures and holds firm to his goals. Even when

Madame and Miss Emily shatter his vision, he never gives up, which can be taken as a good example of perseverance for readers. Thirdly, his attitude towards love also inspires readers to be more rational when they confront the same dilemma in love. Sexual attraction cannot be the source for a lasting relationship while the spiritual communication and supports are the primary force in maintaining a relationship.

In general, Ishiguro attempts to convey hope and strength instead of creating a gloomy atmosphere in *Never Let Me Go* which Ishiguro regards as his most inspiring and pleasant works. Besides, *Never Let Me Go* allows Ishiguro to think about those upright human beings who care for others and are willing to correct their errors. Therefore, this novel expresses humans' positivity instead of their weakness. Through the analysis of Tommy's personalities and his growth, readers gain strength from this character and ponder on their own life in a positive way.

参 考 文 献

[1] Britzman, Deborah P., 2006. "On Being a Slow Reader: Psychoanalytic Reading Problem in Ishiguro's *Never Let Me Go.*" *Changing English: Studies in Culture and Educations*, 13: 307-318.

[2] Ishiguro, Kazuo, 2006. *Never Let Me Go*. New York: Vintage International.

[3] Levy, Titus, 2011. "Human Rights Storytelling and Trauma Narrative in Kazuo Ishiguro's *Never Let Me Go.*"*Journal of Human Rights*, 10.1: 1-16.

[4] Lewis, Barry, 2002. *Kazuo Ishiguro: Contemporary World Writers.* Manchester and New York: Manchester University Press.

[5] Shaffer, Brain W., 1998. *Understanding Kazuo Ishiguro*.Columbia: University of South Carolina Press.

[6] Sim, Wai-chew, 2010. *Kazoo Ishiguro*. London and New York: Routledge.

[7] Storr, Anthony, 1989.*Freud*. Oxford: Oxford University Press.

[8] Teo, Yugin, 2014. *Kazuo Ishiguro and Memory*. London: Palgrave Macmillan.

[9] Wong, Cynthia F., 2015. "Book Review of *Kazuo Ishiguro and Memory*." *Memory Studies*, 8.4: 487-494.

[10] Wong, Cynthia F., and Dr. Hulya Yildiz., 2015. *Kazuo Ishiguro in a Global Context.* London: Taylor & Francis Ltd.

[11] 安东尼·斯托尔. 弗洛伊德与精神分析[M]. 尹莉译. 北京：外语教学与研究出版社，2008.

[12] 郭国良，李春. "宿命"下的自由生存——《永远别让我离开》中的生存取向[J]. 外国文学，2007（3）：4-10.

[13] 谷伟. 泯浮泡影——略论《千万别弃我而去》中"黑尔舍姆"的体制悖论[J]. 外国文学，2010（5）：14-20.

[14] 何爱平. "谈弗洛伊德三重人格理论在文学批评中的应用"[J]. 外语教育教学，2011（2）：98-99.

[15] 李春. 石黑一雄访谈录[J]. 当代外国文学，2005（4）：134-138.

[16] 李厥云. 多元文化下的漫步者：石黑一雄国际化写作研究[M]. 济南：山东大学出版社，2013.

[17] 蒲立昕. 驯服的身体，臣服的主体：评《千万别丢下我》[J]. 当代外国文学，2011（1）：108-115.

[18] 瞿世镜，任一鸣. 当代英国小说史[M]. 上海：上海译文出版社，2008.

[19] 石黑一雄. 千万别丢下我[M]. 朱去疾译. 南京：译林出版社，2005.

石黑一雄《别让我走》替罪羊原型下的主题分析

王若岚

摘　要：本文通过对石黑一雄所著《别让我走》中主要人物克隆人、受捐者以及主要捐献器官的情节分析，通过替罪羊理论的变形运用，得出本文主要探讨的主题——人性本质中的自私是无法逃避的。本文由三个部分组成：引言部分包括文献综述、理论概述以及论文概要三节，简要介绍了国内对《别让我走》的研究概况，简述了法国哲学家勒内·吉拉尔关于替罪羊的理论，陈述了文本结构。第二部分从克隆人以及黑尔舍姆中众人出发，分析了文本中所表现出的人性本质中自私因素的无法避免的存在。第三部分对文章内容进行了简要的总结。

《别让我走》这本小说，通过对克隆因素的运用，深刻而又具有讽刺性地剖析了关于人性本质中自私的不可避免。论文认为，这样的一个主题，既能帮助人类更深刻地认识自我，同时也有助于对自我的改进。

关键词：石黑一雄；《别让我走》；替罪羊；人性自私；克隆人

Abstract：Through the analysis of *Never Let Me Go*，written by Kazuo Ishiguro，and the application of theory of scapegoating，this article attempts to probe into the theme，that is，the selfishness of human cannot be avoided. This article consists of three parts：the introduction part includes literature review，theoretical overview and the summary of the article，which briefly introduces the domestic research on*Never Let Me Go*，and briefly describes the theory of scapegoating of French philosopher René Giral. The second part，from the perspective of clones and other human in Hailsham，article attempts to analyze the inevitable existence of selfishness. The third part gives a brief summary of this article.

Never Let Me Go，by the use of cloning factors，profoundly and ironically analyzes the inevitability of selfishness in the nature of human. Therefore this article argues that such a theme can help humans to understand themselves more deeply，and also contribute to self-improvement.

Key words：Kazuo Ishiguro；*Never Let Me Go*；scapegoating；selfishness；cloning

1 引　言

1954 年 11 月 8 日，石黑一雄生于日本长崎，1960 年随家人移居英国。1983 年开始发表小说，其主要作品有《群山淡景》《浮世画家》和《长日将尽》等。曾获得 1989 年布克奖、2017 年诺贝尔文学奖、大英帝国勋章、法国艺术及文学骑士勋章等多个奖项，与鲁西迪、奈保尔被称为“英国文坛移民三雄”。

石黑一雄与其他少数族裔作家不同，尽管拥有日本和英国双重文化背景，但他从不操弄亚裔的族群认同，而是以身为一个国际主义的作家来自诩。他笔下的主人公总是在对自身命运时感到无可奈何，他们的人生往往建立在一个又一个错误的意义上，但当他们发现这种意义错误时，他们的整个人生也就变得毫无意义，主人公由此变得无措、失据，无法安置自身的位置。

正如诺贝尔评奖委员会对其的赞语，石黑一雄的小说探索了“记忆、时间和自我欺骗”这一其实并不新鲜的文学母题。

1938年，德国科学家首次提出克隆技术的设想。1952年，科学家首先用青蛙开展克隆实验，此后克隆技术的研究不断深入并取得突破性进展。1997年2月《自然》杂志刊登英国科学家伊恩·威尔穆特成功克隆出绵羊“多莉”的消息。这一成果引发了人们对克隆技术可能应用于人类生殖性克隆的广泛关注，克隆人的伦理问题应运而生。由于克隆人涉及社会伦理、科技伦理和生命伦理等诸多方面的问题，因此不仅引发了一场研究者的激烈讨论，也成为文学创作的题材。正是在这样的背景下，石黑一雄推出了他的科幻小说《别让我走》。

小说以女主角凯斯的视角展开，总体分为三个部分，以主人公的生活场所的变化切分。第一部分描写了凯斯，露丝以及汤米三人在黑尔舍姆度过的整个童年时光。在黑尔舍姆他们渐渐懂得要面对的是捐献的宿命。第二部分描写16岁之后三人离开黑尔舍姆去到村舍开始为期两年的过度生活。在村舍他们对自己身份的认知变得明晰，清楚了解了自己要面对的是18岁之后成为看护员然后开始捐献，差不多4次之后就会完成自己的“终结”。第三部分描写三人在医院的交集，残忍的真相一个个被揭开，露丝和汤米相继“终结”，最终凯斯也选择提前结束看护员生活开始捐献并等待自己的“终结”。小说以克隆人的视角展开，在平淡的话语中向我们展现了克隆人短暂的一生。三位主人公从懵懂无知到清楚认知到自己的使命，从对生活充满希望到只剩绝望，小说用平淡的笔调讲述了不平淡的生活，缓缓向我们揭开了一个围绕人性的主题。

在国内，对《别让我走》的研究主要涉及克隆人身份认知以及伦理相关的研究。像桑翠琳这样的批评家主要关注克隆人的身份。浙江大学郭国良和李春的主题论文“‘宿命’下的自由生存——《永远别让我离去》中的生存取向”研究了存在主义。谷伟的文章“沤浮泡影——略论《千万别弃我而去》中‘黑尔舍姆’的体制悖论”揭示了“黑尔舍姆”的体制悖论和隐含其后的社会霸权构建等等。

本文则从法国哲学家勒内·吉拉尔提出的替罪羊理论入手，通过异化的替罪羊推导出小说表现的主题——人性中自私的本质无可避免。

替罪羊原型最早出现在《圣经·旧约》中。上帝耶和华为了考验亚伯拉罕的忠诚，要他把晚年所得的独生子以撒作为燔祭献给上帝。亚拉伯罕十分敬畏上帝，二话没说，就按照上帝吩咐，把儿子带到上帝指定的山上去献燔祭。正当他举刀砍向儿子时，上帝相信了他的忠诚，派天使阻止了他。可是拿什么献燔祭呢？亚拉伯罕抬头一看发现了一只公羊，两只角扣在稠密的树丛之中。他捉了那只公羊，献为燔祭，用来代替他的儿子。这样就产生了替罪羊的原型。

但是随着社会的发展，替罪羊的原型在运用中出现了转变，由最初用羊代替人向上帝献祭转变为由一个人代替他人或集体作为人牺向神献祭，表示赎罪，代人受过以保集体的太平。

在《别让我走》中，最直接让克隆人成为替罪羊的是那个时代高速发展的科学技术和医疗水平本身，而克隆人则因为其本身存在方式的特殊性而被当作异类看待而具有了标签，同时，这些克隆人作为替罪羊的献祭方式是一次次捐献自己的器官，以此达成人类延长寿命的最终目的。

可是，在替罪羊原型中，作为迫害者的选择者本身应该是认为自己是有罪的，从而迫害者选择了带有标记的替罪羊去代替自己完成献祭，即替罪羊的死亡，而净化自身的罪责。因此，这样一个迫害者以及献祭方式与上文推出的形象有着明显出入。

首先，替罪羊存在的前提——迫害者相信自己有罪并且希望能够通过替罪羊的献祭来净化自己的罪责。而科学技术的发展本身是不存在有罪之说的。相反，对这样的技术加以过度利用而忽略伦理界限的人类本身才是有罪的，更确切地说是人性中迫切希望自己能够更长寿而刻意忽略伦理界限的人性中的自私才是作者想要表达出的真实迫害者。其次，替罪羊的献祭方式并不能使迫害者得到净化，他们活着时的每一次献祭都存在揭示这些迫害者本身不顾伦理残害和他们拥有同样基因，同样理性的另一种人类的事实，因而，只有当这些替罪羊最终死亡之后，迫害者才能洗涤其自身的罪责，从而完成净化。即，小说中作者真正想要传递出的迫害者为人类及其本性中的自私，而因为克隆这个因素的存在，克隆人被选择成了替罪羊，他们最终真正的献祭方式也并非捐献器官，而是在他们四次捐献器官之后的死亡。

由此可以推出，作者真正想通过这一替罪羊本身表达出的迫害者是人性中自私的本质，克隆这样的高新科学技术只是其表象。因此，本文将围绕这一主题展开。

论文主体部分主要通过两方面对主题进行探究。一方面对克隆人通过教育获得理性思维，以及他们本身所存在的克隆原型基因影响的综合分析，可以认为克隆人在本质上是和人类无异的个体，因而，在克隆人身上所表现出的人性本质上的自私可以认为是人类共性上的特征；另一方面，论文分析了在黑尔舍姆的作用机制以及在其机制下所表现出的在黑尔舍姆中的众人人性中的自私本质。论文第三部分做了整体上的归纳，再次提出人性本质中自私因素无法避免的论题。

2　克隆人主体人性探究

《别让我走》中，作者刻意引进的克隆因素主要包含两方面原因。一方面，克隆这个因素作为标记替罪羊的标志。用克隆这个因素使克隆人群被人类当作异己看待，从而奠定人类掠夺其器官而不认为自己有罪的基础。另一方面，用克隆的因素作为一个反讽。克隆人在接受了和人类一样的教育之后也获得和人类一样自私的本性，更体现出人性的自私是与生俱来的。因此，本部分主要从克隆人具有人性的两个方面，即理性思维和其基因原型方面进行探讨，再通过对文本内容的分析得出克隆人这个群体因为具有人性之后所表现出的人性中自私的本质特征。

2.1　克隆人理性思维存在

在女主人公凯斯的叙述中，黑尔舍姆的存在和其他任何一所英国寄宿学校是没有太大的差异的。它坐落在一个小村庄上，环境优美。在黑尔舍姆中，生活着一群年龄相仿的学生，还有一群照顾他们生活起居的监护人，这些监护人担当了老师的责任。监护人为学生教授知识，带他们体会诗歌的优美，欣赏绘画的艺术；还给他们开设体育课，甚至还有各种社会生活的模拟实践课；监护人还教育学生之间要相互尊重彼此的劳动成果，重视每个人的创造能力。在这样的培养下，黑尔舍姆的学生懂得欣赏艺术，懂得互相尊重，培养了难能可贵的创造力。

与此同时，学生之间的互动也是那么自然。他们中有各自的小团体，比如女生团体的小头头露丝，她带领一班小女生开展了一个杰拉尔丁小姐的护卫队；又或者，男生群体中总是想尽办法排挤不那么有创造力的汤米。他们中也会有喜欢哗众取宠的劳拉. D，有喜欢出风头的露丝，有才华横溢的苏茜. K，有脾气暴躁的格雷厄姆 •K。当然，在一群正值青春的学生中，不可避免的荷尔蒙也总是存在，汤米. D 和凯斯 • H 之间早在凯斯第一次去安慰被排挤的汤米时就产生。

这些生活在黑尔舍姆的学生，他们和我们一样，在经过 16 年的系统教育之后，拥有了知识，懂得了常识，获得了人类所特有的理性的认知。所以，他们和我们一样，有喜怒哀乐，有爱恨情仇，懂得趋利避害，对未来的生活也充满了向往。

在这样一群克隆人身上，我们每个人都能找到我们自己的影子。他们是我们每个人的缩影。所以，可以发现，这样具有理性思维的克隆人，其实和人类本身并无差异。

2.2 克隆人基因原型影响

这样一群和我们无异的学生，在年满 16 岁之后离开黑尔舍姆到达村舍开始自己的两年过度生活，在那里，他们开始对自己的真实身份有了清晰地认知。

他们逐渐开始正视自己克隆人的身份，于是自然开始渴望寻求自己的原型，想要通过原型的生活区窥探自己内心深处的一种美好愿望。露丝在村舍"老兵"的帮助下，发现一个与自己相似的女白领。可是她很快就发现自己和那个所谓的原型一点也不像，她无助地嘶吼，说自己的原型只可能是社会的渣滓；与此同时，凯斯也在努力寻找自己的原型，因为自身性欲的强烈，她不停地翻阅色情杂志，希望能在那些杂志中寻得自己的原型，但是终究未果。

随着对文本本身的仔细解读，一条条线索逐渐清晰，露丝和校长艾米丽小姐以及凯斯和夫人玛丽小姐之间的关联愈发明显。在小说的第三部分，汤米和凯斯找到夫人的家，看到夫人以及校长艾米丽小姐。此时的艾米丽小姐已经腿脚不便而只能坐在轮椅上，之前仅接受第一次捐献后就腿脚不便的露丝；校长艾米丽小姐说，"只有我在为你们所有的人操心和质问"，露丝也总是"正在尽极大的努力，这不单单是为她自己，也是为了我们所有人"，这样强势的艾米丽校长和露丝又多像。而凯斯和夫人之间的默契更是明显。凯斯一人在寝室听着 never let me go 的磁带，脑海中幻想自己抱着一个孩子转圈，内心渴望自己也有孕育的权力，而看见此景的夫人竟然仿佛能感受一些凯斯自己还未意识到的悲凉，早已泪流满面；在第三部分凯斯和汤米离开夫人家时，夫人深情地抚摸着凯斯的脸，全身一阵战栗并且眼含泪水。这一切不更像是一个"过来人"看着曾经的自己才能表现出的感同身受以及满含眷念么？此外，在文章第一部分，凯斯和露丝两人仅仅因为几匹根本不存在的马就成为关系无比紧密的密友，这样种种的联系难道不是和夫人以及艾米丽校长十分相似么。至于与凯斯和露丝关系十分密切的汤米则更像是被刻意隐藏起来的夫人家中的第四人。汤米和凯斯进门后就听见一个从楼上传来的男声，可是后面这个男人却始终没有出场过，只有一个推着夫人从屋后出现的乔治。这样一个只闻其声不见其人的第四者，我们可否把他当成是和汤米十分酷似的男子，他的出现也许会马上暴露出他是汤米原型的事实，因而他才始终未出现过。

如果这些假设是成立的，那么这些克隆人实实在在的原型就那样存在着，甚至原型的基因中的某些因素还会对他们的生活产生至关重要的影响，那么这样的克隆人在构造上可以说，和人类别无二致。即便是这样的原型假设不成立，这些克隆人也总是存在原型的，他们的基因构造和人类的差异又有什么呢？

于是我们不难得出，和人类拥有一样的基因组成，还和人类一样拥有理性认知的克隆人们和人类，竟然没有本质上的区别，他们的存在就是一个个人类的存在。

2.3 克隆人群体人性本质探究

通过前文我们先后论证了克隆人在生理上和人类无异，并且拥有和人类一样的理性的思维，继而我们可以认为《别让我走》中黑尔舍姆里的克隆人和人类在本质上没有区别，那么在这样一群和人类无异的克隆人身上所表现出的人性中的本质是什么呢？

不难看出，小说中的主人公一直在探寻自己的身份，想要知道自己和外面世界的人们有什么不一样；当他们知道自己真实身份之后又开始努力寻找自己的原型，想通过原型的存在去窥探他们生存的本质，去证明自己生命的本质。他们一直在渴望一个真相，追寻一个机会，可是在这个追寻的过程中，具有人性的克隆人不可避免地表现出人性中本质存在的东西——自私。

首先，这些在黑尔舍姆的克隆人一直处于被管理的状态，他们对自我没有主动的意识，因而也就没有自主的行为，但是这样的状况在露西老师对他们告知了他们真正要面对什么之后便有所改变。在那之后，他们清楚地知道自己不可能去美国，不可能成为演员，不可能成为售货员，也知道自己的存在就是为了等到自己器官成熟之后完成捐献，所以他们也知道露西老师这样的告知也许是不被黑尔舍姆所允许的。可是，在他们得知这样的消息之后，没有一个人为可怜的露西老师的处境考虑过，哪怕是一点也没有。甚至在之后大家知道露西老师“被”离开之后，都不曾有过担忧和后悔，而是“活跃”地谈论这件事，眼中充满了“兴奋”。当时的克隆人已经 16 岁，这是一个足够思考的年龄，可是他们没有一点为露西老师考虑过，只在乎自己知道了真相，只在乎自己又多了一个谈资。

其次，除了表现在群体身上的自私之外，表现在个体身上的自私本性也不难发现。小说的一条主线就是围绕主人公之间的三角恋展开的，而这三角恋的开端便是出于露丝的自私。小说从头至尾都可以读出汤米和凯斯之间的情愫，可是偏偏是汤米和露丝在一起，而凯斯和汤米却只有在最终才终于在一起了不到一年的时间。这期间的因素很多，主要包括两个方面。一方面可能出自于汤米本身的“俄狄浦斯”情节，如“爱之魂—基于三重人格讨论《别让我走》男主人公形象分析”中得出的结论一般，汤米最初接受露丝可能出于本我的性渴望，而和凯斯之间的情愫一直到超我的完善逐渐实现，一直到最终在自我的调节下，平静而不舍地离开。但更重要的另一方面是出于露丝的自私。在第三部分露丝在最终要“终结”之前她向汤米和凯斯坦诚自己是出于自私才破坏了他们，她早看出他们之间的情愫，可是不希望自己被排挤在外，于是她抢先一步和汤米在一起。甚至在以后的过程中，不断地刺激凯斯，在到达村舍之后这样的行为更是变本加厉，刻意使凯斯曲解自己的性欲，使汤米和凯斯之间的关系疏远。可以说，小说中的主线之一的三角恋就是靠露丝的自私在推动。

由此可见，在具有人性的克隆人身上也不可避免地体现出人性中本质上的自私。

3 黑尔舍姆体制下的人性中自私本质探究

黑尔舍姆作为贯穿整本小说的一个存在，其作用主要存在以下三点：首先，其起到地理隔绝的作用，将黑尔舍姆的学生与外界隔离，隔断学生对外的任何可能性，加强了黑尔舍姆本身的权力；其次，黑尔舍姆还有认知隔绝作用，克隆人在黑尔舍姆接受到的教育使他们对自身捐献的使命根深蒂固，从而剥夺了克隆人真正获得主体自由的可能性。此外，黑尔舍姆对于身处其中的监护人或者人类来说，相当于是一个人性避难所，他们通过在黑尔舍姆中对克隆人的照顾和奔走来获得良知上的慰藉，当最终黑尔舍姆破产后，这样的人性避难所的消失更加衬托出小说中人性本质上的自私无可避免的主题。

3.1 黑尔舍姆的地理隔绝作用

小说中对黑尔舍姆地理位置的描述是“黑尔舍姆位于一个四周都是高地的平整山谷中。这就意味从主楼的几乎每个教室的窗口，甚至是从体育馆往外看，你都能有一个开阔的视野，可以清楚地看到又长又窄的道路穿过田野，一直到大门口。”这样的设计类似于边沁的“圆形监狱”，由一个中央塔楼和四周环形的囚室组成，环形监狱的中心，是一个瞭望塔，所有囚室对着中央监视塔，每一个囚室有一前一后两扇窗户，一扇朝着中央塔楼，一扇背对着中央塔楼，作为通光之用。这样的设计使得处在中央塔楼的监视者可以便利地观察到囚室里的罪犯的一举一动，对犯人却了如指掌。同时监视塔有百叶窗，囚徒不知是否被监视以及何时被监视，因此囚徒不敢轻举妄动，从心理上感觉到自己始终处在被监视的状态，时时刻刻迫使自己循规蹈矩。这就实现了“自我监禁”——监禁无所不在地潜藏进了他们的内心。在这样结构的监狱中，就是狱卒不在，由于始终感觉有一双监视的眼睛，犯人们也不会任意胡闹，他们会变得相当的守纪律，相当的自觉。

这样借助于特殊地理环境建立的黑尔舍姆在某种意义上对学生来说就是一种“自我监禁”之所，在这里，学生随时都感觉自己正在被监视，不敢高声说话，不敢随意谈论自己的小秘密，因而每个人都变得小心翼翼。在行动被禁锢的同时，自己的思想也被禁闭的环境限制，变得战战兢兢。

同时，黑尔舍姆的学生和外界接触的方式只有通过一辆辆定期运来外界物资的车辆而已。这样的生活彻底隔绝了学生和外界的联系，使得他们只能被动地接受他们所处的黑尔舍姆的规则，再没有多余的选择。

3.2 黑尔舍姆的认知隔绝作用

除了依凭地理位置对学生造成心理监视作用之外，黑尔舍姆还同时对学生进行认知阻断。

黑尔舍姆与外界的界限只有一排矮小的栅栏，可是这里的学生都很自觉的没有一个人敢去跨越，这除了“自我监禁”的因素外，还得益于黑尔舍姆对学生进行的认知隔绝。在黑尔舍姆流传两则关于这个小树林的传说，一个小男孩和朋友吵架之后跑出去，两天之后尸体被发现绑在林子深处的一棵树上，手脚都被砍掉了；另外一个传说是一个小女孩想看看外面的世界是什么样子的，于是偷偷爬出栅栏，可是之后就再也没能回到黑尔舍姆，不知道去了哪里，再之后就死了，据说灵魂一直在黑尔舍姆外的林子游荡。这样的传说一直弥漫在每一个黑尔舍姆的克隆人耳边，让他们从小就知道外面世界的恐怖，不敢也不愿意跨出黑尔舍姆一步；同时，在黑尔舍姆的每一天都是从校长艾米丽小姐的晨会开始的，她会无数次地重复抽烟对身体的害处，会不厌其烦地提醒学生要注意保持自身身体的健康状态。

谎言重复的次数多了也会成真，在黑尔舍姆持续16年的认知灌输中，学生们对自己身份的认知，对自己责任的认知都逐渐根深蒂固，变得不可动摇。

这样的认知隔绝不仅使学生接受了自己被硬加上的使命之外，在很大程度上限制了克隆人思维发展的可能性，这也解释了为什么克隆人在到达村舍之后可以自由接触外界，可是仍旧没有人愿意那么做，也解释为什么在以后的捐献日子中，尽管很痛苦和绝望可没有一个人想过要逃离。因为这样的思想早在他们幼时就已经被逐渐地抹杀掉了。

4 黑尔舍姆体制下人性本质中自私因素探究

黑尔舍姆在文中的设定似乎是在一个人性缺失的时代中仅存不多的希望唤醒人性的地方了，黑尔舍姆的老师努力照顾学生的生活起居，教授他们知识，顾虑他们的身体健康，告诉他们外界的生活，培养他们的创造力，希望证明他们也是和人类一样拥有灵魂的。可是这样的一个存在真的是这样的么？

首先，黑尔舍姆这样一个地方容不下任何真正考虑学生的监护人的存在。露西老师的出现为他们造成了麻烦，使学生过早过于直白地知道自己的使命，于是露西老师很快被排除出黑尔舍姆。

其次，黑尔舍姆更像是一个传销组织一般的存在。这样一个“学校”传播的知识是学生要注重身体健康的保护，保证器官的良好状态，还编织一个恐怖的外界给学生，禁锢他们行动的同时还一点点入侵他们的思想。

再者，黑尔舍姆的老师都把自己当作时代的卫士，他们为了维护人性而奔走，为了可怜的克隆人付出了年华。可是，通过文中的描述，不难看出，这些监护人对学生都是“冷冰冰”的，没有丝毫感情。热心帮助学生证明灵魂存在的夫人也“怕我们，就如同有人害怕蜘蛛一样”。这样矛盾的情绪出现在一个一心想要帮助克隆人的监护人身上难道不是一种讽刺么？什么样的人才能一遍口口声声证明我看护的是和我们一样的正常人，却又一边深深厌恶并且像惧怕动物一样躲避看护的学生？这样的人性难道不是虚伪的么？或许我们应该说黑尔舍姆的人们不过是为了自身的利益而奔走，他们甚至更为残酷，赋予克隆人灵魂，却在18年后仍旧要他们接受他们不是人，并且永远不可能成为人的事实，然后在他们传播的固化思维之下平静地接受捐赠的命运。更为可笑的是，这样的一群人还在不断被自己的伟大表象所感动，一个连自己都骗过的人，难道不是真的可笑么？

终于，这样的假象也许再也维持不下去了，莫宁戴尔创造出的克隆人更为优秀，可能比人类本身更加优秀，这样的行为彻底激怒了人类。之前为黑尔舍姆投资的人不敢大意了，于是资金链断了，黑尔舍姆关门了。这样的关闭或许意味人类最后为了唤醒人性的尝试的失败，又或者意味人类已经连这块遮羞布都不想再需要了。

对于黑尔舍姆中的艾米丽校长或者是玛丽夫人来说，黑尔舍姆是她们的一项事业，她们为了这项事业游走在各权贵之间为克隆人的短暂权益做着争取，可是最后，该项事业毫无悬念地失败了，一来要归咎于人们不愿意放弃克隆为他们带来的健康长寿；二来更是因为慈善也好，维权也罢，更还有所谓“映射灵魂”的艺术，其实都不过是某些人寻求自我满足的渠道。与克隆技术的实用相比，艺术终究无用。更有甚者，就连“艺术无目的且无功用”的说法都是现代社会的产物，是现代社会运作所必需的意识形态。

在黑尔舍姆中体现出的校长或者夫人的形象确实包含善意的存在，她们愿意为了克隆人的权益去奔走，为他们争取可能的权利，可是更多表现出的是她们人性中的虚伪和自私。她们在为克隆人争取权益的同时却仍旧禁锢他们的思维，让他们为捐献做足了准备，切断了他们其他的可能性。她们所谓的四处奔走游说与其说是为了克隆人的利益，笔者认为更多的是为自己谋得利益，游走于上层资助者之中，然后以造物主的形象出现在克隆人面前，为了表现自己的价值，自私地赋予克隆人短暂的自由然后再将他们永远地打入黑暗。

此外，体现在黑尔舍姆的机制之中的还有对黑尔舍姆进行过资助的“财主”们。他们最初认为证明克隆人的灵魂所在对自己也不会有太大的影响，所以慷慨解囊，可是当莫宁戴尔研究出更高级的克隆人之后，在意识到这些克隆人本身可能是比人类更完善存在的时候，他们为了自身的利益，为了获得高高在上的地位，为了获得更久的寿命，他们毫不犹豫地中断了资助，那些可怜的克隆人再也不在他们的考虑范围之内了。

不难发现，隐藏于黑尔舍姆这样一所乡间寄宿学校之下的是难以隐藏的人性的自私。他们的自私或许出于不同的目的，可是他们的归根却都逃不脱人性的本质。

5 小　结

小说《别让我走》中，通过将克隆人塑造成替罪羊的形象，一步步揭示出人性本质中的自私。通过作者的讲述，我们不难发现，克隆人经过和人类一样的学习，获得了理性思维，与人类一样拥有了灵魂，在本质上已经成为与人类无异的存在，但是一方面，人类本身为了自身的利益忽视克隆人灵魂的存在，体现了人性本身的自私；另一方面，具有了人性的克隆人也在自己的群体中体现出自私的本质，这样的安排进一步加深了主题；同时黑尔舍姆的存在揭示了人性尝试寻找遮蔽所的失去，从而更加凸显出自私这一人性本质的无可避免。

参考文献

[1] 段琦. 经典译林：圣经故事[M]. 南京：译林出版社，2013.

[2] 谷伟. 泅浮泡影——略论《千万别弃我而去》中“黑尔舍姆”的体制悖论[J]. 当代外国文学，2010（5）.

[3] 郭国良. “宿命”下的自由生存——《永远别让我离去》中的生存取向[J]. 当代外国文学，2007（3）.

[4] 梁玉倩. 爱之魂——基于三重人格理论的《别让我走》男主人公形象分析[J]. 海外英语，2013.

[5] 李里. 无处可逃的人生——评《别让我走》[J]. 郑州航空工业管理学院学报（社会科学版），2014（1）.

[6] 石黑一雄. 别让我走[M]. 朱去疾译. 南京：译林出版社，2011.

[7] 钟尹. 替罪羊原型：一个宗教、文学人类学研究模式[C]. 智能信息技术应用学会会议论文集，2015.

《活着》与《老人与海》中主人公的认知模式对比研究
——在“独立”与“互立”间寻求生存希望

陈玥含

摘　要：本论文以“独立”和“互立”这两个认知心理学概念为基础，探讨和分析我国作家余华的《活着》与美国作家海明威的《老人与海》两部作品中主人公认知模式的异同点。众多研究者指出，西方文化崇尚个人自治自足和自我表达，将自己看作是不同于他人和社会环境的独特个体，从而形成“独立型自我”；而许多亚洲文化强调社会等级、群体团结、人际和谐，将个体看作关系网络中的一个，与周边环境不可分割，从而形成“互立型自我”。通过对比分析《活着》与《老人与海》两者间主人公为了求得生存希望，与作品中其他人物和周围环境既相互依存，又不得不各自独立的认知模式，并且因认知模式的差异性存在，而产生了不大相同的结局效果。中西方文学作品人物在面对苦难环境时，共同都表现出双重认知模式，即独立与互立共存，从而寻求生的可能。

关键词：《活着》；《老人与海》；认知模式；独立；互立

1 引　言

在众多已有的文学研究中，研究者对于《活着》和《老人与海》的对比研究，大多表现在两部作品中人物的生存意识、孤独意识和死亡意识等方面，而基于“独立”与“互立”这两个认知心理学概念，对于人物面对艰难环境时的认知模式，即中西方作品中人物的认知模式这一点研究甚少。众多研究者指出，西方文化崇尚个人自治、自足和自我表达，将自己看作是不同于他人和社会环境的独特个体，从而形成“独立型自我”；而许多亚洲文化强调社会等级、群体团结、人际和谐，将个体看作关系网络中的一个，与周边环境不可分割，从而形成“互立型自我”[①]。

在《活着》与《老人与海》两部作品中，前者是国内当代著名作家余华生于20世纪中后期，后者著名美国作家欧内斯特·米勒尔·海明威生于19世纪末期。两个来自不同国度、生于不同年代的作家在分别叙述两部作品时，却碰撞出相似的火花。在两部作品中，主人公都或多或少地表现出“独立”与“互立”的认知模式。本文将“独立”与“互立”看作两种基本的自我认知与文化认知框架。在之前的研究中，“独立”文化中的人被认为习惯于相对整洁有序、目标物清晰的环境，感知时往往聚焦于前景化的目标物，其自我认知框架往往将自我前景化，将周围环境、语境背景化，强调主体的自主性、独立性；而“互立”文化中的人习惯于更复杂交织的环境，感知时注重背景语境及事物之间的联系，其认知框架的前景与背景更容易交融甚至交替，自我的界定更依赖于环境。反映在叙事风格上，“独立”型认知框架在自传性叙事和回忆虚构类故事中细节更丰满，更强调的是那些特殊事件以及自己的主观感受，而“互立”型认知框架产生的自我描述或故事回忆更为笼统，更强调典型的、符合文化规约的事件[②]。

2 《活着》与《老人与海》简介

《活着》是一部长篇小说，是作家余华的代表作。主人公徐福贵嗜赌成性，赌光了家业，一贫如洗，穷困之中的福贵因为母亲生病前去求医，没想到半路上被国民党部队抓了壮丁，等他再回到家，女儿已经成了哑巴，母亲也病了，家里一点吃的也没有。真正的悲剧从此才开始渐次上演。家珍因患有软骨病而干不了重活；儿子因与县长夫人血型相同，为救县长夫人抽血过多而亡；女儿凤霞与队长介绍的城里的偏头二喜喜结良缘，产下一男婴后，因大出血死在手术台上；而凤霞死后三个月家珍也相继去世；二喜是搬运工，因吊车出了差错，被两排水泥板夹死；外孙苦根便随福贵回到乡下，生活十分艰难，就连豆子都很难吃上，福贵心疼便给苦根煮豆吃，不料苦根却因吃豆子撑死……生命里难得的温情被一次次死亡撕扯得粉碎，只剩得老了的福贵伴随一头老牛在阳光下回忆。他的亲人因为天灾人祸先后离他而去，让他孑然一身地活在这个世界上。

《老人与海》是海明威于1951年在古巴写的一部中篇小说，于1952年出版。《老人与海》写的是老渔夫圣地亚哥在海上的捕鱼经历：老人制服大马林鱼后，在返航途中又同鲨鱼进行惊险的搏斗。作品中的形象具有很强的象征意蕴，他用大马林鱼象征人生的理想和人类作为生命本身所不可避免的所具有的欲望，用鲨鱼象征无法摆脱的悲剧命运，用大海象征变化无常的人类社会，而狮子则是勇武健壮、仇视邪恶、能创造奇迹的象征，圣地亚哥则是人类中的勇士与强大势力搏斗的“硬汉子”代表，他那捕鱼的不幸遭遇象征人类总是与厄运不断抗争却无论如何都无法试图去改变命运。“一艘船越过世界的尽头，驶向未知的大海，船头上悬挂着一面虽然饱经风雨剥蚀却依旧艳丽无比的旗帜，旗帜上，舞着云龙一般的四个字闪闪发光——超越极限！”

3 认知心理学中“独立”与“互立”的认知模式简介

认知心理学的研究范围包括感知觉、注意、表象、学习记忆，思维和言语等心理过程或认知过程以及儿童的认知发展和人工智能。本论文中提到的“独立”和“互立”是指人在感知觉时所表现出来的认知特征。“独立”就是指人感知时表现的个体独立性的认知特点，自己决定或选择事物而不受其他外界因素或限制条件的影响，这种认知模式通常表现在成年人的感知当中。自己选择和决定某事物，但也不完全说明成年人就完全具有“独立”的特征，感知觉成熟的青少年同样具有“独立”的认知模式；相反的是，在“互立”的认知模式中，人的感知觉很多时候往往需要依赖外界因素和周围环境来获得个体的满足感、安全感或是成就感，个体在做决定或选择时也需要依赖其他因素的存在才得以实现。这种认知模式大多表现在缺乏社会经验的青少年身上，但也不绝对。这两种认知模式各有特征，处于不同年龄段和人生阶段的个体，在感知觉时会选择不同的认知模式，并且在中西方的价值观里，个体的认知模式也存在明显的差异性。比如，诸多研究者认为，西方人因历史因素和社会因素等一直崇尚个人自治自足和自我表达，将自己看作是不同于他人和社会环境的独特个体，从而形成“独立型自我”；而许多亚洲文化强调社会等级、群体团结、人际和谐，将个体看作关系网络中的一个，与周边环境不可分割，从而形成“互立型自我”。很明显的例子就是“美国梦”与

“中国梦”，前者提倡通过个人努力实现个人价值，后者强调通过集体的努力实现国家富强民主和谐和个人价值。

4 《活着》与《老人与海》主人公认知模式的相似性

4.1 《活着》与《老人与海》主人公的“独立”

《活着》主人公徐福贵本来是地主家的少爷，年轻时不懂事，又赌又嫖，后来龙二设下赌局骗光了他的家产。败光家产后，幸得妻子不离不弃，他也决定发愤图强。但在去给生病的母亲请郎中时被抓了壮丁。后被解放军俘虏，给他返乡钱让其返乡，与家人重逢。本以为就此以后可以安安心心过日子，但又不得不经历三反五反，大跃进的潮流更迭。更加让他惨淡的是，他的儿子有庆因为跑去给县长夫人输血，而被活生生的抽死在了医院。他本想着和那县长拼命的，但是后来却没想到连报仇都不行，因为这县长刚好又是他被抓去当壮丁时的战友春生。再后来他的女儿在生孩子的时候也因为大出血死在了这所医院，他的老婆家珍没过多久也因苦痛的命运而去世，他的女婿因为工地事故也死了，只留下他和他的孙子。但没想到的是，最后连他的孙子也因为吃豆子而被活生生撑死了，只留下他与一头老牛相依为命。

从主人公徐福贵个人整个生命历程来看，他所遭遇的结局具有悲剧性。但在生命过程中仍存有一丝希望，那就是他个人靠心理上的“独立”来表明自己还不是那么脆弱，比如输光了家产还决定靠自己发愤图强来获得重生，并还要支撑家庭重担，要养育母亲和照顾妻子儿女。在母亲去世后不久，妻子家珍也相继离开人世。之后所有的重担全靠福贵这样一位父亲和爷爷的身份来承担。在孙子吃豆子被撑死后，福贵完全就是一个人度过余生了，再也没有亲人的后果，需要他独自靠强大心理来支撑自己活下去。他所经历的三反五反，大跃进的潮流更迭等周围环境是恶劣的，也就是不得不靠“独立”活下去，否则只有死路一条。这些细节都表明福贵还是“独立”的，在内外环境窘迫的情况下，个体还得靠自己“独立”支撑着，才会显得生命虽然脆弱，但并不渺小。

《老人与海》的主人公圣地亚哥在出海的第八十五天后，与一条巨大的马林鱼在离岸很远的湾流中搏斗。老人制服大马林鱼后，在返航途中又同鲨鱼进行惊险的搏斗。这是一场人与自然搏斗的惊心动魄的悲剧。老人每取得一点胜利都付出了惨重的代价，最后遭到无可挽救的失败。但是，从另外一种意义上来说，他又是一个胜利者。因为他不屈服于命运，无论再怎么艰苦卓绝的环境里，他都凭着自己的勇气、毅力和智慧进行奋勇的抗争。大马林鱼虽然没有保住，但他却捍卫了“人的灵魂的尊严”，显示了“一个人的能耐可以到达什么程度”，是一个胜利的失败者，一个失败的英雄。这样一个“硬汉子”形象正是典型的海明威式的小说人物。海明威笔下的圣地亚哥是非常“独立”的，老人拒绝了想要一起前往捕鱼的小男孩马洛林，或许是因为老人的固执，或许是因为老人不想旁人干扰，或许是为了显示自己个体强大的抗争力量，老人都是“独立”形象的存在。

在面对艰难的处境，无论是充满苦楚的社会环境还是恶劣的自然环境，主人公徐福贵和主人公圣地亚哥都用“独立”证明了自己作为个体的价值，不放弃，勇敢面对所遇到的一切。所以，无论是国内的文学作品还是国外的文学作品，作家在体现生命主题时，都表达出主人公的“独立”特征。

4.2 《活着》与《老人与海》主人公的“互立”

《活着》中主人公徐福贵在自己的人生中，虽然接连遭受不好的事情，比如，败光家产后，妻子仍然不离不弃，这就是最大的精神支柱，支撑他继续面对狼狈的生活烂摊子。在母亲和妻子都相继离开人世后，福贵活着的精神支柱中还有儿女和孙子。作家余华把重复发生的死亡事件镶嵌在日常琐碎的生活里，放大了“苦难”的广度和深度，使渺小而软弱的福贵面对巨大的“苦难”形成的力量悬殊，从而产生一种强烈的命运感，最后福贵所有剩余的亲人都一个个死去，只剩下他一个孤零零的老头和一头同样年迈的老黄牛相伴，并且是那样乐观豁达的活着，完全出乎人的意料，也更加彰显了活着的意义和难能可贵。在作品中，福贵已经不仅仅是为了自己而活着，而是为了整个家庭和亲人而活。所以他也不仅仅是“独立”的一个人，也是家庭关系中与亲人，甚至和老黄牛拥有“互立”关系，相互依存。

《老人与海》中主人公圣地亚哥与次要人物小男孩马洛林的关系中，始终保持非一般的朋友关系。小男孩在老人独自出海捕鱼前，时时刻刻跟着老人一起出海捕鱼，并且一起与老人谈论球赛，关心老人的衣食住行。在这种情况下，老人当然也十分乐意和小男孩相处，在物质与精神方面都与小男孩保持亲人一般的“互立”关系。在老人独自出海前，小男孩十分想再次与老人一起出海捕鱼，帮助老人实现捕到大鱼的愿望，但被老人拒绝，而让小男孩与父母的船待在一起，这或许是老人想要保护小男孩的安全问题，才不让其一起出海。但在老人独自出海的过程中，却有好几次表示要是小男孩在自己身边该多好。从这种心理可以看出，老人虽然“独立”，却在面临大海风暴和各种需要对抗的食人鱼面前依然渴望与小男孩马洛林的“互立”关系，想着马洛林在情况可能就不会那么糟。

同样，《活着》与《老人与海》在表达生命和灾难主题时，虽然主人公徐福贵和圣地亚哥都不得不“独立”面对命运遭受的一切，却仍然拥有或渴望拥有“互立”关系，从而使作为生命个体的自己通过拥有精神支柱而变得更加强大。所以在中西方文学表现生命主题的作品中，作家在描写主人公时，都体现其“互立”的特征。

4.3 《活着》与《老人与海》主人公认知模式的差异性

本文作者认为，余华的《活着》和海明威的《老人与海》虽然都不同程度地表现了主人公在面对艰难处境时的“独立”和“互立”，两个结局也有一定的相似性，即悲剧性结局。徐福贵本来是地主家的少爷，身份地位较高，年轻时不懂事，所以才在输光家产后变得不可收拾，这一悲剧也是必然的，就算是破败后，福贵再“独立”，在当时的社会历史环境中，也难以翻身。相反，若是福贵在破败之前，能够在地主身份的前提下，就保持清醒和“独立”，不为周围环境所动摇，就不会遭受家产和地位破败的下场。再者，处理好与家庭亲人之间的“互立”关系，那福贵活着的结局应该不是悲剧色彩的，而是灿烂而美好地活着。

《老人与海》主人公圣地亚哥虽然在独自出海后表现出坚韧勇敢的硬汉形象和抗争精神，但却明显地感受到“独立”面对艰难的孤独感，若是老人圣地亚哥在出海前答应小男孩与其一起，享受捕鱼艰难过程中的“互立”关系，一起并肩抗战，老人圣地亚哥与小男孩一起消灭大马林鱼和鲨鱼，并捕到大鱼，结局就不会那么具有孤独感的悲剧色彩。也就是说，《活着》的主人公徐福贵更加“独立”些，《老人与海》的主人公圣地亚哥更加“互立”些，那么两个主人公的结局都将更好。

5 结 论

在“独立”与“互立”这两个认知心理学概念的基础上，《活着》与《老人与海》的主人公在面对苦难时分别都表现出“独立”和“互立”的双重特征，但又有偏重点，《活着》的徐福贵更偏重于“互立”，《老人与海》中的圣地亚哥更偏重于“独立”。若是两个主人公都在“独立”与“互立”间找寻到平衡点，那结局可能大不相同。通过对比分析《活着》与《老人与海》两者间主人公为了求得生存希望，与作品中其他人物和周围环境既相互依存，又不得不各自独立的认知模式，并且因认知模式的细小差异性存在，而又产生了不大相同的结局效果。进一步发现，中西方文学作品人物在面对苦难环境时，共同都表现出双重认知模式，即独立与互立共存的模式。若是人物在“独立”与“互立”间找寻到平衡点，那么在处于不同的人生阶段都能够很好地面对和处理困难。

注 解

① 众多研究者指出，西方文化崇尚个人自治、自足和自我表达，将自己看作是不同于他人和社会环境的独特个体，从而形成“独立型自我”；而许多亚洲文化强调社会等级、群体团结、人际和谐，将个体看作关系网络中的一个，与周边环境不可分割，从而形成“互立型自我”。这一部分来自于邹涛教授的期刊《任璧莲及其作品人物的认知模式变化——在“独立”与“互立”间寻找平衡》。

② 对于“独立”和“互立”的理解，部分来自于邹涛教授的期刊《任璧莲及其作品人物的认知模式变化——在“独立”与“互立”间寻找平衡》。

参 考 文 献

[1] Markus，H.R. & Kitayama，S., 1991. Culture and the self: Implications for cognition，emotion，and motivation.*Psychological Review*，98：pp224-253.

[2] Matsukawa，Yuko, 1991. *MELUS* Interview with Gish Jen. *MELUS*，18.4. 19 Jan.

[3] 2015<https://www.q Earnest Hemingway，*The Old Man and the Sea*. Foreign Language Press，Beijing，2015. Print.

[4] 邓楠. 国内《老人与海》艺术特色研究述评[J]. 武陵学刊，2015（5）.

[5] 乐黛云. 比较文学与中国——乐黛云海外演讲[M]. 北京：北京大学出版社，2004.

[6] 王宁. 二十世纪西方文学比较研究（上）[M]. 北京：人民文学出版社，2000.

[7] 余华. 活着[M]. 上海：上海文艺出版社，2004.

[8] 邹涛. 任璧莲及其作品人物的认知模式变化——在“独立”与“互立”间寻找平衡[J]. 当代外国文学，2016（1）：22-28.

新批评视域下的《老人与海》的结局合理性分析

廖梦园

摘　要：《老人与海》是一部凝聚海明威高度艺术性和深刻思想的作品，前人对其进行了大量的研究，但很少有人探究小说中的主要意象是如何构建文本的整体意义的。本论文从《老人与海》中两组三角关系出发，即“老人”与“马林鱼”“鲨鱼”之间的矛盾与统一，“老人”与“狮子”“小男孩”之间的矛盾与统一，分析三者分别构成精神世界和现实世界的对立这一有机整体的过程，从而论证该小说的结局合理性，彰显老人的悲剧精神，反映人类追求的宝贵品质，更加深刻地展现该小说自身蕴含的高度艺术性。

本篇论文主要分为四个部分。前两节简要介绍小说内容、理论联系；之后对文中主要人物形象进行分析；第三部分则是对两组三角关系分别的矛盾与统一进行描述，以表现小说的核心内涵，最后两节则是得出两组关系分别构成精神世界和现实世界的对立这一有机整体的结论。

关键词：意象；《老人与海》；有机整体；结局合理性

Abstract: *The Old Man and the Sea* is a work that brings together Hemingway' s highly artistry and profound thoughts. Predecessors have done a lot of researches on it. However, few people have explored how the main images in the novel construct the overall meaning of the text. This thesis starts with two triangular relationships in *The Old Man and the Sea*, namely the contradiction and unity among the old man, the marlin fish and the shark, and the old man, the lion and the little boy. The process of respectively constituting the opposition between the spiritual world and the real world, that is the organic unity, will be analyzed, so as to demonstrate the rationality of the ending of the novel, highlight the tragic spirit of the old man, reflect the valuable qualities pursued by mankind, and finally demonstrate more profoundly the highly artistry the novel itself contains.

This thesis includes four parts. The first two chapters simply introduces the novel's content, relationship between the novel and theory, then analyzes the main character images; The third part is the description of the contradiction and unity of two triangular relationships, to show the core connotation of the novel, and the last part is the conclusion that these triangular relationships respectively constitute the organic unity of the spiritual world and real world.

Key words: Image; *The Old Man and the Sea*; organic unity; the rationality of the ending

1 引　言

《老人与海》是海明威在 1952 年发表的中篇小说。其讲述的故事是一名叫圣地亚哥的老渔夫独自出海打鱼，在一无所获的 84 天后，历经艰辛捕获一只巨大无比的马林鱼，但是在与鲨鱼的殊死搏斗中最终败下阵来，无力回天，马林鱼被鲨鱼几乎吃光。老人最后拖回家的只剩一副光秃秃的鱼骨架。文中他热情地讴歌了人类面对艰难困苦时所显示的坚不可摧的精神力量。故事的最后，小男孩决心一直陪伴老人，学会老人的各种本领，这象征人类这种“永不言败”的精神将世代相传。

“圣地亚哥是海明威所崇尚的完美的人的象征：坚强、宽厚、仁慈、充满爱心，即使在人生的角斗场上失败了，面对不可逆转的命运，他仍然是精神上的强者，是“硬汉子”。“硬汉子”是海明威作品中经常出现的主题，也是作品中常有的人物。他们在外界巨大的压力和厄运打击时，仍然坚强不屈，勇往直前，甚至视死如归，他们尽管失败了，却保持了人的尊严和勇气，有着胜利者的风度。”（《海明威》，3）

前人对该小说进行了大量的研究，研究对象主要有从各理论、各视角出发，对比其不同译本的研究，有从女性主义、生态批评的角度去解读《老人与海》，也有从内容出发，分析主人公的各类形象与性格的文章。相对而言，从新批评角度来解读它的文献较少，更不用说探究小说中的主要意象是如何构建文本的整体意义，由此笔者尝试从此角度出发，对该小说进行解读，试图挖掘该小说中故事叙述与结局安排的独特魅力。

2 理论与文本的关联

选用新批评理论中的有机整体性概念对该小说进行解读主要有以下几方面。

2.1 小说本身

小说的篇幅属于中篇，使用新批评理论可以更容易地充分解读其各形式要素。这是从新批评理论本身的适用性出发，应运而生出使用该理论，对该篇小说进行解读的可行性。

2.2 小说的意象

小说中的意象十分丰富，例如：狮子、马林鱼、鲨鱼、飞鱼、金枪鱼、鲯鳅鱼等等，这有利于从文本出发进行批评分析，而这一点正是新批评家们所倡导的从文学作品本身出发，可以更加直接和客观地了解文本的深层含义。

2.3 小说的写作风格

从该小说的写作风格可以看出，作者海明威采用第三人称的全知全能视角，使用最简洁的语言，平淡地描述事件的发展进程，使其内涵丰富，并力求行文简洁，语词简朴，也就是海明威坚持的冰山原则：“水面上的那一部分占 1/8，在水下的那部分占 7 / 8。你知道的一切都可以删去，这只会强化你的冰山，就是水下的那一部分。”（3）这种独特的写作风格能够吸引人去考量、欣赏该作品的伟大之处。

3 人物形象分析

3.1 老人—站在黑夜与白昼交界处的男人

在别人眼中，老渔夫“圣地亚哥”是一名 84 天都没有捕到鱼的失败者。小说开篇便直接描写老人不顺并且孤独的生活，“He was an old man who fished alone in a skiff in the Gulf Stream and he had gone eighty-four days now without taking a fish.”“The sail was patchedwith flour sacks and，furled，it looked like the flag of permanent defeat.”“But none of these scars（on his hands）were fresh. They were as old as erosions in a fishless desert.”（*The Old Man and the Sea*1）就连唯一陪伴在他身边的小男孩也被迫离开，另谋生计等等，这一系列对老人外表和生存、生活环境的描写都能衬托出老人的惨淡生活。我们此时对他的态度绝对是同情占大多数，这也与后面发生在老人身上精彩的故事形成鲜明的对比。

其实无论在顺境还是逆境（尽管大多数时候都是逆境），老人仍然保持不服输的性格。人物的这一点品质在恶劣的生活境遇中一直是闪光点，是支撑老人精神的主要因素，更一直是我们这些读者在阅读过程中保持希望的主要原因。

老人的另一个明显的个性便是理性与感性共存。说到理性，在他逐渐远离大海的过程中，面对前方未知的风险，与迷失在海上的可能，“That makes no…what I have against me.”（39）“After it is light…too fast.”（44）不管是如何的状况他都能保持清醒的头脑，对局势进行冷静的分析，并给予自己勇气努力，寻找解决问题的办法。在左手抽筋的过程中，他不慌张，不害怕，我们甚至可以说，多次的心理暗示与自我鼓励，使得他的左手加速恢复，在他看来“手是他的兄弟”，“There are three things that are brothers：the fish and my two hands.”（57）而于自己年老的身体的信心也表现了老人对生活与自然的虔诚、热爱。如果不是对自身的信念，又怎么会有对生活的乐观呢？更别说爱自然，爱生命。就像他爱大海，温柔而深沉；他同情海龟，并认为自己如同海龟一样顽强。

后来，当老人终于收获成功的喜悦时，却又无力阻挡新的困境。他一人孤军奋战，精疲力竭，无法抵抗一波又一波鲨鱼的袭击。最后当他仅带回大马林鱼头和脊骨到家时，他已然是缔造了一个神话，那个“Champion”（64）又回来了——他是人们眼中的英雄。在我看来这样的结局悲壮而令人动容，这种结局同时包含圆满与不圆满，但老人的光辉形象已无法撼动。

3.2 小男孩—黯淡生活的色彩与希望

在老人所有的性格背后，提供给他巨大勇气的重要来源就是小男孩的存在。文中对小男孩的单独描写并不算多，但是却用了大量篇幅记录了他与老人的相处与对话。对话中充满了温情，小男孩对他时时倾情照料；即便小男孩被迫离开他，另谋生计，但是他总尽其所能帮助老人、照顾老人、安慰老人、为他赊账、陪他聊天、帮他准备鱼饵，甚至是提前想为他准备好冬天的毛毯。最重要的是，他相信老人——相信他的能力，相信老人身上蕴含的希望。

从老人独自航行的过程中可以看出，他与小男孩无比亲密且信任。不管是毫无收获的时刻，还是有所获得的时刻，他的脑海中总会回荡着“I wish I had the boy.”这句话在文中反复出现。落寞孤寂之时的渴望陪伴，收获颇丰之时的渴望分享，小男孩如黎明的阳光一样，为老人黯淡的生活带来色彩与希望。

4 三者的矛盾与统一——理想与现实的碰撞

4.1 老人、马林鱼、鲨鱼之间的矛盾与统一

4.1.1 老人与马林鱼

老人要捕马林鱼，马林鱼便是老人对某种理想的追求，或是所要达到的一种目的，他势必要捕获他，征服他，这是两者矛盾性的彰显。但是在文中的多处描写中可以看到，他也同

时将马林鱼视为自己的兄弟，（52）他尊重它，崇敬它，（47）这体现了老人对自然的尊重，对理想的尊重，这也是老人的精神的一大亮点。

4.1.2 老人与鲨鱼

老人为实现自己的目标，守护自己的“理想”，要抵抗鲨鱼的凶残进攻，而且鲨鱼的攻击险些使他丧命，这是他们的矛盾性所在。对鲨鱼凶残性的描写反衬出老人的勇敢无畏，正如黑格尔所说：“人格的伟大和刚强的程度，只有借矛盾对立面的伟大和刚强的程度才能衡量出来。”

4.1.3 马林鱼与鲨鱼

鲨鱼要吃马林鱼，两者是天生的敌对关系。但是鲨鱼作为现实环境残酷的代表，作为人们追求理想与目标过程中的破坏性力量，它显示出马林鱼的难得，显示出实现目标过程的艰辛和现实的困难重重。

4.2 老人、小男孩、狮子之间的矛盾与统一

4.2.1 老人与狮子

“狮子”在小说中出现多次，有在老人与小男孩的对话中，也有在老人的睡梦中，或是其幻想与回忆中。在前人的研究里，有人说狮子是力量的象征，宗教信仰的体现，也有人说是意志力、王者与胜利的代表。在我看来，狮子还是老人精神世界的守护神。

首先，在老人与小男孩谈论起狮子的时候，我们可以看出狮子给予老人信念般的力量。尽管连续 84 天没有捕到鱼，但是他仍表现出老当益壮的心态，他坚信他总会成功的。其次，在老人出海的过程中，狮子常常出现在他的睡梦中，他能通过梦见狮子，重获面对一无所获的窘境的勇气，或是征服猎物的理智，使自己的心安定下来，并且重拾信心，保持精神的傲立。这个时候的狮子是老人的精神支柱以及作为慰藉似的陪伴。但是狮子作为精神世界的寄托，又如何不是一种对现实的躲避呢？在梦中和交谈中出现的狮子是虚幻的存在，没有人能保证这种精神世界永远不会崩塌。因此，老人与狮子之间，既有不可调和的对立立场，又彼此站在遥遥相望的两岸，给予源源不断的精神力量。

4.2.2 老人与小男孩

小男孩的存在可以说是一种现实对老人的仁慈关照。小男孩的陪伴使得这位孤独的老人并不是孑然一身，因为小男孩的出现，削弱了老人的孤独感，即便是在小男孩被迫离开他另谋生计，但二人始终惺惺相惜，彼此照应，像真正的家人一样。可是老人在证明自己能力的航海途中，他无法与小男孩同行，这是无法和谐的现实，文中多次出现的“I wish I had the boy”，（*The Old Man and the Sea* 49）深深地表现了老人的孤独和落寞。由此观之，老人和小男孩之间也同样存在矛盾与统一，尽管两者都存在着，小说的核心力量也由此合力彰显。

4.2.3 狮子与小男孩

前面已经提到，狮子是老人精神世界的寄托，小男孩是老人现实中的陪伴者，两者在此基础上都有一个共通点，那就是都给老人带来生活的希望和慰藉。狮子本是群居动物，其存在是对陪伴的向往，对孤独的远离。即便是在精神上给予安慰和力量，它和小男孩一样，都能为老人的生活带来光明。但是狮子的虚幻性存在和小男孩的现实存在，本身就是一种对比：精神世界的不确定性和现实的确定性。综上所述，狮子和小男孩之间既有显著的对比，也有

共同的作用，两者共同反映了老人的真实生活，强化了人物个性。

5 结局合理性分析—胜利与失败的共存

5.1 老人、马林鱼、鲨鱼—合理的存在

老人、马林鱼、鲨鱼三者有机结合，缺一不可，在矛盾与统一中孕育了精神世界与现实的碰撞这一有机整体。尽管结局是老人打败鲨鱼，狼狈地带着鱼头返回，但是在我看来，这样的结局已经给读者最大的心灵慰藉。

5.1.1 仅鲨鱼存在

如果只有鲨鱼，没有马林鱼的存在。有可能老人没有收获，也就没有敌人的出现，或是一路一无所获，只有鲨鱼的攻击，那么这部小说描写的就是一个颗粒无收的更加惨淡的悲剧。但这并不是作者想要呈现的内容，即便没有鲨鱼，也会有 A 鱼，B 鱼等等作为人物实现目标过程中的阻碍出现；没有 A 鱼，B 鱼的出现，收获也没有，敌人也没有，这样的画面也是十分可悲的。因此，小说的悲剧性部分是必然会造就的。

5.1.2 仅马林鱼存在

如果没有鲨鱼的攻击，老人顺利捕获了马林鱼，并安然回归，这是最理想化的结果，但是这样又如何彰显人物在奋斗过程中的硬汉形象，形象地反映人类所追求的价值观-自信与坚强呢？这样的情节安排巧妙地表现了“有得必有失”这一人生常态，传达了作者对生命的写实与尊重。

5.1.3 三者的结合

三者在矛盾激发的过程中，都付出了生命的代价：老人费尽心力捕获马林鱼，但马林鱼被鲨鱼几乎吃个精光；老人赶跑或杀死一些鲨鱼，而自己也差一点在搏斗过程中丧命。这三者就是这样有机地结合起来，作为彼此的矛盾存在，而又逐渐将矛盾和谐化。从某种意义上讲，三者都是失败的勇士，他们虽然彼此克制，但是在面对死亡时都有绝不退缩的勇气。

5.2 老人、小男孩、狮子—合理的存在

5.2.1 老人与小男孩

该小说的结局是在老人回归陆地后，小男孩非常心疼他的遭遇，在他休息后，为他准备妥当各种物品，并决心以后紧紧跟随老人，共谋生计。这是在“失败”的捕鱼之行后，老人能够感到欣慰的事情：他的回归至少不是一场空无一人的等待，也不是一无所获的殊途。

5.2.2 老人与狮子

在回家之后，老人陷入睡梦，他依然能够梦见狮子。狮子——这带给他快乐与力量的存在，没有随着此次捕鱼之行的结束而消失，这也表明他的乐观态度依然存在，他的精神世界依然被守护着。

5.2.3 三者的结合

小男孩、狮子两者在老人回归陆地后都以美好的方式保留着，任何一方的缺失都是一种遗憾。如果在小男孩可以继续陪伴他的同时，他失去了带来心灵力量的狮子，结局会显得突

兀和毫无逻辑。如果依然能梦见狮子，但是小男孩不能继续陪伴他，分享他的快乐与不顺，他的孤独感会更加立体，现实中的失败会在小男孩的缺失面前，显得更加残酷。所以说，两者都是以温情的方式给予老人以抚慰，以美好的陪伴给予老人以希望，也给予读者以希望。

所以可以说，该小说的结局是胜利与失败的共存。胜利是指精神上的胜利，老人虽败犹荣，他的精神值得我们敬佩。而失败是现实中的失败，因为他无法躲过鲨鱼的攻击，顽强抵抗但寡不敌众，最终以失败收场。

6 结　论

正所谓不入虎穴，焉得虎子。人在社会面前如此渺小，对社会险恶与阴暗不可抗，也不可控，这早已暗示了小说悲剧的必然性。但正是通过这些意象之间的对立与统一，分别构成精神世界和现实世界的对立这一有机整体，从而论证了该小说的结局合理性，呈现老人的光辉形象，反映人类伟大的精神文明，深刻地展现该小说自身蕴含的高度艺术性。

在海明威看来，人生是一场打不赢的战争，就像老人那张“用好多面粉袋子补过的旧帆，看上去就像一面永远失败的旗帜”(The sail was patched with flour sacks and，furled，it looked like the flag of permanent defeat.)（*The Old Man and the Sea*1）。但老人始终没有停下追寻的脚步，这是一种面对巨大悲哀的追寻，是一种面对死亡和失败的追寻。我们在圣地亚哥身上看到了巨大的精神力量，在逆境中人的尊严，也看到了悲壮而强烈的生命悲剧意识（《海明威》，104）以及人可以被摧毁，但不能被打败的信心（A man can be destroyed but not defeated.）（*The Old Man and the Sea*，98），这正是老人光辉形象的生动写照。正是在这个意义上他代表了进取的人类的整体，体现了人类的生存价值。这样的结局给予读者的是鼓舞，而不是颓丧，让我们在惋惜的同时，也看到了人性的希望与力量。

参考文献

[1] Ernest Hemingway，2010. *The Old Man and the Sea*.World Book Publishing Company.

[2] Lois Tyson，2006. *Critical theory today*. Routledge.

[3] 何昌邑. 欲望表征的缺失——对《老人与海》的一种拉康式解读[J]. 思想战线，2006（5）.

[4] 黄菁. 试谈斯芬克斯在《老人与海》中的影射[J]. 北方文学，2015（6）.

[5] 黄鸣. 孤独的狂欢——《老人与海》的原型解构[J]. 河南师范大学学报，2012（5）.

[6] 李瑞红，孟晓媛. 海明威[M]. 沈阳：辽宁人民出版社，2014.

[7] 王梦. 论《老人与海》中的象征艺术及其现实意义[J]. 西南民族大学学报，2009（1）.

[8] 夏珺. 认知诗学视阈下的“狮子”、“小男孩”之解析[J]. 黔南民族师范学院学报，2014（4）.

[9] 钟晓菁. 从《老人与海》看海明威的男性世界[J]. 暨南学报，2009（4）.

自我与他者的消解：解构视域下的《幽暗之地》

李　静

摘　要：《幽暗之地》是诺贝尔文学奖获得者约翰·库切的第一部小说，在这部小说中，库切运用高超的写作手法对自我与他者进行消解。透过解构视角，本文剖析了文明与野蛮的本质、理性与疯癫的叙述以及施害与受害的结局这三组二元对立，认为这三组对立的交融消解了殖民者的本我身份与被殖民者的他者身份，解构了殖民者霸权。同时警醒世人，帝国主义和殖民主义的扩张只会伤人伤己。

关键词：自我与他者；解构；约翰·库切；《幽暗之地》

Abstract：In *Dusklands*，the first novel of John Coetzee，the Nobel Prize winner，Coetzee deconstructs self and other with his superb writing skills. In the perspective of deconstruction，this paper makes an analysis of three groups of binary opposition：the nature of civilization and barbarism，the narration of ration and insanity，as well the results of perpetrator and victim，and concludes that the mixtures of the binary oppositions work together to deconstruct the "self" identity of the colonizer，the "other" identity of the colonized，and also the hegemony of imperialist colonizers. Meanwhile，this novel suggests that the expansion of imperialism and colonialism will cause pain to the other and also the self.

Key words：self and other；deconstruction；John Coetzee；*Dusklands*

1 引　言

库切是一位"有道德原则的怀疑论者"（诺贝尔文学奖颁奖词），其首部小说《幽暗之地》就展现了他对殖民主义的强烈反感，对"西方文明中浅薄的道德感"（同上）的质疑。但和其他后殖民作家不同之处在于，库切试图"从他自己的立场，用他自己的声音，找寻到一种言说历史的方式"，（Morphet，16）这与解构主义尝试打破传统言说方式的观念不谋而合。在《幽暗之地》中，库切用其高超的写作手法策划了一场去"西方中心"的自我解构，消解了自我与他者的界限。赛义德在其著作《东方主义》中论述了作为自我的西方与他们眼中作为他者的东方的关系，"西方与东方是一种权利关系，统治关系，一种程度不同的复杂的霸权关系"，（赛义德，见朱刚，503）自我与他者要在这种权利关系中进行博弈。一般来说，在两者的较量中，他者处于劣势，自我与他者变成主从关系。自我通过他者化与自身不同的客体，可以获得心理上的优越感和掌控感，并以此建构自己的形象。在 J. M. 库切的小说《幽暗之地》中，两个主人公泾渭分明地划分自我与他者，以西方文明为自我，非西方文明则为他者。随着小说情节的慢慢展开，自我与他者却从各个层面一点点被瓦解。

小说由《越南计划》（简称《计划》）和《雅各·库切之讲述》（简称《讲述》）两部看似无甚关系的故事构成，以第一人称的讲述手法使读者得以透过两个主人公令人不快的视角，看到作为自我眼中的他者形象。诺奖评委会对此给予较高评价，“《幽暗之地》初次展露了善于移情的艺术才能，这种才能使他一再深入到异质文化中间，一再进入那些令人憎恶的人物的内心深处”。此种写作手法也受到国内外学者的关注，安东尼·乌尔曼将库切与纳博科夫、贝克特进行比较，认为“当暴力作为创作方法中心或者操纵着人类的理解时，这种方法有可能会产生不好的、疯狂的结果”。（Anthony Uhlmann，412）邵凌则认为，库切利用人物的不可靠叙述，可以“指引作者的读者发现表层文本之下的深层生态话语，实现作者的生态言说”。（2015，209）

可是，思考为什么库切要用这样的写作方式展开小说，就一定要结合库切本人对解构殖民霸权所做出努力。研究库切的作品，“不能割裂其作品与现代南非小说创作语境的联系。他的复杂身份及其在后种族隔离时代对身份的追寻、对人性的拷问、对弱者的关注，决定了他为被边缘化的他者代言”。（石云龙，95）把唐恩和库切置于殖民话语结构内，读者得以站在此结构外，洞察他们思维体系和其背后意识形态的局限性和不可靠性，主人公对于自我与他者的界定就得到了自我解构：首先，跟随两位主人公的视角，他们对被殖民者做出的种种暴行得以更全面地揭示，再加上他们面对血腥时的冷漠，这给读者造成更大的心理冲击，解构了文明与野蛮的二元对立；其次，小说的两个部分的叙述特征都是表面理性，实则疯癫，表层文本与深层文本创造的巨大的叙事张力，解构了理性与疯癫的二元对立；最后，深入自我的内心，还可以看到霸权主义对殖民者的异化，解构了自我一向的强势形象，双向揭示了殖民主义的罪恶。

2　本质的解构：文明与野蛮

“文明人”的野蛮与“野蛮人”的文明在《幽暗之地》中慢慢展开，消解了自我与他者对人性本质的界定。正如康拉德在小说《黑暗之心》中刻意模糊文明与野蛮的界限，以此对西方文明所定义的文明提出质疑一样，《幽暗之地》中文明与野蛮的界限也是模糊的，所谓的“思想者”“万物之主”（唐恩和库切的自称）犯下了令人发指的罪行，所谓的野蛮人却表现出具有人性的、文明的一面。

唐恩和库切认为自己是文明的代表，但毫无同情心，需要别人的痛苦来刺激自己麻木的感官。库切通过小说殖民者雅各·库切道出他对野蛮的定义，“野蛮是一种生活方式，蔑视人的价值，从别人的痛苦中得到感官的快乐”。（库切，132）这种野蛮的生活方式在小说两位主人公唐恩和库切身上体现得淋漓尽致。唐恩看到折磨越南人民的血腥的照片，他“颤抖着，流着汗，……心剧烈地跳动着，血液翻腾”，（22）并把它们当作增添想象力的“电脉冲”。更令人心惊的是，唐恩对自己的儿子也是这种态度。在刺伤马丁的时候，唐恩对儿子的称呼由“马丁”变为“那孩子”，说明此时他把自己的儿子也不过当成一个刺激感官的工具而已。他的种种行为很难把他与文明扯上关系。

小说另外一个主人公库切自诩为“万物之主”，却嗜杀成性，宣称“这是一个有死亡因而才是一个生机盎然的世界”。（106）他掠杀成千上万的野生动物，用极其残忍的方式结束布须曼人、霍屯督人的生命。“对库切来说，遗忘的第一步便是暴力发生前，将他者非人化”。（Lynda Ng，424）他把布须曼人放在火上活活烤死就跟他把甲虫肢解，折磨它慢慢死去是一样的心态。在将纳马夸地区的一个霍屯督部落灭族后，他竟然“稍稍冷静下来，感觉心里像海上漂浮着的瓶子那样，有一种晃晃悠悠的愉悦感”。（库切，139）同唐恩一样，他把他者的痛苦只当作感官的刺激物，毫无同情心。两个主人公打着“为你好”以及“把荒野变为果园和农庄”的旗号，对原住民及其居住生态带来毁灭性的打击，并为之洋洋自得，反而与雅各·库切自身对野蛮的定义相契合。从他们的种种行为来看，他们才是真正的野蛮人。

自我眼中的“野蛮人”在与“文明人”种种暴行的对比下，却显现出人性与文明的光辉。坚守机密的越南士兵，在迷幻药的作用下才“神志不清，彻底垮了”，（25）唐恩对自己的白人上司嗤之以鼻，却认为越南营地里精神失常的那些人是“时代的精英，无畏而博爱”。（26）以及库切生病后，悉心照料他的霍屯督妇女，忠心耿耿的霍屯督仆人克劳厄以及英勇赴死的普拉杰，让自大的他有了一闪而过的反思，“那么，这些纳马夸的霍屯督人真的是野蛮人吗？那他们为什么护理我？他们为什么放了我？”（132）这样的描写方式也引起读者深思：文明和野蛮的界限在哪里？什么定义了文明？什么定义了野蛮？也许保尔·威廉斯给出了一个答案，“在对土地、人民和动物进行殖民掠夺时，人与非人之间就没有界限了”。（Paul Williams，16）在唐恩与库切进行殖民扩张时，他们已经与野蛮人无异。正如本书序中所说，“读者在雅各·库切的带领下认识了一种完全异质的文明，本质上并不野蛮的文明”。（陆建德，9）

自我将他者非人化，认为他者是残忍的，野蛮的，未开化的。但在《幽暗之地》中，“所谓的进步是建立在滥杀生命、不计生态代价基础上的，是野蛮的、病态的、扭曲的”，（邵凌，2015，207）而所谓的野蛮人却保留着人性最初的纯真。《幽暗之地》呈现了“文明人”的野蛮行为与“野蛮人”的文明行为，使文明与野蛮在小说中相互交融，呈混杂之势，解构了西方种族主义者所宣扬的“本质决定论”，即种族决定人的本质。

3　叙述的解构：理性与癫狂

这本小说的两个部分是个人经验讲述与官方记录的结合体，是喷涌而出的内心情绪与极度克制的官方报告的结合体，也是极度偏颇与客观公正的结合体。但这些看似对立的二元并非截然分开，他们交融在一起，使叙述产生强大的张力。“叙述者成为反讽的对象，被自己的叙述所解构”。（2015，208）同时，这种张力颠覆了所谓自我的叙述权威，消解了殖民话语权。

唐恩与库切对世界的认知出现偏差，本应该是权威的官方记录也明显与事实不符，体现自我的叙述不可靠。“尤金·唐恩和雅各·库切想尽一切办法遵循他们所搜集文件的数据，读者除了相信他们彻底疯了之外别无选择”。（Lynda Ng，423）唐恩是《越南计划》的叙述者，正文也是他的视角在看，但明显不可靠。他不停地怀疑妻子出轨，别人要伤害他，极端到刺伤自己的儿子。随着小说的展开，读者才知道原来他是一个精神病患者。而“在唐恩执笔的《计划》中，美国智库的可行性报告、政策性建议和精神病患者的内心独白纠结在一起。”（陆建德，4）《越南计划》是越战时期美国将要对越南执行心理战的计划，应当具有严丝合缝的论证，这样的报告竟然由精神病人撰写，其荒诞性可见一斑。《讲述》中的叙述手法比较复杂，但也不可靠。正文部分是库切以第一人称讲述自己的故事，序言部分由他的后人 S. J. 库切撰写，附录部分的证词由库切口述，官方人员代笔。《讲述》正文部分的叙述者库切的叙述是癫狂的，他把“不倦地在证明这些死者为异类，因之其生命也是异类”当作他“一生的成就”，（库切，106）这一点就足以证明他的视角极其偏颇。此外，后记和附录部分本来是为了加强故事的可信性，但省略了库切曾表达过的“过一个白皮肤的布须曼人的生活”的愿望，也忽略了他冷血杀害霍屯督仆人、残忍毁灭霍屯督部落的事实，可以证明所谓官方叙述的偏颇。

小说中展示的西方自我的叙述，深入下去，就能发现不管是个人叙述，还是官方报告都不可靠且掺杂了一定程度的癫狂要素。

理性与癫狂这两种叙述方式的交融能达什么效果？其意义何在呢？“民族本身就是一种叙述，它的不确定性也如同叙述的不可靠性一样”。（王宁，49）为了确保民族的可靠性就必须要确保其叙述的可靠性。话语在对殖民过程中起着非常重要的作用，殖民者通过语言霸权达到文化帝国主义的目的。那么，如何解构帝国主义殖民者话语霸权便成为后殖民时期的关键问题。库切本人一直致力于消解殖民主义话语权，他的做法是让代表自我的叙述变得不可靠，以此达到目的。小说中的主人公语气坚定，尽量让人信服其价值观，还有官方报告为之佐证。但当把主人公的认知缺陷毫无保留地暴露在读者眼前，官方报告又出现明显漏洞时，他们所传达出的价值观越是用令人信服的话语表达出来，其权威性崩坍得越快。正如王宁在评霍米巴巴《民族与叙述》一文中说道：“从殖民话语的内部对其实行压迫，使之带有杂质进而变得不纯，最后其防御机制彻底崩溃，对殖民主义霸权的批判和颠覆也就得以实现”。（50）也就是说，解构殖民话语的有效尝试便是从内部对其进行瓦解，使之带有“杂质”。在《幽暗之地》中，“杂质”指的便是其叙述话语的不可靠性。这样一来，西方自我的可靠性就被瓦解，其殖民话语权威也因此得到消解和颠覆。

历史与民族都是叙述的产物，自我代表的霸权主义决定了什么被铭记，什么被遗忘。一旦殖民内部的话语出现明显漏洞与不可靠，那么其权威性也就被解构了。唐恩与库切以理性、公正的叙述者自居，但认知偏颇，言说混乱。官方记录试图增加他们的可靠性，却暴露出更多的矛盾。唐恩与库切的疯癫叙事解构了传统的殖民者话语的权威形象，官方记录的不可靠进一步消解了“自我”话语的权威性。这是《幽暗之地》对颠覆殖民话语的一次大胆尝试。

4 结局的解构：施害者与受害者

唐恩在刺伤自己的孩子那一刻彻底走向疯狂，被关入精神病院；库切在小说最后表达了自己对人生最后审判的担忧，他或许会终身活在对判决的担忧之中。唐恩的异化和他近距离与越南战争打交道不无关系，库切的异化与近距离接触因殖民扩张产生的死亡紧密相关，他们也是帝国主义和殖民主义的受害者之一。这样一来，一方面解构了自我一贯的强势形象，另一方面也揭示了殖民主义害人害己的恐怖面目。

《幽暗之地》的两个主人公唐恩和库切是被殖民者的施害者之一，但审视他们日记式的独白，便能看到帝国主义扩张导致的战争和殖民给他们所带来的心理创伤。在《越南计划》中，唐恩对自己的疯狂行为进行过反思，他不停地在说“我的崩溃和我的战争背景有关”“无疑我是个病人。我为越南付出了太多”。（库切，47）如果没有帝国殖民的扩张，或许他也不会走到这偏激一步。他疯狂的最终体现的是拿刀刺伤自己的儿子，更加令人吃惊的是，他描述这一切的语气十分冷漠，这种对冷漠源于他长期以来面对血腥的麻木。面对越战中拍摄下的血腥照片时，作为越战计划制定的参与人之一，唐恩只能以一个旁观者的身份来看，努力使自己保持距离，以此逃避良心对自己的审判。长此以往，唐恩的心理知觉渐渐麻木，在伤害至亲时，竟没有一丝丝内疚。战争给他的心理带来很大的损害，而战争的起因是霸权主义的扩张，所以他的创伤源起于霸权主义对他的异化。

库切与唐恩相似，面对屠杀保持着一种麻木的状态，但同时又经受良知的拷问。库切肆意屠杀南非的动物，对布须曼、霍屯督人也是如此。他随意践踏霍屯督人的尊严，“她眼见你杀死她们的男人，在她们眼中代表着力量的男人就像狗一般地被击毙”，（库切，81）对霍屯督人进行报复的方式是灭族，在听见“村庄那边有人厉声尖叫起来，一声接着一声从半英里传来”（139）时，他不过感到一丝心烦而已。同时，库切描述这一切的语气十分漠然，仿佛此刻发生的暴行与他无关，被虐待、被杀害的对象不是人类一般。但暴行之后，他仅剩下的良知对自己进行了无情的拷问，“我也害怕死亡”“我会遭受天谴吗？”（库切，144）库切对此辩解，他“并不比别人更嗜杀戮，只是担当起一个扣动扳机的人”。（库切，144）促使他扣动扳机的幕后黑手实则是殖民主义。对于异族的死亡，当然他自己有不可推卸的责任，但殖民主义更应受到谴责。通过混杂施害者与受害者的角色，《幽暗之地》解构了自我一贯的强势形象。

库切看到了帝国主义带来的战争与殖民不仅给被殖民者带来毁灭性的打击，也给殖民者内心带来了创伤，这正是他与其他后殖民作家的最大不同。《幽暗之地》中，也体现了库切对殖民的一贯看法，“他（库切）将南非社会总结为‘主奴社会’，在这样的社会里，奴隶不自由，主人同样也不自由”，（邵凌，2011，38），这一点从小说名字也可证明。小说起名为“幽暗之地”（Dusklands），貌似与正文两部分无甚关系，笔者认为有两层含义：其一，“幽暗之地”代表南非和越南这两处被殖民的文明与野蛮交汇之地；其二，“幽暗之地”代表这两个主人公的内心。不像康拉德在《黑暗之心》中采用 dark（黑暗）这样绝望的色彩，库切用 dusk（幽暗），光明与黑暗交错的时刻，既指代文明与野蛮的融合，也代表小说中两个以殖民者形象出现的主人公对光明和黑暗，文明和野蛮的反思。这与库切身份的特殊性不无关系。库切出生于南非开普敦，成年后去了英美念书，之后又回到开普敦大学任教，他穿插在不同的文化之中，能够跳出单一的文化结构不受其影响，又能置身于这个结构内部对其进行深入剖析甚至瓦解。但库切这样的写作手法不是在为殖民者进行开脱，反而是想警醒世人，帝国主义与殖民主义的扩张最终也会反噬自身。

综上所述，库切作为南非荷兰裔作家，对于殖民扩张的罪恶感受比较全面。殖民扩张不仅对被殖民者造成沉重的伤害，也会反噬殖民者自身。施害者同时也是受害者，库切用这一手法既谴责了殖民主义对人的异化，也消解了施害者与受害者的身份，解构了“自我”的强势形象。此种写作手法不是为了给殖民者辩解，而是要表达殖民主义带来的伤害是双方的，警醒那些试图继续推行霸权主义的殖民者。

5 结　语

库切的作品是“后殖民、后现代两股思潮相互碰撞的产物”，（2011，36）具有很强的不稳定性，这也给予他作品很强的阐释空间。《幽暗之地》把观察点置于殖民者一方，全方位地展现了他们的视角和暴行：自我眼中的他者是邪恶的，野蛮的，疯狂的，这一切都不同于自我的高尚、文明和理性；暴行的直接呈现也似乎缺少人文关怀，这种方式使库切备具争议，一些学院老师甚至认为在课上教授这本书对学生很危险。尽管如此，却不可否认库切确实创造了“一种新的叙述形式，一种新的想象方式，使得一种新的小说进入到南非文学”，（Morphet，14）并用这种方式“对当下西方文明浅薄的道德观和残酷的理性主义给予毫不留情的批判”（诺贝尔文学奖颁奖词）。

正如库切在其他作品中所做的那样，《幽暗之地》致力于消解自我与他者的界限，体现了他一贯的种族伦理关怀。从库切在这部小说中采用殖民者人物视角开始，边缘与中心便被无限地重新描绘，以此达到去“西方中心”的目的。《幽暗之地》从殖民者与被殖民者的本质，殖民者的叙述话语以及殖民者的结局这三个维度，分别解构了文明与野蛮、理性与疯癫以及施害与受害者这三组二元对立，一步步地消解自我与他者的界限，解构帝国主义殖民者霸权。同时，库切对于殖民主义的深刻洞见使得他看到殖民主义的双向罪恶，并以此警醒世人，霸权主义的扩张不仅会伤害他人，更会反噬自身。

参考文献

[1] Uhlmann，Anthony, 2016. *Dusklands and the meaning of method*，Textual Practice[serial online]. April, 30（3）：399-415.

[2] Ng，Lynda, 2016. *The violence of forgetting：trauma and transnationalism in Coetzee's Dusklands.*Textual Practice [serial online]. May, 30（3）：417-433.

[3] Morphet，Tony, 2004. *Reading Coetzee in South Africa.* World Literature Today [serial online]. January, 78（1）：14-16.

[4] Williams，Paul, 2013. *Hunting Animals in JM Coetzee's Dusklands and Waiting for the Barbarians.*Social Alternatives [serial online]. October, 32（4）：15-20.

[5] J. M. 库切. 幽暗之地[M]. 郑云译. 杭州：浙江文艺出版社，2007.

[6] 邵凌.《幽暗之地》的不可靠叙述与库切的生态言说[J]. 叙事，2015（1）.

[7] 邵凌. 库切与创伤书写[J]. 当代外国文学，2011（1）.

[8] 石云龙. 他者·他性——库切研究[J]. 外语研究，2011（2）.

[9] 王宁. 叙述、文化定位和身份认同——霍米·巴巴的后殖民批评理论[J]. 外国文学，2002（6）.

[10] 朱刚. 二十世纪西方文艺批评理论[M]. 北京：北京大学出版社，2006.

“边缘者的孤独”：《幽暗之地》中的自我他者化

夏谦滢

摘　要：《幽暗之地》作为 J. M. 库切自传式作品风格的滥觞，在库切研究中占有重要的地位。如他其他自传式作品中一样，《幽暗之地》突出的“自我”被置于后殖民的文化语境中，出现他者化的解构特点。本文从后殖民理论中的“他者”与“自我”入手，通过分析尤金·唐恩和雅各·库切分别在精神和行为上的自我他者化，结合作者的创作书稿，认为这一根源来自于作者所处的南非殖民历史背景与文化身份，是自我与他者对抗又同时消解的产物，自我意识被他者化，产生了库切式的“边缘者的孤独”。

关键词：《幽暗之地》；J. M. 库切；自我他者化；孤独；后殖民

1 引　言

诺贝尔文学奖得主，J. M. 库切作品中“他者”与“自我”一直是研究这位南非白人小说家的切入点之一。“他的复杂身份及其在后种族隔离时代对身份的追寻、对人性的拷问、对弱者的关注，决定了他为被边缘化的他者代言。”（石云龙，95）库切的复杂身份是源于他身为南非殖民后裔的血缘，又处于南非特定的后殖民环境中，历史的沉重与文化身份无所皈依的孤独感令他不断反思自己，反思过去，又同时拷问人性。

这一反思的起源为他者的代言，可追溯到 1970 年库切在他的处女作《幽暗之地》的书稿中写道的：“没有人会心怀坚定的被宽恕感再去忏悔。当灵魂依然渴望摆脱过去的束缚，所有更高级的交流形式都变了性质；在新教国家，音乐绘画和信件传记都从一种描写的手段变成表达自我谴责、赎罪和无限忏悔的方式。”（阿特维尔，038）

正如成书于 1974 年的《幽暗之地》乃是库切自传式作品风格的滥觞，这段话也更为明确地表达了库切本人在写作时的初衷来源于“摆脱过去的束缚”与“自我谴责，赎罪和无限忏悔的方式”。作为这一初衷的体现，《幽暗之地》被库切分为两个独立部分进行第一人称的叙述，分别是《越南计划》与《雅各·库切之讲述》。在这两个独立部分中，通过两个明显不同的叙述者，读者仍然能感受到他们灵魂的一种相似共鸣。这两个灵魂，一个是与库切同一时代，正在为美国政府工作，撰写越战计划的“思想者”尤金·唐恩，另一个是遥在南非殖民初期，名为雅各·库切的殖民者，在相似的“自我灵魂”的共鸣中，一者被认为是“思想者”，一者被认为是“行动者”。法国存在主义哲学家让·保罗·萨特曾提出过著名的他人与本体的关系，“他人注视我”这一论说，（萨特，445）因此，在《幽暗之地》中，除了能够明显看到两个不同又有共鸣的“自我灵魂”以外，还能不断看到注视“我”的他人，即“他人，其实就是别人，即不是我自己的那个自我。”（293）

除了对库切作品中他者的形象研究之外，目前国外对《幽暗之地》的研究较多从创作的方法和它的叙事特点进行研究。如 The violence of forgetting：trauma and transnationalism in Coetzee's Dusklands（2016，Lynda Ng）和 J.M. Coetzee’s Dusklands：The meaning of suffering

（2005，Grant Hamilton）对创伤叙事研究，以及 Anthony Uhlmann 在 Duskl and sand the meaning of method 中对《幽暗之地》的写作技巧的研究。值得关注的是，这些研究都与库切本人的创作经历和生平有密切联系，大多参考了库切的自传与访谈。而在国内，专门对《幽暗之地》进行研究的较少，关注度不高，其中有硕士论文《〈幽暗之地〉的疯癫形象和疯癫叙事》，（2016，杜凌）《论《幽暗之地》中的殖民第三空间》，（2012，杜昕）辑刊《幽暗之地：个人型叙事声音解析》（王莎烈，2012）等。可见，国内目前对《幽暗之地》的研究集中在作品的叙事和结构上，对《幽暗之地》与库切的联系以及《幽暗之地》与库切其他作品的关系等探讨得并不多。更多的对《幽暗之地》的研究则散见于对库切的总体研究中，多聚焦在后殖民理论和创伤叙事上，比如《他者·他性——库切研究》，（2011，石云龙）《神话的解构与自我解剖——再论库切对后殖民理论的贡献》，（2011，蔡圣勤）《库切小说中的“属下”形象——后殖民理论视域下的一种阐释》，（2017，王妮，向天渊）《库切与创伤书写》（2011，邵凌）等。

因此，本文在后殖民的语境中，基于萨特存在主义中对“他者”与“自我”定义，通过小说中两个部分的叙述者“自我”：尤金·唐恩和雅各·库切，分析他们一者以精神疯癫被主流社会隔离的边缘他者化，以及另一个在行为上逐渐走向“野蛮”“暴力”的殖民他者化。再结合库切的自传性写作特点以及书稿证据，探究这种自我他者化产生的原因，即殖民历史问题与文化身份问题，找到库切式孤独的起源，一种边缘流散者独有的自传式书写。

值得注意的是，“自我”与“他者”在后殖民语境中多数是二元对立的存在，本文以解构的分析方式论证两者的消解和合一，再通过这一“自我他者化”的创作特点联系到库切的创作出发点，需要作者的自传和评传中第一手材料的支撑。以《幽暗之地》和有关它的书稿笔记作为研究对象，既是对目前国内对库切研究的一点补充，也是为从源头理清库切的创作风格和动机提供了新的思路，即库切的《幽暗之地》通过历史重构的互文形式，既探究了当代流散边缘群体的文化身份产生的孤独感，也在回顾殖民历史中拷问了人性与灵魂，从而形成了他独特的自传式风格与库切式的“边缘者的孤独”。

2 自我他者化的历史互文——尤金·唐恩与雅各·库切

对于“他者”问题的研究，国内学者认为“他者的形成必须发生在二元对立的关系之中，而且对立的双方存在着某种不平等或压迫关系。同者利用武力、语言、意识形态对他者行使霸权，对其进行排挤、支配和控制。他者往往由于各种历史和现实的原因被边缘化、属下化，失去话语权，产生自卑感。”（张剑，127）

在萨特的存在主义中，谈论及他人与“我”的关系时，提出了注视，他认为，“他人注视我并不像他”没于“我的世界存在而是像他的整个超越性走向世界和走向我；他注视我时，他之所以能与我公开，并不由于任何距离，任何实在的或理想的世界对象，任何世界之中的物体，而唯是由于其他人这本性。”（萨特，339）

由此可见，自我的存在依赖于他者的存在，当一个自我被建构时，离不开他者的存在，两者是互相依存的关系。

然而在《幽暗之地》中，虽然存在明显的两个“自我”，尤金·唐恩与雅各·库切，受到小说中其他人物的注视，出现“自我”与“他者”的对立。但是，这种对立并不是纯粹二元的，而是随着小说里“自我”形象的不断变化，一个走向他者化的过程。

首先，在小说的第一个部分《越南计划》中，尤金·唐恩是一个“美国神话”中的“属下”，他不仅是“自我”，也是后来主流社会中的“他者”。“属下”（subaltern）一词来源于安东尼·葛兰西的《狱中札记》，原指“受霸权团体或阶级统治的人”；后经印度“底层人研究小组”的历史学家发展为“南亚社会中普遍的从属态度，不管以阶级、种姓、年龄、性别和职位或以任何其他方式为表现”。（斯皮瓦克，17；转引王妮；向天渊，150）

尤金·唐恩作为一个“自我”，却在叙述中透露着一个属下作为“他者”的悲哀身份。尤金作为上司库切的属下，有着顺从附属的社会关系。他既认为上司“盲目无知”，又不得不“溜须拍马”，竭力讨好。这种矛盾的双重心理正是社会关系带给“自我”的压迫造成的，在上司“注视”下的“我”才是被边缘化，属下化的对象，无法反抗上司的决定，是“失去话语权”的表现。这样身为属下的尤金·唐恩又有着希望某一天取代上司，成为上司库切“毫无二致的复制品”的渴望。

可见，这种对上司库切的表面奉承，内心疏远，又渴望取代的复杂心情，说明尤金·唐恩是一个父权制社会边缘者渴望被主流接纳的人，这也正说明他认为自己是一个需要得到主流承认，被文明驯服的他者。

更能说明尤金·唐恩这一“自我”是边缘他者的，是他后来对越南计划疯狂的执着以及对自身形象的他者化描写。尤金·唐恩在越南计划中刻意注重了模仿父权神话，并攻击“母亲”这一形象，称自己“乘着想象的翅膀，把未来寄托在攻击大地母亲身上。”（库切，41）同时，他与代表着“母亲”形象的妻子玛丽莲矛盾重重，将自己全部的生活重心投入在CT计划的撰写中，时刻想象着击垮压抑他的父权制，最终刺伤了自己的儿子，维护他在家庭中的父权地位。可见他的潜意识中也是既反抗父权制又顺从于父权制，避免被边缘化和排斥，成为“他者”。

然而，这位代表思想者的“我”，在受到社会关系压抑和家庭关系压抑的过程中还是渐渐走向疯癫。最后在他的叙述中，我们看到一个明显的他者化形象：

如果说我这张内在的脸、这具肌肉做的面具有什么特征的话，那么这些特征是极其丑陋的且不为人知的穴居人的脸。好像一个噩梦闯入，在梦中，他眼睛和嘴全缩成了一团。从头到脚，我成了身体反叛的目标。只有腹部的器官还在悠然自在：肝脏、胰腺、肠胃，当然还有心脏，就像还未出生的八爪鱼，互相挤挤挨挨。（库切，11）

一个疯癫的“自我”，在一种内心的“注视”下，他成为一个“他者”，一个与文明相悖的“穴居人”。

在后殖民的语境中，他者是“野蛮”“落后”的象征，“殖民者自认为他们是人类未来理想状态的体现，是正确的自我；原住民则被视为‘他者’，是异类，因此是劣等的，不健全的人。”（Tyson，468）于是，在小说的第二部分《讲述》中，作为“行动者”的库切则通过了对自己行为的叙述，使得他最终成为一个和自己叙述中的布须曼人一样野蛮残忍的“他者”。

首先，库切在描述南非当地的土著居民时，他如此讲道：

布须曼人则是迥异的生番，是充斥着野性的兽类。在产羔季节，有时狒狒会下山来恣意满足贪欲，它们攻击母羊，啮咬小羊的口鼻……布须曼人的天性如出一辙。要是他们对一个农场主嫉恨在信，便趁黑夜潜入农场，把羊只尽可能赶走，剩下的就加以残害，把羊身上的肉一块块割下来，戳瞎它们的眼睛，挑断它们腿上的筋腱。他们一如狒狒般残酷无情，对付他们的唯一办法就是对他们像对野兽一样。（库切，75）

然而，当他患病时却是“野蛮”的，与布须曼人一样同为土著居民的霍屯督人收留了他，并安排人照料。雅各·库切自诩“文明”的殖民者，在一次受到霍屯督少年的嘲笑后竟然愤而咬掉了对方的耳朵，最后被驱逐。在原野流亡的叙述中，雅各·库切对自己行为的叙述也不自觉地透露出他者化的痕迹，他渐渐成为一个“白皮肤的布须曼人”，在原野中释放了自己的兽性，肆无忌惮地发泄杀戮的欲望，撕咬小羊，饮其鲜血。

就这样，雅各·库切的自我化为兽欲的“他者”后，他做出了如之前叙述的布须曼人一样袭击羊的行为，之后率领属下对之前好心收留他的霍屯督部落进行突袭和报复，向同样皈依了白人宗教信仰（基督教）的霍屯督人发动了袭击，在这场屠杀中，雅各·库切化身成为野蛮的“布须曼人”，对同属上帝羔羊的霍屯督人进行了残忍的虐杀，这与他在撕咬小羊时自称“犹如上帝一阵旋风降临一般”，遥相呼应，显得充满对立与矛盾。

邵凌认为，“库切对于自我 / 他者关系的解读受到交互作用下的主体哲学的影响，认为自我不是一个传统意义上的理性的一成不变的主体，不是一个自我生成的封闭而孤立的系统，而是处于与他人和事物的动态联系中。主体与他者不是绝对分离的对立二元，而是彼此渗透、相辅相成的关系，它与他者的交互作用中携带了他者的影子。这样一来，对他者的恶就会反作用于自身，损害自身的道德性与心灵的完整。以主体间性观看种族隔离制度下的主奴关系，库切得出这一不人道的制度降低了黑人的存在、令白人心灵蒙羞的结论。”（邵凌，39）

在尤金·唐恩和库切这两个相隔近 200 年的灵魂接连从思想和行为上由一个文明社会的“自我”转向“他者”时，正好说明了库切对自我和他者关系的解读并非是传统的二元对立，而是两者不断消解，融为一体的关系。这种历史互文的叙述方法都离不开“殖民”这一主题，而深陷在这一主题中，身为白人文明社会的一员却显得无所适从的“自我”则出现他者化的趋向，以至于最后一个思考至疯癫，一个拒绝了思考却行为疯癫。

3 “边缘者的孤独”——自我他者化根源探究

通过对《幽暗之地》中两个“自我”的他者化解读，可以发现两者都同属于殖民意识形态中的殖民者身份，又因为在殖民意识形态内部受到压迫而对“自我”的认定趋向模糊，成为“他者”。那么，探寻这一自我他者化的根源，就需要从创作者本人库切的经历与文化身份谈起。

正如蔡圣勤所谈道的那样：“从解构的选择上，在西方中心的帝国意识内部，库切着手的是对文化身份的质疑，用同批判艾略特的方式一样来批判自己；通过对文化中心论和经典的解构，颠覆了意识形态中核心的二元对立；通过对帝国文学神话及现实主义小说之父的解构，用小历史观颠覆了大历史的宏大叙事；再通过对自我的殖民‘蛮荒’的行为和精神的解剖，彻底颠覆了西方赖以骄傲的文化文明的根基（没有比自我解剖更痛苦同时又更具有说服力的了）。这些其实都是在困境中寻找出路、在不可能性中寻找可能性的一种典型的德里达式的解构。”（蔡圣勤，35）

库切本人的文化身份是南非殖民者后裔，他所经历的后殖民时代特殊的政治环境，种族隔离的社会，无一不带给他深深的思考。

在《幽暗之地》的讲述中，库切如此自称道：

我们都负有罪孽，无人例外，霍屯督人也包括在内。他们死于我的手。可天晓得他们是死于什么他们自己犯下的令人难以想象的罪！上帝的判决就是正义，高深莫测，无可指责。上帝的仁慈并不关乎美德。我只是历史手中的工具？

我会遭受天谴吗？（库切，143）

同样的自问还有尤金·唐恩在最后的叙述：

我正热切地企盼再一次直面人生，但我并不急于从这儿出去。在我抵达我的故事尽头之前，我的整个童年依然有待研究。我的母亲（迄今我还未提起过她）正在夜色下展开她吸血鬼的翅膀。我的父亲正在外当兵。而在美国心脏的一间小隔间里，我沉思着，沉思着，角落里是我的私人盥洗室。我深深盼望着能弄清楚我是谁的过错。（库切，71）

既然《幽暗之地》作为库切在1970年元月一号自传式创作的起点，那么《幽暗之地》中的两个他者化的“自我”所提出的问题又与融进作品之中作者的自我有着怎样的联系？

当他们在自问的时候，令人不得不联想到库切在回首他伍斯特乡下童年岁月的话，这是一段写于《男孩》书稿中的笔记：“走样。我的生活因为南非而年复一年地走样变形。标志：那些西蒙斯敦高尔夫球场上变形的大树。”（阿特维尔，5）

树的比喻与人生的轨迹和走向息息相关。库切融于作品中的自我透露一种“走样”“变形”的悲观，他虽肯定自己的南非乡下经历，但也并不持乐观的态度。他的“自我”在这个时候开始显得有一种与平常的树不一样的自我感知，在他最初的写作意识中，就透露一种游离在主流社会之外的他者感。

因此，这样游离他者感的库切，在写作时也赞成巴尔特的观点，认为写进自传的东西仅应是“躯体在到达生产性状态之前的各种表象，躯体逐步迈向写作的辛苦和快乐过程中呈现的状态。”（阿特维尔，7）持这样的观点，库切在《双重视点》的访谈中更是称道“所有的自传都是写作”。（库切，391）

将自我写于自传起点的《幽暗之地》中，产生的两个自我分别是思想者的尤金·唐恩与行动者的库切。

尤金·唐恩作为首先登场的“自我”，他正好处于和库切同一个时代，同样在美国，同样面对越战。不同的是，现实中的库切因为反对越战而被捕入狱，从此与美国社会无缘，而一手策划CT计划的尤金·唐恩则在这场战争中走向疯狂，被排除在主流社会之外，成为“他者”。可见，尤金·唐恩与库切有着同样被“美国神话”所排斥，游离在社会边缘的经历，这也是这一部分叙述中，作者自我的显现。

作为第二部分登场的雅各·库切，在名义上库切的祖先身处南非殖民的初期，也是库切对自己所负有的文化身份的一种愤怒。在《夏日》的书稿中，他曾如此评价自己当初在《讲述》中描写暴力的段落：“一本有关残忍的书，揭露了各种形式的征服中的残忍。”（阿特维尔，44）“残忍”是库切对那段殖民史的看法，也是他最初面对自己的文化身份之时的一种愤怒和反思。正因如此，回顾那段殖民历史与自己文化身份的库切才会在让创作出来的雅各·库切在最后一昧地行动却不思考，也得不出任何的答案——过去残忍的殖民历史无法回答，自身的文化身份也在面对之时无言以对。

在这样不断面对历史文化身份的自我与现代文明社会中自我的对抗过程中，库切本人的自我在不停地反思和追问，他游离在主流社会之外，成为名副其实的流散者和边缘者，与那些对立的自我抗争。

如果说，库切的《幽暗之地》是“一种大胆的自我解剖”，（蔡圣勤，35）那么给“自我”进行解剖并将之展现的库切本人所要提出的问题正是小说中无论“思想者”还是“行动者”都无法回答的问题，流散的边缘者要何去何从，在承担沉重的历史文化身份后，要如何面对这样的“自我”。

正是这样的无法回答，对那段历史的愤怒和对自己文化身份的感慨，使库切产生了一种流散在主流社会边缘的孤独感，而这一孤独感深深渗透进了他的自传式小说中，从《幽暗之地》开始，生长成为“变形的、走样的”的大树，写出后面更多的自传式作品。就像尤金·唐恩说的那样：“阴暗的自我奔向耻辱和骚乱，而光明的自我则投入恭顺与秩序。阴暗的自我用疑虑压抑光明的自我。这我清楚。它的毒药正在吞噬着我。”（库切，40）

孤独者的灵魂被无从回避文化身份所吞噬，将这样的自我写入小说中，碰撞对立的自我意识接受拷问，消解在二元对立之中，成为“他者”，这正是库切写作的起点，也是他“边缘者的孤独”产生的原因。

4 结　语

库切作为南非殖民者的后裔，他独特的文化身份和特殊的个人经历，不仅使他在历史上处于一个游离边缘者的状态，也在主流社会中处于流散者的状态。通过他的书稿，更为清晰地看到他写作《幽暗之地》的初衷。

在《幽暗之地》中，自我意识的他者化书写既是沉重的笔调，也是内心最深处的叩问，对西方文明的叩问。通过“自我他者化”的方式，在后殖民时期，库切解构了欧洲中心主义为核心的殖民主义意识形态，文明等同野蛮，征服即为残忍。同时也解构了传统的殖民历史，为受压迫的，受损害的南非土著居民发声，直面自己的过去。

他对弱者关注，对人性拷问，渴求摆脱过去的束缚，谴责历史文化身份中的自我，又反思身为文明社会一员，身为白人知识分子的自我。将“自我”置于后殖民的语境，以“他者化”的方式开始了他的自传式写作的起点，同时奠定了他作品中独有的“边缘者的孤独”的基调——无处依偎的灵魂流浪在南非的殖民史中，现代的文明社会中，是边缘流散者自我的永恒孤独。

参考文献

[1] Grant Hamilton. J. M. , 2005. *Coetzee's Dusklands：The meaning of suffering*，Journal of Literary Studies，21：3-4，296-314.

[2] 石云龙. 他者·他性——库切研究[J]. 外语研究，2011（2）：95-100.

[3] 邵凌. 库切与创伤书写[J]. 当代外国文学，2011，32（1）：36-44.

[4] 董亮. 库切研究的新动向：关注作家的作者身份建构[J]. 外国文学研究，2018，40（1）：165-169.

[5] 段枫. 库切研究的走向及展望[J]. 外国文学评论，2007（4）：139-145.

[6] J. M. 库切. 幽暗之地[M]. 杭州：浙江文艺出版社，2013（3）：167.

[7] 张剑. 西方文论关键词 他者[J]. 外国文学，2011（1）：118-127+159-160.

[8] 王妮，向天渊. 库切小说中的“属下”形象——后殖民理论视域下的一种阐释[J]. 当代外国文学，2017，38（3）：149-156.

[9] 蔡圣勤. 神话的解构与自我解剖——再论库切对后殖民理论的贡献[J]. 外国文学研究，2011，33（5）：29-35.

[10] 大卫·阿特维尔. J. M. 库切及其书写的一生：与时间面对面[M]. 董亮译. 哈尔滨：黑龙江教育出版社，2017，3：1-33.

[11] 罗伊丝·泰森. 当代批评理论实用指南[M]. 赵国新等译. 北京：外语教学与研究出版社，2014，3：465-498.

[12] 让·保罗·萨特. 存在与虚无[M]. 陈宣良等译. 北京：三联书店，2007（11）：265-616.

文本世界理论视野下《青春咖啡馆》中的露姬形象探析

常　红

摘　要：《青春咖啡馆》是2014年诺贝尔文学奖获得者、法国当代著名作家帕特里克·莫迪亚诺创作的作品。文本世界理论包含话语世界、文本世界和次级世界三个层次。本文通过对小说中两个主要人物情人罗兰以及女主人公自身的文本世界与次级世界的分析，对露姬形象进行全面解剖，探究露姬不断逃离以及最终选择自杀的原因，

关键词：帕特里克·莫迪亚诺；《青春咖啡馆》；文本世界理论；露姬；次级世界

Abstract: *Youth Cafe* is created by Patrick Modiano, the winner of the 2014 Nobel Prize for Literature and a famous contemporary French writer . The theory of text world includes three levels: discourse world, text world and secondary world. Based on the analysis of the textual world and the secondary world of the two main characters in the novel, the Loren, and the heroine, this paper makes a comprehensive analysis of the image of Rouge and explores the reasons for Rouge's constant flight and eventual suicide.

Key words: Patrick Modiano; *Youth Cafe*; theory of text world; Rouge; secondary world

1　引　言

《青春咖啡馆》讲述了20世纪60年代发生在巴黎塞纳河左岸的拉丁区一家名“孔岱”的咖啡馆里的故事。故事围绕一名年轻女子的失踪展开，全书共分四个章节，每一个章节由一位不同的叙述者讲述这位名为“露姬”的女子的人生故事。他们都以第一人称“我”的口吻向读者讲述露姬短暂的流浪生活。

国内目前对莫迪亚诺的作品的研究主要集中在三个角度：（1）对其小说“逃离、寻找”类主题的分析；（2）对其小说叙事手法的分析，如儿童视角、多视角叙事、模拟侦探小说和运用象征；（3）对其小说结构的分析。然而，针对《青春咖啡馆》一书的文本世界分析却几乎没有。

文本世界理论作为认知叙事学的一个分支，在20世纪90年代中期兴起，为帮助读者更好地认识理论并将理论运用到实践中，本文以诺贝尔文学奖得主帕特里克·莫迪亚诺的作品《青春咖啡馆》为例，给读者展示出要想清晰地认识一个人物形象，可以从其文本世界与次级世界两个方面去理解。论文主要采用举例论证的方法，通过列举书中大量的例子帮助读者在未看到原作的情况下理解文本、分析人物形象，分别从情人罗兰以及女主人公自身的文本世界和次级世界分析和理解露姬的形象以及探究女人主公最终自杀的原因。

2　文本世界理论

文本世界理论（text world theory）（Werth，1999）是认知叙事学的一个分支，该理论将“话

语”（discourse）分为三个概念层次：第一层次为“话语世界”（discourse world），即人类交际的直接场景，包括理解话语产生和理解的所有语境因素；第二层次为“文本世界”（text-world），该世界“是一个指示空间，首先由组成这个世界的话语，尤其是其中的指示和指称因素所决定”；第三层次为文本内“次级世界”（sub-world），指由文本世界内的人物叙述或者想象出来的世界。（唐伟胜，2013）

一般来说，文本世界是最基本的心智世界，其建构需要“世界建构成分”（world-building elements 或 world-builders，简称 WB）和“功能推进成分”（function-advancing elements，简称 FA），其中，“世界建构成分”包含指示信息和指称信息。前者确立文本世界的时间（time，简称 T）和地点（location，简称 L）等，后者确定出现在文本世界的实体，包括人物（characters，简称 C）、物体和抽象概念（objects，简称 O）及其属性、相互关系等。“功能推进成分”主要由命题实现，命题指“对一个简单情景的表征”。（Werth，1999）所有情景要么是路径表达，要么是修饰表达；路径表达与行动和过程相连，修饰表达包括状态、环境和转喻关系等。“功能推进命题”（在叙事语篇中称为“情节推动命题”）引入新信息。

3　从情人罗兰的文本世界理解露姬形象

小说这部分描写的是某天晚上，罗兰、露姬，一对四十岁上下的夫妻应邀到居伊·德·威尔办公室进行聚会。聚会结束后，罗兰和露姬这对之前完全没见过面的陌生人一起离开办公室。按照文本世界理论，地点、人物、概念、功能推进成分的信息更新意味文本世界之间的切换（如图 1～图 2 所示）。

TW1　办公室聚会
WB　　T：某天晚上
L：居伊·德·威尔办公室
C：威尔、罗兰（我）、露姬、一对夫妻
O：文章、蜡烛、电灯等
FA　　罗兰用红色圆珠笔把号码记在了那张纸的下面
罗兰与露姬目光交汇（SW）
威尔目不转睛地凝视着露姬（SW）

图　1

TW2　离开办公室
WB　T：那天晚上
L：花园广场中央
C：罗兰（我）、露姬
O：铁栅栏、林荫大道
FA　罗兰打破沉默，询问露姬居住地址（SW）
两人谈论维嘉书店（SW）

图　2

从 TW1 和 TW2 可以看到地点（L）、人物（C）、物体或概念（O）等世界建构成分（WB）

的变化，同时也发现功能推进命题（FA）的更新。在这两个文本世界中，即在第一次见面时，罗兰已经深深地被露姬这个神秘的女子吸引了，并且不断地制造跟露姬相处的机会以便于进一步了解这个神秘的女子。我们可以看到，在这两个文本世界中，包含许多次级世界（SW），它们对揭示故事背景和人物身份、关系等具有重要意义。TW1 中罗兰的次级世界即直接引语，*“她显得毕恭毕敬的，她的这种严肃认真终于也感染了我”*，首次向读者展现了露姬的形象，同时也体现出罗兰对露姬的喜爱之情。TW2 中的次级世界*“我想找个借口把她留住，不要那么快就和她说再见”*，进一步凸显了罗兰对露姬的感情。总之，文章一开始就把读者带入一个神秘女子和对这个女子一见钟情的罗兰感情线的文本世界中。

接着，镜头由花园广场切换到比尔-阿肯站，两个人由最初的沉默到后来谈论到共同的兴趣爱好，以及露姬迟疑着告诉罗兰她已经结婚的事实。由此，观众继续构建自己的“文本世界”（如图 3 所示）。

TW3　分别

WB　T：那天晚上

L：比尔-阿肯站

C：罗兰（我）、露姬

O：地铁列车、桥、塞纳河

FA　露姬向罗兰讲述她的婚姻（SW）

罗兰问露姬是否可以不回家（SW）

图　3

通过“文本世界”TW3，尤其是 TW3 中罗兰的认知次级世界即“好像她在跟我忏悔一桩罪孽一样。总之，我前世一定认识她”“也许我们俩同时有了同样的想法”，向读者揭示了露姬的身份—已婚以及知道露姬身份后罗兰的表现。在这短短的一晚上，读者看到的是露姬和罗兰相遇、相识，到相爱的感情发展过程。

（1）心想时间都过了那么久，维嘉书店不在了。在巴黎同样再也见不到居伊·德·威尔了，也见不到露姬了……那天晚上真的是在做梦吗？

（2）她只想逃走，逃到更远的地方，用剧烈的方式割断与日常生活的联系，呼吸到自由的空气。

（3）跟我在一起，她什么都不怕。

从上面一段节选中发现，罗兰的文本世界中时间、地点、功能推进成分信息都发生了巨大的变化。露姬没有跟罗兰幸福地生活下去。从前面罗兰和露姬相知相爱的过程中，从罗兰的文本世界和次级世界中；露姬形象为：严谨认真，毕恭毕敬，婚姻不幸，热爱读书等等。她是一个谜一样的女子。但是在这里，露姬的形象更加丰满：她想逃离，不受束缚，追求自由。在罗兰的叙述中，他可以给一直想逃离的露姬安全感，可以让她安定下来。这里体现的露姬形象为跟我们之前构建的文本世界发生了冲突，迫使读者开始调整自己的视角：一方面不断回忆、反思前面的情节；另一方面继续阅读文本，找出事情的真相。

与前面相比，如图 4 所示的文本世界的世界构建成分无论是时间还是地点都发生了较大变化，尤其值得注意的是，指称中除了罗兰和露姬保持连续性外，出现了新的人物-亚娜特，被人称为“骷髅头”。从“骷髅头”这个称呼上读者可以想象出这个新的人物形象。需要注意的是，在这里，新的人物出现，加上罗兰次级世界的描述，*“我本该对她起疑心的……我感觉到她们两个有着共同的秘密”*，读者难免又重新修正我们构建的文本世界。露姬的消失是否与这个新的人物有关？她们之间的秘密是什么？露姬真的是我们之前认知的那个女性吗？

TW4 初遇“骷髅头”
WB T：一个风和日丽的下午
L：圣母院对面的河堤
C：罗兰（我）、露姬、“骷髅头”
O：阳光、河堤、“雪”
FA 露姬和她朝罗兰走来（SW）
罗兰不明白为什么人们叫亚娜特为“骷髅头”（SW）

图 4

（4）我和露姬约好下午五点在孔岱见面。我觉得自己童年和青少年时期的伤口已经彻底痊愈了，从今以后我没有任何一个理由躲藏在一个中立地区了。

（5）他用苍白的声音对我说：“露姬，她从窗户那里跳了下去。”

从节选 4）中读者可以知道他们两个准备好一起过幸福的生活，准备出去旅行，但是从 5）中，我们了解到露姬自杀了。这使我们开始回忆之前的情节，把露姬的消失和她的自杀联系到一起。整篇小说到这里也结束了，作者没有过多地说明露姬自杀的原因。但是我们读者开始怀疑叙述者罗兰的可靠性，因为按照罗兰的次级世界，他和露姬一直是很幸福的，他完全可以给露姬安全感，露姬没有理由选择死亡。

根据文本世界理论中关于世界可达性（Accessibility）和真实性的论述，文本世界是作者和读者可达的，其真实性由作者负责，读者可判断其真实性；而由人物所幻想的次级世界对作者和读者来说是不可达的，其真实性由人物负责。（刘世生、庞玉厚，2011）本文中，罗兰的文本世界以及次级世界说起他们很幸福，但是结局却出乎所有人的意料之外。所以，笔者认为，罗兰这个叙述者是不可靠的，他创造的次级世界也是不可靠的。作者有意把真实的文本世界和罗兰创造的次级世界并置，使读者一时难以判断其真伪，不断地对文本世界进行返回式重构、修正、否定和置换，使露姬的形象的认知也具有片面性。

Gavins 也指出：“通过利用我们的潜意识阅读习惯并由此耍一些干扰性的本体论和认识论戏法，作者可以制造一些十分有趣的概念效果。这些叙事花招只有在读者被成功地哄骗人一种虚假的感觉（他们处于参与者可达的文本世界中，而实际上他们正经历着反映叙述者视角和内心思想的扮演者可达的情态世界里）之后才成为可能。”（Werth，1999）这一点使读者陷入认知误区，需要打破之前的文本世界，建立新的文本世界。“事实上读者只是在按照某种认知优先选择去读解特定的歧义域并在得到‘正确的’读解之后丢弃前面的读解时，才陷入花园路的”。（曼德雷福·雅恩，2002）这虽然是对读者认知的挑战，但这也正是这本小说的魅力所在，花园路叙事实质上就是读者的文本世界和叙述者的次级世界相互混淆，（刘世生、庞玉厚，2011）从而使读者分不清真假。

从“骷髅头”“雪”中，我们可以与毒品联系到一起。当我们都以为露姬结交了恋人和朋友之后会彻底告别孤独和漂泊的人生，她却再一次逃离，没有赴约。不过遗憾的是，正是在罗兰彻底“痊愈”的那个下午，露姬在孔岱咖啡馆自杀了。在罗兰的追述中，露姬的形象为一度吸毒成瘾麻醉自己，不愿受束缚，一直渴望逃离，最后选择最激烈的方式逃离这个纷繁喧扰的尘世——自杀。

4 从露姬的文本世界理解露姬形象

4.1 露姬的文本世界—构建对露姬背景的认知

Werth 对文本世界的界定是："文本世界最初是由语篇本身界定，具体说是由其中的指示和指称成分界定的指示空间。"根据这一理论，笔者认为读者若要进一步理解人物及其作品，他所建构的关于人物的这个文本世界应该属于人物与场景接触的外在世界，而不能首先是人物的内心世界。在进入人物内心世界之前，读者先需要了解有关的外在世界，即确定人物的身份、所处的环境、人物的各种特点等。（唐伟胜，2015）由此，在从露姬的次级世界探索露姬的形象之前，应先通过对露姬文本世界的描写来对露姬的背景做一个全面的了解。

（1）我的本名叫雅克林娜，不叫露姬。

（2）我母亲离世已经四年了，我再也没有什么好怕的了。

（3）母亲年轻来到巴黎的时候，就在红磨坊里找到了一份工作。

（4）随后的三四年里，我常常走同样的路线，同样的街道，可是我越走越远了...那么晚在外面瞎逛并不觉得奇怪。

（5）他们第一次把我抓走时，是在九区，在都外街的街头。

（6）我害怕什么呢，我要去见人。只需要一家咖啡馆就行了。

从上述例子中可以得到几个关于露姬客观形象的基本信息。第一，二，三个例子对露姬真实姓名、露姬母亲的经历及去世的描写为露姬及其周围的环境构建出一个基本的外在世界。在第四，五个例子里，可以看到两处对露姬行为的描写：夜半在路上闲逛，并被警察局抓走。这几处都是作者对露姬的外在世界，即文本世界的进一步构建。由此，读者在不断地整合，联系小说前后对露姬文本世界的描述后，便可以形成对露姬背景的基本认知。

露姬是不幸福的，是一个漂泊者，流浪儿。从小失去父爱，母亲是红磨坊的舞女，她觉得露姬就是当年自己的翻版，不对露姬抱有任何希望。于是，露姬便开始无止境地穿梭在黑暗的街道，孤独地游离在这个城市。在第 6 个例子中，露姬尝试过寻找自己的生活，于是她邂逅了孔岱咖啡馆，融入一群放荡不羁的艺术家的世界里。遇到罗兰和亚娜特，露姬的人生似乎有了光亮。

4.2 露姬的次级世界—构建对露姬内心世界的认知

在对露姬的背景有了基本的认识后，我们可以更深一步进入人物的内心世界。而要实现这一过程必须通过分析露姬的次级世界，以达到对露姬这一形象的全面、真实的认知。

这一段中，露姬所处的外部环境构成了一个完整的文本世界（如图 5 所示）。在文本世界内，人物的内心独白引导读者又进入一个次级世界。根据文本世界界定标准，文本世界是人物采取行动、进行思考的空间，内心独白划归亚文本世界。在第一个次级世界的构造中，读者跟随露姬的内心独白：我害怕走过那个广场，这好像让我所有的一切都从头开始了，我觉得我会晕倒在地。接下来一句是对文本世界的描写："我们没从红磨坊面前经过。"读者跟随露姬的思维活动从刚刚的第一个次级世界迅速撤离返回到原来的文本世界—她和罗兰在布朗西广场上散步。紧接着读者又开始构建第二个次级世界：我想到我的母亲已经离世四年了，她在世的时候，我常常在晚上逃出来，走在林荫大道上。至此，读者完成了对两个次级世界的构建，也就在这一过程中掌握了露姬的思维活动。

WB T 一天晚上
L 布朗西广场
C 罗兰，我

FA 穿越广场
我觉得我会晕倒在地
就好像有人派了罗兰过来

FA 可是，我母亲离世已经四年了
她夜里不在家的时候
我逃出来走在林荫大道上

图 5

第二个例子对文本世界的描写：*时间发生在几年之后一天下午，亚娜特到诺伊利的我家做客，我俩躺在我房间的床上聊天*。到第二段，读者可以很明显地发现与前一段相比发生了时间和空间上的转换。实际上这一段充分描绘了露姬的思想不断游离的过程：她时而想到自己某一次与罗兰在一起时被一束强光照耀而感到眩晕的时刻，时而想到另外一次自己与亚娜特在一起时被同样的一束光照射后的感受，在那一刻她甚至还想到了她的母亲，她觉得她的母亲再也不会来接她了。然而紧接着后面的是亚娜特的一句关心的问话，读者这才反应过来之前一大段的描写其实都是露姬自己的内心活动。也就是说，从第二段话开始，读者被直接置入一个次级世界中，我们可以称其为次级世界（I）；当她的思绪又转换到另一个场景时，我们又会建立次级世界（II）。露姬这一章难懂的原因之一就是读者的思维需要不停地在各个级别的次级世界之间游走穿梭，而这些次级世界都离读者所处的文本世界存在层次上以及级别上的距离，使得读者在认识上难以直接进入（如图 6 所示）。

T 几年之后的一天下午
L 诺伊利 我的房间
C 亚娜特 我
O 床

次级世界 I	次级世界 II
WB	**WB**
T 一天夜里	T 从蒙马特回来
L 康特儿	C 罗兰，我
C 亚娜特，我	O 灯光
O 灯光	
FA	**FA**
强烈的光线	强烈的光线
令我目眩	寻思母亲不会担心我

图 6

4.3 露姬的丰满形象

读者想要对露姬形象有一个全面的理解要综合文本世界与次级世界两个层面以探索露姬这个形象的不同面。罗兰和露姬一样，想要逃离巴黎的漩涡，所以他一直寻找"中间地带"，而露姬对罗兰来说就是这个中间地带，在情人罗兰眼里她是与众不同，独立而又较弱的爱人；在露姬自己看来，她曾经是个常常彻夜不归的都市浪荡儿，现在依然独自流浪，是个旁人眼中的神秘，迷人的女子。在进一步分析露姬的次级世界后，我们可以进一步挖掘出露姬内心的另一面：像是在永远不断地寻找，逃离，再寻找。*"只有在逃跑的时候，我才真的是我自己。"*"雪"这种毒品也营造不出沉醉感，在没有姓名、标准、人际关系的束缚下，她终于成为一个"不存在的雅克林娜"。

从小说中的文本世界和次级世界分析中，读者已形成一个自己熟悉的了解露姬的文本世界。然而在露姬本人的文本世界和次级世界分析中可以看出跟之前形成的露姬形象有很大的不同。读者一方面怀疑罗兰的话是否可靠，另一方面也开始怀疑露姬的可靠性。至此，作者精心设计的花园路叙事起到了一定的效果。陷入信任危机的读者开始调整自己的视角：他们一方面不断回忆、反思前面的情节，一方面跟随故事女主人公露姬去查证事件的真相。根据文本世界理论，读者开始重新评价自己建构的文本世界的真实性，随时准备修正，甚至置换它。这也是作者花重墨从不同视角努力构建露姬这一形象的原因。

5 结　　语

通过上述分析表明，文本世界理论在解读叙事作品方面具有强大优势。它对读者的动态认知过程给出了合理具体的描述，尤其是在处理花园路叙事等特殊现象时显示出巨大的灵活性和解释力。此外需要指出的是，笔者在上述分析中为了更好地展示文本世界理论作为一种认知叙事学方法所具有的适用性和阐释力，有意避免使用叙事学的传统术语。本文的结论认为，文本世界理论以其细致的文本分析、严密的逻辑推理和强大的区分功能为叙事话语的认知研究以及认知语言学研究提供了一种新的视角。（刘世生、庞玉厚，2011）我们有理由相信，文本世界理论将会受到越来越多的认知叙事学家、认知文体学家和认知语言学家的关注。

参 考 文 献

[1] Werth，P. N., 1999. Text Worlds：Representing Conceptual Space in Discourse [M]. London：Longman.

[2] 刘世生，庞玉厚. 认知叙事学初探——以电影《美丽心灵》中的文本世界为例[J]. 外语学刊，2011（2）：45-51.

[3] 曼福雷德 • 雅恩. "说话，朋友，进来吧"：花园路、人工智能和认知叙事学[A]. 戴卫 • 赫尔曼. 新叙事学[C]. 马海良译. 北京：北京大学出版社，2002.

[4] 帕特里克 • 莫迪亚诺. 青春咖啡馆[M]. 金龙格译. 北京：人民文学出版社，2015.

[5] 唐伟胜. 认知叙事学视野中的叙事理解[J]. 外国语期刊，2013（4）：28-36.

[6] 唐伟胜. 叙事层次：概念及其延伸[J]. 外国语文（双月刊），2015（1）：23-29.

从巴赫金的“对话理论”解读《小王子》
——聆听大自然的教导

郭 佼

摘 要：法国作家安东尼·德·圣-埃克苏佩里（Antoine de Saint-Exupéry）的著作《小王子》享誉世界，经久不衰，一个重要的原因是该作品蕴藏丰富而深刻的哲理，这些哲理又是通过童话内外各方的对话得以传达。本文将试着运用巴赫金的“对话理论”，分析《小王子》文本所创造的显性对话和潜性对话、微型对话和大型对话，进而梳理人类与大自然关系的古今发展脉络与现状，重新确立大自然在人类社会发展进程中所占的智慧源泉地位，帮助现代人聆听自然的教导，学会与自然和谐共处。

关键词：安东尼·德·圣-埃克苏佩里；《小王子》；对话理论；人类与自然

Abstract: The masterpiece *The Little Prince*by French writer Antoine de Saint-Exupéry has gained an enduringly world-renowned reputation. One of the important reasons for the success lies in therich and profound philosophies buried in it, which are accomplished through multilateral dialogues both inside and outside the text. With Bakhtin's dialogism, thethesis attempts toexpound the multilateral dialogues created by *The Little Prince*, including the dialogues between little prince and Nature, between little prince and grown-ups, between little prince and the pilot, and between the pilot and the readers.In this thesis, the ancient and present relations of mankind and Nature will be manifested, and one important rule that Nature is a source of wisdom during mankind society development shall be back to realization and be emphasized again. The thesis is designed to help modern people learn from Nature's instruction and live in harmony with Nature.

Key words: Antoine de Saint-Exupéry; *The Little Prince*; Bakhtin's dialogism; mankind and Nature

1 引 言

《小王子》讲述了来自外星球的小王子负气离家游历各个星球，最终降落在地球偶遇狐狸和飞行员的奇幻故事。这篇童话文字简洁却富含哲理，深受大小读者的喜爱。近年来，《小王子》作为畅销书，在中国文学评论界受到大量关注，主要研究方向包括《小王子》文本中的象征、隐喻、“爱与责任”主题、叙事策略和视角、存在主义解读和儿童教育等。现有的运用巴赫金“对话理论”解读《小王子》的研究论文侧重列举了体现“话语对话性”的语句，而对“人与自然关系”这一主题的探讨并未涉及。因此，本文试图用巴赫金的“对话理论”分析《小王子》文本所传达的人与自然的相处之道。

巴赫金在进一步阐发已有的对话理论基础上形成了自己独特的对话主义理论，他将对话上升到哲学的高度，认为“存在就意味着进行对话的交往”。（巴赫金著，白春仁等译，1998）

巴赫金的“对话理论”分狭义和广义的对话：狭义的“对话”指引号内的话语，即两个人或多人之间进行的“纯粹对话关系”，属显性对话；广义的“对话”被巴赫金称为“对话性”，这样的对话关系“存在于各种声音之间、完整的形象之间、小说的完整层面之间（大型对话），而同时在每一句话、每一个手势、每一次感受之中，都有对话的回响（微型对话）”。（转引自李淑敏，2015）有些对话虽不具有直接的话语形式，但对话依然以“潜隐的形式存在，我们将其命之为潜对话”。（张开焱，2000）在这个意义上，人物内心世界的挣扎，或是自我与他人之间的争论，抑或是小说人物的意识冲突，人类所有的行为——包括外在的行动和内在心理活动都具有对话的特征。

《小王子》文本的一个突出特点便是丰富的对话和对话性。正是通过文本精心构造的多边对话空间——小王子与自然、成年人、飞行员“我”的对话以及“我”与读者的对话，在人类与大自然二元对立中，圣•埃克苏佩里展现了古往今来人类与自然相处模式的变化，用历史和现实的经验教训指引现代人回归自然，拥抱自然，遵循自然法则，学会与自然和谐相处。

2　小王子与大自然的对话—敬畏自然，天人合一

来自 B-612 星球的小王子，天真无邪，质朴纯真。他的星球上只有三口火山和一朵玫瑰花，这些便是他拥有的全部，可是小王子生活得非常快乐。他在活火山上做早饭，与那朵玫瑰花儿做伴，观看落日送太阳回家，与大自然十分亲近。小王子和大自然的这种原始默契，与远古淳朴的人类始祖和大自然的相处模式十分相似，尽管小王子与他的玫瑰花儿也有闹别扭的时候。

（1）小王子心想：“如果她看到眼前这片景象，肯定会羞窘得无地自容……她准会使劲地咳嗽个不停，为了逃避这种尴尬，她甚至会倒下装死。而我呢，我就不得不装装样子去照顾照顾她。否则，她为了要让我感到内疚，也许真的会自暴自弃去寻短见……”（安东尼•德•圣埃克苏佩里著，柳鸣九译，2011）

对话（1）在形式上是小王子的内心独白，实际上是一段微型对话。这段微型对话是小王子根据花儿的性格特点，猜测花儿心理，对花儿的行为进行的单方面设想。玫瑰花造作任性，甚至有些虚伪。小王子在心里演练他与玫瑰花的对话，只运用情绪和肢体语言来表达，这比直接描写与花儿纯粹的话语交流更能体现小王子内心对玫瑰花的失望与厌恶。这段独白也为小王子驯服狐狸后对花儿深切的悔恨做了强有力的反衬铺垫。

（2）狐狸开始做出解释：“这是一件好事，可惜已经被忘得一干二净了，‘温驯’意味着建立和谐的关系……”狐狸接着解释，“……如果你使我温驯了，我们两者之间的关系就变得互相依存依恋。那么一来，对我而言，你就是这世上的唯一，而对你而言，我也就是这世上的唯一……”“我开始懂得了，”小王子说，“我拥有那么一朵花儿……我想，可以说她使我温驯了……”（安东尼•德•圣埃克苏佩里著，柳鸣九译，2011）

对话（2）是显性的纯粹对话，可以看出狐狸所代表的大自然对小王子怀着包容怜悯的博爱之心；纯洁善良的小王子也能够懂得大自然那些独特而智慧的话语，尝试着去领会接受狐狸教给他的“驯养”之道——爱与责任。小王子驯养狐狸的方法十分有趣：只需要约在每天的同一时间，很有耐心地坐在草地上和狐狸对视，如此一天天地由远及近……这个过程就是小王子和狐狸心理距离拉近的过程，是驯化的过程。他们之间没有显性的对话形式，却完美诠释了巴赫金定义的“对话性”：“对话性是具有同等价值的不同意识之间相互作用的特殊形

式。”（巴赫金，1992）无须直接而纯粹的话语交流，小王子和狐狸心理上的对话和认同仍然在悄然进行。此处的潜性对话又引出狐狸告诉小王子的秘密——“人只能用心灵去观察，去感受。要知道，光靠肉眼是不可能看到本质的东西的。”（安东尼·德·圣埃克苏佩里著，柳鸣九译，2011）狐狸的一句话“语言是造成隔阂与误解的根由”更是点醒了小王子，使其明白玫瑰花虚伪的话语背后隐藏着对自己深深的爱恋。在用心感受之后，小王子承认自己也一直爱着他的那朵玫瑰花，只怪自己当时不够智慧，不懂得爱与责任的道理而离开花儿铸成遗憾。为此，小王子悔恨不已。

在远古时代，人类从大自然的电闪雷鸣中得到启发，学会钻木取火；他们用树皮遮羞，用石头装饰，伐木建造房屋，捕鱼打猎填饱肚子，而大自然都默默地包容着他们的攫取。小王子能用纯洁的心灵聆听大自然的教导，汲取大自然教给他的“爱与责任”的人生智慧，此举正是象征和重现了人类祖先与大自然亲密互动的过程。在领略大自然的魄力和智慧之后，人类祖先选择遵从“天人合一”的朴素唯物主义思想，明白一切人事应顺乎自然规律，人类文明才得以成形并继续发展。

3 小王子与成年人的对话—远离自然，走向异化

小王子负气离开他的星球后，先后拜访了六个住着成年人的小星球。大人们住在自己的星球上，小王子的到访与之形成了围绕人性与欲望的对话关系：成年人的眼中只有自己的欲望，他们接受着小王子所代表的淳朴人性的拷问。细品这种对话关系，能够让人更清楚地认识到成人世界的急功近利，荒唐可笑。

巴赫金认为：“语言是针对对话者的，就是说话语生存于两个人之间，它既出于说话人，同时又连接对话人，即他人，并回应他人对答的言语。”（转引自胡经之，2003）《小王子》文本中有很多国王与小王子的显性对话，但笔者认为国王实际是在与自己对话，或者用巴赫金的话来说，是在与小王子的对话中，由小王子即“他人”的质问揭示国王内心的隐秘矛盾：一方面，国王明白“权威首先要建立在理性之上”，知道他自己能做的不过是“要求每个人去做他能够办得到的事情”，但在纠结徘徊之余，他仍被权力蒙蔽，认为权力高于一切，哪怕手中的权力徒有虚名。在小王子看来，国王的行为是自欺欺人，不可理喻的。

第四个星球上的生意人心中只有数字化的财富欲望，他拥有五亿零一百六十二万二千七百三十一颗星星，但他不满现状，企求更多的拥有。可笑的是，拥有得再多，生意人也不曾认真地去了解欣赏这些星星；相反，小王子只拥有过一朵玫瑰花儿，他天天给花儿浇水，听花儿唠叨抱怨。小王子与生意人的财富观念和人生态度也形成了对话关系：生意人只在乎收获，小王子则更看中付出。对话在如此迥异的意识间进行，注定只有冲突和对抗。小王子欣赏第五个星球上的点灯人，因为他勤劳务实。无奈点灯人的星球自转速度逐年加快，点灯的指令却没改变，还是每一分钟点一次灯接着又熄一次灯，这使点灯人一秒钟也休息不了。可见，点灯人已经被异化成一台点灯机器，这讽刺了现代人在快节奏的物质生活中，已经无法放慢脚步去亲近自然，一有空闲就只想睡觉，没有心情观赏唯美的日出日落。

最后降落在地球上，小王子遇见了迎来送往的扳道工和卖解渴丸的商贩。在与他们的显性对话中，小王子见识到现代人与大自然之间难以跨越的鸿沟。现代科技的发展日新月异，给人类带来便利的同时也使人类疏远了大自然，割裂了人类与大自然的天然联系。火车的发明，省去了人们长途跋涉疲惫，本可以让人们轻松地观赏沿途的自然风景，但火车里的人们

“在车厢里睡大觉呢，要不就是在打哈欠”“只有那些小孩把脸紧贴着玻璃窗朝车外观看”（安东尼·德·圣埃克苏佩里著，柳鸣九译，2011）。解渴丸的发明更是为了消除人类的自然属性，试图割裂人与大自然的天然联系，似乎人的自然属性已然成为人类发展的阻碍。然而实际上，这样的科技显示出一种反自然规律的极端倾向，将人类异化成麻木工作的机器，是人类的一种悲哀。

（3）“和地球人在一起，也是孤独的。”蛇说。

花儿曾经有一天见过一支商队经过，她答道：“人吗？的确有……但现在谁也不知道在什么地方可以找到他们，他们随风漂泊。他们没有根，这对他们很不利。”（安东尼·德·圣埃克苏佩里著，柳鸣九译，2011）

作者借由小王子、蛇和花儿之间的对话，揭示了现代人物质生活日趋丰富，精神世界退入荒原的困境。国王、生意人、地理学家、扳道工和解渴丸商贩这些成年人都代表文明飞速发展的现代人，他们的意识和价值观综合起来就是现代人的自然观：将自然置于人类的统治之下，视大自然为征服对象，日渐远离自然，背离自然；而小王子所代表的则是与大自然有着和谐关系的人类祖先。在完全对立的意识相互碰撞后，小王子无法理解现代人的行为原则，这使他深感孤独和忧伤。

4 小王子与飞行员“我”的对话—回归自然，不忘初心

小王子在对现代人彻底绝望之前，在撒哈拉沙漠与飞行员“我”相遇。小王子请“我”为他画一只绵羊，几经努力后“我”画了一只装在盒子里的羊。正是这只羊开启了我们之间的对话，可是起初的对话并不顺利。

（4）“不，不，我什么都不相信！我只是随便说说，我现在正忙着呢，我正在忙要紧的事！”他惊呆地盯我一眼。“要紧的事！”……“你现在说起话来，真像那些成年人。”（安东尼·德·圣埃克苏佩里著，柳鸣九译，2011）

关于“要紧的事”的一番显性对话表明——“我”与小王子的价值观念冲突很大。成人与儿童二元世界的对立十分明显：有着纯洁心灵的儿童以博爱的观念看待万物，这与大人们的“合目的的理性”观念是格格不入的。除了众多的显性对话，小王子与“我”之间还存在不少大型对话。“大型对话”指的是小说结构上的、完整形象之间、完整层面之间的对话，是小说各部分之间、作品人物之间的一种潜在的对话关系。（何健敏，2012）文本中“大型对话”的一个例子就是小王子与“我”对待毒蛇的不同态度和感情的对话关系。小王子来到地球上与毒蛇相遇并与之结成要好的伙伴。毒蛇怜悯小王子孤单无助，小王子对毒蛇也毫不畏惧，二者的和谐相处再次突显小王子与大自然的亲密无间。可在成年人“我”的意识里，毒蛇是大自然凶猛而可怕的捕食者，是邪恶的代表，靠近毒蛇就意味靠近死亡。“我”忌惮毒蛇，无法像小王子那样与毒蛇对话，正是因为现代人与大自然的平等关系不复存在。小王子与“我”的这一大型对话暗中对比了儿童与成人对待万物生命和大自然的态度和观念，作者并未就谁对谁错明确表态，而是留给读者自己去感悟。

在与小王子进行深入的对话和交流后，“我”与小王子、大自然的隔阂渐小，距离拉近，童心也逐渐被唤醒。小王子只看一眼就能懂得我画的那幅“蛇吞象”的简笔画；“我”安慰他说那只羊“也不是那么小呀……瞧！它在箱子里睡着了……”在大漠之中，成年人是不会想到去寻找水井的，因为希望渺茫，但在小王子的坚持带领下，他们找到了那口延续生命的水井。

（5）“你听，”小王子说，“我们唤醒了这口井，它开始歌唱了”

“其实，他们所要追求的东西，很可能就藏在一朵孤零零的玫瑰花中，或者在少许一点水里……”“的确如此。”我答道。（安东尼·德·圣埃克苏佩里著，柳鸣九译，2011）

这口水井滋润了“我”与小王子濒临绝望的心田，带给我们生存的希望，还使“我”与小王子在彼此的生命中变得独特而有意义，就像那朵玫瑰花对于小王子，小王子对于狐狸的意义一样。而这就是小王子从狐狸（大自然）那里学到的“驯养”智慧。通过寻找水井这件事，小王子又将“驯养”智慧教给了“我”，让“我”学着去相信自然，回归自然。可见，大自然永远都是人类文明的智慧源泉，指引着人类社会的不断发展。

在科技文明迅猛发展的今天，现代人改造自然的痕迹日渐显著，过度膨胀的自信使人类妄想征服自然。作为飞行员的“我”换个视角于高空俯视大地，才明白人类相比于浩瀚的宇宙和神奇的大自然仍然显得卑微渺小。人类想要“统治”宇宙，主宰自然，无疑是自不量力的做法。

5 结论：“我”与读者的对话—寄予希望，和谐共存

《小王子》的终章里，飞行员“我”与读者分享小王子造访地球后离开的故事，推测小王子最终有没有回到他的星球上，他的那朵花儿有没有被小绵羊吃掉……其实这是“我”试图与读者进行的一种对话。

（6）请你们仰望天空，请你们发问吧：绵羊有没有把那朵玫瑰花吃掉？你们只要关心这样的问题，你们看万物时就会有全然不同的感受……

请仔细观赏这一景致，为的是，如果有朝一日你们有机会去非洲旅行，……只要是这么一个小男孩，你们准会猜出他是谁了。如果你们真是碰上了他，那可要请你们想着我呀，请你快快写信告诉我他回来了，别让我总是沉浸在悲苦的思念之中……（安东尼·德·圣埃克苏佩里著，柳鸣九译，2011）

这种对话向独白、向非对话形式渗透的现象被称为“对话性”。（刘雨，2001）独白形式的话语还可以分为有听众的独白和孤立的独白。（凌建侯，2012）对话（6）就属于有听众的独白，但并不要求立刻得到回答。可以看出，“我”那些带着强烈祈使语气的话语，因为使用了第一人称复数“我们”和第二人称“你”“你们”，能够感召每一位关心小王子命运的读者参与进来，号召每一位读者思考人生的真谛。通过这些有听众的独白，“我”引导读者去思考“绵羊与花儿”的自然命题，感叹大自然的奇妙与智慧，倡导人们适时放下手中繁忙的工作投入大自然的怀抱，去看沙漠和星星，亲近自然，回归自然，体会大自然赋予人类的本真。通过与读者的这番对话，“我”将人与自然和谐发展的希望寄予读者，期盼他们像小王子一样汲取大自然的智慧，重新确立大自然在人类发展道路上的智慧之源地位，聆听自然的教导，创造人类文明可持续发展的辉煌明天。

小王子驯养狐狸是在沙漠里，与“我”相遇是在沙漠里，最后的离开也是在沙漠里，而沙漠是最能代表大自然的意象之一。故事情节的如此安排，意在表明大自然就像智慧的母亲，人类则是顽皮的孩子，敬畏自然是现代人应该继承的传统思想。在笔者看来，小王子最后选择离开，也是尊重自然，顺应自然规律的一种体现，因为儿童终究要长大成人，人类社会也在不断地向前发展，如此一想，对小王子的离去也就少了些悲伤，多了份释然。庆幸的是，小王子教会了飞行员聆听大自然智慧的奥秘——即“最重要的东西要用心灵去感受”，而飞行

员又将其传递给了广大读者。笔者坚信，《小王子》的读者们带着小王子的赤子精神和大自然的智慧重新出发，会更加合理地建设人类文明，人与大自然的和谐发展也将指日可待。

参 考 文 献

[1] 安东尼·德·圣埃克苏佩里. 小王子：汉英对照[M]. 柳鸣九译. 南京：译林出版社，2011.

[2] 巴赫金. 巴赫金全集第五卷[M]. 白春仁译. 石家庄：河北教育出版社，1998.

[3] 巴赫金. 陀思妥耶夫斯基诗学问题[M]. 北京：生活·读书·新知三联书店，1992.

[4] 何健敏. 运用巴赫金的对话理论解读《暗恋桃花源》[J]. 长春教育学院学报，2012，28（4）.

[5] 侯瑞琴. 从巴赫金话语对话性角度解读《小王子》[J]. 山西农业大学学报（社会科学版），2015，14（5）.

[6] 胡经之. 西方文艺理论名著教程（下卷）[M]. 北京：北京大学出版社，2003.

[7] 李淑敏. 巴赫金对话理论视角下的《等待野蛮人》[J]. 漯河职业技术学院学报，2015，14（6）.

[8] 凌建侯. 文学话语的对话性分析[J]. 社会科学家，2012（7）.

[9] 刘雨. 巴赫金对话理论与中国现代小说的对话性[J]. 东北师大学报，2001（5）.

[10] 张开焱. 放开人格——巴赫金[M]. 武汉：长江文艺出版社，2000.

Magic Realism in Yellow Back Radio Broke-Down

谢诗阳

摘　要：《黄后盖收音机破了》是非裔美国作家伊斯米尔·里德“新伏都”美学思想和表意系统的初次登场，里德在这部小说中建构了一个伏都教重写历史的魔幻小镇，揭露了美国的种族歧视氛围和社会政治腐败现实。伊斯米尔·里德将小说根植于非洲传统文化，吸收了之前以加西亚·马尔克斯为首的魔幻现实主义作家的创作思想、艺术风格和理论基础，将非洲本土伏都教元素和拉美魔幻现实主义手法相结合，创造出独到的魔幻式美学效果。本论文通过文本细读的方式，对小说中魔幻现实主义的并置、魔幻现实主义的模棱两可以及魔幻现实主义的象征物等进行挖掘、探讨、分析，揭示荒诞闹剧背后的传统观、文化观、历史观，给读者以启迪：复兴民族传统的根本途径是破除单一文化主义和本质主义，提倡融合开放、异质多元的文化。

关键词：《黄后盖收音机破了》；魔幻现实主义；伊斯米尔·里德；伏都教

Abstract: Ishmael Reed is an African-American writer, and *Yellow Back Radio Broke-Down* (1969) is the debut of his neo-hoodoo aesthetic ideas and signifying system. In this novel, the writer constructs a magic town where Hoodoo rewrites history and discloses racial discrimination as well as political corruption in American society. Ishmael Reed roots this novel in African traditional culture, absorbs creating ideology, artistic character, theoretical basis and combines Hoodoo elements and Latin-American Magic Realism, creating unique magic aesthetic effect. Through close reading, the paper makes a detailed analysis on magic realist elements in this novel such as magic realist juxtaposition, magic realist ambiguity and magic realist symbolic objects, revealing views on tradition, culture and history behind the absurd chaos, and delivering the enlightenment that the fundamental approach to rejuvenate national tradition is do away with *monoculturalism* and essentialism, promote inclusive, open, heterogeneous, and diversified culture.

Key words: *Yellow Back Radio Broke-Down*; magic realism; Ishmael Reed; hoodoo

1　Introduction

Yellow Back Radio Broke-Down is Ishmael Reed's second novel in which at the first time he describes hoodoo magic. It is the debut of Reed's neo-hoodoo aesthetics ideas and signifying system.Happening in an American western town Yellow Back Radio, the story is about a black cowboy named Loop Garoo Kid's revenge. Through practicing hoodoo magic, Loopbeats Drag Gibson who is the representative of autocracy and tyranny.

Some researches abroad are from the perspective of critical theories, exploring colorful cultural and historical ideologies the writer projected into imageries and scenes. Jack Hicks analyzed Loop the protagonist in his*Cutting Edges: Young American Fiction for the 70s* (1973) . Celebrated

Afro-American literary critic Henry Louis Gates pointed Reed's concerns in his paper "The Signifying Monkey: A Theory of Afro-American Literary Criticism"(1988). Bernard. W. Bell in his book *The Afro-American Novel and Its Tradition* (1987) praised that Reed "is not only one of the most talented and most controversial artists in America, but also the chief proponent of the black postmodernism" (24). Joe Weixlmann thought that deconstruction of traditional western novel form and ideologies hide behind was one salient feature in Reed's novel. While in China, researches about *Yellow Back Radio Broke-Down* are still in its early phase, existing much deficiency. Lin Yuanfu's "Ishmael Reed and His Works On*Yellow Back Radio Broke-down*" (2004) summarizes that Ishmael Reed mocked idea of democracy and freedom under capitalist system.Lin Yuqing's "How Hoodoo and Neo-HooDooism Work in *Yellow Back Radio Broke Down*" (2013) pointed Ishmael Reed's aims in using neo-hoodooism. In all, researches about *Yellow Back Radio Broke-Down* have not been extensively unfolded.

As a literary genre, since Franz Roh used the Germany word "Magischer Realismus" (9) to describe a painting style in 1925, magic realism has evolved into a significant writing style that was first used by Latin American writers then spread across literary circle to do creation of collective consciousness by "opening new mythical and magical perspectives on reality". (727) Up to now, magic realist works are often related to various characteristics, and corresponding artistic techniques behind.

First comes the hybridity and mysticality. Magic realism combines local religion, legends, folklores, and even superstitions with western biblical prototype, borrowing several literary techniques such as symbolism, expressionism, surrealism and stream of consciousness. The second feature is ambiguity. The author reaches ambiguity from two aspects: giving characters more than more identities to make them the representative of different themes, or using shift of narrative perspectives, makingthe narrative fragmentary and subjective.The third feature is disorder. It is achieved by juxtaposition that can be divided into two aspects: juxtaposition of fancy and reality, and anachronism in times. Through this method, magic realists inject such magic realist elements as hybridity, mysticality, ambiguity and disorder into their works, aiming to expose and attack colonialism, military dictatorship, and rigid religious rules in times of one specific area, and reflecting people's political awakening; and more broadly exhibit given concepts of history, culture and tradition.

2 Magic Realist Symbolic Objects in *Yellow Back Radio Broke-Down*

The same as every magic realist, Reed is also a master of symbolism, and he attempts to present the truth in a magic symbolic way. In *Yellow Back Radio Broke-Down*, there are mainly two kinds of magic realist symbolic objects: instruments that Loop uses to cast hoodoo spells; and the anthropomorphic iron-jawed hogs.

2.1 Hoodoo Religious Instruments

In traditional hoodoo religious ceremony，there are some instruments the wizards use to work spells or to summon hoodoo gods. In *Yellow Back Radio Broke-Down*，though not exactly the same as traditional hoodoo instruments，Loop not only uses some objects as vehicles to interconnect the real world and the hoodoo mystical system，but also take them as symbols of neo-hoodoo aesthetic thoughts，or other mythological archetypes. By using such magic realist symbols，Ishmael Reed delivers his aesthetic judgements and views towards religion and culture to readers.

When Zozo Labrique is dying，she puts a mad dog's tooth（26）in Loop's hands and tells Loop that it would bring him connaissance. And in the following plots，the mad dog's tooth appears several times as the important media between Loop Garoo Kid and the hoodoo magic world. Together with the altar covered with cloth，a tapestry of a heart to each side of which were drawings of serpents（61），a small doll made of feathers，hair，snake skins and pieces of bone，which bore a resemblance to Drag（62），a laced canopy embroidered with such emblems as skulls，crossbones，swords，serpents and hearts（63），they are used in a grotesque way become hoodoo instruments. Among them，some of them are actually innovative for traditional hoodoo. That is to say，on the first level，the hoodoo magic instruments in the novel symbolize the mixture of traditional hoodoo spirits and new elements of the era. Reed makes everyday use the miraculous thing that can arouse magic power. This technique of defamiliarization on the one hand uncover the mystique of common things，while on the other hand emphasizes the syncretism and inclusiveness of hoodoo. Hoodoo is a flexible and developing religion，so，it works under any new circumstances. On the second level，these instruments are symbols of Ishmael Reed's multicultural view. Through connecting common objects with hoodoo religion，Reed encloses mystiques of things in real life，producing magic realist effect.

2.2 Anthropomorphic Object：Iron-jawed Hogs

Magic realist writers are good at personifying things，they give things features that are exclusive of human being and by this way strengthen magic realist effects. In *Yellow Back Radio Broke-Down*，the landlord Drag Gibson sets a torture device to punish the betrayer—a swine pit（113），where there are iron-jawed hogs which feed on human beings. Commonly，hogs are animals without mind，Reed personifies them and makes them think and talk. At the end of the story，Ishmael Reed arranges a conversation about Drag Gibson between two pigs in the swine pit. One pig says that "Yeah that guy was real tasty，especially the bull's sperm on top of his jughead. Wow，that dish was better I'll bet than those heads we got cheated out of they stole for that traveling lecture room".（175）Drag Gibson，a cold-blooded tyrant，however，he is eaten by animals like himself—greedy and bloody thirsty. At the level of word meaning，"hog" can be used to describe the people who is greedy and selfish. The exaggeration of flaws of human beings and the anthropomorphism of animals put the two kinds of species together and make them kill each other. This arrangement enlarges the absurdity of the real world，and digs out the similarity between human society and animal world，thus produce magic realist effects.

The anthropomorphism of these hogs nakedly exposes individualism that has become a mainstream world view in white society. Different from collectivism of Africans, Indians or other nationalities, individualism possibly leads to egoism. Hogs in the story are personalized to make them the concretization of such features as greed, apathy, individualism and materialism, which are originated from industrialization and would give rise to absolutism and dictatorship.

3 Magic Realist Juxtaposition in *Yellow Back Radio Broke-Down*

Yellow Back Radio Broke-Down is one of the representatives of Reed's neo-hoodoo aesthetics. Because Yellow Back Radio is a fictional town, though things in it are abnormal, all of these gain readers' acceptance. Reed puts many celebrities from past in the town and exaggerates their characteristics to mock them, thus create magic realist impression. At the same time, he injects hoodoo magic that is taken as granted by people live in the town. This presupposition naturally blurs the border between reality and fancy.

3.1 Anachronism of the Past, the Present, and the Future

Ishmael Reed deliberately mistakes historical events and corresponding characters to attain satire and irony, enclosing the absurdity of things happened as well as behaviors of the characters. He disrupts timeline to make things impossible happens, parodying the past and producing magic realist effect.

Ishmael Reed summons many historical characters in the small-town, and most of them are pioneers in American westward movement who devoted much to build this new land. In the introduction of Loop Garoo Kid, one of his characteristics is that "he was a mean night tripper who moved from town to town quoting Thomas Jefferson and allowing bandits to build a flophouse around his genius. (9) Thomas Jefferson is the third president of US who is a most influential Founding Father of the United States. One of his labels is freedom for he pursuing Classical Liberalism and scheming Virginia Statute for Religious Freedom and other policies. Here, Loop's idol is Thomas Jefferson and he can't agree with Jefferson's quotations more. And for this reason, Loop allows bandits to build a flophouse, which may not good news for ordinary people. The deliberate anachronism seems to tell readers that the great man who is known for his tremendous contribution to the USA, actually has a dark side—spares no expense to tame America, and shelters the illegal who destroyed the native habitats. Intimation of the bloody pioneering history in America is similar to Latin American writers' exposition of colonist history in their land, both branded with painful memories on the native people's heart.

Ishmael Reed mentions more than one generation of American president in *Yellow Back Radio Broke-Down*, he puts them together as they are still alive at the same time to confuse readers' consciousness towards times."Magic realism is a mode suited to exploring... boundaries, whether the boundaries are onto logical, political geographical, or generic." (5) John Quincy Adams, the sixth president of the USA, also appears in *Yellow Back Radio Broke-Down*. Though this name is just mentioned once, Reed puts Thomas Jefferson and him together, making them contemporary. The juxtaposition of different generations in Yellow Back Radio，makes the town an epitome of the USA since its constitution，blurs readers' conception about times in reality. At the same time，reasonable parody rewrites the past，exhibits the cruel nature as well.

After breaking down the past，Reed exaggerates the present with fragmentary characters and plots by narrating apocryphal history. That is to say，the present is the rewriting of the past that may influence the future. Magic becomes the clue，connecting the plots，which makes the fictional history reasonable and acceptable. "Magical realism at its best opposes fundamentalism and purity；it is at odds with racism，ethnicity and the quest for tap roots，origins and homogeneity".（22）"One of the unique features of magical realism is its reliance upon the reader to follow the example of the narrator in accepting both realistic and magical perspectives of reality on the same level".（3）When Loop and his 86-D circus are confused with the situation where there are no adults except a crowd of children camp around. One of children tells them how they drove these evil adults away with magic pills：

One day we found these pearl-shaped pills in a cave of a mountain. They're what people ages ago called devil's pills. We put them in the streams so that when the grown-ups went to fill their buckets they swallowed some. It confused them more than they were so we moved on them and chased them out of town.（16）

"Devil's pills" do not exist in real world，but Reed makes it a tool to try to remedy governor's behaviors in the fictional world，because it is difficult for him to fix flaws in reality. This action firstly connotes that Reed denies rationalism and materialism's prior position in American society. Reed injects magic elements into the depressed children' fighting back to the autocratic grownups to warn the whole society to stop to retrospect the origin，and not to lose tradition. Secondly，Reed constructs a new system，in which the metaphysical is more powerful than the material，proclaiming that the power of faith is far stronger than nowadays people considered.

By using magic，Reed indicates that such kind of humanism is nonexistent not only in history，but also in modern America. That's the reason that he images a utopian "Anarchotechnological Paradise"—Seven Cities of Cibola（17）as the ideal destination for the children when they depart from European-style American town Yellow Back Radio.

Helicopter is an invention from the future for Chief Showcase who live in the early century，while technological paradise is a product of highly developed science and technology in the future.When Loop Garoo Kid is insulted by "the neo-social realist gang"（34）leaded by Bo Shmo，he is rescued by Chief Showcase，the only surviving Indian chief，who is on his way to Europe with a "Flying Brush Beeve Monster"（37）In order to relive the young man's puzzlement，Chief Showcase tells Loop：

I created it to get around in，made it from spare parts I found in desert ghost towns. I also used a new kind of plant called plastic I discovered growing in the hills like wildfire… I call it a helicopter，lots of mileage on very little fuel，but I wouldn't be surprised if bad medicine steals the patents and calls them his own. Honkie. Devil.（38-39）

Firstly，for Chief Showcase，helicopter is a creation from future；secondly，in history，it is not created by him. Reed makes the representative of tradition the creator of new things to exhibit his view on tradition and history, which is more diversified, inclusive, and up-to-date. At the same time, Reed puts plastic as "a new kind of plant" that covers a mystic color on conventional objects with techniques of defamiliarization.

3.2 Juxtaposition of Reality and Fancy

In *Yellow Back Radio Broke-Down*, the protagonist Loop Garoo Kid controls his opponents with hoodoo magic, accelerating deconstruction of Yellow Back Radio. With the help of hoodoo religion, Reed juxtaposes reality and fancy naturally.The plotting that Loop beats Drag Gibson is in fact the symbol that African cultural tradition and black people's independent spirit can compete with Jewish Christianity—the foundation of American cultural hegemony.

During the process of revenge, Loop's hoodoo magic disturbs radio waves of Yellow Back Radio, which brings chaos to the town, plunging it into a magic realist condition:

Town lying about fifty miles from here—Video Junction. Everybody dead except for the kids up in the mountains dancing and smoking injuntobaccy and some women arriving to a shindig on the backs of obscene goats.... Then everybody got on the ground. They was gnashing their teeth and rolling over each other and the air got all hot and funky... She didn't yell but said some furriner jaw-breaking word, exquisite exquisite, said it over and over again. (55)

With Loop's magic power becoming stronger, people in the town or nearby are becoming crazy. This surreal scene likePaul D in the haunted house in Toni Morrison's *Beloved* (1987), or people with insomnia and amnesia in Macondo in Gabriel García Márquez's *One Hundred Years of Solitude.*When people are under curses, they smoke "injuntobaccy" and have some atavistic behaviors. That is to say, under the manipulation of hoodoo, they go back to their origin that is closely related to Indian civilization. Hoodoo magic provides people room for reflections about history as well as culture.Ishmael Reed combines hoodoo religion and American social reality to form a magic western town, where marginal religions or cultures can compete with mainstream culture. Loop's revenge relies on mysterious religious power of hoodoo.The juxtaposition of fancy and reality triggered by hoodoo magic reflects Reed's strict criticism for history. It's an ultimate criticism to reality rather than a kind of fiction.

As Salman Rushdie says, "sometimes we feel that we straddle two cultures; at other times, that we fall between two stools". (15) One chair is traditional culture, while another is local society.The construction of Yellow Back Radio on enlightening sense is a lash on backward cultural condition in local society.Influenced by imagism and impressionism, Reed's magic town presents artistic surrealistic features, which also reflect hoodoo's inclusiveness as well as his multicultural view.

4 Magic Realist Ambiguity in *Yellow Back Broke-Down*

Ambiguity is a feature of magic realist works that is always presented from more than one aspect in order to enhance magic effect. In *Yellow Back Radio Broke-Down*, magic realist ambiguity mainly embodies from two aspects: one is the ambiguity in narrative, while the other is the ambiguity in characters' identities.

4.1 Ambiguity in Narrative

Ishmael Reed on the one hand implies native slangs，prophetic words，fragmentary narrative and subjective narrative in Yellow Back Radio Broke-Down，on the other hand deliberately deletes quotation marks and hybridizes more than one text genres together such as western fiction and broadcast to innovate narrative.

4.1.1 Narrative Method

Except for Loop Garoo Kid and Chief Showcase，other characters such as Drag Gibson and his men，and historical characters are modern Americans. However，their words mix up with black or Indian slangs. This absurd feature on the one hand satires their ignorance and disrespect to tradition and culture，on the other hand gives readers a sense of illusion，using characters based on reality to imagine a more multicultural world.When Drag mentions the president of the USA，he calls him “the Great White Father”（57），and says：“the president in the East，is probably getting jealous of me cause I’m so fine and the top man and all. They just need an excuse to get the cavalry in here and start up a grand jury”.（57）“The Great White Father” is an address that Indian people call the American president during the initial stage of the USA. In the most cases，they use it to satire the superiority and monopoly on power of the president. Yellow Back Radio is the reduced version of American society，so，Drag Gibson is an incarnation of the USA president who yearns for absolute power. Drag shares same features with an autocratic dictator，and he even can be deemed as the exaggeration of “the president in the East”. However，he ironically names the American president like the Indian native people，which produces exquisite irony. Making one find fault with himself through the way he sniffs at，Ishmael Reed equivocates characters’ narration to deliberately increases unreliability. In this way，Reed achieves ridiculous and satirical effect，at the same time，leads readers to take a look at the real world.

Prophecyis a frequent narrative method in magic realist works. Ishmael Reed arranges some prophetic plots in *Yellow Back Radio Broke-Down*，providing inspiration through magic way.When the circus sees the dead advance man，above the man’s head，there is a “hoodoo rock”（14）. Then，ZozoLabrique says：“I have a funny feeling that everything isn’t all right down there.”（14）Things happen afterwards testify that Zozo like a hoodoo witch who can utter predictions through intuition. And when she is dying，she gives some instruments to Loop and tells him：“It’s a mad dog’s tooth it’ll bring you connaissance and don’t forget the grisgris，the mojo，the wangols old Zozo taught you and when you need more power play poker with the dead”.（26）Like the role of ÚrsulaIguarán in *One Hundred Years of Solitude*，or Baby Suggs in *Beloved*，Zozois a prophet or a woman with wisdom and knowledge in *Yellow Back Radio Broke Down*. Though she doesn’t live a long life like the formertwo，she plays an irreplaceable role in Loop’s revenge—it is her who teaches Loop the hoodoo magic. Prophetic plots on the one hand magnify senses of human beings，and reveal the mystique of objects；on the other hand，reflect its charm and its close relation with everyday life.

Plots in *Yellow Back Radio Broke-Down*are fragmented but combines to an organic whole. Ishmael Reed breaks the convention of narrative continuity，linearity and order of traditional discourses to give readers a captivating effect and exhibit social diversity.AmaryllChanady states that magical realism is an "amalgamation of a rational and an irrational world view". (21) Firstly, scenes in the text shift frequently, so dialogues and characters accordingly change like watching a movie. Loop Garoo Kid is expelled by his Father and joins a circus, beginning a new journey. The destination is a town named Yellow Back Radio. Then suddenly comes the second scene, the Banker, the Marshal, and the Doctor send a visit to Drag Gibson, asking for help. However, the aim and the cost are also the town Yellow Back Radio. The whole narrative seems scattered and leaping, but all plots lead to the same object. Fragmentary narrative has progressive layers of bedding, until the climax. Secondly, representational times disappear in the whole story. Times are broken, so readers need to participate in the storytelling to judge which scenes happened earlier, which are happening now, and which will happen later.By this way, Reed weakens conventional elements of a novel to break traditional narrative, exhibiting innovativeness and pluralism of neo-black aesthetics. Lastly, the ending of the story is open. In this story, the fragmentary narrative ending for one thing, invites readers to imagine varied possibilities, which makes the construction of theme more colorful, for another, shows the harmonicity of hoodoo religion.

There are many characters in*Yellow Back Radio Broke Down*, the shift of different narrative points of view delivers information from different opposite positions. And subjective narrative from characters increases the unreliability and ambiguity of the text.The use of such narrative techniques which "assume that there are multiple versions of a story, emphasizes the possibility of expressing multiple perspectives in the text".(85)In the text, less voice-overs than characters' statements appear. And characters' words alternately and fluently appear without any notices, just like plots of a film. Through this magic realist narrative method, firstly, distance between readers and characters is narrowed; secondly, subjective narrative in *Yellow Back Radio Broke-Down* exhibits things from multiple angles, making both characters and events three-dimensional full. Round subjective narrative like the harmonic mixture of African traditional music with stereoscopic sound effect and black jazz with improvisational switches and performances.

4.1.2 Techniques Strengthening the Effect of Narrative

Apart from such narrative methods as Indian or black slangs, prophetic plotting, fragmentary narrative and subjective narrative, Ishmael Reed uses some techniques to strengthen the effect of narrative, and at the same time to deepen miraculous impression. Firstly, the whole text lacks quotation marks.When readers come into contact for the first time with the novel, it may be difficult to distinguish the voice-over and the conversations for there are no quotation marks. Readers can only tell them apart by contexts and characters' names, which sometimes emerge. Reed utilizes postmodern literary narrative techniques to deconstruct traditional narrative form and convey his aesthetic thought. Secondly, Reed conceals dialogists to increase difficulty for readers to get the connotation of the text, which forces readers to make a careful study on hoodoo metaphorical system hidden in the text. The mystique of the dialogue pattern echoes the magic realist story content.Thirdly, Ishmael Reed uses two small circles to present shifts of different scenes and plots, among which the left one is solid and while the right one is hollow. The obscure notice is unconventional and revolutionary，showing Reed's ingenuity and revolting artistic thoughts.

Besides，the genre of the text is ambiguous and miscellaneous. It shares features with parodic historical novel，western fiction and radio play.First of all，this novel like a big party where not only historical personages from different times，fictional characters living in different areas，but also historical events，fictitious events converge together. Among the limited descriptions of the environment，there is a typical one："The street was a dumpheap of Brueghel face，of Hogarth faces，of Coney Island hot-dog kissers，ugly pusses and sinking mugs，whole precincts of flat peepers and silly lookers".（104）Brueghel Pieter's paintings depict peasants' life and their revolutionary struggles to connote politics of the times. Through this metaphor，wild and sluggish street with atmosphere in tension can be noticed. William Hogarth painted to uncover and satire social injustice，which is trenchant in depicting the real world. Coney Island is the earliest large-scale amusement park in America. Until the 1960s，it was not as prosperous as it was initially built. Besides these metaphors，the rough portrayal of characters--"hotdog kissers，ugly pusses"，"flat peepers and silly lookers"，reflects people's indifference and vulgarity. The declined and deteriorating situation provides readers a stark and desolate feeling in the sensation of the town Yellow Back Radio.

Ishmael Reed hides quotation marks and identities of the speakers，at the same time，he deliberately gives very few voice-overs，which makes the whole text to look like a playscript. Based on dialogues and commentaries，radio play makes full use of sound effects to strengthen atmosphere. When Loop Garoo Kid appears and flogs the hypocritical Preacher，who always plays with words. Loop queries him angrily：

（CRACK！）Whenever you say something like that.（CRACK！！ CRACK！！）In the future. Check out some sources.（CRACK！！ CRACK！！）Motherfucker！！（CRACK！ CRACK！）Ask your mama.（CRACK！）Yo wife.（CRACK！ CRACK！）Guillaume Apollinaire.（CRACK！ POP！ CRINKLE！ SNAP！）Anybody you want to ask.（CRACK！）But get your information right next time.（NICK！）O. K.？（103）

Firstly，brackets and words written in capital letters are the simulation of sound，which used to vividly deliver Loop's anger and his increasing magic power. With these emphasizing marks，readers can intuitively and visually get the context like listening to a radio play. Secondly，Ishmael Reed uses repetition to impress readers. Repeated word "CRACK" gives prominence to Loop's hoodoo magic power while repeated sentence pattern "ask sb." highlights Loop's violent emotion.These features make the *Yellow Back Radio Broke-Down* to read like a script of radio play，strengthening narrative effects.

4.2 Ambiguity in Characters' Identities and Related Mythological Prototypes

In magic realist works，the writer always endows characters multiple identities with deep connotations.Ishmael Reed deliberately complicate and equivocate characters' identities，on the one hand，produces magic realist effects，one the other hand，concretizes abstract concepts through characterization，enclosing issues in reality.

4.2.1 Multiple Identities of Loop Garoo Kid

Loop Garoo Kid， who is the central character in *Yellow Back Radio Broke-Down*， is the most complex figure. Firstly， he appears as a black cowboy with rebellious spirit. Different from traditional protagonist， Loop seems like the incarnation of evil spirit. He plays childish pranks on government organization， flirts with women， and makes the Pope cry from exasperation. All these features make him the evil spirit of hoodoo， who dares to challenge fixed social order. LoopGaroo Kid becomes a hybrid of black cowboy and hoodoo spirit. Ishmael Reed combines traditional cowboy culture and black culture to create a highly inclusive character， thus making Loop a typical representative of his neo-hoodoo aesthetics and the view of a more diversified culture.

On the one hand， cowboysare always labelled such tags as freedom， ambition， or more passively， expansionism. Though they made great contributions to develop the USA， at the same time， they deprived native people's rights and brought disasters to them. So， the identity of cowboy has the more negative meaning—the oppressor. While on the other hand， slave trade brought black people traumatic and miserable life. They were for a long time in a passive and oppressed position. Ishmael Reed combines the two opposite identities into Loop Garoo Kid， making him a symbol of hoodoo harmonicity， which has the ability to defuse cultural conflict.

From the religious point of view， Loop Garoo Kid has similarities with both Christ Jesus and Hoodoo Dambala. First of all， Loop is molded as an unfilial son and abandoned man， who is expelled by Father after a quarrel， betrayed by his so-called friends after them gaining benefits from him， and teased by any insignificant objects. As recorded， Jesus is son of God， here Loop Garoo Kid becomes another son of God.Loop's experience seems like another version of Jesus's： born with nobleness， betrayed by closest relatives， becomes the scapegoat of human beings' sins.Then， Loop Garoo Kid shares the same characteristic with Dambala， the chieftain of hoodoo spirits. Dambala is the incarnation of snake and its symbolic color is white. According to hoodoo religion， a complete person includes two parts： ti-bon-angel and gro-bon-angel. The former means the cherub of virtue， while the latter is the archangel of virtue. Loop born with some symbolic birthmarks： "born with a caul over his face and ghost lobes on his ears..." （9） The caul on Loop's face like another head of him， which endows him double consciousness and double perception. With the increasement of Loop's hoodoo magic power， his appearance changes： "A white snake moved around Loop Garoo'sneck， green with envy. It frowned above its pink eyes and whistled its pink tongue". （68） It is more and more obvious that Loop is the incarnation of the chieftain of hoodoo spirits Dambala.Christianity is the orthodox religion in western world， while hoodoo is disparaged as paganism. The doubled religious identity strengthens the mystique of Loop's identity and manifests the charm of hoodoo， exhibiting Reed's inclusive cultural view.

What's more， Loop's behaviors symbolize Dionysian spirit.Dionysus is one of the Olympus Twelve in ancient Greek mythology who spreads happiness and love， gives impetus to establish laws and build civilization in ancient society， thus maintaining world peace.Loop Garoo Kid in this novel is depicted as a joker who once immersed himself in amusement： "Once a wild joker he cut the fool before bemused Egyptians， dressed like Mortimer Snerd and spilled french fries on his lap at Las

Vegas' top of the strip".（9）Loop seems to have background of Egyptian civilization，and his appearance is important for "bemused Egyptians". According to the record，Dionysus and his sacrifice were first introduced into Greece from Egypt. That is to say，Loop and Dionysus share similar background. Mortimer Snerd，the comic puppet，is famous for its clownish bumpkin image. Loop is fond of amusing people by dressing like a joker and behaving like a comedian. This feature tallies with Dionysus，who is the incarnation of joy.

4.2.2 Multiple Identities of Other Characters

Besides Loop Garoo Kid，identities of other characters in *Yellow Back Radio Broke-Down* also fraught with uncertainty and ambiguity. Their intricate identities show Ishmael Reed's complex or even contradictory attitude towards some existing epistemologies. And at the same time，characters' mysterious backgrounds make the story pattern complicated and confusing，deepening the magic realist theme.

Chief Showcase，is the last surviving native American in the town Yellow Back Radio，who is deliberately kept on by the autocratic landlord Drag Gibson for gags.（89）He firstly appears as an Indian chief living in the early 19th century with "The Flying Brush Beeve Monster" from the future. In this story，Chief Showcase is creative，kind，tolerant，and resourceful. He invents helicopter with materials he finds in deserted ghost cities and "a new kind of plant called plastic"，（39）he saves Loop Garoo Kid and sends him to Video Junction，（43）he keeps calm and patient about his revenge for genocide."Showcase" means a box that is used for showing objects in public places，such as store or museum.Reed takes it as the last Indian people's name，suggesting that Chief Showcase survives to be used as a sample and exhibition of Indian living fossil.Ishmael Reed blends traditional character image and modern spirits to create Chief Showcase，making him a symbol of the bitter history of native Indian，the relic of Indian culture，a glimmer of hope for Indian civilization like his elder cousin Chief Cochise，and the possibility that native Indians are capable of rewriting history.More broadly，with the amazing creativity and imagination，Chief Showcase dares to try and successes in inventing objects，which satires the prim conservative such as Bo Shmo. It makes Showcase the representative of advancing time spirit.

Drag Gibson is the number one villain in the story. He is greedy and never satisfied with his lands and possessions；he is selfish and merciless，he murders his ex-wife and feeds his mail order bride to the iron-jawed hogs；and he is autocratic，even shows contempt for the federal government. Above all，Drag Gibson is a completely tyrant，who is indifferent to anything except for himself.When Drag Gibson and his followers mention people who have different racial backgrounds，they call them heathens（20）or infidels.（56）And they call native Indians "injuns"，（53）while the Chinese "chinee"，（58）which are offensive words for the native Americans and Chinese people. In a dialogue between Drag Gibson and Skinny McCullough，Skinny calls God "a gila monster"（45）And Drag replies "Those Protestants，so lazy with allegory".（45）From the perspective of religion，Drag Gibson and his followers are narrow-minded dogmatism. So，Drag is the representative of religious extremists and the spokesman of Christianity；While from the perspective of race，Drag Gibson adopts a hostile attitude towards other kinds of people，which makes him a merciless racist. Yellow Back Radio is the miniature of American society, while Drag Gibson is the incarnation of dictatorial ethos in such society.What's more, the depiction of Drag Gibson's behaviors shows his queer leaning. He tends to be a homosexual. The detailed depiction of Drag's kissing with a male horse portrays a pervert who is crazy about material desire. And the reason he prefers this abnormal green horse may be the horse is very similar to himself. They are both queer. The word "queer" mostly refers to a homosexual, especially man. Ishmael Reed puts them together to deliver the information that Drag is also the representative of the grotesque in American society. He is an aggregation of grotesque and absurdity in American society.

Zozo Labriqueand Mustache Sal are two significant female characters in this story. Zozo Labrique is a hoodoo mambo and she is also black. It is her, who teaches Loop Garoo Kid the hoodoo magic, and offers prophecies. And when she is dying, she gives Loop such hoodoo instruments as a mad dog's tooth and poker, and warns Loop don't toforget hoodoo spells she taught him before. Zozo is the guide who inspires Loop on hoodoo magic, and the "charter member of the American Hoo-Doo Church". (10) The same as Baby Suggs in *Beloved* and ÚrsulaIguarán in *One Hundred Years of Solitude*, ZozoLabrique is an older prophet with wisdom in her field. Because Zozo is the ancestor of hoodoo, the teacher of Loop, so, it can be said that Zozo is the incarnation of traditional hoodoo religion, the origin of neo-hoodoo. What's more, Zozo is also the representative of traditional African women who"wore a full skirt and a bandana on her head. Her face was black wrinkled and hard. The sun suddenly appeared, causing the gold hoops on her ears to sparkle". (12) She is the representative of traditional African women who are maltreated and marginalized. And she is the strong black female image as far as Reed concerns. When Loop summons hoodoo Loa, in his spells, he calls Zozo as "ZozoLabrique Marie Laveau the Great Improvisers". (63) In Loop's eyes, Zozo is the real master of hoodoo.She is the incarnation of hoodoo spirits.

Mustache Sal is a controversial female character in this story. Outwardly, she is giddy, greedy, and even nymphomaniacal. She flirts with any possible men and marries to Drag in order to possess his wealth. Among the hoodoo divinities, Erzulie Freda is the spirit of love and beauty, who symbolizes sex in hoodoo religion. And she wears three wedding rings from her husbands, one of which is from Damballa. In *Yellow Back Radio Broke-Down*, Mustache Sal is the ex-girlfriend of Loop. And one of Loop's identities is the hoodoo Dambala. Concluding from all above, Mustache Sal is the embodiment of the hoodoo spirit Erzulie Freda. In addition, different from the female bar keeper Big Lizzy, Sal doesn't discriminate and she equally accepts men of different races. Though Sal seems superficially frivolous, she doesn't like the western tyrant Drag, his people, and the prevailing racially discriminatory atmosphere in American society Drag represents. She is highly racially inclusive, which makes her a representative of multiculturalism. In contrast to the Hurdy Gurdy girls and Drag's ex-wife, Mustache Sal behaves independently and intelligently. She has his own ideas and she clears her goals. She plays around Loop, Showcase and Drag, keeping her wits about her all the time. Sal designs stratagem to murder Drag Gibson without fear and hesitation. Though she fails, her cleverness and capability make her a new woman with advanced minds in her times. Through the audacious depiction of new woman, Ishmael Reed shows his appreciation towards female with self-consciousness.

5 Conclusions

Not like most African American writers，Ishmael Reed abandons the traditional method，through which it backtracks traumas to accuse slavery and to restore blackness. So，in *Yellow Back Radio Broke-Down*，he doesn't concentrate much efforts on depicting the painful slave past of African Americans，and emphasizing the miserable experiences. Thus，the novel path makes Ishmael Reed a dissenter in African American literature. On the contrary，Reed adopts African traditional religion，which is the representative of black culture as a lever to pry up American society—where the white culture dominates. Through applying such hoodoo creeds as syncretism，synchronism and inclusiveness，Reed constructs a space，where the hoodoo magic is predominant among other religions，especially the Christianity，which is deemed as prior in white world；and at the same time，by injecting magic realist juxtaposition，ambiguity，and images，Reed deconstructs the history that is written by the white."History is always ambiguous. Facts are hard to establish，and capable of being given many meanings. Reality is built on prejudices，misconceptions and ignorance as well as on our perceptiveness and knowledge".（25）The magic realist parody of history exhibits black aesthetics reflected from hoodoo religion. The returning to origin makes Reed a root-seeker as well.

Through parodying history with hoodoo magic，Ishmael Reed reveals in this story that the fundamental approach for the revival of national tradition and culture is to break awaymonoculturalism and essentialism，to advocate integrated and open，heterogeneous and diversified culture.

参考文献

[1] Bell，Bernard. W., 1987. *The Afro-American Novel and Its Tradition*. Amherst：University of Massachusetts Press.

[2] Bowers，Maggie Ann, 2004. *Magic（al）Realism*. New York：Routledge.

[3] Chanady，Amaryll Beatrice, 1985. *Magical Realism and the Fantastic：Resolved Versus Unresolved Antinomy*. New York：Garland.

[4] Cooper，Brenda, 1998. *Magical Realism in West African Fiction：Seeing with a Third Eye*. London：Routledge.

[5] García Márquez，Gabriel, 1967. *One Hundred Years of Solitude*. New York：Harper Collins.

[6] Gates，Henry Louis, 1988. *The Signifying Monkey：A Theory of Afro-American Literary Criticism*. New York：Oxford University Press.

[7] Hicks，Jack. *Cutting Edges：Young American Fiction for the '70s*. New York：Holt，Rinehart and Winston，Inc.，1973.

[8] Morrison，Toni, 1987. *Beloved*. New York：Alfred A. Knopf.

[9] Reed，Ishmael, 2000. *Yellow Back Radio Broke-Down*. Chicago：Dalkey Archive Press.

[10] Rushdie，Salman, 1991. "Imaginary Homelands." *Essays and Criticism 1981-1991*. London：Granta，8-21.

[11] Weixlmann，Joe, 1991. "African American Deconstruction of the Novel in the Work of Ishmael Reed and Clarence Major." *Melus* 17：4，57-79.

[12] Zamora，Lois and Wendy B., 1995. *Faris. Magical Realism：Theory，History，Community，Durham*. NC and London：Duke University Press.

[13] 林元富. 历史·神话·虚构·幻想——伊斯米尔·里德和他的〈黄后盖收音机破了〉[J]. 外国文学，2004（6）：12-15.

[14] 蔺玉清. 论《黄后盖收音机的解体》中的伏都宗教与“新伏都”[J]. 山东外语教学，2013（4）：79-83.

从原型-神话批评分析《最蓝的眼睛》中男性形象神话原型

黄　丹

摘　要：托妮·莫里森是美国有名的黑人作家，她的作品真实反映了黑人解放后黑人群体的真实生活状况。《最蓝的眼睛》是她小说的开山之作，小说通过多个视角描写黑人女孩佩克拉在追求蓝色的眼睛（白人文化）过程中遭受的悲惨遭遇，最终失而不得的结局。本文通过运用弗莱神话-原型批评的“后站”方法，宏观分析人物形象，分别找出乔利和皂头牧师神话原型，即哈迪斯和奥顾瑞斯，进一步说明分析人物原型对理解小说黑人文化缺失主题的引导作用。

关键词：《最蓝的眼睛》；托妮·莫里森；神话-原型批评；诺思诺普·弗莱

Abstract: Tony Morrison is a famous black writer as her work reflects the real status-quo of the black group. *The Bluest Eyes* is his first work which describes the sad events when pursuing the white culture but no results delivered. This paper uses the “post-station” method of Frye mythology-prototype criticism to analyze the characters in a macroscopic way and find out the mythical prototypes of Jolly and Pastor，namely Hades and O’Guris，further explaining the analysis of the character prototype to understand the novel.

Key words: *The Bluest Eyes*；Tony Morrison；mythology-prototype criticism；Northrop Frye

1 引　言

非裔美国作家托妮·莫里森在美国颇具盛名，她于1993年获得诺贝尔文学奖，她的文学功底深厚，本科时代专门学习古典文学和英语。她的小说作品风格独特，想象新奇，但小说主题意韵丰富，故一经出版就引起广泛的关注。其主要作品有《最蓝的眼睛》《秀拉》《所罗门之歌》《柏油马路》《宠儿》《爵士乐》《仁爱》等。她的作品主要表现亲情和母爱，且作品大多都发生在黑人白人群体之间或者男性与女性之间。之前的国内外研究都重视对其小说中女性形象的分析和解读，不可否认的是，莫里森作品中的女性形象精神饱满，人物性格鲜明。但细读她的作品文本，可以发现她作品中的男性形象在不多的笔墨中也刻画得令人印象深刻，人物个性明显，而这些男性形象对全书的主题有着突出的表现力。

《最蓝的眼睛》是她的第一部小说作品，出版于1970年。《最蓝的眼睛》通过不同人物的视角转换从多维度视角展现了黑人女孩佩克拉的悲惨命运。佩克拉从小遭受各种不平等的待遇，受到黑人社区人们的排挤和欺侮，而她却把自己这些遭遇归结为她没有一双蓝色的眼镜，她天真地认为只要自己有一双蓝色的眼睛，所有人都会对她有截然相反的态度，并会友好地接纳她。为此，她一直幻想拥有一双像白人一样蓝色的眼睛，甚至去找牧师乞求一双这样的眼睛，但牧师却诱骗她毒死了院子里的狗，为此她大受打击，而在这之前她已遭到家中父亲的强暴并怀有身孕，精神压力巨大，处于崩溃边缘。最终这两者造就了她精神的崩溃，她变成一个成天幻想自己已经拥有蓝色的眼睛的疯人。笔者认为导致小说主人公的悲剧结局的一个重要因素就是群体中的男性人物，尤其是佩克拉的生父乔利和皂头牧师。因此笔者认为分析这两者形象神话原型对理解女主人公的悲剧结局，进而理解小说黑人文化缺失主题具有引导性作用。

由于深受古典文学的影响，莫里森的小说人物原型大都由神话故事异化而来，故要更好地理解小说文化内涵和小说人物形象性格，必须分析小说的人物神话原型，从源头入手，更好地把握其文化内涵。国内外都从不同的角度对《最蓝的眼睛》进行了研究。国内研究主要是围绕引起主人公佩克拉的悲惨命运的原因背景等做分析和探究莫妮森独特的写作手法。国外研究主要是从莫妮森这部作品所引起的社会影响角度看这部作品。虽有研究从弗莱神话-原型批评分析《最蓝的眼睛》中部分主人公形象，但都忽略小说男性形象神话原型的分析，而小说男性人物是导致主人公悲剧结局的重要人物，必须予以重视。故而本文拟从弗莱神话-原型批评理论出发，结合小说情节分析《最蓝的眼睛》中的主要男性形象神话原型，进而得出人物形象原型分析引导读者对文化缺失主题的理解的结论，以期对后来的研究者提供一点借鉴作用。

2　主要男性形象神话原型分析

2.1　乔利神话原型分析

弗莱结合人类学和心理学把文学与神话联系在一起，从神话、仪式这些被视为积淀人类祖先原始经验和原型意象的形式出发，认为文学是神话仪式的表现，是神话的复活与再现。弗莱所理解的神话，实际上是故事、情节或叙事，只不过在人类社会抽象思维尚未形成之前，文化只有故事的形态，而最早的神话即是关于神祇的故事。作为故事，神话总具有潜在的文学性。他这一观点实际上就是把神话故事文学化。神话往往保留着语言的象征意义，不同的神话意象象征不同的寓意。了解不同神话故事寓意对于了解故事的文化和思想内涵都有重要的意义，这就使得神话像意象一样具有可交流性。在古希腊神话故事中有这样的一个关于冥王哈迪斯的神祇故事：哈迪斯与波塞冬、宙斯都是兄弟，为瑞亚所生。珀耳塞福涅乃是宙斯和德墨忒尔的女儿，也就是冥王的侄女，但冥王哈迪斯垂涎其美貌，便与宙斯共谋设下圈套，在地母神盖亚的协助下以美艳的水仙为诱饵，把正在草地上嬉戏的珀耳塞福涅劫持至冥府施行强暴并逼迫其做了冥后。德墨忒尔寻女未果，一怒之下施展神威，令种子深埋大地寸草不生，人间饥荒成灾，直接威胁奥林匹斯山诸神的供奉。无奈之下宙斯只得让步，派神使赫尔墨斯去冥界带回珀尔塞福涅。然而老奸巨猾的哈迪斯在神使到达前说服珀塞福涅吃了六颗石榴籽，从而迫使她一年之中要有三分之一的时间留在冥府，其余的时间则回到地上和母亲团聚。珀耳塞福涅在冥界时，忧郁的母亲遭受丧女之痛而疏于农事，大地毫无生机，人们忍受严冬的酷寒和死寂；她回到地臣母女相聚时，春天亦随之而来，草木复苏一派勃勃生机，于是有了一年四季春夏秋冬的轮回，珀耳塞福涅也因此被尊为春之女神。根据弗莱在《批评的剖析》中提出神话“移用”，即移用的基本原则：在神话中可以通过隐喻来表明具有同一性的，在浪漫故事中却只能通过明喻的某些方式联系起来；类比，有意义的联想、偶然相伴出现的意象等等。通过阅读文章情节，不难发现，佩克拉父亲乔利与冥王哈迪斯有着相似性，乔利的形象可以看作是哈迪斯神人物的移用和变形。首先，从对象关系上来看，小说主人公佩克拉和乔利的关系是亲生父女关系，而哈迪斯和珀耳塞福涅是侄父关系，他们这两者的结合都属于是乱伦关系；其次，从方式手段上来看，《最蓝的眼睛》中有一段叙写乔利如何强暴佩克拉，他的心理活动以及他的强迫行为，正是这些强迫行为和强迫手段给佩克拉的心理留下深深的阴影，构成佩克拉最后疯掉悲剧的一个主要因素。在希腊神话中，哈迪斯通过劫持然后强暴珀耳塞福涅，进而胁迫后者成为冥后，为后边的母亲寻找的故事铺垫。因此，两者使用的手段都是相似的，通过强有力的，在对象非自愿的情况下达成两性关系。最后，两者所代表的社会或者神界地位上来看，乔利是一家之主，乃是一家的希望，他在当时的家庭中所代表的就是黑人男性不可挑战的父权。例如，他在家中不赚钱，而由他的妻子赚钱养家，同时其他人对此还不敢有任何意见；哈迪斯乃是冥界之王，他在冥界就代表至高无上的权威和权力，其他人不可逾越和质疑。通过以上的对比，笔者认为冥王哈迪斯就是乔利的神话原型，莫里森根据时代的要求和小说的需要对哈迪斯的形象进行移位变形，从而更好地展现了佩克拉所处的悲惨境地。正如弗莱所言，神话意象的世界。通常是用宗教中天堂或者乐园的概念表现出来的，而且这个世界是神启式的，即一个完全隐喻的世界，在这个隐喻的世界里，每一个事物都意指其他的事物，似乎一切都处在一个单一的无限本体之中。乔利神话原型是哈迪斯的分析增强了小说中乔利所代表的父权形象，同时在《最蓝的眼睛》中，乔利这个人物形象所意指的是当时黑人群体中的黑人男性，这群人代表社会的权威，但是在思想上却和乔利一样，缺乏积极上进精神，心中缺少对周围亲人的爱和关心，内心没有黑人文化精神的支撑和文化信仰，一味只认同白人文化，盲目追随白人文化，丧失自身的文化自信。

2.2 皂头牧师神话原型分析

弗莱把神话视作一种文化模式，表达人类如何塑造他们建立起来的文明史以及对该行为的思考：“神话作为一个完整体系，按自己方式解释了某个社会的宗教信仰、历传统，关于宇宙的思考。”因此，按照弗莱所说，通过寻找人物形象的神话原型，从神话中探寻人物所表现的社会宗教信仰等，这对理解小说社会背景和小说主题都大有裨益。而在《最蓝的眼睛》小说的叙述中，皂头牧师的形象主要是通过他自己的回忆自述呈现的，他是一个落魄贵族家庭中的私生子，并以此为荣，付出一切努力来保持自己的落魄贵族身份，接受教育，最后当上牧师。做牧师之后，他自己做的勾当，他自己都认为是不准确的，但是还是继续下去做了。他的这一系列行为导致他欺骗佩克拉，最终使佩克拉遭受心理打击和心理欺骗，致使她崩溃。在罗马神话中，有一个这样的卜算者叫奥顾瑞斯，通过鸟飞的方向进行预卜未来，他自己也知道自己的卜算是骗人的，但是他仍旧为别人卜算，当然也有很多人要找他卜算。笔者认为这个卜算者与皂头牧师至少有三点相似之处；第一，从职业的相上来看，皂头牧师的职业就是牧师，帮助信徒忏悔，达成他们的愿望，而奥顾瑞斯的职业是卜算者，为那些相信通过卜算预测命运的人占卜。第二，从他们的职业道德素养上来说，皂头牧师本身文化修养是比较高，值得尊敬的，但是其道德修养是不足的。他自己都认为自己是神棍，认为自己的行为不正确，但是仍然一直这样错误的做。奥顾瑞斯知道自己的占卜是欺骗性的，却仍装作自己的占卜是真的一样，欺骗前来的占卜者，这两者的职业素养道德都是毋庸置疑地急需提高。第三，从他们代表的信仰层面来看，皂头牧师代表人们对上帝对基督的虔诚的信仰，而奥顾瑞斯则代表当时罗马人对巫术的敬仰和相信，认为命运都在上天手上。结合弗莱所提出来的神话“移位”基本原则，笔者认为《最蓝的眼睛》中皂头牧师形象的神话原型就是奥顾瑞斯，且奥顾瑞斯在整个罗马神话中提及较少，这也暗示奥顾瑞斯在整个神话之中的地位较轻，微不足道。但这二者共同代表的意义值得去探究，他们都代表信仰，但这种信仰都是欺骗性的，是不值得提倡而且可能是导致信民们崩溃的，这也就是说我们应该改造这种信仰或者放弃这样无用的信仰，进而寻找新的有利于我们自身的信仰。

3 神话原型分析对理解小说主题的引导作用

小说主题是小说的中心命题，关系小说对当时社会的影响，对特定读者的震撼。但文学作品同时又是隐晦含蓄的，它需要文学批评者通过不同的方式解读小说的内涵，揭示小说的主题，从而使读者能够清晰地理解和认识小说深藏的内涵。本文对小说中男性形象的分析正是起着这样的作用，所分析的男性形象与小说主人公的悲剧性结局都有直接的关系，因而这样的解析对于小说文化缺失主题的理解具有引导作用，并且能够帮助读者追溯文化源头。

原型分析通过对小说形象的解读，使读者明确小说人物所具有的人物特征，从而为引导读者理解小说主题做铺垫。本文前两部分对小说中两位男性人物神话原型进行了分析，认为希腊神话中的哈迪斯是乔利的神话原型，罗马神话中的奥顾瑞斯是皂头牧师的神话原型。乔利在小说中是黑人社会权威的代表，他的价值导向和价值观念对整个黑人群体都是举足轻重的，而他的文化价值取向却是信仰白人文化，摒弃黑人文化的，这对黑人文化的发展来说是十分不利的；同时也正是因为他一味追求白人文化，但白人文化却不接纳黑人，导致自己心中价值信念丢失，行为放荡不羁，没有观念支撑最终直接导致女儿的悲剧，这也恰恰印证了原型哈迪斯的身份之寓意。哈迪斯是冥界之王，是地狱的代表，地狱代表万劫不复和黑暗，恰恰乔利对于佩克拉来说就是地狱就是黑暗的地府。借助原型分析，可以清楚地看到黑人群体由于自身文化的缺失而导致群体中其他人物的不幸命运。同时，皂头牧师也代表社会的信仰，代表黑人群体的信念，皂头牧师在《最蓝的眼睛》中是一直相信自己生父的贵族身份，并且也一直在努力维持自己所认为的高贵血统。这体现他对白人文化是深深的信仰，但是从小说的结局来看，神父这种欺骗性的行为也是导致小说黑人女孩凄惨命运的动因之一。这暗示这样对白人文化的信仰是不可相信的，是误导的。既然现有的白人文化信仰不可相信，那么就必须要探寻黑人文化的信仰，否则像女主人公这样的不幸命运就将一直持续下去。就像神话原型中的奥顾瑞斯，相信他占卜未来结果的人会追随他所谓的占卜结果而去规划未来，这可能也会导致他们的悲剧结局。通过对这两者的原型寓意分析，笔者发现导致黑人不幸命运的都是黑人自身文化信仰的问题，而这就引导我们走向文章的主题，即探求黑人文化的根，相信黑人文化的力量，通过改变自身的信仰，为自己发声，从而改变黑人的命运。无论之前对乔利还是对皂头牧师的原型分析，可以看出黑人命运的不幸之源在于黑人对自己文化信仰的缺失。那么要改变黑人命运就要改变黑人群体的信仰，寻找自己的本真的黑人文化信仰，这样才能一步步改变命运。这一结论与《最蓝的眼睛》小说的文化缺失主题相符，是基于小说人物情节的基础上借助原型批评的宏观方法引导出来的。因此，对《最蓝的眼睛》主要男性形象的原型分析对小说文化缺失主题的理解具有引导作用。

4 结　语

莫里森小说《最蓝的眼睛》独具新意，小说情节构思巧妙，叙述结构新奇而又富有深意，小说主题意义深远，对黑人社会甚至美国社会影响深远。本文通过使用弗莱神话-原型批评的方法，对小说主要男性形象神话原型进行分析，认为乔利的神话原型是希腊神话中的冥王哈迪斯，而皂头牧师的神话原型则是罗马神话中的一位占卜者奥顾瑞斯。在这基础之上，笔者通过进一步分析发现，对人物神话寓意的分析对理解该小说黑人文化缺失主题具有引导作用。

参考文献

[1] Frye，Northrop, 1997. *Anatomy of Criticism*.Oxfordshire：Princeton University Press，Print.

[2] Morrison，Toni, 2002. *The Bluest Eye*.New York：HOLT RINEHART AND WINSTON，Print.

[3] 李元俏. 从神话原型批评看《最蓝的眼睛》中的乔利形象[J]. 长安学刊，2016（2）：88-89.

[4] 鲁刚. 古希腊罗马神话词典[J]. 郑述谱编译. 北京：中国社会科学出版社，1984：113-118.

[5] 牛志远. 浅谈神话原型批评理论. 文体艺术，2010（2）：113-114.

[6] 诺思洛普·弗莱. 批评的剖析[M]. 陈慧，袁宪军，吴伟仁译. 天津：百花文艺出版社，2002：150-151.

[7] 唐小霞. 希腊神话视阈下《最蓝的眼睛》人物原型解读[J]. 辽宁工程技术大学学报（社会科学版），2013（4）：402-406.

[8] 吴持哲. 诺思洛普·弗莱文论选集[M]. 北京：中国社会科学出版社，1997：115-116.

非洲作家阿依·克韦·阿尔马赫国内外研究述评

常　红

摘　要：阿伊·克韦·阿尔马赫是非洲最具意识形态倾向的作家之一。他的著作具有传记性、社会性、政治性、历史性和思想性，包括对所有殖民机构和活动的猛烈攻击，揭示了非洲如何能够走上复兴和发展道路的社会愿景。其创作手法的多样性和作品主题的广泛性引起国内外学界的关注，马克思主义、存在主义、神话批评、后殖民主义批评等各种理论和视角都可以用来解读阿尔马赫的作品。本文对迄今阿尔马赫国内外研究做一综述并阐明其研究意义。

关键词：阿依·克韦·阿尔马赫；非洲；研究综述

1　引　言

阿依·克韦·阿尔马赫（Ayi Kwei Armah，1939—）是非洲加纳小说家，为非洲大陆小说创作的发展做出了巨大贡献。早年在阿奇莫塔大学接受教育，之后去往哈佛大学学习社会学。他曾在加纳、坦桑尼亚、莱索托和美国担任教师，还在阿尔及利亚、墨西哥和巴黎担任记者。自1982年以来，他一直住在塞内加尔首都达喀尔附近的普罗波，并未返回其家乡加纳。从《美好的人尚未诞生》（1968）到《碎片》（1970）、《为什么我们这样有福？》（1972）、《两千个季节》（1973）、《治疗者》（1975）、《欧西里斯崛起》（1995），他始终用散文小说作为媒介来审视非洲问题的复杂性和严重性。对他来说，殖民主义是一种“征服后的欧洲战略”，目的是让非洲不发达和依赖欧洲（Armah，213）。加纳第一任总统夸梅·恩克鲁马曾试图沿着社会主义道路发展的决策遭受到系统性的挫败，1966年的军事政变彻底阻断了这一发展道路。在《美好的人尚未诞生》小说中，阿尔马赫对加纳在不稳定、贫穷、腐败、粗放积累和消灭消费的背景下取得进展的前景做了冷静和悲观的评价，然而，作者后期作品中出现话语转换。在内容和叙事风格上，《欧西里斯的崛起》承认了非洲发展和解放的可能性，同时摆脱了殖民主义强加给非洲的“差异性”负担，认为这些负担是殖民主义强加于它的（Adeoti，2）。除了阿尔马赫之外，后殖民时期的非洲作家，如本·奥克里、恩吉·瓦·蒂永奥、恩戈齐·阿迪奇等，他们都用小说作为一种激进的抗议手段来揭示殖民时期的黑暗与痛苦。阿尔马赫的艺术创作源于他对非洲大陆命运的关注和使命，重视非洲当代局势的诊断和社会重建。他创造了“一部战斗文学，一部革命文学”，扮演“人民的觉醒者”的角色。（Fanon 179）为真正的非殖民化进行革命斗争，重建一个健康的非洲大陆。

2　国外关于阿依·克韦·阿尔马赫研究状况

2.1　写作风格研究

2011年亚历山大·卡卡拉巴（Alexander Dakubo Kakraba）在《当前社会科学研究杂志》

上发表了《阿依·克韦·阿尔马赫小说〈美好的人尚未诞生〉中的粗俗语言：一种治疗工具》。作者指出阿尔马赫在这部小说中的语言是如此粗俗，甚至有时是非常粗俗，以至于他有意识地引起读者的注意。作者认为正是阿尔马赫非常规语言的力量，言语的辱骂和粗俗的言语，使这部小说充满强大的治疗效果。叙述者和作者的声音可以强烈地辱骂或侮辱那些令人讨厌的人物。通过对小说中粗俗语言的功能分析，作者得出“他用令人讨厌的语言来惩罚社会上的邪恶和堕落的领导人和人民……旨在彻底改造一个如此颓废的社会……也是他作为一名作家的独创性表现出来的标志。”（Kakraba，312）

2014 年约翰·埃米克（Dr. John Emike）在《全球人类社会科学杂志：艺术与人文心理学》上发表《阿依·克韦·阿尔马赫小说〈美好的人尚未诞生〉的文体评价》。文章通过对《美丽的人尚未诞生》的文体评价，考察了非洲小说中的语言使用，揭示了小说家运用各种文体特征来表达作者的主题关注。文章分别论述了小说中使用的各种文体方法：第三人称全知视角、回忆、时间删节、语篇衔接手段、拟人、隐喻等，并结合小说中的具体案例来分析这些文体特点。作者表明当读者能够找到作家的世界时，文学作家的作品就会成功。当读者和小说作家在一个语言共同体中(阿尔马赫小说的背景-加纳是一个语言共同体)，有效的交流就实现了。

2015 年谢里夫·阿米纳（Charef Amina）在穆罕默德·海尔比斯克拉大学发表了硕士论文《阿依·克韦·阿尔马赫小说〈美好的人尚未诞生〉的腐败》。文章第三部分详细分析了在这部小说中阿尔马赫各种语言工具来阐释腐败主题。比如作者指出进行时态是阿尔马赫在他的小说中使用的一种叙事手法，这种手法被用来显示连续性，描述加纳各地腐败和污秽的不断扩张，表明加纳政治和个人的道德逐渐衰败；省略是另一种帮助阿玛描绘小说中普遍存在的腐败、腐朽和厌恶的技巧，它是通过使用标记省略而产生的，这些省略几乎是在小说的每一部分，阿尔马赫使用标记省略号来表示腐败行为不容易说出；阿玛喜欢用粗俗的语言来表现加纳存在的严重腐败，这种语言是一种工具，用来吸引读者对令人震惊和令人厌恶的问题的关注，它反映了人物粗俗行为及对历史事件的解读。阿尔马赫在《美丽的人尚未诞生》中使用了许多叙事技巧，这些技巧使他能够清晰地讨论取代道德的腐败程度。通过使用闪现和倒叙，他能够倒转到悲伤时期的不同记忆中，甚至是进入社会的未来。尽管使用了进行时态来表现国家腐败现象的继续发展，但从侧面也预示着阿尔马赫的读者们仍在继续前进。因此，阿尔马赫在小说中实现了自己的艺术目标。

2.2　作品主题研究

2.2.1　统治精英的腐败

1998 年摩西·阿伊沃（Moses Ayivor）在开普敦大学发表了博士论文《阿依·克韦·阿尔马赫小说中的非洲缺陷》。论文指出阿尔马赫的五部小说都有一个占主导地位的主题：非洲被自己的统治精英所背叛。（Ayivor，247）然后作者分析了这五部小说同一主题的持续复现。在《美好的人尚未诞生》中，以库姆森为代表的统治精英不断地剥削压迫贫苦大众，从中获取利益；在《我们为什么这样有福？》中，阿尔马赫否定了非洲领导阶层，把非洲革命民族主义解放运动的领导人描绘成自私的政治人物，仅仅是为了享受奢侈的生活，而非洲人民却生活在贫困和暴乱之中；在《碎片》中，阿尔马赫的重点是非洲领导人倾向于与欧美公司的密切合作，以剥削他们自己的人民；在《两千个季节》中，阿尔马赫肢解了像上帝一样的非洲国王的形象，他认为过去那些神奇的传说不过是由当权者在意识形态上创造出来的，并为暴政而服务的工具而已；在《治疗者》中，阿尔马赫指出古代非洲统治精英的邪恶本性。作者通过分析这五部小说里面具体的人物、情节来展现非洲统治阶层的腐败和不作为，但是也肯定了加纳第一任总统夸梅·恩克鲁马对教育事业做出的正确决策，让加纳普通人民都能够接受教育。

2015年谢里夫·阿米纳（Charef Amina）在穆罕默德·海尔比斯克拉大学发表的硕士论文《阿依·克韦·阿尔马赫小说〈美好的人尚未诞生〉的腐败》中第二部分重点着墨论述了这部小说的腐败主题。腐败是一个消极的名词，它意味社会的普遍腐朽和道德松弛，它在没有纪律和强有力的道德准则的地方蓬勃发展。本文通过研究这部小说解释了独立后非洲大陆存在的主要问题——那里存在着道德败坏的现象，缺乏能够妥善治理国家的有道德的领导人。因此，本文对小说中所涉及的腐败现象进行了考察，严厉批评后殖民时期腐朽的价值观，但还是客观评价了夸梅·恩克鲁马政府执政期间对加纳建设做出的贡献。本文指出小说腐败的主题存在于领导人治理国家和人民的方式中，在加纳和所有非洲国家，这一现象被认为是有益的，也是实现繁荣的唯一手段。本文首先指出在《美丽的人尚未出生》中，阿尔马赫已经表明非洲政治家确实腐败。在小说文本中，作者使用了库姆森这个角色，他就是腐败的领导，这些政客为了富足自己而窃取公共资金的方式，牺牲社会上的普通民众。此外，作者还分析了小说中表现腐败主题的象征符号，比如奇奇多鸟和生锈的公交车等等。作者指出要在加纳取得成功，一个人必须是一个小偷和腐败。

2.2.2 重建非洲的愿景

1991年钦耶尔·恩瓦胡尼亚（Chinyere Nwahunanya）在《现代小说研究》上发表了《理想的愿景：阿尔马赫的〈两千个季节〉》。文中论述了前殖民时期和殖民时期非洲的社会历史和社会经验，指出了社会解体的原因和非洲悲剧的根源。通过分析小说中人物科兰奇在社会内部腐化中的作用，阿尔马赫对作为西非问题根源的殖民时期的西非领导人做了最严厉的评论。对于阿尔马赫来讲，领导人的贪婪和无知将非洲人民推向白人剥削者的统治之下。同时，作者还表明阿尔马赫并未对这样的社会现状表现出彻底的悲观和绝望，而是提出将过去的创伤转变为现在积极的潜力来改造社会，把所有这些意义投射到小说主人公的话语和年轻人的革命活动上，试图给出一个新的推动力。阿尔马赫强调将"道路"作为一种有远见的理想，这种道路意味着解决非洲问题的一种精神，这也是一种乌托邦式的愿景，因为它可以作为复兴的后盾，也可以作为指引的灯塔，为规划非洲社会和精神健康的未来方向指明了方向。

2014年阿尔伯特·萨基（Albert A. Sackey）在《勒贡人文杂志》上发表了《读阿依·克韦·阿尔马赫的〈为什么我们这样有福？〉》，文章指出这部小说呈现了文学、历史和神话的复杂组合，通过对主要人物的研究，探索小说中体现的乌托邦、爱、种族以及暴力来总结出非洲解放的障碍与紧迫。本文分析出被同化的非洲人有两种选择——留在边缘，不再孤独，或者转移到中心，拥抱一种"无所不在的孤独"。主人公莫丁选择变换到中心，并付出生命的代价。然后作者分析了次要人物和他们在这个两极对立的世界中所扮演的各种角色。比如杰斐逊夫人，杰弗逊教授的妻子，莫丁的"导师"。杰斐逊夫人是"最幸福的人"之一。她的生活充满了物质上的充实，但她像许多"最幸福"的美国女性一样，她们的生活包括单调乏味的装腔作势和挫折感。每个人都面临同样的困境——无法感觉，无法在他们萎缩的生活中体验情感的实现，他们的世界就是地狱。然后，作者指出非洲所有革命的方式：自由是经过漫长而血腥的斗争后获得的；但非洲独立随之而来的是对普通人民真正的奴役，而他们的辛劳和无私的牺牲有助于赢得独立。财富和权力集中在少数机会主义者手中；其余人口生活在赤贫和肮脏之中。（Sackey，99）最后，作者对比分析了阿尔马赫的其他几部小说主题，指出重建非洲的道路是团结和友好，而不是分裂和敌对，回归非洲道路绝非易事，需要非洲人民内部团结起来对抗白人带来的诱惑和软化，努力寻找自己的解脱之路。

2017 年穆斯塔法教授（Pro.Mustapha）在第七届欧洲学术界国际会议上提交了论文《阿依·克韦·阿尔马赫〈欧西里斯崛起〉的回归与变化》。文章首先描述了阿尔马赫这部小说中跨大西洋奴隶贸易的历史背景，然后论述小说主人公阿斯特，一位非裔美国历史学者，如何寻找她的非洲身份。她还致力于为非洲的福祉做出贡献，成为改革非洲教育体系的基层组织的一员。穆斯塔法教授指出身份和变化是阿尔马赫认为重建非洲的关键问题所在，在《欧西里斯崛起》这部小说中，阿尔马赫展示了身份认同的追求与教育体制改革之间的相互联系，认为这是改变非洲大陆发展不足的治本之道，因为教育是非洲大陆政治、社会和文化问题的主要基础。

2.3 新的研究视角——女性主义批评

从阿尔马赫作品以往的研究中可以看出，学者们更偏向于对语言风格和主题的研究，而对于小说中出现的众多女性的作用却鲜少提及。2013 年福阿德·马米（Fouad Mami）在《语言文学研究》上发表了《阿依·克韦·阿尔马赫小说中欲望的文化诗学或女性原则》，从非洲辉煌历史的核心—母系氏族制度出发，探索其文学创作的欲望文化诗学。在《两千个季节》（1973）中，阿尔马赫提到了妇女的统治，与男性统治相比，妇女统治的特点是和平与繁荣，但是却被混乱和暴力吞噬掉了。在《治疗者》（1975）中，阿约亚和阿拉巴·杰西瓦两个女性对登苏产生了一些神奇和持久的影响。在非洲，有些男人可以有四个或者更多的妻子，每个妻子只是男人的附属品。而在小说中仍会出现“为什么女人不能带领祈祷者……”这样的质疑。而阿斯特拯救了杰奎琳，使她免于在《欧西里斯崛起》（1995 年）中成为第四任妻子的命运。但是辛克·埃基亚诺说：“你想让每个女人都有一个男人吗？非洲人一直都是一夫多妻制的。”（153）福阿德·马米发现了欲望在阿尔马赫小说中的首要地位，指出“非洲妇女所遭受的苦难”加剧了这种小说的语境。（Mami，142）然而，尽管许多妇女在非殖民化斗争中与男性同行并肩战斗，但在许多独立的非洲国家，女性的边缘化仍在继续。

福阿德·马米在文章第二部分开始论述性别与政治，还指出阿尔马赫并不是第一个提到欲望至上的人。1988 年伍·穆贝丁在《非洲的发明》一文中提出“希腊范式的力量”，指的是早期希腊地理学家和旅行者对利比亚人、埃塞俄比亚人和其他非洲黑人的消极态度的起源。随着西方价值观和伦理道德的胜利，非洲和东方被视为一个被征服的女性身体，任凭其侵略者希腊阳刚之气的摆布和发行暴力。提到这个欲望起源的目的就是论证从《我们为什么这样有福》（1972）开始，阿尔马赫就将希腊关于父权制社会结构下的欲望的观念与他所认为的非洲母系结构进行比较，认为非洲本质上不同于资本主义的欧洲，因为希腊的暴力遗产和最大利益形成了非洲和欧洲之间的永久裂痕。紧接着，福阿德·马米阿尔分析了阿尔马赫几部小说里面的恋人关系，如在《碎片》（1970），巴科与胡安娜的爱情保持完整的情况下，这种力量是可以完全控制他的精神的，哪怕只是一小段时间。但正是在胡安娜缺席的情况下，巴科终于屈服于他曾经抱怨过的社会现实。作者总结出阿尔马赫的“欲望”文学表达旨在将爱情和爱情的产生归因于一种思想，而这样的思想构成了他预见的非洲社会蓝图的基础。接下来，作者分析了小说中被“扭曲”的欲望或“希腊范式”的欲望。为了解释帝国主义的观念牢牢扎根于希腊范式，作者指出莫丁的母系性倾向使他很容易被父权主义者虐待，而这个父权主义者的代表就是莫丁的白人女友艾米。而最后，莫丁的死亡也是跨文化、跨民族的最终后果，得不到任何可能的救赎。从文化上讲，他从不把痛苦当作宣泄，因为根据阿尔马赫的说法，非洲人没有宣泄的权力。因此，任何涉及非洲男子与美国妇女的关系，如莫丁和艾米的关系都是注定的，只能是破坏性的。像艾米这样的人所能做的就是剥夺这个非洲男人的尊严，剥夺他作为非洲人的身份。

在文章第四部分，福阿德・马米以神话与隐喻的角度来分析女性对非洲大陆的作用。阿尔马赫将失去的非洲母系制度包装成大量的符号，承载着他的欲望哲学，将其视为一种治愈力量，这在小说《《欧西里斯的崛起》中的主人公名字符号中尤其体现得出来。作者最后指出，阿尔马赫在他的三部小说中精心编织了与女性相关的符号，以表达他对非洲妇女的崇敬。对阿尔马赫来说，非洲妇女对社会团结的热情使母系因素成为建设现代非洲的可行选择，体现了阿尔马赫由悲观到积极的一个创作转变。

3　国内关于阿依・克韦・阿尔马赫研究状况

与国外研究相比，国内对于该研究领域仍处于待挖掘阶段，甚至可以说是有待开垦的处女地。首先，国内对于作家名字“Ayi Kwei Armah”的翻译尚无定论，也没有专门的词条来对这个作家进行详尽的介绍；其次，阿尔马赫迄今为止共有 7 部小说、一本自传《作家的雄辩》和散文集《牢记被肢解的大陆》，但目前为止在国内并没有相关的中文译本，造成文学作品接受的滞后，甚至在国内都只能买到几本英文版作品，其他的资料更是寥寥无几。此外，国内关于阿尔马赫作品研究的期刊文章仅有两篇，2018 年才出现一篇硕士论文，尚未研究阿尔马赫的博士论文，也没有一部专门研究阿尔马赫及其作品的专著。

2010 年张毅在《兰州教育学院学报》上发表的《阿尔马赫与他的人生三部曲》，主要从三个方面来进行研究。首先，对作家阿尔马赫的生平进行详细的介绍，正是他这种海外求学的经历、亲身体验西方虚伪的价值观以及重建非洲的愿景使得他的作品里面带有浓厚的自传色彩；其次，作者分别对《美好的人尚未诞生》《碎片》《为什么我们这样有福》这三部作品的主人公进行分析，这些正面人物也都有各自的缺陷，最终这些主人公的结局都是悲惨的，体现了在这段时间阿尔马赫对于加纳以及非洲发展的悲观情绪；最后，张毅还对这三部曲的主题思想进行了探索，揭示了东方与西方、现实与理想、个人与社会的深刻矛盾，抒发了作者对建立一个“新世界”——一个非洲人真正当家做主，非洲人赖以自豪的心灵家园的强烈渴望。（张毅，24）2011 年颜志强在《外国文艺报》上发表了《加纳文坛怪杰艾伊・奎・阿尔马赫：非洲精神的书写者》，首先作者对阿尔马赫文学观形成相关的求学经历、政治观点、革命思想等进行了详细的阐述，其次提出了阿尔马赫的创作分为前后两段：写个人的存在主义时期和写集体记忆的泛非主义时期，并以具体的代表作品来阐释这两个创作阶段的特点，着重介绍分析阿尔马赫后期的作品《治疗者》和《两千个季节》，并赞扬阿尔马赫作为一个守望家园的作家，在语言、意象、结构、印刷方面都做了民族化的努力。（颜志强，1）2018 年赵敏在中国知网上发表了硕士论文《荒诞世界中的选择与希望——存在主义视角下解读〈碎片〉和〈美好的人尚未诞生〉》，首先，作者把阿尔马赫这两篇前期作品中体现的思想与萨特的存在主义进行比较研究，找出两者的相通之处；其次，作者分析了两部小说中的主人公在那样混沌的社会背景下为追求自由而做出的选择以及各自的结局；最后，作者分析了阿尔马赫的生平经历，探索是否这两部作品体现的是完全悲观主义，并通过文本细读找出小说里面体现的乐观

思想和希望。作者认为，阿尔马赫在悲伤的基调中，并没有完全丧失对美好生活的向往。（赵敏，1）

加纳文学在非洲和世界有一席之地，首先是因为有阿尔马赫。值得欣慰的是，2016 年钟明和孙妮在《重庆交通大学学报》上发表了《国内外阿依·克韦·阿尔马赫研究述评》，说明国内部分学者已经开始注意到加纳作家阿尔马赫的重要地位和研究价值。钟明和孙妮首先按照时间顺序介绍国外最先开始介绍和研究阿尔马赫的专著以及文章，然后从历史、文化研究视角，对比研究视角以及马克思主义与同性恋研究视角来介绍研究阿尔马赫作品的相关文章。与钟明和孙妮的研究述评不同之处在于，本文对于国外研究主要关注的是小说语言风格研究和主题研究，侧重于文本分析。此外，本文还介绍了国外学者对于阿尔马赫作品的新视角研究——女性主义批评，并指出阿尔马赫编织的女性符号代表了其由悲观向乐观的转变。

因此，从现有的资料来看，国内对于阿尔马赫的研究尚处于起步阶段。非洲作为发展中国家最多的大陆，其辽阔的土地，丰富的资源，多元而悠久的历史文化以及经济社会特别的贫穷与欠发展状态，使非洲拥有和中国同样的最为巨大也更为持久的发展需求。中非合作论坛北京峰会上，习近平主席提出共筑更加紧密的中非命运共同体。值得欣喜的是，国家领导人提出中非全面合作的发展战略也使得国内学界开始了解和注意非洲作家和作品，通过研究本土作品来揭示非洲身份认同和民族复兴的渴求。而在后殖民主义众多作家中，阿尔马赫利用小说作为媒介创造的革命和战斗文学，始终将重建非洲大陆作为自己的使命和责任，不仅指出政府领导人的不作为、腐败，社会经济发展依然被殖民垄断等问题，也为复兴非洲大陆提供了可能性，即寻求身份认同和改革教育制度，以解决非洲大陆的不发达状况（Mustapha 2）。因此，加深对阿尔马赫作品的研究，可以透过本土作家的视角更加深入地了解加纳独立后以及整个非洲大陆的发展和现状，加深中非全面合作，实现两大文明的协同复兴。

4 结　　语

无论是口头的还是书面的文学艺术都有能力为变革创造必要的刺激。在其虚构性上，文学提出了不同的存在主义视角、惯性问题及其解决方案。正如索因卡提醒我们的那样，“文学的社会功能之一是对过去进行有远见的重建，以形成一个社会方向”，（1976：106）阿尔马赫的小说正是文学思想和社会力量交融的场所。对其作品进行深入的研究可以对非洲问题的本质和成因形成一个整体的了解，这对于当代社会发展方向也是一项重要的探索。因此，研究阿尔马赫的作品可以加深对非洲大陆的了解，更有效地加强全方位中非合作，也可以为第三世界国家如何保持身份、文化、政治、经济独立提供借鉴意义。

参 考 文 献

[1] Adeoti，Gbemisola, 2005. *The Re-Making of Africa：Ayi Kwei Armah and the Narrative of an（Alter）-native Route to Development* [J] Africa Media Review，（13）：1-15.

[2] Armah，Ayi Kwei, 1995. *Osiris Rising：A Novel of Africa Past，Present and Future*[M]. Popenguine：Per Ankh.

[3] Armah，Ayi Kwei, 1979. *Two Thousand Seasons*[M]. London，Ibadan：Heinemann.

[4] Ayivor，Moses, 1998 A *Saga of Black Deglorification：The Disfigurement of Africa in Ayi Kwei Armah's Novels*，[D]. University of Cape Town.

[5] Fanon，Frantz, 2011. *The Wretched of the Earth*[A]. New York：Grove Weidenfeld，179.

[6] Kakraba，Alexander, 2011. *Ayi Kwei Armah ' s Vulgar Language in the Beautyful Ones are not Yet Born，a Therapeutic Tool*[J]. Current Research Journal of Social Sciences，(4)：306-313.

[7] Mami，Fouad, 2013. *The Cultural Poetics of desire or the Feminine principle in Ayi Kwi Armah's novels*[J]. STUDIA UBB PHILOLOGIA，LVIII，(3)：141-163.

[8] Mustapha，Benzahra, 2017. *Regaining Original Identity and Change in Ayi Kwei Armah's Osiris Rising*[J]. Moulay Ismail University，1-9.

[9] Sackey，Albert, 2014. *Reading Ayi Kwei Armah's Why are We so Blest ?* [J]. Legon Journal of the Humanities，(25)：76-103.

[10] 颜志强. 加纳文坛怪杰艾伊・奎・阿尔马赫：非洲精神的书写者[N]. 文艺报，2011（5）.

[11] 张毅. 阿尔马赫与他的人生三部曲[J]. 兰州教育学院学报，2010（6）：23-24.

[12] 赵敏. 荒诞世界中的选择与希望——存在主义视角下解读《碎片》和《美好的人尚未诞生》[D]. 电子科技大学，2018.

[13] 钟明，孙妮. 国内外阿依・克韦・阿尔马赫研究述评[J]. 重庆交通大学学报（社会科学版），2016，16（2）：93-96.

社会心理学视角下“先生”的形象分析
——以夏目漱石《心》为对象

黄玉珊

摘　要：小说《心》发表于大正三年（1914 年）4 月，是日本近代文坛巨匠、批判现实主义作家夏目漱石后期代表作之一。夏目漱石借先生的遗书为我们展现了明治时代知识分子的内心。小说中的先生在青年时期失去父母后，被叔父这个唯一的亲人骗走了家产，后又在追求爱情的过程中，背叛了自己的好友。先生先失去了亲情，又为了爱情背弃友情，最终走向了自杀。小说充满了对人物内心的细节刻画，线索层层铺垫，展现出主人公在经历重大事件后心理的变化。在被叔父骗走家产后，失去了对所有人的信任，对社会的看法变得消极，这也导致在友情和爱情面前，他不顾一切地选择了爱情，然而孤独感和负罪感却使他产生严重的自我认同危机。作为一个失去自我的人，先生感到迷茫、困惑、痛苦。自杀让我们看到时代之于先生的无奈和无助。

关键词：心；社会心理学；友情；爱情

1 引　言

夏目漱石被称为“国民大作家”，在日本近代文学史上享有很高的地位。他所创作的《我是猫》《少爷》等作品广为人知。夏目漱石的文学作品通常体现出强烈的道德意识和对现实的深刻批判。本文将探讨的《心》是他的代表作之一，小说将先生的过往和内心想法娓娓道来，同时，又留下许多值得读者去慢慢品读思考的细节。小说中的先生在青年时期失去父母后，被叔父这个唯一的亲人骗走了家产，不再信赖任何人，后又和好友 K 爱上同一个人。先生在不顾一切地争取爱情的过程中，没料想到 K 会自杀。在失去亲情后，先生相继失去友情、爱情，过着行尸走肉般的生活，最终以明治天皇驾崩为契机结束了自己的生命。正如小说的名字《心》，故事中先生的行为选择都是围绕他的心理变化进行的，通过分析先生的心理，可以使先生的人物形象更为清晰。

目前国内主要围绕“明治精神”和“利己主义”来探讨夏目漱石的《心》，此外，将小说主人公“先生”的自杀与明治精神结合来考察的研究也很多。曹志明（2013）分析了先生的自杀和明治精神之间的联系，并认为先生的自杀使日本的传统道德观念传递到下一代人身上。孙萍（2016）从主观和客观两方面分析了先生自杀的原因。日本除了分析《心》中的人物和现象，还关注作品在日本国内外的接受情况。现今，国内外已有大量对《心》的研究，然而，对先生自杀的原因还没有形成统一的意见，在探讨先生死因的时候，大多数研究都着眼于明治精神等社会历史背景方面的问题，而忽视将先生推向死亡的一系列事件背后的社会心理及个人心理原因。小说第三部分“先生与遗书”是全书中唯一一个以先生为第一人来叙述的部分，这个部分能够最为贴近地观察先生的心理。

先生的行为和他的心理联系紧密，而作为具有社会属性的存在，他的心理是难以和他当时所处的环境分离的，由此，本文将试图结合社会心理学，分析先生的过去对他的心理活动及行为的影响，以此还原先生的人物形象并探寻遗书的字里行间中透露的信息。

2 先生的往事

“先生和遗书”中，过半的内容都是先生对过去的回忆，而这些过去的经历对先生现在的性格影响巨大，也和先生后来选择自杀有着密不可分的联系。现在，笔者将整理原文，理清先生的过去经历和现有性格的关系。

“由于家里有钱，自幼生活倒是悠闲自在。”（下· 三）

先生生长在一个富裕的家庭，小时候的性格大方随和，后来性格发生了转变。

“我记得叔父欺骗了我，与此同时，我深深觉得其他人也一定会欺骗我。”（下· 九）

先生的父母去世之后，叔父成了先生可以依靠的亲人，深得先生的信赖，然而叔父却骗走了先生父母留下的财产，背弃了先生对他的信任。当时尚且年轻的先生受到了打击，感到世上的任何人都不值得相信，也就是说，先生失去了对人的信任。

之后，先生不再和叔父一家一同居住，自己找了住宿，那是一位寡妇和她女儿共同生活的房子。先生渐渐地对小姐产生了感情，却又一直怀疑小姐和夫人别有用心，对她们抱有戒备心理。先生的朋友 K 由此登场。先生在利用 K 打破这种窘境，一方面可以试探夫人和小姐，另一方面也能帮助到自己的好友。K 受先生的好意邀请搬了进来，和先生住在同一个屋檐下。令先生意想不到的是，K 也喜欢上了小姐，K 主动将自己的想法告诉了先生，这让先生感到惊慌失措，生怕 K 抢走了小姐。这时的先生面临的是爱情和友情的选择，结果，先生选择了满足自己的感情而背弃友情。他一直没有告诉 K 自己也喜欢小姐，将这份感情隐藏在了心底，还用 K 说过的话中伤他，“精神上没有上进心的人是傻瓜”。这让 K 产生了更加消极的情绪，心情低落。除此之外，先生还急忙找到夫人，向她表明了心意，请求夫人将女儿许配给自己，赶在 K 之前得到小姐。先生在做这一系列行为的时候，恐怕从未想到过 K 会自杀，但先生一心只想着要达成自己的愿望，即使在发现 K 自杀以后，先生首先做的事情是为了保全自身名誉，查看 K 的遗书中是否有对自己不利的内容。

上述内容为先生的遗书中提到的对先生的人生产生了重大影响的往事，大致可以分为两个部分。第一部分：先生被自己信赖的叔父骗走了财产，转而变得不相信任何人。第二部分：受之前叔父的事情影响，先生在和小姐、夫人以及 K 的交往中，也缺乏对他们的信赖感。

Markus 和 Kitayama 提出了“独立性自我”(independent self)和“互赖性自我”(interdependent self)。他们认为，“独立性自我”强调个体内在特征的完整性和唯一性，在此基础上表现出他人的区别性与独立性，它激励和推动个体去实现自我，发展独特的自我潜能，表达个体特殊的需要和权利。而“互赖性自我”强调个体与他人的联系与依赖，这种有关自我知觉的信息一般来自重要他人以及自我与他人的关系方面。互赖性的情感体验更多来自社会、与他人之间的关系等较外在的因素，独立性自我的情感体验更多来自自身内部①。

年少时先生与叔父的交往中，我们可以看到先生表现出明显的“互赖性自我”，由于父母的去世，叔父成了可以依靠、信赖的重要的人，这使得先生依然有家人照料，有归属感，而

① Markus H, Kitayama S. 1991, Culture and self: Implications for cognition, emotion, and motivation. Psychological Review, 98:224-253

先生的这种心理是童年时期对叔父的美好印象的延续，即由固有印象形成的对叔父的信任。当叔父欺骗先生，也就意味他背离了先生的固有认知，同时，先生的自我认知也发生了改变。叔父对于先生来说原本是很重要的人，这样的人对先生的背叛，使得先生自我认知的改变拓宽到对他人及社会的认识，继而出现对他人的不信任。先生在失去叔父这个唯一可以信赖的人后，也就没了强烈的互赖关系，这迫使先生依据自己内在的思想、情感和活动来组织和建构行为和心理，比起“互赖性自我”“独立性自我”在先生身上的比重更大。此时的先生深感焦虑、无助，他虽然不信任小姐和夫人，但又怕 K 会先行抢走小姐，为了满足自己的情感，不顾忌 K 是否受到伤害，向夫人提亲。这也是先生急于探明自我的一种表现，失去了一切的他，不能再让别人夺走什么，以至于即便是好友，他也丝毫不客气。但后来他意识到，自己的所作所为和叔父一样，因此，感受不到幸福，并且开始认为，这个世界上连自己也是不可信的，出现了自我认同危机。这种“决策后失调”（即，由于做出决策而产生的认知失调）导致先生不仅对人类和社会感到失望，还失去了活下去的动力。先生在决定提亲的时候，并没有想到后果，也就造成实际发生的情况不同于他的料想。这影响到他的自我认同。随着心理防线的一点点坍塌，他便产生了自杀的想法。

“我和妻子面面相对时，会忽然被 K 吓到。妻子仿佛处在我和 K 中间一般，K 伴随着妻子，如影随形，无法驱散。我对妻子没有任何不满之处，但仅由于这一点，我不禁想疏远她。”（下· 五十二）

“我只是深刻感受到了人类的罪恶。正是这种感觉让我每个月都去到 K 的墓前，是这种感觉让我照顾妻子的母亲，也是这种感觉命令着我善待妻子。（中略）我产生了应该自己了结自己的想法。”（下· 五十四）

可以看出，在背离了友情后，先生并没能享受爱情，只有孤独感和罪恶感在他心中久久无法消散。先生无法应对自我认知的失调，并且这种失调在他内心日益累加，使他的自我认同危机感日益加重。先生深感人类的罪恶，只是为了妻子保留自己的生命。先生用到“人类的罪恶”一词，而不是将其简单地归结为自己的罪恶，似乎是在表达会发生那些事情并不全是自己的错。遗书中也没有表明，先生认为 K 的死是因为他造成的。这或许是先生应对自我认知失调的防御机制，以此减轻内心的痛苦。总之，先生还没有找到足够的理由令他立刻结束自己的生命。

遗书讲述了先生的过去经历，也诚实地展现了先生内心的黑暗。前文都是由和先生偶然结识的“我”在进行叙述，而遗书这一部分的叙述视角发生了改变，从前文的他人变为先生本人。相对于读者来说，先生的距离就更近了。先生冷静地讲述自己的一生，这使得遗书像一部自传，可以想见，先生这么写不光是为了给别人看，也是想要在自杀前再度回顾一下自己的过去。

3　先生的自杀

明治天皇驾崩，乃木大将殉死，便是先生自杀的契机。

“我回答妻子：‘假如自己殉死，就殉死明治精神’。”（下· 五十六）

那么，先生口中所说的“明治精神”究竟为何物？从时代背景考虑，明治时期，西方的文化和技术不断传入日本，这些文化和技术对日本来说，无疑都是新鲜的事物，这让日本社会各个方面都迎来了巨变。在这样的时代环境下出生的知识分子受到的不仅是日本传统文化的影响，还有西方近代思想的影响。日本社会也在这两种文化的相互碰撞间不断向前迈进。同时，也让明治时代成为充满矛盾冲突的时代。这样的时代背景对先生的心理产生了深刻的影响。

先生在评价明治时代的时候这样说道："在这个充满自由、独立和自我的现代出生的我们，作为牺牲，都不得不品尝孤独的滋味。"（上・十五）先生用到了"自由""独立""自我"这些积极的词汇去形容明治时代，但是后半句在谈到这个时代对于每个人的影响时，又用的是"牺牲""孤独"这样消极的词汇。由此，可以看到先生内心的矛盾。先生在和小姐结婚之后，内心一直充满强烈的罪恶感和孤独感，一方面是因为前文分析到的种种经历所造成的自我认同危机，另一方面也与时代相关，是明治时代给先生内心带去了矛盾纠结。

传统文化环境下，人们的自我认同较为单一稳定，而东西文化的冲突也造成自我的多样性。先生由于决策后失调的影响，自我认同出现分裂。这也就解释了先生身上表现出的"独立性自我"和"互赖性自我"这两种自我（通常，"独立性自我"在西方个人主义文化社会中比较典型，而"互赖性自我"更常见于东方文化[①]）。先生一直沉溺在过去，逃离不出来，丧失了生活的意义感和方向感，负面情绪让他毫无作为，这样的先生看不见自己的未来。之所以会这样，正是因为先生在传统文化环境中成长，要求他重视和谐，重视与他人的关系，即便失去所有的亲人也不建立新的社交关系，他也无法抛开道德的桎梏和社会对他的评价。西方近代思想带给他的是更多的纠结和迷惘，先生身上的"独立性自我"和"互赖性自我"始终互相冲突，难以得到平衡。明治时代随着天皇的驾崩而终结，严重缺失自我认同感的先生产生了要随同时代的结束而结束自己的生命的想法。对于人来说，由于能够意识到自己是一个独立实体，孤独与生俱来，然而又都会希望与人相联系。没有了亲情、友情和爱情，人生也就没有意义可言，先生在这个时机自杀，把明治精神作为殉死对象，只是为他的死亡增添了一个理由。

"就像我不能理解乃木大将死去的理由，你大概也没办法想明白我自杀的理由，如果确是如此，那可能是由于时势变化给人带去了人的变化，这是没办法的事情。抑或是由于个人天生的性格不同造成的。"（下・五十六）

以上是书中关于先生自杀理由做出的说明。这段先生的话语中没有道出明确的理由，但可以看出，先生认为自杀和他个人天生的性格有关系。先生会提到"天生的性格"是由于他对人性的失望。他很厌恶叔父的所作所为，自己也本不该做出类似的事，然而，在背弃友情的那一刻，他意识到自己和叔父一样，是个不值得被信赖的小人。先生无法理解，也无法接受这个事实，他没办法怪罪别人，但出于防御心理，他又不想承认这是自己主动做出的选择，因此，"天生的性格"成了最好的掩护。而在考虑性格，我们不得不考虑他的家庭背景、身边的人、生活环境、教育等因素，因为一个人性格的养成绝不会是由他个人所左右的，而是在各种复杂因素的影响下逐渐形成的。因此，与其说他的自杀是由于"天生的性格"决定的，不如说是后天形成的心理造成的。

---

①Markus H, Kitayama S. 1991, Culture and self: Implications for cognition, emotion, and motivation. Psychological Review, 98: 224-253

“我是愿意写的。即便不谈义务我也是想写的。不妨说，我的过去只是我个人的经历，归我个人所有。生前不把它送给别人，可谓遗憾。我多少还有这样的愿望。”（上·二）

“为了让你能更大限度理解这个莫名其妙的我，我才写了这么多。”（上·二）

“我的努力不单是为了实现对你的约定，更多的是因为我受到自身要求的驱使。”（下·五十六）

由上可以看出，先生写遗书的理由有三。第一，先生希望自己的过去可以化为经验留给别人。第二，为了解答“我”的疑问。第三，写遗书是先生对自己的要求。虽然失去活下去的意义，也没有人际方面的顾虑，先生想做并且能够做的只有对自己内心进行安抚，这也表明他在突破道德底线后，还在努力自我救赎。通常，遗书中写的都是留给家人朋友的遗言，或者遗产的分配处置问题。不过，先生的遗书却明显不同于通常的遗书，他有着自己的目的。这份遗书不仅让读者对先生的形象有了更清楚的了解，还留给读者许多值得思考的地方。而先生对写这份遗书的理由做了说明，却没有对自杀的理由进行解释，这也可以看出，先生写遗书的目的在于让我们关注他的经验以及背后反映的问题。

4 结　语

故事原本可以随着先生自杀而结束，然而通过出自先生本人的遗书，读者可以以先生的视角去回顾整个事情经过，并得以窥视其内心。先生的死不能单纯归结于孤独感与罪恶感，或是明治精神，而应考虑各个方面的因素。在明治时代这个受西方影响巨大的时代，先生经历了亲人背叛，这使他突然失去可以依赖的关系，被迫转向心理独立，然而在追寻自我的过程中，他背弃了友情，也没能享受爱情，一步步坍塌的心理防线将他推向崩溃，出现严重的自我认同危机，也正是这种内心的孤独、无助、纠结等一系列负性情绪的不断堆积，让他无法作为正常的具有社会属性的人生活下去，更无从适应明治时代社会的变化。作为一个失去自我的人，深感迷茫、困惑、痛苦，自杀就成了他的唯一出路。夏目漱石没有写明死因，更多地在遗书中描写先生在自杀之前的过去经历，这是为了让读者的视线集中在先生身上。遗书让先生有了坦白的机会，也让读者注意到先生所写下的经验和这些经验背后的先生这个人物所代表的众多人。先生只是那个充满矛盾的时代中内心矛盾纠结的知识分子中的一个。夏目漱石借先生的遗书描绘了明治时代知识分子的内心，并向读者传达：没人可以抵抗时代给人们内心带去的矛盾和孤独。

注：文中译文均由笔者译自《心》，集英社，1991

参考文献

[1] Markus H，Kitayama S., 1991，Culture and self：Implications for cognition，emotion，and motivation. Psychological Review，98：224-253.

[2] 曹志明. 夏目漱石的“明治精神”——再论夏目漱石《心》中先生之死[J]. 外语学刊，2013（3）.

[3] 马俊杰. 刍议自我认同危机的释放途径——以社会心理学为视角[J]. 科技资讯，2010（14）.

[4] 孙萍. 夏目漱石小说《心》的主人公自杀悲剧探源[J]. 辽宁工业大学学报（社会科学版），2016（2）.

[5] 杨宜音. 自我与他人：四种关于自我边界的社会心理学研究述要[J]. 心理学动态，1999（3）.

从《刺青》来考察谷崎润一郎的审美情趣

何 露

摘 要：谷崎润一郎是日本近代耽美派的作家。在他将近半个世纪的创作生涯中，创作出许多对日本文学界很有影响力的作品。他不仅获得过诺贝尔文学奖的提名，而且他还是日本当选美国艺术院、美国文学艺术协会的名誉会员的第一人。谷崎润一郎经历了明治、大正、昭和三个时期，虽然创作风格发生了变化，但是在早期作品中所体现出的审美意识贯穿于他整个创作生涯。本文围绕谷崎润一郎的早期代表作《刺青》来研究他一直贯彻的审美意识：即追求官能美、东方美以及日本传统之美。

关键词：谷崎润一郎；刺青；审美意识

第1章 はじめに

19 世紀前期、フランスから始まってきた耽美主義は当時のヨーロッパで盛んでいた。耽美主義とは芸術と美がこの上ない高い地位を持ちあげられ、美の唯一の目的がそのもの自身だということである。19 世紀後半、ヨーロッパでの耽美主義は徐々に衰えていくが、その中に含まれた芸術思想や芸術表現などがアジアに多大な影響をあたえ、とりわけ日本の文壇に大きな変化を引き起こした。20 世紀初期日本でさかんに流行ってきた自然主義文学に反して、耽美主義が登場した。

谷崎潤一郎は耽美派の代表者のひとりとして、一生にわたり、独特の文学作品を大量に創作した。そのためか、日本文学史では彼が活躍していた時代を「大谷崎」「谷崎朝」と呼ぶようになった日本国内だけではなく、海外でも高い地位と評価を得た。耽美派の隆盛期は 5、6 年しか流行っておらず、大正中期頃から、新しく文壇に登場する新現実主義や芸術派などにより、徐々に注目されなくなる。しかし、耽美派の代表者とする谷崎潤一郎はこれまで培ってきた創作理念を簡単に諦めずになくなるまで貫こうとしたといえる。

谷崎潤一郎の創作は三つの段階に分けられる。まず、1910 年に発表された「刺青」から 1923 年関西に引越すまでの時期を第一段階といえよう。この時期の作品群は官能的および耽美的な美を求め、男性と女性が虐待しあっていく過程の中で快感を探るという内容を多く描かれている。これらの作品から見られるように、彼は情感より、官能のほうが人間にとってもっとも真実な美であることに重視していた。

次に、1905 年の『少将滋幹の母』の発表まで第二段階といえよう。1923 年，関東大震災後、谷崎潤一郎は関西に引越した。歴史があさい東京に比べ、関西は悠久の歴史を持ち、日本伝統的な美が至る所まで表現されている。谷崎潤一郎は言うまでもなく、芸術至上と主調してきた衝撃をうけ、これまで異なった創作方法を取り入れようと次から次へ新しい作品を書いた。『卍』『春琴抄』『細雪』はこの時期の作品である。これらの作品は、初期の「官能」「肉体」な美から日本の伝統的な美を求めよう谷崎潤一郎の創作姿勢を容易にうかがうことができよう。

最後に、1950 年から彼がこの世を去るまでの間を第三段階といえよう。その時に発表された『少将滋幹の母』は谷崎潤一郎が「悪魔主義」に戻る作品と見なされている。その後、発表された『鍵』『瘋癲老人日記』などは老人の視点から、露骨的な描写によって主人公の心理活動を描かれている。おそらく老人になった谷崎潤一郎はつねに、生と死を考えようになり、作品を通じて生命の真理を探ろうとしていた。

このように、谷崎潤一郎の創作方法は主に二つに分けることができる。初期と晩期の作品群は「悪魔主義」を中心に描かれ、中期の作品は日本の伝統的な美を中心に描かれている。

日本で谷崎潤一郎及び作品についての研究は長い歴史を持ち、今まで豊かな成果を収めてきた。例えば、佐藤春夫の「潤一郎、人及び芸術—谷崎潤一郎の悪魔主義」、三島由紀夫の「谷崎潤一郎について」、伊藤整の「谷崎潤一郎の文学」などがある。それに対して、我が国で谷崎潤一郎の文学に関する研究もずいぶん前から始まったのである。斉珮の「谷崎潤一郎の耽美主義文学の世界について」、王麗君の「谷崎潤一郎の文学世界での耽美主義について」などが例として挙げられる。

本研究で取り上げられる「刺青」は、谷崎潤一郎初期における代表作の一つである。谷崎初期作品についての研究の中で多くな研究者はこの作品に焦点をあて、さまざまな角度から論じできた。例えば、藤原智子「谷崎潤一郎『刺青』論」は「刺青」の本質を実証しようとするものであり、高田育子の「『刺青』の＜女＞」は登場人物である女性形象化に焦点をあて、谷崎文学の本質を探ろうとしたものである。これらの先行研究の中で初期における谷崎潤一郎の美意識について論じられているものもあるが[①]、主にマゾヒズム、サディズム・フェティシズムを中心に検討されてきた。しかし、中期作品に見られる日本伝統な美への追求がいきなり現れるはずがなく、すでに初期作品、特に「刺青」の中でも見られる。

本研究では、「刺青」を分析することを通じて、作品に見られる谷崎潤一郎の美意識を見つけ出し、これらの美意識は彼の初期作品のみならず、その後の彼の文学生涯にも多大な影響を与えたことをあきらかにしたい。

第2章　「刺青」について

2.1　創作背景

1868 年の明治維新以来、欧米の政治制度や科学技術とともなって文学思想も次第に日本文壇に進出するようになった。19 世紀の末期、資本主義制度の弊害が少しずつ露出するのにつれて、日本の社会は物欲の溢れ、民衆の不安に満たした。それまで文学界で提唱してきた自然主義は読者の要求に満足できなくなった。一方、ヨーロッパですでにこの問題を解決されている。その解決方法と見られる耽美主義は日本の文学者にも希望を与え、芸術至上主義を主調する人が現れるようになった。谷崎潤一郎はその中の一人である。

---

① 李韜瑾の「谷崎润一郎的初期审美意识—以《文身》为例」は「追求江户情调」、「对美的崇拜和女性至上思想」、「恶魔主义的萌芽」の角度から谷崎潤一郎の初期の美意識を研究した。任向欣の「试探谷崎润一郎作品中的美意识」は「女性形象刺青前后的眼神、动作、语言的变化」について分析した。

谷崎潤一郎は少年時代から、日本の古典のみならず、漢文及び東西の哲学書などをぬく読み続けていた。浮世絵や草紙などを通し、日本の伝統的な美意識も身についたことは容易に想像つく。文学好きであった谷崎潤一郎は1908年に東京帝国大学国文科に入り、第二次『新思潮』の創刊に加わり、1911年そこで「刺青」を発表した。「刺青」が発表された頃、夏目漱石や森鴎外などによる反自然主義的な文学が盛大に行われた時期である。こうしてみれば、「刺青」は時代の潮流に従って創り出されたものと言える。

2.2 「刺青」のあらすじ

「刺青」は1910年（明治43年）11月に雑誌『新思潮』①に発表された。作品の内容を以下のとおりである。

主人公の清吉は江戸時代の刺青師で、ふさわしい美女の輝いた肌に自己の魂を刺し込みたいという願いを抱き、このような女を探し続けてきた。ちょうど四年前の夏のある夕べに、深川の料理屋平清の前を通りかかった時に、偶然真っ白な駕籠にすわっている女の素足を見かけ、この足を持った女こそが長年にわたって探し求めてきた女性だと信じていた。4年間、彼はずっと探してきたが、残念なことに、見つけなかったのである。また一年が過ぎ、その年の春のある朝、その女は姉芸者の使いとして清吉の家を訪ねてきて、清吉は帰ろうとする娘に暴君紂王の寵妃の末喜を描いた絵と「肥料」を題とした絵を見せた。前者の絵は現在の彼女の心が映っていることであり、後者の絵は彼女の将来を示していることであると、清吉は彼女にかかつた。絵を見せられた彼女は動揺せずにはいられなかった。なぜかというと、これらの絵は自分の思いをよく反映されているからである。清吉は絵のような女に実現させるために、恐ろしかった女に麻酔剤をかがせ、背に女郎蜘蛛を刺した。その仕事をし終わった後、清吉の心は空虚で刺青こそが自分の生命のすべてであると思う。一方、この女の場合は、刺青される前と打って変わって、清吉を見下げていた。

第3章　美意識の考察てついて

本章では、作品に基づき、「刺青」に見られる谷崎潤一郎の美意識を検討してみる。

3.1 官能美への追求

「刺青」は反自然主義の立場から徹底して、官能美を追求したものと見られてきた。世の中、女性であれば誰でも自然界の摂理である官能美を備えている。一方、男性は美しく官能する女性の見ることに喜びを覚える生命体である。「刺青」の中で、主人公である清吉はどのようにしてその喜びを覚えたのだろう。

清吉は刺青師として若いなのに、腕利きがもっとも優れている人である。そのため、多くの人は彼を慕ってやってくる。そう言っても、やってくる人々は必ず彼に刺青してもらえるわけではない。「彼の心を惹きつけるほどの皮膚と骨組みとを持つ人でなければ」②彼

---

① 『新思潮』は、日本の文芸雑誌である。1907年（明治40年）小山内薫創刊したが振るわず挫折。以後、帝大生復活され、東京大学系の同人誌として後に続いた。谷崎潤一郎が1910年参加して「誕生」や「刺青」などを発表した。（https://ja.wikipediaorg/wiki 新思潮、2016年5月25日）

② 伊藤整編『日本現代文学全集43』講談社より、1980年5月、25頁。

は刺青をやらない。このような良心がある青年には、人の知らない秘密がある。それは、刺青される人の苦痛による快楽を覚えることである。

「彼が人々の肌を針で突き刺す時、真紅に血を含んで脹れ上がる肉の疼きに堪えかねて、大抵の男は苦しき呻きごえを発したが、その呻きごえが激しければ激しいほど、彼は不思議に云い難き愉快を感じるのであつた。刺青のうちでも殊に痛いと云われる朱刺、ぼかしぼり、―それを用うることを彼は殊更喜んだ。一日平均五六百の針に刺されて、色上げを良くするため湯へ浴つて出て来る人は、皆半死半生の体で清吉の足下に打ち倒れたまま、暫くは身動きさえ出来なかつた。その無残な姿をいつも清吉は冷やかに眺めて、

「嘸お痛みでがしょうなあ」

と云いながら、快さそうに笑つている。」[①]

引用文は少し長くなつたが、他人に苦しみを与えることにより、自分が快感を覚えた清吉の姿は生々しく現れている。清吉にとつて、愉快を感じるのはほかではなく、その「呻きごえ」と「無残な姿」ということに注意されたい。相手は女性にしろ、男性にしろ、聴覚と視覚から快感を覚えることは彼にとつてもつとも大切であつた。

また、清吉には宿願があつた。その宿願というのは「光輝のある美人の肌を得て、それへ己れの魂を刺り込むことであつた。」[②]その宿願はなかなか適わなかつたが、彼は容易に捨てなかつた。ようやく五年目の時に、一年目前から偶然見かけた女の足の持ち主が彼のところにやつてきた。芸妓から寄こされた使の者でありながら、彼女の顔は「長い月日を色里に暮らして、幾十人の男の魂を弄んだ年増のように物凄く整えてい」[③]る。そして、彼は娘に二本の画幅を見せた。二本の画に描かれてある女性たちの性分を持つていいることを感じさせられた娘は「後生ですから、早くその絵をしまつて下さい」[④]と恐ろしくこんかんしたが、彼は聞き入れなかつた。どこらか、恐ろしがる娘の姿を見ると、いつも「意地の悪い笑いが漂つてい」る。おそらく、彼女の恐る恐るとした姿とこんかんは彼にとつて、「呻きごえ」と「無残な姿」に等しいことであろう。

ここまでの考察からわかるように、清吉は他人の「呻きごえ」と「無残な姿」を聴覚と視覚によつて快感を覚えている。言い換えれば、人を虐げることを通して、快感を覚えることといえよう。ところで、作品の中で、彼は虐待者として一貫されていない。作品の最後の部分では娘の最初の「肥料」になつた彼は、被虐待者として描かれている。しかし、「肥料」になつたのは、外から与えられた圧力ではなく、彼自ら選んだ道である。彼はそれを実現するために、彼の魂を打ち込んだのである。換言すれば、虐待者であろうと、被虐待者であろうと、彼は他者による喜びを感じることができたといえよう。

このような他人を虐げることと他人に虐げられることを通して快感を感じることから、谷崎潤一郎は官能的な美意識への追求がはつきりわかる。精神や思想などの代わりに、生

①伊藤整編『日本現代文学全集 43』講談社より、1980 年 5 月、26 頁。

② 同①，27 頁。

③ 同①，29 頁。

④ 同①，32 頁。

理官能のような実感が芸術そのもので、官能への刺激こそが美の実体である。それに、これを達成するために犠牲した人々への悲哀も官能美の伝えへ拍車をかけた。

一方、自己虐待、自己を壊した行為は谷崎潤一郎からすれば、快感を引き起こさせただけでなく、病的な官能美から人間の心底にある原始的な美、真実の美も探させることである。

3.2　東洋美への追求

「刺青」は西洋の耽美主義の影響を受けて書いた作品と見られてきたが、作品のところどころに散りばめられている日本の江戸情緒や中国の古い文化を重視してはいけない。谷崎潤一郎は関西に転居してから、伝統的な美をえがくようになった。その初期でもすでにその要素があった。

まず、「刺青」にあった江戸情緒を考察してみる。文章の冒頭では次のとおりに書いていた。

「それはまだ人々が愚と云う貴い徳を持っていて、世の中が今のように激しく軋み合わない時分であった。」①

「刺青」が発表された当時の日本では、西洋文明は積極的に受け入れていたが、日本の伝統文化は軽蔑されがちであった。西洋文明と伝統文明の間の「激しく軋み合わない」時期に、谷崎潤一郎は時代の潮流に迎合せず、皆に敬遠された江戸時代を背景に作品を書いたのである。それは、おそらく長年培ってきた知識からの影響であろう。江戸子として生まれた谷崎潤一郎は少年時代から、江戸時代の文化を代表とする歌舞伎や浮世絵や浮世草子などへの接触を通じて、江戸文化の栄養をとり、多大な影響を受けてきた。

江戸時代で、商品経済の発展につれ、商人の地位があがり、士農工商の身分制度を破ろうとする商人が現れてきた。彼らはさまざまな形を通して、主調したい思想を取り入れたのである。例えば、浮世絵、俳句、浮世草子などと見られる。それらによって、町人文化が盛んに流行るようになった。その中、刺青という活動も町人文化の一つとして、人々の生活の中で活躍していた。「誰も彼も挙って美しからんと努めた揚句は、天稟の体へ絵の具を注ぎ込むまでになった。芳烈な、或は絢爛な、線と色とがその頃の人々の肌に躍った。」②から見ると、当時の人々は刺青を肉体の美の現れの手段として認めていた。「馬道を通りお客は、見事な刺青のある駕籠舁を選んで乗った。吉原、辰巳の女も美しい刺青の男に惚れた。博徒、鳶の者はもとより、町人から稀には侍なども入墨をした。」③人々は籠を選ぶ時に、「見事な刺青のある」ものを選び、刺青のある男は女性に人気がある。また、刺青をするのは博徒、鳶の者ではなく、武士の中でも入墨した人もいる。ここからも分かるように、江戸時代では女性にしろ、男性にしろ、また、どのような階級にある人にしろ、皆は刺青することを好んでいたのである。江戸文明の一つと見られる刺青が作品の主題に選ば

① 伊藤整編『日本現代文学全集43』講談社より、1980年5月、24頁。

② 同①。

③ 同①。

れたことから、谷崎潤一郎の江戸情緒への心境をうかがうことができる。

次に、作品における中国の古い文化を見てみよう。谷崎潤一郎は中国の文学から多く影響を受けた日本作家の一人である。彼が小学生の頃から、稲原清吉に「大学」、「論語」、唐詩宋詞などを教えてもらい、漢文素養を身につけた。また、中華料理屋を開いた友達の笹沼源之助との付き合ってから、中国に関わるものにますます興味を持つようになったと言われている。彼の作品に中国の要素を見つけることができる、無論、「刺青」は例外ではなかった。

清吉は女に入墨をを刺そうとした時、彼女に二本の巻物を見せた。一つは「肥料」を題とする美人の足元で斃死した男たちの絵で、もう一つは中国の暴君紂王の寵妃、末喜の姿を描いた画である。

「瑠璃珊瑚を鏤めた金冠の重さに得堪えぬなよやかな体を、ぐったり勾欄に靠れて、羅綾の裳裾を階の中段にひるがえし、右手に大杯を傾けながら、今しも庭前に刑せられんとする犠牲の男を眺めている妃の風情。」①

中国の桀王と紂王は寵姫に溺れた暴君としてよく知られている。『列女伝』によると、紂王の寵姫は妲己で、桀王の寵姫は末喜である。ここで、谷崎潤一郎は「紂王の寵姫、末喜」という差と書いたのは、おそらく覚え間違ったただろう。そう言っても、谷崎潤一郎が中国の文学への理解の深さを抹殺することができない。ただ 150 文字で、末喜の贅沢さと残忍さが現れている。一般的に、谷崎潤一郎の中国趣味は中国の古典である「論語」から材を取り書いた「麒麟」を始めとされるが、「刺青」の中にある中国要素も彼の初期の美意識の現れといえよう。

3.3　伝統的な美への追求

「幽玄」「侘び」「寂び」などの美意識は日本の伝統的なもので、谷崎潤一郎が関西に引越してから、彼の主な文学主張となったと見なされている。しかし、初期における作品の中にも日本伝統の美学意識が見つけられる。「刺青」の中に、欠けていることこそ美であるという美意識が潜んでおり、「悪魔主義」と混ぜて彼の特別な美意識を表している。

日本人は昔から、一部分が欠け、不完全なものを好んでいた。『枕草子』、『方丈記』と合わせて日本三大随筆と評価されている『徒然草』の 82 段により、「不具なるこそよけれ」、「すべて、何も皆、事のととのほりたるは、あしき事なり。」「前賢の作れる内外の文にも、章段の欠けたる事のみこそ侍れ。」②などの文章から、完璧に整えてしまうことに比べ、不揃いで残欠のほうが面白いと考えられている。今にしても、日本の建築物や日本人が平日に使っている器や花瓶などはわざと何か残欠がある様子とされ、満月より、日本人は残月がさらに美しいものと思っている。また、映画や小説の結局の大多数が悲劇の場合も多い。他国にとって不運を象徴する残欠は日本国民が古来から暗黙のうちに認められる美で、谷崎潤一郎も自然にその美意識を身につけ、作品を通じて残欠の美を提唱した。

---

① 伊藤整編『日本現代文学全集 43』講談社より、1980 年 5 月、30 頁。

② 吉田兼好『徒然草』より。（http://roudokus.com/tsurezure/082.html、2016 年 5 月 25 日）

「入れ墨とは、針・刃物・骨片などで皮膚に傷をつけ、その傷に墨汁・朱・酸化鉄などの色素を入れ着色し、文様・文字・絵柄などを描く手法、および、その手法を使って描かれたものである。」[①]一旦針で皮膚に刺青すると、なかなか消せるものではない。たとえ、除去手術ができても、心身に与えられたダメージは容易に消せない。現在の日本では、入れ墨を入れた者には様々な制限がある。普通な人のように公衆浴場に入場することさえ出来なければ、公務員、自衛官などの職種にも採用されない。しかし、江戸時代では、皆が入れ墨を肉体の美の象徴とされ、「時々催される刺青会では参会者おの肌を叩いて、互いに奇抜な意匠を誇り合い、評しあった。」[②]現在においては、刺青は人間に不完全を引き起こすが、谷崎潤一郎の小説では独特な魅力を持ち、入墨をしていなければむしろ恥であると見なされるほどである。言い換えれば、残欠こそが美しい物である。

清吉は女の背に女郎蜘蛛という絵柄を刺し込んだ。しかし、なぜ桜や菊など女性にふさわしいものではなく、怖い女郎蜘蛛を選んだのか。実は、絡新婦について日本各地にいろいろな伝説が伝わっている。それは美しい女の姿に化ける絡新婦は自分の美貌を利用し男たちを誘惑してから、三日後彼らの首級を取り食べるという話である。その女が絡新婦のように男性を征服したのを望んでいた清吉は彼女の意志を問わず、むりやりに麻酔剤をかがせ、自分長年の願いを遂げた。その娘にとって、そんな醜く悪らつな絡新婦を自分の真っ白な疵なき肌に刺されたのは受け入れがたく、生涯さえ補えなかった欠陥である。しかし、文末に「折から朝日が刺青の面にさして、女の背は燦爛とした。」[③]と書いているように、その女は女郎蜘蛛の刺青のおかけで、剣のような瞳を輝かし、自己脱皮を実現できたのである。いわば、絡新婦の刺青が本来その女一生に伴った残欠に見なされるが、ここでは彼女の美の分身として二人とともに生きていく。

第4章　終わりに

本稿は「刺青」を中心に谷崎潤一郎の独特な美意識を検討してみた。これまで「刺青」を研究際に、官能美への追求および「悪魔主義」に焦点を与えてきたが、作品に潜んでいる東洋美、および「かけていることこそ美である」という日本の伝統美意識を見つけ出すことができた。谷崎文学において、初期のみならず、中期、晩期にいたるまで、それらの美意識は一貫しており、時には、官能美が中心になれ、時には日本の伝統美が中心になる。その独特な美意識には、日本文学史で、他人に替えられない根強い魅力があるのを認めなければならない。それらの美意識はその後の作品にどのように織り交ぜられていくのか、今後の課題の一つとしてもっていきたいと思う。

---

① フリー百科事典『ウイキペディア（Wikipedia）』による入れ墨の解釈。（https://ja.wikipedia.org/wiki/入れ墨、2016年5月25日）

② 伊藤整編『日本現代文学全集43』講談社より、1980年5月、24頁。

③ 同②，41頁。

参考文献

[1] 郝周绍. 谷崎润一郎“异端”审美意识浅析[J]. 太原城市职业技术学院学报，2012（4）.

[2] 隽雪艳. 日本人的美意识与无常思想[J]. 日本学刊，2008（4）.

[3] 李韬瑾. 谷崎润一郎的初期审美意识——以《文身》为例[D]. 文教资料，2012（8）.

[4] 李芸德. 论谷崎润一郎作品中的美意识[D]. 佳木斯教育学院学报，2013（8）.

[5] 刘静娜. 论谷崎润一郎的唯美文学意识[D]. 辽宁大学，2013.

[6] 林绿. 试论谷崎润一郎《刺青》中的女性形象与刺青图案[J]. 现代语文，2011（2）.

[7] 卢茂君. 试论《刺青》的技巧探索与形式创新[J]. 焦作大学学报，2010（10）.

[8] 缪霞. 残缺与永恒——浅析谷崎前期作品美学意识[J]. 湖北广播电视大学学报，2009（10）.

[9] 皮俊珺. 谷崎文学的“美意识”萌芽之初探[J]. 天津外国语学院学报，2002（3）.

[10] 齐珮. 谷崎润一郎的唯美世界[D]. 吉林大学，2004.

[11] 任向欣. 试谈谷崎润一郎作品中的美意识——以《刺青》为中心[J]. 语文学刊，2015（8）.

[12] 王丽君. 试论谷崎润一郎作品中的唯美主义[D]. 中国海洋大学，2009.

[13] 曾真. 谷崎润一郎唯美主义文学论[D]. 湘潭大学，2003.

[14] 高田育子「『刺青』の＜女＞」、(http://ci.nii.ac.jp/naid/40016253874、2016年5月25日）.

[15] 三島由紀夫「谷崎潤一郎について」、『豪華版日本文学全集 12』解説、河出書房、1966年10月、248頁.

[16] 藤原智子「谷崎潤一郎『刺青』論」、(http://ci.nii.ac.jp/naid/110002556697、2016年5月25日）.

[17] 伊藤整「谷崎潤一郎の文学」、『近代文学研究叢書—谷崎潤一郎研究』、八木書店、昭和47年11月、519頁.

[18] 佐藤春夫「潤一郎、人及び芸術—谷崎潤一郎の悪魔主義」、『現代日本文学大系 30』解説、筑摩書房、昭和53年11月、546頁.

日本人缩小意识中隐含的扩大心理研究
——以日本传统文学为例

韩文丽

摘　要：长期以来，日本受地理条件和自然资源的制约，在东方大地的一隅产生了自己独树一帜且极具本民族特色的文化特质，即尊崇缩小。韩国学者李御宁在其著作《日本人的缩小意识》中指出，无论是对于任何事物日本人都倾向于将其缩小。日本人的这种缩小意识不仅渗透在折扇、便当、袖珍书等最常见的生活用品上，在日本人耳熟能详的《桃太郎》《一寸法师》等民间故事的主人公塑造及日本和歌、俳句、庭园、茶室等传统文学和庭院建筑方面都体现出日本人的缩小意识。通过这些体现日本人缩小意识的典型事例，可以发现日本人独有的心理特征。因此，本文首先将试图从日本传统文学入手去审视日本人的缩小意识，并剖析日本人的缩小意识中隐含的独特的扩大心理追求。其次，结合日本的国情分析缩小意识及其心理特征形成的原因。

关键词：缩小意识；民间故事；俳句；扩大心理

Abstract: For a long time, Japan, restricted by geographical conditions and natural resources, has developed its own unique cultural characteristics with its own national characteristics in the corner of the eastern land, that is, reverence and narrowing. The Korean scholar Lee O-Young, in his book, "Japanese shrinking consciousness", puts forward another new definition of Japanese worship and shrinking aesthetic consciousness, that is, the Japanese "shrinking consciousness". The Japanese people's consciousness of shrinking not only permeates the most common daily necessities, such as folding fans, benches, pocket books, etc. In the Japanese familiar with "Taotaro", "one inch mage" and other folk stories of the protagonist shaping and Japanese harmony, haiku, garden, teahouse and other traditional literature and courtyard architecture aspects of the Japanese reflected the consciousness of shrinking. Through these typical examples of Japanese shrinking consciousness, we can find the unique psychological characteristics of Japanese. Therefore, this thesis will try to examine the Japanese people's shrinking consciousness from the Japanese traditional literature, and analyze the unique expanding psychological pursuit implied in the Japanese people's shrinking consciousness. Secondly, combined with the national conditions of Japan to analyze the reasons for the formation of shrinking consciousness and psychological characteristics.

Key words: Shrink consciousness; Folk story; Haiku; Expand psychology

1 绪　论

韩国学者李御宁在《日本人的缩小意识》一书中首次提出缩小意识的概念。"缩小意识"是指日本人擅长将生活中的大多数事物缩小化的文化特性。即日本人善于将大的事物缩小，并在小东西中表现出雄大的感觉，同时捕捉其中所蕴含的美感。观察日本人的生活，我们可以发现有诸多的事物都表现出缩小意识。如日本生产的小巧轻便的电子产品、庭园、茶室、折扇、便当等。

日本人的这种缩小意识是一种特色鲜明的日本文化风格。缩小意识及其心理特征对日本的国家经济、科技创造，对民族文化的打造及国民日常生活审美也都产生了至关重要的影响。在当今全球化的背景下，对于缩小意识的深入研究，有助于我们了解日本国民心理及社会文化的形成原因，有助于促进中日两国在文化层面的理解和包容。《日本人的缩小意识》一书列举了各种各样包含日本人缩小意识的事物和表现，例如，折扇、庭园、盆栽、人偶等，得出缩小意识是日本人所持有的特性。这本书对本文梳理日本人的缩小意识的具体事例提供了翔实和广泛的资料，有非常重要的参考价值，但并未对日本人缩小意识的成因以及深层心理做出详细的分析。此后的先行研究也都着重介绍缩小意识在日本人生活、文学的外在表现上，并未对缩小意识背后的心理动机展开深入的分析和研究。鉴于此，本文旨在研究日本民族在缩小的审美意识中隐藏的心理诉求。

2　日本人的缩小意识

说起日本人的缩小意识，首先想到日本最古老的和歌集《万叶集》，其中歌颂吟咏的自然景观多是香久山、耳梨山等低矮幽美的小山；吟诵的植物也都是小巧精致的花朵居多。到了平安时期（760—1191），清少纳言所著《枕草子》中「美しきもの」列举了众多娇小可爱的小事物，得出「何もかも、ちいさきものはいと美しい」的结论。因此，“うつくしい”在古语中多指对娇小可爱的小事物产生的喜爱之情。“缩小”作为一种审美意识也是从很早的时期就活跃于日本文化之中。

日本民族缩小意识的确立与日本的地理环境及资源的匮乏有关。我们知道日本作为岛国，四面环海，国土面积狭小，且日本地形多以山地为主，但没有雄伟的高山。就是在这样的自然环境中，日本本土皆是小巧而纤丽的景观，这在无形中培养了日本民族的缩小的意识形态。受土地面积及地质地貌的局限，日本长期处于资源短缺的状态，这一现实国情促使日本将环保节能作为长期贯彻的方针政策来开展本国的生产生活。日本国民深知本国资源短缺的现状，为了响应国家的政策方针，便将缩小意识渗透于日常生产生活的方方面面，使得缩小意识从文化层面走出并深入地渗透于生活的各个层面。此外，日本四季分明，花开花落秋去春来都有条不紊地进行在明显的季节更替中。长此以往，那些细小事物和景物的变化皆能引起日本人的注意，这也就在无形中训练了他们发现细小之美的敏感度。日本人也在四季微妙的变化和生命律动的日夜感受中，将本民族的审美意识同自然密切结合，形成了日本民族特有的缩小的审美意识。

3　传统文学中的缩小意识

文学是一个民族文化和审美意识的折射和重要栖息地。因此，本文将从代表日本传统文学的民间故事和俳句的角度剖析日本人的缩小意识。

3.1　民间故事中的缩小意识

民间故事是指由劳动人民创作并传播的，具有虚构内容的口头文学作品，是庶民文化的最佳表现之一。它的内容讲述多为人与人之间的种种关系，体裁广泛又充满幻想，且非常贴近生活。民间故事之所以有许多脍炙人口的名篇自创作能流传至今，是因为民间故事是群众将生活智慧和哲理及自己对生活理想和愿景以一种大众喜闻乐见、易于接受的形式创作出来的艺术产物。韩（2008）认为，“民间故事是一个民族古代生活习俗、民族心理、审美意识和文化价值取向的综合反映”，不难看出民间故事是了解一个民族的审美意识的重要素材。本文将从三个日本最具有代表性的民间故事中探讨缩小意识。

《一寸法师》是在日本广为流传的民间故事，是讲一对老夫妇生下一个拇指大的婴儿，便取名为一寸法师。一寸法师虽然身材娇小但本领奇大，独自一人外出去体验生活，获取成就。遇到危险挺身而出，最后用自己的智慧打败了高大强壮的魔鬼，并获得一个万能宝槌，使自己身材变大成为朝廷重臣后迎娶了公主，并和自己的父母幸福的生活在一起。

《桃太郎》的故事也是家喻户晓，讲述一位老婆婆将捡到的桃子带回家并抚育了从桃子里诞生的桃太郎。桃太郎生来很小，但是见风就长大，很快就成为一个身强力壮的小伙子，并用糯米团子收容了狗、猴、雉鸡后，一起前往鬼岛为民除害的故事。

《竹取物语》的故事在日本也是无人不晓。一位老爷爷在上山砍竹时在竹子中发现一个巴掌大的可爱小女婴——辉夜姬，带回家抚养后辉夜姬快速成长，在很短的时间内出落成远近闻名的绝世美女。她用自己的智慧拒绝了天皇五位贵公子的求婚，最后升天。

上述三个日本民间故事在主人公的塑造方面有共同的特点，就是主人公都是身材娇小，但却本领非凡的人物。他们凭借自己的勇敢和智慧，用自己微小的力量同邪恶或强大的势力做斗争以追求最终完美的结局。这充分地展示出日本人的缩小意识在民间故事这一传统文学形式中的渗透，其中，被紫式部称为物语文学鼻祖的《竹取物语》中，当老爷爷发现辉夜姬时，感叹道“三寸ばかりなる人、いとうつくしうてゐたり。”（只有三寸大小的小女孩真是美丽得惹人怜爱啊）老翁面对只有巴掌大的主人公时，由衷地感叹“うつくし”。这是日本人的缩小意识在文学创作中的最为直观地反映，也可以说明民间故事正是日本民族缩小意识的一个剪影，日本人就是在这样的小事物、“小人物”中发现美，并在精神层面感悟到美。

3.2 俳句中的缩小意识

俳句也将日本人的缩小意识淋漓尽致地体现在其中，日本人通过俳句向世人完美地展现出日本文化细致入微又精美绝伦的别样美感。

俳句被称为世界上最短的诗歌，只有 17 个假名组成，通过季语和切字，以“象征”“暗示”等艺术手法让世人充分领略日本民族将大千世界浓缩进纸页方寸之间的深厚功力。来看松尾芭蕉的名句“よく見れば なづな花咲く 垣根かな（凝目仔细看，荠菜白花隐隐现，独放篱笆边）”，即为仔细瞧篱笆的下边，发现绽放的小小的荠菜花。荠菜花外形小巧玲珑，篱笆边的荠菜花更是微不足道，这也只是俳句歌咏众多花草中的一个小事物。夏目漱石的俳句“菫ほどの小さき人に生まれたし（小小紫丁香，生来如你为我愿，默默路旁站）”中，描写的紫丁香也同样是娇小的花朵，也作为作家捕捉和关注的对象。可以发现上述两首俳句所例证的花朵都有一个共同点，即花朵较小。所以我们可以知道在日本人独有的审美意识、即缩小意识的作用下，日本的诗人才擅长发现大自然中不会被轻易发现的、隐秘的美感。俳句通过其 17 个假名的格式以及绝大多数的吟咏对象皆为小巧事物这一事实，我们可以看出俳句是日本人缩小意识在文学中最直观的一大体现。

日本人这种感受细微小事物的心绪也体现在俳句的意境格局的架构方面，俳句的意境可以说是对缩小意识的极致体现。

首先以松尾芭蕉的代表作“古池や 蛙飛び込む 水の音”（古池冷落一片寂，忽闻青蛙跳水声，激起水声响）为例。这首诗以其幽微深远的意蕴被视为日本俳句中的名篇佳作。古池塘、青蛙、水，三个自然界中极为普通的存在仅作为这首诗的三个意象被作者巧用便勾勒出一幅自然界的灵动的画像。再看与谢芜村的句作，“春の海終日のたりのたりから”（终日悠悠是春海，波光潋滟浪花柔）这首诗的意象只有一个，即是春天波动的海洋。我们可以看到俳句所容纳的意象为数不多，这是其缩小意识在俳句的又一体现。

因此我们可以深刻地理解日本民族自古以来钟情并擅长将自己对缩小意识的推崇和喜爱之情融入民间故事、俳句等日本传统文学之中，也再次领略在日本传统文学中，日本人的缩小意识担任何等重要的角色。

4 缩小意识隐含的扩大心理

一个民族在某种意识萌芽之后再经过时间的不断推移，使得该意识在文化、文学及日常生活中产生深厚的底蕴和积淀，最后逐渐形成该民族一种稳定的和具有鲜明风格的审美心理。本章节将重点探讨缩小审美意识中隐含的日本民族的心理特征。

上述的日本民间故事中列举了三个体现缩小意识的人物。一寸法师、桃太郎、辉夜姬的共同特点即为身材娇小却拥有神通广大的力量，娇小的身躯迅速变大变强，或者以小博大，以娇小的身躯去挑战和降服那些体格力量、权势地位比自己强大的对象。这些人物形象明显反映出日本民族的心理特征，即喜爱“小中求大”。祝大鸣（2009）认为日本人这种由小变大、以弱胜强的人物塑造，实则为日本人扩大性格的作用和影响。笔者认为这也是日本民族赋予虚构的人物形象中的精神寄托，即渴望扩大的心理追求。日本国土面积狭小，自然资源匮乏，自然灾害频发。自古以来，日本人在适应和克服这种恶劣的自然环境的过程中产生了试图改变、试图争取的顽强意识。同时，用自己的智慧创造小的事物，发现生活中微不足道的美。但日本民族并没有停留在缩小的自我欣赏层面，而是在这审美倾向中加注本民族试图以小博大、小中求大，不断想扩大的心理追求。

日本诗人仅通过17个字的诗句创作便在诗意世界中描绘出一幅又一幅大千世界的画卷，在纸页的方寸之间就能向读者展开一幅幅意境恢宏的画面。诗人通过俳句的意境构造，给读者架构的画面要么是精巧纤丽的古潭一隅，要么是广阔纵深的浩瀚汪洋。诸如此类的俳句在日语中不胜枚举，俳句都是通过寥寥数字便做到将读者与广阔的自然巧妙联结，使读者通过纸页上的17字便得以在顷刻间领略大自然的风华绝代。所以说俳句的意境构造也巧妙地向世人传达日本民族对于缩小意识的喜爱和推崇。

俳句的季语是表示季节的咏题。通过季语直接体现一年四季的风情时令。在俳句中甚至有“无季不成句”的说法，并且俳句对季节与季物的区别相当精细。正如松尾芭蕉描写春秋的两首典型俳句：“うぐいすや柳やぶの前”（啼莺在何处，柳后或薮前）、“菊の香や奈良には古佛達。”（重九奈良风光好，古佛常伴菊花香）这两首俳句中明显带有“柳”“菊”这样象征季节的“季物”，作者便是借用季物将大自然的季节感和缩小为首的审美意识浓缩进俳句之中。所以通过各种各样带有季语的简短的俳句我们便可以在各色诗中体会大自然一年四季的轮回，万物荣枯。

日本民族运用俳句这样简短的描写，将自然界中的动与静，寂与响重现在纸面上，余韵悠长。通过俳句的“季语”“切字”将日本一年四季的变化和风情体现得淋漓尽致。诗人将一幅幅完整的景色浓缩进短短17个字中，在一年四季的时间纵向和完整广阔的意境空间的横向上向世人展示日本民族善用缩小意识的文学功力及缩小意识背后所蕴含的在时间和空间上延展扩张的心理特征。通过俳句的短短17字便将大自然的四季浓缩，将自然景物的辽阔缩小于三两个意象，这些都是日本民族试图在俳句中追求的一种“扩大”的渴望。

日本民族的缩小意识中隐藏的扩大心理可以从以下两个方面得以验证。首先，从军事方面来看，以中日甲午战争为例，120年前中日两国的实力，无论在经济上还是军事上，中国都更胜一筹。中国当时的GDP超过日本，北洋舰队主力舰和总吨位超过日本，陆军数量超过日本。再看日本，明治维新后，日本的实力虽大幅上升，但与中国相比仍有差距。在第二次世界大战前，世界公认无论经济实力还是军事实力，日本都不如中国。但是在这场战争中中国还是以惨败收场。究其原因，从外部因素来看，还是源于日本并未受制于本国自身的缺陷，而是动用最大的能量在对外扩张中做出奋力一搏。当时日本作为一个弱小国能战胜中国，这绝对是众多日本以小博大的历史事件中最为典型的一场战役。

其次，第二次世界大战后日本迅速复苏，走上依靠高科技产品占领国际舞台的道路。日本依靠独有的缩小意识在科学技术领域不断创新，研发了一系列现代化的袖珍产品，这些产品在小巧精致的外形里潜藏丰富强大的功能和内涵。袖珍产品为日本打开高科技产业的国际市场，为本国赢得更多的话语权。日本擅于研制外形小巧而功能强大的产品，以电子产品的“小”来攻取世界经济及政治的“大”舞台，这便是证明日本人的缩小意识中所隐含的“小中求大”的心理特征的又一强有力的例证。

这两个实例非常直观地表现出日本民族的缩小意识，一是以自我国家的各种与“小”有关的特征为美，也可以理解为日本民族自我欣赏与自豪的心理；二是可以体现出日本人对“缩小”的喜爱并未只停留在表面上，而是在缩小意识中时刻穿插顽强的扩大意识。

5 结束语

如前所述，缩小意识是日本民族特有的审美意识，贯穿于日本民族的发展历史之中，并渗透于文化和生活的各个方面。日本受自然地理状况及资源短缺的限制产生了缩小意识，但背后却潜藏日本民族渴求强大，力图扩张的心理追求。正如美国著名学者鲁思·本尼迪克特提出的日本人极其鲜明的矛盾性格一样，日本试图扩大的欲望有多么强烈，反之，他对于缩小的喜爱就有多么鲜明，日本民族通过事物性质上的反向来巧妙而含蓄地表达自己真正的心理追求和主张，这既符合日本人矛盾性格的表现特点，也呼应了日本人含蓄美的主张。这也充分说明日本人在缩小的审美意识中寄托了“小中求大”的心理追求。

参考文献

[1] 高階秀爾. 日本人の美意識[A]. 王宣琦. 武汉大学出版社，2004：1-10.
[2] 韩若冰. 日本民间童话故事“桃太郎”的文化解读[J]. 民俗研究，2008（21）.
[3] 李御寧.「縮み」志向の日本人[M]. 学生社，1982.
[4] 李兆忠.“大日本”与“小日本”[J]. 世界知识，2002（15）.
[5] 李御宁. 日本人的缩小意识[M]. 张乃丽译. 济南：山东人民出版社，2003.

[6] 鲁思·本尼迪克特. 菊与刀[M]. 北京：商务印书馆，2001.

[7] 王洁. 日本人的扩大意识[J]. 开封教育学院学报，2015（4）.

[8] 于长敏. 日本民间故事及其文化内涵[J]. 日语学习与研究，2004（3）.

[9] 于海英. 浅析日本人“以小为美”的民族文化意识[J]. 文化艺术研究，2010（23）.

[10] 杨红，王景杰. 论日本人“以小为美”的审美意识与文化特性[J]. 重庆大学学报（社会科学版），2006（5）.

[11] 祝大鸣. 日本民族对立统一的性格特征——以扩大与缩小性格为例[J]. 日语学习与研究，2009（2）.

[12] 赵冬梅，亷煜. 从大小看日本人的审美意识[J]. 文学教育（下），2014（10）.

[13] 张琳. 浅谈日本人的缩小意识[J]. 考试周刊，2011（90）.

[14] 張婉婉. 日本人の審美意識—もののあわれの形成した原因への探り[D]. 西安外国語大学，2011.

翻译研究

存异伦理视角下文化负载词的翻译研究
——以葛浩文英译《蛙》为例

毛晓燕

摘　要：伴随20世纪60年代的“文化转向”（cultural turn）以来，译者的主体性地位日益凸显。同时，自20世纪90年代以来，“翻译伦理”的概念随之发展，成为不可挡的趋势。所谓的“伦理”一词，在《辞海》中给出这样的定义：“处理人们相互关系所应遵循的道德和规则。”（1989：578）所谓翻译伦理，即是“翻译的主体行为‘人’在翻译活动中所遵循的道德准则”，包括作者、读者、出版社、源语言、目的语等因素。针对翻译伦理，国内外众多学者对其进行了研究总结，其中一种主张建立尊重语言和文化差异的存异伦理随即出现。这种“存异伦理”（Ethics of difference）是由美国著名翻译理论家劳伦斯·韦努蒂（Lawrence Venuti）提出的。他声称：“我所支持的伦理立场是这样，它敦促翻译在阅读、写作和评估各方面对语言和文化的差异表现出更多的尊重。”（Venuti，1998）他的这一翻译伦理研究对于译者的翻译实践有着一定的指导作用。因此，本文试图从韦努蒂（Venuti）的“存异伦理”（Ethics of difference）角度出发，从保留源语言“异质”文化和考虑到目标语读者的阅读兴趣之间的平衡，旨在通过对葛浩文英译本《蛙》进行存异理论视角解析，以此验证产生于西方后殖民批评语境下的存异伦理亦能在中国文学外译的背景下找到其发展的适用性。本文将在采用举例分析法对原文本和译本进行对比分析的基础之上，探寻葛浩文尤其在处理文化负载词所遵循的翻译存异伦理观，并着重解析译者为实现这一伦理观所采取的具体翻译策略和理念，由此从中得到一些启示，对中国文学作品如何更好地传播进入外语世界具有重要的借鉴和参考意义。

关键词：存异伦理；葛浩文；《蛙》；文化负载词翻译

Abstract: With the cultural turn of the 1960s, the translator's subjectivity has become increasingly prominent. Since the 1990s, the concept of “translation ethics” has developed, which became an unstoppable trend. The so-called “ethics” gives such a definition in *CiHai*, “the morals and rules that should be followed in dealing with people's mutual relations.” (1989: 578) Furthermore, the so-called translation ethics is the “moral codes that the subjective behavior of the translation ‘human’ should follow in translation activities”, including authors, readers, publishers, source language, and target language. In response to the ethics of translation, many scholars at home and abroad have carried out research and summarization, one of whom advocates the establishment of one kind of ethical ethics that respects language and cultural differences. This “Ethics of difference” was proposed by the famous American translation theorist Lawrence Venuti. He claimed, “The ethical position I support is this point that it urges the translation to show more respect for existed language and cultural differences in these aspects of reading, writing and evaluating, etc.” (Venuti, 1998) and his researches on translation ethics have a certain guiding role for translators' translation practice. Therefore, this paper tries to balance between the “heterogeneous” culture of the source language and the reading interest of the target language readers from the perspective of Venuti's "Ethics of difference". Through the analysis of Howard Goldblatt's English translation of *Frog* from the perspective of Ethics of difference，this paper verifies that the Ethics of difference，which was produced in the context of western post-colonial criticism，can find its applicability under the background of translation of Chinese literature. Based on the comparative analysis of the original text and the translated version，this paper will explore the translation ethics existing in Howard Goldblatt's translated version *Frog*，especially in dealing with culture-loaded words，and also focus on the specific translation strategies and concepts adopted by the translator to achieve this ethics. Thus this can help usobtainsome enlightenment from it，and this will have significant reference for how our Chinese literature better spread into the foreign language world.

Key words: Ethics of difference; Howard Goldblatt; *Frog*; Translation of culture-loaded words

1 引 言

伴随 20 世纪 60 年代的“文化转向”（cultural turn）以来，译者的主体性地位日益凸显。而伦理性是翻译存在的一个侧面、一种途径。有人群的地方就有人际关系，就有人际关系的规范，因而就有伦理。翻译伦理研究产生于 20 世纪 80 年代中叶，以 1984 年贝尔曼正式提出“翻译伦理”（ethics of translation）这一概念为标志。（Berman，1992）同时，自 20 世纪 90 年代以来，“翻译伦理”的概念随之发展，成为不可挡的趋势。同样，随着文化全球化的浪潮席卷而来，世界上越来越多的民族文化正不可避免地被卷入这一浪潮之中，而作为文化碰撞和交融的重要阵地，翻译也不可避免地需要应对文化全球化所带来的伦理问题。这一浪潮使得各个国家和民族之间的语言和文化交往日益密切，也给翻译带来了愈发激烈的语言和文化异质冲击。在这样的背景之下，翻译无法避免面临伦理选择问题，即是翻译不得不思考和决定应当如何对待语言和文化的他者。按照译界普遍公认的说法，“翻译伦理”这一概念在西方译界的诞生至今尚不足 30 年，至于中国译界，相关的研究更是近十年才逐渐兴起。

在 20 多年的时间里，西方的翻译伦理研究涌现出一批代表性知名学者和有影响力的著述，提出一系列的基本概念和核心术语。这既标志着翻译伦理研究的阶段性成果，也体现了其蓬勃发展的势头。而在西方翻译伦理研究领域里，贝尔曼、韦努蒂、皮姆、切斯特曼的成果最为显著，影响范围也是最广，其中贝尔曼期望通过伦理规约促使翻译凸显异质，要求翻译对异质表现出欢迎和尊重的态度。（Berman，1992）他试图通过“变形系统”这一方式来建构一种迎向异质的翻译伦理模式。而韦努蒂竭力发掘被掩盖的弱势民族的声音，以抵制西方霸权话语，为此提出“差异伦理”的概念，试图通过在翻译活动中凸显差异来消解欧美中心主义的话语霸权。皮姆致力于研究译者伦理，他的翻译伦理思想旨在改善文化间性，为此他极力推行“文化间性”这一概念，主张将译者伦理的重心放在改善文化间的关系上。同样对于切斯特曼而言，翻译伦理也是其重要的研究对象，他提出了一套基于价值的翻译伦理模式，还提出一个重要的伦理概念——“解放性翻译”，并肯定和强化了翻译的职业伦理意识。近年来，西方的翻译伦理理论逐渐被引入中国，并引起越来越多人的兴趣。在这股潮流下，一批中国学者相继投身于翻译伦理研究，取得了重要的成绩，在中国“翻译伦理”一词最早出现于《中国翻译》1998 年第 1 期《国外翻译新书简介》一文中。（杨镇源，翻译伦理研究，p. 206）随着中国翻译伦理研究的迅速升温，一些中国译学界知名专家纷纷投身于翻译伦理研究，在各类理论专著或期刊论文中阐述了自己的翻译伦理理论，提出了“翻译伦理学”“译者职责”“伦理转向”等相关概念。

鉴于之前众多学者对葛浩文《蛙》英译本的研究来看，更多是从译者本身的主体性地位以及译者文化身份认同视角来看译本所采用到的翻译策略，而本文试图从外部原因视角探索，而译者不再是单一的主体，更多关注到其他各个行为主体形成影响翻译活动的种种关系要素，包括译入语、译入语文化以及读者期待视野等要素，即构成的这张伦理网络便使得翻译的存在呈现出不可忽视的伦理性。而本篇论文即是基于翻译伦理理论中的一个重要部分——韦努蒂（Venuti）的“存异伦理”（Ethics of difference）角度出发，从保留源语言“异质”文化和考虑目标语读者的阅读兴趣之间的平衡视角来看，本文旨在通过对葛浩文英译本《蛙》进行存异理论视角解析，以此验证产生于西方后殖民批评语境下的存异伦理亦能在中国文学外译的背景下找到其发展的适用性。本文将在采用举例分析法对原文本和译本进行对比分析的基础之上，探寻葛浩文尤其在处理文化负载词所遵循的翻译存异伦理观，并着重解析译者为实现这一伦理观所采取的具体翻译策略，包含归化、异化等翻译策略，同时指出其翻译活动体现出“异化翻译”“僭越性忠实”和“对抗式翻译”这三大翻译伦理理念。

本篇论文主要分为五个部分。第一部分简要介绍莫言《蛙》和译者葛浩文以及《蛙》英译本；第二部分介绍韦努蒂“存异伦理”理论相关概念；第三部分根据葛浩文（Howard Goldblatt）和季进的访问录等资料解读《蛙》英译本中所体现的韦努蒂“存异伦理”理念；第四部分根据“存异伦理”理论中的三大核心概念，即“异化翻译”“僭越性忠实”和“对抗式翻译”，解析葛浩文《蛙》英译本中的文化负载词的翻译；第五部分是结语部分，通过对葛浩文英译本《蛙》进行存异理论视角解析，探寻发现译者所遵循的翻译存异伦理观，并着重解析译者为实现这一伦理观所采取的具体翻译策略，以此验证产生于西方后殖民批评语境下的存异伦理亦能在中国文学外译的背景下找到其发展的适用性，由此从中得到一些启示，对中国文学作品如何更好地传播进入外语世界具有重要的借鉴和参考意义。

2　莫言《蛙》、译者葛浩文及其译本简介

作为中国首位诺贝尔文学奖获奖者的作品之一，《蛙》对世界文坛产生的影响当然值得人们去发掘研究，而作为把《蛙》推向世界文坛的英译本无疑也同样值得人们去发掘研究。也许因为其面世的时间还比较短，所以目前学者们对其英译本研究还比较少。目前国内对于莫言作品的翻译研究主要从翻译作品特定视角分析，作品中艺术特色以及针对非英文译本的研究，而国外对莫言英译本的研究大致可从三个方面来看，分别是使用政治批评的视角分析作品主题、人物形象以及语言特色，莫言作品艺术特色分析以及利用比较文学的对照研究视域。莫言，原名管谟业，中国当代著名作家，是第一个获得诺贝尔文学奖的中国籍作家。他自1980年以一系列乡土作品崛起，充满“怀乡”以及“怨乡”的复杂情感，被归类为“寻根文学”作家，其作品深受魔幻现实主义影响，代表作有《红高粱》《檀香刑》《丰乳肥臀》等，其中《蛙》获第八届茅盾文学奖。2012年莫言获得诺贝尔文学奖，颁奖词称莫言“用魔幻般的现实主义将民间故事、历史和现代融为一体”。《蛙》是莫言酝酿十多年、笔耕四载、三易其稿，潜心创作的第11部长篇小说，将书信、元小说叙事和话剧融为一体，以中华人民共和国成立近60年波澜起伏的农村生育史为背景，通过讲述从事妇产科工作50多年的乡村女医生姑姑万心的人生经历，在形象描述国家为控制人口增长、实施计划生育国策所走过的艰巨而复杂

的历史过程的同时，成功地塑造了一个生动鲜明、感人至深的农村妇科女医生形象，并结合计划生育过程中的复杂现象，剖析了以叙述人蝌蚪为代表的知识分子卑微、尴尬、纠结、矛盾的精神世界。

葛浩文（Howard Goldblatt），美国著名汉学家，是2012年诺贝尔文学奖得主莫言作品的英文译者，目前是英文世界地位最高的中国文学翻译家，他的翻译严谨而讲究，让中国文学披上了当代英美文学的色彩。葛浩文翻译了包括萧红、姜戎、莫言等20多位名家的50多部作品，出生于美国的葛浩文在翻译时一方面多采用归化式翻译，对原文有适量增减和改动；在另一方面因受其文化身份的影响，他将归化与异化相结合，以便更好地为西方读者服务，同时在译者对文本的解读上，他的文化身份使他可以更好地解读中国特色文化背景下的各种文化词汇，从而在本土化的翻译下，更好地促进跨文化上的交流。由此葛浩文在译莫言作品时既发挥了译者的主体性，又保留了原作的文化色彩，将《蛙》惟妙惟肖地展现给世人，在2014年由其翻译出版的《蛙》在面向英语国家读者中取得了较大的成功。

3　韦努蒂（Venuti）“存异伦理”介绍

伦理是人类思想对于终极价值的一种深沉的追寻。伦理有别于道德，道德是调节人类行为的一系列行为规范，属于实践的范畴，而伦理则属于思想的领域。英文的ethics源自古希腊语ethos，意为“本质”“人格”“风俗”“习惯”，所探讨的就是人与人之间关系的问题，任何人类行为、学科都会涉及伦理问题。正如Jeffrey M.Green所说：“一旦涉及到翻译，不得不考虑到作者、读者、出版社等。”可见，翻译和伦理的关系就不言而喻了。自从1984年，贝尔曼在一次国际学术研讨会上第一次提出“翻译伦理”的概念之后，更是在其后出版的《异的考验》一书中进一步阐述了这一思想，认为翻译伦理的核心就是尊重原作中的语言和文化差异，而其目的则旨在通过引入差异来丰富自身。而美国解构主义翻译理论家劳伦斯·韦努蒂从法国哲学家列维纳斯以及贝尔曼那里“借来”翻译伦理，又从中衍生出存异伦理（ethics of difference）。“存异伦理”（ethics of difference）是由美国著名翻译理论家劳伦斯·韦努蒂（Lawrence Venuti）所提出的，他声称：“我所支持的伦理立场是这样，它敦促翻译在阅读、写作和评估各方面对语言和文化的差异表现出更多的尊重”，（Venuti，1998）由此指出存异伦理的实质要求是对他者发自内心的尊重态度。

韦努蒂认为翻译的功能就是对异质性的吸收，好的翻译必须致力于保留语言文化差异，他把这样的伦理称为“存异伦理”。他在《翻译的耻辱》一书中认为，“作为翻译行为主体的译者不管主观意愿如何，在客观上本土体系和机构剥削、利用外国文本和文化的共谋”，他将这一事实称为“翻译最令人不堪的奇耻大辱”。（Venuti，1998：4）由此他提出翻译伦理目标就是反对“同一化”，反对文化殖民霸权主义。翻译存异伦理提倡的是通过异化来保留原语文本及文化的异质性，但这并不是要让翻译摆脱归化，关键是译者要改变翻译的本族中心主义方向。此外，他在此书中对存异伦理进行了进一步的解构，提出了“因地制宜伦理”（the ethics of location），即根据实际语境的历史和社会状况来判断翻译的价值内涵，而非在翻译策略上偏执于一隅。（Venuti，1998：188-189）他认为好翻译不局限于归化翻译或是异化翻译，只要能因地制宜促进文化更新和变化的就是好翻译。

4 葛浩文《蛙》英译本体现的“存异伦理”

翻译活动很大程度上会受到翻译伦理的制约和影响，韦努蒂提出的“存异伦理”就是翻译伦理中非常重要的理论之一。莫言的小说在全世界的文化输出与其英语译者葛浩文的关系密不可分，而作为莫言作品的首席英语译者，葛浩文很好地保留了莫言原作中的异质成分，同时又考虑到英语读者兴趣，做到两者之间的平衡，这点也是韦努蒂所强调的文化间的不平衡现象，通过打破这一现象以此抵制西方本族文化中心主义和自恋主义，更好地实现跨文化交流的目的。

小说《蛙》是以中华人民共和国成立近60年波澜起伏的农村生育史为背景，其中涉及中国实行计划生育国策等富有中国国情和民族特色。而小说《蛙》魔幻现实主义的创作方式，民族性的中国特色叙述特点都带有大量的异质文化色彩，很好地体现了中国的东方色彩和异域文化色彩。同时，译者在翻译过程中，其翻译策略的选择也受到存异伦理的影响。首先，在称谓和人名的翻译上，葛浩文并不单一局限于采用归化或是异化的翻译策略，而是选择了较为灵活的译法，比如文中主要人物“姑姑”的译法就有aunt和Gugu两种译法，这种归化和异化相结合的译法就很好地做到了韦努蒂“存异伦理”所主张的尊重语言和文化差异的翻译伦理理念。其次，在诸如“走资派”“贫下中农”等这些在中国特殊时期的特定表述的文化词汇，译文更多的是使用异化策略，让读者自己去了解中国历史。这样的翻译策略不仅很好地保留了中国文化的特色，而且还有利于中国文化在英语世界的传播，并且在一定程度上动摇了西方英语主导国家的霸权地位，更好地实现各国间跨文化交流的目的。还有译者对原小说魔幻现实主义的写作手法以及独特的兼书信体与叙述体的叙述方式，更有一些四字成语、歇后语以及比喻等修辞手法都很好地保留了下来，这些都是中国文学的很重要体现，也是翻译“存异伦理”理念的重要体现与影响。

5 “存异伦理”视角下文化负载词的翻译

5.1 “异化翻译”

针对莫言作品英译本的读者，葛浩文在翻译过程中对于原文中的文化负载词采取了不同的翻译手段，使译文尽量保留中国文化特色，又符合英语表达习惯，从而实现翻译的文化交互功能。本文将从“存异伦理”理论的“异化翻译”“僭越性忠实”和“对抗式翻译”这三个翻译原则分别来分析葛浩文在处理原文中的文化负载词时所采用的具体翻译策略，探究葛浩文的翻译风格。

从异化翻译来说，韦努蒂提倡采用的异化翻译并不是一种策略，而是一种态度，这是在译文中所表达的对外语文本和外国文化的一种道德态度。（郭建中，2008：3）而对于韦努蒂而言，通过不同的翻译策略可以产生异化的翻译效果，采用这种异化翻译是为译文增加其可读性，同时让读者注意到外语文本中语言和文化的异质性。这一点也正是葛浩文在翻译莫言《蛙》的过程中所注意到的，不管是他采用归化还是异化的翻译手法，葛浩文在考虑读者兴趣以及理解度上都是有意愿在译文中向读者传达原文的异质成分。

《蛙》中部分文化负载词源语和目标语对比如表1所示。

表 1

牛鬼蛇神	Ox-ghosts and snake-demons	火冒三丈	The flames were thirty feet high
如果他敢伤……一根毫毛	Harmed a hair of	绵里藏针	A needle tucked into cotton
千杯不醉	Drink a thousand cups without getting drunk.	根红苗红	Your roots are red and your limbs are straight
“语录歌”	“A Song of Quotations”	“风暴造反团”	“Window Rebel Corps Commander”

在对上述这些文化负载词进行翻译的过程中，译者葛浩文之所以采用异化的翻译策略，正是因为尊重中外两种语言和文化的差异存在，于是这些译入语很好地保留了原文的形式和文化内涵。这种持有异化态度的译者不仅向目标语读者传达出原文的异质成分，也使得这些读者有机会去品析中国暗含的独特文化色彩，更便于达到跨文化交流的目的。

5.2 “僭越性忠实”

“僭越性忠实”这个理念是韦努蒂借用刘易斯的《翻译的效果实施》一文中的一词，他认为这种旨在打破熟悉感、制造不安的僭越性忠实标志译文与原文之间存在僭越、模糊的关系，打破传统忠实观的狭隘标准，客观上推动翻译对语言文化的重塑。（Venuti，1998：204）（如表 2 所示）

表 2

中华人民共和国成立前	Before the establishment of the People’s Republic	大羊栏小学	Great Sheep’s Pen Elementary School
打架闹得鸡犬不宁	Fought like cats and dogs	神仙般的日子	Live a magical life
别卖关子	The suspense is killing me	投胎转世	a reincarnation of
鬼门关口	The gate of Hell	吃了安心丸	Put her mind at ease
狗特务	Dog of a spy	断了他们财路	They’d be out of work.
盛夏的天气	In the dog days of summer	下九流	Work of lower classes
水漫金山	Flooded streets	黄道吉日	A fine，auspicious day
刺刀见红	When push came to shove	“活阎王”	“Living Queen of Hell”

这里，“打闹得鸡犬不宁”翻译成“fought like cats and dogs”，而不是“fought like dogs and chicken”；还有“吃了定心丸”的译文是“put her mind at ease”，而不是“taking mind-easing pills”；

“水漫金山”是用“flooded streets”来表达，而不是“water flooding the Jinshan Temple”等等。这些例子译者都是采用归化的翻译策略，葛浩文删译了原文富含的大量文化信息，这些正是对于读者而言是完全陌生的。针对这些文化负载词的处理，葛浩文从目标语读者的接受度和译本的可读性这两个角度出发，他采用的是外语国家地道的表达习惯语和俗语来表达同等的意思，以便于目标语读者去理解。通常意义上来讲，译者在对这些重要的文化信息进行处理时，将会先弄明白一级、二级词汇以及那些不可删译的词语，然后再严格评估整个文本的翻译风格。正因为译者决定采取何种翻译策略都将对目标语的文本产生极大的影响。在《蛙》的英译本中，这种看似毫不忠实于原文形式和文化内容，并且带有所谓“强制性暴力”翻译的僭越性忠实，这种貌似做到对译入语的“僭越性忠实”却更好地让读者产生浓厚的阅读兴趣。虽然译者删除了原文中富含的众多文化信息，但却以此使读者避免了对这些文化信息产生困惑和理解的问题。

5.3 “对抗式翻译”

举例 1

原文：家里人都围着上去教他，有的掐人中，有的捏虎口，有的拍胸膛。（莫言，2012：35）

译文：Some pinched the spot over his upper lip；someone else pinched the spot between his thump and finger，and a third person thumped him on the chest.

举例 2

原文：炕头上摞着王仁美娘家送来的四条新被子，两条新褥子，两条毛毯，两个枕头，几乎顶着纸天棚。

译文：Piled high at the head of a kang were four new quilts，two bed mats，two woolen blankets，and two pillows，all from Renmei’s family；they nearly touched the ceiling.

举例 3

原文：大人物之所以能成为大人物，就是能忍受常人不能忍受之苦难，之屈辱，比如能忍胯下之辱的韩信，比如能忍陈蔡之饥的孔夫子，比如能吞下自己粪便的孙膑……（莫言，2012：272）

译文：Important people become important by enduring the suffering and humilation that defeats ordinary people. Examples like General Han Xin，who drank the cup of humiliation；or like Confucius，who endured hunger from Chen to Cai；or Sun Bin，who ate his own faces…（Mo Yan，2014：302）

上面三个例子在译文中十分常见，因原文背后特殊的中国文化特点，所有的译文都没有对这些进行合适的解释说明，比如第一例中的“人中”和“虎口”在传统中医里是身体进行急救的关键部位，而译文也只是进行其所处位置说明而已；在第二例中，所有王仁美娘家送来的被子、褥子、毛毯、枕头都是传统“嫁妆”中的部分物品，而在山东很流行这一文化习俗。在第三例中也是，译者针对原文中的“胯下之辱”“孔夫子”“韩信”和“孙膑”等词语，译者并没有解释词中所谓的“屈辱”指的是什么，同时也没有对“韩信”“孙膑”等中国历史上的名人进行标注说明。正是因为如此，葛浩文采用归化的翻译策略，为了实现可读性的目标，译者删译太多蕴含的文化信息。这些与之前例子不同的更是，译者没有进行解释性的标注，给读者留下众多思考和了解的空间。这种改变传统通顺流畅的翻译话语策略，而是采用一种“对抗式”的话语策略来翻译原文，彰显出中西方两种语言和文化的差异存在。韦努蒂强调翻译要“译者显身”这一点也在葛浩文身上得到鲜明体现。译者这种尊重语言和文化差异的伦理态度能让读者注意到这种文化差异并会有所了解，从而真正实现跨文化交际的目的。

6 结　语

鉴于之前众多学者对葛浩文《蛙》英译本的研究来看，更多是从译者本身的主体性地位以及译者文化身份认同视角来看译本所采用到的翻译策略，而本文试从外部原因视角探索，而译者不再是单一的主体，更多关注其他各个行为主体形成影响翻译活动的种种关系要素，包括译入语、译入语文化以及读者期待视野等要素，即构成的这张伦理网络便使得翻译的存在呈现出不可忽视的伦理性。而本篇论文即是基于翻译伦理理论中的一个重要部分——韦努蒂（Venuti）的“存异伦理”（Ethics of difference）角度出发，从保留源语言“异质”文化和考虑目标语读者的阅读兴趣之间的平衡视角来看，本文旨在通过对葛浩文英译本《蛙》进行存异理论视角解析，以此验证产生于西方后殖民批评语境下的存异伦理亦能在中国文学外译的背景下找到其发展的适用性。本文通过采用举例分析法对原文本和译本进行对比分析，探寻葛浩文尤其在处理文化负载词所遵循的翻译存异伦理观，并着重解析译者为实现这一伦理观所采取的具体翻译策略，包含归化、异化以及两者结合处理的翻译策略，而在其实施的策略中蕴含“异化翻译”“僭越性忠实”和“对抗式翻译”这三大翻译伦理理念。

参考文献

[1] Howard Goldblatt, 2014. *Frog*[M]. Beijing：Penguin Group（Australia）in associate with Penguin（Beijing）Ltd.

[2] Venuti，Lawrence, 1998. *The Scandals of Translation：Toward an Ethics of Difference*，London & New York：Routledge.

[3] Venuti，Lawrence, 2004. *The Translation's Invisibility：A History of Translation*（1sted）[M]. Shanghai：Shanghai Foreign Language Education Press.

[4] 郭建中. 韦努蒂访谈录[J]. 中国翻译，2008（3）.

[5] 蒋童. 韦努蒂的异化翻译与翻译伦理的神韵[J]. 外国语（上海外国语大学学报），2010（1）.

[6] 季进. 我译故我在——葛浩文访谈录[J]. 当代作家评论，2009（6）.

[7] 葛浩文. 葛浩文随笔[M]. 史国强编，闫怡恂译. 北京：现代出版社，2014.

[8] 莫言. 蛙[M]. 上海：上海文艺出版社，2012.

[9] 刘亚猛. 韦努蒂的“翻译伦理”及其自我解构[J]. 中国翻译，2005（5）.

[10] 申连云. 尊重差异——当代翻译研究的伦理观[J]. 中国翻译，2008（2）.

[11] 孙际惠. 从翻译存异伦理探讨儒家概念词英译——以“仁”为例[J]. 焦作大学学报，2010（4）.

[12] 杨镇源. 翻译伦理研究[M]. 上海：上海译文出版社，2013.

[13] 张景华. 翻译伦理：韦努蒂翻译思想研究[M]. 上海：上海交通大学出版社，2009.

从“音美”角度看《古诗十九首》的英译
——以《青青河畔草》和《迢迢牵牛星》为例

张　玲

摘　要：《古诗十九首》是中国古代文人五言诗选辑。全诗语言朴素自然，描写生动真切，具有浑然天成的艺术风格，被誉为“一字千金”和“五言冠冕”。本文从诗歌翻译“三美”理论中的“音美”角度出发，对许渊冲教授英译的《古诗十九首》中《青青河畔草》和《迢迢牵牛星》这两首诗译文中“音美”的再现进行详细分析，探讨如何在译文中再现原诗的“音美”以更好地体现原诗的风貌和神韵。

关键词：《古诗十九首》；音美；诗歌翻译

Abstract: *Nineteen Old Poems* is an anthology of five-character poems of ancient Chinese literati. The language of the anthology is natural and simple and the description is vivid，owning a natural artistic style, and known as “a single word worthy of a thousand pieces of gold” and “the best of five-character poems”. From the perspective of “beauty in sound” in the theory of “three beauties”，this paper makes a detailed analysis of the reproduction of “beauty in sound” in *Green，Green Riverside Grass She Sees* and *Far，Far Away the Cowherd Star* of *Nineteen Old Poems* translated by professor XuYuanchong. The purpose of the paper is to explore how to reproduce the “beauty in sound” of the original poem in the translation to better reflect the style and essence of the original poem.

Key words: *Nineteen Old Poems*；Beauty in Sound；poetry translation

1 引　言

“《古诗十九首》产生于东汉末期，它标志着五言诗在发展中达到成熟的阶段。”（马茂元，1981：8）它是乐府古诗文人化的显著标志，深刻地再现了文人在汉末社会思想大转变时期，追求的幻灭与沉沦、心灵的觉醒与痛苦，抒发了人生最基本、最普遍的情感和思绪。游子和思妇是《古诗十九首》的基本内容。“在艺术上，《古诗十九首》文温以丽、意悲而远的风格，被誉为‘一字千金’和‘五言冠冕’。”（曹旭，2002：2）诗歌的风格特征除了“情真、景真、事真、意真、澄至清，发至情”（曹旭，2002：3）外，还具有极高的音美特征。《古诗十九首》善用“从《诗经》发展而来重张叠句的复沓形式。古诗善用叠字，如《青青河畔草》中的‘青青’‘郁郁’‘盈盈’‘皎皎’‘娥娥’‘纤纤’，被顾炎武《日知录》誉为和《诗经·卫风》‘河水洋洋’一样连用六叠字‘亦极自然，下此即无人可继’。”（曹旭，2002：3）虽然《青青河畔草》《迢迢牵牛星》两篇都是只有十个句子的短诗，在这短短的十个句子里，每首诗都有六句“是用形容词开头，而且这些形容词都是用叠字组成的。可是由于运用的巧妙，它使我们一点也不感到单调、呆板，而是从不同的词性里极其生动地、形象地赋予所形容的事物以颜色、声音和意态，这是后来诗论家推为绝调的。”（马茂元，1981：39）至于《古诗十九首》目前的研究现状，对其英译研究比较少，且研究多集中于宏观、整体性的描述，而微观、个案的深入研究较少。本文从诗歌翻译“三美”理论中的“音美”这一角度出发，深入详细分析由许渊冲教授翻译的《古诗十九首》中的其中两首——《青青河畔草》和《迢迢牵牛星》，探讨这两首诗英译本所体现的“音美”以及如何在译文中再现原诗的音美以更好地体现原诗的风貌和神韵。

2 许渊冲先生“诗歌翻译音美论”

许渊冲先生提出诗歌翻译“三美”论，即诗歌翻译应当传达出原诗的意美、音美和形美，并且认为中国古典诗歌是“意美”“音美”和“形美”的完美结合，译文中应尽可能地再现原诗的“三美”。虽然音美在“三美”论中并不是居于第一位的，但是译诗只有准确、完美地再现了原诗的音美，才能更好地服务于原诗的意美。翻译诗歌“宁可继承 Giles 诗体译文的传统，而不可采用 Waley 的散体译法。……而传达原诗的‘音美’，则远远胜过了散体。”（许渊冲，1984：64）

“诗要有节调、押韵、顺口、好听，这就是诗词的音美。……中国诗主要是七律和五律；七律译成英语可以考虑用亚历山大体，也就是指每行十二个音节的抑扬格诗句；五律可以考虑用英雄体，也就是指每行十个音节的抑扬格诗句。”（许渊冲，1984：55）“‘音美’首先是押韵。……如果没有押韵，也不可能保存原诗的风格和情趣。押韵诗要传达原诗的‘音美’，并不一定要求和原诗‘音似’。”（许渊冲，1984：69）这里的押韵并不是指“译诗用词的声音和原诗用的字声音相近”，（许渊冲，1984：70）而是指在符合译入语诗歌押韵规则的前提下，尽可能地再现原诗的押韵特点。

“‘音美’除了押韵外，还有个重复的问题，首先是叠字的问题。”（许渊冲，1984：70）对于如何实现叠字的“音美”，在多数情况下，许先生采用了以重复译重复的方法。但有时，在诗歌中重复的字并没有连在一起，而是出现在诗句中，这时许先生认为可以将其译成内韵。除了押韵和重复的问题之外，还有一个重要的问题，就是如何翻译诗歌的节奏。吕叔湘在《英译唐人绝句百首》的《赘说》中写道：“英文诗也有和中文诗的平仄相当的节奏，就是轻音和重音的配置。”（许渊冲，1984：72）因此，许先生在翻译时，基本采用一轻一重的抑扬格。

3 原诗的音美

3.1 《青青河畔草》原文及其音美

《青青河畔草》

青青河畔草，郁郁园中柳。
盈盈楼上女，皎皎当窗牖。
娥娥红粉妆，纤纤出素手。
昔为倡家女，今为荡子妇。
荡子行不归，空床难独守。

这是一首描写思妇自述内心寂寞苦闷的诗。此诗运用第三人称的写法，写出少妇渴望爱情，渴望夫妻相依相偎，甚至举案齐眉的平凡生活。“在结构上，此诗通篇排偶，句句发声，环环相扣，上下句互相说明。尤以六句叠字句法令人赞叹。”（曹旭，2002：8）叠字指两个相同的字重叠起来而构成的一个词，其形式整齐，音节和谐，表意生动，具有天然的节奏感和曲折回环的音乐美。“这类词……如果运用得好，它往往可以从最简单的字面里传达出客观事象的意态和神情，增进情感的强度，显示出回环复沓的音节之美。”（马茂元，1981：116）

本诗中六个叠字词，“可以分成三个类型，而在每一类型之中彼此间又有所区别：‘青青’和‘郁郁’同样是形容植物的生机畅茂，但‘青青’是人所看到的草的颜色，而‘郁郁’则是人所感到的柳的意态；‘盈盈’和‘皎皎’同样是形容人的丰姿，但‘盈盈’是指仪态，而‘皎皎’则指风采；‘娥娥’和‘纤纤’同样是形容人的容貌，但‘娥娥’则比较抽象地赞叹‘红粉妆’的美好，‘纤纤’则十分具体地刻画出‘素手’的形状。”（马茂元，1981：116）此外，这六个叠字词还有平仄声调上的变化，极富音乐节奏美。“青青”（平声），“郁郁”（仄声），“盈盈”（平声），“皎皎”（仄声），“娥娥”（平声），“纤纤”（平声）。这样一平一仄声调上的变化所体现出的音美可谓深得诗心。

3.2 《迢迢牵牛星》原文及其音美

《迢迢牵牛星》

迢迢牵牛星，皎皎河汉女。
纤纤擢素手，札札弄机杼。
终日不成章，泣涕零如雨。
河汉清且浅，相去复几许？
盈盈一水间，脉脉不得语。

这首诗借天上的牛郎、织女双星，被银河阻隔而不得会面的悲剧来写人间离别之感和夫妻不得团聚的悲哀。“本篇和《青青河畔草》一样，十句之中也有六句用叠字组成的形容词开头。‘迢迢’是星空的距离，‘皎皎’是星空的光线，‘纤纤’是手的形状，‘札札’是机的声音，‘盈盈’是水的形态，‘脉脉’是人的神情。词性不同，用法上极尽变化之能事，然而都显得确切不移，自然生动。和《青青河畔草》篇是异曲同工的。”（马茂元，1981：132）此外，这首诗中的六个叠字词同样具有平仄的音乐节奏美。“迢迢”（平声），“皎皎”（仄声），“纤纤”（平声），“札札”（平声），“盈盈”（平声），“脉脉”（仄声）。这样的平仄音韵上的变化使诗歌读起来朗朗上口，极具音乐美感。

4 译诗的音美

4.1 《青青河畔草》译文及其音美

Green，green riverside grass she sees；
Lush，lush the garden’s willow trees.
Fair，fair，she waits in painted bower；
Bright，bright like a window-framed flower.

In rosy，rosy dress she stands；
She puts forth slender，slender hands.
A singing girl in early life；
Now she is a deserted wife.
Her husband's gone far，far away；
How to keep lonely bed each day！

首先是六个叠字词的翻译。许先生采用了重复译重复的方法。将“青青”译为“green，green”；“郁郁”译为“lush，lush”；“盈盈”译为“fair，fair”；“皎皎”译为“bright，bright”；“娥娥”译为“rosy，rosy”；“纤纤”译为“slender，slender”；这样不仅再现了原诗的回环复沓的音乐美，同时，这六组词也体现了头韵，从而更好地传达了原诗的音美。其次是尾韵。原诗每行结尾的汉字几乎不与下一行结尾的汉字押韵，而许先生的译文每两行结尾的单词都是押韵的。比如，“sees”—“trees”，“bower”—“lower”，“stands”—“hands”，“life”—“wife”，“away”—“day”。这样在原诗每行结尾并不押韵的情况下，许先生也尽可能地将译文押韵，以倍增其译文的音美。

4.2 《迢迢牵牛星》译文及其音美

Far，far away the Cowherd Star；
Bright，bright riverside Weaving Maid.
Slender，slender her fingers are；
Clack，clack her shuttle's tune is played.
She weaves all day，no wed is done；
Like rain her tears drop one by one.
Heaven's River's shallow and clear；
The two stars are not far apart.
Where brimful，brimful weaves appear；
They gaze but can't lay bare their heart.

首先，六个叠字词的翻译除了最后一句里的“脉脉”没有采用以重复译重复的方法，其余五个叠字词都采用了以重复译重复的方法。将“迢迢”译为“far，far”，“皎皎”译为“bright，bright”，“纤纤”译为“slender，slender”，“札札”译为“clack，clack”，“盈盈”译为“brimful，brimful”，这样来再现原诗的音美。这些重复的词同样地也押了头韵。其次是尾韵。与《青青河畔草》这首诗一样，此诗每行结尾的字与下一行结尾的字也几乎不押韵。但为了更好地体现诗歌的音美特征，许先生在翻译此诗时，同样地注重了尾韵的翻译。译文所展现的尾韵为：ababccdede，这样便使得原诗的音美在译文中得到强化，更有力于体现原诗的音美。

综上所述，《青青河畔草》和《迢迢牵牛星》这两首诗的译文都生动形象地再现了原诗的音美特征；此外，译文中所出现的尾韵更进一步增强了原诗的节奏感和曲折回环的音美。

5 结 语

《古诗十九首》以游子和思妇为基本内容，风格率真质朴，不事雕琢，温柔敦厚，颇具独特的审美意趣，反映了当时的哀愁与苦闷，有极其现实的社会历史意义。整个《古诗十九首》中的诗歌可谓字字珠玑，句句优美，其中在音韵上最为突出的两首诗——《青青河畔草》和《迢迢牵牛星》两篇都是只有十个句子的短诗，但在这短短的十个句子里，每首诗都有六句包含叠字，但是由于词汇的巧妙运用，它使读者一点也不感到单调、刻板；相反，这两首诗中的叠字从不同的词性里极其生动地、形象地赋予所形容的事物以颜色美、声音美和意态美。

在许渊冲的译文里，他采用了以重复译重复的方法来翻译原诗中的叠字，这样既再现了原诗回返复沓的音美特征，又用头韵增强了译诗的节奏感；此外，这两首诗译文中所采用的尾韵，也进一步增强了原诗的节奏感和曲折回环的音美特征，从而更好地再现原诗的“音美”。由此观之，为了更好地在译文中再现原诗的“音美”，根据译入语的押韵规则，在不损害原诗意美、音美、形美的情况下，可以增加尾韵、头韵、抑扬格等多种手段来强化原诗的“音美”。“音美”最重要的便是押韵。因为中英文的差异，并不一定要求和原诗“音似”，而是要求在符合译入语诗歌押韵特点的前提下，尽可能地再现原诗的押韵特点，以倍增其“音美”，从而更好地体现原诗的风貌和神韵。

参考文献

[1] 曹旭. 古诗十九首与乐府诗选评[M]. 上海：上海古籍出版社，2002.

[2] 马茂元. 古诗十九首初探[M]. 西安：陕西人民出版社，1981.

[3] 徐日宣，潘智丹. 从许渊冲法译唐诗看译诗理论中“音美”的传达[J]. 外语与外语教学，2011（1）：57-61.

[4] 许渊冲. 翻译的艺术[M]. 北京：中国对外翻译出版公司，1984.

[5] 许渊冲译. 汉魏六朝诗一百五十首[M]. 北京：北京大学出版社，1996.

[6]（梁）钟嵘. 诗品[M]. 周振甫译注. 北京：中华书局，1998.

《虬髯客传》英译本中主要人物肖像描写比较研究

伍永晔

摘　要：唐传奇《虬髯客传》在中国民间广为流传，“风尘三侠”红拂女、李靖、虬髯客个性鲜明的侠客形象亦深入人心。《虬髯客传》的英译本同样也对人物肖像描写进行了精心的翻译。该文以三位重要人物的肖像描写为例，对三个译本的翻译进行分析和探讨，探求《虬髯客传》人物肖像描写英译的关键要素和翻译策略，对古典小说人物肖像描写的英译提供现实指导意义。

关键词：肖像描写；《虬髯客传》；英译本

Abstract：*The Tale of the Curly-Bearded Guest*，an article from Literary Tales of the Tang，spreads widely among the people in China.The three romantic characters of this story，a girl with a red whisk，Li Jing and the curly-bearded guest，all have impressed readers with their extraordinarychivalrous images. The three different English translation versions also take much work on the translation of the portraiture of main characters. Taking the portraiture of main characters for example，this paper compares and studies the three different English translation versions，hoping to find out the key elements and translation strategies of portrait description in English of *The Tale of the Curly-Bearded Guest*；what's more，to provide practical guidance for English translation of portrait description in classical novels.

Key words：portrait description；*The Tale of the Curly-Bearded Guest*；English translation versions

1 引　言

《虬髯客传》是唐代著名的传奇小说，相传为唐末道士杜光庭所做。这篇传奇中的三个主要人物，红拂女、李靖和虬髯客，后世称为“风尘三侠”。该文在人物形象的塑造上取得了巨大的成功。红拂女的机智俏丽，李靖的沉着英俊，虬髯客的豪迈卓异，相映成趣，给予后人留下深刻印象。此外，对文皇的描写虽着墨不多，但气象不凡的翩翩少年形象亦是跃然纸上。本文将以周劲松、杨宪益与戴乃迭夫妇以及 Wang Jing 三个《虬髯客传》英译本为研究范本，比较分析其中主要人物肖像描写的翻译。

本文选择的三种译本分别为：取自《大中华文库》（中英对照）系列翻译丛书《唐代传奇选》中的杨宪益、戴乃迭《虬髯客传》译本；William H. Nienhauser Jr. 所编 *Tang Dynasty Tales：a guided reader* 中 Wang jing 译本：*“Qiuran Ke Zhuan” 虯髯客傳*（*The Tale of the Curly-Bearded Guest*）；电子科技大学周劲松出版的《翻译基础十二讲》上的《虬髯客传》译本。文中简称“杨、戴译本”“Wang 译本”和“周译本”。

肖像描写即描绘人物的面貌特征，它包括人物的身材、容貌、服饰、打扮以及表情、仪态、风度、习惯性特点等。肖像描写的目的是以“形”传“神”，刻画人物的性格特征，反映人物的内心世界。描是描绘，写是摹写。描写就是用生动形象的语言，把人物或景物的状态具体地描绘出来。写文章只有通过描写才能做到“绘声绘色”“活灵活现”“栩栩如生”“历历在目”“惟妙惟肖”。肖像描写是对人物的外貌特征进行描写，通过描写人物的五官或者其不同时期的变化来揭示人物的思想性格，表达作者的爱憎，加深读者对人物的印象，表达作者文学创作的主旨。好的肖像描写不仅仅是用文字给我们描绘出一个人的外在形象，还应该通过人物的外在形象为我们展示出他的思想、性格和气质。显然《虬髯客传》原文在肖像描写这一点上做得非常出色，其对人物的肖像描写虽字数不多，但却将人物形象与特征刻画得淋漓尽致，令读者过目不忘。但是这对于译者来说却是一个极大的挑战，如何将短短几字文言文翻译成英语，并使英语读者欣然接受，成为翻译《虬髯客传》一大亟待解决的难题。

2　主要人物肖像描写比较分析

《虬髯客传》中对主要人物红拂女的肖像描写共有6处，本文选取典型的3处进行比较研究。原文对于李靖的肖像描写共有 2 处，但均为侧面描写，通过虬髯客之口向我们描绘了李靖的形象。故本文对李靖的肖像描写暂不讨论。原文对于虬髯客的肖像描写共有 2 处，这 2 处在文中出现的时间空间距离不同，显示虬髯客的身份不同，具有很强的研究性。原文对于文皇李世民的肖像描写有2处，这2处描写亦十分经典，具有很强的研究性。

2.1　红拂女肖像描写比较分析

例 1　原文：当公之骋辩也，一妓有殊色，执红拂，立于前，独目公。

周译本：When Lijing was vehemently in his speech，his very gesture，however minute，failed no touch of the eyesight of the one among the beautiful girls who was holding a red whisk and standing ahead.

Wang 译本：While Li Jing was presenting his argument convincingly，a singing girl with exceptional beauty holding a red whisk in her hand stood in front[of the maids].

杨、戴译本：Now while Li had been discoursing brilliantly，one of Yang’s maids-- a very beautiful girl who was standing in front of them holding a red whisk-- had watched him intently.

此处为红拂女第一次在文中登场，原作者并未对其外貌进行过多的描写，仅用“殊色”二字对其进行描绘。考虑到后文中红拂女还会多次出现，而且后文对其外貌描写更为惊艳与具体。所以此处的翻译既要做到让英语读者能够感受红拂女是一个外貌出众的女孩，又不能对其外貌进行过分夸张的刻画与赞扬，让读者的注意力在第一时间只集中到她的美貌上。可以看到三个译本都没有在此处进行过多的发挥，周版最为简洁，只使用了“beautiful”一词简单带过。Wang 版和杨、戴版则多加了一个表示程度的修饰词。前者使用的是“exceptional beauty”，表示红拂女的美貌在众多歌女中是比较突出的，给人惊鸿一瞥之感。后者则在“beautiful”前面多加了“very”进行修饰，增加了读者对于红拂女形象的直观感受。但总体来讲，红拂女的第一次出现侧重于她对李靖的一见倾心，而非她出众的美貌，故三个译本在此处都以直译为主，未多加刻画。

例 2　原文：脱衣去帽，乃十八九佳丽人也。素面华衣而拜。

周译本：Overcoat off and hat down，a girl of amazing beauty of about 18 years old was standing before his eyes and greeted him with a deep bow. Taken by the surprise，Lijing bowed back all in a fluster. The girl wearing no cosmetics on the face but really luxurious clothes on the body explained:

Wang 译本：Taking off her coat and removing her cap，she appeared to be a beauty of eighteen or nineteen years old. She was in gorgeous clothes with no make-up on her face， and bowed to him.

杨、戴译本：When she took off her outer gown and cap，he saw she was a beautiful girl of about nineteen with a fair complexion， dressed in bright clothes.

此处为原文中第三处对红拂女的肖像进行描写，也是第一次直接细致地刻画红拂女的外貌。此处为著名的“红拂夜奔”桥段的开端，红拂女紫衣掩面深夜投奔李靖时，第一次与李靖正面相识的场景。因此，此处的翻译应该突出红拂女素面华衣的外貌重点，即使未施粉黛但却依然年轻漂亮，宛若仙女。周版较之例 1 的描写增加了形容词“amazing”。后两者则均侧重于对其年龄和素面华衣的描写，注重于从整体描写中来突出红拂女的年轻貌美。即使素面也不会被华美的衣裳夺去光芒，依然能使人将注意力集中到她这个人身上，而不是衣服上面。

例 3　原文：观其肌肤仪状、言词、气性，真天人也。

周译本：but to his greatest satisfaction the girl was found to be really a stunner with good manners and eloquence and temperament.

Wang 译本：Observing her skin and manner，conversation and disposition，it seemed that she was indeed a lady from Heaven.

杨、戴译本：He found her an angel in complexion， manner， speech and character.

此处为文中第四处对红拂女进行肖像描写。此处是从李靖的角度出发，通过与红拂女的第一次畅谈后，李靖对红拂女的直观感受与所思所想。原作者使用“肌肤”“仪状”“言词”“气性”四个词语简洁明了地将红拂女的肖像概括出来，用“真天人也”的感叹总结其气质的超凡脱俗、言谈举止的大方得体和个人形象的美丽惊艳。在翻译此句时，不仅要保留原文的简洁精炼，同时还要表现出李靖对美丽聪慧的红拂女的赞叹之情与爱慕之心。在简洁精炼这一点上，三个译本的处理方式大致相同，选择的都是“manner”“conversation”“character”等精炼的词语。但是在“真天人也”的翻译上则有出入。周版使用的是“really a stunner”，而且添加了对李靖的内心描写“to his greatest satisfaction”。二者搭配，将红拂女的美丽生动形象地刻画在英语读者面前。Wang 版则直接表示“she was indeed a lady from Heaven”，直接翻译更为直观。杨、戴版本与 Wang 版类似，直接将红拂女描写成“angel”。

2.2　虬髯客肖像描写比较分析

例 1　原文：公方刷马，忽有一人，中形，赤髯如虬，乘蹇驴而来。

周译本：Out of the door，Lijing was about to groom their horses，before he found a man of middle height characterized by a beard of fiery bristles coming up on the back of a lame donkey.

Wang 译本：Suddenly，a mid-sized man whose red bears was [curled]like a dragon approached them，riding a lame donkey.

杨、戴译本：when suddenly a man of medium height with a curly beard rode up on a sorry-looking donkey.

此处为虬髯客第一次出场，“中形，赤髯如虬”，虽仅有六个字，却意蕴颇丰：仅“中形”二字即给人以不同于一般英雄豪杰、身材魁梧的独特感觉，且与他的“蹇驴”相呼应，以形象的不完美衬托性格的豪爽不羁；“赤髯如虬”则更塑造了他独一无二的形象，“赤”是五行中的火和八卦中的离所代表的颜色，也是血的颜色，象征热烈、奔放、革命和斗志，“髯”乃“颊须也”，亦给人张扬豪放之感，“虬”意为龙子有角者，此处将虬髯客的髯比作“虬”，一则写出他的胡须卷曲的形态，二显出他的不凡气魄，三隐隐暗示他惊世之才以及想当皇帝的雄心壮志。当然，英译本不可能通过短短几个词语便表达出中文里面这些深刻的含义，所以此处翻译只要做到忠实原文，突出虬髯客红胡子的特征和他放荡不羁的豪侠性格即可。综合比较三个译本也均采用直译的方法，言简意赅地向读者刻画虬髯客的侠客形象。

例 2　原文：乃虬髯纱帽裼裘而来，亦有龙虎之状，欢然相见。

周译本：Lijing heard somebody calling “Brother Third is coming” and found Fiery Bristles approaching in a gauze cap with the fur coat on the body unbuttoned.

Wang 译本：It was the Curly-Bearded Guest，who came in wearing a gauze cap and brown fur coat. He demonstrated the bearing of a dragon and a tiger.

杨、戴译本：He came in wearing a gauze cap，with a fur coat thrown over him，his whole appearance magnificent and kingly.

此处是文中对于虬髯客的第二处外貌描写。其位置位于文章靠后部分，这个时候虬髯客已经认定“此世界非公世界”，自己的大作为在他方，欲将所属家产全部赠予李靖与红拂女。此处虬髯客的外貌描写点明了虬髯客的另一重身份：纱帽是古代君主、官员戴的帽子，而裼裘与李世民的穿着相同，一反虬髯客的江湖游侠形象，言简意赅地点明他有雄心壮志、渴望建功立业的形象。所以，此处的翻译应该彰显出虬髯客衣着形容的华贵及其必能成就一番伟业的轩昂气宇。综合比较三个译本的翻译，笔者个人更加偏好于杨、戴译本，“his whole appearance magnificent and kingly”，这里的“magnificent”和“kingly”用得极为巧妙。与 Wang 版直接点名“dragon”与“tiger”不同，“magnificent”和“kingly”从侧面烘托出虬髯客的“龙虎之状”，既符合中文读者的理解，也能将文章本意完整地传达给英文读者。

2.3　文皇李世民肖像描写比较分析

例 1　原文：使回而至，不衫不履，裼裘而来，神气扬扬，貌与常异。

周译本：He was found an eccentric wearing no shoes or gown but a fur garment；nevertheless he was an illuminating with a mien quite different from the ordinary people.

Wang 译本：He did not wear a robe or shoes，and was wearing his silk garment which partially covered with his fur coat. His spirit was high and his appearance different from ordinary people.

杨、戴译本：Presently Li Shimin arrived，wearing neither coat nor shoes，but with a fur coat thrown over him. He was overflowing with good spirits，and his appearance was very striking.

文皇李世民虽不是《虬髯客传》中的主人公，但事实上却是原作者真正想要讴歌与赞扬的人。文皇才是应天命而生的“真命天子”，是“the choosing one”，故其肖像描写应突出与凡人不同之处。在翻译上，也要尽可能的夸张，让读者能够在第一时间感受文皇身为真命天子的特殊性。原文作者在此处使用了四个四字词语来描写文皇，具有音韵美与节奏感。如果在翻译过程中也能做到节奏感便是极好的。综合比较三个译本，周版在对此处进行翻译时使用的是“；”将“不衫不履，裼裘而来”与“神气扬扬，貌与常异”分割开来，用“nevertheless”巧妙衔接衣着与神态的对比。后两个版本则使用的是“。”，将“不衫不履，裼裘而来”与“神气扬扬，貌与常异”划分为两个句子进行翻译，中间并无衔接词。此处，笔者个人更加偏好于周版的翻译，衔接词的使用让译文更加紧凑，也带有节奏感。

例 2　原文：俄而文皇到来，精采惊人，长揖而坐。神气清朗，满坐风生，顾盼炜如也。

周译本：After a while，the fated person came in and greeted everyone in reverence. He was seated，with no superfluous movements，but all at once，the whole situation was permeated with his vigor and energy，which was not only powerful enough to set every one ablaze，but looming so dense and dignified that every one was dimmed.

Wang 译本：He made a long bow and sat down. His charisma was so clear and expression so serene that everyone present was influenced and the room filled with splendor. When he looked around，he was very graceful.

杨、戴译本：When Li Shimin arrived，his appearance struck awe into them all. He bowed and sat down，looking so serene and talking so well that the atmosphere seemed to freshen and splendour to be shed all around.

此处为对文皇李世民的第二处肖像描写。此时，为了再次确认李世民是否真的为“the choosing one”，虬髯客、道兄与李靖再次来到刘文静府上。为了为后文道士看到文皇本人后顷刻惨然，对虬髯客直言“此世界非公世界，他方可也。勉之，勿以为念”做铺垫，同时也再次突出文皇作为真命天子，无论是从气质、长相还是言谈举止上都与众不同、超凡脱俗的特征，原作者在此处使用了较为夸张的词语对其进行描写。在翻译的过程中，应该保持原文中的夸张成分，甚至可以更加夸张，以突出唐传奇故事的戏剧性。综合比较三个译本，译作者都在词汇的选择和句型的构成上下了很大的功夫。周版使用“permeated”一词来形容文皇的“满座风生”，Wang 版则选择的是“influenced”和“filled”，杨、戴版本选择的是“freshen”和“shed”，可谓各有各的风采。结构上来讲，周版使用了“not only...but”句型和前肯后否的结构，还使用了“but all at once”等短语，使得句子结构多样化，读来妙趣横生，不会单调乏味。后两者则按照原文顺序选择了正常的翻译结构，没有做过多的变化，但也遵从了翻译通顺与忠实原文的原则。此处的翻译，笔者个人认为 Wang 版与另外两版相比要稍逊一筹。

3 结　　语

著名武侠小说作家金庸先生评价《虬髯客传》时称赞：“这许多事情或实叙或虚写，所用笔墨却只不过两千字。每一个人物，每一件事，都写得生动有致。艺术手腕的精炼真是惊人。当代武侠小说用到数十万字，也未必能达到这样的境界。”（金庸，1994）《虬髯客传》中人物肖像描写对于塑造人物整体形象意义重大，成功的描写使人物形象跃然纸上，在读者头脑中形成生动的视觉感受。毫无疑问，原作的描写极其成功，通过实例分析发现，三个译本总体上也居功至伟地向译文读者尽力呈现了原文的表达效果，总体遵从翻译“信、达、雅”的原则，多采用直译，着重体现原文的文化内涵和语言特征。在直译无法完全体现原文文化负载内容时，也适度加入有主观感情色彩的词语，以帮助译文读者理解，采用增译的方法将我国文言文的特殊魅力展现在外国读者面前。当然各个版本的译文各自也有值得商榷之处，但总体来讲，瑕不掩瑜，我们在对译文进行分析批评时，仍需对三个版本译作者的努力与坚持致以崇高的敬意。

参考文献

[1] Extract Pages From William H. Nienhauser Jr.，2010. Tang Dynasty Tales：A Guided Reader， New Jersery et al.：World Scientific.

[2] 金庸. 金庸作品集[M]. 北京：生活·读书·新知三联书店，1994.

[3] 浅析唐传奇《虬髯客传》中虬髯客的形象塑造[J]. 文学教育（下半月），2017（7）.

[4] 唐代传奇选[M]. 杨宪益，戴乃迭译. 北京：外文出版社，2007.

[5] 周晨译. 唐人传奇选译[M]. 成都：巴蜀书社，1990.

[6] 周劲松. 翻译基础十二讲[M]. 成都：电子科技大学出版社，2016.

《虬髯客传》两种英译本中李靖人物形象和传统礼仪对比分析

杨亚婷

摘　要：《虬髯客传》属于唐代传奇，是唐代豪侠小说的集大成者。虬髯本有争夺天下之志，但见李世民器宇不凡，知不能匹敌，遂倾其家财资助李靖，使辅佐李世民成就功业。本文选取这篇小说的两种英译版本，即杨宪益、戴乃迭译本和 William H. Nienhauser Jr.所编 *Tang Dynasty Tales: a guided reader* 中的 Wang Jing 译本，通过举例分析得出两种译本中李靖人物形象以及体现出来的传统礼仪的不同，从而总结出一些翻译心得和技巧。

关键词：《虬髯客传》；李靖人物形象；传统礼仪；英译对比

Abstract: *The Tale of the Curly-Bearded Guest* is a legend of Tang Dynasty and it integrated the essence of novels that describe heroes and warriors in Tang Dynasty. The curly-bearded guest was ambitious and inclined to the govern the whole kingdom until he saw Li Shiming, because Li was excellent and had an air of emperor. So the curly-bearded guest gave all of his asset to Li Jing and asked him to support Li Shiming. This thesis referred to two translations, one is Yang Xianyi and Dai Naidie's version, and the other is Wang Jing's version, collected in William H. Nienhauser Jr's *Tang Dynasty Tales: a guided reader*. By citing examples and analyzing sentences, the differences of the character of Li Jing and the traditional etiquette embodied in the two translations are found. It's the writer's hope that this thesis can summarize some elicitation and skills of translation.

Key words: *The Tale of the Curly-Bearded Guest*; the character of Li Jing; traditional etiquette; comparison of two translations

1 作品简介

唐王朝的统治者在创造辉煌的盛世之后，从“安史之乱”开始走上动荡的下坡路，晚唐时出现藩镇割据的局面。当时各地藩镇势力强大，而且互相敌视，除了招兵买马加强军事实力之外，还把蓄养刺客作为牵制和威慑对方的秘密武器，游侠之风因之在社会上盛行。而神仙方术的蔓延又赋予这些侠客超现实的神秘色彩。乱世之中的人们对现实不满，又找不到出路，便寄希望于那些锄强扶弱、伸张正义的侠客。不畏强暴、本领非凡的侠客就成了人们心目中的英雄，受到人们的敬重和爱戴，关于他们的传奇故事也就应运而生。在这种背景下，晚唐传奇出现了以《虬髯客传》为代表的豪侠传奇。

《虬髯客传》讲述了隋炀帝临幸江都，司空杨素掌大权，生活奢侈糜烂。一天，布衣书生李靖献策求见杨素，两人相谈无果。杨素府上有一名家妓张氏，手持红拂，在李靖离去后查得李靖投宿的驿站，当夜就投奔李靖，共结连理，离开京师去太原。一日，二人到一客栈投宿，一个满脸虬髯的人闯入窥看红拂女梳头，红拂女看出虬髯客的不凡，当机立断与虬髯客结为兄妹，并且引丈夫李靖与虬髯客相识。李靖、虬髯客相见甚欢，并且相约在太原相见。三人抵达太原后，李靖引虬髯客通过刘文静见李世民。虬髯客本有争夺天下之志，见李世民神气不凡，知不能匹敌，便放弃逐鹿中原的意图，并再次约定李靖择日相见。李靖携红拂女至虬髯客府第，与虬髯客夫妇相见。虬髯客将全数家产赠予李靖以助李世民争天下，自己则带妻子离开。贞观十年，李世民已是天下之主，李靖官至左仆射平章事，虬髯客则入扶馀国自立为王。

2 两种译本中李靖人物形象对比分析

本文选择了两种英译本，即杨宪益、戴乃迭译本和 William H. Nienhauser Jr.所编 *Tang Dynasty Tales: a guided reader* 中的 Wang Jing 译本，后文简称“杨译本”和“Wang Jing 译本”。首先要分析的是在这两种译本中李靖形象的不同，以下是举例说明。

第一，Wang Jing 译本中的李靖较杨译本更勇敢。

例 1.

原文“公前揖曰：‘天下方乱。英雄竞起。公为帝室重臣，须以收罗豪杰为心，不宜踞见宾客。’”

译文

杨译本：“Li approached and said with a bow，‘The empire is in a turmoil and the bold are contending for power. As chief councillor to the imperial house，Your Highness should be thinking of how to rally good men，and should not receive visitors sitting.’”

Wang Jing 译本：“Li Jing stepped forward，bowed to him，and said，‘The world is in turmoil at this moment and the heroic fellows all have risen to compete for the throne. You，sir，are a mighty minister of the imperial court，with heavy responsibilities.You ought occupy yourself with thoughts of congregating and collecting extraordinary people. It is inappropriate to receive guests while reclining on a couch.’”

这两段译本中，有两处可以体现 Wang Jing 译本中的李靖更勇敢。一为“前”字的翻译，杨译本翻译成“approached”，Wang Jing 译本翻译成“stepped forward”。作为汉语母语的我们，当读到“approached”和“stepped forward”时，感觉明显不同。“approached”意为“接近，走近”，仅客观说明了李靖从离杨素有一段距离的某处渐渐接近杨素，对他的气宇神态未作很好地表达。而“stepped forward”意为“迈步，向前走”，我们可以感受到当李靖看到杨素如此傲慢待客时，他内心的不满，于是李靖奋身前行，意欲指出杨素的错误。“stepped forward”很好地描绘出李靖在面对一个比自己地位高得多的朝廷官员时，仍然不畏权势，敢于上前的勇敢情状。第二处就是对“不宜踞见宾客”的翻译。杨译本为“should not receive visitors sitting”，Wang Jing 译本翻译成“It is inappropriate to receive guests while reclining on a couch”。前者意为“不应该坐着接见宾客”，后者意为“靠在长榻上接见宾客是不对的”。不难看出，“不应该”和“不对的”表达出来的建议力度有所不同。“不应该”建议的成分较多，即不要这么做为好，而“不对的”不仅包含希望对方不要这么做的意思，还有隐含的批评之意。可见，虽然两种译本李靖都指出杨素做法的不妥，但在 Wang Jing 译本中，李靖确实勇敢不少。

例 2.

原文“曰：‘烈士不欺人，固无畏。’促鞭而行。”

译文

杨译本："'Such a brave fellow will not deceive us,' they said. 'We need not worry.' After asome time they whipped up their horses and left."

Wang Jing 译本："They said，'A marvelous man does not deceive people and we have nothing to fear.' They simply spurred their horses with their whips and went on."

在这两句话中，对"促鞭而行"的翻译可以看出 Wang Jing 译本中的李靖更勇敢。杨译本对这句话的翻译是"After some time they whipped up their horses and left"，Wang Jing 译本则为"They simply spurred their horses with their whips and went on"。联系这两句话的上文我们知道，李靖和红拂女对虬髯客的奇怪作为又惊又怕，虬髯客又提出太原一会，他们更是不知道该不该动身。杨译本的"After some time"，即"过了一会"李靖和红拂女才骑马离开，暗含李靖夫妇在虬髯客这个不速之客离开后需要一段时间来平复心情，内心的害怕之情比较浓厚。而 Wang Jing 译本中的"simply"这个词，说明李靖夫妇仅仅简单地骑上马就走了，根本不用花时间平复，可见，该译本中李靖确实比较勇敢。

第二，Wang Jing 译本中的李靖较杨译本考虑得更周全。

例 3.

原文"数日，亦闻追讨之声，意亦非峻。乃雄服乘马，排闼而去。"

译文

杨译本："...and for a few days a half-hearted search was made for her. They Li and the girl dressed in fine clothes and fled on horseback from the capital to Taiyuan."

Wang Jing 译本："After several days，having not heard news that [Minister Yang had sent out people to] search for the girl，he considered the situation not very serious. Only then did he have her put men's clothes，mount a horse，and gallop [with him] out through the gate，planning to return to Taiyuan."

这几句话中，有两处可以看出 Wang Jing 译本中的李靖是一个考虑较为周全的人。第一是对"意亦非峻"的翻译。杨译本中对"意亦非峻"几乎没有处理，仅翻译到"他们听说有些许追讨红拂女的消息，然后穿上华丽的服装离开"，根本没有突出李靖对情势的分析，究竟在什么情况下可以离开呢？虽然刚开始追查红拂女的风声不严重，但万一越来越严重的话，他们此刻离开岂不是更危险？杨译本这样处理就显得李靖比较冒失。而 Wang Jing 译本则是"he considered the situation not very serious. Only then did he..."即"李靖认为情况还不算严重，确认之后，他才……"这样处理可以看出李靖在带红拂女出逃前是思考过的，确认安全才离开，是一个考虑比较周全的人。第二处是对"雄服"的翻译。杨译本是"fine clothes"，Wang Jing 译本则是"men's clothes"。前者是"华丽的服装"，后者是"男人的服装"。虽然我们对"雄服"的理解可以多种，但是，李靖和红拂女在出逃之时穿"华丽的衣服"其实是欠妥的。在古代，老百姓穿得都很朴素，只有达官贵人才穿得珠光宝气，华服装生，若出逃之人衣着华丽，岂不是引人注目，暴露身份吗？相反，李靖让红拂女穿上"男人的服装"躲避追捕显得更合理。所以，这一点也可以看出在 Wang Jing 译本中，李靖考虑事情比较周全。

第三，Wang Jing 译本中的李靖较杨译本更有礼貌。

例 4.

原文"因刘文静可见之。然兄为何？"

译文

杨译本：“We can arrange an interview through Liu. But why do you want to see him？”

Wang Jing 译本：“It is possible to see him through Wenjing；however，my elder brother，what do you want to do？”

这个例子中，Wang Jing 译本里的“my elder brother”就是区别所在。我们知道，在上文中，红拂女和虬髯客以兄妹相称，李靖自然而然也得叫虬髯客一声哥哥。在杨译本中，虬髯客和李靖的对话里并未出现李靖对虬髯客的尊称，所以，Wang Jing 译本中的李靖是一个更有礼貌的人。

例 5.

原文“曰：‘靖虽贫，亦有心者焉。’”

译文

杨译本：“‘I may be poor but I am no fool.’ said Li.”

Wang Jing 译本：“Li Jing said：‘Although I am poor，I am also a man with ambition.’”

这两句话里，杨译本说“我可能比较穷，但是我不傻”，情感色彩比较重，细细一推，可能会让人觉得李靖认为虬髯客在说自己穷、傻才发问，然后李靖自辩“我可能是穷，但可绝对不傻”，使得整个谈话气氛不是很和谐。但是 Wang Jing 译本为“我虽然穷，但也有抱负”，首先李靖直接承认了自己经济状况不好，再平述说自己有理想抱负，除去了一定的辩论色彩，显得谦逊有礼。

第四，Wang Jing 译本中的李靖较杨译本更有内涵。

例 6.

原文“客曰：‘观李郎仪形器宇，真丈夫也。’”

译文

Wang Jing 译本：“He said to Li：‘Judging by your looks and behaviour，you are a stout fellow.’”

Wang Jing 译本：“He further said：‘Master Li，Judging from your appearance and demeanor，you are a real man.’”

从“真丈夫”的翻译来看，Wang Jing 译本中的李靖更有内涵。杨译本的“真丈夫”是“a stout fellow”，即“一个强壮的人”，强调的是身体上的男性特征。而 Wang Jing 译本的“a real man”，即“一个真正的男人”，强调的则是李靖的内在和气质等方面，显得李靖更有内涵。

第五，Wang Jing 译本中的李靖较杨译本更真实。

例 7.

原文“诈谓文静曰：‘有善相者思见郎君，请迎之。’”

译文

杨译本：“...told him，‘A good fortune-teller wants to meet Li Shimin. Will you send for him？’”

Wang Jing 译本：“Li Jing lied to Wenjing saying，‘There is a man who excels in reading face and longs to meet the gentleman.’”

这里对“诈”字的翻译可以看出，Wang Jing 译本中的李靖更真实。“诈”杨译本为“told”，即“告知，告诉”，是一个中性词，无褒贬；而 Wang Jing 译本的“诈”是“lied”，即“说谎”，是贬义词。照理说《虬髯客传》是武侠小说，里面的风尘三侠本该品质完美，怎么会“说谎”呢？但是，说谎就是说谎，这只是真实的人物形象体现而已，毕竟人无完人。所以，Wang Jing 译本让李靖人物形象从刻板印象中抽离开，变得更真实起来。

3　两种译本中传统礼仪对比分析

两种译本中，Wang Jing 的译本较杨译本更丰富地体现出中国传统礼仪。

从称呼看（以下均为译本中出现频率较多称呼实例）。

虬髯客对李靖的称呼：Li（杨译本）；Master Li（Wang Jing 译本）

虬髯客对红拂女的称呼：Your（指李靖的）wife（杨译本）；The first younger sister（Wang Jing 译本）

李靖对虬髯客的称呼：You（杨译本）；My elder brother（Wang Jing 译本）

红拂女对虬髯客的称呼：My cousin（杨译本）；Third brother（Wang Jing 译本）

道士对虬髯客的称呼：You（杨译本）；Sir（Wang Jing 译本）

不难看出，Wang Jing 译本中人物之间的称呼比杨译本里的客气得多，“you”之类的称呼几乎没有。在中国古代，礼仪等级是十分讲究的，Wang Jing 译本很好地体现了这一点。

从虬髯客的仆人传话场景看。

例 8.

原文“既毕，传云：‘三郎来！’”

译文

杨译本：“After they had washed they changed into rich and strange garments，and then their host was announced.”

Wang Jing 译本：“After Li JIng and the lady had washed and organized themselves，they were invited to change into clothes which were again precious and extraordinary. After finishing this，a message was pressed on that ‘The Third Master has arrived.’”

我们都知道，在中国古代，当某位大人物登场时都会有“某人驾到！”或“某人到！”这样的宣语以彰显人物的崇高地位和无比尊贵。在这里，虬髯客登场时也是如此，杨译本用被动的方式一笔带过虬髯客的出场，十分平淡，轻描淡写。而 Wang Jing 译本则采用直接引语的方式，一声“三郎到！”让读者马上能想象虬髯客出场时侍婢罗列，无比宏伟的气势，生动地体现出中国古代的传统礼仪。

从虬髯客邀请李靖做客一段看。

例 9.

原文“虬髯曰：‘计李郎之程，某日方到。到之明日，可与一妹同诣某坊曲小宅相访。李郎相从一妹，悬然如罄。欲令新妇祗谒，兼议从容，无前却也。’”

译文

杨译本：“To Li the curly-beared man said：‘The day after you arrive，come with your wife to my humble lodgings. I know you have no property. I want to introduce my wife to you and talk things over. Be sure not to fail me.’”

Wang Jing 译本：“The Curly-Beared Guest said：‘Master Li，calculating your itinerary，you won’t arrive until a such-and-such a day. The day after your arrival，you may visit a small residence in a certain　quater with the first younger sister. Master Li，I regret that you had to follow us to and fro，and the first younger sister had nothing in her possession [as her dowry].’ I would like my humble wife to meet you and chat with you at ease. Please do not decline.’”

这一段有两处可以分析。第一，是对“一妹”的翻译。杨译本译作“your wife”，即你的（李靖的）妻子；Wang Jing 译本则为“the first younger sister”，即“我的（虬髯客的）一妹”。看似没什么讲究，实则不然。杨译本中，虬髯客是将红拂女与李靖归在一起，说她是李靖的妻子，与自己拉开了距离。而 Wang Jing 译本中，虬髯客就把红拂女和虬髯客自己联系在一起，说她是自己的一妹，拉近了与红拂女的联系，自然而然地与李靖也亲近了。在古代，长幼有序，家中排行是很重要的，虬髯客用“我的一妹”就体现出传统礼仪。另外，“一妹”更有利于促进人际关系和谐亲密，也是古代传统礼仪的目的之一。

第二是对“新妇”的翻译。杨译本为“my wife”，即“我的妻子”，属于叙述，无别的意义。Wang Jing 译本为“my humble wife”，可以理解成“我的贱内”。我们知道，中国古代人说话都十分谦逊，例如，日常生活中经常会说到“欢迎光临寒舍”等这样的委婉语。这里的“贱内”就是同样的例子，比单纯的“我的妻子”更带有传统礼仪的味道。

4 结　语

本文主要举例讨论了在杨译本和 Wang Jing 译本中，李靖人物形象和传统礼仪的不同，认为在 Wang Jing 译本中，李靖更勇敢，考虑得更周全，更有礼貌，更有内涵，更真实，且 Wang Jing 译本更好地体现出中国传统礼仪。

通读本文后会有一种比较推崇 Wang Jing 译本的感觉，但是并非如此。本文将两种译本的细节之处进行分析，不是为了区分这两种译本孰优孰劣，而是单纯钻研字句，从中得出翻译经验而已。首先，翻译没有统一的标准来判断优劣，只要译者有自己的理由，谁又能说他的处理方式不对呢？其次，顺着本文思路走，杨译本里李靖的人物形象就不如 Wang Jing 译本中的那么鲜明，但是，有没有可能这都是 Wang Jing 译本的添加与发挥，而杨译本是为了尊重原文，还原李靖本来就不那么鲜明的人物形象呢？又者，杨译本之所以对传统礼仪的体现不那么充分，有没有可能是想保留原小说里不拘小节侠义风情，而故意如此的呢？可见，换一种思路，两种译本又能擦出不一样的火花。

参考文献

[1] William H., Nienhauser Jr., 2010. *Tang Dynasty Tales：A Guided Reader* [M].New Jerseryetal.：World Science.

[2] 董晓华. 论语篇连贯与翻译策略[J]. 英语广场，2018（10）.

[3] 王晓晶. 杨宪益先生的翻译思想及其成就探究[J]. 兰台世界，2018（8）.

[4] 袁晓亮. 戴乃迭合译和独译行为对比研究[J]. 齐齐哈尔大学学报，2018（9）.

[5] 杨宪益，戴乃迭. 唐代传奇选[M]. 北京：外文出版社，2007.

从文学文体学视角评析《虬髯客传》两译本的可读性和灵活性

施　瑞

摘　要：本文基于《虬髯客传》的两个英译本，先从文学文体学角度来分析比较两个译本的可读性和灵活性，分别从词汇、句法两个方面来总结哪种翻译方式更适用于再现原文风格，让读者更加容易接受。为了能进行更加细致和深刻的分析，本文选取《虬髯客传》中几个经典人物的片段作为分析对象。

关键词：文学文体学；可读性；灵活性；《虬髯客传》

Abstract: Based on the two English translation versions of *The Men with Curly Beard*, this paper analyses the two versions from the perspective of literary stylistics to compare two versions of readability and flexibility. And from vocabulary and syntax, this paper summarizes what kind of translation method is more applicable to express the meanings of the source text, and easier to be understood by readers. In order to carry out a more detailed and deep analysis, this paper selects some fragments of classic characters in *The Men with Curly Beard* as the analysis objects.

Key words: library stylistics; readability; flexibility; *The Men with Curly Beard*

1 引　言

《虬髯客传》是唐传奇的代表作之一，被视为武侠小说的鼻祖。译文选取周劲松（2016）和杨宪益夫妇（2007）的译本（下文简称周译和杨译）。两个译本出于不同的翻译目的、翻译技巧和翻译风格，都有鲜明的风格。本文从文学文体学的视角，从词汇、句法等方面分析两个译本中的几个经典场景，解析各个译本的可读性和灵活性，从而总结怎样的翻译方式能更好地体现《虬髯客传》这一类传奇故事的生动性，辨别出哪种翻译模式才能更形象生动地刻画出原文中个性鲜明的人物形象。

广义和狭义的文体中都强调了语言的运用。因此，文体必须通过三个方面的因素得以体现出来：体裁，语体，风格。（童庆炳，1994）在翻译之前，要对原文的文体进行分析，作为译文风格的指导，使得译文尽量与原文风格保持一致。文章的语境也要根据上文的语境来确定其意义。意义是复杂的。一个词不仅有直接的、表面的、字典上的意义，还有内涵的、情感的、牵涉许多联想的意义。（王佐良，1986）这也是翻译中的“忠实”。《虬髯客传》属于唐传奇，是现代概念上小说的前身。对原文进行分析可以看出：首先，《虬髯客传》主要讲述一个时代里以“风尘三侠”为主的侠士故事，所以原文中人物的塑造，故事的讲述、铺陈都是重点，译文应形象生动地再现这些人物形象和情节，增强可读性。其次，在形式上，《虬髯客传》用语简洁明快，三言两语间就紧凑地刻画出人物形象，铺开了整个故事，古文用语简明，鉴于英汉语言的差别，译文应适时增强灵活性，才能更好地再现原文的文体意义。

2　文学文体学理论简介

文学文体学评估是文学译本的一种重要的理论，申丹教授（1998）认为文学文体学旨在阐明文学作品中语言形式的主题意义和审美价值，语言形式则是作者寻求达到主题和美学意义的方法。文学翻译中如果对作品的文体意义和语言形式所具有的意义，那么就很容易出现“假性等值”现象。为避免这样的现象，译者需要先对原文本的文体意义和语言形式内涵有深入的理解。申丹教授（1998）认为文体风格是在美学意义或者主题意义驱动下的选择，Leech（1981）也讲到文体学就是为了研究作者为何选择这种特殊的表达方式。

下面将从词汇和句法两个方面统计原文的客观数据，分析原文风格和语言形式的内涵来评估两个译本的可读性和灵活性。

3　文学文体学视角下两个译本的实例分析

《虬髯客传》是一篇典型的唐传奇小说，其文体形式丰富。全篇以简洁明快的语言，重点塑造了红拂女、李靖以及虬髯客三个不同的侠士形象，世人称之为“风尘三侠”。此外，故事情节跌宕起伏，寥寥数笔铺陈出整个故事。考虑到唐传奇是古文小说，原文中许多隐含意义或者表现原文主题意义的语言形式，加之英汉语言之间有明显的差异，所以译文应当灵活地展现原文的主题，增强小说的可读性。

3.1　可读性

翻译的可接受性是翻译工作的核心，即翻译是为读者服务的，译文需要明白易懂，为面向的读者所接受，这也是译文的可读性。影响译文可读性的因素有很多，本文将站在文体学的角度，从词汇长度、句子长度方面来考察两个译本的可接受性。以杨素出场、红拂夜奔这几个刻画人物形象的片段为例。

3.1.1　词汇

首先本文选取《虬髯客传》中第一段描写杨素的场面，统计词语长度，分析比较三个译文版本的用词特点，再选取实例进行说明。

《虬髯客传》开篇第一段中的“素骄贵……扶危持颠之心”，一共用 73 个字，三句话讲述杨素的背景，形象地刻画出杨素的人物形象。文字简洁但内涵丰富，杨素本人奢贵自奉、位高权重的形象跃然纸上。

根据表 1 的词长和词数统计可知，杨宪益、戴乃迭的译文最为简洁，周译的字数最多。2～5 个字母的简单词汇在两个译本中的占比都是最大的。如果定义 1～5 个字母的词长为该段中的简单词，那么周译中，简单词汇占比约为 76.5%，杨译中，简单词汇占比约为 75.3%；而长难词占比极少，甚至没有。由此推断，简单词汇在两个译本中占大部分的内容，所以对多数读者而言，在词汇上的要求很低，三个译文的可读性都很高。

两个译本的词汇虽然都集中在简单词汇部分，但是其中还是有一定的差别。将 9 以上的词长定义为长难词的话，那该选段中，周译的长难词为 12 个，杨译中长难词有 7 个。对比之下，两个译本中，杨译贯彻了简洁的风格，用词简单，长难词最少，周译居中。单从这一点来看，杨译最易被读者所接受，从文本整体字数上看，周译的发挥是最多的。

表 1　杨素出场段落的字数统计

	周译	杨译
词长	词数	词数
1-letter word	5	2
2-letter word	35	21
3-letter word	34	18
4-letter word	28	16
5-letter word	12	13
6-letter word	16	7
7-letter word	12	4
8-letter word	7	5
9-letter word	6	5
10-letter word	4	1
11-letter word	0	0
12-letter word	1	1
13-letter word	0	0
14-letter word	1	0
总计	149	93

例 1　每公卿入言，宾客上谒，未尝不距床而见，令美人捧出，侍婢罗列，颇僭于上。

周译：Yangsu paid no respect to the rituals a man of royal service should abide by and went so far as to lie down casually on a couch to handle official businesses and receive guests，no matter they were officials of high ranks or common folks of urgent appeals. There was hardly a time when he was not seen coming into the drawing room on the couch in the myriad of beautiful girls and surrounded by a host of servants at his call.

杨译：He received both officials and guests seated on a couch，and went about supported by beautiful maids，in his behavior usurping the emperor's prerogatives.

这是直接描写杨素出场时的排场，描绘杨素的奢贵自奉，原文用 29 个字写尽杨素前呼后拥，位高权重的场景，此处的笔墨是浓厚的。就字数上来看，周译最多，82 个词，杨译最简。周译着重刻画场景的生动性和故事性，让读者在画面上更容易接受；杨译基本采用直译，切合原文精简的用词方式，在文字上最简单易读。所以，在读者可接受性上，杨译最高，其次周译。

3.1.2　句子

在阅读的过程中，句子的长度也是影响可读性的一个因素。两位译者采用不同的方式翻译《虬髯客传》，语言风格各不相同。下面将《虬髯客传》中经典的“红拂夜奔”作为选段，统计每个译本中句子的平均长度，分析句子长度对可读性的影响。选段内容为“公归逆旅……而窥户者无停履”。

表2 红拂夜奔的句长统计

	周译	杨译
词数	314	260
句数	17	18
每句平均词数	18.5	14.4

通过表2可以得出，两个译本的句子平均长度有较大差别。周译中平均每个句子包含18.5个词，句子最长，杨译较短，句子平均长度为14.4个词，总体用词最少，保持一贯的简洁风格。由此可见，周译中多用长句，句子中包含的信息较多，或者是描写较为细腻，读者需要对长句有一定的把握才能更流畅地阅读。杨译保持一贯精简的风格，句子也多为简单句，节奏明快。所以，单就句子的难易程度来看，杨译的可读性更强，其次周译。

例2 脱衣去帽，乃十八九佳丽人也。素面华衣而拜。公惊答拜。曰："妾侍杨司空久，阅天下之人多矣，无如公者。丝萝非独生，愿托乔木，故来奔耳。"

周译：Overccat off and hat down，a girl of amazing beauty of about 18 years old was standing before his eyes and greeted him with a deep bow. Taken by the surprise，Lijing bowed back all in a fluster. The girl wearing no cosmetics on the face but really luxurious clothes on the body explained："I have been in service of Premier Yang too long and seen people too many there，but I can find no one your superior."

杨译：When she took off her outer gown and cap，he saw she was a beautiful girl of about nineteen with a fair complexion，dressed in bright clothes. She bowed to him，and he returned the bow.

"I have served Yang Su for a long time，" said the girl，"and seen many visitors. But there has never been any one like you. The vine cannot grow by itself，but needs a tree to cling to. So I have come to you."

这一片段是红拂女正式亮相的描写，原文人物形象刻画就在这一眼之间，所以译文需要展现出红拂举手投足的美和言辞之间的智慧。红拂夜访李靖，气氛紧张，时间有限，句子节奏整体较快，但因为红拂所说的一段话对故事情节有至关重要的推动作用，所以，在此处，节奏明显放慢。这一片段，周译用了78个词，3句话描绘了红拂出场的这一片段，整体来讲，句子较长，句意更加连贯。句子虽然很长，但是在处理的过程中，周译使用了简洁有力的短语和适当的间隔停顿，比如"Overcoat off and hat down"，让译文有了原文的节奏感。在杨译中，句子的平均长度与王译相差无几。杨译用了80个词，6句话描绘了这一场景，杨译处理句子时，用简单短语和逗号将句子划分清楚的同时，也把握了整体的节奏，比如："dressed in bright clothes"和"She bowed to him，and he returned the bow"等，句子简洁明快。

综合可知，周译中句子较长，句意连贯，阅读起来有一定的难度，但通过小词和断句处理，刻画细腻，节奏把握得很好；杨译句子连贯，语言简洁有力，句子短断句多，整体节奏较快，易于阅读，读者最容易接受，但是描述太过朴素，失去了初见红拂女时的惊艳，与原文要表达的内涵不符。

3.2 灵活性

在翻译中，受翻译目的、翻译风格、文本理解等因素的影响，不同的译者对同一个文本、同一个段落甚至同一句话的处理都截然不同。《虬髯客传》主要讲述乱世之中，侠义之士的故事，重点对其中风格各异的人物形象进行刻画。在文体学的角度，译文都应当体现原文的文体意义，即在人物塑造、情节刻画等主题意义上符合原文的主题意义。在处理古文句子时，两个译本都灵活地运用句子重组和增译的翻译技巧来再现原文的主题意义。

3.2.1 重组

《虬髯客传》是用文言文写成的，而文言文的句法结构转换英文句子，很多不能照直译，不能按照原文的顺序和句子结构来翻译，否则会造成逻辑上的混乱，不能很好地表现原文，也不能让读者理解译文。所以在译文中灵活地调整语序，拆分组合句子，能够帮助译文更好地还原故事的生动性。两个译文有自己的处理方式，下面举例说明。

例 3　乃雄服乘马，排闼而去。将归太原。

周译：Despite that，the two decided to leave for Taiyuan on the horseback with the girl wearing a man's clothes.

杨译：Then Li and the girl dressed in fine clothes and fled on horse-back from the capital to Taiyuan.

在原文中，“乃雄服乘马，排闼而去”和“将归太原”是两句话，但是两个译文都选择了将其合并为一句。这样的处理会使得据以更加连贯，若是按照原文的句子结构来译，那么译文就会显得拖沓，文言文是简洁明快的，译文若是节奏上拉得太长，也不符合原文的整体风格。所以当句子形式与文章风格相冲突的时候，应以内容和原文的风格为重，而不是拘泥于原文的句法结构。在这一点上，两位译者都有相似的想法，但是他们的具体处理又是不同的。周译对“乃”字的理解有所不同，译为“despite that”，并且调整了语序，把“将归太原”提前了，没有译“排闼”。杨译同样也是忽略了“排闼”这个动作，按照原文语序直译。两个译本都有抓住原文的主题意义，着重体现李靖和红拂女决心携手奔现太原，一展宏图的豪气和潇洒。

例 4　素娇贵，又以时乱，天下之权重望崇者，莫我若也，奢贵自奉，礼异人臣。

周译：Arrogantly confident and deeming nobody his match as regards to power and fame against the turbulent times，Yangsu paid no respect to the rituals a man of royal service should abide by and went so far as...

杨译：Now Yang Su，that proud noble，plumed himself on the fact that in those unsettled times no one in the empire had greater power or prestige than he. Giving free rein to his love and pride，he ceased to behave like a subject.

这句话是开篇第一段直接对杨素的描写，原文句子很长，内容丰富，也是第一段的重点，所以用的笔墨较多，而两位译者处理的方式不同。杨译选择了断句的处理方式，将“奢贵自奉，礼异人臣”断为一句，作为前面描写的总结。在句子形式上，用适当的短语和停顿来处理句子，杨译更加契合原文的节奏。周译不但没有断句，反而合并了句子，将这一句和下面的“每公卿入言，宾客上谒，未尝不距床而见”合并在一起，把描写“素娇贵”的内容放在一起来译，在这点上，杨译处理得妥当些。但周译的句子非常连贯，在画面感上把杨素置于句子的中心位置，表现出原文中杨素的娇贵自负。

3.2.2　增译

《虬髯客传》整个篇幅只用了两千余字，文字虽精简，但整个故事的起承转合，每个人物的举手投足、风格气度都跃然纸上。原文中省略了很多内容，英文译文若是要表现出原文的生动性就不能严格按照原文直译，少不了根据原文增加一些译文。增译是翻译中常见的技巧，根据译者对译文理解的翻译的目的，每位译者的发挥方式和空间不同，也会带给译文不一样的风格。

例 5　隋炀帝之幸江都也，命司空杨素守西京。

周译：It was some time in the last few years of the Sui Dynasty. Whilst EmperorYangdi was on his inspection tour to the city of Jiangdu（presently Yangzhou），Premier Yangsu was in charge of the garrison at the city of Xijing（presently Xi'an）at His Majesty's request.

杨译：When Emperor Yang of the Sui Dynasty（605-618）visited Yangzhou，Councillor Yang Su was ordered to guard the West Capital.

这是整个故事的开篇第一句，原文是直接进入故事主题，没有铺垫，但是在英文中显然会很突兀，不符合小说故事的叙述方式。周译没有直译这句话，也做了一些增译的处理，加入了“It was some time in the last few years of the Sui Dynasty”，就好像是《三国演义》的第一句“话说天下大，合久必分，分久必合”，把读者带入那个时代中，然后缓缓展开整个故事。而且周译采用古英语中的“whilst”，将唐传奇的历史感译出来了。杨译直接以“When”开头，随后将主语切换到杨素，开门见山的叙事，这样就少了周译的带入感。

综合来看，从内容和用词上来看，周译用增译的技巧开启整个故事，明显更有代入感，使译文更有故事性。杨译只是简单增加了句子的逻辑关系，局限在字句里。

例 6　末年愈甚，无复知所负荷，有扶危持颠之心。

周译：As Yangsu lost himself in the ostentation and extravagance more and more and committed himself to his responsibility less and less with days gone by，such afrequent scene has turned from offensive to aggressive and the idea of risking for an usurpation became the frequent load on his mind.

杨译：He became worse，too，in his old age when，forgetting his duty to his sovereign，he made no attempt to save the realm from utter ruin.

这是第一段的最后一句，总结杨素的奢贵自奉到达收不住的地步。全篇对杨素的重点描写就到此结束，所以这一段对于杨素人物形象的塑造是至关重要的，也为后面的故事情节做了铺垫。杨译采取了简单直接的处理方式，直接增补出“sovereign”，在断句上做了处理，但是连续用短语和逗号进行停顿，破坏了句子整理的连贯性和流畅性。周译在这部分的增译比较明显，补充出很多细节部分，比如“末年愈甚”增译为“As Yangsu lost himself in the ostentation and extravagance more and more and committed himself to his responsibility less and less with days gone by，such a frequent scene has turned from offensive to aggressive”，将“末年愈甚”的内容具体化和生动化。在选词用句上，也独具一格，用“from offensive to aggressive”细化了“愈甚”的程度，将杨素一发不可收拾的娇贵描绘得淋漓尽致。在发挥的这一部分来看，周译虽然没有遵守原文简约的行文风格，但是抓住了原文想要传递给读者的人物形象，是可取的增译方式。

例 7　客曰：“观李郎之行，贫士也。何以致斯异人？”

周译：Back in the room，the guest asked：“Brother Li，it seems by your appearance you are not that rich，how should you have such an extraordinary girl in your company？”

杨译：“You seem a poor fellow，” the stranger remarked to Li. “How did you get hold of such a marvellous girl？”

这是虬髯客喂完他的驴之后，问李靖的话，直接用“客曰”就开始了两人的交谈，没有任何细节描写，但按照常理来说，这样突兀甚至带有一点冒犯意味的问题，当事人一定有自己的心理特征，或者与上文喂驴之间有过渡的内容。杨译将虬髯客的这段问话独立成句，与上文的喂驴隔开，首先就显得不是那么突兀，然后调整句子顺序，“seem”要使语气委婉一些，用“remarked”译“曰”比“said”更有感情。周译在译文中增加了“Back in the room”，自然地进行了衔接和空间转换，合情合理。在处理句子的过程中，增加了具体描写，比如“that rich”“in your company”，使得虬髯客的问话更符合情理，更真实可信。所以总的来说，杨译将问话独立成句的方式可以作为衔接句子和翻译对话句子的一种方式，将动作细化也是值得学习的，周译加入合理的过渡成分和具体描写，使得整个故事更加流畅生动。两种灵活的增译方式为灵活处理译文的可取之处。

4 总　结

在分析总结《虬髯客传》的两个译本之后，可见两个译本都有自己特别的风格。周译灵活多变，文字细腻，在内容上高度还原了原文的故事性；杨宪益、戴乃迭的译文精简干练，流畅稳妥，在文字风格和节奏上与原文一致。

就可读性来讲，周译的描写最为细腻，笔墨最多，遣词造句最为讲究，所以需要读者有一定的阅读水平；王译句式简单，少长难句多简单句，在选词用字上，简单词的比例也与其他译本相差不大，占比很大，所以在词句上都比较容易理解，可读性比较强。杨宪益、戴乃迭的译本用词最少，句子长度适中，节奏明快，难词极少，言简意赅，所以不论在内容上还是句子风格上都比较容易被大多数读者接受。站在读者的角度，最容易接受、可读性最强的应该是杨宪益、戴乃迭的译本。

在灵活性上，周译中句子的重构和内容的增译最多，对原文细节的描绘和逻辑性的考量也最多，译文生动，具有极强的故事性。在语言风格上，尽量将读者带入古代唐传奇的风格，贯彻小说式叙事方式，间或使用古英语，充分还原了《虬髯客传》唐传奇的生动性；杨宪益、戴乃迭的译文贯彻了简洁明快的风格，对句子的切分、节奏和逻辑把握得很好，处理灵活，文字最有效率，内容和形式上的流畅度很高。总的来说，周译最为生动，细致地给读者展现了一个传奇故事；杨宪益、戴乃迭的译本最为朴实流畅，在形式上和节奏上与原文高度契合。

这样看来，可读性和灵活性貌似是相悖的，因为遣词造句简单，发挥的空间就被限制了，其实不然。因为通过调整句式，用不同的节奏，短句小词也能让译文生动灵活，眼前一亮，起到画龙点睛的作用。值得借鉴的是两个译本鲜明的风格，在翻译过程中，我们要根据原文的主题意义使用不同的翻译技巧，不仅在词句内容上要有所考量，还要站在整体的角度上看待问题和文章风格，充分发挥现象，理解原文内容，这样译文才能兼具可读性和灵活性。

对比分析两个译本，因整个文本很长，所以只挑选了其中具有代表性的段落进行举例说明，例子不够全面，但是希望能给以后做此类翻译的译者带来一些启发。

参考文献

[1] Leech，G. & M.Short，1981. *Style in Fiction：A Linguistic Introduction to English Fictional Prose*. Beijing；Foreign Language Teaching and Research Press.

[2] 杜光庭. 虬髯客传. 百度阅读网电子书在线阅读，2014.

[3] 申丹. 文学文体学与小说翻译[M]. 北京：北京大学出版社，1998.

[4] 童庆炳. 文体. 与文体的创造[M]. 昆明：云南人民出版社，1994：63-64.

[5] 王佐良. 英文文体学论文集[M]. 北京：外语教学与研究出版社，1986：98.

[6] 唐代传奇选[M]. 杨宪益，戴乃迭译. 北京：外文出版社，2007.

[7] 周劲松. 翻译基础十二讲[M]. 成都：电子科技大学出版社，2016.

动态对等在人物形象翻译中的适用性探讨
——以《虬髯客传》为例

于　晶

摘　要：动态对等是奈达翻译理论中的经典，自问世以来对广大译者的翻译实践起到了很好的指导作用。特别是在文学翻译中，译者常常采用动态对等来处理诸多翻译过程中的问题。本文通过从肖像描写、行动描写和心理描写三个角度举例，从动态对等的词汇、句法和篇章对等上来分析《虬髯客传》的三个英译本中人物形象的刻画描写，认为动态对等理论在文学翻译中有较强的适用性，动态对等效果从词汇、句法和篇章上依次递增。希望本论文对后来此类文本研究的相关译者能有一定促进作用。

关键词：文学翻译；人物形象；动态对等；《虬髯客传》

Abstrct: Dynamic equivalence is quite classic in Nida's translation theory. Since its emergence, it has been an excellent guidance in translation practice of the majority of translators. Especially in literary translation，dynamic equivalence is often used by translators to deal with many problems in translation process.This paper analyzes the portrayal of the characters in the three English versions of *Fiery Bristles* from the perspectives of portrait description，action description and psychological description on the basis of lexical equivalence，syntactic equivalence and textual equivalence. The theory has strong applicability in literary translation，and the dynamic equivalence effect increases from vocabulary，syntax to text. This paper is expected to help the relevant translators do research on such texts .

Key words: literary translation；character images；dynamic equivalence；*Fiery Bristles*

1 引　言

美国翻译理论家、语言学家尤金·奈达（Eugene A. Nida）提出了翻译动态对等理论，对翻译界产生了深远影响。后来不少知名学者都对这一理论进行了分析和探究。但是，动态对等在文学作品中人物刻画方面的研究却很少有人涉足。所以本文将探讨动态对等在文学作品中人物形象翻译中的适用性。

文学作品不同于其他非文学作品，在翻译过程中要遵循更加苛刻的原则，对意思表达、兴文成句有更高的标准。文学翻译固然是翻译，但是作为译者，不应忘记文学。“文学，从本质上说，是一种艺术：文学翻译，自然也该是一种艺术实践。”（罗新璋，1990：291）因此文学翻译过程中不仅要达到基本的翻译对等，译者更要揣摩原文作者的内涵和深意，努力完整传达原文中所包含的文化意义，所以动态对等理论常常被用于文学翻译。

人物是文学作品，尤其是小说的灵魂，是小说的核心内容。小说中的人物是表达作者思想的媒介，发展、影响情节，因此小说中人物形象描写不可忽略。人物描写语句的主要作用是“描绘人物的形貌以及内心世界，使人物活动的环境具象化”。（杨仕章，2004：115）在翻译描写类言语时，要选择恰当的语句来表达，使得译文生动传神，带入读者，使读者身临其境。人物的一颦一笑、一举一动都暗含原文作者的意图，因此人物描写至关重要。为了刻画出栩栩如生的人物形象，一般通过肖像描写、行动描写和心理描写等直接描写手段，使得人物形象塑造得更加丰富。译者在翻译过程中要把握好小说人物整体形象的塑造，在翻译选词和行文的过程中一定要结合文章背景、具体语境，考虑到个体特性，选择最适合的词汇、句子结构，在译文中描绘出最符合原文作者意图的人物形象。

2　唐传奇和《虬髯客传》简介

《虬髯客传》是唐末的传奇小说。传奇小说是文言短篇小说为主的一种新型小说，真正代表了唐代小说的最高成就。唐传奇的出现和成就标志中国古典小说达到一个全新的境界。（吴庚舜等，1995：520-522）唐传奇在艺术上有了很大的创造和提升，实际上是已具规模的小说。就内容而言，唐传奇偏向广阔的社会现实生活，这和以往那些说神道鬼和记载名人轶事的小说不一样。唐传奇的题材多样，包括恋爱故事，历史或现实的宫廷、官场、藩镇、商贾、农人生活故事以及许多高人、僧道、异人故事。就艺术而言，传奇小说结构精巧繁复，语调丰富多变，细节特色鲜明，人物刻画精致细腻，戏剧冲突引人入胜。传奇小说的语言并不追求简单精炼，而是充分铺陈且用必要的词藻进行修饰，所以语言上有美感，篇幅上较为舒展。

作为一部意义重大的唐末传奇小说，也是一部艺术成就相当高的豪侠小说，《虬髯客传》中就充分体现了这些特点，人物关系充满了戏剧冲突，故事情节环环相扣，故事叙述充满悬念。这篇小说大约作于唐末，叙述了“风尘三侠”李靖、红拂女和虬髯客之间的传奇故事，其中主要人物刻画得相当成功，英俊勇武的李靖、聪慧机智的红拂女、豪爽剽悍的虬髯客在一言一行中跃然纸上。《虬髯客传》的情节及人物描写颇为精彩，所以如何传达原文的文化意义是一个挑战，其中红拂的勇敢机智，虬髯的豪爽慷慨刻画尤为鲜明突出，文笔亦细腻生动，艺术成就在唐传奇中属于上乘。接下来我们将通过《虬髯客传》中的人物形象翻译探讨去检验动态对等的适用性。

本文选择的三个译本分别为杨宪益、戴乃迭译本（2007），William H. Nienhauser Jr. 所编《Tang Dynasty Tales：a guided reader》（2010）中 Wang Jing 译本和周劲松①译本（2016），以下文中简称“杨译本”“Wang Jing 译本”和“周译本”。

3　动态对等理论

奈达将翻译定义为“翻译，就是指从语义到文本在译语中用最贴切而又最自然的对等语再现原语的信息”。（Eugene A.Nida，1969：12）奈达提出“翻译即交际”的观点，并确立了动态对等的翻译原则，获得了译界的广泛认可。在这一理论中，奈达认为动态对等是指“与源语言最接近的、最自然的对等的语言”，（Eugene A.Nida，1964：166）其中，“对等”是指与源语言的信息对等，是核心；“最自然”是对译语而言，用译语中最自然的表达；“最接近”是指在“自然”的基础上选择与原文意义最接近的译文。奈达在《翻译理论与实践》中表示，

① 周劲松，电子科技大学外国语学院副教授，主要研究方向为翻译学、文艺学、符号学等。

在动态对等的翻译中，译文读者对译文的反应应和原文读者对原文的翻译大体一致。

在“动态对等”中的对等包括四个方面：（1）词汇对等；（2）句法对等；（3）篇章对等；（4）文体对等。（郭建中，2000：67）因此，根据奈达的理论，译者在文学翻译中应以动态对等的四个方面作为翻译的原则准确地在目的语中再现源语的文化内涵。文学作品具有特殊性，它是一种以原作为基础的再创作，其基本任务在于创造能给译作读者带来艺术美的言语产品，因此在翻译过程中对语言的表达提出了更高的要求，译者在翻译文学作品时尤其要注重译文的遣词造句以及行文结构。

4 《虬髯客传》中人物形象翻译的动态对等

奈达的动态对等包括词汇、句法、篇章和文体四个方面。文体上的动态对等，只有在同时掌握源语和目的语两种语言的特征，且能熟练运用两种语言的情况下才能真正实现，译者才能创造出真实体现源语风格的翻译作品。不同文体的翻译作品有着各自独特的语言特征。作品语言风格的不同就意味所蕴含的文化因素也各不相同。《虬髯客传》是一篇影响颇深的唐传奇文言短篇小说，而中国古代的小说类型多样，单是文言短篇小说就分为传奇体、笔记体和志怪体，宋代又出现白话小说。所以，这部小说的翻译其实是两种语言之间的跨时空翻译，具有天然的不对等性。再者，译者要面向读者，都采用现代英语来翻译这篇文言小说，这就更难达到文体上的对等。因此，本文接下来主要是从词汇、句法和篇章对等上来探究《虬髯客传》三种译本中，人物形象在肖像描写、行动描写和心理描写上的刻画。

4.1 人物肖像翻译与动态翻译

肖像描写“是通过描写人物的容貌、衣饰、姿态等外部特征刻画人物形象”，（胡显耀，2009：215）一般会用大量形象化的描写语句。因此在翻译肖像描写时要注意突出人物性格，强调塑造形象的生动性。肖像描写翻译时要达到“形肖性似”，（杨仕章，2004：119）可以在加深人物形象吸引力的同时，揭示人物性格。

例 1 其夜五更初，忽闻叩门而声低者，公起问焉，乃紫衣带帽人，杖揭一囊。公问谁。曰：“妾，杨家之红拂妓也。”公遽延入。脱去衣帽，乃十八九佳丽人也，素面画衣而拜。

周译本：Deep in the darkness at about 4 o’clock that night，he was awakened by a fit of knocking at the door with whispers. Vaguely it was somebody in purple dress and hat along with a package at the end of a long road. “Who is that？” he asked. “It’s me，the courtesan holding the red whisk at Yangsu’s house.” Lijing invited her into the room. Overcoat off and hat down，a girl of amazing beauty of about 18 years old was standing before his eyes and greeted him with a deep bow. The girl wearing no cosmetics on the face but really luxurious clothes on the body explained...

Wang Jing 译本：That night，at the beginning of the fifth watch，he suddenly heard someone knocking softly on the door. Li Jing got up and asked who it was. It was someone in purple clothes，wearing a cap，and carrying a sack tied on a stick.Li Jing asked who it was. The person said，“I am the singing girl with the red whisk from Yang’s residence.” Li Jing immediately invited her in. Taking off her coat and removing her cap，she appeared to be a beauty of eighteen or nineteen years old. She was in gorgeous clothes with no make-up on her face，and bowed to him.

杨译本：That night，just before dawn，there was a soft knocking at Li's door，and when he got up he found a stranger there in a cap and a purple gown，who was carry a stick and a bag. Askedd who he was，the stranger said，"I am the maid with the red whisk in Councillor Yang's house." Then Li quickly let her in. When she took off her outer gown and cap，he saw she was a beautifulgirl of about nineteen with a fair complexion，dressed in bright clothes，she bowed to him.

这一小段话描写的是红拂女夜访李靖的场景。原文用了“紫衣带帽”“佳丽”“素面画衣”等来描写红拂女的容貌衣饰。此处的“素面画衣”是指未施脂粉且衣着华丽，但是杨译本却直接译为“a fair complexion”，译文读者阅读时并不能像原文读者一样感受到人物的未施粉黛惊为天人，但是周译本和 Wang Jing 译本在目的语中找到具有对应意义的词和表达，实现了意义对等，译文读者可以充分体会到原文的含义。所以，译者可以用译语中另一个词语来表示被指示物的形式，或者以牺牲形式上的同一性来体现对等功能。（Eugene A.Nida，1964：167）从肖像描写的词汇上来看，译者可以在译语中找到传达原文意义的词汇，是能够轻松地实现动态对等的。

从句子层面来看，原文多为描述故事情节的陈述句，长短句交替。在描写人物时，多用判断句，而且主语有所省略。以“脱去衣帽，乃十八九佳丽人也，素面画衣而拜”这句为例。Wang Jing 版本将“素面画衣”单独译为句子的主干部分，杨版本采用介词短语做后置定语，周版本则是灵活地将“素面画衣”放到后面做非谓语修饰主语。这三个译本没有被原句所束缚而是选择译语中最自然的表达方法，进行了符合英语句法规范的相应调整，实现源语与译语在信息上的对等，充分体现了文学翻译中的动态性。奈达认为，译者有义务调整词序，并调整语法。语法的修改是比较容易的，因为许多语法的变化是由译语的强制性结构决定的。译者虽然不能在译语中找到完全对等的句式，但是可以通过动态调整句式结构，完整再现原文意义。

同时，译者在分析本小段时不能只分析语言本身，而要在特定的篇章中看语言所体现出的意义和作用。比如小说中关于“衣”的译法，应根据上下文可以做出动态调整，本例的“衣”应是长袍或者外套类的衣服，而不是像 Wang Jing 译本中的“clothes”这种泛指。译文所传达出的信息在上下文语境下的得体性不仅仅和词汇的所指意义有关，还和文化背景相关联。本例中“五更”这一体现中国文化的词汇就值得译者仔细思考。古人把夜里四十刻分为四段共五个节点，这些节点被称为“更”，一夜即有“五更”，第五更在三到五点。周译本取了中间值译为“about 4 o'clock”，杨译本译为“before dawn”也比较恰当地表达了大概时间；Wang Jing 译本直接译为“at the beginning of the fifth watch”，在译本中加脚注详细解释了“五更”的含义，读者可以大概了解到有关文化背景。译者注意到译文信息在语境中的适用性及体现的意义和功能，在篇章中用贴近译文的表达传递出与原文最对等的信息。

4.2 人物行动翻译与动态翻译

行动描写语句会应用大量动词、副词等，连贯流畅地将人物行为表现出来，因此在翻译时，要选择适当的词汇，构成符合人物形象的语句。行动描写，或者动作描写，通常大量为动词，翻译时需要在译入语中找到“等值的、富有表现力”的动词，活泼地再现人物形象。（胡显耀等，2009：215）

例 2　每公卿入言，宾客上谒，未尝不踞床而见，令美人捧出，侍婢罗列，颇僭于上。

周译本：Yangsu paid no respect to the rituals a man of royal service should abide by and went so far as to lie down casually on a couch to handle official business and receive guests，no matter they were officials of high ranks or common folks of urgent appeals. There was hardly a time when he was not seen coming into the drawing room on the couch in the myriad of beautiful girls and surrounded by a host of servants at his call.

Wang Jing 译本：Every time minister and high-ranking officials came to confer with him，or retainers and guests paid visits，he would always receive them reclining on a couch. He ordered beautiful women to surround him and accompany him when he went out，and maid to line up and wait on him.

杨译本：He received both officials and guests seated in a couch，and went about supported by beautiful maids，in his behavior usurping the emperor's prerogatives.

本例中连用了好几个动词来描写杨素的骄横跋扈和骄奢淫逸，译者要选择富有表现力的动词或表达来生动再现人物形象。但是由于中英语言的差异性，在文学翻译中，要想在两种语言中达到词汇意义上的完全对等几乎是不可能的，因此，这就需要译者使用不同的形式来表达相同的意义。（Eugene A.Nida，1964）Wang Jing 译本则是按照原文顺序直译下来，显得略微生硬冗长。杨版本最特别，简短两行就将原文完整解释出来，在体现人物特点这一点上一带而过。周译本省略“入言”“上谒”这两个动词，而是用了“lie down casually on a couch to handle...and receive...”来表现杨素的傲慢无礼，“casually”更是巧妙地塑造了人物的傲慢形象。在刻画人物的行动描写方面，译者经过仔细推敲，可以达到较为理想的动态翻译效果。

例句中罗列了一连串动词，且省略主语，没有任何表逻辑的关联词。译者应考虑好如何在最接近原文信息的情况下衔接处理这些动词，需要考虑主句从句的次序和组合，构成符合英语语言规范并生动再现人物形象的句子。三个译本都将这一长句一分为二，译为两个主句。不同的是，周译本对这句进行了增译，“Yangsu paid no respect to the rituals a man of royal service should abide by”，直接指出杨素这一行为根本没有遵守臣子礼节，贴近译语并给读者以深刻印象，使译文读者对译文的理解与原文读者对原文的理解基本相同。

本句位于小说开端，渲染氛围，并为下文做铺垫，因此译者在这种特定的情景语境中要表达出本句在篇章段落中所起到的效果。杨译本句子简单，Wang Jing 译本最忠实原文，起到为下文做铺垫的作用，但是周译本不仅在词汇和句法上选择了贴近原文而又自然对等的译语，还注重文化差异带来的影响，采用了“重创”这一翻译技巧来解决文化差异。想要兼顾意义最接近原文和译语最为自然这两者，需要译者正确处理语言在语境中体现的意义和功能。

4.3 人物心理翻译与动态翻译

人物心理描写包括思考、联想等，大多言语细腻，因此在翻译过程中，要仔细体会人物的情感，体现出丰富的内心和情感的波动，营造出符合原文的意境，引起读者共鸣。心理描写方式多种多样，大多意在展示人物丰富的内心世界，译文要体现人物的心理变化。

例 3　使回而至，不衫不履，裼裘而来，神气洋洋，貌与常异。虬髯默然居末座，见之心死。

周译本：He was found an eccentric wearing no shoes or gown but a fur garment；nevertheless he was an illuminating with a mien quite different from the ordinary people. Struck dumb at the first sight，Fiery Bristles at the end of the tea table only felt his heart was sinking.

Wang Jing 译本：Shortly after，Emperor Taizong arrived. He did not wear a robe or shoes，and was wearing his silk garment which partially covered his fur coat. His spirit was high and his appearance different from ordinary people. The Curly-Bearded Guest sat at the end of the table in silence. When he saw the Emperor，his ambition vanished.

杨译本：Presently Li Shimin arrived wearing neither coat nor shoes，but with a fur coat thrown over him. He was overflowing with good spirits，and his appearance was very striking. The curly-bearded man，sitting silently at the end of the table，was struck from the moment of his entry.

小说中，虬髯客看到神采飞扬、仪态异于常人的李世民，就知道自己无法与之抗衡，所以“默然”“心死”，将虬髯客从充满希望到彻底失望的动态的心理活动展现出来。如何在译文中用寥寥几词自然贴切地表达出虬髯客的失望，值得译者仔细斟酌。杨译本和周译本都用“stuck”形容虬髯客初见李世民时震惊的状态，不同的是周译本直接对虬髯客的心理进行了描写——“only felt his heart was sinking”，特别是“sinking”这一词——使译文读者能够同原文读者一样体会虬髯客的这种“心死”心理。Wang Jing 译本用“vanished”达到了同样的效果。词汇的翻译不是语言中单个符号的翻译，而是涉及两种语言符号所表达出来的信息效果对等的动态翻译，在人物心理活动描写中尤其如此。

奈达认为“内容第一，形式第二”，提倡翻译着眼于原文的内容和意义，不必拘泥于形式。（Eugene A.Nida，1964）在文学翻译中，译者不必完全禁锢在原文句式中，可以做出一定调整。在例句的第一句中，周译本灵活运用分号，并用“nevertheless”连接第二句，将读者重点放在第二句，领略到李世民的独特风姿。Wang Jing 译本和杨译本一样，增译了李世民到来这一动作，将原句断句译为两句，使译文结构有逻辑性而不会太冗长。这种句法上的动态对等既符合译语语言规范，又传达了原文信息。

Wang Jing 译本和杨译本都特指出主语为李世民，考虑到上下文语境以及译文读者的需要。而且这两个译本都在句首添加描写他到来的动作，更好地处理了篇章结构。而周译本则有所欠缺，既没有特指出主语，也没有衔接上下文的表达，可能会给读者带来困扰。因为读者对译文的总体印象不仅包括文字所指的对象、所表达的事件的抽象内容和所展现的关系，还包括表达这些方面时采用的方法和逻辑顺序。在人物心理描写方面，译者特别注重将人物心理动态活动传递出来，就需要用最贴切最自然的译语将原文信息传递出来。

5 结　论

本文以《虬髯客传》三个译本中的人物形象描写翻译为例，探讨动态对等理论在文学翻译中的适用性。动态对等不要求原文形式与译文形式、原文信息与译文信息达到完全对等，而是注重译语读者对译文的反应和原语读者对原文的反应尽可能一致。在文学翻译中，动态对等有较强的适用性，特别是在翻译文化词汇和语法结构以及处理篇章情节时，动态对等效果依次递增。因此，在《虬髯客传》中，动态对等的适用性较强。但是，在翻译这部小说的文体方面运用动态对等，因缺乏较强的概括力，不能很好地体现原作文体风格，有所欠缺。所以，译者在文学翻译中要根据原作特点灵活使用翻译策略，充分理解原文作者的内涵和深意，努力完整传达原文中所包含的文化意义。

参考文献

[1] Eugene A.Nida, 1964. *Toward A Science of Translating*[M]. Leiden：Brill.

[2] William H. Nienhauser Jr, 2010. *Tang Dynasty Tales：a guided reader*[M]. Singapore：World Scientific.

[3] 郭建中. 翻译中的文化因素：异化与归化[J]. 上海外国语大学学报，1998（2）：12-18.

[4] 胡显耀. 高级文学翻译[M]. 北京：外语教学与研究出版社，2009.

[5] 罗新璋.“似”与“等”[J]. 世界文学，1990（2）：289-291.

[6] 谭载喜. 新编奈达论翻译[M]. 北京：中国对外翻译出版公司，1999.

[7] 吴庚舜，董乃斌. 唐代文学史（下）[M]. 北京：中国人民大学出版社，1995.

[8] 杨仕章. 篇章翻译概要[M]. 哈尔滨：黑龙江人民出版社，2004.

[9] 唐代传奇选[M]. 杨宪益，戴乃迭译. 北京：外文出版社，2007.

[10] 周劲松. 翻译基础十二讲[M]. 成都：电子科技大学出版社，2016.

从操纵论看《诗经》英译
——以《桃夭》三个译本为例

詹　廷

摘　要：《诗经》作为我国最早的诗集，是我国古代文学的瑰宝，也是中国文化的源泉。在我国文化中有着举足轻重的地位，其文化价值吸引许多学者来研究，其中《桃夭》是中国历史上第一首描写婚礼的歌曲，描述了桃树鲜花朵朵、果实累累以及枝繁叶茂的景象。从操纵论视角下比较许渊冲、理雅各和庞德的三个译本，主要从意识形态、诗学和赞助人三个方面进行比较，分析造成译文差异的深层原因，探索对翻译产生的影响以及指导意义。

关键词：操纵理论；意识形态；诗学；赞助人

Abstract：As the earliest anthology in China，*Shijing* is the treasure of ancient Chinese literature and the source of Chinese culture. It plays a significant role in Chinese culture，and its cultural value attracts many scholars to study. Among them，*Taoyao* is the first nuptial song in Chinese history，depicting the peach blossoms，the fruit and the leaves. Based on the perspective of Manipulation Theory，Xu's，Legge's and Pound's English versions are compared. It mainly analyzes the translation from three aspects：ideology，poetics and patronage. And the aim is to analyzes the underlying causes of translation differences and explore the influence and guiding significance of translation.

Key words：Manipulation Theory；ideology；poetics；patronage

1 引　言

《诗经》是中古代诗歌开端，收集了西周初年至春秋中叶的诗歌，反映了周初至周晚期的社会面貌，分为《国风》《雅》《颂》三部分。《国风》共收录周王室的乐官在诸侯国采集到的民歌民谣，“民歌大都淳朴自然，反映了古代人民各方面的生活、劳动斗争、思想感情、喜怒哀乐”，（许渊冲，2012：394）其中《雅》又分为《大雅》与《小雅》，前者记录了帝王事件，多用于朝廷庆典；后者则记录了贵族的生活，大部分是西周贵族宴会使用的乐章。《颂》用于宗庙祭祀，主要内容是赞美王室祖先的丰功伟绩。《诗经》的表现手法主要是赋、比、兴。《诗集传》中写道：“赋者，敷陈其事而直言之也”，即直叙其事；“比者，以彼物比此物也”，即比喻；“兴者，先言他物以引起所咏之词也”，即引发开头。在形式上，《诗经》中叠句与叠字居多，例如，《关雎》中的“窈窕淑女”重复了四次，《樛木》中每句都以“南有樛木”开头等；叠字如《硕人》中的“洋洋”“活活”“发发”和《大车》中的“槛槛”“啍啍”等，叠字的使用在演唱时更有节奏感，语音上和谐悦耳，韵律协调，具有传情达意的特点，从而形成特定的表达效果。

2 《桃夭》原文与三个译本

《桃夭》是《国风》周南中的第八篇。根据当时的规定，女子与男子要在春季桃花盛开的时候结婚，因此全篇都在以桃花、桃果和桃叶进行描写。《桃夭》这首诗歌也是"中国历史上第一首关于婚姻的歌曲"。（许渊冲，2012：19）。全诗共三章，每一章分为四个小句，第一章用"桃之夭夭，灼灼其华"起兴，同时还用鲜艳的桃花比喻待出嫁女子的娇媚，给人一种强烈的色彩感；第二章写桃子果实累累，象征女子早生贵子和子孙满堂的祝愿；第三章桃叶茂盛祝愿女子能够操持家庭。《桃夭》中用桃花比喻女子这一用法给后人留下深刻的影响，以后的许多诗人也用桃花来比喻美人，如大家熟知的"去年今日此门中，人面桃花相映红""依旧桃花面，频低柳叶眉"等都是运用桃花来形容女子美丽的颜容。整体上，《桃夭》在语言上朴实平淡，叠句和叠字的使用增添音乐趣味，让诗歌具有节奏感。

原文：桃之夭夭，灼灼其华。之子于归，宜其室家。
桃之夭夭，有蕡其实。之子于归，宜其家室。
桃之夭夭，其叶蓁蓁。之子于归，宜其家人。

许渊冲译本：
The peach tree beams so red，
How brilliant are its flowers
The maiden's getting wed，
Good for the nuptial bowers.

The peach tree beams so red；
How plentiful its fruit
The maiden's getting wed；
She's the family's root.

The peach tree beams so red；
Its leaves are lush and green.
The maiden's getting wed；
On household she'll be keen.

James Legge 译本：
The peach tree is young and elegant；
Brilliant are its flowers.
This young lady is going to her future home.
And will order well her chamber and house.

The peach tree is young and elegant；

Abundant will be its fruit.
This young lady is going to her future home.
And will order well her house and chamber.

The peach tree is young and elegant;
Luxuriant are its leaves.
This young lady is going to her future home.
And will order well her family.

Ezra Pound 译本：
O omen tree，that art so frail and young，
so glossy fair to shine with flaming flower;
that goest to wed
and make fair house and bower;

O omen peach，that art so frail and young，
Giving us promise of such solid fruit，
Going to man and house
To be true root.

O peach-tree thou art fair
As leaf amid new boughs;
Going to bride:
to build thy man his house.

3 翻译操纵论

安德烈·勒菲弗尔（Andre Lefevere，1945—1996）是国际著名翻译理论家、比较文学家和翻译家。他是当代西方比较文学和翻译研究领域十分重要的理论人物，其一生著作颇丰，涉及比较文学和翻译理论，撰写、主编十几部著作，翻译十多部译作，主要著述有《翻译、历史与文化论集》（*Translation，History and Culture*）、《翻译、改写及对文学名声的制控》（*Translation，Rewriting and the Manipulation of Literary Fame*）、《翻译、历史与文化资料书》（*Translation/History/Culture：A Sourcebook*）等，还发表了上百篇论文。这些开拓性的著述，提出翻译的研究应当具有开放性，文化、社会、意识形态等因素都应该被考虑在内，传统意义上的翻译方法应该在其后。此外，他还提出需要重新审视原文、译文、译者等的角色定位，需要确立一种新的学科范式。（刘军平，2009：415）在《翻译、改写及对文学名声的操纵》一书中，他提出："翻译是对原文文本的改写。所有改写者不管出于什么目的，都反映了某种意识形态和诗学。通过操纵文学，改写在特定的社会以一种特殊的方式而起作用。改写即操纵，以行使权力的形式出现。从积极方面来讲，改写有助于某种文学和社会的进化。"（Lefevere，2010：vii）在勒菲弗尔看来，任何的翻译活动都不可能与原文相等同，即使再忠实于原文的

译作也是一种改写，属于翻译策略中的一种，对于不忠实原文本的翻译也可能是意识形态的操纵所造成。操纵论将这些因素主要分为三个方面：意识形态、诗学和赞助人。意识形态主要从社会、政治等方面来影响译者的翻译活动；诗学指译者进行翻译活动时所处的文化体系，译者会根据当时所处的环境对译本进行改变，达到让目的语读者接受的目的；赞助人则从始至终会影响整个翻译过程和译者的活动，勒菲弗尔对于赞助人的描述是“可以理解为某种力量（个人，机构），这种力量可以推进或阻碍文学的阅读、写作和改写”。（Lefevere，2010：15）操纵论中的这三个因素在翻译活动中相互联系和相互影响，使得译本丰富多彩，“翻译不仅只是翻译意义，更重要的是翻译文化”。（刘军平，2009：421）

4　操纵论视角下译本分析

《桃夭》中对桃花、果实和桃叶的描写以及其深层意义带有浓厚的中国文化，三位译者的翻译也各具特色。以操纵论的三因素为指导，将译本置于更广阔的层面进行分析和探讨，从而深入了解三个译本的差异。

4.1　意识形态

意识形态是指反映特定经济形态、特定阶级或社会集团利益和要求的观念体系，其基本内容包括人们的政治、法律、道德、哲学、艺术、宗教观点等等。而译者们由于其自身经历的差异会产生不同的意识形态，因此在翻译时会有不同偏重点，这与译者的文化传统、教育程度、对文本的理解和态度等都有关联。在一定程度上，意识形态影响翻译目的与策略的选择。

许渊冲在《诗经》英译本的序中写道：“《诗经》在国内虽然非常重要，但在国外并不广为人知。”他致力于将中国文化推广到国际上，希望世界能够了解中国文化的价值，为中国文化登上世界文坛开辟道路。基于这一目的，他的译文力求能够接近原文所表达的韵味，让读者尽可能体会到原汁原味的《诗经》。理雅各作为一名传教士，自身责任就是传教，他为了实现在中国更好地实现传教目的，就需要了解这个国家的历史文化和社会结构。在这种责任和目的形成的意识形态下，理雅各以这样的初衷开始翻译《诗经》。埃兹拉·庞德是 20 世纪英美文坛具有影响力的诗人，他主张的意象主义认为诗歌翻译是一种艺术，要求诗人用高度凝练的意象生动地展现事物，并将诗歌与诗人的思想感情相融合。

纵观三个译本，从整体上看许渊冲与理雅各译本更贴近原文，庞德作为意象派诗人，他在翻译中并没有完全追求内容与形式的对等。三位译者在不同意识形态的影响下，选择了不同的翻译策略。

例 1　之子于归

许渊冲译：The maiden’s getting wed

理雅各译：This young lady is going to her future home.

庞德译：that goest to wed、Going to man and house、Going to bride

“之子于归”是原文中的叠句，分别都重复了三次，其意思为“此女子即将出嫁”，许渊冲和理雅各分别译为“getting wed”与“going to her future home”，从字面上就能清晰了解女子即将嫁人的意思。庞德的翻译可以看作是总—分—分的概念，其中“wed”“man and house”“bride”分别对应婚姻、男性与女性。婚姻是一个整体，男性和女性则是组成婚姻的分支，在此庞德采用意译的策略，加入了自己的认知。

例 2　室家、家室、家人

许渊冲译：the nuptial bowers、the family's root、household

理雅各译：chamber and house、house and chamber、her family

庞德译：house and bower、true root、his house

“室家、家室、家人，迭词，义同。因避复而变文”。（袁梅，1985：88）许渊冲与庞德在翻译中都进行了一些意译，“家室”他们都表达一种家庭根基的意思。许渊冲将“室家”译为“the nuptial bowers”，将其本意缩小了。理雅各在形式和意思上完全对等与原文，室与家的位置调换也体现在译文中 chamber 与 house 的换位。

4.2　诗学

诗学形态分为两类：一是各种文学的手法、体裁、中心思想、人物原型和场景以及象征；二是文学在整个社会中扮演的角色或者应当扮演何种角色。勒菲弗尔认为后者是在主题选择时具有影响力。诗学影响译者对翻译技巧的使用。

例 3　“华-家”“实-室”“蓁-人”

许渊冲译：“flowers-bowers”“fruit-root”“green-keen”

理雅各译：“flowers-house”“fruit-chamber”“leaves- family”

庞德译：“flower-bower”“fruit- root”“boughs-house”

《桃夭》是一首韵体诗，正是叠词、叠句与押韵产生了节奏感，也是核心之处。例 3 中分别是三处押韵，许渊冲与庞德的译文也在相同处押韵，具有音乐感，许渊冲的译文除了在叠句和押韵处于原文一致，并且在“桃之夭夭”与“之子于归”上也押韵，其中“red-wed””押韵让译文节奏感更强，为译文添彩；理雅各的译文只是在叠句上与原文一致，但在对修饰桃花、桃子和桃叶的形容词上押韵，分别使用了“brilliant”“abundant”“luxuriant”，虽然与原文押韵处不一样，也能给读者带去节奏感。

诗学中一个观点说的是：文学在整个社会中扮演的角色或者应当扮演何种角色，这一点影响着译者决定选择哪种与社会主流相关作品主题并且是否能引起注意，这与第一个因素，即意识形态相关联。译者赋予译本定位和价值，但是何种定位与何种价值是译者的意识形态所决定的。三个译本中，许渊冲译本读起来“韵味十足”，诗歌叠句和押韵也是为演唱时增加节奏感和音乐感而服务，许译本也抓住了这一特点；理雅各译本在选词和句式结构上忠实原文，从最基本点着手；庞德译本则运用意象来翻译，赋予了诗歌新的生命力和特点。译本是诗学的一种表现形式，微观角度看是对不同译者特点的体现，从宏观角度上看则是反映当时目的语的需求。从上面可以看出，译者在语言风格、翻译策略、思想上都有着差异，正是这些差异让译文在社会环境下扮演不同的角色。相同处是三位译者的翻译活动都是带有自己的目的和意图，即使形成的结果不一样，却都帮助了译本的传播。还有一点则是当译者选择一种诗学形态后，就会在长时间内坚持，使其具有稳定性，这可以从三位译者的翻译中看出来，甚至于是影响译者一生的翻译活动。

4.3　赞助人

赞助人是个人或者团体，如宗教团体、政党、社会阶层、出版商和大众媒体等等。他们尝试规范文学系统与其他系统间的关系，从而形成一种文化和社会。可以说赞助人一直在操纵着整个翻译过程，影响着译者。勒菲弗尔认为赞助人基本包含三个元素：意识形态成分、经济成分和地位成分。对于译作的形式和主题的选择及发展会受到意识形态的限制，勒菲弗尔所讲的意识形态并不局限于政治，还包含规则、惯例、信仰等。如同前面所提到的，意识形态影响作品的风格、主题、内容等，译者的意识形态也会受到赞助人的干预和影响；经济成分则是让作家、翻译家们能够确保生活，可能会以提供佣金或者指定一些职位等不同的方式。译者接受了赞助人的委托就要完成任务，勒菲弗尔认为“赞助人的接纳表明一个特定支持团体与生活方式的融合”，（Lefevere，2010：16）译者就会受到赞助人的要求，会有所限制，他们会给译者规定翻译的主题方向和范围，译者的主体性在这时便不再那么强烈，同时也需要有赞助人出版书籍才能达到译者的意识形态要求。赞助人拥有权力和资金，相较于诗学，他们更看重意识形态的问题，因此，赞助人可以说是代表了他们所在时期的主流意识形态。

许渊冲先生为传播中国经典文化翻译，理雅各为了更好地传教，从而开始了解中国文化而翻译，庞德对于翻译诗文有独到的见解，通过提炼原文的内容而不局限于形式。这三位译者在翻译《诗经》时都出于不同的目的，他们在翻译时要受目的的限制。此外，他们的角色则不仅仅是翻译家，还要承担文化传播者、传教士、意象派诗人的责任。这些都会在翻译过程中影响甚至控制译者的活动，最终对译文产生影响，形成在形式、体裁、翻译策略上的不一样。赞助人的存在必然会对翻译活动和译者产生影响，并且这种影响从赞助人介入就开始了。“毫无疑问，一部作品的翻译出版不仅仅是译者的个人行为，从译著的选择、出版，甚至到接受，都有赞助人这个‘看不见的手’在背后起作用”，（刘军平，2009：422）所以赞助人是从头到尾操纵整个翻译过程，他们的要求会让译者妥协某些条件，因此可以看出，赞助人施加的力量对译者和译作可能有着积极的作用，也可能会起到消极的作用，有时为了迎合主流意识形态，译者可能就会选择放弃一些自身的风格特点，从而形成更符合目的语读者的习惯、主流社会的意识形态以及文化风格等。

5 结　语

翻译作为一项交流工具，从来就不是与原文机械、生硬地对应而已。随着文化转向的到来，勒菲弗尔将翻译置于更广的层面进行探讨，不再只是考虑原文和译文之间相对应的关系，延伸至意识形态、诗学和赞助人的大环境中，研究这三个方面对译者、翻译活动、译作的影响。理解翻译过程中各个因素的操纵，可以让我们能够更好地了解翻译活动的实质，还能够让译者对目的语社会和文化有更深的认识。《诗经》作为我国的经典文化，是一块瑰宝，在进行翻译时不应该只局限于内容，本文虽不能以一个例子窥全局，却也通过对三个译本的比较分析，得出了操纵理论对于译者翻译活动产生的影响。作为译者，在翻译任何体裁的文本都不应只局限于文字上的关系，还应考虑意识形态和社会环境等宏观层面。中国诗歌蕴含丰富的中国传统文化和思想，语言风格鲜明，极具特点，这对译者来说并不容易，需要扎实的文字功底，还需对中国古诗歌文化有所了解和认知。作为译者，应当肩负起将中国经典文化传向世界的责任和义务，弘扬与传承中华文明，进一步促进中西文化的交流。

参考文献

[1] Lefevere，Andre, 2010. *Translation，Rewriting and the Manipulation of Literary Fame* [M]. Shanghai: Shanghai Foreign Language Education Press.

[2] Lefevere，Andre, 2010. *Translation/History/Culture：A Sourcebook* [M]. Shanghai：Shanghai Foreign Language Education Press.

[3] 陈敬艳. 勒菲弗尔及其操纵论[J]. 现代妇女（下旬），2013（6）.

[4] 廖七一. 当代西方翻译研究原典选读[M]. 北京：外语教学与研究出版社，2010.

[5] 理雅各.《诗经·国风》译释：汉英对照[M]. 上海：上海三联书店，2014.

[6] 刘军平. 西方翻译理论通史[M]. 武汉：武汉大学出版社，2009.

[7] 傅斯年.《诗经》十讲[M]. 北京：新世界出版社，2017.

[8] 许渊冲. 许译中国经典诗文集：《诗经》（汉英对照）[M]. 北京：五洲传播出版社，2012.

[9] 袁梅. 诗经译注[M]. 济南：齐鲁书社，1985.

《二十世纪的女性》英译汉实践报告

李文瑾

摘　要：本文为一篇翻译报告，所选原文为斯·杰·克莱恩博格（S. J. Kleinberg）所著的《20 世纪的女性》（“Women in the Twentieth Century”）。作者介绍了 20 世纪这一百年间，在两次女权运动和两次世界大战的影响下，美国女性通过不懈努力，在工作、家庭、教育等领域角色和地位的变化。作者通过将西班牙裔美籍女性、拉丁美裔美籍女性、亚裔美籍女性、非裔女性与白人女性相比，展现了她们在教育、工作领域受到的种种不公平待遇，揭示了 20 世纪美国普遍存在的种族歧视现象。从 20 世纪初，美国女性与男性相比，受教育机会较少、工作限制较多、薪资较低。到 21 世纪初美国女性拥有更多机会接受良好教育、从事高薪职业，表明了随着时代发展，美国女性的地位显著提升并且受到越来越多的社会尊重。

本翻译报告共分为四部分。第一部分为引言，旨在对翻译项目的背景、意义与报告结构进行介绍。第二部分为原文分析，包括作者介绍、原文内容介绍以及文体风格分析。第三部分为翻译难点与翻译方法阐释，包括翻译之前的准备工作，翻译过程中遇到的问题、以泰勒三原则为依据的翻译方法。如：主被动转换、词性转换、重组法以及翻译之后的修改过程。第四部分总结翻译过程中的经验教训以及仍待解决的问题。

关键词：翻译报告；女性地位；主被动转换；词性转换；重组法

Abstract: This is a translation report.The source text of this project, “Women in the Twentieth Century”, is taken from *Modern American Culture* edited by Christopher Bigsby. In the text, the author S. J. Kleinberg introduced American women’s changing roles and status in job, family and education under the influences of two feminist movements, two world wars and their restless efforts during the twentieth century. By comparing the Spanish, Latina, Asian American women as well as African American women with white women, the author unveils the prevailing racial discrimination by analyzing the unfair treatment they have confronted. In the early twentieth century, compared with men, they suffered from less education opportunities, more work restrictions and less payment. However, with their unremitting efforts and struggles, American women have more opportunities to better education, higher-paid work. Additionally, their status has achieved a remarkable rise and they have received increasing respect from the society.

This translation report consists of four parts. The first part introduces the background, significance and structure of the translation project. The second part is the analysis of the original text, including the background of the author and the lexical and textual styles of the original text. The third part illustrates difficulties in translation and discusses with abundant examples the three principles of Tytler and strategies including conversion of voices, conversion of word classes and restructuring applied to the translation. The fourth part is the summary of lessons drawn from the translation project.

Key words: translation report; the status of women; conversion of voices; conversion of word classes; restructuring

1 Introduction

The source text of this project, "Women in the Twentieth Century", is written by S. J. Kleinberg, an American writer, whose works, such as *Retrieving Women's History*, *The Shadow of the Mills*, havewon her a lot of awards and attention. In this text, Kleinberg illustrates American women's changing roles and status through complex events of the twentieth century, including long-term trends such as urbanization and immigration, shorter-term political events including wars and economic booms and busts, and various sociopolitical movements, unveiling the prevailing racial and sexual discrimination in the twentieth century. With time passing by, the status of American women has witnessed a remarkable rise and they received increasing respect from the society.

The significance of the translation project lies in two points. Firstly, the source text itself cannot be missed for its content. The author elaborately depicts the changing course of American women's role and status chronologically and makes a detailed introduction to the events which have exerted tremendous influence on women and enables the Chinese readers to have a comprehensive understanding of the history of American women in the twentieth century. Secondly, sexual and racial discriminations are hotspot issues of worldwide concern and are worth of making more Chinese readers available to the educational and work conditions of women, thus having a full-scale comprehension of the American culture.

This translation project, completed in Sichuan International Studies University, lasts for more than five weeks, during which the translator has gone through several steps to bring about a satisfactory translation, including the selection and reading of the source text, search of background information, translation and text modification with the assistance of the supervisor.

Apart from introduction and conclusion, this report mainly consists of two chapters. The first chapter is the analysis of the original text, including the background of authors and lexical and syntactic styles of the original text. The second chapter illustrates difficulties in translation and discusses with abundant examples the three principles of Tytler and strategies including conversion of voices, conversion of word classes and restructuring applied to the translation.

2 Analysis of the Original Text

2.1 Introduction of the Author

S. J. Kleinberg is a professor of American history at Brunel University, West London. As Chairperson of Society for the History of Women in the Americas, she is co-convenor of the Gender and History in the Americas Seminar at the Institute for Historical Research and editor of History of Women in the Americas. Her research on women in the twentieth-century US remains ongoing with publications including *Retrieving Women's History*, *The Shadow of the Mills*, *The Practice of U.S. Women's History*, *and Widows and Orphans*.

Her research focuses on the impact of economic and social change on women's roles inside and outside the home, principally in the United States in the nineteenth and twentieth century and in distinctive urban settings such as Pittsburgh, Fall River and Baltimore. She investigates how diverse economic structures led to distinctive gendered social welfare and child labor policies in those cities. Her present research is on how middle-aged women's lives changed during the twentieth century and women's migration patterns within the Americas, primarily between Cuba and the US.1

2.2 Introduction of the Content

The original book, Modern American Culture, offers a comprehensive, authoritative, and accessible overview of the cultural themes and intellectual issues that drive the dominant culture of the twentieth century.It explores the social, political, and economic forces that have made America what it is day and shows how these contexts impact upon twentieth-century American literature, cinema, and art.

The selected text "Women in the Twentieth Century"illustrates American women's changing roles and status through complex events of the twentieth century, including long-term trends such as urbanization and immigration, shorter-term political events including wars and economic booms and busts, and various sociopolitical movements. It firstexamines women's lives in the Progressive Era. Next, the author investigates theimpact of the Great Depression and World War II on women. What follows is the interrogation of their "survival in the doldrums", the years in which Americanwomen supposedly returned todomesticity, although political activism in the civil rights and peace movements and rising levels of employmentmeant that women accomplished much in these years. Finally, it turns to the Women's Liberation Movement, the demographic andeducationalchanges of the last three decades of the twentieth century, looking at women's activities outside the home, the backlash against feminism, and the continued ambivalence about gender roles. In the course of the twentieth century, the status of American women has witnessed a remarkable rise and they received increasing respect from the society.

3 Analysis of the Style

The source text is typical of a narration that elaborates the changing roles and status of women in chronological order with simple, plain words, complicated grammatical structure and rigorous style.

3.1 Lexical Features

On the lexical level, the source text is abundant with simple, plain words and abbreviations of institutions and organizations. For example:

Joined by women from other ethnic groups these unskilled women relied upon community networks and support from the Industrial Workers of the World in asuccessful strike which coined the rallying cry, "give me bread, but give me roses, too." The WTULsupported the strikers, although the AFL did not.[2]

In the paragraph above, all the words employed are simple, plain and widely used. There exits three proper nouns and abbreviations, namely, "Industrial Workers of theWorld", "WTUL", short term of "Women's Trade Union League" as well as "AFL", the abbreviation of "American Federation of Labor", adding to the preciseness and reliability of the content it describes.

3.2 Syntactic Features

On the syntactic level, a large number of long and complex sentences characterized by complicated grammatical structure have been employed. For example:

In 1900, the Census recorded about 3 percent of married white women as holding jobs, compared with 26 percent of African American wives, additionally, manyworking-class and immigrant women contributed to their families' well-being by taking in boarders, washing, or sewing.[3]

The sentence listed above is a complex one with subordinated clause connected with past participle"compared with" and the conjunction"additionally" is used to connect two clauses. The second complex sentence is composed of postpositive attributive "contributed to", featuring the distinctive difference between the Chinese and English languages. English is a hypotactic language with dependent or subordinate construction or relationship of clauses with connectives, whereas Chinese is a paratactic one characterized by the arrangement of clauses one after another without connectives to show their relations.

4 Analysis of the Translation Practice

4.1 Translation Difficulties

The first difficulty the translator met in the translation project is to have a better understanding ofthe American culture and its social and cultural background. The United States is a multi-national country with immigration across the world, thus its society being shaped by various cultures. In the twentieth century, when referring to the status and roles of women, the translator should take into consideration the economic and social impact, instead of merely focusing on the linguistic transference. Susan Bassnette once said, "Language is the heart within the body of culture, and it is the interaction between the two that results in the continuation of life-energy."[4]

The second obstacle that lies ahead is the complex sentence structure. The source text employs large quantities of long and complex sentences. Nida pointed out that: "So far as English and Chinese are concerned, the most important difference linguistically is the contrast between hypotaxis and parataxis."[5] English is a hypotactic language with dependent or subordinate construction or relationship of clauses with connectives, whereas Chinese is a paratactic one that the arranging of clauses one after another without connectives showing their relations. Translation, as defined by Eugene A. Nida, consists in reproducing in the receptor language the closet natural equivalent of the source text, first in terms of meaning and secondly in terms of form.[6] Because of the distinctive difference between Chinese and English, it is not easy to analyze the sentence structure of long and complicated sentences, thus making it difficult to convey the full and complete meaning of the original content.

Thirdly, looking up the precise authoritative Chinese translated version of proper nouns and abbreviations of eras, acts and institutions has taken great efforts and time. When translating proper nouns, such as "Progressive Era", "The Chinese Exclusion Act", "The Gentlemen's Agreement with Japan", "the Sixth Circuit of the US Court of Appeals" and so on, the translator picked up the most authoritative and widely accepted one from various Chinese translated versions.In consideration of the ambiguity of the abbreviations, for example, AFL (American Federation of Labor and American Football League), WPA (World Parliament Association), WPA (Works Progress Administration and With Particular Average), the translator picked up the precise meaning based on their contextual meaning and cultural background.As for other abbreviations, such as WTUL, NAWSA, WAC, and EEOC, the translator has looked into professional dictionaries to find the widely accepted Chinese translated names.

4.2 Translation Strategies

Most theorists agree that flexible strategies are used by translators when they encounter translation difficulties and literal translation does not work. When appropriate strategies are applied, the translated text can be intelligible for the target readers and make them accessible to Chinese readers. Three strategies frequently adopted in the translating process are conversion of voices, conversion of word classes and restructuring.

4.2.1 Conversion of Voices

The passive voice is frequently used in the English language, whereas the Chinese has a trend to use active voice. When there is no need, improper to mention the conductor or anyone wants to shirk the responsibility, people will naturally turn to the passive voice. On the contrary, the Chinese passive form marked by "被" is traditionally felt to be an "inflictive voice", mainly expressing things unpleasant or undesirable to the subjective person.[7] Therefore, when facing passive voice in English, the translator often convert them into active ones in Chinese. For example:

TT: United by their biology, but <u>divided</u> by class, race, ethnicity, place of birth, locale, education, religion, social values, and political beliefs, women, no less than men, constituted a varied group.[8]

ST：女性虽然有一样的生理特征，但阶级、种族、民族、出生地、居住地、教育背景、宗教信仰、社会价值和政治信仰<u>各不相同</u>，女性因此和男性一样，构成了一个多样化的群体。

With no application of the translation strategy, conversion of voice, the sentence above might be translated into 但被阶级、种族、民族、出生地、居住地、教育背景、宗教信仰、社会价值和政治信仰区分。Violating the translation criteria of smoothness，the translated version is unidiomatic，and Chinese readers may find it difficult to grasp the original meaning. After the passive voice "divided" being converted into active voice，the translated version is 但阶级、种族、民族、出生地、居住地、教育背景、宗教信仰、社会价值和政治信仰各不相同，being intelligible to Chinese readers and achieving the fluency and smoothness of the target text. What follows is another example：

Joined by women from other ethnic groups the seunskilled women relied upon community networks and support from the Industrial Workers of the World in asuccessful strike which coined the rallying cry，"give me bread，but give me roses，too."[9]

这些身无技能的妇女与其他种族的妇女并肩作战，依靠社区网络和来自世界工业工人组织的支持，在一场成功的罢工中发出了"给我面包，但也给我玫瑰花"的呼喊。

If it had been translated directly with no use of conversion，the original sentence would have been translated as 这些身无技能的妇女被其他种族的妇女加入，whichis unidiomatic and does not conform to Chinese expressions. However，it can be translated as 这些身无技能的妇女与其他种族的妇女并肩作战，conforming to the language convention that Chinese has a tendency to use active voice，whereas English passive voice.

4.2.2 Conversion of Word Classes

English and Chinese are two distinctive languages with its own features. Broadly speaking，English is a static language，featuring the predominance of nouns over verbs，with more use of nouns，adjectives，adverbials and prepositions. On the contrary，Chinese is a dynamic language，which often employsverbal phrases and subject-predicate structure. Therefore，when dealing with the English-Chinese translation，many of those static words should be converted into dynamic ones. For example：

A desire to assimilate Native Americans into mainstream US society resulted in the Bureau ofIndian Affairs sending many young Native Americans to boarding schools aconsiderable distance from their reservations.[10]

印度事务局抱着渴望同化印第安人使他们融入美国主流社会的想法，将许多年轻的印第安人送到离他们居留地很远的寄宿学校学习。

English has a preference for static words，such as nouns，adjectives，adverbials and prepositions to indicate movements，where asverbs or subject-predicate structures find their wider use in Chinese. In translation，therefore，the conversion of English nouns into Chinese verbs becomes one of the techniques employed for smooth representation in idiomatic Chinese.[10] In the sentence above，"a desire to assimilate" is translated into 渴望同化，which makes the expression intelligible for the receptors. What follows is another example：

Betty Friedan stated that ever since World War II, there had been an attempt "to get women back into the home by glorifying feminine fulfilment – woman's fulfilment as a wife and mother – as the sole aim and justification of woman's existence." [11]

贝蒂·弗里丹表示自第二次世界大战以来，人们试图"通过赞颂女性作为妻子和母亲的付出让她们回到家中，并将其视为女性存在的唯一目的和理由。"

The most remarkable distinction between Chinese and English lies in that English is inclined to use static words, especially action nouns and other abstract nouns while Chinese has a preference for verbs or multi-verbal forms. In this sentence, the noun "attempt" is translated into the verb 试图, which is idiomatic in Chinese.

4.2.3 Restructuring

Restructuring refers to the necessary or inevitable change of word-order or the logical rearrangement of expression in a sentence in conformity with the standard or good usage of the target language on account of syntactic differences between the source language and the target language. What is quite natural in order in one language may seem in another language awkward in arrangement; each language has its own peculiarities in word-order or logical arrangement of expression. The natural order in English may seem the inverted or irrational order in Chinese or vice versa, hence the necessity of restructuring in translation.[12] For instance:

In 1900, the Census recorded about 3 percent of married white women asholding jobs, compared with 26 percent of African American wives, additionally, many working-class and immigrant women contributed to their families' well-being by taking in boarders, washing, or sewing.[13]

1900 年，据人口普查记载，相较于 26%拥有工作的非裔美籍妻子，约 3%的已婚白人妇女拥有工作。此外，许多工薪阶层和移民妇女通过接受寄宿、洗衣或缝纫等方式帮助他们的家庭改善生活。

The past participle "compared with", functioned as adverbial clauses denoting comparison may precede or follow the main clause, while it's contrary to that in Chinese. In the source text, the past participle "compared"denoting comparison is put behind "married white women". Nevertheless, according to the idiomatic Chinese expression, 与 26%拥有工作的非裔美籍妻子相比 is put ahead of "married white women", conforming to the Chinese sentence order.Additionally, when the preposition structure "by…" means the methods to do something, in English it can both be put in the beginning or the end of the sentence structure. However, it is usually placed in the beginning of the sentence structure, thus 通过接受寄宿、洗衣或缝纫等方式 precedes 帮助他们的家庭改善生活.Another example is presented below:

It completely ignored the physically arduous jobs done by women of color on farms orin kitchens，nor did it regulate the hours they worked cleaning offices or in other “non-industrial” employments.[14]

它完全忽视了有色人种妇女在农场或是厨房里艰苦劳累的工作，也没有规定她们打扫办公室或在其他“非工业”岗位工作的时间。

The past participle，functioning as postpositive attributive，may precede or follow the main clause，whereas in Chinese，it is placed before the noun to modify it. In the sentence above，“done by women of color” is used to modify “jobs”，therefore，the translator inverses their orders as 有色妇女在农场或是厨房里艰苦劳累的工作. As“they worked cleaning offices or in other ‘non-industrial’ employments” is an attributive clause，under the same rule，the translator put its translated version precede “the hours”.

5 Conclusions

Translation can be defined as the reproduction or recreation of the original message in the target language.It is not only a linguistic transference but also a medium of intercultural communication. In order to meet the translation criteria of “faithfulness” and “smoothness” in this project，the translator upheld the three principles of translation proposed by Alexander Fraser Tytler，a famous British translation theorist.

To achieve the full and complete conveying or transmission of the original content in the target language，the translator looked up large quantities of information on economy，culture，politics，religions and customs of the U.S. society. Moreover，it takes great efforts and energy to acquire the background information of the major events and their impacts on women in the twentieth century，such as the Great Depression，WWII，and Women’s Liberation Movement.Because of the long and complex sentences employed by the author，the translator read the source text for many times in order to classify their structures.

After grasping the ideas of the original work，the translator tried to reproduce the style and manner of the original textin the translated text. Style is a way of expressing something that is characteristic of the author，lying in the writer’s choice of words，phrases as well as the sentence structures. As a narration of the changing roles and status of women in the twentieth century，the author resorted to simple and plain words，as well as long and complex sentences to elaborate the history. Therefore，the translator turned to concise and plain Chinese words to reproduce its rigorous style. Additionally，although having been concerned with the destiny of American women，the author took an objective attitude to their development，with no injection of her individual emotions and comments. Therefore，the translator is obliged to objectively reproduce the faithfulness of the content of the source text.

However，there is no denying that some deficiencies still remain in both the translation and the report.First，because of the translator’s limited proficiency of analyzing the complex sentence and grammatical structures，some of the restructuring Chinese sentences are not idiomatic and some Chinese words employed in the translated text are not always effective enough. Second，because of the inadequate knowledge reserve of the American culture and society, the translator sometimes cannot have a comprehensive comprehension of the original work, thus failing to find the precise correspondence in Chinese. Last, the translated words and sentences sometimes lack seriousness and rigorousness.

In order to become a qualified translator, one must be proficient in the two languages, have an abundant knowledge reserve of the Chinese and western cultures and have a good master of translation skills and principles by continuously practice and accumulation.As the old Chinese saying goes: "No matter how high the mountain is, one can always ascend to its top".Therefore, there isno limit to the further learning of translation, and the translators should unwaveringly strive for the improvement of the translated text.

Notes

1. https://theconversation.com/profiles/jay-kleinberg-226645.

2. S. J. Kleinberg, "Women in the Twentieth Century," in *The Cambridge Companion to Modern American Culture*, ed. Christopher Bigsby (Cambridge: Cambridge University Press, 2006), 196.

3. Ibid., 197.

4. Susan Bassnette, *Translation Strategie* (London: Routledge, 2002), 23.

5. EugeneA.Nida, *Language, Culture and Translating* (Shanghai: ShanghaiForeign Language Education Press, 1993), 125.

6. Eugene A. Nida and Charles R. Taber, *The Theory and Practice of Translation* (Shanghai: Shanghai Foreign Language Education Press, 2004), 12.

7. https://wenku.baidu.com/view/e00b484ba8956bec0975e3f9.html

8. S. J. Kleinberg, 195.

9. Ibid., 197.

10. Ibid., 196.

11. Ibid., 202.

12. https://wenku.baidu.com/view/248c4a1ba300a6c30c229fee.html

13. S. J. Kleinberg, 196.

14. Ibid., 198.

15.贾德江. 英汉语对比研究与翻译[M]. 长沙：国防科技大学出版社，2002：130.

参考文献

[1] Bassnette, Susan, 2002. *Translation Strategies*. London: Routledge. https://wenku.baidu.com/view/e00b484ba8956bec0975e3f9.html.

[2] Kleinberg, S. J., 2006. "Women in the Twentieth Century." In *The Cambridge Companion to Modern American Culture*. Ed. Christopher Bigsby. Cambridge: Cambridge University Press.

[3] Nida, Eugene A., 2001. *Language and Culture: Context in Translating*. Shanghai: Shanghai Foreign Language Education Press.

[4] Nida, Eugene A., and Charles R. Taber, 2004. *The Theory and Practice of Translation*. Shanghai: Shanghai Foreign Language Education Press.

[5] Tytler，Alexander Fraser, 2012. *Essay on the Principles of Translation*. Amsterdam：John Benjamins Publishing Company.

[6] 方梦之，毛忠明. 英汉-汉英应用翻译综合教程[M]. 上海：上海外语教育出版社，2008.

[7] 贾德江. 英汉语对比研究与翻译[M]. 长沙：国防科技大学出版社，2002.

[8] 连淑能. 英汉对比研究[M]. 北京：高等教育出版社，1993.

[9] 马会娟，苗菊. 当代西方翻译理论选读[M]. 北京：外语教学与研究出版社，2009.

[10] 谭载喜. 西方翻译简史[M]. 北京：商务印书馆，2004.

《十大探险胜地》英译汉项目报告

詹　廷　刘　夏　刘芸均

摘　要：近年来，中国出境游客的数量不断攀升。旅游文本不仅有助于为游客提供更多的信息，还有利于增加旅游景点的知名度，但有时语言障碍会让旅行者的出行变得困难。英语作为世界上使用最广泛的语言，也已成为国际旅游中最常用的服务语言。为了满足中国游客的需求，大量的外国旅游文本被翻译成中文。然而，由于中英语言和文化习俗的差异，旅游翻译存在许多问题。本报告在弗米尔目的论的指导下，从目的原则、连贯原则和忠实原则三方面对译文进行分析。从词语与句法层面入手，译者根据自身的目的采取对应的翻译方法以弥补原文与目的语之间的差异。本文旨在为旅游文本的翻译提供参考价值，更好地造福中国游客。

关键词：旅游文本；目的论；弗米尔

Abstract：In recent years，the number of outbound tourists in China has been rising. The tourism text not only helps to provide more information for tourists，but also helps to increase the visibility of tourist attractions. But sometimes language barriers make tourists' travel difficult. As the most widely used language in the world，English has become the most commonly used service language in international tourism. In order to meet the needs of Chinese tourists，a large number of foreign tourist texts have been translated into Chinese ones. However，due to differences between Chinese and English language and cultural customs，there exists some problems in tourism translation. Under the guidance of Vermeer's Skopos Theory，this report analyzes the target text in terms of the three principles of purpose，coherence and faithfulness. Starting from the level of words and syntax，the translator adopts corresponding translation methods according to his own purposes to make up for the difference between the original text and the target language. The purpose of this report is to provide reference value for the translation of tourist texts，and to better benefit Chinese tourists.

Key words：tourist texts；Skopos Theory；Vermeer

1　项目描述

本部分主要介绍项目背景和项目意义。项目背景主要包括地点、人物、周期、分工等。项目意义包括原文涉及的行业现状以及对同一类型文本的指导价值等。

1.1　项目背景

为了帮助学生更好地完成论文写作，学校特设了翻译论文写作课程，让学生更好地了解翻译论文写作流程和相关规范。课堂上，学生分为 8 个小组，各自抽取一份文本进行翻译并完成项目报告。

本组翻译文本为 *Top Ten Places for Traveling*，英文总字数为 600，翻译目标语为中文，需要在一周内完成此项任务。在翻译前，小组成员首先共同确定原文本属于旅游类文本，随后参考一些平行文本，找出此类文本的共性与原文本的特性。在翻译后，组员各自分别阅读其他组员的翻译，指出问题并进行集体讨论。对任务的分析和总结将在目的论的指导下进行。

1.2 项目意义

近年来，越来越多的中国游客出国旅游，出境旅游已成为一种新的时尚。英语作为世界上使用最广泛的语言，也已成为国际旅游中最常用的服务语言。为了满足中国游客的需求，使他们更好地欣赏旅游景点的自然美和西方的异域文化魅力，大量的外国旅游景点被翻译成中文。然而，由于中英语言和文化习俗的差异，旅游翻译存在许多问题。因此，本文旨在为旅游文本的翻译提供参考价值，更好地造福中国游客。

2 翻译过程

翻译并非一蹴而就，而是环环相扣。因此，在翻译过程中，译者要做好各个环节的工作，这样才能保证翻译质量。对于整个翻译过程的描述，本章主要从译前准备、译中流程和译后审校三个部分进行。

2.1 译前准备

翻译小组在正式翻译之前开展了一系列准备工作。首先是平行文本的准备：小组成员阅读原文并查找相关资料，确定此文本为旅游类文本。因此，组员利用 CNKI、维普、万方等网站查找平行文本，从这些文本中总结出此类文本的特点以及一些常用的翻译方法。其次是翻译工具的准备：由于原文中出现了许多国家名称和地名，通过网上检索，对专有名词进行了查阅和翻译，本次翻译借助了一些网络工具和实体工具，如：谷歌翻译、百度翻译、CNKI 翻译助手、《汉英大辞典》《陆谷孙英汉大辞典》等等。

2.2 译中流程

做完充分的准备工作之后，小组成员便正式着手翻译。由于原文本篇幅较短，翻译时间较为充足，小组成员经讨论后决定每人先各自在目的论的指导下独立进行翻译。小组成员分别将翻译过程中遇到的难点标注出来，以便最后进行讨论。翻译时组员借助各种网上翻译助手，使用了纸质和电子词典，并查找了相关文献。组员各自翻译完毕后，再进行整合讨论。

2.3 译后审校

审校是翻译全过程的一个重要环节，是确保译文质量的最后关口。翻译完成后，小组成员第一遍对照原文校对各自的译文，检查有无疏漏、误译的地方；第二遍脱离原文审校，检查有无生硬拗口的地方，再针对争议处以及各自翻译过程中遇到的难点进行讨论，并提出解决方案。通过一系列的讨论，本组确定了译文的初版。随后，核查译文内容是否流畅，全文风格是否一致，前后术语是否统一。最后，检查是否有拼写、标点等小错误。审校工作结束后，确定译文的最终稿。

3 文本分析

译者在进行翻译前，大量的翻译准备是不可或缺的。通过对平行文本与原文本的阅读，总结出其共性与特性之处，能让翻译工作事半功倍。

3.1 英语旅游文本分析

旅游文本是指旅游（接待）一线人员（尤其是导游翻译）在工作中经常碰到的、约定俗成的那些应用型文本。（陈刚，2004）由于旅游活动涉及社会的许多领域和部门，如旅行社、住宿业、餐饮业、交通客运业、旅游用品和纪念品销售行业等，因此英语旅游文本的涉及面也很广泛。从广义上来讲，英语旅游文本可以划分为旅游专业文本和普通文本。旅游专业文本是针对旅游领域内专业人士，例如，旅游研究论文；旅游普通文本是针对普通大众（潜在的旅游者）的文本，其中包括旅游标识语（告示标牌）、导游词、旅游广告、旅游宣传册、旅游宣传单、旅游指南、旅游景点介绍等。（丁大刚，2008）

词汇特点：（1）英语旅游文本的词语选择非常严谨，常常使用大量经过精心选择的关键词，这些关键词一般简短扼要、清晰明了、一语中的；（2）旅游是一门交叉学科，因此也就造成了旅游英语的词汇具有词汇量大和跨学科的特点，其专有名词除了地名外可能涉及历史、地理、艺术、建筑等等；（3）表达信息时使用相对简单的词汇，旅游文本属于宣传类文本，要达到在广大读者群中的宣传目的，争取更多的读者游览所宣传介绍的景点或享受所宣传的旅游服务，旅游文件就必须使用一定的简单词汇，因为读者的受教育程度不一。（丁大刚，2008）

句法特点：（1）简单句短促有力，读起来朗朗上口。作为一种宣传材料，旅游文本使用短句可以更好地发挥其宣传作用；（2）旅游文本属于呼唤类文本，即号召读者采取行动，享受某一旅游服务或游览某一旅游景点，因此旅游文本中会使用一些祈使句来增加号召和呼唤的语气；（3）疑问句的功用主要在于提出问题，启发读者思考。旅游文本中经常使用疑问句（包括一般疑问句和特殊疑问句），目的在于启发读者，引起注意，从而发挥旅游文本的号召作用。同时，疑问句就像对话，使读者读起来增加亲切感，即旅游文本使用疑问句可以更好地贴近读者。（彭萍，2010）

3.2 原文本分析

随着旅游业的发展，市场上出现了各种各样的旅游信息类文本：有常见的“必看之地（must-sees）”的旅游观光指南，也有一些较为专业的旅游文本，例如，美食游、自驾游、徒步游的旅游手册。为旅游者提供一些有关旅游景点的信息，属于参考资料。通常情况下，读者（或潜在的旅游者）是在做出旅游的决定之后采取阅读旅游文本，目的是从中获得更多有关旅游景点的信息。本项目的翻译文本是一篇冒险类旅游指南。

词汇层面：（1）使用大量专有名词。旅游文本宣传的大多是旅游景点，因此旅游文本中就会出现很多的地名和景点名称，如 Leh、the Grand Canyon 等。（2）使用第二人称代词。在旅游文本中的第二人称代词不是特指某个人，而是一种泛指。第二人称代词用在广告宣传文体中可以拉近与读者的距离，使读者产生一种亲近感，从而更好地宣传推介产品或服务。（彭萍，2010）（3）使用描述性很强的词汇。在介绍宣传景点时都会使用一些描述性很强的形容词或动词，以渲染所介绍的景点之美，从而达到说服读者来旅游景点旅游的目的，（彭萍，2010）

如 breathtaking、fantastic 等。(4) 使用形容词的比较级和最高级。旅游文本属于宣传广告类型，而广告在使用形容词时往往会倾向于其比较级或最高级，以示其优势，如 one of the best places 等。

句法层面：（1）原文本句式灵活，以简单句为主。表达清楚明了，用简短的一句话介绍旅游景点及其特点，让读者能够在短时间内了解旅游目的地，同时也能给他们留下深刻的印象，从而达到旅游文本宣传的目的。(2) 句型多样。为了突出景点的特色，原文本使用了陈述句、祈使句、倒装句等句式，使行文更加丰富和具有吸引力。

4 理论基础

翻译实践的成功离不开翻译理论的指导。旅游指南是一种宣传文本，为游客提供旅游景点的信息。在目的论的正确指导下，根据所选翻译文本的特点，该小组通过合理的翻译技巧对译文进行了恰当的处理和改变。

4.1 目的论概念

目的论的德文是 Skopostheorie，原文来自于希腊语 Skopos，意为“目的”“目标”“意图”“功能”。目的论的英文对应的是 Skopos Theory。翻译目的论的定义是：“在目的语背景下，为目的语的目的，和目的语环境读者，生产一个文本”。(Christiane，1997)

弗米尔最早在《普通翻译理论基础》(Groundwork for a General Translation Theory，1978) 中提出了目的论理论，旨在将理论和实践相结合来解决实际问题。该理论认为决定翻译步骤的一个主要的原则就是其整个翻译活动的目的。费米尔认为在翻译领域里有三个可能的目的。它们分别是：在翻译过程中翻译者的主要目的，在翻译条件下目标文本的交流目的以及在特定的翻译策略和步骤中所产生的目的。目的论强调翻译的互动和语用特征，认为目的语文本的形式应当首先由功能，即由目的语语境中要达到的目的来决定。

4.2 目的论三原则

目的论者认为，译者必须根据翻译之目的来制定策略。由于语言和文化差异的存在，译文不可能和原文的各方面都达到一致。要么有所保留，要么有所变动。保留多少，改动多少就要视翻译目的而定。目的论理论主张，译本的预期目的决定翻译的方法和策略，在翻译过程中应遵循三个总体原则，即目的论原则（Skopos rule）、连贯原则（coherence rule）和忠实原则（fidelity rule）。(刘军平，2009)

（1）目的原则，指的是所有翻译活动应该遵循的第一条主要原则就是“目的原则”。换言之，整个翻译过程包括翻译方法和策略的选择都是有翻译行为所要达到的目的决定的。

（2）连贯原则，指的是译文必须符合内文连贯（intratextual coherence）的要求，是针对译文内部及其与译入语文化之间的关系而言的。

（3）忠实原则，指译文与原文之间应符合互文连贯（intertextual coherence）的要求，是针对译文文本与原文文本之间的关系而言的，近似于我们通常所说的译文应忠实于原文的说法。

5 案例分析

本项目以目的论为理论基础，从目的论三原则出发，采取不同的处理方式来翻译文本。

针对旅游文本的特性，如何正确地把握目的语的特点和表达习惯，同时采用适当的翻译技巧，译者需要仔细斟酌。

5.1 目的原则

在目的论中，目的法则是其第一大原则。（仲伟合、钟钰，1999）目的法则决定了整个翻译行为，在目的法则中，"目的""目标"意味着翻译者的目的和目标必须要完整准确地表达出来。（马蓉，2011）译者在翻译这篇旅游指南时应当时刻遵循目的原则，译文应体现原文本的特性，以达到吸引游客的目的。

ST	Doesn't matter whether or not you reach the top or not：we're sure the view from each peak is as breathtaking as from the top
TT	无论你是否到了珠峰顶都无关紧要：我们确信每个峰顶的景色与其一样令人叹为观止

ST	The creatures found in this region are not found anywhere else in the world
TT	这个地区的生物在地球上是独一无二的

原文本属于旅游类文本，其目的是为冒险者提供信息，并吸引他们去体验。但中文与英文在表达上差异较大，为了达到吸引旅游者这一翻译目的，译者采用**四字格**，将"breathtaking"和"not found anywhere else"分别翻译为"叹为观止"与"独一无二"两个四字成语。"成语的积极修辞作用在于能根据原文的要求达意传神，收到很好的语言效果"，（刘宓庆，1985）在表达上更加具有力度和感染力，能为译文增添光彩，达到吸引游客的目的。

5.2 连贯原则

根据目的论的连贯性法则，译者应当采取灵活的翻译方法，使得译文在目的语的文化和语言环境中通顺、连贯、有意义，方便目的语读者理解。

ST	Never will your adventure diary be complete without an attempt to scale the world's highest mountain
TT	如果没有尝试过攀登世界最高峰，那么你的历险记永远不会完整
方法	介词短语前置

ST	What makes it stand out from other locations are its breathtaking lagoons，rainforest，mountains，and even the volcanoes
TT	那令人叹为观止的泻湖、雨林、山脉以及火山等一系列景观，使得它脱颖而出
方法	主语从句后置

以上两个例子中，第一个例子为部分倒装句，译者在翻译时将介词短语前置，第二个例子的主语为从句，翻译时将主语从句后置。如按照原文结构进行翻译，译文则显得生硬拗口，不符合汉语的表达习惯。

因为在句子形式上，"英语重形合，汉语重意合。英语注重运用各种有形的联结手段达到语法形式与逻辑形式两个方面的完整，概念指代分明，句子组织严密，层次明确，句法功能呈外显特征。而汉语通过句子之间的内部逻辑关系来表达英语中那些连接词所表达的意思”。（钟书能，2017）在信息的表达顺序上，“英文句子的表述中重心通常在前，而汉语句子的表述重心通常在后”。（罗左毅，2012）

鉴于以上中英文之间的差异，为了符合中文表达以及句子意思的连贯和通顺，译者在处理此两个例子时都对原文句子进行了语序调整，从而更加符合目的语读者的阅读习惯。

5.3 忠实原则

忠实原则指译文与原文之间应符合互文连贯的要求，是针对译文文本与原文文本之间的关系而言的，近似于我们通常所说的译文应忠实于原文的说法，其中忠实的程度和形式取决于译文的目的和译者对译文的理解。

ST	The Grand Canyon isn't just a heritage site
TT	科罗拉多大峡谷不仅仅是一处文化遗产

ST	Choosing the right destination is crucial to an adventurous vacation
TT	选择正确的目的地对于冒险度假来说至关重要

在旅游类文本中，常使用大量的专有名词和简单句，原文本中出现了大量的地名和简单句，对于地点名的翻译则是查询词典和网络资料；简单句短促有力，表达意思清晰简洁，因此在翻译此类句子时，采用了**直译**的方法，而“采取原语的表达方式，往往能够更加准确、更加充分地传达原文的意思”，（孙致礼，周晔，2010）这样会让游客容易抓住文本的主要信息。

6 总结反思

结论：本次翻译项目原文为旅游类文本，其原文本特征正如前文所提及，译者在翻译时既要保留旅游文本的风格，也要充分考虑目的语读者的阅读习惯，使其译文能够有足够的吸引力，达到旅游文本的宣传效果。因此，译者根据原文的词汇、句法等特点，以目的论为指导，采取不同的翻译方法。

词汇层面：对于地名、景点名等专有名词通过查找相关资料，采用约定俗成的译法，保证译文的准确性；对于描述性强的词汇采用四字成语，使行文简短有力，富有节奏感和美感，从而更加具有吸引力；对于形容词+介词的结构，将形容词转换为动词，使语言更加简洁生动。

句法层面：对于倒装句以及各种从句等，适当调整语序，使译文更具有连贯性，更加通顺；对于简单句采用合并法，使译文更符合汉语表达方式，避免冗余繁杂。

不足：对文本的特征分析不够深入，对此旅游类及其他实用性文本缺乏翻译经验，以后应多注重实践实用型文本翻译；理论知识装备不足，平时应多涉猎各种理论，以备不时之需；双语功底不足，今后应多阅读双语读物，不断提高完善自己对语言的掌控能力。

参考文献

[1] Nord，Christiane, 1997. *Translation as a Purposeful Activity：Functionalist Approaches Explained*[M]. Manchester：St. Jerome Publishing Litd.

[2] Graham. MS. Dann, 1996. *The Language of Tourism：A Sociolinguistic Perspective* [M]. Wallingford：CAB International.

[3] 陈刚. 旅游翻译与涉外导游[M]. 北京：中国对外出版公司，2004.

[4] 丁大刚. 旅游英语的语言特点与翻译[M]. 上海：上海交通大学出版社，2008.

[5] 连淑能. 英汉对比研究[M]. 北京：高等教育出版社，2010.

[6] 刘宓庆. 文体与翻译[M]. 北京：中国对外翻译出版公司，1985.

[7] 刘军平. 西方翻译理论通史[M]. 武汉：武汉大学出版社，2009.

[8] 罗左毅. 英汉实用翻译教程[M]. 南京：南京大学出版社，2012.

[9] 马蓉. 翻译目的论在旅游翻译中的应用——以宁夏旅游英译为例[J]. 中国商贸，2011（33）.

[10] 彭萍. 实用旅游英语翻译：英汉双向[M]. 北京：对外贸易经济大学出版社，2010.

[11] 孙致礼，周晔. 高级英汉翻译[M]. 北京：外语教学与研究出版社，2010.

[12] 钟书能. 英汉翻译技巧[M]. 北京：对外经济贸易大学出版社，2012.

[13] 仲伟合，钟钰. 德国的功能派翻译理论[J]. 中国翻译，1999（3）.

目的论视角下《伊豆的舞女》两个中译本的比较研究

吴崔娟

摘 要：从日本的大正到昭和年间，川端康成一直是活跃在日本文坛顶端的作家之一。明治32年出生于大阪市的川端康成在3岁时因父母双亡便成为孤儿，随后养育自己的祖父母又相继离世，15岁便成为真正的天涯孤儿。虽然他将悲惨遭遇寄情于文学创作中，但是血缘亲情的离去仍然对他的文学创作有着深刻的影响。《伊豆的舞女》是川端康成早期的代表作，讲述了心理扭曲的主人公通过伊豆的旅行，认识了舞女一行人，对舞女从肉体的渴望到后来心理的净化，最后达到精神升华的故事。《伊豆的舞女》在中国有很多译本，在此之中，1996年叶渭渠的译本和2011年林少华的译本最具有代表性。笔者将以目的论为基础，比较各自的差异，分析叶译和林译的风格和特征。

关键词：译本；目的论；受众；目的

1 序 論

1.1 問題提出

川端康成は日本近現代文学史において、代表的な作家である。『伊豆の踊り子』は川端康成の初期の有名な作品で、彼が新人作家になったきっかけと思われている。『伊豆の踊子』は川端康成が19歳のときに伊豆旅行の実体験をもとに綿密な筆致で書き上げた作品である。彼は性格の歪んだ「私」が「踊子」に対しての肉欲的欲ばりの卑劣な心理から心理的浄化、精神的昇華を遂げた人性の更生おりを現す。作者の川端康成は新奇な言葉を用い、景色などの側面から人物の豊かな心理活動を表す。一見してわかりやすく、素朴な言葉だが、実はその中には作者の深い意味を含んでいる。そういう特別な筆致は時期的な特徴を反映している。この作品は日本の優れた短編小説として、多くの訳本に翻訳された。中国でも訳本が多い。そのうち、林少華と葉渭渠の中国語訳本がある。川端康成の文学作品が中国に紹介される過程では、翻訳者の葉渭渠の力は無視してはいけないのである。翻訳者の林少華も日本文学の翻訳には重要な地位を占めている。先行研究では「论叶渭渠和林少华《伊豆舞女》的翻译技巧」、「林少华的“审美忠实”及其译作《伊豆舞女》」二篇の研究資料しかない。しかし、『伊豆の踊り子』において、二人の訳本の翻訳方法と風格がかなり異なっている。その差異が生じる原因と背景についての研究はほとんどないのである。それゆえ、本稿はその空白を補うことができる。

1.2 研究の意義と方法

先行研究の中で、『伊豆の踊り子』の言葉、主題、人物、自然環境についての研究が多いが、翻訳の視角から見るこの小説を検討する論文は少ないのである。それゆえ、本稿では、『伊豆の踊り子』の訳本の中に、差異が大きいな二つの訳本を研究対象として、スコポス理論を援用し、二つの訳本に存在する差異を検討する。研究の方法としては、まず、原作と二つの訳本を十分に読み込んだ上で、二つの訳本の差異を見つける。次に、系統的にスコポス理論を用い、自然環境と人物描写二つの面から、、林少華の訳本と葉渭渠の訳本を比較し、各訳本の風格や特徴などを究明する。

2　スコポス理論

伝統的な翻訳理論では翻訳が簡単に語彙を等価する行為と見られている。そのゆえ、伝統的な翻訳理論の指導で、起点テキストと目標テキストの間での異文化差を無視してしまう可能性がかなり高いということがある。しかし、20世紀70年代から機能主義的翻訳理論①が伝統的翻訳理論の不足を補足した。機能主義的翻訳理論は学者のライス（Katharina Reiss）による発展し始め、その以降、何人もの学者に整われていた。ライスの生徒としてのフェルメール（Hans J. Vermeer）は、翻訳行為で最も重要なことは「翻訳の目的」だと考えていた。翻訳の時は、言葉の面にこだわるわけではなく、ある目的を含む人間活動、あるいわ異文化交流の行為として行わねばならないのである。これは、機能主義翻訳理論の核心であるスコポス理論のはじめと思われていた。フェルメールの一般翻訳理論の規則を三つの部分をスコポスルール、結束性ルール、忠実性ルールと分けていた。スコポスルール：翻訳というコミュニケーション行為は、目的（スコポス）により決まり、相手との関係に依存するものである。受容者は目的に含まれる重要な要素で、つまり、目的は受容者に依存するということである。結束性ルール：目標テクストが受容者の状況において十分に意味をなし、解釈可能であれば、その翻訳は成功したと言える。忠実性ルール：翻訳は起点テクスト[翻訳元言語テクスト]と関連する訳出を目指す。スコポス理論によれば、翻訳の方法と方略を決定するのは翻訳の予期の目的である。異なる文化が違っている風俗習慣や価値観を持っているので、翻訳行為は特定の文化環境において、翻訳の目的の指導で、翻訳を行わねばならないのである。スコポスルールを守るとする前提の翻訳の過程では、訳者は異文化の要素を考えて、受容者の受け入れやすい翻訳手段を決めている。いわば、機能主義翻訳理論のスコポス理論では何よりも翻訳の目的が一番重要で、結束性ルールと忠実性ルールはスコポスルールに従属するということである。スコポス理論は翻訳を人間行為の一つだと考え、文学翻訳だけではなく、通訳でも多くの翻訳行為に適用できる一般的な理論を目指す。伝統的な原文志向の等価理論の制限を突破し、機能主義翻訳理論の核心であるスコポス理論は、原文の単語や文章単位を等価する翻訳理論の不足を補足し、新しい視角から翻訳行為を説明し、翻訳理論の世界で新しい革命をもたらしたのである。

3　『伊豆の踊り子』について

3.1　『伊豆の踊り子』の紹介

『伊豆の踊子』は川端康成の初期の代表作として、1926年に『文芸時代』に載られた。川端康成が実生活の体験をもとにして第一人称の視点から、旅芸人一行との付き合いを題材に創作した。この作品が性格の歪んだ私の主人公が卑劣な心理で踊子に対しての肉欲的欲ばりから心理的浄化、精神的昇華を遂げた人性の更生おりを現した。作品において孤独や憂鬱な気分から逃れるために、伊豆へ一人旅に出かけた「私」は、修善寺から湯ケ島や天城峠を越えて湯ケ野、下田へと向かう旅芸人と道連れになったことにより、「踊子」によって代表される旅芸人一行からの好意や友情、人間的温情に感動して孤児根性に歪んでいた心が癒された。

3.2 『伊豆の踊り子』の二つの訳本について

川端康成は日本の新感覚派の代表作家で、大量な作品を創作した。ノーベル文学賞を受賞した日本人の作家である川端康成は日本だけでなく、世界中の広い範囲に好まれて、国際的に有名になっていた。彼の代表の作品が多国で出版されて、各国の訳者や学者の研究対象となった。20世紀80年代初期、中国において、川端文学のブームがいきなり巻き起こった[②]。それ以来、川端文学の翻訳が絶えなく出版されるようになってきた。『伊豆の踊り子』という代表作も何度と翻訳された。1996 年に、中国社会科学出版社によるり、葉渭渠の「川端康成文集伊豆の踊り子」が初めて出版された。それ以降、ほかの出版社がこの作品を何度も出版した。2011 年に、青島出版社により、林少華の訳文も出版された。上記の紹介からわかるように、葉渭渠の訳文は最初出版された訳文として、その価値は見逃せない。時代の流れとともに、言葉も変わっているわけで、林少華の訳文は最新の訳文として、過去の訳文と異なる点が最も多くのではないだろうか。だから、多くの訳文から、この二つの訳文を選んだのである。

4 スコポス理論から見た『伊豆の踊り子』の二つの中訳本の比較

本研究ではスコポス理論を基づき、葉渭渠と林少華の中訳文を自然環境と人物描写二つの面から比較する。

4.1 自然環境の面から見た実例の比較

例 1 「重なり合った山々や原生林や深い渓谷の秋に見とれながらも、私は一つの期待に胸をときめかして道を急いでいるのだった。」

叶译：“重叠的山峦，原始的森林，深邃的幽谷，一派秋色是在让人目不暇接。可是我的心房却在猛烈的跳动。因为一个希望在催促我赶路。”

林译：“重重叠叠的山峦，原森林，深谷的溪流——我出神的看着这山间秋色却又急急赶路——一种期待感使得胸口砰砰直跳。”

この文は主人公の私が旅芸人に会いたいという気持ちを持ちながら、道を急いでいる様子を表した。一人の旅で寂しく感じている主人公は旅芸人に好奇心を持って、彼らと道連れになれないかという期待で、周りの美しい景色を無視して、旅芸人の休んだ茶屋へ急いでいた。高く険しい山なみの自然環境は私の胸をときめかしている期待を強調した。林訳に「重なり合った山々や原生林や深い渓谷の秋」を「重重叠叠的山峦，原森林，深谷的溪流」とそのまま翻訳した。言語の意味から見ると、林訳は翻訳の忠実性を守った。換言すれば、起点テキストの言葉、形式を目標テキストでの最も似ていた表現で表した。文脈を分析すると、私が芸人たちを追いかけるために、秋の美しさを鑑賞する余裕もなかった。葉訳に三つの五字言語（重叠的山峦，原始的森林，深邃的幽谷）ガ大自然の壮大さを表している同時に、私の心の強い期待も表現してきた。語境の意味から見ると不安で緊張している雰囲気に、葉訳の勢い訳文が適切である。

例 2　「トンネルの出口から白塗りのさくに片側を縫われた峠道が稲妻のように流れていた。この模型のような展望の裾のほうに芸人たちの姿が見えた」

叶译：“山路从隧道出口开始，沿着崖边围上一道刷成白色的栏杆，像一道闪电似地伸沿过去，极目展望，山麓如同一副模型，从这里可以窥见艺人们的倩影。”

林译：“山路从隧道出口如同一道闪电沿着一侧白漆栅栏流淌下去，就在这模型般的远景下端，那伙艺人出现了。”

これは旅芸人が茶屋から出発した後、私が彼たちに追いかけていた時、前方から見る景色に対する描写である。その時、私が旅芸人と道連れになったわけではないが、旅をきつかけとして彼たちが付き合つてくれると期待しながら、道を急いでいた。不安でいても、何を期待していた微妙な気分で、周囲の景色も明るくかわつてきた。林訳は忠実に原文景色を訳出した。語彙も語順も全部原文のままに表現した。目標言語の受容者に起点テキストの言葉、形式などを直接に表現した。そうすると、受容者は起点言語を自分の慣用の言葉や語順だけではなく、新しい考え方で原文を理解できる。林訳と比べると、葉訳は意訳の翻訳手段を利用した。目標言語の受容者の立場から考えると、起点テキストを目標テキストに訳する過程で、語彙だけではなく、語順なども適度に調整した。例えば、原文の長い文を訳する時、いくつかの短い文で取り替えて、受容者にとつて、読みやすい形式を表した。原文の中で、「姿」という言葉があつた。『スーパー大辞林』によると、「姿」が人の体つき、外観からとらえた体の格好の意味である。葉訳は「倩影」という言葉を使つて、「姿」もとの意味を

表す上で、私が旅芸人に抱いた好意も自然に訳出した。旅芸人たちの前向きの状態が私を引き寄せた。そのため、つぎの旅は彼たちと体験するつもりで、道を急いでいた。

例 3　「秋空が晴れ過ぎたためか、日に近い海は春のようにかすんでいた。」

叶译：“秋空分外澄澈，海天相连之处，烟霞散彩恍如一派春色。”

林译：“也许因为秋天的天空晴过头了，靠近太阳的海面像春天一样烟雾蒸腾。”

この例文は私が道連れの旅芸人と一緒に旅の故郷の下田へ進んでいる過程で見た秋の景色であつた。、その時、しばらく海が見え隠レしていたが、彼たちの懐かしい故郷だから、親しんでいた。秋空もすつきり晴れて、海も春のように霞んで、明るい雰囲気か漂つていた。林訳は原文の語彙と語順を直接に翻訳した、原文を忠実して、目標源語の中での等価した言語を使つて、晴れ秋をそのまま描写下。目標言語の受容者にはこの直接に訳出した分を通して、原文の形を理解した上で描写された秋の景色の様子も想像できる。葉訳は林訳より、忠実性だけだはなく、結束性も考えに入れた、まずは、受容者の読む習慣を考えて、原文の長い文を短くした。次は、原文の言葉をこだわらないで、目標言語の中でもつとふさわしい言葉を探して、起点言語を翻訳した。晴れ空と霞んでいた海という美しい秋を受容者に真に迫つていて、生きているかのように正確に伝えられた。

4.2　人物描写の面から見た実例の比較

例 1　「踊子は十七くらいに見えた。私にはわからない古風の不思議な形に大きく髪を結つていた。それが卵型の凛々しい顔を非常に小さく見せながらも、美しく調和していた。」

叶译："舞女看上去约莫十七岁光景。她梳理一个我叫不上名字的大发髻，发型古雅而又奇特。这种发式把她那严肃的鹅蛋形脸庞衬托得更加玲珑小巧，十分匀称，真是美极了。"

林译："小舞女看上去十七八岁。头发梳得胀鼓鼓的，在我眼里形状古老得不可思议。尽管这使得她那清秀的鸭蛋形脸庞看起很小，却又相得益彰。"

この文は姿を描写したは。私には彼女の姿が絵姿のようで、不思議でも、美しく調和していた。それまでは、踊り子たちを二度見た私は彼女に朦朧な愛を抱いていた。例文の中で、「古風」という言葉は、『スーパー大辞林』によると、三つの意味がある。一つ、昔風の流儀や習慣、また、古めかしいさま。二つ、漢詩で、古詩。三つ、自派の俳諧を当流と呼んだ談林派が貞門派の俳諧をさしていつた。古流。ここでは、第一の意味が似ていた。葉訳の「古老」は「古風」の概念の意味から目標テキストの言葉で等価した言葉を用いた。すなわち、起点言語の「古風」をそのまま目標言語の「古老」と訳出した。充分に原文を忠実した。葉訳を分析すると，林訳より葉訳ほうがほかの意味が訳文に入っていた。「古雅」という語彙は古老の意味を表している他には、美しい、典雅などの感じがある。私には、踊り子髪型が古風な感じより、優雅さの印象が深かつた。目標言語の受容者に対して、必ず起点原文の等価した言葉を使うだけではなく、柔軟に適切な表現で、私の心理活動を忠実に表すことが大切である。だから、語境の視点から見ると、葉訳のほうがもつとふさわしい。

例 2　「若桐のように足のよく伸びた白い裸身を眺めて、私は心に清水を感じ、ほうっと深い息を吐いてから、ことこと笑った。子供なんだ。」

叶译："洁白的裸体，修长的双腿，站在那里宛如一株小梧桐。我看到这幅景象仿佛有一股清泉荡涤着我的心。我深深地吁了一口气，扑哧一声笑了。她还是个孩子呐。"

林译："望着她那双腿如小梧桐树一般笔直的白皙裸体，我觉得仿佛有一股清泉从心头流过，如释重负地深深呼了一口气，呵呵笑了起来。还是个孩子！"

この文は若桐のように足のよく伸びた白い裸身の踊子には、私は心で清水を感じて、頭がぬぐわれたように澄んで、微笑がいつまでもとまらなかつたという主人公の私の状態である。子供のような踊子は心からの明るい笑顔を「私」に見せて、心の汚れを拭いてくれた。清純無垢な踊子に対する「私」は彼女に肉体的欲望が一瞬感に消えて、邪念が完全に絶つて、心も浄化された。不幸な生い立ちで、孤児根性の本質を持っていた「私」は心が踊子の単純と素朴で癒されて、世間の純粋、美しさ、暖かさを感じた。「若桐のように足のよく伸びた白い裸身を眺めて、私は心に清水を感じ、ほうっと深い息を吐いてから、ことこと笑った。子供なんだ。」この例文では、子供のようなしぐさで私を呼んでいる単純な姿が私の前に突然現れた。林訳によると、直訳の翻訳方法で、その姿を直接に描写した。簡潔な言葉、同じ語順で原文を踊り子の天真爛漫の様子を描いた。林訳と違つて、葉訳が意訳の手段を使つて、目標言語の受容者の受け入れやすい表現で翻訳した。一つの文を句読点を使って、三つの文分けていた。つまり、長い文を短くして、もっと読みやすい形で表現した。受容者の状況において、もつと、原文の形をなし、理解できる訳文を訳出した。すなわち、スコポス理論の結束性を指導として、原文の伝えたい意味を忠実翻訳した上で、訳文の形式を目標言語の習慣のように訳出したのである。そういう美しい姿には私は心に清水を感じた。林訳は「流过」という言葉で私の心理活動を表しした。葉訳は「荡涤」という言葉を私の気持ちを訳出した。「荡涤」には流れるの意味が入っている。しかも汚れを洗い落とすという意味も含んでいる。その汚れは私が前に踊り子に対して起きた邪念を指していた。だから、ここは清水が私の心を流れるだけではなく、邪念の汚れも取り除いた。

例3 「乗船场に近づくと、海際にうずくまっている踊子の姿が私の胸に飛び込んだ。傍に行くまで彼女はじっとしていた。黙って头を下げた。」

叶译："快到码头，舞女蹲在岸边的倩影赫然映入我的心中。我们走到她身边以前，她一动不动，只顾默默地把头耷拉下来。"

林译："靠近码头的时候，蹲在海边的小舞女形象飞进我的胸口。直到我走到她身旁她也一动不动，只是低头不语。"

これは私との別れに対して、踊り子のがっかりした姿であった。短い旅だが、私は踊り子とお互いに朦朧な愛を生み出した。これからもう出会う機会がないと思ったら、前に一緒に作ったいい思い出も苦しく感じていた。だから、私に対して、いっぱいなことを話したくても話せない踊り子はただ黙って頭を下げた。林訳に「子の姿が私の胸に飛び込んだ」を「小舞女形象飞进我的胸口」と訳出した。この起点テキストと目標テキストを比較したら、翻訳の忠実性がわかっていた。訳文は完全に原文の言葉を目標言語での等価した言葉で取り替えた。目標言語の受容者にとっては、読む習慣と違ったが、よく考えると、作者の描写した場面が理解できる。林訳と比べると、葉訳は意訳の翻訳手段で原文を訳出した。また、この例文では、踊り子は私には単純で美しい様子を見せていた。葉訳の「倩影」という言葉は「姿」の優雅さを表現してきた。「飛び込む」は急いで中に入り込むという意味があるが、林訳の「飞进」より葉訳の「映入」は受容者にとって、理解しやすい。「映入」と「倩影」という目標言語は踊り子の美しい姿を生き生きと描写してきた。

5 結　論

本稿では、先行研究の成果を踏まえ、スコポス理論に基づいて、『伊豆の踊り子』二つの中訳本を比較研究した。例文を通して、原文の自然環境と人物描写という二つの面から考察検討した。スコポス理論を用いて、語彙、語順など面から訳文を比較する過程で、葉訳と林訳の間に異なる翻訳特徴も明らかに明確した。上述の例文の分析から見ると、同じ文学作品であるが、葉渭渠と林少華の中訳文が独自の特徴を持っている。林訳は原作の内容と形式などを大切にし、そのまま起点テキストの語彙と語順を翻訳した。すなわち、スコポス理論の視点から見れば、林訳が忠実性ルールを十分に守って、直訳の翻訳手段を利用した。受容者の場合には、林訳を読むと、原作の中に入った作者の創作風格と異文化の差がわかるようになるのではないだろうか。林訳に対して、葉訳では十分に訳者の創造力を発揮した。多種多様な美的な中国語の多用した。受容者の立場から考えた上で、原作の内容と形式を適当に調整して、起点テキストを翻訳した。異文化のため、異なる言語の間には、大きな差がある。そのゆえ、訳者は受容者に原作の内容や精神などを伝える過程では、最もふさわしい翻訳手段を選択する。葉訳のほうが、起点テキストを目標テキストに翻訳するには、受容者の読む習慣と中国語の特徴を考えて、意訳という翻訳手段を用いた。

目的性がスコポス理論の核心として、ほかの翻訳ルールを指導する。また、訳者が生活する社会環境、役者の知識と語学力などは翻訳の目的にも大きな影響を与える。本稿では、二つの中訳文を比較した結果、直訳の翻訳手段を利用する林訳と意訳を多用する葉訳は翻訳の目的の指導で、翻訳手段、翻訳風格などが異なる表現を表していた。

参考文献

[1] 卞建华. 传承与超越功能主义翻译目的论研究[M]. 北京：中国社会科学出版社，2008.
[2] 川端康成. 川端康成著作选释 《伊豆的舞女》《雪国》[M]. 林璋，王成注释. 北京：商务印书馆，2011.
[3] 川端康成. 伊豆舞女[日]川端康成著[M]. 林少华译. 青岛：青岛出版社，2011.
[4] 刘婧. 川端康成和《伊豆的舞女》[J]. 文学翻译，2008（10）.
[5] 卢娟. 林少华的“审美忠实”及其译作《伊豆舞女》[D]. 辽宁大学，2013.
[6] 吴文洁. 心灵的旅程——读川端康成《伊豆的舞女》[J]. 考试周刊，2016（79）.
[7] 相莉，徐凤. 论叶渭渠和林少华译《伊豆舞女》的翻译技巧[J]. 重庆第二师范学院学报，2008（3）.
[8] 叶渭渠. 川端康成文集伊豆的舞女[M]. 北京：中国社会科学出版社，1996.
[9] 张艳丽.《罗生门》与《鼻子》的汉译本对比研究基于功能目的论分析[D]. 沈阳师范大学，2014.

目的论视域下的励志性人物自传翻译策略探析
——以路英勇译《五体不满足》为例

张　娇

摘　要：汉斯·弗米尔是德国功能学派的主要代表人物之一。他提出的“目的论”将翻译研究从原文中心论的束缚中摆脱出来，为西方翻译理论做出了重要贡献。“目的论”的核心理念为：翻译的目的决定翻译的策略和方法。众所周知，励志性人物自传旨在通过作者的自身经历来感染、鼓舞读者。因此，励志性人物自传翻译不必拘泥于一字一句地对应，其主要目的是通过一些翻译手段使译文更加自然贴切、简单易懂，减少读者的“阅读障碍”，让其轻松地领略到文章精神所在。

本文以乙武洋匡著，路英勇译的励志性人物自传《五体不满足》为研究对象，从“目的论”的视角出发探析了其主要翻译策略。不难发现译者是在尊重原文的基础上，通过调整语言表达方式、增加修饰成分、将固有名词翻译得更加明确直白等手段来尽量消除译文“异质性”。

关键词：目的论；《五体不满足》；励志性人物自传翻译

1　绪　　论

关于“翻译”，有的人主张忠实于原文的一字一句。有的人却认为不应该拘泥于形式，表述自然，意思传达到即可。归根结底，这终究不过是一场以原文为中心的“直译”与“意译”之争。跳出这个单一的“怪圈”，德国功能派学者汉斯·弗米尔提出的“目的论”，将翻译研究从原文中心论的束缚中摆脱出来。他认为翻译的目的决定翻译的策略和方法。励志性人物自传旨在将作者的精神传达给每一位读者。接下来笔者将在“目的论”的视域下去浅析路英勇译的励志性人物自传《五体不满足》的翻译策略。

2　《五体不满足》简介

《五体不满足》被誉为“媲美《假如给我三天光明》的成长杰作”。该书由一位名叫乙武洋匡的日本人根据自身经历写成的自传。乙武洋匡生来就没有四肢，但是他以顽强的毅力和乐观的心态克服了行动上的不便，不仅能生活自理，还能写字、跑步、游泳、爬山、打球等，他脸上永远洋溢着灿烂自信的笑容。

1998 年 10 月，《五体不满足》于讲谈社（出版社名称）出版之后，以席卷之势登上日本各大畅销榜第一名，并创下日本史上单次加印 50 万册的最高纪录。在书中他写道：“身体障碍只意味着生活不便，绝非不幸！”他坚毅的性格和乐观的生活态度如同冬日暖阳温暖和鼓舞了万千读者。

《五体不满足》在日本刚出版后，次年在中国便出版了刘子倩译的面向台湾读者繁体中文版《五體不満足》。同年 9 月，山东文艺出版社又出版了郅颙译的简体中文版《五体不满足》。

由此可见《五体不满足》在中国也受到了极大的关注与欢迎。为了响应广大读者的要求，作者又在原来的基础上增加了内容，于 2001 年 4 月讲谈社又出版了《五体不满足完全版》。因此 2001 年以后出版的译本均是针对《五体不满足完全版》的翻译。为了更加直观清晰地将各大译本展现出来，笔者将其整理为如表 1 所示。

表 1

书名	语言	出版时间	出版社	译者
五體不滿足	繁体中文	1999 年	圆神出版社	刘子倩
五体不满足	简体中文	1999 年 9 月	山东文艺出版社	郅 颙
No One's Perfect	英语	2004 年	Kodansha（讲谈社）	不 详
五體不滿足完全版	繁体中文	2007 年 4 月	圆神出版社	刘子倩
五体不满足	简体中文	2010 年 9 月	南海出版社	路英勇

值得注意的是郅颙是路英勇的笔名，即时隔 11 年之后路英勇再次翻译了《五体不满足》，其中 2010 年出版的《五体不满足》获亚太 APPA（出版商协会）优秀奖。

目前国内针对励志性自传《五体不满足》翻译风格的研究几乎没有。刘子倩译的繁体中文版和路英勇译的简体中文版有何异同？路英勇 11 年之前译的《五体不满足》的翻译风格与十年之后又有怎样的对比？对此笔者怀有浓厚的兴趣。但是限于篇幅，暂且先以 2010 年 9 月南海出版社出版的路英勇译的简体中文版《五体不满足》为研究对象。从弗米尔的目的论视角出发去探析该人物传翻译的翻译策略。

3 目的论简介

Skopos 一词源自希腊语，意为“目标”或“目的”。该词于 20 世纪 70 年代由德国功能派学者汉斯·弗米尔引入翻译理论。弗米尔认为译文必须要符合预定的目的，即他所说的必须“功能充分”。因此，弄清楚翻译原文的目的以及译文的功能对于译者而言尤为重要。翻译“目的论”的核心就是“目的决定手段”。弗米尔提出的“目的论”中有以下三大原则。

3.1 目的原则

在弗米尔的三大原则中，目的原则是其首要原则。翻译的目的在于使译文在目标文化中发挥作用，并且能够以目标读者所期望的形式呈现，以满足他们的阅读需求。因此，翻译技巧与策略的选择是由翻译行为所要达到的目的决定的。

3.2 连贯原则

连贯原则强调译文必须符合译文读者的情况，为译文读者所理解。即译文必须将译文读者的需求、背景、文化水平考虑在内，让读者看得懂。

3.3 忠信原则

忠实原则强调原文和译本必须连贯，关注原文与译文之间的关系。虽然它要求译本应当忠实于原文，但强调其忠实的程度和形式仍然由翻译行为的目标以及译者对原文的理解所决定的。

4 《五体不满足》的写作意图

在《五体不满足完全版》（乙武洋匡 2001b）原文的后记中，其作者乙武洋匡写道：

「だからこそ，声を大にして言いたい。「障害を持っていても，ボクは毎日が楽しいよ」。健常者として生まれても，ふさぎ込んだ暗い人生を送る人もいる。そうかと思えば，手も足もないのに，毎日、ノ一天気に生きている人間もいる。関係ないのだ、障害なんて。

そうしたメセツジを伝えるためにも、この本のタイトルをあえて『五体不満足』という、少々、ショツキングなものとした。五体が満足だろうと不満足だろうと、幸せな人生を送るには関係ない。そのことを伝えたかつた。」①

（乙武洋匡 2001b：264）

由此可见，作者写《五体不满足》，旨在通过描述自己的亲身经历来鼓励每一位读者。这是作者的写作目的，同时也应是译者的翻译目的。目的论主张“翻译目的决定翻译策略和方法”。对于励志性的自传翻译更应如此，重要的是如上述提到的那样“译文必须将译文读者的需求、背景、文化水平考虑在内，让读者看得懂。”只有读者轻松读懂译文，才能领略到这部励志性人物自转的精神所在。接下来将从弗米尔的“目的论”视角出发，浅析路英勇译的人物自传《五体不满足》的翻译策略。

5 书名的翻译

由前文中的表 1 可知，此书的中文译本皆是借用日语原著的书名，直接将其翻译为“五体不满足”。对于“五体不满足”这个译名，在《咬文嚼字 2000 年第 4 期》杂志的“『五体不满足』要满足什么”一文中胡连荣写道：“封面上的《五体不满足》这个书名却十分让人费解，见过作者的人或许能猜出几分，因为他是个坐在轮椅上的残疾人。而对绝大多数中国读者来说，不读完全书恐怕无人能解其中味。”

日本权威辞书《广辞苑》中对“五体”解释如下：

①身体を構成する五つの部分。即ち筋・脈・肉・骨・毛皮、頭・両手・両足。または頭・頚・胸・手・足。転じて、全身。またその五つ部分からなる体。②書体で古文・大篆・小篆・八分・隷書の称。また、篆・隷・真・行・草。中文中有一个“五体投地”的成语，这里的“五体”即是指人的头和四肢。这与日语“五体”释义中的①相符合。大多数的中国读者或许能够猜测出“五体”所指意思。但是在中文中“满足”一词则常用于某种条件或者是某种需求得到满足的情况下。因此大多数的中国读者单看“五体不满足”这几个字是很难理解其含义的。然而日语中的“满足”还有“完整”的意思，“五体不满足”即“五体不完整”。但是绝大多数中国读者并不知道这一点。那为何中文译者均将其直接翻译为“五体不满足”呢。

胡连荣曾在这篇文章中提议将其翻译为“生命的奇迹”。这与路英勇以及刘子倩直接翻译

① （日）乙武洋匡著，路英勇译.《五体不满足》，南海出版社，2010 年 9 月. 路英勇译为：但我要大声宣告：“我是残疾人，但是我生活的每一天都是快乐的。”谁也不能否认，有的人身体健康，但他的人生却是忧郁昏暗的；有的人身有残疾，却拥有美好幸福的生活。人生与残疾毫无关系。”正是为了传达这种认识，我才把这本书起名为《五体不满足》。

的“五体不满足”哪个更好？笔者不敢妄加评论。但是，如上述作者乙武洋匡在后记中提到的那样，“五体不満足”这几个字虽然有些扎眼，但是他就是想要告诉大家生活是否幸福跟你身体是否完整毫无关系，所以故意将其命名为“五体不满足”。或许中文译者就是为了传达作者的这种意志，才将其原原本本地翻译为“五体不满足”。正如德国功能学派另一位重要学者克里斯蒂安·诺德所说的那样：“译文目的应与原文作者之目的兼容。”

6　正文翻译中的再创作

读完路英勇的译本，不难发现译者并不是完全对照着原文进行翻译，而是站在读者的角度，对译文做了一些调整，使其表达更加自然贴切、浅显易懂，以至于中国读者能够轻松地读懂译文。

6.1　语言表达方式的调整

将译文与原文进行比较之后，发现路英勇翻译时，对译文语言表达方式做出了调整，并经过一番润色，转换成更符合中文表达习惯的句子，如表 2 所示。

表　2

	原文	路英勇译	笔者译
例1	平凡な夫婦の、平凡な出産。	一位平凡的母亲，一次平凡的分娩	一对平凡夫妻的平凡生产
例2	自分のお腹を痛めて産んだ子供（乙武洋匡 2001b：4）	从自己身上掉下来的肉	自己经过阵痛生下的孩子
例3	真の厳しさとは、真の優しさである。（乙武洋匡 2001b：32）	严师如慈父	真正的严厉才是真正的温柔
例4	「チヨ、チヨツト待つて、何百人もあるんだから、そんなんじゃ誰が正しいかわからないんじゃないの」と先生が遮る。（乙武洋匡 2001b：94）	老师莫名其妙连忙否定说：“不行，不行！有好几百人呢，那样做，怎么能知道谁答得对，谁答得错？”	老师连忙打断说道：“等，等一下，因为有好几百人，若是那样做，不就不知道谁答正确了吗”

如表 2 所示笔者试图将上面四个例子对照原文进行直译，中国的读者虽然能读懂这样的直译，但总觉得这样的语言表达有些欠妥当。简而言之，一看译文就知道是被翻译过来的，带有浓浓的“翻译腔”。

反之，路英勇却将例 1、例 2 和例 3 分别翻译为：“一位平凡的母亲，一次平凡的分娩”“从自己身上掉下来的肉”“严师如慈父”，不仅将原文的意思传达到了，并在尊重原本意思的基础上进行了“再创作”，使其表达显得更为通畅自然，更加符合中国人的表达习惯。再如例 4 中的“チヨ、チヨツト待つて”是日本人用于打断别人说话时很典型的日式表达，直译为“等，请等一下”，因为日本人很少直接否定一个人的观点。而译者则是按中国人的说话方式将其翻译成“不行，不行”。此外，“そんなんじゃ誰が正しいかわからないんじゃないの”也是日语中一个很委婉柔和否定的表达方式。若是如笔者那样直译为“若是那样做，不就不知道谁

答正确了吗”，这对于中国人来说这句话是不完整的。而路英勇将其翻译为“那样做，怎么能知道谁答得对，谁答得错”则十分符合中国人直接明了的说话方式。

6.2 修饰成分的增加

表 3

	原文	路英勇译
例5	「オギャー、オギャー」火が付いたかのような鳴き声とともに、一人の赤ん坊が生まれた。元気な男の子だ （乙武洋匡 2001b：2）	“啊……啊……”像是被火烧着，痛苦的叫喊声急促而尖利。伴着叫喊，一个婴儿呱呱坠地：一个精神十足的男婴
例6	ボクの姿を見つけると、みんなアリのように群がってきた （乙武洋匡 2001b：15）	他们目不转睛地盯着我看，一会儿，我的周围就聚集了一大堆孩子，就像争抢食物的蚂蚁
例7	そんな親や先生方の心配をよそに、僕は必要以上に「たくましく」育っていくのだった…… （乙武洋匡 2001b：16）	由于父母和老师的悉心照料，我顺利地成长，健康地成长，生命的步伐坚实而轻快……

表 3 中有下画线（下画线由笔者注）的译文，在原文中均找不到与之对应的句子，这是译者在翻译时结合语境添加的修饰成分。若将例 5 中的“火が付いたかのような鳴き声”、例 6 中的“みんなアリのように群がってきた”、例 7 中的“「たくましく」育っていくのだった……”直译，则分别为“像被火烧着一样的啼哭声”“大家向蚂蚁一样向我围过来”“茁壮成长”。不难发现这样的直译未免有些“生硬干瘪”。而路英勇的译文中，则分别添加了“声急促而尖利”“像争抢食物的”“生命的步伐坚实而轻快”这样的修饰成分，使译文变得更加生动形象，更加符合中国人的阅读习惯。

6.3 固有名词的翻译

固有名词：名词下位分类的一种，指特定的人或事物所专有的名称，如人名、地名、国名、书名、公司名、团体名等，如表 4 所示。

表 4

	原文	路英勇译
例 8	江戸川区	东京江户川区
例 9	サリドマイド（乙武洋匡 2001b：2）	导致胎儿畸形的药物
例 10	雨のひなまつり （乙武洋匡 2001b：137）	雨中的三月三

表 4 例 8 中的地名“江戸川区”，直译则为“江户川区”。大多数中国读者单是看到“江戸川区”这四个大字，对其地理位置并无直观感受。然而当读者看到路英勇译的“东京江户川区”几个字时就会立刻知晓“江户川区”的大概位置，不至于对其茫然无知。例 9 中的“サ

リドマイド”，中文名称：酞胺哌啶酮，反应停①，是一种安眠药。若是直接将其译为酞胺哌啶酮或者反应停，由于日常生活中很少看到或者听到，想必大多数的读者很难知其意。反之译者将其翻译成“导致胎儿畸形的药物”，浅显易懂，也就消除了读者的阅读障碍。其次，例10中的“ひなまつり”是日本传统节日之一。即3月3日，有女孩子的人家搭设坛架，摆上偶人及其用具，供摆棱形年糕、白酒、桃花等的仪式。中文常将其译为“女儿节”。实际上此“女儿节”并非中国传统节日的“女儿节”。在中国，农历三月三日被认为是轩辕黄帝的诞辰，作为纪念便把这一天定为“上巳节”，又称之为“女儿节”。毕竟日本的“女儿节”与中国的“女儿节”有着本质的不同，若是将“ひなまつり”译为“女儿节”恐是缺乏严密性，或许译者正是基于这样的考虑，才直接将“ひなまつり”译为其举行时间“三月三”以保证其准确性，不给读者造成误解。

通过表2～表4中译文与原文对比的例子，不难发现译者在翻译的时候是站在目标语读者的角度，在保证准确性的基础上，对译文做出一些调整，进行了二次创作，使译文表达更加流畅自然、生动形象，以便读者能够轻松看懂译文。

7 结　　论

本文在目的论的指导下，对路英勇译的《五体不满足》译文进行了简单分析，发现相较于原文译文做了不少的改动。例如，将原文的语言表达方式进行调整使其转换为更为中式的表达、增加修饰成分使译文变得更加生动形象，更符合中国人的阅读习惯、将固有名词翻译得更加浅显易懂。总之，译者始终站在读者的角度，将读者的需求、背景、文化水平考虑在内，在注重准确性的同时进行了“再创作”。

综上所述，笔者认为励志性人物自传翻译与其他的人物自传和文学作品的翻译都有所区别。若是普通的人物自传翻译只需要准确无误的传达原文信息即可，若是文学作品翻译则是要保持原文的语言风格才不致使其文学性受损。但是励志性人物自传旨在通过作者自身经历来鼓舞读者，因此，翻译励志性人物自传时，为了让读者都能轻松看懂，领略其精神所在，做出一些调整、再创作是可行的。

参考文献

[1] 乙武洋匡. 五体不满足[M]. 東京：講談社，1998，10.

[2] 乙武洋匡. 五体不满足完全版[M]. 東京：講談社，2001，4.

[3] 乙武洋匡. 五体不满足[M]. 郅颙译. 济南：山东文艺出版社，1999.

[4] 乙武洋匡. 五体不满足[M]. 路英勇译. 海口：南海出版社，2010.

[5] 胡连荣. 《五体不满足》要满足什么[J]. 咬文嚼字，2000（4）.

[6] 吉米里·芒迪. 翻译学导论：理论与应用第三版[M]. 李德凤等译. 北京：外语教学与研究出版社，2014：117-120.

[7] 马万平. 析汉斯·费米尔的目的论[J]. 语文学刊·外语教育教学，2010（3）.

① 西德开发的一种安眠药，现已证实妊娠初期服用该药，会产生海豹肢体症等畸形（短肢畸形）儿，目前已禁止制造和使用。

从《罗生门》中文译本看翻译策略和原因
——比较鲁迅译本和林少华译本

李杨红

摘　要： 芥川龙之介是日本大正时代具有代表性的作家之一，在日本近代文学史上占有重要的位置。芥川龙之介的处女作《罗生门》在中国为人们所熟知，曾被19位作家翻译。最早的中文译本是1921年鲁迅翻译的版本，而出版次数最多的则是林少华版本。

本论文首先对《罗生门》的鲁迅和林少华的译本进行了具体的比较，分析各自使用的翻译策略。然后根据两译本所处的时代背景和译者的翻译观，探明各自选用不同翻译方略的原因。

关键词： 罗生门；鲁迅；林少华；翻译策略；原因

1　はじめに

芥川竜之介は日本の大正時代に活躍した「新思潮派」の代表的な作家であり、日本近代文学史において重要な地位を占めている。1915年に発表した短編小説『羅生門』は芥川竜之介の処女作であり、芥川龍之介の諸作品で最も有名である。『羅生門』は平安時代を背景とした作品である。天災地変に襲われた平安京は人影もないが、主人から暇を出されて途方に暮れた下人が一人羅生門で雨宿りをする。死人ばかりの羅生門の中である老婆が飢え死にしないように女の死体から髪の毛を抜き、かつらをつくろうとしている。下人はその老婆の着物をはぎ取って夜の闇に消えていく。この物語は資本主義社会の醜さを暴き出し、利己主義を皮肉に表現している。簡潔な言葉を通じて、恐ろしい環境や登場人物の動作と心理を生き生きと描写した。まさに日本の優れた短編小説の代表作である。

『羅生門』は多くの国の言語に翻訳されており、中国に紹介されてからすでに19種類の中国語訳が出版されている。この数は中国における『羅生門』の魅力を肯定し、中国に読者が多いことへの裏付けになるだろう。最初に出版されたのは魯迅の中国語訳（以下魯訳と略す）である。魯訳は1921年6月に「晨報副刊」に載せられ、1923年には『現代日本小説集』に収録された。そして、再出版の回数が最も多く、現在広く読まれているのは林少華による中国語訳（以下林訳と略す）である。1997年に漓江出版社から出版されて以来、何回も再出版された。したがって、本研究では中国初の中国語訳である魯訳と再出版の回数が最も多い林訳を研究対象として取り上げる。

翻訳回数が多いだけ『羅生門』に関する研究も盛んに行われてきた。中国語訳をめぐる研究も多数ある。例えば、洪（2017）はイデオロギーという要因から『羅生門』の林少華と魯迅の中国語訳の翻訳プロセスを研究した。翻訳は特定の社会の下で行われる行為であるため、その社会の歴史コンテクスト、文化及びイデオロギーの影響を受けると指摘された。邵（2017）はスコポス理論に基づき、『羅生門』の異なる時代の魯迅、楼適夷、林少華の中国語訳を比較し、意味伝達の状況によりスコプス理論の効果に達したかどうかを検討した。これらの先行研究には、魯迅と林少華の翻訳特徴を論じたものは見られたが、その原因に注目した研究が少ないと言えよう。したがって、翻訳者の置かれた時代背景と翻訳観を踏まえ、その原因を究明するのが本稿の目的である。

2　魯訳と林訳の比較分析

本節では、主に文章の基本をなす語彙とセンテンスのレベルから代表的な例を取り上げ、比較分析し、魯訳と林訳の翻訳方略を検討する。

2.1　語彙の翻訳

魯訳と林訳から翻訳が異なる語彙を探し出し、以下の表にまとめた。

番号	原文	魯訳	林訳
1	（蟋蟀）一匹	一匹	一只
2	市女笠	市女笠（注释：市女笠是市上的女人或商女所戴的笠子）	高斗笠
3	揉烏帽子	揉乌帽子（注释：乌帽子是男人的冠，若不用硬漆，质地较为柔软的，便称为揉乌帽子）	三角软帽
4	胡麻	胡麻	芝麻
5	面皰	面疱	粉刺
6	検非違使	检非违使（注释：古时的官，司追捕，纠弹，裁判，诉讼等事）	按察使
7	帯刀	带刀（注释：古时春宫坊的侍卫之称）	禁军
8	仏具	佛具	祭祀用品
9	旧記	旧记	旧书记载
10	平安朝	平安朝（注释：西历七四九年以后的四百年间）	平安年间（注释：平安时期，日本古代断代史之一，从 794 年迁都平安京（现京都）开始，持续 400 年）
11	足音	足音	蹑手蹑脚
12	檜皮色	桧皮色	柏树皮色
13	菜料	菜料	做菜

この表を見ると、二つの中国語訳で翻訳が最も異なる語彙は日本独特な文化を反映した漢字語彙が半分を占めている。魯訳は殆ど原文から漢字語彙をそのまま借用し、それに日本独特な語彙には注を付け、その意味を補足した。それに対し、林訳は現代中国語に既存する言葉に置き換えた。また、注をつけたのは「平安朝」一つだけである。

いくつか例をあげる。例えば、「蟋蟀が一匹とまっている」での「匹」は、日本語では獣、鳥、魚、虫など体の大きな動物から小さな動物までを数える助数詞であるが、中国語の「匹」は古くから主に馬など大型の動物を数える助数詞として使われる。魯訳は日本語の助数詞をそのまま借用し、「蟋蟀」のような小型の昆虫に使っている。林訳は「匹」を現在昆虫など小さな体の動物によく使われる「只」に訳した。

原文：羅生門が、朱雀大路にある以上は、この男のほかにも、雨やみをする市女笠や揉烏帽子が、もう二三人はありそうなものである。

魯訳：这罗生门，既然在朱雀大路上，则这男子之外，总还该有两三个避雨的市女笠（注）和揉乌帽子（注）的。

林訳：其实这罗生门位于朱雀大路，按理，除他以外，也该有两三个头戴高斗笠或三角软帽的避雨男女。

「市女笠」と「揉烏帽子」は平安時代から現れた日本上流社会の服飾である。「市女笠」とは、女性が外出時に使った頂に高い布子のある菅の笠であり、「揉烏帽子」とは、薄く漆を塗って柔らかにもんだ男性が被った烏帽子を指すように、「市女笠や揉烏帽子」は単なる服飾だけではなく、女性と男性がいることも示唆している。これらの語彙は日本独特の表現であるため、中国語には正確に対応する語彙がない。魯訳は二つの語彙をそのまま借用し、注釈で笠と帽子の形と使用者の性別までを説明している。林訳では「市女笠」を「高斗笠」に、「揉烏帽子」を「三角軟帽」に訳しているので、性別は表示されていないが、センテンスの最後に「避雨男女」と説明を入れている。つまり、「市女笠や揉烏帽子」をまず一般的な表現に翻訳し、後で「男女」がいることを補足したが、どれが男性用でどれが女性用であるかについては明示されていないため、原作とは異なる雰囲気を出していると考えられる。

「それが胡麻をまいたようにはっきり見えた」の「胡麻」はゴマ科の一年草のことである。中国では現在林訳のように「芝麻」としか知られていないが、資料を調べたところ、唐の時代までは「胡麻」として使われた記録が残されている。魯訳は「胡麻」をそのまま引用しているが、古典に詳しい知識人たちには「胡麻」の意味を正確に読み取ったのではないかと推測する。

他の語彙の解釈は、紙面の関係で割愛する。

2.2 センテンスの翻訳

次は、センテンスレベルから魯訳と林訳の翻訳を比較する。

例1 ある日の暮れ方のことである。一人の下人が、羅生門の下で雨やみ　を待っていた。

魯訳：是一日的傍晚的事。有一个家将，在罗生门下待雨住。

林訳：暮色时分，罗生门下。一个仆人正等待雨的过去。

これは作品の冒頭で、雰囲気が決まる重要な場面である。魯訳は原文の読点の位置をそのまま移し、原文の語彙を最大限に再現したため、日本語と中国語本来の特徴と構造による語順の差はあるものの、原文と中国語訳では語彙がほぼ一対一に対応している。さらに、主語省略が目立つのが日本語の特徴であるが、魯訳ではその特徴も踏襲され、「是一日的傍晚的事」と主語がない表現になっている。中国語として自然な文章とは言えない。その一方で、林訳は原文の語順を調整し、「罗生门下」を前に移して、物語の時間と場所を印象づけている。また、物語の時間と場所がそれぞれ四字からなっているため、対句のようなリズムを作り出しており、中国語の言い方に適し、簡潔でインパクトがある。

例2　下人の眼は、その時、はじめてその死骸の中に蹲っている人間を見た。桧皮色の着物を着た、背の低い、痩せた、白髪頭の、猿のような老婆である。

魯訳：那家将的眼睛，在这时候，才看见蹲在死尸中的一个人。是穿一件桧皮色衣服的，又短又瘦的，白头发的，猴子似的老妪。

林訳：仆人的眼睛这是才看清死尸中间蹲有一个人，一个身穿丝柏树皮色衣服的白发老太婆，又瘦又矮，混如猴子。

これは下人が初めて老婆に会い、外見を描写した文である。下線を引いた文には日本語の特徴が二つ反映されている。一つは主語の省略で、もう一つは「老婆」の前に五つの節からなる長い修飾語がついたことである。日本語は膠着語で、語順が比較的自由であるため、主語の省略が多く、長い連体修飾語がつけられることが多い。魯訳は原文のように、主語が省略され、「桧皮色の着物を着た、背の低い、痩せた、白髪頭の、猿のような」にあたる中国語が連体修飾語として「老婆」の前に使われている。林訳はまず、二つのセンテンスを一つのセンテンスにし、文のつながりを強めている。また、五つの節からなる連体修飾語のうち、「桧皮色の着物を着た」だけを修飾語として残し、残りの四つは「老婆」の後で述語として表現している。中国語は日本語と異なり孤立語であるため、語順と構造が厳密であり、長い連体修飾語がつくことがまれである。林訳は中国語の習慣に合わせるように調整し、巧妙に老婆のイメージを描いている。

例3．云わばどうにもならない事を、どうにかしようとして、とりとめもない考えをたどりながら、さっきから朱雀大路にふる雨の音を、聞くともなく聞いていたのである。

魯訳：说起来，便是抱着对于没法办的事，要想怎么办的一种毫无把握的思想，一面又并不听而自听着那从先前便打着朱雀大路的雨声。

林訳：也就是说要为根本无法可想之事而想方设法。他一边沉浸在漫无边际的思绪里，一边似听非听地听着朱雀大路持续已久的雨声。

例3　では、魯訳は原文に倣い、一つの文に翻訳された。また、「どうにかしようとして」、「聞くともなく聞いていた」はそのまま中国語に当てているように思われる。林訳は「想方设法」や「似听非听」の四字熟語で訳し、中国語としての洗練さが表現されている。

以上のように、魯訳と林訳を比較すると、魯迅は直訳という方略をとり、林少華は意味伝達と中国語としてのロジックを重要視する意訳をとっていることが分かる。直訳とは、外国語を別言語に翻訳する際に、原文の文法構造にこだわり、起点言語と目的言語が一対一の対応関係をなし、原文の表現の特徴をできる限り再現しようとする。意訳とは、原文の一語一語に拘らず、作者の意図するところや起点言語の聞き手の心に起きるはずのことを深く理解し、その中身をできるだけ忠実に再現しようとした翻訳だと言える。筆者の統計では、魯訳ではほぼ98パーセントの文が直訳という翻訳方略を用い、林訳では86パーセント近くの文が意訳の翻訳方略を使うことが明らかになった。魯訳は原文の字句や文法に忠実に翻訳し、漢字語彙をそのまま借用し、センテンスの順番と読点の位置が原作とほぼ同じである。魯迅は表現上の特徴を失わないという前提に立ち、注を付ける形で意味伝達も重要視している。その一方、林少華の中国語訳は原文の字句や文法に拘らず、原文を読み解き、それが中国人読者に伝わるように、日本文化を表す語彙は中国に既存する似たような表現に入れ替えた。センテンスの順番を変え、四字熟語など豊かな表現を多用し、中国語として洗練された文章に翻訳した。林訳は語彙の表現が豊富であり、語彙の処理が巧みであり、表現が洗練、流暢である。

3　原因の分析

翻訳は真空状態で行われる行為ではなくて、特定な時代の中で作り上げた作品であると言えよう。同一作品でも時代により、また翻訳者により異なる作品として現れることがある。つまり、時代が異なると、翻訳に求めるものが異なり、翻訳者が異なると、翻訳に対する態度と目的も異なると考えられる。したがって、本節では、主に翻訳が行われた時代背景、及び翻訳者の翻訳観を踏まえて、魯訳と林訳が異なる翻訳方略を取った原因を解明する。

3.1　魯訳の時代背景と魯迅の翻訳観

魯迅の中国語訳は1921年6月14日に「晨報副刊」に掲載された。当時、中国では陳独秀を中心に優秀な知識者が新文化運動を提唱した。外国文化を吸収し、中国の古い文化を改造し、外国文学を大いに引き受けるということである。国家存亡の危機に際し、日本に留学した魯迅は医者をやめて一生文学に携わり、文学を手段として中国人を無知から救ようと思った。このような背景の下で、魯迅は積極的に翻訳を行った。魯迅の本格的な翻訳は1909年の翻訳小説集『域外小説集』から始まった。直訳を試みた画期的な翻訳作品集である。それ以降、魯迅は「寧信而不順」(すらすら読めることよりも寧ろ忠実であること)を中心とする翻訳観を確立し、直訳の翻訳方法を主張した。できるだけ原文に忠実し、エキゾチックを保ち、決して中国人の固有な考え方と読者の好みに合わせるために削除したり書き直したりしない。原著の権威を取り出し、外国文化の吸収や中国の固有文化の改造に大きな役割を果たした。

また、魯迅は中国語と外国語の比較を通じて、中国語の紛らわしい語彙と厳密ではない文法が外国の思想と文化を受け入れるのを妨げると指摘した。中国語自体の「欠陥」を変えるために、外国語の語彙や文型をそのまま中国語に導入し、最大限に白話文を普及させようとした。したがって、魯迅は直訳、さらには硬訳を提案した。つまり、「硬訳」だと、元々のニュアンスも失わず、固有の文型に新しい要素を添え加え、外来文化を自分のものにすることが可能になる。(魯1930年3月1日に、発表した「『硬訳』と『文学の階級性』」)。

3.2　林訳の時代背景と林少華の翻訳観

林少華は1997年に『羅生門』の中国語訳を完成した。改革開放のおかげで中国が様々な領域において急激な発展を遂げた時期である。市場経済により、生活が豊かになり、外国文学や文化に興味を持つ人が大勢現れた。出版社は販路を打開するために、読者の好みに合わせて外国の名著を中国に紹介してきた。林訳は1997年に漓江出版社から出版されて以来、何回も再翻訳、再出版されてきた。

林少華は『ノルウェーの森』の翻訳者としても知られており、美しい中国語で翻訳するのがその特徴である。『羅生門』の中国語訳においても四字熟語を多用し、中国語として自然で流暢な翻訳文を作り上げた。林少華は中国古典に造詣が深く、漢字がこの世で最も美しい文字だと考えている。さらに、翻訳については、硬い翻訳調を好まず、銭鍾書が提案した「化」を推賞する。「化」とは原文の深層の感情をよく理解した上で、自分の言葉に変えて読者に伝えることである。目標言語の読者に翻訳された作品であることを意識させないような翻訳文を求めている。（林1998年1月に、発表した『「和臭」要不得』）。

また、林少華は四字熟語を多用し、美しい中国語に翻訳した原因を次のように指摘した。日本文学はまるで味が薄い日本料理のように薄いからこそ美しいのである。もし、中国語訳が日本と同じく薄いなら、中国人は必ずしも美しいと思わないだろう。薄い味を好む日本と好まない中国との間に存在する美意識の格差を縮めるために、可能の範囲で調整した（林2013年に、発表した『落花之美』）。林訳は中国と日本との美意識の格差を埋めるために、中国人読者の好みに適する読みやすい文章を作り上げたといえよう。

4 終わりに

以上のように、魯訳と林訳を比較すると、それぞれ直訳と意訳の翻訳方略を取ったことが判明した。新文化運動直後に翻訳された魯訳は外来文化を吸収し、中国語の「欠点」を補うために直訳を行った。その一方、改革開放以降、中国が急速に発展した時期に翻訳された林訳は、読者の需要を重要視し、より多くの読者に日本文学を読んでもらうために意訳を行った。また、中国古典に造詣が深く、翻訳調を好まず、美しい翻訳文を好む林少華の翻訳観も反映されている。

参考文献

[1] 单海林. 直訳手法から見る魯迅の異化翻訳:『羅生門』の中国語訳の比較を通して[J]. 東アジア日本語教育日本文化研究，2015（18）：351-369.

[2] 洪分芳. 論意識形態対『羅生門』両個漢訳本的操控[J]. 広州外語外貿大学，2017.

[3] 芥川竜之介. 文春文庫[M]. 日本：文藝春秋，1997.

[4] 芥川竜之介. 罗生门[M]. 林少华译. 桂林：漓江出版社，1997.

[5] 芥川竜之介. 罗生门[M]. 林少华译. 上海：上海译文出版社，2010.

[6] 林少華.「和臭」要不得——村上春樹文集翻訳随筆[J]. 出版広角，1998（1）：63-64.

[7] 林少华. 落花之美[M]. 青岛：青岛出版社，2013.

[8] 魯迅. 萌芽月刊[M]. 上海：光華書局，1930.

[9] 南海.『羅生門』の九種の漢訳文をめぐって[J]. 福井大学教育地域科学部紀要，2014，5：25-34.

[10] 邵雷宇. 従目的論看『羅生門』的漢訳——以魯迅・楼適夷・林少華訳本為例[D]. 華中師範大学，2017，5.

[11] 许渊冲. 翻译的艺术[M]. 北京：五洲传播出版社，2006：31-34.

[12] 谢飒. 浅议鲁迅的翻译思想[J]. 短篇小说：原创版，2012（12）：21-22.

[13] 止庵. 现代日本小说集[M]. 北京：新星出版社，2006，12.

浅析日本电影片名的翻译方法

樊一霖

摘　要：近年来，随着中日交流的日益频繁，许多经典优质的日本电影被陆续引进国内电影市场。电影不仅是人们娱乐、消遣的手段，也是了解该国家风土人情和民族文化的方式之一。电影片名是电影内容的高度浓缩，而且电影片名中带有本国特有的文化印记。对于外国电影来说，一个翻译精准巧妙的片名非常重要，促使日本电影在我国得到良好的发展，带动我国电影市场的国际化就应该重视包括片名在内的电影翻译。本论文整理了近 5 年（2013—2018）中国官方引进并且已经上映或正在排档的日本电影共计 40 余部，分类和分析我国在引进日本电影时所采用的翻译方法，总结了我国引进的日本电影片名的翻译现状。

关键词：日本电影；片名；翻译方法

Abstract: In recent years, with the increase of Sino-Japanese exchanges and economic development, many classic Japanese films have been introduced to the domestic film market in order to meet the spiritual and cultural needs of the public. For foreign films, a precise and skillful translation of the title is particularly important. It is not only a means of entertainment, but also a way to understand the local conditions and customs of the country and it's national culture. There is different cultural background and linguistic expression habits between China and Japan, thus the title of the film has its own unique cultural imprint. Therefore we should attach importance to the translation of film titles so as to make Japanese films gain their popularity and to promote the internationalization of the Chinese film market .This thesis collates 40 Japanese films which have been introduced by the Chinese authorities in the past five years（2013—2018）. Trying to analyzes the translation methods adopted by the Chinese authorities and study the translation of foreign film titles introduced into China in the past five years.

Key words: Japanese film; film title; translation method

1 引　言

近年来，随着频繁的国际交流和电影行业的蓬勃发展，许多经典优质的日本电影被陆续引进到国内电影市场。如今，外国影视作品不仅是人们娱乐、消遣的手段，也是了解该国家的风土人情和民族文化的方式之一。一部外国电影能否被接受和认可，除了电影的主题是否能够吸引中国的观众这一因素外，包括电影片名在内的翻译质量也不容忽视。促使日本电影在我国得到良好的发展，带动我国电影市场的国际化就应该重视包括片名在内的电影翻译。借助良好的片名翻译增强受众群体对电影的初步观感，增强日本电影对观众的吸引力，为日本电影经济、社会效益的实现提供相应的保障。那么，如何翻译出一个好的电影片名着实考验译者的语言功底和文化素养。

2 电影片名的特点

电影是一种大众的艺术，服务对象是广大观众，而不是少数专家，因此片名尽量使用通俗易懂的词汇，避免使用晦涩艰僻的词语词汇，或者专业性过强的术语。同时，为了保证高票房和收视率，片名需要足够的吸引力，使观众产生浓厚的兴趣。

首先，近年来日本上映的电影片名不会局限于长度，如『昼顔』仅有两个汉字的电影，也有如『打ち上げ花火、下から見るか？横から見るか？』较长的电影片名。

其次是句式，既有如『8年越しの花嫁』最为常见的句式，也有疑问句式，如『打ち上げ花火、下から見るか？横から見るか？』。

最后是片名所使用的语言，常见的是汉字，或汉字加假名，还有一部分采用了英文或外来语。如『シン・ゴジラ』『サバイバルファミリー』『Kingsglaive Final Fantasy XV』『ONE PIECE FILM GOLD』『BORUTO -NARUTO THE MOVIE-』等。

中国电影的片名很少使用英语或音译词汇。汉语博大精深，汉字具有强大的组词功能，因此仅仅使用汉字足以表达电影的内涵。

中国电影片名使用成语较多。成语式片名可以分为两种表现形式：一种是完全使用原成语作为片名，不做任何改动，如《邪不压正》（2018）、《英雄本色》（2018）、《金蝉脱壳》（2013）、《后会无期》（2014）等，这些四字成语已为广大观众所熟悉，在电影片名中加以运用，很容易引起观众的兴趣和认同；另一种是对原成语中的个别字、词进行替换或改动，我们且称之为成语式结构的变式，如：《猛虫过江》（2018）（改编自猛龙过江）、《剩者为王》（2015）（胜者为王）、《胆笑心惊》（2018）（胆战心惊）、《梦寐以球》（2018）（梦寐以求）等，这些四字成语的变式为电影作品提供了丰富的象征意味，为观众创造了广阔的联想空间，同时也增添了片名的趣味性。

3 日本电影片名的翻译方法

为了研究日本电影片名的翻译特点和翻译现状，笔者调查了2013—2018年10月中国官方引进并且已经上映或正在排档的日本电影，共计40部。在这里将按照其翻译方法进行分类分析。

3.1 直译

近五年中国引进40部日本电影中，有25部电影的片名采用了直译如表1所示。

近年来的日本电影片名多采用直译的方法。所谓直译，指日语和中文的单词和表达基本对应。如，『名探偵コナン ゼロの執行人』《名侦探柯南：零的执行人》、昼顔《昼颜》等都是逐字逐句对日文进行翻译，未进行任何加工与修改。而『8年越しの花嫁』译为《跨越8年的新娘》，日语和中文也基本对应，只是因为中文和日语之间的差异致使语序略有变动而已。

究其原因，首先，近年来中日交流频繁，日本电影在国内拥有较高的人气，有着较强的观众基础，观众能够看懂、明白其含义。其次，中日两国在悠长的历史进程中相互借鉴相互交融，使得两国的语言、文化、风俗等方面存在许多共同点，比如，使用汉字，即使直译也能够清晰地表达原名想表达的含义和韵味。直译还能够保存原作的手法，因而能达到与原文近似的语言效果，更好地传达原作的“异域风味”。

表 1

原名	译名	原名	译名
8年越しの花嫁	跨越8年的新娘	メアリと魔女の花	玛丽与魔女之花
名探偵コナン ゼロの執行人	名侦探柯南：零的执行人	ポケモン・ザ・ムービー XY&Z ボルケニオンと機巧のマギアナ	精灵宝可梦：波尔凯尼恩与机巧的玛机雅娜
今夜、ロマンス劇場で	今夜在浪漫剧场	名探偵コナン 業火の向日葵	名侦探柯南：业火的向日葵
シン・ゴジラ	新哥斯拉	聲の形	声之形
GODZILLA 怪獣惑星	哥斯拉：怪兽行星	銀魂	银魂
万引き家族	小偷家族	ドラえもん のび太の南極カチコチ大冒険	哆啦A梦：大雄的南极冰冰凉大冒险
サバイバルファミリー	生存家族	君の名は	你的名字
昼顔	昼颜	名探偵コナン 純黒の悪夢	名侦探柯南：纯黑的恶梦
ちびまる子ちゃん イタリアから来た少年	樱桃小丸子：来自意大利的少年	寄生獣	寄生兽
クレヨンしんちゃん 爆睡！ユメミーワールド大突撃	蜡笔小新：爆睡！梦境世界大突击	寄生獣 完結編	寄生兽：完结篇
ドラえもん 新·のび太の日本誕生	哆啦A梦：新·大雄的日本诞生	聖闘士星矢 Legend of Sanctuary	圣斗士星矢：圣域传说
ビリギャル	垫底辣妹	STAND BY ME ドラえもん	哆啦A梦：伴我同行
Kingsglaive Final Fantasy XV	最终幻想15：王者之剑		

此外，还有两个特殊的直译，第一个是『ビリギャル』，中文官方译为《垫底辣妹》，虽然词意、语序都和原名一样，但是在“妹”前加了“辣”字，更加切合影片中女主人公由原来的不良少女改头换面变成努力学习的好学生，人物形象的反差较大，更能够凸显辣妹逆袭的电影主题。

第二个则是『STAND BY ME ドラえもん』《哆啦A梦：伴我同行》和『Kingsglaive Final Fantasy XV』《最终幻想 15：王者之剑》。翻译遵循了原文的词意，但是却把片名的前后两个单词调换顺序，换了顺序后更加符合汉语的语序，把观众已经知道的信息放在前面，更能突出是系列影片中的一部。

3.2 明晰化

明晰化作为一种翻译中的普遍现象，指将源语中可以通过上下文语境推导出的隐含信息表达出来，使译文更加明确。明晰化策略指在翻译过程中，将源语信息中隐含信息、抽象信息，或由于文化或作者行文风格等差异造成理解困难的信息以更清楚的方式呈现出来，使用这一策略能使译文更易于理解，共有5部影片采用了明晰化策略。

例1 『ドラえもん のび太の宝島』

影片以加勒比海为舞台，讲述了为了寻找大航海时代海盗们隐藏的梦幻宝藏，大雄和小伙伴们极其巧合地在太平洋中心找到一座藏有金银财宝的新的岛屿，从而展开了宏大的冒险。

这部电影官方译名为《哆啦A梦：大雄的金银岛》，乍一看仿佛是简单的直译，但实际上，将“宝島”译成“金银岛”。若单纯地搬来汉字直译为“宝岛”，很有可能会在一定程度上引起大家的误解，因为在我国，提起“宝岛”两字，很多人的第一印象可能便是“宝岛台湾”或“藏有宝物的岛屿”。而“金银岛”，顾名思义，让人感觉是有着金银财宝的岛屿，更加切合电影内容。“金银岛”结合电影内容进行调整，表达得更加清楚明白。

例2 『三度目の殺人』

电影讲述的是精英律师重盛为30年前就有前科的杀人犯辩护，做好败诉的心理准备后，他却在与当事人接触过程中发现他动机不足，怀疑他不是真凶而展开的故事。

这部电影在中国的官方译名为《第三度嫌疑人》。若按日文片名直译来则应该是“第三次的杀人”，从“杀人”变成“嫌疑人”，了解电影内容，不难发现使用了明晰化策略。从剧情简介中可以看出，三隅虽然曾经有过前科，但在此次案件中并非真正的凶手，给出的三版证词也是一直在改变，这只能算是我们所说的“嫌疑人”，但若译为“第三次杀人”，则会让观众认为这个人杀过三次人，产生误解。

例3 『BORUTO -NARUTO THE MOVIE-』

官方译名为《火影忍者剧场版：博人传》。该影片是《火影忍者》的第11部剧场版作品，围绕漩涡鸣人和宇智波佐助一代忍者的后辈在经历历练、突破重重困难中成长并且和父辈一起战胜新的敌人大筒木桃式和大筒木金式的故事。

《火影忍者》是一部中国观众并不陌生的动漫，堪称“90后”的童年回忆之一。但是绝大多数的中国观众都不知道其日语名字，更别提英文名称了。把英文“NARUTO”翻译为中文“火影忍者”能够让观众清楚这是哪个系列的影片。此外，在翻译“BORUTO”这个单纯的人名时加了“传”字，便能够清楚地让中国观众明白这是围绕剧中的一个人物博人展开的故事。

例4 『ドラゴンボールZ 復活のF』

官方译名为《龙珠Z：复活的弗利萨》。该片是鸟山明的漫画作品《龙珠》的第19部剧场版动画，讲述了悟空与贝吉塔等众人开始了与弗利萨的宿命之战。与上面提到的《火影忍者剧场版：博人传》同为中国观众熟知的动画的剧场版。“ドラゴンボール”自然是译为大家熟知的“龙珠”；“復活のF”译为“复活的弗利萨”，即“F”改为人名“弗利萨”。抽象的字母“F”可以有多种解读方式，可以是暗号，或某种标记，或某个人物的代号。“弗利萨”一目了然，就是反派的名字，能够使观众了解影片出场的人物。

例5 『ONE PIECE FILM GOLD』

该片是《航海王》系列的第13部剧场版，讲述了路飞率领的草帽海贼团在黄金城遭到了算计，索隆被抓，为了救索隆，草帽一伙展开了与黄金城统治者泰佐洛对决的故事。

官方译名为《航海王之黄金城》。通过对该系列之前的了解，“ONE PIECE”可以轻松地译为“航海王”，而“GOLD”直译过来则是“黄金”，若译为“航海王之黄金”则会让观众感到困惑。而结合影片内容可知，“GOLD”是一座城堡的名字，而影片讲述的也是在黄金城发生的故事。那么译为“航海王之黄金城”十分合理。此外，日语片名中的“FILM”在翻译过程中被删去了。电影院放映的即是电影，因此不必强调是“FILM”。如果加上“电影版航海王之黄金城”，反而有些累赘，此处使用的则是接下来要阐述的减译法。

3.3 减译

减译指删去不符合目标语思维习惯、语言习惯和表达方式的词，以避免译文累赘冗长，有 4 部影片使用了减译的翻译方法。

例 1 『銀魂 2 掟は破るためにこそある』

官方译为《银魂 2》，省略了“掟は破るためにこそある”（“规则是要打破的”）。《银魂》这部影片曾经在中国上映过，有一定的观众基础。直接翻译为《银魂 2》，观众同样能知晓是《银魂》之系列剧。如果不省略，在译名中加上“规则是要打破的”不符合中文片名的表达习惯，反而会让观众感到疑惑，不知所云。

例 2 『DESTINY 鎌倉ものがたり』

官方译为《镰仓物语》，该片改编自西岸良平的推理漫画，讲述了住在镰仓的推理作家一色正和与爱妻亚纪子一同破解奇怪案件，当亚纪子被妖怪带走后，正和奋不顾身闯进黄泉拯救妻子的故事。省去了“DESTINY”（“命运”），简洁明了地提示影片重点讲述的是在镰仓发生的故事。如若不省略，译为《命运：镰仓物语》，重点则为“命运”，与影片主题不符。

例 3 『劇場版 ソードアート・オンライン -オーディナル・スケール-』

官方译为《刀剑神域：序列之争》，是由小说改编而成的电视动画《刀剑神域》系列动画电影。剧情为原创，讲述了原作小说第 7 卷圣母圣咏篇与第 9 卷 Alicization 篇之间，即电视动画第二季《刀剑神域 II》之后的故事。

作为系列电影，其有《刀剑神域》的翻译基础，也有广泛的观众基础，其名称中的“ソードアート・オンライン”便可按照之前的名称“刀剑神域”进行翻译。“-オーディナル・スケール-”（Ordinal Scale）指“序列之争”。中文片名删减了“劇場版”，因为官方作为电影引进，并在电影院上映，因此“劇場版”有画蛇添足之嫌。

例 4 『打ち上げ花火、下から見るか？横から見るか？』

中文译为《烟花》，这是有浓郁日本青春电影风格的动画电影，讲述的是暑假某个海边小镇，在烟花晚会之前，在同学们热热闹闹的聊着“升空的烟花从侧面看是圆的？还是平的”这样的话题时，奈砂向暗恋自己的典道发出了一起私奔的邀请后发生的时光倒流等一系列故事。可以说烟花绽放是整个故事开始的背景，但不是主题。在翻译成中文时，如果不进行省略，译为《升起的烟花，从下面看？还是从侧面看？》未免过于冗长，同时有些喧宾夺主。并且这句话也不符合中国人的语言习惯，同样汉语中“烟花从哪边看比较好”缺乏电影标题该有的美感。

以上几部影片都是在不破坏原文表达意思的前提下，对其进行删减，从而得到符合中国人的语言习惯及倾向性的片名。

3.4 转换

转换指翻译过程中为了使译文符合目标语的表述方式和习惯，便于中国观众接受，改变或调整原来的叙事方式或视点，有 6 部影片使用了转换的手法。

例 1 『君の膵臓をたべたい』

该影片讲述的是志贺春树偶然发现高中同班同学山内樱良所写的秘密日记“共病文库”

（即患病日记），从而得知她身患胰脏绝症的秘密。性格天差地别的两人也因此走近，一同度过了樱良生命中最后一段时光。

影片的官方译名为《念念手纪》，乍一看是与原文标题毫不相干的翻译，但其实不然。原片名直译为“我想吃掉你的胰脏”，虽然说是与文章内容相关，胰脏被“吃掉”，樱良就不会死。但在中国，“我想吃掉你的胰脏”让人联想到恐怖片，而不是青春片。反而是“念念手纪”，使人清楚地明白这是一部经典的日本青春电影。同时，“手纪”也与电影中一切的起源——患病日记有关。

例 2 『君と 100 回目の恋』

官方译为《与君相恋一百次》，该片讲述了陆为拯救青梅竹马的爱人葵海，不断使用秘密方法回到过去，试图改变命运的奇幻爱情故事。把片名从名词转换为动词，突出很多次的恋爱，如果直译为“与君第一百次的爱恋”给人感觉则只是指“第一百次”。

例 3 『ミックス』

官方译为《恋爱回旋》，该片讲述了曾经是天才乒乓球少女的多满子，年近三十却恋爱、工作都一事无成，她与梦想受挫、一无是处的前职业拳击手组成混合双打搭档，通过“乒乓球”创造“奇迹”的故事。

原文的“ミックス”既有混合双打的意思，也有男女主人公齐心合力通过乒乓球创造奇迹的意思。直译为“混合双打”过于直白，不足以表达电影主题。“恋爱回旋”将恋爱故事和乒乓球的“回旋”特征融为一体，扣紧主题，也吸引观众的眼球。

例 4 『ナミヤ雑貨店の奇蹟』

该片讲述了在僻静街道旁的一家杂货店，只要写下烦恼投进店前门卷帘门的投信口，第二天就会在店后的牛奶箱里得到回答后发生的一个个奇妙的故事。翻译为《解忧杂货店》，与原文相比，删去了杂货店的名字，突出了杂货店的“功能”和主题，使观众对影片的内容有大致的了解。

例 5 『続・深夜食堂』

官方译为《深夜食堂 2》。《深夜食堂》改编自安倍夜郎的同名漫画，以坐落在小胡同里的深夜食堂为舞台，讲述了各路食客在食堂里得到心灵慰藉的故事。那么作为其续集依然延续了系列作品的设定，手艺精湛阅历丰富的食堂老板和一群老食客们串联起三个独立的暖心小故事。

如果按照日文原名对其进行直译，则译为“续·深夜食堂”，这种说法并不符合中国人的语言表达习惯。而译为《深夜食堂 2》不仅符合中文的语序，也能强调这是电影《深夜食堂》的续集。

例 6 『詩季織々』

该动画电影是中日合拍电影，以北京、广州和上海三个中国城市为舞台，讲述了以“衣食住行”为主题的《一碗乡愁》《霓裳浮光》和《纤雨初晴》这三个青春短篇故事。

如果直译为《诗季织织》是一个很抽象的带有艺术气息的名称，但却让观众无法理解。而官方译为《肆式青春》，“肆”的本意为放肆、肆意，此处放在片名中并不合适。笔者认为大写的“四”的意思。影片中有三个故事，片名说四个，所以最后少的一段青春故事应该是观众自己的青春，每个人通过这部电影或多或少都会回忆起自己的青春故事。此处体现的是视点的转换，站在观众的角度来进行翻译。

4 结　论

综上所述，我国近五年在翻译引进日本电影时，采用的是以直译为主，多种翻译方法并存的翻译策略。考虑到中日语言文化的相似性等因素，多数采用了直译的翻译方法，但此处的直译也并非是简单地一一对应，而是进行了艺术的加工。采用直译的电影片名或是原片名较为简单易懂，或是在中国已有一定的观众基础，直译可以最大限度上保留其原片名的形式和意义。

但是，直译并不适用于所有影片。一些在中国没有观众基础，或是思维习惯、语言表达和文体等与中文有差异的日文片名在翻译时如果采用直译可能会造成误解，所以还需要采用其他技巧，如明晰化、减译、转换等。

明晰化策略是一种比较新颖的翻译方法，以前大多只用于英文片名的翻译中，现在也借鉴到日文片名翻译里，是一个很大的进步。与直译相比，明晰化能更清楚地表原片名要传递的信息，但译者要把握好明晰化程度。明晰化一旦过度，则会包含译者过多主观性，失去原文风格的味道，甚至违背翻译“忠实于原文”的准则。而减译与转换也能够使译文更加通顺流畅、地道可读，符合中文的表达习惯，更易于中国观众理解和接受。

总体来说，我国随着引进日文电影数量的增多，对片名翻译的把握也越来越精准娴熟，使用的翻译方法也变得多样化，符合本国的语言习惯及观众的喜好。

随着电影艺术的普及，观众对日本电影片名翻译的要求也越来越高，所以这依然是一项重大的工程。想要切实做好电影片名的翻译工作，不仅需要牢记电影片名的翻译原则，还要了解电影本身的内容以及体裁，结合日本文化和我国实际情况，找到之间的共同点和契合处，之后运用适当的翻译方法进行翻译。

参 考 文 献

[1] 包惠南. 文化语境与语言翻译[M]. 北京：中国对外翻译出版公司，2001.

[2] 卢志君，覃江华. 电影片名翻译研究在中国（1984—2015）[J]. 外国语文研究，2017（8）.

[3] 兰立亮. 日本电影片名的汉译问题[J]. 电影评介，2008（8）.

[4] 奈达 • 泰伯. 翻译理论与实践[M]. 上海：上海外语教育出版社，2004.

[5] 宁之寿. 谈电影片名的翻译[J]. 中国科技翻译，1997（1）.

论叶渭渠译《母亲的初恋》的翻译特点
——兼论谭晶华的中译本

邓雨洁

摘　要：叶渭渠是川端康成作品在中国译介和研究的主要学者之一，其译作研究具有重要的参考意义。本文将川端康成发表于1940年的短篇小说《母亲的初恋》的叶译本（1994）作为研究对象，旨在通过翻译实例分析以及比较谭晶华的中译本（2015），探讨叶渭渠的翻译风格以及翻译特点。

关键词：《母亲的初恋》；川端康成；叶渭渠；翻译特点

川端康成（1899—1972）是日本著名作家、新感觉派的代表作家，曾于1968年获得诺贝尔文学奖，是日本第一位，亚洲第三位获得诺贝尔文学奖的作家。他一生创作了一百多篇小说，除1968年获得诺贝尔文学奖的《古都》《雪国》《千只鹤》外，主要作品还有《伊豆的舞女》《名人》《舞姬》等。川端康成的许多小说被翻译到世界各国，深受各国人民的喜爱。20世纪80年代初，川端康成的作品成为中国翻译家争相译介的对象。1981年7月，上海文艺出版社出版了韩侍桁翻译的《雪国》，同年9月，山东文艺出版社出版了叶渭渠、唐月梅翻译的《雪国·古都》。这样，叶渭渠与韩侍桁成为最早接触川端康成作品译介的翻译家。叶渭渠于1989年写出了一部近20万字的专著《东方美的现代探索者——川端康成评传》（中国社会科学出版社），这是由中国学者撰写的第一部系统介绍和研究川端康成的学术著作，也是中国第一部日本作家研究专论[1]。在中国的日本文学研究界，叶渭渠有“川端康成研究之王”的称誉，日本著名学者千叶宣一曾这样评价：“以他的专著《东方美的现代探索者——川端康成评传》及译作的成果足以证明他居于外国包括欧美在内的川端康成文学研究的第一位”。时至今日，提到川端康成的翻译和研究不得不提到叶渭渠。鉴于叶渭渠对川端康成研究的专业性和系统性，叶渭渠的翻译特点值得我们研究和借鉴。1994年，叶渭渠将短篇小说《母亲的初恋》翻译成中文，并收录在《世界婚恋小说丛书·日本卷》中，这是《母亲的初恋》第一次传入中国。2015年，谭晶华也翻译了《母亲的初恋》，并收录在川端康成短篇小说集《爱的人们》中。本文选取叶渭渠翻译的《母亲的初恋》，通过实例分析与谭晶华译本的对比，探讨叶渭渠的翻译风格以及翻译特点。

1　原著及译者简述

1.1　《母亲的初恋》简述

《母亲的初恋》是川端康成发表于1940年的短篇小说，主要描写了电影编剧佐山在青年时期曾经和一位叫民子的女人有过一段恋情，后来民子却将佐山抛弃。多年之后，佐山事业获得了成功，而民子却生活潦倒并最终病逝。出于好心，佐山收养了民子同其他男人生下的女儿雪子，并为雪子筹办婚礼。但在这期间雪子却对养父佐山产生了纯真而克制的初恋之情。小说看似平淡，却构思精巧。小说中会话场景较多，用词也比较日常。虽说长句偏多，但句内停顿十分明显，读起来简单易懂。

1.2 译者简介

叶渭渠（1929—2010）是中国著名的日本文学研究家、翻译家。1952 年就读于北京大学东方语言文学系，主修日本语言文学。大学毕业后被分配到当时的国务院对外文化联络局做秘书，1972 年被调到人民文学出版社做编辑，并开始着手翻译。20 世纪 80 年代初，叶渭渠开始转向对川端康成作品的译介。1981 年 9 月，山东文艺出版社将叶渭渠译出的《雪国》和唐月梅译出的《古都》合为《古都・雪国》出版。此后，叶渭渠继续译出川端康成的一系列作品，如《母亲的初恋》《致父母的信》《温泉旅馆》《参加葬礼的名人》《南伊豆纪行》《名人》《花的圆舞曲》《川端康成小说选》《花的圆舞曲》等。在叶渭渠的努力与带动下，川端康成作品的译介成为 20 世纪 80 年代初中国的日本文学翻译中的热点，1985 年还迎来了川端作品翻译的丰收年："这一年总共出版了七八个川端康成作品的译本……川端康成获得诺贝尔奖的几个作品——《雪国》《千鹤》《古都》等都有了译本，而且是两个以上不同的译本。"[2]1989 年，叶渭渠撰写了《川端康成评传》，融会了叶渭渠多年翻译和研究川端康成作品的体会，资料很丰富，对作品分析深入细致，观点剀切祥明，堪称我国读者全面了解川端康成的必读书[2]。此外，20 世纪 90 年代，叶渭渠主编了四套川端康成的作品丛书，分别是 1996 年中国社会科学出版社出版的《川端康成文集》（全十卷）；1996 年东北师范大学出版的《川端康成集》（全三卷）；1998 年漓江出版社出版的《川端康成作品》（全十卷）；1999 年中国文联出版社出版的《川端康成少年少女小说集》（全两卷）。作为中国的川端康成文学翻译与研究的集大成者，叶渭渠在关注川端康成的同时，也在密切注视日本文学的最新动态。1991 年与唐月梅和日本学者加藤周一合作主编了《日本文化与现代化丛书》（全十卷）。之后又独自撰写了《日本文学散论》《日本古代文学思潮史》《日本文学思潮史》等。自 20 世纪 70 年代到 21 世纪初，叶渭渠在日本文学的翻译与研究领域一直笔耕不辍且硕果累累，为日本近现代文学在中国文学研究领域的传播和接受做出了重要贡献，并被日本《图书新闻》称作"中国的日本文学最先的领悟者和阐释者。"[1]

2 《母亲的初恋》中译本中的实例分析

《母亲的初恋》是一篇短篇小说，日常会话描写较多，且句式多为短句，人物描写时也多用具象化描写。本章节将通过具体的例句解析，探讨叶渭渠的翻译特点。为了更直观全面地探讨叶渭渠的翻译风格，笔者在分析叶渭渠译本中的例文时，将参考谭晶华的译本进行对比分析。

例 1　解放と独立との強い感じのなかに、婚礼の翌朝は目覚めさせてやりたいというのが、佐山の心づくしであった（p.14）。

叶译：佐山的用意，就是要让他们在婚礼的第二天早晨，能在解放和独立的强烈感受中睡醒过来。（p.172）

谭译：佐山真心诚意地希望雪子于新婚翌日的清晨在一种强烈的解放和独立的感受中醒来。（p.5）

例 1 中，“……のが、佐山の心づくしであった”是判断句，而主语中包含较长的定语从句，即“解放と独立との強い感じのなかに、婚礼の翌朝は目覚めさせてやりたいという”。叶渭渠在翻译这句话时，保留了判断句的句子形式，译为“佐山的用意，就是……”，而且仿照原文的节奏加了两处标点符号。而谭晶华将“佐山の心づくし”的名词改为“佐山真心实意地希望……”的动词，并且删除原文中的标点，没有停顿，直接调整为一句长句。

例 2　佐山は雪子の手を見た。水仕事でそれほど荒れているらしくはなかった。色白だからでもあるが、なんとしても、十九という若さであった。首のういういしいふくらみなどは、ぼうっと温かいものが匂って来そうだ。（p.11）

叶译：佐山看了看雪子的手。虽然干了厨房的活计，但她的手还不怎么粗糙。她的皮肤洁白，可能是个原因，不管怎么说，她正是芳龄十九的年轻姑娘。那柔嫩而又丰满的玉颈，仿佛漾出一股温馨，迎面扑来。（p.171）

谭译：佐山看着雪子的手，好像并没有因为干活而显得粗糙，或许她本来就皮肤白皙，怎么说她还只是个十九岁的年轻姑娘，佐山觉得她的娇嫩丰腴的颈项处散发出一股温柔的馨香。（p.4）

例 2 的原文由四个短句组成，每一句都不长，而且第三个短句和第四个短句中分别使用逗号停顿。叶渭渠的翻译不增不减地译成了四个短句，可以说是与原文高度一致，在原文中容易找到对应的内容。第四句叙述的视角也与原作保持一致，对“首のういういしいふくらみなど”进行了客观叙述。谭译则改变了原文的句式结构，将原文的四个短句揉合在一起，译成了一个长句。而且对第四句的视角进行了调整，补充了“佐山觉得”，凸显了出佐山的感受。

例 3　そう思って佐山が見ていると、雪子は小皿にしゃくったつゆを、ちらちら舌を出して味わってみながら、楽しそうに目を細めている。（p.9）

叶译：他看了看雪子，只见她微微地伸出舌头，尝了尝舀到小碟里的汤，高兴得眯起眼睛。（p.170）

谭译：他瞅着雪子，见她高兴得眯缝着眼睛，不时伸出舌头去品尝舀到小碟子里的汤水。（p.3）

原文中出现在句末的“楽しそうに目を細めている”一句用于形容雪子的神态，叶译与原文一致放在了句末。谭译则改变了句子的语序，采取倒译的翻译技巧将表示神态的句子提到了前面。如此一来，两个译本的意思就出现了偏差，叶渭渠的译文表示雪子之所以高兴，是因为品尝了碟子里的汤。谭晶华的译本可以理解为雪子微笑着品尝汤。叶译在形式上接近原文，而谭译在内容上接近原文。

例 4　民子は長年の無理がたたって、体にひびが入り、今は医者がよく起きて働いているとあきれるほど、心臓と腎臓とが悪く、さっきも時枝に見つかって逃げ出すと、眼が見えなくなって、くらくら倒れたのだそうである。（p.21）

叶译：民子长年受煎熬，积劳成疾，甚至连医生都感到吃惊，她怎么还能经常起来干活。她心脏病和肾病都非常严重，刚才她被时枝发现时，本想溜走，可没想到眼前一片漆黑，昏沉沉地栽倒在地。（p.177）

谭译：长年的打拼劳累使民子的身体垮了，心脏病、肾脏病都很严重，以至于医生看了都感到惊讶，她居然还能起床工作！刚才被时枝发现后一跑，眼前发黑，晕晕乎乎地摔倒了。（p.10）

对照原文和叶渭渠的译本，我们不难发现叶译的叙事顺序同原文完全一致。但由于两种语言的差异，相同的顺序所表达的意思不尽相同。原文中“今は医者がよく起きて働いているとあきれるほど”的后面有标点符号，但实际修饰的是标点符号后面的“心臓と腎臓とが悪く”，表示心脏病和肾病的严重程度，而叶译本在“她怎么还能经常起来干活”结束，并以“她心脏病和肾病都非常严重”开启新的话题，因此前后两句看起来并没有直接的联系。谭译则对语序进行了调整，将表示结果的“心脏病、肾脏病都很严重”一句提到了前面，将表示严重程度的“以至于医生看了都感到惊讶，她居然还能起床工作”放在后面。这符合中文的表达习惯。

例 5　お勝手から手を拭き拭き出て来た雪子は、敷居際にちょっと膝をついて聞いていたが、頬を赤らめるほどでもなくて、うつ向いたまま、また煮物の方へ立って行った。(p.9)

叶译：边擦着手从厨房里走出来的雪子，微曲着双膝，跪坐在门框边上侧耳恭听，但还不至于红起脸来。她依然低着头，站起来向厨房那边走去。(p.169)

谭译：雪子擦着手从厨房里走出来，跪在门边听时枝说话。她并没有羞得脸红，然后，低着头起身又去做饭。(p.2)

例 5 有两处需要关注的翻译。首先是 “お勝手から手を拭き拭き出て来た雪子”一句，“雪子”前面有定语从句，叶渭渠的翻译也仿照原文保留了定语从句，而谭译将“雪子”提到前面，而原文中的定语从句成为表示动作行为的谓语，跟后面的系列动作一气呵成。其次，“膝をついて”表示“跪”，叶译先直译为“微曲着双膝”，然后加了“跪”的动作，原文的形式和内容都表达出来了。谭译则采用了意译的方法，直接将“膝をついて”翻译成“跪”。

例 6　雪子はうなずいた。

「母ちゃんが……」

「母ちゃんが？」

「佐山さんによろしくって言いました。」(p.33)

叶译：雪子点点头。

“母亲她……”

“母亲她？……”

“她说向佐山先生问好。”(p.184)

谭译：雪子点点头。

“我妈妈……”

“妈妈怎么了？”

“妈妈说要向佐山先生问好。”(p.18)

例 6 是佐山和雪子之间的简短对话。第二个“母ちゃんが？”显然是省略的问句，佐山想知道雪子接下来说的话。叶译与原文一致，只翻译为“母亲她？”后面的话省略了，而谭译译为“妈妈怎么了”，加译了“怎么了”一词，改成完整的问句。

通过上述 6 个例句的对比分析，我们不难看出叶译最大的特点就是采用直译，在形式上尽可能地忠实于原文，与原文保持一致。照搬原文的叙事顺序、标点符号，乃至省略方式等特点都一一反映出来，从形式上最大限度地还原原著的作品风格。因为篇幅关系，这里只选取了 6 个例句，总体而言，叶译倾向于直译。而谭译则通过顺序调整、合译、减译、加译等翻译技巧，对句子的语序以及内容进行了调整，使译文更符合中文表达习惯。

日语和汉语属于不同的语言体系，有着不同的篇章结构和特点，采用直译的翻译策略能够保持和追求形式上的忠实，但难免会出现译文不够流畅，或表达不准确等问题。笔者认为这是译者有意为之，是学者型翻译家叶渭渠的翻译风格，其目的在于让中国的读者接触川端康成的文章风格和书写特征。叶渭渠作为川端康成小说最早译者之一，翻译了大量川端康成的小说，并且在翻译作品时尽可能地忠实于原文，力求将原著的风格特征传达给国内读者。叶渭渠曾谈道："对待日语中的汉字，不能完全用我国汉字的同样字义来解读。这是日本语言在'汉字文化圈'中所具有的独立位置所决定的……"那么同样在翻译新感觉派作家的作品时，应该注意其为了强调主观感受所使用的感觉语言，如果仅仅为了汉语习惯或文句通顺而翻译就会失去其艺术特征[1]。这正是叶渭渠传达川端康成作品的内容和思想的同时，尽量使译作在表现形式上贴近原著的原因。

3 总　结

叶渭渠作为研究和翻译川端康成作品的主要学者，他的译作具有十分重要的研究意义。通过《母亲的初恋》中译本的对比分析，发现叶译主要采取直译，尽量保留原文的句式以及结构特点，尤其是在断句以及语序上几乎与原文一致，尽可能地保留了原著的书写特点。笔者想借鲁迅的话，总结和解释叶渭渠的翻译特点。"只求易懂，不如创作，或者改作，将事改为中国事，人也化为中国人。如果还是翻译，那么，首先的目的，就在博览外国的作品，不但移情，也要益智，至少是知道何地何时，有这等事，和旅行外国，是很相像的：它必须有异国情调，就是所谓洋气。其实世界上也不会有完全归化的译文，倘有，就是貌合神离，从严辨别起来，它算不得翻译。"[3]

参考文献

[1] 甘丽娟. 叶渭渠与日本近现代文学的翻译[J]. 日本研究，2011（2）：103-108.

[2] 王向远. 王向远著作集（第三卷），日本文学汉译史[M]. 银川：宁夏人民出版社，2007.

[3] 鲁迅. 且介亭杂文二集[M]. 南京：译林出版社，2013.

[4] 蔡茂友. 母亲的初恋[M]. 谭晶华译. 北京：华夏出版社，1994.

[5] 川端康成. 爱的人们[M]. 谭晶华译. 上海：上海译文出版社，2015.

[6] 川端康成. 愛する人間[M]. 新潮文库，1951.